COMMUNITY POLICING:
PARTNERSHIPS FOR PROBLEM SOLVING

FOURTH EDITION

LINDA S. MILLER
Former Executive Director of the Upper Midwest Community Policing Institute

KÄREN M. HESS
Normandale Community College, Bloomington, Minnesota

THOMSON
WADSWORTH
Australia • Canada • Mexico • Singapore
Spain • United Kingdom • United States

THOMSON
WADSWORTH™

Acquisitions Editor:
Jay Whitney

Assistant Editor:
Jana Davis

Editorial Assistant:
Jennifer Walsh

Technology Project Manager:
Susan DeVanna

Marketing Manager:
Terra Schultz

Marketing Assistant:
Annabelle Yang

Advertising Project Manager:
Stacey Purviance

Project Manager, Editorial Production:
Matt Ballantyne

Art Director:
Vernon Boes

Print/Media Buyer:
Judy Inouye

Permissions Editor:
Sarah Harkrader

Production Service:
Shepherd, Inc.

Photo Researcher:
Suzie Wright

Copy Editor:
Carey Lange

Cover Designer:
QYA Design Studio

Cover Image:
Copyright © Bernd Obermann/Corbis

Text and Cover Printer:
Quebecor World–Kingsport

Printed in the United States of America
1 2 3 4 5 6 7 08 07 06 05 04

For more information about our products, contact us at:
Thomson Learning Academic Resource Center
1-800-423-0563
For permission to use material from this text or product, submit a request online at
http://www.thomsonrights.com
Any additional questions about permissions can be submitted by email to
thomsonrights@thomson.com

Library of Congress Control Number: 2004108868
ISBN: 0-534-62888-5

Wadsworth/Thomson Learning
10 Davis Drive
Belmont, CA 94002-3098
USA

Asia
Thomson Learning
5 Shenton Way #01-01
UIC Building
Singapore 068808

Australia/New Zealand
Thomson Learning
102 Dodds Street
Southbank, Victoria 3006
Australia

Canada
Nelson
1120 Birchmount Road
Toronto, Ontario M1K 5G4
Canada

Europe/Middle East/Africa
Thomson Learning
High Holborn House
50/51 Bedford Row
London WC1R 4LR
United Kingdom

Contents in Brief

Contents

SECTION II

BUILDING RELATIONSHIPS AND TRUST 133

Preface

Welcome to *Community Policing: Partnerships for Problem Solving, Fourth Edition.* The complex responsibilities of departments embracing the community policing philosophy are challenging. Changes in technology and society continually present new challenges to police officers, requiring them to be knowledgeable in a wide variety of areas.

Community policing offers one avenue for making neighborhoods safer. Community policing is not a program or a series of programs. It is a philosophy, a belief that working together, the police and the community can accomplish what neither can accomplish alone. The synergy that results from community policing can be powerful. It is like the power of a finely tuned athletic team, with each member contributing to the total effort. Occasionally heroes may emerge, but victory depends on a team effort.

Community policing differs from earlier efforts such as team policing, community relations, crime prevention programs or Neighborhood-Watch programs. Community policing involves a rethinking of the role of the police and a restructuring of the police organization. Its two core concepts are community–police collaboration and partnerships and a problem-solving approach to policing. These dual themes are present throughout the text.

Changes in This Edition

The structure and focus of the fourth edition is completely revised based on reviewer suggestions and changes in the challenges facing the police. Section I is basically unchanged other than being updated. Section II, which had six chapters, now has three chapters. The chapters on communication (Chapters 6 through 10) have been compressed into one chapter (Chapter 6). A new chapter (Chapter 7) on building partnerships has been written. The third section on community policing in the field has been expanded. The two chapters that discussed youths and gangs (formerly Chapters 9 and 14) have been rewritten into one chapter on youths (Chapter 12) and one chapter on gangs (Chapter 13). The chapter on crime and drugs (formerly Chapter 15) has been split into two chapters (Chapters 10 and 11) and introduced earlier in the section. Finally, a discussion of terrorism has been added to the chapter on violence, now Chapter 14.

Organization of the Text

This text discusses in Section I the evolution of community policing and the changes in our communities and our law enforcement agencies which have occurred. The section then examines the problem-solving approach to policing and how community policing might be implemented.

The text emphasizes in Section II developing the interpersonal skills needed to build good relationships with all those the police have sworn "to serve and protect." This includes those who are culturally, racially or socioeconomically different from the mainstream, those who are physically or mentally disabled and those who are elderly. It also includes youths, both as victims and as offenders, gangs and gang members, and victims of crime. In addition, building partnerships and interacting effectively with members of the media are vital to the success of community policing.

Section III describes community policing in the field. It begins with a look at early experiments in crime prevention and the evolution of community policing strategies. The remainder of the section is entirely new material dealing with community problems ranging from traffic to crime and the fear of crime. It then takes a close look at the drug problem bringing youths into community policing, addressing the gang problem, finally understanding and preventing violence, including domestic violence, workplace violence and terrorism. The final chapter explains what research has found and explores what the future might hold for community policing.

New to This Edition

The fourth edition has been completely updated with over 250 new cites published between 2000 and 2004 and over 60 new terms. Several new figures, tables and photographs have been added. The following additions have also been made to the fourth edition.

- Chapter 1 The Evolution of Community Policing—Descriptions of August Volmer's and O. W. Wilson's contributions to the policing profession; commissions established to examine police services; and the three generations of community policing.
- Chapter 2 Inside Police Agencies: Understanding Mission and Culture—A changing police culture; and use of force and the police image.
- Chapter 3 Understanding and Involving the Community—Communities, crime and displacement; white flight; population trends; and community justice.
- Chapter 4 Problem Solving: Proactive Policing—Community policing compared to problem-oriented policing; qualitative and quantitative data; process evaluation and impact evaluation; the least-effort principle; and the IACP's Community Policing Awards.
- Chapter 5 Implementing Community Policing—Union support; analyzing the community; skills needed by officers in a problem-oriented policing environment; and community empowerment.
- Chapter 6 Communicating Effectively—One on One—Racial profiling.
- Chapter 7 Building Partnerships: The Glue of Community Policing—A new chapter discussing the core components of community partnerships, the four dimensions of trust, the kinds of beats and shifts that enhance partnerships, impediments to a shared vision and common goals, the benefits of partnerships, the purposes served by citizen police academies and key collaborations that may be overlooked.

- Chapter 8 Forming Partnerships with the Media—Results of a national survey on the police–media relationship, victim privacy rights, differing perspectives, the PIO triangle, five interview failures, factors affecting the police–media relationship, comments by the FBI's police–media relations expert, marketing community policing and publicity as a means to prevent crime.
- Chapter 10 Safe Neighborhoods and Communities: From Traffic Problems to Crime—Traffic problems including traffic and safety, corridor safety programs speeding in residential areas, street racing, red light running, impaired drivers and nonuse of seat belts; defining characteristics of Safe Communities; addressing disorder concerns, reducing citizen fear of crime; what the Office of Community Oriented Policing Services (COPS) does; the importance of place; side effects of place-focused opportunity blocking; partnerships to prevent and reduce crime and disorder; strategies to prevent burglaries, shoplifting, robbery at ATMs, assaults in and around bars, street prostitution and thefts of and from vehicles.
- Chapter 11 Community Policing and Drugs—The core principles of the National Drug Control Strategy, the mission of the National Drug Intelligence Center; drug control specialists; Lead On America; federal grant programs aimed at the drug problem; drug-free community funding; open and closed drug markets; drugs in apartment complexes; strategies for getting impaired drivers off the road; Freeway Watch; underage drinking; binge drinking on college campuses; strategies to discourage irresponsible marketing of alcohol; rave parties; the gateway theory; and the liberal and conservative crime control strategies.
- Chapter 12 Bringing Youths into Community Policing—Connecting youths and the community; crime in schools; the bullying circle; *Indicators of School Crime and Safety 2002*; types of threats; the FBI's four-prong threat assessment; personality traits and behaviors of school shooters; characteristics of effective schools and how school–law enforcement partnerships contribute; the three P's for dealing with school violence; lockdowns; school mock disaster exercises; and the 8% problem.
- Chapter 13 The Challenge of Gangs: Controlling Their Destructive Force—The Seattle study; National Youth Gang Center publications; criminal activity by type of gang; early precursors of gang membership; the GRIP program; recognizing the presence of gangs; collaborative gang initiatives; providing alternatives to gangs.
- Chapter 14 Understanding and Preventing Violence and Terrorism—Hate crime on college campuses; the seven-stage hate model; citizen firearms safety programs; right-to-carry laws; the link between animal abuse and domestic violence; barriers to multiagency collaboration; and terrorism, including definitions, international and domestic terrorism; the police response/responsibility; keys to combating terrorism; and partnerships to prevent terrorism.
- Chapter 15 What Research Tells Us and a Look to the Future—Impediments to experimental design; the action research model; when experimental designs are

appropriate; use of case studies; what communities should value in police departments; and a look toward the future, including time line predictions.

Chapters 10 through 14 conclude with award-winning examples of problem-solving partnerships in action.

How to Use This Text

This text is a carefully structured learning experience. The more actively you participate in it, the greater your learning will be. You will learn and remember more if you first familiarize yourself with the total scope of the subject. Read and think about the Table of Contents, which provides an outline of the many facets of community policing. Then follow these steps for *triple-strength learning* as you study each chapter.

1. Read the objectives at the beginning of the chapter. These are stated as "Do You Know?" questions. Assess your current knowledge of the subject of each question. Examine any preconceptions you may hold. Look at the key terms and watch for them when they are used.
2. Read the chapter, underlining, highlighting or taking notes—whatever is your preferred study method.
   a. Pay special attention to all highlighted information:

   > Two themes apparent in the various definitions of community policing are problem solving and partnerships.

   The key concepts of the text are highlighted in this way and answer the "Do You Know?" questions.
   b. Pay special attention to the terms in bold print. The key terms of the chapter appear this way the first time they are defined.
3. When you have finished reading the chapter, read the summary—your third exposure to the chapter's key information. Then return to the beginning of the chapter and quiz yourself. Can you answer the "Do You Know?" questions? Can you define the key terms?
4. Then read the Discussion Questions and be prepared to contribute to a class discussion of the ideas presented in the chapter.

By following these steps, you will learn more information, understand it more fully and remember it longer.

A Note: The material selected to highlight using the triple-strength learning instructional design includes only the chapter's key concepts. Although this information is certainly important in that it provides a structural foundation for understanding the topic(s) discussed, do not simply glance over the "Do You Know?" highlighted boxes and summaries and expect to master the chapter. You are also responsible for reading and understanding the material that surrounds these basics—the "meat" around the bones, so to speak.

Exploring Further

The text also provides an opportunity for you to apply what you have learned or to go into specific areas in greater depth through discussions, InfoTrac College Edition Assignments and Community Projects. Complete each of these areas as directed by the text or by your instructor. Be prepared to share your findings with the class.

Good learning!

Acknowledgments

A number of professionals from academia and the field have reviewed the previous editions of *Community Policing: Partnerships for Problem Solving* and provided valuable suggestions. We thank them all: James S. Albritton, Marquette University; Michael B. Blankenship, Memphis State University; W. D. Braddock, Boise State University; William Castleberry, The University of Tennessee at Martin; Vincent Del Castillo, John Jay College of Criminal Justice; Burt C. Hagerman, Oakland Community College; Robert Ives, Rock Valley College; Deborah Wilkins Newman, Middle Tennessee State University; James E. Newman, Rio Hondo Community College; Willard M. Oliver, Glenville State College; Carroll S. Price, Penn Valley Community College; Charles L. Quarles, University of Mississippi; Mittie D. Southerland, Murray State University; B. Grant Stitt, University of Nevada-Reno; Gregory B. Talley, Broome Community College; and Gary T. Tucker, Sinclair Community College.

The following reviewers contributed numerous suggestions to the fourth edition: Alan Kraft, Seminole Community College; Jeanne Stinchcomb, Florida Atlantic University; Bernadette Jones Palomobo, Louisiana State University–Shreveport; William King, Bowling Green State University; and Deborah Jones, California State University–San Bernadino.

We greatly appreciate the input of these reviewers. Sole responsibility of all content, however, is our own.

We extend a special thank you to Christine M. H. Orthmann for her careful proofreading of the revised manuscript and the supplemental materials. Additional special thanks go to Jay Whitney, our editor; Matt Ballantyne, production editor at Wadsworth Thomson Learning; and Peggy Francomb, production editor at Shepherd, Inc. Finally, we thank our families and colleagues for their continuing support and encouragement throughout the development of *Community Policing: Partnerships for Problem Solving*.

Linda S. Miller
Kären M. Hess

Foreword

A democratic society has to be the most difficult environment within which to police. Police in many countries operate for the benefit of the government. The police of America operate for the benefit of the people policed. Because of that environment, we are compelled to pursue ways to advance our policing approach, involve people who are part of our environment and enhance our effectiveness. Our policing methodology is changed or molded by trial and error, the daring of some policing leaders, the research and writing of academicians and the response of our communities to the way we do business.

Over the past 30 years, we have tried a variety of approaches to doing our job better. Some have remained. Many have been abandoned, thought to be failures. They may, however, have been building blocks to our current policing practices and for what is yet to come. For instance, the community relations and crime prevention programs of the 1960s and the experiments with team policing in the 1970s are quite visible in the business of community policing. So should be the knowledge gained from research such as that conducted in the 1970s and 1980s associated with random patrol, directed patrol, foot patrol, one-officer/two-officer cars and the effectiveness (or lack thereof) of rapid response to all calls for service. If we look at our past, we should not be surprised at the development and support of community policing as the desired policing philosophy in our country today. It merely responds to the customers' needs and their demand for our policing agencies to be more effective. And therein lies the most important outcome of community policing—effectiveness. Yes, we have responded to millions of calls for service, made millions of arrests and added thousands to our policing ranks. If we're honest about it, however, we may be hard-pressed to see the imprint of our efforts in our communities. Community policing, involving problem solving, community engagement and organizational transformation, can contribute significantly to the satisfaction of the community policed and to those policing.

This text provides insight into the meaning of community policing and presents many dimensions necessary to consider when developing a community policing strategy. Its content should help readers to understand the practical side of community policing, recognize the community considerations that need to exist and develop methods applicable to their unique environments.

Donald J. Burnett
General Partner
Law Enforcement Assistance Network

About the Authors

This text is based on the practical experience of Linda S. Miller, who has spent 26 years in law enforcement and the expertise of Kären M. Hess, who has been developing instructional programs for 30 years. The text has been reviewed by numerous experts in the various areas of community policing as well.

Linda S. Miller is the former executive director of the Upper Midwest Community Policing Institute (UMCPI) as well as a former sergeant with the Bloomington (Minnesota) Police Department. She was with the department 22 years, serving as a patrol supervisor, a crime prevention officer, a patrol officer and a police dispatcher. Ms. Miller has been a member of the Minnesota Peace and Police Officers Association, the International Police Association, the Midwest Gang Investigator's Association, the International Association of Women Police and the Minnesota Association of Women Police. She was a member of the People-to-People's Women in Law Enforcement delegation to the Soviet Union in 1990. She is a frequent presenter to community groups and is also an instructor.

Kären M. Hess holds a PhD in English and in instructional design from the University of Minnesota and a PhD in criminal justice from Pacific Western University. Other West/Wadsworth Thomson Learning texts Dr. Hess has coauthored are *Criminal Investigation* (Seventh Edition), *Criminal Procedure, Corrections in the 21st Century: A Practical Approach, Introduction to Law Enforcement and Criminal Justice* (Seventh Edition), *Introduction to Private Security* (Fifth Edition), *Juvenile Justice* (Fourth Edition), *Management and Supervision in Law Enforcement* (Fourth Edition), *Police Operations* (Third Edition) and *Seeking Employment in Criminal Justice and Related Fields* (Fourth Edition).

She is a member of the Academy of Criminal Justice Sciences, the American Association of University Women, the American Correctional Association, the American Society for Industrial Security, the American Society for Law Enforcement Trainers, the American Society of Criminologists, the Association for Supervision and Curriculum Development, the International Association of Chiefs of Police, the Minnesota Association of Chiefs of Police, the National Institute of Justice, the Police Executive Research Forum and the Text and Academic Authors Association, which has named her to their Council of Fellows.

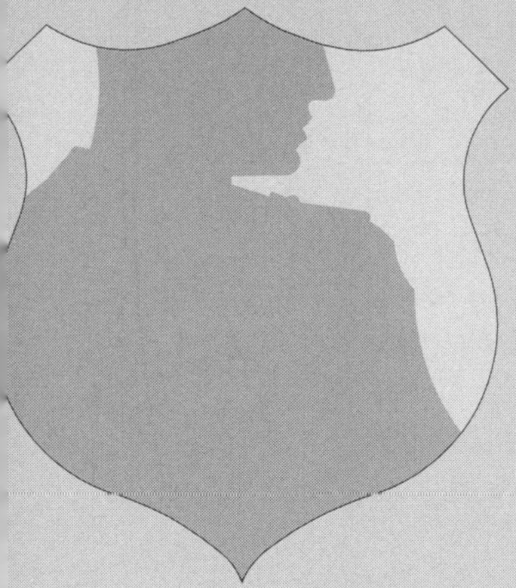

Section I

AN OVERVIEW

Chapters in this Section:

The community and the police depend on each other. The common police motto—"To serve and protect"—suggests a target population of individuals who require service and protection. Most police departments stress the importance of community relations, and many have taken community relations beyond image enhancement and crime prevention programs and have started involving the community in policing itself.

This section begins with a discussion of the evolution of police–community relations. Since people first came together in groups, they have had some responsibility for ensuring that those within the group did as was expected. The U.S. method of "preserving the peace," modeled after that used in England, has evolved through several stages. The relationship between the community and its police has been severely strained at times, and attempts to improve it have taken several forms. Recently, emphasis on improved public relations and crime prevention has expanded to a more encompassing philosophy of community policing, including problem-solving policing in many jurisdictions (Chapter 1).

Next an in-depth look at the police is presented (Chapter 2). Who are the people behind the badges? How have they changed over the years? How might they change in the future? How does the public generally view the police? What aspects of the police role contribute to this view?

The focus in Chapter 3 is on the people and agencies involved in community–police relations. Who are the members of a community? How do communities differ? How have they changed over the years? What future changes might be anticipated? What aspects of a community must be understood by those working within it? What is expected of community members? What do community members expect?

This is followed by an examination of problem-solving policing, a key component of the community policing philosophy (Chapter 4). The section concludes with a discussion on implementing community policing guidelines and cautions (Chapter 5).

CHAPTER 1

The Evolution of Community Policing

The police are the public and the public are the police.

—Sir Robert Peel

DO YOU KNOW?

- When "modern" policing began?
- What Sir Robert Peel's principles emphasize?
- What the three eras of policing are?
- What the police relationship with the community was in each era?
- What the professional model of policing emphasizes?
- What some common types of crime prevention programs are?
- What community policing is?
- What two themes are apparent in the various definitions of community policing?
- What four essential dimensions of community policing are?
- What three generations of community policing have been identified?

CAN YOU DEFINE?

community policing
community relations
frankpledge system
hue and cry
human relations
paradigm
paradigm shift
patronage system
proactive
professional model
progressive era
public relations
reactive
reform era
spoils system
"thin blue line"
tithing
tithing system

Introduction

Community policing did not just magically appear as a panacea for society's ills. It has been centuries in its evolution and may indeed be merely a steppingstone to yet another form of policing in the future. As society's needs change, so do the methods it uses to "keep the peace."

Police departments, and to a lesser extent sheriffs' offices, in the United States report that they are involved in community policing. Sixty-eight percent of local police departments and 55 percent of sheriffs' offices had a community policing plan in 2000. Two-thirds of all police departments (Hickman and Reaves, 2003a, pp.14–15) and nearly two-thirds (62 percent) of sheriffs' offices were using full-time community policing officers (Hickman and Reaves, 2003b, pp.14–15).

Although no one has been able to define community policing in a way that satisfies everyone, most will agree that it includes two vital components. A problem-solving approach to crime and disorder and partnerships involving both the police and the community in solving the problems. Without solving the problems it encounters, the police are doomed to handling the same problems and suspects again and again. Without community partnerships, the police's chances for successfully solving the problems also are slim. A community without input

During the community era of policing, demonstrations still challenge law enforcement across the country. Here a large crowd demonstrates in San Francisco on March 20, 2004, to mark the one-year anniversary of the Iraq war.

and ownership in the solutions will unintentionally or even intentionally undermine police efforts.

What constitutes community policing varies from location to location. Chief Brown (2001, p.56), Hudson (Ohio) Police Department, provides one way of viewing community policing:

> The essence of community policing is to return to the day when safety and security are participatory in nature and everyone assumes responsibility for the general health of their community—not just a select few, not just the local government administration, not just the safety forces, but absolutely everyone living in the community.
>
> Community policing in its simplistic form is the development and fostering of a working relationship and a cooperative spirit between community and its law enforcement agency to better serve the community's needs and service expectations. It encourages and promotes to the maximum extent possible, an environment of safety and security for all persons residing in the community, working in the community, visiting the community or merely commuting through it.

This chapter begins with a brief history of policing and its evolution in the United States. This is followed by an examination of three strategic eras of policing and the paradigm shifts that occurred. Next the influence of public relations, community relations and crime prevention programs is explored. The chapter concludes with an in-depth look at community policing, including definitions, major features, potential problems and the incorporation of a problem-solving approach.

A Brief History of Policing

Throughout history societies have established rules to govern the conduct of individuals and have devised punishments for those who break the rules. The earliest record of an ancient society's rules to control human behavior dates back to approximately 2300 B.C., when Sumerian rulers codified their concept of offenses against society. Since then such rules have been modified and adapted. According to Wrobleski and Hess (2003, p.4):

> The beginnings of just laws and social control were destroyed during the Dark Ages as the Roman Empire disintegrated. Germanic invaders swept into the old Roman territory of Britain, bringing their own laws and customs. These invaders intermarried with those they conquered, the result being the hardy Anglo-Saxon.

The Anglo-Saxons grouped their farms around small, self-governing villages that policed themselves. This informal arrangement became more structured under King Alfred the Great (A.D. 849–899), who required every male to enroll for police purposes in a group of 10 families, known as a **tithing.** The **tithing system** established the principle of collective responsibility for maintaining local law and order.

The tithing system worked well until 1066, when William the Conqueror, a Norman, invaded and conquered England. William, concerned about national security, replaced the tithing system of "home rule" with 55 military districts called shires,[1] each headed by a Norman officer called a reeve, hence the title shire-reeve (the origin of the word *sheriff*). William also established the **frankpledge system,** which required all free men to swear loyalty to the king's law and to take responsibility for maintaining the local peace.

By the seventeenth century, law enforcement duties were divided into two separate units, a day watch and a night watch. The day watch consisted of constables who served as jailers and fulfilled other government duties. Citizens worked on the night watch. Each citizen was expected to take a turn watching for fires, bad weather and disorderly individuals. Some towns also expected the night watchman to call out the time.

If a watchman or any other citizen saw a crime in progress, he was expected to give the **hue and cry,** summoning all citizens within earshot to join in pursuing and capturing the wrongdoer. Preserving the peace was the duty of all citizens.

By the end of the eighteenth century, most people with sufficient means paid others to stand their assigned watch for them, marking the beginning of a paid police force and, in effect, the original neighborhood watch.

The system of day and night watchmen was very ineffective. Because wealthy citizens could avoid the watch duty by hiring someone to take their place, those they hired were hesitant to invoke their authority against the well-to-do. According to Richardson (1970, p.10), by the mid-1700s New York City's night watch was "a parcel of idle, drinking, vigilant snorers, who never quelled any nocturnal tumult in their lives . . . but would, perhaps, be as ready to join in a burglary as any thief in Christendom."

London, suffering from the impact of the Industrial Revolution, was experiencing massive unemployment and poverty. It had become a disorderly city with enormous, crime-ridden slums and a significant juvenile delinquency problem. Some citizens had even begun to carry weapons for self-protection. In an attempt to address the problems, Parliament convened five parliamentary commissions of inquiry between 1780 and 1820. When Sir Robert Peel was appointed home secretary, he proposed that London appoint civilians, paid by the community, to serve as police officers. The Metropolitan Police Act was passed in 1829 and modern policing began.

The Beginnings of "Modern" Police Forces

"Modern" policing began with the formation of the London Metropolitan Police, founded by Sir Robert Peel in 1829.

Peel set forth the following principles on which the police force was to be based:

- The duty of the police is to prevent crime and disorder.
- The power of the police to fulfill their duties is dependent on public approval and on their ability to secure and maintain public respect.
- Public respect and approval also mean the willing cooperation of the public in the task of securing observance of the law.

[1]A shire is equivalent to a U.S. county.

- The police must seek and preserve public favor not by pandering to public opinion but by constantly demonstrating absolutely impartial service to law.
- The police should strive to maintain a relationship with the public that gives reality to the tradition that the police are the public and the public are the police.
- The test of police efficiency is the absence of crime and disorder, not the visible evidence of police action in dealing with these problems.

Peel's principles emphasized the interdependency of the police and the public as well as the prevention of crime and disorder.

As Gehrand (2000, p.111) notes: "Peel also recognized that the police were only successful at their jobs when they elicited public approval and assistance in their actions without resorting to force or the severity of law. These beliefs hold true today. No police department can control crime and disorder without the consent and voluntary compliance by the public."

Peel envisioned a close police–citizen relationship that helped the police maintain order in London. As originally envisioned by the architects of London's Metropolitan Police—acknowledged to be the first modern police department—a police officer's job was primarily crime prevention and social maintenance, not crime detection. Police were to serve as local marshals who actively maintained order by interacting with the neighborhoods they served.

Policing in the United States

Those who came to America in 1620 and their descendants, through the American Revolution, rejected the British Crown's rule that permitted British soldiers to take over homes and to have complete authority over the colonists. Our founders wanted to ensure that no such power would exist in the newly created nation. As former Chief Justice of the U.S. Supreme Court Warren E. Burger (1991, p.26) stated: "The Founders, conscious of the risks of abuse of power, created a system of liberty with order and placed the Bill of Rights as a harness on government to protect people from misuse of the powers." Nonetheless, the system of policing and maintaining order in the northern part of the United States was modeled on the police system developed in England.

At the time the Metropolitan Police Force was established in London, the United States was still operating under a day-and-night-watch system similar to the one that had been used in England. In the 1830s several large cities established separate paid day watches. In 1833 Philadelphia became the first city to pay both the day and night watches. Boston followed in 1838 with a six-officer police force. In 1844 New York City took the first step toward organizing a big-city police department similar to those that exist today across the country when it consolidated its day and night watches under the control of a police chief. The police department was modeled on the London Metropolitan Police and Peel's principles. Other cities followed the example set by New York. By 1857 Boston, Chicago, New Orleans, Newark, Cincinnati, Philadelphia and Baltimore had consolidated police departments modeled on London's Metropolitan Police. The new police chiefs of these departments faced the beginning of tremendous personnel problems among their officers. Early professionals found security services in disarray.

> What those first chiefs of police found in their newly consolidated forces was a motley, undisciplined crew composed, as one commentator on the era described it, principally of "the shiftless, the incompetent, and the ignorant." Tales abounded of police officers in the 1850s who assaulted their superior officers, who released prisoners from the custody of other officers, who were found sleeping or drunk on duty, or who could be bribed for almost anything (Garmire, 1989, p.17).

Despite these problems, and because there were also many honest, dedicated police officers, the citizens considered the police a source of assistance. Early police officers' duties included more community assistance and service than often imagined. Even at the beginning of the twentieth century, law enforcement was one of the only government-sanctioned services to help citizens 24/7. Welfare, parole, probation and unemployment offices did not exist. Police in New York, for example, distributed coal to the poor, monitored the well-being of vulnerable citizens, served as probation and parole officers and helped establish playgrounds.

It was more than a decade after the formation of the first police forces in the United States that attempts were made to require police officers to wear uniforms. Police officers' well-known resistance to change was apparent even then. The rank-and-file reaction against uniforms was immediate. Police officers claimed that uniforms were "un-American" and "a badge of degradation and servitude." In Philadelphia, police officers even objected to wearing badges on their coats. It was a bitter four-year struggle before they were finally persuaded to wear a complete uniform.

In 1856 New York City required its officers to be uniformed, but each local ward[2] could determine the style of dress. As a result, in some sections of the city, police officers wore straw hats, whereas in others they wore felt hats. In some wards summer uniforms were white "duck" suits; in other wards they were multicolored outfits.

Policing in the Southern States

Policing in the South had different origins—the slave patrols found in the Southern colonies and states. By 1700 most Southern colonies, concerned about the dangers the oppressed slaves could create, had established a code of laws to regulate slaves. These codes prohibited slaves from having weapons, gathering in groups, leaving the plantation without a pass or resisting punishment.

Predictably, many slaves resisted their bondage. According to Foner (1975) the resistance usually consisted of running away, criminal acts and conspiracies or revolts. Compounding the problem, in some Southern states slaves came to outnumber the colonists. For example, in 1720 South Carolina's population was 30% white and 70% black (Simmons, 1976, p.125). As Reichel (1999, p.82) notes, the white colonists' fear of the slaves as a dangerous threat led to the development of special enforcement officers with general enforcement powers as a transition to modern police. Dulaney (1996) contends that these slave patrols were the first truly American police system. He notes that by 1750 every Southern colony had a slave

[2]A ward is an administrative division of a city or town.

patrol that formally required all white men to serve as patrollers. In actuality, however, the patrollers were generally poor white men.

In most colonies and states, patrols could enter any plantation and break into slaves' dwellings, punish slaves found outside their plantation, search, beat and even kill any slaves found to be violating the slave code. Asirvatham (2000, p.2) suggests:

> Twentieth-century Southern law enforcement was essentially a direct outgrowth of the 19th-century slave patrols employed to enforce curfews, catch runaways, and suppress rebellions. Even later on, in Northern and Southern cities alike, "free men of color" were hired as cops only in order to keep other African-Americans in line [enforcing Jim Crow laws supporting segregation]. Until the 1960s black cops, by law or by custom, weren't given powers of arrest over white citizens, no matter how criminal.

The evolution of law enforcement in both the North and South is often divided into three distinct eras.

The Three Eras of Policing

Three major paradigm shifts have occurred in the evolution of policing in the United States. A **paradigm** is a model or a way of viewing a specific aspect of life such as politics, medicine, education and even the criminal justice system. A **paradigm shift** is simply a new way of thinking about a specific subject. Kelling and Moore (1991, p.6) describe these paradigm shifts as specific "eras" of policing in the United States.

The three eras of policing are political, reform and community.

The Political Era (1840 to 1930)

The political era extended into the first quarter of the twentieth century and witnessed the formation of police departments. During this era police were closely tied to politics. This was very dissimilar to the situation in England, where the police were centralized under the king, and the police chief had the authority to fire officers. In the United States the police were decentralized under the authority of the municipality in which they worked. The chief had no authority to fire officers; therefore, the police were often undisciplined. "The image of 'Keystone Cops'—police as clumsy bunglers—was widespread and often descriptive of realities in U.S. policing" (Kelling and Moore, p.9).

Police officers usually lived in their community and were members of the majority group. Since foot patrol was the most common policing strategy used, officers became close to the public.

During the political era the police sought an intimate relationship with the community.

During this era chiefs of police were politically appointed and had a vested interest in keeping those who appointed them in power. Politicians rewarded those who voted for them with jobs or special privileges. This was referred to as the **patronage system,** or the **spoils system,** from the adage "To the victor go the spoils."

In 1929 President Herbert Hoover appointed the National Commission on Law Observance and Enforcement to study the criminal justice system. Hoover named George W. Wickersham, former U.S. attorney general, as its chairman. When the report was published in 1931, it became one of the "most important events in the history of American Policing" (Walker, 1997, p.154). The Wickersham Commission focused two reports on the police. Report 11, Lawlessness in Law Enforcement, described the problem of police brutality, concluding that "the third degree—the inflicting of pain, physical or mental, to extract confessions or statements—is extensively practiced." Specific tactics included protracted questioning, threats and intimidation, physical brutality, illegal detention and refusal to allow access of counsel to suspects (National Commission on Law Observance and Enforcement, 1931, p.4). Report 14, The Police, examined police administration and called for expert leadership, centralized administrative control and higher standards for personnel—in effect, for police professionalism. The inefficiency and corruption of the police led to the second era of policing, the reform era.

The Reform Era (1930 to 1980)

The **reform era** is often referred to as the **progressive era.** August Vollmer and O.W. Wilson are usually attributed with spearheading the reform movement that called for a drastic change in the organization and function of police departments.

August Vollmer is sometimes referred to as the father of American policing. He was elected to be the Berkeley city marshall in 1904, a position changed to chief of police in 1909. Vollmer was chief until 1932. During his tenure at Berkeley, Vollmer created a police force that became a model for the country. His innovations included radios in patrol cars, a fingerprint and handwriting classification system, a workable system for filing and using MO files, motorcycles and bicycles on patrol, and a police school at his department. Vollmer believed police should be trained professionals who were also social workers with a deeper responsibility to the community than simply fighting crime. Vollmer's book, *The Police and Modern Society* (1936), is still a classic in law enforcement. Vollmer also helped create the first college police program at the University of California at Berkeley (Central Missouri State University Web site).

O.W. Wilson, a protégé of Vollmer, continued the move toward the professionalization of the police. One of Wilson's greatest strengths was his firm belief in honest law enforcement. He was very aware that the police had little control over the root causes of crime, but developed the concept of preventive patrol. Wilson's most noted works are *Police Administration* (1950) and *Police Planning* (1957) (Central Missouri State University Web site).

One basic change during this era was to disassociate policing from politics, which was accomplished in a variety of ways. In Los Angeles, for example, the chief of police position became a civil-service job that required applicants to pass a civil-service test. In Milwaukee the chief of police was appointed for life by a citizen commission.

With the disassociation of policing from politics came a change in emphasis in the police role as citizens began to equate policing with fighting crime. The police considered social-service-type functions less desirable and avoided them when possible.

The relationship between the police and the public also changed during the reform era. As Kelling and Moore (p.12) note: "Police leaders in the reform era redefined the nature of a proper relationship between police officers and both politicians and citizens. Police would be impartial law enforcers who related to citizens in professionally neutral and distant terms." *Dragnet,* one of the first and most popular police shows ever televised, depicted this era perfectly. The main character, Sgt. Joe Friday, typified the impartial and distant reform-era officer with his often-repeated line, "Just the facts, ma'am." The public viewed the police as professionals who remained detached from the citizens they served.

During the reform era the police relationship with the community they served was professionally remote.

During this era the concept of the **"thin blue line"** developed. This phrase refers to the line that separates law-abiding, peaceful citizens from the murderous, plundering villains who prey upon them. The phrase also suggests a distance between the police and the public they serve. The thin blue line describes the dangerous threats to communities, with police standing between that danger and law-abiding citizens. It suggests both police heroism and isolation.

Adding to the distancing of police from the public during the reform era was the replacement of foot patrols with motorized patrols. O. W. Wilson's preventive patrol by squad car coupled with an emphasis on rapid response to calls for service became the dual focus of policing during this era. The police image became one of officers roaring through city streets in high-powered squad cars, lights flashing and sirens wailing. The police were viewed as professional crime fighters. Consequently, policing during the reform era is often referred to as the professional model.

The **professional model** emphasized crime control by preventive automobile patrol coupled with rapid response to calls.

The problems the first police administrators faced did not change much, but under the professional model their answers did. Many police methods were challenged during the 1960s, when social change exploded in the United States as the result of several significant events occurring almost simultaneously.

The civil rights movement began in the late 1950s as a grassroots movement to change the blatantly unequal social, political and economic systems in the United States. Confrontations between blacks and the police, who were almost completely male and white, increased during this time. Representing the status quo and defending it, the manner in which the police handled protest marches and civil disobedience often aggravated these situations.

Punctuated by the assassinations of President Kennedy, Malcolm X, Martin Luther King, Jr., Medgar Evers and Robert Kennedy, the events of the decade were, for the first time in history, documented in detail and viewed by millions of

Americans on television. The antiwar movement, based on college campuses, was also televised. When demonstrators at the 1968 Democratic convention in Chicago were beaten by the Chicago police, the demonstrators chanted: "The whole world is watching." Watching what was later termed a police riot, Americans were shocked.

Plagued by lack of training and confronted by a confusing array of social movements as well as an emerging drug culture, the police became the "enemy." Officers heard themselves referred to as "pigs" by everyone from students to well-known entertainers. They represented the status quo, the establishment and everything that stood in the way of peace, equality and justice. Police in the 1960s were at war with the society they served. Never had the relationship between the law enforcement community and the people it served been so strained.

In addition to the questionable way police handled race riots and antiwar demonstrations in the sixties, several big-city police departments were charged with corruption at that time. The 1960s changed the face of the United States, and law enforcement was no exception. Studies in the 1970s on corruption and criminal behavior among police agencies brought great pressure on the entire criminal justice system to change its methods, attitudes and image. Media coverage of law enforcement practices educated the public, who ultimately demanded change.

Understanding Community Policing (1994, pp.6–7) describes the social and professional "awakening" that occurred during the 1960s and 1970s:

> Antiwar protestors, civil rights activists, and other groups began to demonstrate in order to be heard. Overburdened and poorly prepared police came to symbolize what these groups sought to change in their government and society. Focusing attention on police policies and practices became an effective way to draw attention to the need for wider change. Police became the targets of hostility, which ultimately led police leaders to concerned reflection and analysis. . . .
>
> A number of organizations within the policing field also became committed to improving policing methods in the 1970s. Among those on the forefront of this movement for constructive change were the Police Foundation, the Police Executive Research Forum, the National Organization of Black Law Enforcement Executives, the Urban Sheriffs' Group of the National Sheriffs' Association and the International Association of Chiefs of Police. These organizations conducted much of the basic research that led police to reevaluate traditional policing methods.

Commissions Established to Examine Police Services According to Barry (1999): "One measure of the turmoil in U.S. cities and the controversy surrounding police practices in the 1960s and early 1970s was the proliferation of blue-ribbon commissions during that period. Five national commissions were formed to examine various aspects of police services and the criminal justice process and make recommendations for reform."

- The President's Commission on Law Enforcement and Administration of Justice was influenced by urban racial turmoil. An outgrowth of its report published in 1967 and 1968 was the Safe Streets Act of 1968 and the Law Enforcement Assistance Administration, which provided significant funding for police-related programs.
- The National Advisory Commission on Civil Disorders (popularly known as the Kerner Commission) was also inspired by the riots and other disorders in many U.S. cities in the summer of 1967. Its report examined patterns of disorder and prescribed responses by the federal government, the criminal justice system and local government.
- The National Commission on the Causes and Prevention of Violence was established after the assassinations of Martin Luther King, Jr. and Robert Kennedy in 1968. Its report, "To Establish Justice, To Insure Domestic Tranquility," was published in 1969.
- The President's Commission on Campus Unrest was established following student deaths related to protests at Kent State and Jackson State universities in 1970.
- The National Advisory Commission on Criminal Justice Standards and Goals issued six reports in 1973 in an attempt to develop standards and recommendations for police crime control efforts.

In response to the negative police image that emerged during the 1960s, several departments across the country established programs to enhance their relationships with the communities they served. These programs included public-relations programs, community-relations programs and crime prevention programs.

Efforts to Enhance Relations between the Police and the Community To avoid confusion, it is helpful to distinguish among public relations, community relations and human relations because these terms are used frequently throughout this text and in other literature on policing.

- **Public relations:** Efforts to enhance the police image—"We'll tell you what we're doing, but leave us alone to fight crime."
- **Community relations:** Efforts to interact and communicate with the community—team policing, community resource officers and school resource officers
- **Human relations:** Efforts to relate to and understand other people or groups of people—the focus of Section Two

Public-relations efforts are usually one-way efforts to raise the image of the police. These efforts by police departments include hosting departmental open houses and providing speakers for school and community events. Many police departments have established a public-relations office or division and have assigned specific officers to the public-relations effort. Such efforts reflect the growing recognition by police administrators that they need public support.

In the past several decades, especially in the late 1970s and also as a result of the widening gap between the police and the public, many police departments began community-relations programs. Unlike public-relations efforts, which were primarily one-to-one communications, often media generated, community-relations programs sought to bring the police and community closer through isolated police tactics such as team policing and community resource officers. Efforts to enhance community relations also frequently involved citizens through crime prevention programs.

Crime Prevention Programs

Crime prevention programs that enlist citizens' aid include Operation Identification programs, neighborhood- or block-watch programs and home- and automobile-security programs.

Such programs, which continue to be strategies used in many community policing efforts, are discussed in detail in Section Three.

The Law Enforcement Assistance Administration (LEAA) Another response to the negative image of the police was the establishment of the Law Enforcement Assistance Administration in 1968. Over the next several years LEAA provided billions of dollars to the "war on crime," funding studies and programs for law enforcement. LEAA awarded more than $9 billion to state and local governments to improve police, courts and correctional systems, to combat juvenile delinquency and to finance innovative crime-fighting projects. Tens of thousands of programs and projects were supported with LEAA funds, and millions of hours were applied to identify effective, efficient, economical ways to reduce crime and improve criminal justice.

Although the consensus among law enforcement officials today is that LEAA was mostly mismanaged, there was also a very positive aspect of LEAA. This was the Law Enforcement Education Program (LEEP), which provided thousands of officers with funding for higher education.

The Courts The courts also had a major impact on criminal justice during the 1960s. Several legal decisions limited police powers and clarified the rights of the accused. In 1961 *Mapp v Ohio* extended the exclusionary rule to every court and law enforcement officer in the country. The exclusionary rule, established in 1914 in *Weeks v United States,* mandated that federal courts must refuse to consider evidence obtained by unreasonable, and therefore unconstitutional, search and seizure, no matter how relevant the evidence was to the case.

In 1963 in *Gideon v Wainwright* the Supreme Court ruled 9 to 0 that the due process clause of the Fourteenth Amendment requires states to provide free counsel to indigent (impoverished) defendants in all felony cases. The next landmark case came the following year in *Escobedo v Illinois* (1964), when the Court ruled that if individuals confess without being told of their right to have a lawyer present and are then allowed to have a lawyer present during questioning, the confessions are not legal.

In 1966 this right to have a lawyer present, and at public expense if necessary, and other rights were reaffirmed in what is probably the best-known Supreme Court case—*Miranda v Arizona.* The Court held that evidence obtained by police during custodial interrogation of a suspect cannot be used in court unless the suspect is informed of the following four basic rights *before* questioning:

- The suspect's right to remain silent
- The right of the police to use in a court of law any statement made by the suspect
- The suspect's right to have an attorney present during questioning
- The suspect's right to have a court-appointed attorney before questioning if he or she cannot afford one

Another landmark decision was handed down in 1968 in *Terry v Ohio*. This case established the right of police officers to stop and question a person to investigate suspicious behavior and to frisk that person if the officer has reason to believe the person is armed:

> The police have the authority to detain a person for questioning even without probable cause to believe that the person has committed a crime. Such an investigatory stop does not constitute an arrest and is permissible when prompted by both the observation of unusual conduct leading to a reasonable suspicion that criminal activity may be afoot and the ability to point to specific and articulable facts to justify the suspicion. Subsequently, an officer may frisk a person if the officer reasonably suspects that he or she is in danger.

Other Problems and Challenges during the Progressive Era Despite this decision, reported crime increased and the public's fear of crime intensified. An influx of immigrants added to the problems of major cities. The deinstitutionalizing of mental patients in the 1970s brought thousands of mentally disabled individuals into the mainstream of the United States, often without means to support themselves. This, coupled with the return of many Vietnam veterans who found it difficult to reenter society, resulted in a large homeless population.

Another challenge to the effectiveness of the professional model was the Kansas City Preventive Patrol Study. This classic study found that increasing or decreasing pre ventive patrol efforts had no significant effect on crime, citizen fear of crime, community attitudes toward the police, police response time or traffic accidents. As Klockars (1983, p.130) notes: "It makes about as much sense to have police patrol routinely in cars to fight crime as it does to have firemen patrol routinely in fire trucks to fight fire."

Many law enforcement officials view the Kansas City Preventive Patrol Study as the beginning of a new era in policing. It was considered by police as the first experimental design used in policing and, as such, was a landmark. It set the stage for further research in policing and is viewed as the first true movement in the professionalization of policing. Its findings are also controversial. There were real problems with the research design and implementation of this study; however, it called into question many assumptions about policing. It concluded what many police officials already knew but did not want publicized for fear of the impact on police budgets. Other research conducted in the 1970s also questioned police effectiveness:

> Research about preventive patrol, rapid response to calls for service, and investigative work—the three mainstays of police tactics—was uniformly discouraging.
>
> Research demonstrated that preventive patrol in automobiles had little effect on crime, citizen levels of fear, or citizen satisfaction with police. Rapid response

> to calls for service likewise had little impact on arrests, citizen satisfaction with police, or levels of citizen fear. Also, research into criminal investigation effectiveness suggested that detective units were so poorly administered that they had little chance of being effective (Kelling, 1988, p.4).

By the mid-1970s the general period of reform in policing in the United States slowed. Many promising reforms, such as team policing, had not caused any major changes. (Chapter 5 discusses team policing and its demise.) The reform movement was called into question by two articles: Herman Goldstein's "Problem-Oriented Policing" article in 1979 and James Q. Wilson and George L. Kelling's "Broken Windows" article in 1982.

Other reasons for reevaluating police methods were the changing nature of the people who became police and their frustration with the traditional role of the patrol officer. Although patrol was given lip service as the backbone of policing, it was seen as the least desirable assignment. A change was needed at the patrol level to attract more highly educated and less militaristic recruits. The patrol officer had to become important to the department in accomplishing its mission.

Finally, many businesses and individuals began to hire private security officers to ensure their safety. The public assumed that the police alone were unable to "preserve the peace." While some called for greater cooperation between public and private policing, others argued that the public should collaborate with all policing efforts.

A combination of the dissatisfaction with criminal justice and the role of patrol officers, research results, the trend toward private policing and the writings of Goldstein and Wilson and Kelling led to the third era of policing—the community era.

The Community Era (1980 to Present)

In the 1980s many police departments began experimenting with more community involvement in the "war on crime." Also during this decade several cities tested Goldstein's problem-oriented approach to policing. The emphasis in many departments began to shift from crime fighting to crime prevention.

According to some historians, the community era had its roots in the Kerner Commission Report, released in February 1968 by the President's National Advisory Committee on Civil Disorder. The report condemned racism in the United States and called for aid to black communities to avert further racial polarization and violence.

Gradually law enforcement has become more responsive to the public's desire for a different kind of policing. Today there is considerable citizen–police interaction and problem solving. Although still resistant to change, police agencies are now more likely to respond to the needs and wishes of the communities they serve. The significant changes in the way police address sexual assault, domestic violence, sexual abuse of children, drunk driving and missing children attest to this new responsiveness. The public wants the police to be proactive; citizens want police to try to prevent crime in addition to apprehending criminals after they have committed a crime.

> During the community era the police sought to reestablish a close relationship with the community.

Highlights of the three eras of policing are summarized in Table 1.1.

Table 1.1 The Three Eras of Policing

	Political Era 1840s to 1930s	*Reform Era 1930s to 1980s*	*Community Era 1980s to Present*
Authorization	politics and law	law and professionalism	community support (political), law and professionalism
Function	broad social services	crime control	broad provision of services
Organizational design	decentralized	centralized, classical	decentralized, task forces, matrices
Relationship to community	intimate	professional, remote	intimate
Tactics and technology	foot patrol	preventive patrol and rapid response to calls	foot patrol, problem solving, public relations
Outcome	citizen, political satisfaction	crime control	quality of life and citizen satisfaction

SOURCE: Summarized from George L. Kelling and Mark H. Moore. "From Political to Reform to Community: The Evolving Strategy of Police." In *Community Policing: Rhetoric or Reality,* edited by Jack R. Greene and Stephen D. Mastrofski. New York: Praeger Publishers, 1991, pp.6, 14–15, 22–23.

The community era is referred to by many names: community policing, community-oriented policing (COP), neighborhood policing and the like. Currently the term **community policing** is most commonly used. At the heart of most "new" approaches to policing is a return to the ancient idea of community responsibility for the welfare of society—police officers become a part of the community, not apart from it. A comparison of traditional policing and community policing is made in Table 1.2.

Although community policing is considered innovative, one of its central tenets of involvement with and responsiveness to the community is similar to the principles set forth by Sir Robert Peel in 1829 when he established the London Metropolitan Police and stated: "The police are the public and the public are the police." Policing has strayed so far from these principles in the past century that the concepts central to community policing seem fresh and sensible today.

Community Policing Defined

Whereas traditionally policing has been **reactive,** responding to calls for service, community policing is **proactive,** anticipating problems and seeking solutions to them. The term *proactive* is beginning to take on an expanded definition. Not only is it taking on the meaning of anticipating problems, but it is also taking on the Stephen Covey slant, that of accountability and choosing a response rather than reacting the same way each time a similar situation occurs. Police are learning that they do not obtain different results by applying the same methods. In other words, to get different results, different tactic are needed. This is the focus of Chapter 4.

According to Frazier (2000, p.1): "Community-oriented policing is proactive, solution-based, and community driven. It occurs when a law enforcement agency and law-abiding citizens work together to do four things:

- Arrest offenders
- Prevent crime

Table 1.2 Comparison of Traditional Policing and Community Policing

Question	*Traditional Policing*	*Community Policing*
Who are the police?	A government agency principally responsible for law enforcement.	Police are the public and the public are the police: the police officers are those who are paid to give full-time attention to the duties of every citizen.
What is the relationship of the police force to other public service departments?	Priorities often conflict.	The police are one department among many responsible for improving the quality of life.
What is the role of the police?	Focusing on solving crimes.	A broader problem-solving approach.
How is police efficiency measured?	By detection and arrest rates.	By the absence of crime and disorder.
What are the highest priorities?	Crimes that are high value (e.g., bank robberies) and those involving violence.	Whatever problems disturb the community most.
What, specifically, do police deal with?	Incidents.	Citizens' problems and concerns.
What determines the effectiveness of police?	Response times.	Public cooperation.
What view do police take of service calls?	Deal with them only if there is no real police work to do.	Vital function and great opportunity.
What is police professionalism?	Swift, effective response to serious crime.	Keeping close to the community.
What kind of intelligence is most important?	Crime intelligence (study of particular crimes or series of crimes).	Criminal intelligence (information about the activities of individuals or groups).
What is the essential nature of police accountability?	Highly centralized; governed by rules, regulations and policy directives; accountable to the law.	Emphasis on local accountability to community needs.
What is the role of headquarters?	To provide the necessary rules and policy directives.	To preach organizational values.
What is the role of the press liaison department?	To keep the "heat" off operational officers so they can get on with the job.	To coordinate an essential channel of communication with the community.
How do the police regard prosecutions?	As an important goal.	As one tool among many.

SOURCE: Malcolm K. Sparrow. *Implementing Community Policing.* U.S. Department of Justice, National Institute of Justice. November 1988, pp.8–9.

- Solve ongoing problems and
- Improve the overall quality of life"

The Upper Midwest Community Policing Institute (UMCPI) provides this definition: "Community policing is an organization-wide philosophy and management approach that promotes community, government and police partnerships; proactive problem solving; and community engagement to address the causes of crime, fear of crime and other community issues."

Community policing is a philosophy that emphasizes working proactively with citizens to reduce fear, solve crime-related problems and prevent crime.

McCarthy (n.d., p.1), a community policing officer for the Braintree Police Department, says: "Community policing is a collaborative effort between the police and the community that identifies problems of crime and disorder and involves the community in the search for solutions. It is founded on close, mutually beneficial ties between police and community members."

As Kelling (1994) points out: "Whether one calls community policing a philosophy, a strategy, a model, or a paradigm, it is a complex set of ideas that simply cannot be put into a simple one-sentence definition that will encompass all three elements to everyone's satisfaction."

Running through these definitions are two basic themes: police–community partnerships and a proactive, problem-solving approach to the police function.

These two themes are also incorporated throughout this text.

Some criminologists go beyond defining community policing to describe its key features as well as its essential elements.

Features of Community Policing

Trojanowicz and Bucqueroux (1994, pp.131–132) state what they perceive to be the goal of community policing as solving problems—improved relations with citizens is a welcome by-product. Several major features associated with it are regular contact between officers and citizens; a department-wide philosophy and department-wide acceptance; internal and external influence and respect for officers; well-defined role including both proactive and reactive policing—a full-service officer; direct service—the same officer takes complaints and gives crime prevention tips; citizens identify problems and cooperate in setting up the police agenda; police accountability is ensured by the citizens receiving the service in addition to administrative mechanisms; the officer is the leader and catalyst for change in the neighborhood to reduce fear, disorder, decay and crime.

The chief of police is an advocate and sets the tone for the delivery of both law enforcement and social services in the jurisdictions. Officers educate the public about issues (like response time or preventive patrol) and the need to prioritize services. Increased trust between the police officer and citizens because of long-term, regular contact results in an enhanced flow of information to the police. The officer is continually accessible in person, by telephone or in a decentralized office with regular visibility in the neighborhood.

Officers are viewed as having a stake in the community. They are role models because of regular contact with citizens (especially youth role models). Influence is from the bottom up—citizens receiving service help set priorities and influence police policy, meaningful organizational change and departmental restructuring—ranging from officer selection to training, evaluation and promotion. When intervention is necessary, informal social control is the first choice. Officers encourage citizens to solve many of their own problems and volunteer to assist neighbors. Officers encourage other service providers like animal control, firefighters and mail carriers to become involved in community problem solving. Officers mobilize all community resources, including citizens, private and public agencies and private businesses. Success is determined by a reduction in citizen fear, neighborhood disorder and crime.

Identification and awareness of these features has allowed law enforcement departments nationwide to implement the principles and philosophy of community policing. In fact, community policing has come a long way since publication of the first edition of this text in 1994. Frazier (p.2) notes that currently 87% of the country is served by a department that practices community policing. In addition, a national network of 28 regional community policing institutes and the Community Policing Consortium (comprised of IACP, NOBLE, PERF, NSA and the Police Foundation) has trained over 100,000 law enforcement personnel and community members in the principles of community policing.

Four Essential Elements of Community Policing

Cordner (1999, p.137) suggests: "It [community policing] started out as a fuzzy notion about increasing police–citizen contact and reducing fear of crime, then settled into a period during which it was seen as having two primary components—problem solving and community engagement." He provides a framework consisting of four dimensions for viewing community policing and determining whether the essential elements are in place.

Four dimensions of community policing are the philosophical, strategic, tactical and organizational dimensions.

The Philosophical Dimension

Many advocates of community policing stress that it is a philosophy rather than a program; and it does have that important dimension. The three important elements within this dimension are citizen input, a broadened function and personalized service. Cordner (p.138) contends that citizen input meshes well with an agency that "is part of a government 'of the people, for the people, and by the people.' " A broadened police function means expanding responsibility into areas such as order maintenance and social services, as well as protecting and enhancing the lives of our most vulnerable citizens: juveniles, the elderly, minorities, the disabled, the poor and the homeless. The personal service element supports tailored policing based on local norms and values as well as on individual needs.

The Strategic Dimension

A philosophy without means of putting it into practice is an empty shell. This is where the strategic dimension comes in. This dimension "includes the key operational concepts that translate philosophy into action" (Cordner, p.139). The three strategic elements of community policing are reoriented operations, a geographic focus and a prevention emphasis.

The reorientation in operations shifts reliance on the squad car to emphasis on face-to-face interactions. It may also include differential calls for service. The geographic focus changes patrol officers' basic unit of accountability from time of day to location. Officers are given permanent assignments so they can get to know the citizens within their area. Finally, the prevention emphasis is proactive, seeking to raise the status of prevention/patrol officers to the level traditionally enjoyed by detectives.

The Tactical Dimension

The tactical dimension translates the philosophical and strategic dimensions into concrete programs and practices. The most important tactical elements, according to Cordner, are positive interactions, partnerships and problem solving. Officers are encouraged to get out of their vehicles and initiate positive interactions with the citizens within their beat. They are also encouraged to seek out opportunities to partner with organizations and agencies and to mediate between those with conflicting interests, for example, landlords and tenants, adults and juveniles. The third essential element, problem solving rather than responding to isolated incidents, is the focus of Chapter 4.

The Organizational Dimension

Cordner's fourth dimension, the organizational dimension, is discussed in Chapter 5.

Other Views of the Elements of Community Policing

Maguire and Mastrofski (2000) examined the dimensionality of the community policing movement and found that the number of dimensions underlying the community policing movement varied significantly according to the source of the data:

- Skolnick and Bayley (1988) described the four recurring elements of community policing found internationally: community-based crime prevention, reorientation of patrol activities, increased police accountability and decentralization of command.
- Bayley (1994) defined community policing using four dimensions: consultation, adaptation, mobilization and problem solving.
- Bratton (1996) defined community policing as the three p's: partnership, problem solving and prevention.
- Rohe, Adams, Arcury, Memory and Klopovic (1996) use three dimensions separating community policing from traditional policing: shared responsibility, prevention and increased officer discretion.
- Roth and Johnson operationalized community as articulated by the COPS office using four dimensions: problem solving, community partnership building, preventive interventions and organizational change.
- Maguire and Katz used four additive community policing indices measuring patrol officer activities, management activities, citizen activities and organizational activities.

- Maguire, Uchida, Huhns and Cox (1999) used a three-dimensional model of community policing: adaptation, problem solving and community interaction and engagement.

Clearly, just as there is no one definition of community policing that will satisfy everyone, there is no one way to look at how community policing is viewed in practice. In addition, the evolution of community policing itself should be considered.

The Three Generations of Community Policing

Oliver (2000) contends that community policing has become the "paradigm of contemporary policing, evolving significantly over the past 20 years." He (p.367) notes: "That which was called community policing in the late 1970s and early 1980s only somewhat resembles community policing as it is practiced today." Oliver describes three generations of community policing.

The three generations of community policing are innovation, diffusion and institutionalization.

First Generation: Innovation (1979 through 1986)

The innovation generation also marked the beginning of the community era previously described. Influences on this first generation have been described: Goldstein's focus on problem solving coupled with Wilson and Kelling's broken window theory. Says Oliver (p.375): "The innovation stage of community policing was primarily characterized by a few isolated experiments in a small number of major metropolitan areas across the United States that were testing specific methods of community policing, generally in a small number of urban neighborhoods."

Second Generation: Diffusion (1987 through 1994)

As the experiments in community policing showed indications of success, the concepts and philosophy of community policing began to spread among American police departments. According to Oliver (p.376): "Community policing during the diffusion generation was largely organized through various programs that consisted of newly created units or extensions of previously existing organizational units." A good example of such programs was Baltimore County, Maryland's, Citizen Oriented Police Enforcement (COPE) program.

Third Generation: Institutionalization (1995 to Present)

Says Oliver (p.378): "This specific term [institutionalization] is used to denote the fact that community policing has seen widespread implementation across the United States and has become the most common form of organizing police services." In September 1994, President Clinton signed into law the Violent Crime Control and Law Enforcement Act, allocating almost $9 billion to hire, equip and train 100,000 police officers in community policing. The Office of Community Oriented Policing Services (COPS) was created and began funneling grant money to state and local law enforcement agencies. Through the already existing community Policing Consortium and newly created Regional Community Policing Institutes (RCPIs), training on Community policing became available for agencies throughout the country.

Researchers Zhao et al. (2003) examined changes in law enforcement organizational priorities related to three core functions of policing—crime control, the maintenance of order and the provision of services—during the era of community policing. They analyzed the changes by using data from three national surveys of more than 200 municipal police departments conducted in 1993, 1996 and 2000. They found that police core-function priorities remained largely unchanged, but that the systematic implementation of COP programs reflects an all-out effort to address all three core functions at a higher level achievement. They (p.716) conclude: "Our analysis showed that the extent of implementation of COP is a statistically significant predictor of all core functions of policing. On the basis of the analysis presented here, we argue that COP can be characterized as a comprehensive effort by local police simultaneously to control crime, to reduce social disorder and to provide services to the citizenry." A basic difference, however, is that they no longer seek to do it alone, but rather through partnerships and problem solving.

SUMMARY

"Modern" policing began with the formation of the London Metropolitan Police, based on principles set forth by Sir Robert Peel. His principles emphasized the interdependence of the police and the public as well as the prevention of crime and disorder.

Policing in the United States has had three distinct paradigm shifts or eras: political, reform and community. During the political era the police sought an intimate relationship with the community. During the reform era the relationship was professionally remote. During the community era the relationship was again perceived to be intimate.

During the 1960s and 1970s relations between the police and the public were extremely strained. In an effort to improve relations, many police departments instituted public-relations programs whose goal was to improve the image of the police. Many departments also began crime prevention programs that enlisted the aid of citizens, including programs such as Operation Identification, neighborhood or block watches and home- and automobile-security programs.

Community policing is a philosophy that emphasizes working with citizens to reduce fear, solve crime-related problems and prevent crime. Two basic themes consistent in the various definitions of community policing are police–community collaboration and a problem-solving approach to the police function. Four dimensions of community policing are the philosophical, strategic, tactical and organizational dimensions. The three generations of community policing are innovation, diffusion and institutionalization.

Discussion Questions

1. From the perspective of law enforcement, what are the strengths and weaknesses of each of the three eras of policing? Answer this question from the perspective of a citizen.
2. What lessons should community policing advocates learn from history?
3. Are any community policing strategies being used in your community? If so, which ones?
4. What advantages does community policing offer? Disadvantages?
5. How is the relationship between the police and the public typically portrayed in popular television programs and movies? In the news media?
6. How might the historical role of the police in enforcing slavery in the South and later segregation contribute to present-day police-minority relations?
7. Can you see any evidence of the patronage or spoils system of policing in the twenty-first century?
8. What is the relationship of community policing and problem-solving policing?
9. Is community policing being implemented in law enforcement agencies in the United States and to what extent?
10. Have you witnessed any examples of the "thin blue line"?

InfoTrac® College Edition Assignments

- Use InfoTrac College Edition to help answer the Discussion Questions when appropriate.
- Find an article on community policing and outline it. Be prepared to discuss your reaction to the article with the class.
- Read and outline the encyclopedia selection on Sir Robert Peel OR read and outline the article on the "thin blue line."
- Search community relations and pick one selection that relates directly to community policing.

Community Project

Individually or in a self-formed group, visit your local police department to obtain any printed material they have on community policing.

References

Asirvatham, Sandy. "Good Cop, Bad Cop." *Baltimore City Paper,* May 2000.

Barry, Daniel Patrick. *Handling Police Misconduct in an Ethical Way.* Unpublished Thesis, University of Nevada, Las Vegas, December 1999.

Brown, Jim. "Community Policing: Reality Check." *Law and Order,* April 2001, pp.55–58.

Burger, Warren E. "Introduction." *The Bench & Bar of Minnesota,* May/June 1991, p.26.

Central Missouri State University. *August Vollmer.* http://www.cmsu.edu/cj/august.htm

Central Missouri State University. *O. W. Wilson.* http://www.cmsu.edu/cj/o_w.htm

Cordner, Gary W. "The Elements of Community Policing." In *Policing Perspectives: An Anthology,* edited by Larry K. Gaines and Gary W. Cordner. Los Angeles: Roxbury Publishing Company, 1999, pp.137–149.

Dulaney, W. Marvin. *Black Police in America.* Bloomington, IN: Indiana University Press, 1996.

Foner, P. S. *History of Black Americans: From Africa to the Emergence of the Cotton Kingdom.* Westport, CT: Greenwood, 1975.

Frazier, Thomas C. "Director's Notes: A Definition of Community Policing." Washington, DC: Office of Community Oriented Policing Services, April 2000.

Garmire, Bernard L., ed. *Local Government Police Management.* Mimeographed. Published by the International City Management Association, *Law and Order,* August 1989.

Gehrand, Keith. "University Policing and the Community." *Law and Order,* December 2000, pp.111–117.

Hickman, Matthew J. and Reaves, Brian A. *Local Police Departments, 2000.* Washington, DC: Bureau of Justice Statistics, January 2003a. (NCJ 196002)

Hickman, Matthew J. and Reaves, Brian A. *Sheriffs' Offices, 2000.* Washington, DC: Bureau of Justice Statistics, January 2003b. (NCJ 196534)

Kelling, George L. "Police and Communities: The Quiet Revolution." *Perspectives on Policing,* June 1988.

Kelling, George L. "Defining Community Policing." *Subject to Debate,* April 1994, p.3.

Kelling, George L. and Moore, Mark H. "From Political to Reform to Community: The Evolving Strategy of Police." In *Community Policing: Rhetoric or Reality,* edited by Jack R. Greene and Stephen D. Mastrofski. New York: Praeger Publishers, 1991, pp.3–25.

Klockars, Carl B. *Thinking about Police: Contemporary Readings.* New York: McGraw-Hill, 1983.

Maguire, Edward R. and Mastrofski, Stephen D. "Patterns of Community Policing in the United States." *Police Quarterly,* March 2000, pp.4–45.

McCarthy, John. "Definition of Community Policing." Braintree Police Department Home Page, no date.

National Commission on Law Observance and Enforcement. *Report on Lawlessness in Law Enforcement.* Washington, DC: Government Printing Office, 1931.

Oliver, Willard M. "The Third Generation of Community Policing: Moving through Innovation, Diffusion and Institutionalization." *Police Quarterly,* December 2000, pp.367–388.

Reichel, Philip L. "Southern Slave Patrols as a Transitional Police Type." In *Policing Perspectives: An Anthology,* edited by Larry K. Gaines and Gary W. Cordner. Los Angeles: Roxbury Publishing Company, 1999, pp.79–92.

Richardson, J. F. *The New York Police.* New York: Oxford University Press, 1970.

Simmons, R. C. *The American Colonies.* New York: McKay, 1976.

Trojanowicz, Robert and Bucqueroux, Bonnie. *Community Policing.* Cincinnati: Anderson, 1994.

Understanding Community Policing: A Framework for Action. Washington, DC: Bureau of Justice Assistance, August 1994.

Walker, Samuel. *Popular Justice: A History of American Criminal Justice,* 2nd ed. New York: Oxford University Press, 1997.

Wrobleski, Henry M. and Hess, Kären M. *An Introduction to Law Enforcement and Criminal Justice,* 7th ed. Belmont, CA: Wadsworth Thomson Learning, 2003.

Zhao, Jhong "Solomon"; He Ni; and Lovrich, Nicholas P. "Community Policing: Did It Change the Basic Functions of Policing in the 1990s? A National Follow-Up Study." *Justice Quarterly,* December 2003, pp.697–724.

CHAPTER 2

Inside Police Agencies: Understanding Mission and Culture

The strength of a democracy and the quality of life enjoyed by its citizens are determined in large measure by the ability of the police to discharge their duties.

—Herman Goldstein

DO YOU KNOW?

- What a mission statement is?
- What police spend the majority of their time doing?
- How the makeup of the police force has changed in recent years?
- What characteristics are attributed to the police subculture?
- Where the police image comes from?
- What a negative contact is?
- What the public expects of the police?
- What dilemma faces law enforcement?
- When agencies or officers exercise discretion?
- How discretion fits into the community policing philosophy?
- What three ethics checks are?

CAN YOU DEFINE?

discretion
mission statement
negative contacts
911 policing
police culture
selective enforcement

Introduction

Although "police officers" are the professionals discussed in this chapter, the concepts reviewed apply equally to those with different titles such as deputies or sheriffs. Although this chapter focuses on police officers as professionals, always remember that police officers are first and foremost people. They are sons, daughters, mothers, fathers, brothers, sisters, aunts, uncles, neighbors and friends. They may belong to community organizations, attend local churches and be active in politics. Their individual attributes greatly influence who they are as police officers.

This chapter begins by discussing why we have police and how this is expressed through mission statements including the two sometimes conflicting roles of law enforcement and service to the public. Next the chapter describes who the police are and some characteristics of their culture. This is followed by a discussion of the police image and public expectations of the police. Then the role of police discretion and use of force are discussed. The chapter concludes with an examination of ethics and policing.

The Police Mission

Why do most law enforcement agencies exist? What is their mission? The answer is obvious to those who say the purpose is to catch "bad guys." Others believe the purpose is

A sign at a community policing mini-station in Dearborn, Michigan, spells the word Police *in English and Arabic. Dearborn is home to the largest Arabic community outside the Middle East.*

to prevent crime, maintain order or protect the public. There are those who believe writing out a mission statement is baloney because it is just words. As one police chief said in response to the question, what is your mission statement: "Look at our badge. It says it." Nonetheless, articulating the reason for an agency's existence helps its members focus on the same goals and determine how to accomplish their purpose.

A **mission statement** is a written declaration of purpose.

A mission statement is a "road map" that delineates how an agency will arrive at a desired destination. Without it, a law enforcement agency can wander, appearing inconsistent, inefficient and purposeless. The mission statement defines what the agency's commitment is to the community it serves and how it views its relationship with the community. A mission statement can reveal rather accurately the state of police–community relations. The importance of mission statements is summarized quite eloquently by Lewis Carroll's Cheshire cat in *Alice in Wonderland:* "If you don't know where you're going, it doesn't matter which way you go."

A mission statement can also focus a police department's energies and resources. Will the department continue to be reactive and focused on fighting crimes that have already occurred or proactive, focused on identifying problems and attacking them? As Wilson and Kelling (1989, p.49) note, a community-oriented policing philosophy requires redefining the police mission: "To help the police become accustomed to fixing broken windows as well as arresting window-breakers requires doing things that are very hard for many administrators to do." Consider the following mission statement of the Aurora (Illinois) Police Department:

> We, the Aurora Police Department, exist to serve all people within our jurisdiction with respect, fairness and compassion. We are committed to the prevention of crime and the protection of life and property; the preservation of peace, order and safety; the enforcement of laws and ordinances; and the safeguarding of constitutional guarantees.
>
> With community service as our foundation, we are driven by goals to enhance the quality of life, investigating problems as well as incidents, seeking solutions and fostering a sense of security in communities and individuals. We nurture public trust by holding ourselves to the highest standards of performance and ethics.
>
> To fulfill its mission, the Aurora Police Department is dedicated to providing a quality of work environment and the development of its members through effective training and leadership.

The mission statement of the Los Angeles Police Department is much shorter, but similar in meaning:

> It is the mission of the Los Angeles Police Department to safeguard the lives and property of the people we serve, to reduce the incidence and fear of crime, and to enhance public safety while working with the diverse communities to improve their quality of life. Our mandate is to do so with honor and integrity, while at all times conducting ourselves with the highest ethical standards to maintain public confidence (www.LAPDonline.org).

How are mission statements developed? A committee, composed of members of the community and police officers, assesses various police functions. Why would a law enforcement agency include input from the community when it develops its mission statement? Community input improves police–community relations and increases the likelihood of an agency accomplishing its missions.

The public identifies the services it expects from its police department. If those expectations go unmet, the department generally suffers loss of financing and political support as well as increased interference in day-to-day operations.

Developing a mission statement that reflects an agency's commitment to the community it serves can be the vehicle to positive, meaningful police–community relations as well as to a more effective police department. This mission statement in large part determines where the agency places its priorities.

Some departments also develop a vision statement, which is more philosophical and embodies the spirit of the department. The Fresno Police Department has the following vision statement: "We will be a model law enforcement agency, nationally accredited, and viewed internally and externally as professional, enthusiastic and trustworthy. We are committed to rewarding our employees for creativity, hard work and being responsive to the needs of our community. We will treat our employees and our citizens with dignity and respect, continually striving to meet their needs. We will operate with fiscal prudence as we effectively manage our resources, while providing the highest level of service and protection to our citizens. The mission of the Fresno police department is to provide a professional, effective and timely response to crime and disorder in our community" (Fresno PD Web site).

From the preceding examples, it is clear that such statements require thought and reflect how a department views itself. Closely related to the mission statement are the goals and objectives set by a department. Programs emphasizing a service philosophy may not sit well with some police officers. For example, in one police department, its Neighborhood-Oriented Policing (NOP) program was perceived as more social work than police work and was referred to as "Nobody on Patrol." To avoid such perceptions, top management should emphasize that the community policing philosophy enhances their ability to detect and apprehend law violators. In fact, community policing is tougher on crime than traditional policing because it relies on citizens helping the police and sharing responsibility for their neighborhood.

Fighting Crime versus Service to the Public

Police departments are often divided on whether their emphasis should be proactive or reactive. Every department will have officers who are incident oriented (reactive) and believe their mission is to do 911 **policing.** That is, they are incident driven—reactive—and may speak disparagingly of the community policing officers as social workers.

Is the best police officer the one who catches the most "bad guys"? Certainly police departments will continue to apprehend the "bad guys." The crimes they target may, however, contribute to negative police–community relations. The police usually focus on certain kinds of crime, particularly common crimes such as burglary, robbery, assault and auto theft. The police expect that offenders who commit these crimes might flee or try to avoid arrest in some other way. Police may need to use force to bring offenders to justice.

Police officers generally do not enforce white-collar crimes. They would not, for example, investigate or arrest a businessperson for insider trading, price fixing or cheating on income taxes. White-collar crime involves those who are in business, the professions or public life—those who tend to be relatively well-to-do, powerful people.

Common crimes can conceivably be committed by anyone, rich or poor. The vast majority of these crimes, however, are committed by those from society's lowest socioeconomic level. Those at or near the poverty level include the majority of our minority populations.

As Klockars (1985, p.57) notes, since the police officers' domain is the streets: "Those people who spend their time on the street will receive a disproportionate amount of police attention . . . particularly people who are too poor to have backyards, country clubs, summer homes, automobiles, air conditioning, or other advantages that are likely to take them out of the patrolman's sight."

These facts contribute to the impression that the police are focused solely on the kind of crime poor people and minorities commit, hence, the impression that they are hostile to those who are poor or members of minority groups. This negative impression does little to foster good community relations.

Police work involves much more than catching criminals. It is a complex, demanding job requiring a wide range of abilities. Studies suggest that 80 percent of police officers' time is spent on nonenforcement activities. The vast majority of the problems police attend to are in response to citizen requests for service.

The majority of police actions have nothing to do with criminal law enforcement but involve service to the community.

Service to the community includes peacekeeping; preventing suicides; looking for lost or runaway children or vulnerable adults; protecting children and other vulnerable people; maintaining public safety; assisting motorists with disabled vehicles; dealing with emergencies and crisis situations, such as vehicle crashes and natural disasters; delivering death notifications; resolving conflicts; preventing crime; and educating the public.

Rowell (2000, p.1) suggests that community policing officers view citizens as clients because these officers have both protector and servant roles. Defining exactly what police work entails is almost impossible. Most would agree, however, that people have always called the police for help. They call not only about criminal matters but also about a variety of situations where they perceive a need for government intervention. The police respond to such calls and usually take whatever action is needed. It has been said that the police are the only social-service agency available 24/7, and they make house calls.

Neighborhood Cops or Special Ops?

The proactive or reactive controversy can be seen in the parallel development of two contradictory models in policing in the last decade: community-oriented policing (COP) and special weapons and tactics (SWAT) teams.

Robinson (2000, p.14) notes that COP grew out of the public's dissatisfaction with police forces seen as "occupying armies" rather than public servants. In contrast, SWAT teams were established in Los Angeles to control the riots of the 1960s. Such teams are by nature reactive. Since that time SWAT units have grown rapidly with the majority of departments serving cities with populations over 50,000 having paramilitary units.

The so-called militarization of local law enforcement is in part a consequence of efforts to combat a growing drug problem. In addition, as a result of 9/11, the public is more aware of the need for such units and funding is more readily available. Glick (2000, p.42) contends: "Despite critics' complaints that tactical teams are a threat to the nation itself, SWAT callouts are usually for defensive purposes and the majority end without a gun battle." SWAT teams should be viewed as a line of defense, not offense, suggests Glick. He (p.44) concludes: "They are peace officers—husbands and fathers, wives and mothers, and they are preparing for the unthinkable. One day they may be asked to rescue their own children, in addition to the lives of others, including suspects." A balance is certainly needed, however, between crime fighting and providing services to citizens.

Who Are the Police?

Traditionally, police officers have been a fairly homogeneous group: white, male, with a high school education and a military background. This has changed somewhat; police officers have become a more heterogeneous group, although police are still overwhelmingly white males.

> Today police departments have more minority and female officers. The educational level of the officers is much higher, and fewer have military experience. More officers are also as interested in helping people as they are in fighting crime.

Such changes in the makeup of the police force are fundamental to the community policing philosophy. As police departments become more representative of the communities they serve, they will be better able to understand the problems they must address. As officers become better educated, they will be better equipped to devise solutions to community problems. However, one impediment might be the existing police culture.

The Police Culture

Law enforcement agencies, not unlike most other organizations, develop a unique organizational **police culture** consisting of informal values, beliefs and expectations that is passed on to newcomers in the department. Adcox (2000, p.20) suggests: "This informal police culture exercises powerful influence over the conduct of employees separate from and sometimes at odds with the formal rules, regulations, procedures and role authority of managers." An agency's true culture is the behavior that occurs when supervisors or visitors are not present.

The police have tremendous power over the citizens they serve and protect as expressed at the Southwest Law Enforcement Academy in a commencement address by Walls (2003, p.17): "Two hundred and twenty-six years ago our ancestors fought the entire overwhelming might of the British empire at seemingly insurmountable odds for freedom of speech, of religion, of assembly; for freedom from unreasonable searches and seizures; and for all of the other 'freedoms' implied or mentioned in the Constitution. In American society, nothing is more sacred to us than our freedom. And, in an American society, only one segment of that society is given the authority, the power and the responsibility to take that freedom away—the police. So, I say to you today that there is *no greater responsibility* than to be entrusted with the freedom of an entire free society."

In addition, police may face a life-threatening situation at any time. Their lives may depend on each other. They experience situations others would not be likely to understand. As a result, they have developed their own culture or value system. According to Goldstein (1990, pp.29–30):

> The strength of the subculture grows out of the peculiar characteristics and conflicting pressures of the job: the ever-present physical danger; the hostility directed at the police because of their controlling role; the vulnerability of police officers to allegations of wrongdoing; unreasonable demands and conflicting expectations; uncertainty as to the function and authority of officers; a prevalent feeling that the public does not really understand what the police have to "put up with" in dealing with citizens; a stifling working environment; the dependence that officers place on each other to get the job done and to provide for their personal safety; and the shared sense of awareness, within a police department, that it is not always possible to act in ways in which the public would expect one to act.

The police culture has been characterized as clannish, secretive and isolated. As McErlain (2001, p.87) suggests: "A 'Code of Silence' exists today in the law enforcement profession. Those who would suggest that some law enforcement officers today no longer hide behind the banner of loyalty are either naïve or concealing reality, contributing to the problem and enabling others to do the same." He notes: "Some progress has been made in tearing down this age-old problem, but in many ways a police culture that exalts loyalty over integrity still exists."

Ferrell (2003, p.9), however, looked at internal affairs investigation in the Houston Police Department from 1992 to 2002 and found that in seven of the eleven years examined, more than 50 percent of all the complaints investigated were generated by internal officer complaints as opposed to external citizen complaints. He also reports that statistics from 15 departments from among the nation's 50 largest cities showed similar results. He concludes: "These statistics would tend to indicate that the blue wall or code of silence exits only in the minds of the Hollywood movie directors."

Trautman (2001, p.68) reports on a study conducted by the National Institute of Ethics (NIE) which asked 3,714 officers and recruits from throughout the country to provide insight about the "most secret element of any profession: direct participation in the code of silence." Of the 1,116 officers who participated (42 percent), 532 or 46 percent said they had witnessed misconduct by another employee but had not taken action. Of these officers, 47 percent said they had felt pressure to take part in the code of silence from the officers who committed the misconduct.

A culture also involves core beliefs held in common. Such beliefs in the police culture may include the following:

- Police are the only real crime fighters.
- No one understands them or what police work is all about.
- They owe 100 percent loyalty to other officers.
- They must often bend the rules to win the war against criminals because the courts have given criminals too many civil rights.
- The public is unappreciative and quick to criticize.
- Patrol is the worst assignment.

In addition, police work is often unpleasant. Police often have to deal with ugly situations and antisocial behavior. Police are lied to, spit upon and sworn at. They see unspeakable atrocities. Because of their shared experiences and unique exposure to their community, many police officers develop negative characteristics as coping mechanisms.

Conventional wisdom holds that two dominant characteristics of the police culture are isolation and a "them-versus-us" worldview.

Such isolation and "them-versus-us" worldview conflict with a community-oriented philosophy of policing. As communities move toward a return to foot patrol and an emphasis on improving police–community relations, police isolation and their worldview are likely to change.

Paoline et al. (2000, pp.578–579) describe other aspects of the "conventional wisdom" surrounding police culture:

- Officers cope with the danger and uncertainty of their occupational environment by being *suspicious* and *maintaining the edge.*
- Officers cope with the organizational environment by taking a *lay-low* or *cover-your-ass* attitude and adopting a *crimefighter* or *law-enforcement* orientation. . . . Thus the police culture stresses law enforcement or "real" police work over order-maintenance or service roles.
- The problems that officers confront in their working environment, as well as the coping mechanisms prescribed by the police culture, produce the defining characteristics of the police culture: *social isolation* and *group loyalty.*

Paoline et al. studied police culture in the Indianapolis, Indiana, and St. Petersburg, Florida, police departments and found that the conventional wisdom of police culture is overdrawn. They note that research now questions it more directly. They (p.601) report that many officers have significant attitudes and outlooks that vary from those of the traditional police culture. While almost all view law enforcement as an important responsibility and believe a good officer patrols aggressively, at the same time, many hold contradictory attitudes. For example, many do not consider law enforcement as their most important duty. Many also expressed at least some reservations about aggressive patrol. Most also accept responsibility for handling incidents of disorder and many to handling problematic conditions for which police executives only recently have assumed responsibility as a part of problem solving. Many officers also expressed confidence in being able to gain citizens' cooperation.

Having looked at how the police often see themselves, now focus on how the public often views the police.

The Police Image

How does the public view the police?

- The handsome, relatively realistic cops of *NYPD Blue* and *Homicide?*
- Unselfish, fearless heroes who protect the weak and innocent? Dirty Harrys?
- Hard-hearted, brutal oppressors of the underclass?
- Corrupt abusers of power, who become part of the criminal world?

Our society has varied images of law enforcement professionals. As noted in Chapter 1, that image is greatly affected by how the public perceives the criminal justice system within which the police function. Many Americans believe in an ideal justice system in which fairness and equality are guiding principles, truth and justice prevail, and the accused is innocent until proven guilty. Law enforcement professionals are part of this idealized vision; many view police officers and sheriff's deputies as unselfish, fearless, compassionate protectors of the weak and defenseless, who can uncover the truth, bring the guilty to justice and make things "right."

In contrast, others in our society see a criminal justice system that is neither fair nor just. Some individuals point out that the system employs officers who are overwhelmingly white, middle-class males. They also believe that some officers abuse their power and, in some cases, also abuse those with whom they come in contact in the line of duty.

The most recent Gallup Poll (2000), which rated the honesty and ethical standards of 45 occupations, ranked police officers eighth, tied with dentists, college teachers and engineers—very respectable company. The top seven rankings, in order, went to nurses, druggists/pharmacists, veterinarians, medical doctors, grade school and high school teachers, clergy and judges. As some might suspect, the lowest ranking went to car salesmen, preceded by telemarketers.

Sources of the Police Image

An individual's opinion of the police is based on many factors, possibly including television programs, movies, newspapers, magazines, books, the opinions of friends and family, level of education, neighborhood, economic status, disabilities, gender, minority group membership and, most important, contacts with the criminal justice system.

The police image is affected by individual backgrounds, the media and citizens' personal experiences with the criminal justice system.

The media can greatly impact public opinion. The police image is affected by the manner in which television and newspaper stories present crime and law enforcement activities. Improving police–media relations is the focus of Chapter 8.

An additional source of the police image is the folklore surrounding citizen interaction with police. People tend to embellish their contacts with the police. In addition, many stories people tell about contacts with the police are actually not theirs but a contact that a friend of a friend had. Unfortunately, few if any of these stories can be traced to their origin, but in the meantime, police end up with a negative image. Further, police seldom run in the same social circles where the stories are recounted and therefore have no means of defending themselves, their co-workers, their departments or their actions.

Yet another contributor is police work itself. Police officers are charged with some of society's most distasteful and dangerous tasks and are allowed to use reasonable force to affect arrests. They are even permitted, under strict circumstances, to use deadly force. This ability, however, creates a paradox for the police image—using force to achieve peace. Nonetheless, the nature of police work and the power they are legally permitted to use make the police extremely powerful and contribute to their image.

The police image is also shaped by appearance and police actions.

The police image is further affected by the police uniform and equipment. The uniform most police officers wear is a visible reminder of the authority and power bestowed upon them. In fact, officers know that the uniform plays a major part in their ability to gain cooperation and compliance from the public. Much of their authority comes simply from what they are wearing. People recognize and react to visible symbols of authority. According to Johnson (2001, p.27): "The crisp uniform of the police officer conveys power and authority. When officers put on their uniforms, citizens believe that they embody stereotypes about all police officers. Research has suggested that clothing has a powerful impact on how people perceive each other. The police officer's uniform has a profound psychological impact on others, and even slight alterations to the style of the uniform may change how citizens perceive them. . . . Citizens in the presence of a person in a police uniform cooperate more and curb their illegal or deviant behaviors." The uniform and its trappings—patches, badges, medals, mace, nightsticks, handcuffs and guns—can be overwhelmingly intimidating and can evoke negative public responses. Reflective sunglasses and handcuff or gun tie tacks can add to this negative image.

Officers' behavior also has a direct impact on their image. One behavior that may negatively affect the police image is accepting gratuities, no matter how small, such as free coffee.

The manner in which police exercise their authority also has an impact on the police image. The attitude of law enforcement officers, their education, their personal image of policing, discipline, professionalism and interaction with the community have enormous impact on the public's perception of the police.

Seemingly innocent and humorous police novelty items have caused major confrontations between police and the communities they serve. Some police product companies produce calendars, posters, T-shirts and mugs that support, encourage and make light of police brutality. Almost always meant to be humorous, the public may not share the same sense of humor. Such items can be immensely destructive to police–community relations. Particularly offensive examples include slogans such as "Brutality, the fun part of police work" and takeoffs on the Dirty Harry line, "Go ahead, make my day."

A few years ago a black suspect died in police custody as the result of a carotid hold applied by police officers during a struggle. In response to the black community's anger and concern, the chief of police issued an order prohibiting the carotid hold. Already in severe conflict with their chief over several other issues, two officers produced and sold T-shirts within the department that said, "Don't choke 'em, smoke 'em." The T-shirts went on sale the day of the suspect's funeral. It is not difficult to understand how destructive this was to the police image and community relations in that city as well as in other cities where the media reported these events.

In contrast to this unfortunate incident is the Hug-a-Bear Program that many departments now use. Plush teddy bears are used to calm traumatized children whom officers encounter in the course of fulfilling their duties. The bears, sometimes donated to the department by community organizations, are often carried in patrol cars and have been invaluable at accident scenes, in child-abuse situations and at the scene of fires. Programs such as this can reduce the effect of negative contacts people may have with the police.

Personal Contacts

Individual encounters with citizens most often determine the citizens' image of police work. One factor that contributes to a negative police image and difficulty in maintaining good community relations is what police commonly refer to as negative contacts.

Negative contacts are unpleasant interactions between the police and the public. They may or may not relate to criminal activity.

Although officers have many opportunities to assist citizens, much of what they must do causes people unhappiness. Many people have police contact only when something goes wrong in their lives. Citizens commonly interact with the police when they receive a traffic citation, have an illegally parked vehicle towed, have a loud party terminated, have been victimized, discuss a child who is in trouble with the law, have a domestic "disagreement" broken up, are arrested for driving while intoxicated (DWI) or some other offense, or receive a death notification. Many more possible scenarios in which citizens become angry or disillusioned occur daily because of the actions police officers must take to perform their duties.

For the most part, the police have no way to eliminate negative contacts and still perform their duties. A major challenge of law enforcement is to build good community relations despite the often adversarial nature of the job. The fact that many negative contacts take place between police and noncriminal individuals, the so-called average citizen, makes the task especially difficult.

More positive contacts are needed. For example, the Fremont (Nebraska) Police Department has put a new spin on the phrase "gotcha." In Fremont, officers observing young people doing something good (for example, wearing a bike helmet or picking up litter) give out tickets for soda pop and French fries at local fast-food restaurants. This works best for bike patrol officers. As one such officer said, "Young people have a totally different perception of police officers on bikes with their black shorts and yellow shirts" ("Rewarding Good Deeds," 2000, p.9).

Public Expectations

Otherwise law-abiding citizens who receive traffic tickets or who are arrested for DWI often believe they should be excused and that the police should concentrate on "real" criminals. Most police officers feel that citizens want the law enforced to the letter except when it comes to themselves.

The public commonly demands that the police crack down on crime, on drunk drivers and even on traffic violations. For many police departments, the majority of their complaints involve traffic problems. Citizens often demand that police enforce speed laws near their homes. Inevitably, when the police respond by issuing citations to violators, some of those who want the laws to be strictly enforced are ticketed; they often feel betrayed and angry. Somehow they see their own violation of the speed law as different from that of teenagers or "outsiders," and they feel they deserve a break. Most police officers have been asked, "Why don't you spend your time catching real criminals instead of picking on citizens?"

People expect the law to be enforced except when enforcement limits their own behavior.

Citizens become incensed when crime flourishes and hold the police responsible for combating crime. They hear it constantly referred to as a "war on crime" or "war on drugs," and since 9/11 a "war on terrorism," which demands an all-out attack by police on criminals and terrorists. Like American soldiers in Vietnam, however, the police are fighting a war they cannot win because it requires assuming social responsibilities that belong to politicians rather than to police.

The police are placed in the dilemma of being expected to win the wars on crime, drugs and terrorism but are given no control over the causes of these problems. The police cannot win these wars alone.

Klockars (1991, p.244) also holds this view:

> The fact is that the "war on crime" is a war police not only cannot win, but cannot in any real sense fight. They cannot win it because it is simply not within their power to change those things—such as unemployment, the age distribution

> of the population, moral education, freedom, civil liberties, ambitions, and the social and economic opportunities to realize them—that influence the amount of crime in any society. Moreover, any kind of real war on crime is something no democratic society would be prepared to let its police fight. We would simply be unwilling to tolerate the kind of abuses to the civil liberties of innocent citizens—to us—that fighting any kind of a real war on crime would inevitably involve.

In addition, when citizens have a problem, they expect the police to help resolve it. In fact, police sociologist Egon Bittner (1974) states that we have police for just that reason—because "something-ought-not-to-be-happening-about-which-something-ought-to-be-done-NOW!" The NOW portion of Bittner's explanation refers to the police's unique ability to use force to correct a situation. Klockars (1985, p.16) notes that Bittner purposely did not refer to the situation as illegal because the police are called upon in many situations that do not involve an illegality. Bittner left the purpose of police involvement wide open: Something ought to be done.

People also expect the police to help them when they have a problem or when someone else is causing a problem.

What actions, if any, the police take in response to citizens' requests is usually up to the individual officer's discretion.

Police Discretion

The police have awesome power—to use force, to lock people up and even to take someone's life. Police have broad discretionary powers. According to Adcox (p.16):

> **Discretion** is making a decision based on individual choice or judgment and is influenced by a number of factors. These factors include not only the law and established organizational guidelines, but also individual personal values and beliefs, as well as the values, beliefs and norms of one's peers and work groups [emphasis added].

Each agency exercises discretion when it establishes its mission, policies and procedures. Each officer exercises discretion when deciding whether to issue citations or make arrests when laws are violated.

Officers make those choices based on a variety of reasons such as these:

- Is there evidence to prove a violation in court?
- Will a good purpose be served by arrest or citation, or is police contact sufficient to end the violation?
- What type of crime and suspect are involved?
- What circumstances exist at the time?

Officers would probably not arrest a stranded motorist in a blizzard who, in danger of freezing to death, breaks into an alarmed commercial building. Nor would they be likely to arrest a driver who develops chest pain and breathing difficulty and drives through a stop sign in an attempt to maneuver off the road. In these cases the value of police discretion, or **selective enforcement,** is clear. It makes sense to most people not to enforce the letter of the law.

Police discretion also poses a problem for police, however, because citizens know that officers can act subjectively. The person an officer tickets or arrests may feel discriminated against. The public is also concerned that discretion gives the police too much freedom to pick and choose when and against whom they will enforce the law. Citizens worry that discretion allows the police too much room to discriminate against some and overlook the violations of the wealthy and powerful.

Police agencies and officers have broad discretion in deciding which laws to enforce, under which circumstances and against whom. Some people believe the law should be enforced consistently and in every instance. Most officers, however, believe that such police action would soon be unacceptable, far too harsh and virtually impossible.

Community policing functions well when officers have the discretion to make the decisions necessary to help solve community problems. Officers working in the community are usually more informed about the problems and community members and are often more connected and trusted by community members. However, the increased officer discretion necessary for community policing is a concern to many police administrators who fear loss of control of their officers.

The police are not the only players in the criminal justice system to exercise discretion. Prosecutors exercise discretion when determining priorities for prosecution and in plea negotiations. Judges exercise discretion in preliminary hearings, exclusionary rulings and sentencing. Parole boards, parole officers, probation officers, corrections officials and prison guards also exercise discretion.

Reasons for Police Discretion

Police departments are bureaucracies subject to rules and regulations that may contribute to irrational and inappropriate behavior. Such regulations limit an officer's ability to use common sense or act in a humane way in certain situations. Such limitations subject the officer to critical media coverage and adverse public opinion. For example, the police strictly upheld the law and towed a car containing a crying and screaming paraplegic girl because the vehicle was parked 15 minutes too long in a restricted zone. Millions of Americans and Canadians viewed this episode on national television.

Discretion is necessary for a number of reasons. The statute books are filled with archaic or ambiguous laws. Some laws are almost never enforced, and no one expects them to be. There are not enough police to act on every violation. They must select which laws they will enforce. Police prioritize the offenses they act upon. Crime is of more concern than a violation of a regulation, and felonies are a greater threat than misdemeanors. The police act accordingly. Discretion is important to maintaining good community relations. If the police were to enforce the letter of the law, community resentment would soon follow. Community standards influence how the police enforce laws. In most urban areas, significant changes have occurred in the past several years in enforcing drunk-driving laws. Now violators are routinely arrested and charged; the police rarely overlook this kind of violation.

Changes in Police Discretion

Law enforcement has responded to an increased public awareness of the dangers of tolerating drunk driving. Agencies, as well as individual officers, have a mandate from the public to strictly enforce DWI laws. Police discretion in this area is limited.

Similar changes have occurred in other areas as well. The public has ceased tolerating crimes that occur among family members. Once among the laws the public knew police would not enforce, laws against spouse beating and the physical and sexual abuse of children are now strictly upheld. Again, a significant change in police discretion has occurred in this area. Community policing has also had a great impact on police discretion. Officers are trusted to use good judgment in everyday activities with fewer limits and restricting rules.

Community policing emphasizes wider use of officer discretion.

In *Terry v Ohio* (1968), the Supreme Court recognized the role that discretion plays in policing. It granted police authority to stop and question people in field interrogations. Research has found this tactic to significantly reduce crime.

The Downside of Police Discretion

Officers usually work independently without direct supervision and have tremendous power to decide what action they will take, who they will arrest and which laws they will enforce. Unfortunately, some police officers may use their discretion illegally to obtain bribes or payoffs.

Discretion and the Police Image

Unless the police exercise their discretion with care, the community may complain about an actual or perceived abuse of power or discrimination in the way police enforce the law. If the community believes the police overlook violations committed by a certain segment of society or strictly enforce laws against another, severe community-relations problems will develop.

A police agency's policies, procedures and priorities and the manner in which it equips and assigns its officers indicate how that agency will exercise discretion. Individual officers have the greatest amount of discretion. Police officers have wide discretion in matters of life and death, honor and dishonor in a tension-filled, often hostile environment. In addition, within the police bureaucracy, discretion increases as one moves down the organizational hierarchy. Thus, patrol officers—the most numerous, lowest ranking and newest to police work—have the greatest amount of discretion. All officers should be acutely aware of the power they wield and the immense impact the exercise of discretion has on the community and the police–community relationship.

Although officers often operate independently, it is important to remember that the community watches how officers perform their duties. The public notes how and when officers enforce the law. Citizens may form opinions about their police department and about all officers in that department based on an individual officer's actions. Perhaps the most critical discretionary decision an officer can make is when and how much force to use.

Use of Force

Police officers are trained and equipped to overcome the resistance they can expect to encounter as they perform their duties. Certain types of criminals, usually those who commit common crimes, are likely to try to evade arrest and require the police to find and forcibly take them into custody. Police deal with noncriminal situations that can also require overcoming resistance. Suicidal individuals may require forceful intervention. So might out-of-control mental patients.

Langan et al. (2001, p.1) report on a 1999 national survey of contacts between police and the public. Among their findings were that in 1999, 43.8 million persons age 16 or older had at least one face-to-face police contact (21 percent of all people in this age range). Contact for whites was 17 percent higher than for blacks and 32 percent higher than for Hispanics. The rate of contact for males was 20 percent higher than for females, but varied with age (those ages 18 to 29 had a rate of contact 160 percent higher than those age 50 or older). About half of all the police contacts were the result of a traffic stop. One in five had reported a crime. Three percent were suspects of a crime. Of all people having contact with police, "less than half of 1 percent of the population age 16 or older were threatened with or actually experienced force during the contact."

A study by Terrill and Reisig (2003, p.291) on police use of force found that officers were significantly more likely to use higher levels of force when suspects are encountered in disadvantaged neighborhoods and in neighborhoods with higher homicide rates. Another study by Garner et al. (2002, p.705) used police officer self-report data from 7,512 adult custody arrests in six jurisdictions. The researchers concluded that "physical force was used by police in less than one-sixth of the custody arrests, and in most instances the force was of the lower or most moderate level. Suspect characteristics such as race generally were not related to the use of force." They also found that the amount of force used was related to whether the officer was dispatched or if the event was officer initiated. In addition, Garner et al. report that "more force was likely to be used if the officer called for backup or if there were several officers on the scene."

The use of force by the police encompasses a wide range of possible actions, from the officer's mere presence to the use of deadly force. The police presence affects a majority of citizens. The police uniform and squad cars are symbols of the officer's power to enforce the law and bring violators to justice—by the use of force if necessary. The visual image of power and authority created by the uniform and equipment facilitates the officer's ability to gain public compliance. The police image is also affected, either positively or negatively, by whether a department develops an authority-heavy image. Care must be taken not to develop such an intimidating image that it alienates the community.

Controversy on the use of force by police is almost always discussed in terms of police brutality, which is considered a problem by a large segment of the public. The extent of the problem is perceived differently among urban and suburban, rich and poor, and minority and majority populations. Valid reasons exist for why different people have different perceptions of the problem. One reason is the job the police are required to do differs from community to community.

First recall that because the police must intervene in crimes where apprehension is likely to be resisted, most of their enforcement efforts are directed toward "common" criminals. In contrast, white-collar criminals are unlikely to flee or resist. They tend to see their situation as a legal dilemma to be won or lost in court. White-collar criminals are relatively wealthy and have a career and a place in the community; they have too much to lose to simply flee. Because police enforcement efforts focus on common criminals, who are frequently poor, the most use of force by the police will be directed against this part of the population.

Citizens in white suburban areas are more likely to see the police in more positive circumstances when they report a crime and have been victimized; when they need assistance after an automobile crash, in a medical emergency, when their child is lost or when their car has run out of gas; and when they have locked themselves out of a car or home—or want their home watched.

In each scenario the police are there to lend assistance. Citizens in suburban areas may never see a police officer use force. The most negative experience they are likely to have with a police officer is receiving a traffic ticket.

When people from these widely separated communities talk about the police, it seems as though they are speaking of entirely different entities. On the one hand, police may be referred to as brutal, racist aggressors whereas others describe them as professional, helpful, efficient protectors. Which is the true picture of the police?

While the public has many stereotypes of the police, those stereotypes are shattered or reinforced each time a citizen has personal contact with a police officer. Each individual police contact can have a positive or negative impact on police–community relations.

Most citizens understand and support law enforcement officers' obligation to enforce the law and to use appropriate force when necessary. All officers have a duty to the profession to encourage public support by professional behavior respectful of each citizen's rights. Sometimes, however, public support of the police does not exist in a community. Lack of support may be the result of the unique characteristics of coercion.

Ethical Policing

The tremendous power that policing has over people's lives requires that police officers represent good over evil. To maintain the public trust, police must be men and women of good character who hold foremost the ideals of fairness and justice. The manner in which police use their discretion to enforce the law and solve problems determines whether the public views the police as ethical.

The ethical way to act is not always clear. Unfortunately, the police have often not been given appropriate guidance in ethical decision making. Given the complexities of enforcing the law in an increasingly diverse population, it is inadequate to teach rookie officers the technical skills of policing and then send them into the community under the assumption they will do the "right thing."

A move toward higher ethical standards is perhaps reflected by the decision of many police departments to require their police officers to have a college education. There is an increasing need to begin a dialogue within the police community on ethics—what ethical behavior is and how to achieve it in the profession.

One simple adage, set forth by Blanchard and Peale (1988, p.9), might serve as a starting point for a discussion on ethics: "There is no right way to do a wrong thing." They (p.20) suggest three questions that can be used as personal "ethics checks."

Three ethics-check questions are:

- Is it legal?
- Is it balanced?
- How will it make me feel about myself?

The first question should pose little problem for most officers. The focus of the second question is whether the decision is fair to everyone involved, in the short and long term. Does the decision create a win-win situation? The third question is perhaps the most crucial. Would you mind seeing your decision published in the paper? Would you feel good if your friends and family knew about your decision? Ethical behavior by individual officers and by the department as a whole is indispensable to effective police–community partnerships.

Ethical Dilemmas

Ethical dilemmas are often rooted in the ends-versus-means controversy. Adcox (p.19) explains that the tendency of police to place ends over means is not new: "There is ample historical evidence to suggest that similar police values, beliefs and practices have existed since the inauguration of modern policing in the United States." Historically, some officers have valued results over duty and principle with "the standard measurement of good police work [becoming] goal achievement, with all else being secondary" (Adcox, p.19).

As Thompson (2001, p.77) notes: "The American public readily understands and recognizes that the police are entitled to special privileges and exceptions relative to obeying the laws." They can exceed speed limits and violate traffic laws to enforce the law. They can carry concealed weapons and own or have access to weapons that are restricted to citizens. Sometimes this leads new recruits to receive a message that says they are above the law. As Thompson (p.79) suggests: "Officers need to know the limitations on their behavior. . . . Equality under the law is the foundation of American criminal justice. If law enforcement officers believe they are above the law, then this subverts the very essence of law enforcement and criminal justice in our society."

A belief that officers are above the law, coupled with the code of silence previously discussed can leave officers in ethical dilemmas. A study by the National Institute of Justice, The Measurement of Police Integrity, surveyed 3,235 officers from

30 departments and found that the majority of respondents said they would not report a fellow officer for accepting free gifts, meals or discounts, or for having a minor traffic accident while under the influence of alcohol ("How Do You Rate?" 2000, p.1). These behaviors were not considered major transgressions by the respondents. Three behaviors they did find serious were accepting a cash bribe, stealing money from a found wallet and stealing property from a crime scene.

Closely related to unethical behavior as a result of believing that the ends justify the means is actual corrupt behavior.

Police Corruption

Since policing began, corruption in law enforcement has been a problem. Strandberg (2000, p.100) notes: "Corruption takes on many forms, and something seemingly insignificant can put an officer on a slippery slope, leading to major crimes." This sentiment is echoed by Trautman (2000, p.65): "Research repeatedly confirms that most scandals start with one employee doing relatively small unethical acts and grow to whatever level the leadership allows."

This parallels the broken window theory of crime. According to Adams (2000, p.2): "If the toleration of minor law violations leads to more serious crime on the street, it would also follow that the toleration of minor law violations by the police will lead to more serious crime on the force." He suggests that if we free police from limits on their behavior: "We create a culture within police departments that the end justifies the means. This culture, in turn, increases antagonism between the police and the communities they serve, escalating the violence that is perceived to be necessary to keep the peace." It can also lead to corruption.

When discussing police corruption, some believe that it is just a few "rotten apples" that give a department a bad name. Trautman suggests: "The 'rotten apple' theory that some administrators propose as the cause of their demise is usually nothing more than a self-serving, superficial façade, intended to draw attention away from their own failures."

Byers (2000, p.4) describes the "venerable 'rotten barrel theory' of police corruption" which suggests that unethical, illegal behavior is pervasive throughout a department and can be traced to top management. A "few bad apples can spoil the whole bunch."

Swope (2001, p.80) also suggests that perhaps the problem is not in "bad apples" but in bad barrels: "It is the barrel, the culture of the police organization, that can cause the root shaking scandals that periodically face some police organizations."

The importance of management and of ethical officers within the department in curbing corruption cannot be underestimated. Among the most important forms of corruption, according to Strandberg, is adherence to the code of silence. It might be viewed as the No. 1 barrier to lasting improvements in police–community relations, especially in communities of color where such misconduct has been more prevalent (p.100).

The scandals rocking the Los Angeles Police Department illustrate the emphasis on ends over means and on the code of silence. Hundreds of criminal convictions may be questioned due to a police-corruption scandal involving allegations of officers framing innocent people, lying in court and shooting unarmed suspects.

Cortrite (2000, p.8), a police officer for over 30 years in a department bordering the LAPD, suggests that the underlying problem is the LAPD culture. He contends that the LAPD has touted itself as the greatest department in the world. This has led to a feeling that officers can do whatever they want without having to answer to the public, politicians or even the courts. Such an attitude has created not only arrogance but also complacency. Their second cultural mistake, says Cortrite, "is their command and control management style." He feels officers who do not meet supervisors' expectations have been given suspensions of draconian proportions, such as six months off without pay. In addition, their policies-and-procedures manual encompasses several thick volumes. Cortrite sees the culture as one "based on fear and lack of trust."

Cortrite concludes: "The huge majority of cops are highly ethical people. Trusting them more with the responsibility to maintain the ethical standards of the organization will empower them to eliminate any unethical conduct from their midst."

Investigative Commissions

Historically law enforcement administrators or local officials have responded to police-corruption scandals by calling for investigative commissions as discussed in Chapter 1. Monahan (2000, p.79) reports that many police chiefs or politicians convene an investigative commission or board of inquiry following a scandal. For example, the Knapp Commission, convened in 1972 by Mayor John Lindsay, was a response to alleged corruption in the New York City Police Department. This commission uncovered widespread corruption. But 20 years later, the Mollen Commission found many of the same corruption issues had resurfaced.

The scandal involving the videotaped beating of Rodney King resulted in the Christopher Commission. A new chief was appointed who implemented many of the reforms recommended by the commission, but they were not institutionalized. Monahan (p.83) notes: "That the reforms did not become a permanent part of the organization is made clear by the Rampart scandal." This scandal led to formation of yet another commission, the Rampart Board of Inquiry.

The lesson to be learned from the investigative commissions, says Monahan (p.84), is that too often the implemented reforms are only temporary: "Changes were temporary because too much was dependent on the appointment and characteristics of the incoming police administrator. Departments did not internalize the reforms so that with the passage of time, or once the chief left, the officers reverted to their corrupt behavior."

Police corruption is an issue to be faced and dealt with. In a department where corruption is tolerated, the public trust will fade. As Fulton (2000, p.250) asserts: "The public trust is a most valuable commodity. You can't touch it or see it, but when you walk into a community, you can feel when it's there and when it's not. Without the public trust, a police department is hollow and ineffective."

Summary

Community policing will require a change in mission statement, departmental organization and leadership style. A mission statement is a written declaration of purpose. Departments must find in their mission a balance between fighting crime and service to the public. The majority of police actions do not involve criminal law enforcement, but rather are community-service oriented.

Ethics and integrity are crucial to good policing. Community policing depends on community trust and involvement, which can be gained only by professional, ethical policing. Today's police departments have more minority and female officers. The educational level of the officers is much higher, and fewer have military experience than in years past. Most officers are also as interested in helping people as they are in fighting crime. A dominant characteristic of the police subculture is isolation and a "them-versus-us" worldview.

The police image is affected by individual backgrounds, the media and personal experiences with the criminal justice system. It is also shaped by how police look—their uniform and equipment—and by what they do. Negative contacts are unpleasant interactions between the police and the public. They may or may not involve criminal activity.

People expect the police to enforce the law unless it adversely affects them. People also expect the police to help them when they have a problem. The police face the dilemma of being expected to win the wars on crime, drugs and terrorism without having control over the causes of these problems. The police cannot win these wars.

Police use of discretion and force will profoundly affect police–community relations. Each agency exercises discretion when it establishes its mission, policies and procedures. Each officer exercises discretion when deciding whether to issue citations or make arrests when laws are violated. Community policing emphasizes wider use of officer discretion. Police discretion and authority to use power are balanced by the responsibility to act ethically. Three questions to check police ethical standards are: (1) Is it legal? (2) Is it balanced? and (3) How will it make me feel about myself?

Discussion Questions

1. What is the image of the police in your community? What factors are responsible for this image? Could the police image be made more positive?
2. What expectations do you have of law enforcement agencies?
3. Does police discretion frequently lead to abuse of alleged perpetrators?
4. Are police officers now more violent and less ethical than their predecessors?
5. Does the image of law enforcement affect officers' ability to get the job done?
6. How do you explain the development of the two contradictory models in policing: community-oriented policing (COP) and special weapons and tactics (SWAT) teams? Can they coexist?
7. What should be a department's ideal balance between fighting crime and service to the community?
8. Have you witnessed police exercise their discretion? How did it impress you?
9. Do you think mission statements are valuable for an organization or are they only window dressing? How do they affect the organization? Compare the Los Angeles Police Department's mission statement with what appears to be the reality. Does this work?
10. What decisions commonly made by police officers involve ethical considerations?

InfoTrac College Edition Assignments

- Use InfoTrac College Edition to help answer the Discussion Questions when appropriate.
- Research and outline at least one of the following topics: *mission statement, police discretion, police culture, police ethics* or *police corruption* **OR** read and outline "The Psychological Influence of the Police Uniform" by Richard R. Johnson.

Community Project

Visit a police department and obtain a copy of the mission statement and, if possible, an organizational chart. Be prepared to discuss how these fit with the discussion in this chapter. **OR** go on the Internet and find a police department of interest and record the mission statement.

References

Adams, Noah. "Broken Windows Theory of Policing." *All Things Considered.* National Public Radio, March 7, 2000.

Adcox, Ken. "Doing Bad Things for Good Reasons." *The Police Chief,* January 2000, pp.16–28.

Bittner, Egon. "Florence Nightingale in Pursuit of Willie Sutton: A Theory of Police." In *The Potential for Reform of Criminal Justice,* edited by H. Jacob. Beverly Hills: Sage, 1974, pp.17–44.

Blanchard, Kenneth and Peale, Norman Vincent. *The Power of Ethical Management.* New York: Fawcett Crest, 1988.

Byers, Bryan. "Ethics and Criminal Justice: Some Observations on Police Misconduct." *ACJS Today,* September/October 2000, pp.1, 4–8.

Cortrite, Mike. "What's the LAPD's Problem? It's the Culture!" *Law Enforcement News,* June 15, 2000, p.8.

Ferrell, Craig E., Jr. "Code of Silence: Fact or Fiction?" *The Police Chief,* November 2003, pp.9–11.

Fulton, Roger. "Preventing Corruption." *Law Enforcement Technology,* Vol. 27, No. 12, December 2000, p.250.

Gallup Poll, 2000. "Honesty and Ethics in Professions." http://www.gallup.com/poll/indicators/indhnstyethcs.asp

Garner, Joel H.; Maxwell, Christopher D.; and Heraux, Cedrick G. "Characteristics Associated with the Prevalence and Severity of Force Used by the Police." *Justice Quarterly,* Vol. 19, No. 4, 2002, p.705.

Glick, Larry. "The Paramilitary: A Product of 'Parareportage.'" *Police,* Vol. 24, No. 4, April 2000, pp.42–44.

Goldstein, Herman. *Problem-Oriented Policing.* New York: McGraw-Hill Publishing Company, 1990.

"How Do You Rate? The Secret to Measuring a Department's 'Culture of Integrity.'" *Law Enforcement News,* October 15, 2000, pp.1, 6.

Johnson, Richard R. "The Psychological Influence of the Police Uniform." *FBI Law Enforcement Bulletin,* March 2001, pp.27–32.

Klockars, Carl B. *The Idea of Police.* Newbury Park: Sage Publishing Company, 1985.

Klockars, Carl B. "The Rhetoric of Community Policing." In *Community Policing: Rhetoric or Reality,* edited by Jack R. Greene and Stephen D. Mastrofski. New York: Praeger Publishing, 1991, pp.239–258.

Langan, Patrick A.; Greenfeld, Lawrence A.; Smith, Steven K.; Durose, Matthew R.; and Levin, David J. *Contacts between Police and the Public: Findings from the 1999 National Survey.* Washington, DC: Bureau of Justice Statistics, February 2001. (NCJ 184957).

Los Angeles Police Department Board of Inquiry into the Rampart Corruption Incident. *Final Report* (Executive Summary), March 28, 2000. http://www.LAPDOnline.org

McErlain, Ed. "Acknowledging the Code of Silence." *Law and Order,* January 2001, p.47.

Monahan, Francis J. "Investigative Commissions Implemented Reforms Prove Ephemeral." *The Police Chief,* October 2000, pp.79–84.

Paoline, Eugene A.; Myers, Stephanie M.; and Worden, Robert E. "Police Culture, Individualism and Community Policing: Evidence from Two Police Departments." *Justice Quarterly,* September 2000, pp.555–570.

"Rewarding Good Deeds Is Just the Ticket." *Law Enforcement News,* June 15, 2000, p.9.

Robinson, Patricia A. "Neighborhood Cops or Special Ops? Policing in the New Millennium." *The Law Enforcement Trainer,* March/April 2000, pp.14–16, 45.

Rowell, James D. "The Pro-Active Approach to Crime Fighting." *The Law Enforcement Trainer,* March/April 2000, pp.8–10.

Strandberg, Keith W. "Light Dawns on the Dark Side." *Law Enforcement Technology,* July 2000, pp.96–104.

Swope, Ross. "Bad Apples or Bad Barrel?" *Law and Order,* January 2001, pp.80–85.

Terrill, William and Reisig, Michael D. "Neighborhood Context and Police Use of Force." *Journal of Research in Crime and Delinquency,* August 2003, pp.291–321.

Thompson, David. "Above the Law?" *Law and Order,* January 2001, pp.77–79.

Trautman, Neal. "How Organizations Become Corrupt: The Corruption Continuum." *Law and Order,* May 2000, pp.65–68.

Trautman, Neal. "Truth about Police Code of Silence Revealed." *Law and Order,* January 2001, pp.68–76.

Walls, Kelly G. "Not a Token Effort." *FBI Law Enforcement Bulletin,* July 2003, pp.16–17.

Wilson, James Q. and Kelling, George L. "Making Neighborhoods Safe." *The Atlantic Monthly,* February 1989, pp.46–52.

CHAPTER 3

Understanding and Involving the Community

I believe in the United States of America as a government of the people, by the people, for the people.

—American Creed

DO YOU KNOW?

- How U.S. citizens established the "public peace"?
- What a social contract is?
- How to define community?
- What the broken window phenomenon refers to?
- What demographics includes?
- What role organizations and institutions play within a community?
- What power structures exist within a community?
- What issues in the criminal justice system affect police–community relations?
- How the medical model and the justice model view criminals?
- What restorative justice is?
- How citizens and communities have been involved in community policing?

CAN YOU DEFINE?

bifurcated society
broken window phenomenon
community
community justice
demographics
displacement
diversion
formal power structure
ghetto
heterogeneous
homogeneous
incivilities
informal power structure
justice model
medical model
NIMBY syndrome
plea bargaining
privatization
restorative justice
social capital
social contract
syndrome of crime
tipping point
white flight

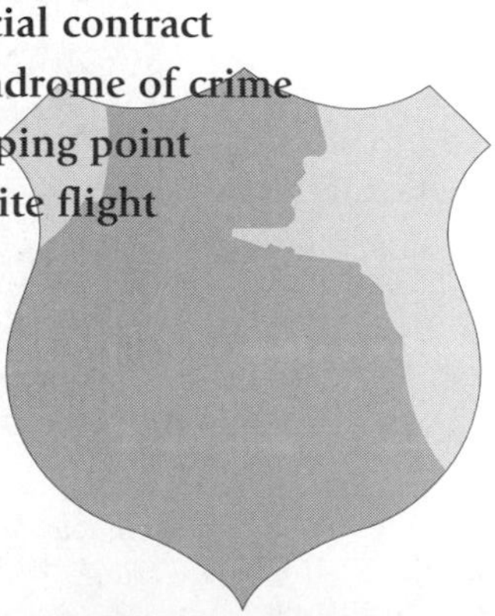

Introduction

The opening sentence of the American Creed, adopted by the House of Representatives on April 3, 1918, uses language attributed to Abraham Lincoln in his address at Gettysburg, November 19, 1863: "We here highly resolve that these dead shall not have died in vain; that this nation, under God, shall have a new birth of freedom; and that government of the people, by the people, and for the people, shall not perish from the earth." The philosophy implicit in the American Creed is central to the concept of "community" in the United States. Each community is part of a larger social order.

The U.S. Constitution and Bill of Rights, as well as federal and state statutes and local ordinances, establish the "public peace" in the United States.

In the United States individual freedom and rights are balanced with the need to establish and maintain order. The United States was born out of desire for freedom. In fact, former President Jimmy Carter noted: "America did not invent human rights. In a very real sense, it is the other way around. Human rights invented America."

The importance of individual rights to all citizens is a central theme to the following discussion of community. Citizens have established a criminal justice system in an effort to live in "peace," free from fear, crime and violence. As the gatekeepers to the criminal justice system, the police have an inherent link with the public, as Sir Robert Peel expressed in 1829: "Police, at all times, should maintain a relationship with the public that gives reality to the historic tradition that the police are the pub-

Wilson and Kelling's broken window theory holds that signs of disorder such as this vandalized window, left uncorrected, indicate that no one cares and that this neighborhood will tolerate crime.

lic and the public are the police; the police being the only members of the public who are paid to give full-time attention to duties which are incumbent on every citizen in the interests of community welfare and existence."

To ensure the peace, citizens of the United States have also entered into an unwritten social contract.

The **social contract** provides that for everyone to receive justice, each person must relinquish some freedom.

In civilized society, people cannot simply do as they please. They are expected to conform to federal and state laws, as well as local rules and regulations established by and for the community in which they live. Increased mobility and economic factors have weakened the informal social contract that once helped to keep the peace in our society. As a result the police, as agents of social control, have had to fill the breach, increasing the need for law-abiding citizens to join with the police in making their communities free from fear, drugs, crime and terrorism.

Correia (2000, p.5) suggests that the traditional law enforcement model of policing strongly reflected a classical liberal theory of democratic governance, emphasizing the rights and responsibilities of the individual. In contrast, community policing is driven by "communitarian values and philosophical principles, in which community values and needs are paramount in political and civic activities." He notes: "This philosophical shift to communitarian principles requires fundamental changes in citizen-to-citizen and citizen-to-government relations in law enforcement."

This chapter begins with definitions of community and social capital as well as lack of community. This is followed by a look at crime and violence in our communities and an explanation of community demographics. Next the organizations and institutions within a community, the public–private policing interaction and the power structure within a community are described. Then the role of the criminal justice system in community policing and restorative justice are discussed. The chapter concludes with an explanation of citizen and community involvement in community policing.

Community Defined

What does the word *community* bring to mind? To many people it conjures up images of their hometown. To others it may bring images of a specific block, a neighborhood or an idyllic small town where everyone knows everyone and they all get along.

Community has also been defined as a group of people living in an area under the same government. In addition, community can refer to a social group or class having common interests. Community may even refer to society as a whole—the public. This text uses a specific meaning for community.

Community refers to the specific geographic area served by a police department or law enforcement agency and the individuals, organizations and agencies within that area.

Police officers must understand and be a part of this defined community if they are to fulfill their mission. The community may cover a very small area and have a limited number of individuals, organizations and agencies; it may perhaps be policed by a single officer. Or the community may cover a vast area and have thousands of individuals and hundreds of organizations and agencies and be policed by several hundred officers. And while police jurisdiction and delivery of services are based on geographic boundaries, a community is much more than a group of neighborhoods administered by a local government. The schools, businesses, public and private agencies, churches and social groups are vital elements of the community. Also of importance are the individual values, concerns and cultural principles of the people living and working in the community and the common interests they share with neighbors. Where integrated communities exist, people share a sense of ownership and pride in their environment. They also have a sense of what is acceptable behavior, which makes policing in such a community much easier.

Community also refers to a feeling of belonging—a sense of integration, a sense of shared values and a sense of "we-ness."

Research strongly suggests that a sense of community is the glue that binds communities to maintain order and provides the foundation for effective community action. It also suggests that shared values, participation in voluntary associations, spiritual or faith-based connectedness and positive interaction with neighbors indicate a strong sense of community and correlate with participation in civic and government activities (Correia, p.9).

Harpold (2000, pp.23–24) describes six types of neighborhoods that exhibit different levels of "well-being" of which community policing officers should be aware. The *integral neighborhood* has well-manicured lawns and well-maintained buildings and shows a high level of pride. Citizens interact and support one another and also link to outside organizations. The *parochial neighborhood* residents share similar values and cultures, insulating themselves and taking care of their own, usually without involving the police. The *diffuse neighborhood* residents have much in common but seldom interact, limiting their ability to problem-solve.

The *stepping-stone neighborhood* consists of small single-family residences, townhouses and apartments whose residents tend to move out quickly. Nonetheless, they tend to get involved in community organizations and to assume leadership positions. The *transitory neighborhood* residents either move often or have little in common and, hence, the neighborhood lacks cohesion. Finally, the *anomic neighborhood* is characterized by isolation and alienation. Residents have resigned themselves to accept criminal victimization as a way of life. Recognizing what type of neighborhood a community policing officer is involved in will help determine what strategies might be most appropriate, as discussed in Section Three of this text.

Social Capital

Communities might also be looked at in terms of their **social capital.** Coleman (1990, p.302) developed this concept, which he defined as: "A variety of different entities having two characteristics in common: They all consist of some aspect of a social structure, and they facilitate certain actions of individuals who are within the structure." Coleman saw the two most important elements in social capital as being trustworthiness, or citizens' trust of each other and their public institutions, and obligations, that is, expectation that service to each other will be reciprocated.

Social capital can be found at two levels: local and public. *Local social capital* is the bond among family members and their immediate, informal groups. *Public social capital* refers to the networks tying individuals to broader community institutions such as schools, civic organizations, churches and the like as well as to networks linking individuals to various levels of government—including the police. According to Correia (p.53): "Taken together, the concepts of sense of community and social capital go a long way toward describing the strength of a community's social fabric."

Community Factors Affecting Social Capital

Correia reports on a study using Community Action Support Teams (CASTs) and the community factors affecting social capital in six cities: Hayward, California; Davenport, Iowa; Ann Arbor, Michigan; Sioux City, Iowa; Pocatello, Idaho; and Ontario, California. Data came from self-administered mail surveys, direct observations and interviews. Of the 22 hypotheses tested, 7 were supported by the data (pp.34–35):

1. Trust in others depends on the level of safety an individual feels in his or her environment. Therefore, the higher the levels of perceived safety, the higher the levels of local social capital will be.
2. The lower the levels of physical disorder, the higher the levels of perceived sense of safety will be.
3. Females will hold lower levels of perceived safety than males.
4. The higher the levels of public social capital, the higher the levels of collective action will be.
5. The more individuals trust one another, the more likely they will be to engage in collective activities. Consequently, the higher the level of local social capital, the higher the level of engagement in collective action will be.
6. The more individuals trust one another, the more likely they will be to interact. Therefore, the higher the levels of local social capital, the higher the levels of neighboring activity will be.
7. The higher the levels of civic activity, the higher the levels of public social capital will be.

Correia concludes (p.41):

> Effective community policing may be limited to those areas with high levels of social cohesion; most likely, these areas do not need community policing as badly as others. This suggests that communities lacking high levels of Putnam's social capital, yet with high levels of community policing activity, are possibly beyond repair; their stocks of social capital cannot be replenished without extraordinary effort, nor can their strained social cohesion be repaired exclusively by police efforts. Consequently, this method of law enforcement may in fact raise more expectations than it is able to satisfy.

In effect: "Social capital is a prerequisite to citizen engagement in community efforts" (Correia, p.48). The implications of this significant finding are discussed in Chapter 5.

Sociologists have been describing for decades either the loss or the breakdown of "community" in modern, technological, industrial, urban societies such as ours. Proponents of community policing in some areas may be missing a major sociological reality—the absence of "community"—in the midst of all the optimism about police playing a greater role in encouraging it.

Lack of Community

Community implies a group of people with a common history and understandings and a sense of themselves as "us" and outsiders as "them." Unfortunately, many communities lack this "we-ness." In such areas, the police and public have a "them-versus-us" relationship. Areas requiring the most police attention are usually those with the least shared values and limited sense of community. When citizens are unable to maintain social control, the result is social disorganization. All entities within a community—individuals as well as organizations and agencies—must work together to keep that community healthy. Such partnerships are vital, for a community cannot be healthy if unemployment and poverty are widespread; people are hungry; health care is inadequate; prejudice separates people; preschool children lack proper care and nutrition; senior citizens are allowed to atrophy; schools remain isolated and remote; social services are fragmented and disproportionate; and government lacks responsibility and accountability.

Broken Windows

In such unhealthy communities, disorder and crime may flourish. In a classic article, "Broken Windows," Wilson and Kelling (1982, p.31) contend:

> Social psychologists and police officers tend to agree that if a window in a building is broken and is left unrepaired, all the rest of the windows will soon be broken. This is as true in nice neighborhoods as in run-down ones. Window-breaking does not necessarily occur on a large scale because some areas are inhabited by determined window-breakers whereas others are populated by window-lovers; rather, one unrepaired broken window is a signal that no one cares, and so breaking more windows costs nothing. (It has always been fun.)

The **broken window phenomenon** suggests that if it appears "no one cares," disorder and crime will thrive.

Wilson and Kelling based their broken window theory, in part, on research done in 1969 by a Stanford psychologist, Philip Zimbardo. Zimbardo arranged to have a car without license plates parked with its hood up on a street in the Bronx and a comparable car on a street in Palo Alto, California. The car in the Bronx was attacked by vandals within 10 minutes, and within 24 hours it had been totally destroyed and stripped of anything of value. The car in Palo Alto sat untouched. After a week Zimbardo took a sledgehammer to it. People passing by soon joined in, and within a few hours that car was also totally destroyed. According to Wilson and Kelling (p.31): "Untended property becomes fair game for people out for fun or plunder, and even for people who ordinarily would not dream of doing such things and who probably consider themselves as law-abiding."

Broken windows and smashed cars are visible signs of people not caring about their community. Other less subtle signs include unmowed lawns, piles of accumulated trash and graffiti, often referred to as **incivilities.** Incivilities include rowdiness, drunkenness, fighting, prostitution, abandoned buildings, litter, broken windows and graffiti.

Incivilities and social disorder occur when social control mechanisms have eroded. Increases in incivilities may increase the fear of crime and reduce citizens' sense of safety. They may physically or psychologically withdraw, isolating themselves from their neighbors. Or increased incivilities and disorder may bring people together to "take back the neighborhood."

It is extremely difficult to implement community policing when the values of groups within a given area clash. For example, controversy may exist between gay communities and Orthodox Christian or Jewish communities in the same area. Do each of these communities deserve a different style of policing based on the "community value system"? Do "community" police officers ignore behavior in a community where the majority of residents approve of that behavior but enforce sanctions against the same behavior in enclaves where that behavior causes tension? These are difficult ethical questions.

Another factor that negates a sense of community is the prevalence of violence. We live in a violent society. The United States was born through a violent revolution. The media emphasize violence, constantly carrying news of murder, rape and assault. It seems that if a movie or television program is to succeed, at least three or four people must meet a violent death. The cartoons children watch contain more violence than most adults realize. Children learn that violence is acceptable and justified under some circumstances. Citizens expect the police to prevent violence, but the police cannot do it alone. Individuals must come together to help stop violence and in so doing can build a sense of community.

Communities and Crime

Although traditional policing has most often dealt with high crime levels by stricter enforcement (zero tolerance), "get-tough" policies and a higher police presence, police usually have little ability to change things for the better in the long run. Cracking down on crime usually results in **displacement.** The community in which the crackdown occurs may be temporarily safer; however, forced by the increased police presence and increased likelihood of arrest, criminals usually just move their operations, often a few blocks or miles away making adjacent communities less safe. Policing efforts can develop into an unending game of cat and mouse.

Traditional police tactics often fail because the causes of crime in communities are complicated and linked to a multitude of factors including environmental design; housing age, type and density; availability of jobs; residents' level of education;

poverty level, family structure, demographics (average age of residents, ethnic and racial makeup of the community), mobility and perhaps other unidentified factors. Such complicated underlying causes require creative solutions and partnerships. Police who form alliances with organizations and agencies associated with education, religion, health care, job training, family support, community leaders and members can often affect the underlying factors in criminal behavior and community decay.

A theory called the ecology of crime explains how criminal opportunities are created in neighborhoods. Just like a natural ecosystem, a neighborhood can hold only a certain number of things. Add too many and the system will collapse. This is similar to the **tipping point,** the point at which an ordinary, stable phenomenon can turn into a crisis. For example, a health epidemic is nonlinear; that is, small changes can have huge effects and large changes can have small effects—in contrast to linear situations when every extra increment of effort will produce a corresponding improvement in result.

This principle of nonlinearity is captured in the expression, "That's the straw that broke the camel's back." The principle can be applied to the phenomenon of **white flight,** the departure of white families from neighborhoods experiencing racial integration or from cities experiencing school desegregation. Depending on the racial views of white residents, one white neighborhood might empty out when minorities reach 5 percent of the neighborhood population, while another more racially tolerant white neighborhood might not tip until minorities make up 40 or 50 percent. Communities need to recognize when they are approaching the tipping point or the threshold in a given situation. In addition to understanding the complex concept of community, it is also important to assess the demographics of the area.

Community Demographics

Demographics refers to the characteristics of the individuals who live in a community.

> Demographics include a population's size, distribution, growth, density, employment rate, ethnic makeup and vital statistics such as average age, education and income.

Although people generally assume that the smaller the population of a community, the easier policing becomes, this is not necessarily true. Small communities generally have fewer resources. It is also difficult being the sole law enforcement person, in effect, on call 24 hours a day. A major advantage of a smaller community is that people know each other. A sense of community is likely to be greater in such communities than in large cities such as Chicago or New York.

When assessing law enforcement's ability to police an area, density of population is an important variable. Studies have shown that as population becomes denser, people become more aggressive. In densely populated areas, people become more territorial and argue more frequently about "turf." Rapid population growth can invigorate a community, or it can drain its limited resources. Without effective planning and foresight, rapid population growth can result in serious problems for a community, especially if the population growth results from an influx of immigrants or members of an ethnic group different from the majority in that area.

The community's vital statistics are extremely important from a police–community partnership perspective. What is the average age of individuals within the community? Are there more young or elderly individuals? How many single-parent families are there? What is the divorce rate? What is the common level of education? How does the education of those in law enforcement compare? What is the school dropout rate? Do gangs operate in the community? What is the percentage of latchkey children? Such children may pose a significant challenge for police.

Income and income distribution are also important. Do great disparities exist? Would the community be described as affluent, moderately well off or poor? How does the income of those in law enforcement compare to the average income? Closely related to income is the level of employment. What is the ratio of blue-collar to professional workers? How much unemployment exists? How do those who are unemployed exist? Are they on welfare? Do they commit crimes to survive? Are they homeless? Are there gangs?

The ethnic makeup of the community is another consideration. Is the community basically homogeneous? A **homogeneous** community is one in which people are all quite similar. A **heterogeneous** community, in contrast, is one in which individuals are quite different from each other. Most communities are heterogeneous. Establishing and maintaining good relations among the various subgroups making up the community is a challenge. Usually one ethnic subgroup will have the most power and control. Consider the consequences if a majority of police officers are also members of this ethnic subgroup.

The existence of ghettos in many of our major cities poses extreme challenges for law enforcement. A **ghetto** is an area of a city usually inhabited by individuals of the same race or ethnic background who live in poverty and, to outsiders, apparent social disorganization. Consequently, ghettos, minorities and crime are frequently equated. Because ghettos are the focus of many anticrime efforts, this is often perceived as a clear bias by law enforcement against members of racial or ethnic minorities.

Poverty, unemployment, substandard housing and inadequate education have all figured into theories on the causes of crime. They are often part of the underlying problems manifested in crime. However, as Reiman (2001) points out, our criminal justice system tends to focus on those who commit street crimes and who are also usually poor. They are arrested more often and are given more severe sentences. Those who commit economic crimes such as those perpetrated by the CEOs of several large corporations in the past few years are not as often prosecuted, and the penalties are seldom as severe. He contends that our criminal justice system should focus attention on those who commit crime against the environment, who commit infractions in the workplace and who create more long-term damage to the economy than those who are prosecuted for street crimes.

A Rapidly Changing Population

Communities have been undergoing tremendous changes in the past half century. In 1950 the white population made up 87 percent of the population. The white population has declined from 80 percent in 1980 to 69 percent in 2000.

The greatest growth has been in the Hispanic population, growing from 6 percent in 1980 to double that in 2000. The black population grew by 1 percent. According to PRB Hispanics are projected to outnumber blacks early in the 21st century. Figure 3.1 shows racial and ethnic composition of the United States in 1999 and the projected composition in 2025.

PRB contends: "Over the next 25 years, minority concentrations are projected to increase in all parts of the country, but especially in the South, Southwest and West. By 2025, minority groups are expected to account for over 50 percent of the population in four states (Hawaii, California, New Mexico, Texas) and the District of Columbia." The PRB also projects that if the current trends continue, almost half of the U.S. population will be nonwhite by 2050. These distinctions may be blurred, however, by the growing rate of intermarriage among whites, blacks, Hispanics and Asians.

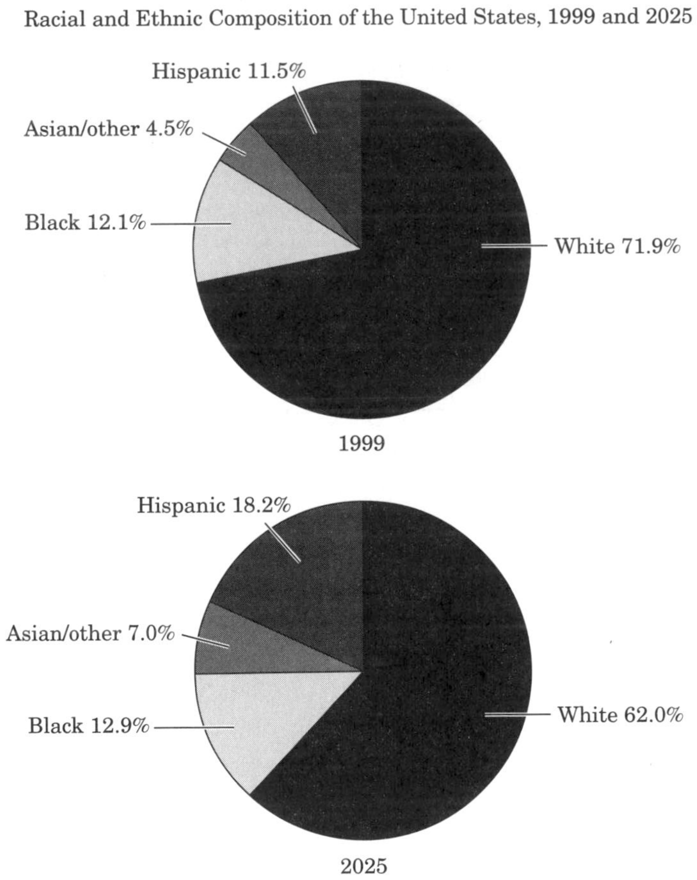

Figure 3.1 Racial and Ethnic Composition of the United States, 1999 and 2025

Note: White, black, and Asian/other categories exclude Hispanics, who may be of any race. The Asian/other category includes American Indians, Eskimos, Aleuts, and Pacific Islanders. Totals may not add to 100 due to rounding.

In addition to a change in ethnic makeup, the United States is also experiencing a widening of the gap between those with wealth and those living in poverty. The middle class is shrinking, and the gap between the "haves" and the "have nots" is widening, resulting in a **bifurcated society.**

The following trends in the United States are likely to continue: The minority population will increase, and white dominance will end; the number of legal and illegal immigrants will increase, and the elderly population will increase. As Peed (2003, p.11), director of the COPS office, stresses: "It is important to remember that community policing means building close partnerships with every facet of every community. It is even more important to realize that community policing makes that possible."

Organizations and Institutions

In addition to understanding the demographics of the community and being able to relate to a great variety of individuals, community policing officers must also be familiar with the various organizations and institutions within the community and establish effective relationships with them. A strong network of community organizations and institutions fosters a cohesiveness and shared intolerance of criminal behavior and encourages citizens to cooperate in controlling crime, thereby increasing the likelihood that illegal acts will be detected and reported. These networks and partnerships are essential, for no single organization or group is able to address all the problems and concerns of a community alone. All the organizations and groups working beyond their individual capacity are unable to do more than apply localized, specific band-aid solutions to the total community problems.

Organizations and institutions can play a key role in enhancing community safety and quality of life.

A good relationship between the schools in the community and the police is vital to maintaining order. Other organizations and institutions with whom police officers should interact effectively include departments of human services, health care providers, emergency services providers and any agencies working with the youth. Communities may also have libraries, museums and zoos that would welcome a good relationship with the police. Such cooperation often poses problems, however, as Wilson and Kelling (1989, p.52) note:

> The problem of interagency cooperation may, in the long run, be the most difficult of all. The police can bring problems to the attention of other city agencies, but the system is not always organized to respond. In his book *Neighborhood Services,* John Mudd calls it the "rat problem": "If a rat is found in an apartment, it is a housing inspection responsibility; if it runs into a restaurant, the health department has jurisdiction; if it goes outside and dies in an alley, public works takes over." A police officer who takes public complaints about rats seriously will go crazy trying to figure out what agency in the city has responsibility for rat control and then inducing it to kill the rats.

In other words, if responsibility is fragmented, little gets accomplished.

The Public–Private Policing Interaction

A good relationship between the private security industry and the police is also becoming more important. Many communities and even police departments are using **privatization**, contracting with private security agencies or officers to provide services typically considered to be law enforcement functions. Examples of privatization include prisoner transport and prisoner housing.

Many police departments are also relinquishing responsibility for responding to home security alarms to private security firms. The number of false alarms generated by private alarm systems is staggering and severely depletes the resources of many police departments. As one municipality with a population of approximately 45,000 reports:

> When properly installed, used and maintained, alarms can be a real asset to a community. When misused or neglected, they become a liability. In 1999, the [Apple Valley (Minnesota) Police Department] responded to over 1200 false alarms and billed $14,000 for this service. . . .
>
> Responding to false alarms wastes time and money for officers who are sworn to protect. . . . Repeat false alarms also create a level of complacency for the officers responding ("To Be or Not to Be," 2000, p.1).

The need for public and private police forces to establish good working relationships was recognized by the National Institute of Justice in the early 1980s when it began urging cooperation between the agencies and established the Joint Council of Law Enforcement and Private Security Association. The International Association of Chiefs of Police (IACP) has also recognized this need for cooperation by establishing a Private Sector Liaison Committee (PSLC).

Unfortunately, police often view private security employees as poorly trained, poorly paid individuals who could not land a police job. Names such as "rent-a-cop" and "cop-in-a-box" add to this negative perception. Despite this image, private security plays a major role in safeguarding Americans and their property.

The Power Structure

Most communities have both a formal and an informal power structure.

> The **formal power structure** includes divisions of society with wealth and political influence such as federal, state and local agencies and governments, commissions and regulatory agencies.

The public can usually readily identify the formal power structure. Often policy decisions made at the federal and state level directly affect local decisions. In addition, federal and state funding can directly influence local programs.

> The **informal power structure** includes religious groups, wealthy subgroups, ethnic groups, political groups and public interest groups.

The public cannot as readily identify the informal power structure, which includes banks, real estate companies and other large and influential businesses in a community. The informal power structure is not merely a few people controlling the masses; rather, the control groups are entire subcultures that influence other subcultures. It has been alleged that 400 families control the wealth of the United States, affecting every other subculture. Awareness of the way informal groups, especially wealthy and political groups, exercise their ideologies is important. How informal group pressure is forced into an organization's formal structure is key to understanding why the community at large often conflicts with the criminal justice system.

Wilson and Kelling (1982, p.34) suggest: "The essence of the police role in maintaining order is to reinforce the informal control mechanisms of the community itself. The police cannot, without committing extraordinary resources, provide a substitute for that informal control." Law enforcement personnel must understand the different subgroups within their jurisdiction and the power struggles that occur among them. They must also be aware of this reality: Democracy does not always ensure equality.

The Criminal Justice System

Many people equate policing or law enforcement with the criminal justice system when, in fact, it is only one part of this system. The other two components, courts and corrections, are much less visible in most communities. Because the police are the most visible component of the system, however, they often become the criminal justice system in the eyes of the community.

In the criminal justice process, the role of law enforcement is to prevent, detect or act on reports of law violations, to apprehend suspects reasonably believed responsible for such violations and to bring those suspects or defendants before a court of law. The court then assesses the charge and the evidence as presented by both the prosecution, for which the police officer may be a witness, and the defense to determine the defendant's guilt or innocence. If found guilty of the charge the offender may be sentenced by the court to confinement in a correctional facility or be allowed to return to the community under supervision.

This three-part system provides a procedure of checks and balances intended to ensure that no person is accused of a crime and then deprived of freedom without every reasonable step being taken to guarantee fairness and equity throughout the process, guarantees consistent with the Fourteenth Amendment requirements of the "due process" and "equal protection" clauses. The courts are often criticized by the public as being the weak link in the criminal justice process, letting too many offenders off easy and allowing wealthy defendants to buy their way out of convictions. Those who criticize judges usually do so based on whether they agree with a judge's procedures and sentencing practices. Critics must remember though that the system is designed to work the way it does. After all, if we assumed that everyone arrested by the police is guilty of a crime, there would be no need for prosecutors, judges, juries or courtrooms. The accused could be taken directly to prison.

Many people have a limited understanding of the role the courts and corrections play in crime control. Indeed, at times various components of the criminal justice system seem to work against each other. When the perception or the reality is that criminals are not being convicted or are being released early from prison, some people demand more police and ask why they are not doing their job.

Members of the law enforcement community often become frustrated by such attitudes and incidents. Decisions made in court can discourage officers, who may become cynical and wonder why they work so hard to make arrests when they see cases dismissed or plea bargained. Officers may also become frustrated when those who are convicted are given a light sentence or probation. Officers may be further aggravated by what they view as inadequacies of the corrections system, aware of the many career criminals whose behavior has not improved even after they have been through prison, probation, parole, halfway houses and rehabilitation programs. Officers are not alone in their disappointment, however. The public, too, can be frustrated by the performance of the courts and corrections.

The public may have a negative opinion of the courts because of their failure to process cases promptly, their inconsistency in plea bargaining and the long tenure accorded to judges. Many believe that the courts provide "assembly-line" justice, and the legal process is filled with delays. Aspects of the correctional system that have impeded good public relations include failures to reform offenders, the early release of recidivists and the growing prison population.

To help overcome negative opinions and improve public relations, agencies within the criminal justice system are now actively seeking partnerships with others in the community. Many communities now have community prosecution, community courts, community corrections and even **community justice.** As Clear and Karp (2000, p.21) explain: "Community justice might be best described as an ethic that transforms the aim of the justice system into enhancing community life or sustaining community. To achieve that aim, the community partners with the justice system to share responsibility for social control."

Jurik et al. (2000, pp.293–294) note that community partnerships have become increasingly popular and that: "Crime prevention partnerships that join criminal justice agencies to work with business, university or other community members have been a prominent part of this trend." They studied a community–criminal justice partnership between a western university (WU) and a juvenile corrections agency (JCA) over four years. They (p.313) concluded:

> Partnerships offer the promise of an organizational niche to work partially inside, partially outside and partially across large bureaucracies. From this niche, change agents may circumvent obstacles faced by others working entirely in or outside of existing organizations. In a partnership model, change agents may more easily develop a nexus of support for transforming organizations and communities.
>
> With regard to the inculcation of a community research-service ethos at WU, the WU-JCA partnership was highly successful. Faculty members and students became involved in the community, a service learning curricula was adopted, and spin-off community service and research opportunities prospered at WU. The

commitment of resources by several top WU administrators greatly encouraged this community-oriented ethos.

What constitutes good criminal justice administration is open to debate.

Controversial Issues

Numerous controversial issues related to the effectiveness of the criminal justice system affect police–community partnerships. Although many issues are outside police officers' appropriate sphere of action, they affect the system as a whole. Therefore, police officers need to be aware of these issues and their potential impact.

Controversial issues in the criminal justice system that affect police–community partnerships include plea bargaining, diversion, sentencing, rehabilitation, community alternatives to prisons, victims' rights and capital punishment.

Plea bargaining is a practice by which prosecutors charge a defendant with a less serious crime in exchange for a guilty plea, thus eliminating the time and expense of a trial. **Diversion** is a system operating in most states that removes juvenile status offenders and delinquents from the jurisdiction of the courts, when possible. This practice evolved because, once juvenile delinquents are labeled, they may act out and perpetuate that negative role.

Within the courts, judges often have considerable discretion in sentencing. When the community perceives sentences as too lenient, it sparks controversy. Police officers often believe that sentences are too light for serious crimes. Issues within the corrections component of the criminal justice system include locating alternative correctional facilities within the community. These alternatives become especially controversial when a community must determine the location of the facilities. Citizens often have the **NIMBY syndrome**, that is, "not in my backyard."

A growing number of people are protesting the treatment of victims by the criminal justice system. The law enforcement community has responded to this protest in a number of ways, as discussed in Chapter 7. In addition, the debate continues on the merits and effectiveness of capital punishment as a deterrent to crime and a form of retribution.

Another controversial issue in the criminal justice system is that it has operated reactively, concentrating its efforts on fighting crime to keep the "public peace" and allowing police officers to function as armed social workers. Many believe the system has been shortsighted, focusing almost exclusively on detecting individual offenses and specific ways to eliminate each crime instead of concentrating on developing strategies to proactively attack the syndromes of crime. A **syndrome of crime** is a group of signs, causes and symptoms that occur together to foster specific crimes. The syndromes of crime are central to problem-oriented policing, discussed in detail in Chapter 4.

Yet another issue within the criminal justice system has been a shift in basic philosophy from a medical model to a justice model.

The **medical model** sees those who break the law as victims of society; the **justice model** views lawbreakers as responsible for their own actions.

No longer will society take the blame for individual criminals. Justice is served by having individuals be responsible for their own actions and suffer the consequences when they break the law. This change in philosophy is likely to enhance relations between those in the criminal justice system and law-abiding citizens.

In addition, a new meaning has been attached to the medical model, equating it with the way health maintenance organizations (HMOs) are approaching medicine from a preventive stance. As Harpold (p.23) notes:

> Police departments would do well to take their cues from the medical profession. Physicians know a great deal about disease and the nature of injuries; they treat patients based on the collective knowledge and experience in the treatment of illness. They observe the symptoms present in the patient, diagnose the disease, prescribe the treatment, then monitor the patient's progress. At the same time, they practice preventive medicine and educate the public. To treat the causes of illness in the community, the police must do the same.

The medical model supports the restorative justice approach being taken by some communities.

Restorative Justice

Restorative justice can be traced back to the code of Hammurabi in 2000 B.C. This type of justice holds offenders accountable to the victim and the victim's community, rather than to the state. Rather than seeking retribution (punishment), it seeks restitution—to repair the damages as much as possible and to restore the victim, the community and the offender. Under common law, criminals were often required to reimburse victims for their losses. Beginning in the twelfth century, however, under William the Conqueror, crimes were considered offenses against the king's peace, with offenders ordered to pay fines to the state. This tradition was brought to the United States. In the 1970s, reformers began trying to change the emphasis of the criminal justice system from the offender back to the victim. The Victim Witness Protection Act of 1982 marked the reemergence of the victim in the criminal justice process.

Restorative justice advocates a balanced approach to sentencing that involves offenders, victims, local communities and government to alleviate crime and violence and obtain peaceful communities.

Table 3.1 summarizes the differences between the traditional retributive approach to justice and restorative justice. Figure 3.2 illustrates the restorative justice approach.

The most common forms of restorative sentences include restitution (payments to victims) and community service. Other restorative justice practices include victim impact statements, family group conferences, sentencing circles and citizen reparative boards.

Helfgott et al. (2000, p.5) conducted a pilot study of citizens, victims and offenders participating in a restorative justice program at the Washington State Reformatory. The results showed that the program was effective in meeting the four

Table 3.1 Paradigms of Justice—Old and New

Old Paradigm Retributive Justice	*New Paradigm Restorative Justice*
1. Crime defined as violation of the state	1. Crime defined as violation of one person by another
2. Focus on establishing blame, on guilt, on past (did he/she do it?)	2. Focus on problem solving, on liabilities and obligations, on future (what should be done?)
3. Adversarial relationships and process normative	3. Dialogue and negotiation normative
4. Imposition of pain to punish and deter/prevent	4. Restitution as a means of restoring both parties; reconciliation/restoration as goal
5. Justice defined by intent and by process: right rules	5. Justice defined as right relationships; judged by the outcome
6. Interpersonal, conflictual nature of crime obscured, repressed; conflict seen as individual vs. state	6. Crime recognized as interpersonal conflict; value of conflict recognized
7. One social injury replaced by another	7. Focus on repair of social injury
8. Community on sidelines, represented abstractly by state	8. Community as facilitator in restorative process
9. Encouragement of competitive, individualistic values	9. Encouragement of mutuality
10. Action directed from state to offender: • victim ignored • offender passive	10. Victim's and offender's roles recognized in both problem and solution: • victim rights/needs recognized • offender encouraged to take responsibility
11. Offender accountability defined as taking punishment	11. Offender accountability defined as understanding impact of action and helping decide how to make things right
12. Offense defined in purely legal terms, devoid of moral, social, economic, political dimensions	12. Offense understood in whole context—moral, social, economic, political
13. "Debt" owed to state and society in the abstract	13. Debt/liability to victim recognized
14. Response focused on offender's past behavior	14. Response focused on harmful consequences of offender's behavior
15. Stigma of crime unremovable	15. Stigma of crime removable through restorative action
16. No encouragement for repentance and forgiveness	16. Possibilities for repentance and forgiveness
17. Dependence upon proxy professionals	17. Direct involvement by participants

SOURCE: Howard Zehr. *IARCA Journal,* March 1991, p.7. Used by permission of the International Association of Residential and Community Alternatives.

goals established: "The seminar provided a safe environment for inmates to begin making amends for their crimes and for victims to heal, facilitated constructive communication between polarized groups, and encouraged participants to develop creative ways of thinking about justice and strategies for dealing with crime."

Citizen Involvement in the Law Enforcement Community

Once upon a time, when food resources in a village were seemingly gone, a creative individual—knowing that each person always has a little something in reserve—proposed that the community make stone soup.

Restorative Justice

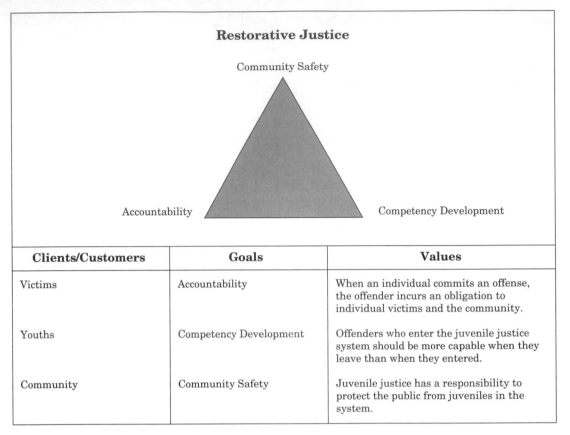

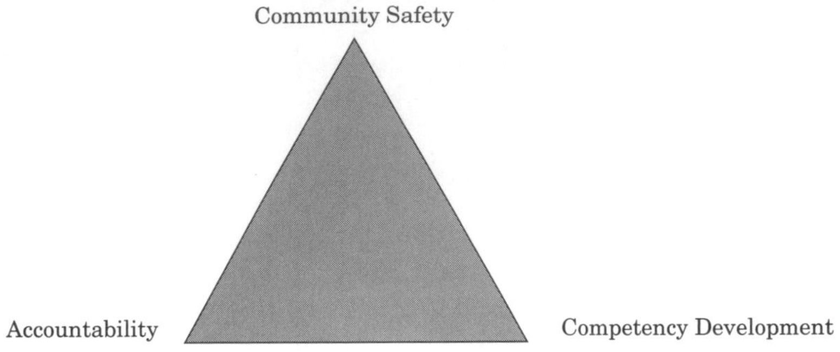

Clients/Customers	Goals	Values
Victims	Accountability	When an individual commits an offense, the offender incurs an obligation to individual victims and the community.
Youths	Competency Development	Offenders who enter the juvenile justice system should be more capable when they leave than when they entered.
Community	Community Safety	Juvenile justice has a responsibility to protect the public from juveniles in the system.

Figure 3.2 Restorative Justice Approach

Adopted from D. Maloney, D. Romig and T. Armstrong. 1998. *Juvenile Probation: The Balanced Approach,* Reno, NV: National Council of Juvenile and Family Court Judges.

SOURCE: Shay Bilchik. *Guide for Implementing the Balanced and Restorative Justice Model.* Washington, DC: Office of Juvenile Justice and Delinquency Prevention, December 1998, p.6.

After a stone was set to boil, people in the community were asked if they had "just a little something" to improve the soup. One person found a carrot, another brought a few potatoes, another a bit of meat and so on. When the soup was finished, it was thick and nourishing. Such is the situation in our communities today. Because resources are stretched to the limit, people tend to hold on to their time, talent or money. These self-protective actions leave most groups without enough resources to effectively handle community problems. Perhaps it is time to adopt the "stone soup" stance of cooperation.

Community members have a high interest level in their local police departments and have been involved in a variety of ways for many years. This involvement, while it accomplishes important contact, should not be mistaken for community policing. It usually does not involve the partnerships and problem-solving activities of community policing.

Citizen involvement in the law enforcement community and in understanding policing has taken the form of civilian review boards, citizen patrols, citizen police academies, ride-alongs and similar programs.

Civilian Review Boards

The movement for citizen review has been a major political struggle for over 40 years and remains one of the most controversial issues in police work today. As Farrow (2003, p.22) explains: "Basically, the concept is defined as a procedure under which law enforcement conduct is reviewed at some point by persons who are not sworn officers." Supporters of civilian review boards believe it is impossible for the police to objectively review actions of their colleagues and emphasize that the police culture demands police officers support each other, even if they know something illegal has occurred. Opponents of civilian review boards stress that civilians cannot possibly understand the complexities of the policing profession and that it is demeaning to be reviewed by an external source. Walker (2001, p.21) outlines the history of civilian review as falling into three broad periods:

> Between the 1920s and the mid-1950s, oversight first emerged as a radical idea, and after World War II was eventually embodied in a few experimental agencies. In the second period, from the late 1950s through the 1960s, civilian review as it was called, became one of the major demands of civil rights leaders. Extremely bitter conflicts over this issue erupted in Philadelphia and New York City. The demise of review boards in those two cities by the end of the decade appeared to signal the death of citizen oversight. The third period began with the quiet revival of oversight in 1969 with the creation of the Kansas City Office of Citizen Complaints and continues to the present day.

Currently, most departments handle officer discipline internally, with department personnel investigating complaints against officers and determining whether misconduct occurred. Finn (2000), however, notes that the 1990s showed a "considerable increase" in citizen oversight of the police. He (p.22) describes the four main types of oversight systems:

- Citizens investigate allegations of police misconduct and recommend a finding to the head of the agency.
- Officers investigate allegations and develop findings. Then, citizens review and recommend that the head of the agency approve or reject the findings.
- Complainants may appeal findings established by the agency to citizens who review them and make recommendations to the head of the agency.
- An auditor investigates the process the agency uses to accept and investigate complaints and reports to the agency and the community the thoroughness and fairness of the process.

In Favor of Civilian Oversight Citizens who demand to be involved in the review process maintain that internal police discipline is tantamount to allowing the "fox to investigate thefts in the chicken coop." According to these citizens, police protect each other and cover up improper or illegal conduct. Citizens believe that this perpetuates abuses and sends a message to brutal officers that their behavior will be shielded from public scrutiny.

In some larger cities, police have lost the power to investigate complaints against fellow officers. The trend is toward more openness and citizen involvement in these matters. Officers should assume they will be required to be more accountable for their actions. Officers may be held to a higher standard and will need to be prepared to justify their use of force in certain situations.

Finn (p.26) describes ways citizen oversight can benefit police agencies, including "bettering an agency's image with the community, enhancing an agency's ability to police itself, and, most important, improving an agency's policies and procedures." He (p.27) concludes: "If both sides make a sincere and sustained effort to work together, citizen oversight can help law enforcement administrators perform their jobs more effectively and with increased public support."

Walker (p.3) believes the problem of police misconduct is not a matter of a few rotten apples but of failed organizations. He suggests citizen oversight is "a means . . . for changing police organizations in order to reduce officer misconduct." Walker (p.4) defines citizen oversight as "a procedure for providing input into the complaint process by individuals who are not sworn officers." He (p.15) suggests:

> It [citizen oversight] represents a form of political control by adding a new mechanism for direct citizen input into police matters. It resembles the judicial control of police behavior by creating a quasi-judicial process of investigating and adjudicating complaints. It incorporates aspects of professional police management by strengthening the disciplinary process. And it parallels community policing by emphasizing citizen input into policing.

Walker (p.16) summarizes the arguments of advocates for citizen oversight:

- Police misconduct is a serious problem and internal police complaint procedures fail to address this problem.
- Citizen oversight will provide more thorough and fair investigation of complaints than those conducted by the police themselves.
- Citizen oversight agencies will sustain more complaints.
- Oversight agencies will result in more discipline of guilty officers.
- More disciplinary actions will deter police misconduct more effectively than internal police procedures.
- Complaint review by oversight agencies will be perceived as independent and will provide greater satisfaction for complainants and also improve public attitudes about the police.
- Citizen oversight will help professionalize police departments and improve the quality of policing.

In Opposition to Civilian Oversight Theoretically, citizen review boards offer an efficient and effective means of identifying officer misdeeds and reconciling them to the satisfaction of the community at large. However, although civilian review boards may be good in theory, they are often poor in reality. They frequently fail to operate objectively, lack impartial or specialized agents to conduct essential investigations, and are devoid of any enforcement power needed to carry out their recommendations. Furthermore, the people who volunteer to serve on the board are not necessarily representative of the community and, in many cases, are "vocal rabble rousers" who wish to impose their values on the community. Opponents to civilian review boards cite such shortcomings as reasons to do without these ineffectual entities.

Police often maintain it would be unfair to allow those outside police work to judge their actions because only police officers understand the complexities of their job and, in particular, how and when they must use force. They stress that few citizens understand such concepts as "command presence" and "verbal force" so often necessary in high-risk encounters. As one police sergeant put it: "The public should walk a mile in our combat boots before they judge us."

Walker (p.17) also summarizes the arguments of opponents of citizen oversight who believe that oversight achieves none of its goals and often makes matters worse:

- Police misconduct is not as serious a problem as people allege.
- Police officers are capable of and do in fact conduct fair and thorough investigations.
- Police internal affairs units sustain a higher rate of complaints than do citizen oversight agencies.
- Police departments mete out tougher discipline than oversight agencies.
- Internal police disciplinary procedures deter police misconduct more effectively than oversight agencies.
- Internal police disciplinary procedures provide greater satisfaction to complainants and the general public.
- External citizen oversight agencies harm policing by deterring effective crime fighting by police officers and also by undermining the managerial authority of police chief executives.

Opponents also argue that police should have full responsibility for managing their own conduct just as other professionals such as physicians and lawyers do.

Striking a Balance Successful resolution of this issue requires that the concerns of both the community and the police be addressed. The desired outcome would be that the police maintain the ability to perform their duties without the fear that they will be second-guessed, disciplined or sued by those who do not understand the difficulties of their job. The key, according to Walker (p.21) is that successful oversight agencies do more than simply investigate complaints: "They take a proactive view of their role and actively seek out the underlying causes of police misconduct or problems with the complaint process."

Citizen Patrol

Community policing is rooted in law enforcement's dependence on the public's eyes, ears, information and influence to exert social control. In some communities citizens' attempts to be those eyes and ears have emerged in the form of citizen patrols. Some citizen patrols have formed as part of partnerships with the local police department, some independent of police partnerships and some in the face of police opposition. It is difficult for citizen volunteers, especially those in citizen patrols formed in spite of police opposition, to win the respect, trust and support of the police, who often have strong opinions about civilian involvement in what they consider police business or see them as critics of department efforts.

Citizen patrols are not new. The sheriffs' posses that handled law enforcement in America's Wild West have evolved to present-day citizen patrols, reserve police programs and neighborhood-watch groups. Many of the citizen patrols established throughout the country focus on the drug problem. For example, the Fairlawn Coalition in Washington, DC, established nightly patrol groups to walk the streets of Fairlawn and act as a deterrent to drug trafficking. Wearing bright orange hats, the citizen patrols drove drug dealers from their positions simply by standing out on the streets with them and later by bringing in video cameras, still cameras and much publicity. The citizen group decided not to invite the Guardian Angels or Nation of Islam to help them, fearing their aggressive tactics could escalate into violence. They chose instead to include men and women aged 40 and older to create a presence on the street but to pose no threat to the physical well-being of dealers.

The Blockos in Manhattan, New York, used a similar approach. To combat street-level drug dealing in their middle-class neighborhood, residents held some meetings and decided to go out into the street as a group and stand near the dealers. They also had a graphic artist provide posters to announce their meetings, and a member persuaded the *New York Times* to publish a story on their efforts.

Another tactic was used in Manhattan by a group called 210 Stanton, referring to the address of a building that was headquarters of a major drug-selling operation. Community patrol officers guarded the entrances to the building, requiring all visitors to sign in. If the visitors were going to the apartment where the drug dealing was occurring, officers accompanied them. In addition, information provided by residents helped solidify the case against the apartment where most of the drug dealing was taking place. Search warrants were issued, charges filed and the resident convicted.

In Arizona, ranchers near the Mexican border have formed the American Border Patrol (ABP), a citizens' patrol group whose goal is to help the official U.S. Border Patrol by finding and detaining illegal immigrants crossing into America from Mexico. They claim to have apprehended and turned over about 10,000 illegal immigrants to the Border Patrol in the past five years. Federal law enforcement agencies are not enthusiastic about the patrols. The U.S. Border Patrol does not comment on the matter but clearly is against any citizen activities beyond observing illegal activity and calling them for help.

Some citizen groups have exchange programs to reduce the chance of retribution by local drug retailers. Such exchange programs provide nearby neighborhoods with additional patrols while reducing the danger. Local dealers are less likely to recognize a vigil-keeper who lives in another neighborhood.

Citizen Police Academies

Another type of community involvement is through citizens' police academies designed to familiarize citizens with law enforcement and to keep the department in touch with the community. Police academies, which are popular with police departments and citizens, have the benefit of building community support for law enforcement and of helping citizens understand the police. They are not, however, community policing initiatives.

The first recorded U.S. citizen police academy (CPA) began in 1985 in Orlando, Florida. This program was modeled after a citizen police academy in England, which began in 1977. Such academies help a community's residents become more familiar with the day-to-day operations of their police department and to understand the procedures, responsibilities and demands placed on their officers.

The Sedgwick County (Kansas) Sheriff's Department Citizen Police Academy has won national recognition. Its 13-week program's purpose is: "To develop a harmonious working relationship between members of the community and law enforcement while at the same time opening a mutually supportive avenue for communication" (Sedgwick County Sheriff's Department Web site). Table 3.2 presents a typical agenda of a 12- to 13-week CPA.

The San Luis Obispo County (California) Sheriff's Citizen Academy provides community members with an inside look at the sheriff's office, law enforcement ethics, criminal law, investigations, patrol procedures, communications, crime prevention, drug enforcement and drug education.

Citizen police academies are not without limitations. First, even if attendees sign hold-harmless waivers, the agency may still be sued if a participant is injured or killed while attending the academy. Second, officers and administrators may resist an academy, feeling law enforcement activities should not be open to the public. Third, an agency may feel its resources could be better used.

Typical requirements for admission to a citizen police academy include a minimum age of 21 years, living or working in the department's jurisdiction and no prior felony convictions or misdemeanor arrests within one year of application.

Aryani et al. (2000, p.17) stress: "Like the police academy, success of the CPA depends on the administrative support, the strength of the curriculum and staff members, and the selection of students." They (p.21) conclude: "Citizen police academies represent a vital part of community-oriented policing. CPAs keep the public involved by making them part of the police family."

Some departments, such as in Waco, Texas, and Hartford, Wisconsin, have a Citizen Police Academy Alumni Association to provide an opportunity for continued education in law enforcement and related fields. They also allow participants to have a more interactive association with the police department.

Table 3.2 Typical Agenda of a 12- to 13-Week CPA

I. Administration and Professional Standards
- Introduction and welcome from the chief
- Administrative information and department overview
- Officer selection
- Ethics
- Internal affairs
- History of policing

II. Operations
- Field training
- Patrol procedures
- Communications
- Ride-alongs
- Traffic law and radar operation
- Accident investigations
- Officer safety/use of force
- Driving while intoxicated enforcement
- K-9 operations
- Firearms
- Tactical demonstrations

III. Investigations
- Child abuse/family violence
- Narcotics
- Criminal investigations

IV. Legal Issues
- Criminal justice system
- Juvenile law
- Probation/parole
- Corrections

V. Crime Prevention
- Drug Awareness Resistance Education/Gang Resistance Education and Training Program
- Neighborhood Crime Watch
- Citizens on Patrol
- Auto theft prevention
- Target hardening/insurance reduction surveys

VI. Special Topics
- Federal and state criminal justice system and agencies
- Economics of crime
- Criminology
- Citizen police academy alumni association information
- Forensic hypnosis
- Emergency medical services
- Special weapons and tactics

SOURCE: Giant Abutalebi Aryani et al. "The Citizen Police Academy: Success through Community Partnerships." *FBI Law Enforcement Bulletin,* May 2000, p.19. Reprinted by permission.

A twist on the citizens' academy is the Teen Citizen Academy of the Arroyo Grande Police Department. Designed for youths 13 to 18 years old, the academy provides an overview of topics such as gangs, drugs, weapons safety and personal safety.

Ride-Along Programs

Ride-along programs are a popular, yet controversial, means to improve police–community relations and get citizens involved in the efforts of the department and its officers. These programs are designed to give local citizens a close-up look at the realities of policing and what police work entails while giving officers a chance to connect with citizens in a positive way.

Many ride-along programs permit any responsible juvenile or adult to participate, but other programs have restrictions and may limit ridership. Participation by officers in a ride-along program is usually voluntary. Whether riders are allowed to use still or video cameras during a ride-along varies from department to department. Many departments also require their riders to dress appropriately.

Despite the numerous benefits of ride-along programs, some departments do not get involved for legitimate reasons such as insurance costs, liability and concerns about the public's safety. Some departments ask participants to sign a waiver exempting the officer, the department and the city from liability.

Sometimes a ride-along does more than foster police–community relations. In Denver, for example, officers who take clergy as riders have help with death notifications as well as a number of other situations, such as handling runaways, emotionally disturbed persons, victims of natural disasters, persons threatening suicide, substance abusers, child-abuse victims and victims of sexual assault. Boston's ride-along program with probation officers helps the police identify lawbreakers and gather information from those traveling in the same circles as offenders.

CAUTION: Citizen involvement in understanding and helping to police their communities is very important, but it, in itself, is NOT community policing. At the heart of the community policing philosophy is an emphasis on partnerships and on problem solving, the dual focus of the remainder of the text.

SUMMARY

Community policing must begin with an understanding of what communities are and how they function. Citizens of the United States have established the "public peace" through the U.S. Constitution and Bill of Rights, as well as through federal and state statutes and local ordinances. They also adhere to a social contract, which states that for everyone to receive justice, each person must give up some freedom.

Community refers to the specific geographic area served by a police department or law enforcement agency and the individuals, organizations and agencies within that area. Community also refers to a feeling of belonging—a sense of integration, a sense of shared values and a sense of "we-ness." The broken window phenomenon suggests that if it appears "no one cares," disorder and crime will thrive.

Understanding a community requires police to know about its demographics. Demographics include population or size, distribution, growth, density and vital statistics such as average age, education and income as well as employment rate and ethnic makeup. Three important changes that will alter the demographics of our communities are (1) white dominance will end, minorities will increase; (2) the elderly population will increase; and (3) the number of legal and illegal immigrants will increase.

Organizations and institutions can play a key role in enhancing community safety and quality of life. The private security industry can also play an important role in improving a community's well-being.

Operating within each community is a power structure that can enhance or endanger police–community relations. The formal power structure includes those with wealth and political influence: federal, state and local agencies and governments, commissions, regulatory agencies and power groups. The informal power structure includes religious groups, wealthy subgroups, ethnic groups, political groups and public interest groups.

Also operating within communities and affecting the police–community relationship tremendously is the criminal justice system, including the courts and corrections. Controversial issues in the criminal justice system that affect community policing include plea bargaining, diversion, sentencing, rehabilitation, community alternatives to prisons, victim's rights and capital punishment. The criminal justice system is moving away from a medical model of criminality to a justice model. The medical model sees those who break the law as victims of society; the justice model views lawbreakers as responsible for their own actions.

Restorative justice advocates a balanced approach to sentencing that involves offenders, victims, local communities and government to alleviate crime and violence and obtain peaceful communities. Other forms of citizen or community involvement include civilian review boards, citizen patrols, citizen police academies and ride-alongs.

Discussion Questions

1. How would you describe your community?
2. What instances of broken windows have you seen in your neighborhood? Other neighborhoods?
3. Can you give examples of the NIMBY syndrome?
4. What major changes have occurred in your community in the past 10 years? In your state?
5. Who is included in the power structure in your community?
6. Do you favor the medical model or the justice model for dealing with criminals? Why?
7. How extensively are the services of private security used in your community? Do they cooperate with or compete against the local police?
8. Do you favor use of civilian review boards? Why or why not?
9. Which seems more "just" to you: retributive justice or restorative justice?
10. What factors are most important in establishing a "sense of community"?

InfoTrac College Edition Assignments

- Use InfoTrac College Edition to help answer the Discussion Questions as appropriate.
- Select one of the following assignments to complete and share with the class.
  - Locate and outline two articles dealing with community leadership.
  - Research and outline your findings of at least one of the following subjects: *broken windows, ghettos, restorative justice* or *social contract.*
  - Read and outline one of the following articles:

    "The Citizen Police Academy: Success through Community Partnerships" by Giant Abutalebi Aryani et al.

    "Getting Along with Citizen Oversight" by Peter Finn

    "A Medical Model for Community Policing" by Joseph A. Harpold

Community Project

Use your telephone directory to determine what city services or community resources are available locally. Select one to contact and determine what relationship (if any) exists between it and your local police department.

References

Aryani, Giant Abutalebi; Garrett, Terry D.; and Alsabrook, Carl L. "The Citizen Police Academy: Success through Community Partnerships." *FBI Law Enforcement Bulletin,* May 2000, pp.16–21.

"Citizen Police Academy Alumni Association, Waco, Texas." www.accesswaco.com/community/ groups/ Citizens Police Academy/ index.html

Clear, Todd R. and Karp, David R. "Toward the Ideal of Community Justice." *NIJ Journal,* October 2000, pp.20–28.

Coleman, J. *Foundations of Social Theory.* Cambridge: Harvard University Press, 1990.

Correia, Mark E. *Citizen Involvement: How Community Factors Affect Progressive Policing.* Washington, DC: Police Executive Research Forum, 2000.

Farrow, Joe. "Citizen Oversight of Law Enforcement: Challenge and Opportunity." *The Police Chief,* October 2003, pp.22–29.

Finn, Peter. "Getting Along with Citizen Oversight." *FBI Law Enforcement Bulletin,* August 2000, pp.22–27.

Harpold, Joseph A. "A Medical Model for Community Policing." *FBI Law Enforcement Bulletin,* June 2000, pp.23–27.

Helfgott, Jacqueline B.; Lovell, Madeline L.; Lawrence, Charles F.; and Parsonage, William H. "Results from the Pilot Study of the Citizens, Victims, and Offenders Restoring Justice Program at the Washington State Reformatory." *Journal of Contemporary Criminal Justice,* February 2000, pp.5–31.

Jurik, Nancy C.; Blumenthal, Joel; Smith, Brian; and Portillos, Edwardo L. "Organizational Cooptation or Social Change?" *Journal of Contemporary Criminal Justice,* August 2000, pp.293–320.

Peed, Carl. "Connecting with Minority Communities." *The Police Chief,* May 2003, pp.10–11.

Reiman, Jeffrey. *The Rich Get Rich and the Poor Get Prison: Ideology, Class and Criminal Justice.* Needham Heights, MA: Allyn & Bacon, 2001.

"Sedgwick County Sheriff's Department Citizen Police Academy." www.sedgwick.ks.us/sheriff/CPA/index.html

"To Be or Not to Be . . . ALARMED!" *Apple Valley City News,* Summer 2000, p.1.

Walker, Samuel. *Police Accountability: The Role of Citizen Oversight.* Belmont, CA: Thomson/Wadsworth Publishing, 2001.

Wilson, James Q. and Kelling, George L. "The Police and Neighborhood Safety: Broken Windows." *The Atlantic Monthly,* March 1982, pp.29–38.

Wilson, James Q. and Kelling, George L. "Making Neighborhoods Safe." *The Atlantic Monthly,* February 1989, pp.46–52.

Additional Resource

National Citizen Police Academy Association, President Michael Koster, 630-801-6563.

Chapter 4

Problem Solving: Proactive Policing

A problem well stated is a problem half solved.

—Charles Kettering

Do You Know?

- How problem solving requires changes in the ways police treat incidents?
- How efficiency and effectiveness differ? Which is emphasized by community policing?
- What the first step in a problem-solving approach is?
- What four stages of problem solving are used in the SARA model?
- What three areas problem analysis considers?
- How the magnet phenomenon occurs?
- What the purpose and goal of the DOC model is?
- What crime-specific planning is?
- What the focus of crime mapping is?
- What two barriers to problem solving are?

Can You Define?

analysis (in SARA)
assessment (in SARA)
creativity
crime-specific planning
displacement
DOC model
effectiveness
efficiency
geographic profiling
hot spots
impact evaluation
incident
innovation
killer phrases
least-effort principle
magnet phenomenon
mediation
mental locks
problem-oriented policing (POP)
problem-solving approach
process evaluation
qualitative data
quantitative data
response (in SARA)
scanning (in SARA)

Introduction

The Community Oriented Policing Services Office stresses: "Engaging the community without problem-solving provides no meaningful service to the public. Problem solving without [partnerships] risks overlooking the most pressing community concerns. Thus the partnership between police departments and the community they service is essential for implementing a successful program in community policing" (*Problem-Solving Tips,* 2002, p.3).

A **problem-solving approach** involves identifying problems and making decisions about how best to deal with them. A basic characteristic of community policing is that it is proactive rather than reactive, meaning it involves recognizing problems and seeking their underlying causes.

To illustrate, a man and his buddy, who could not swim, were fishing on a riverbank when a young boy floated past, struggling to stay afloat. The fisherman jumped in and pulled the young boy from the water. He resumed his fishing, but within a few minutes another person came floating by, again struggling to stay afloat. Again, the fisherman reacted by jumping in and pulling the person to safety. He then resumed his fishing and again, within minutes, another person came floating by. The fisherman got up and started heading upstream. His buddy called after him, "Where are you going?" To which the fisherman replied, "I'm going to find out who's pushing all these people into the river!"

It is usually more effective to get to the source of a problem rather than simply reacting to it. This chapter focuses on a problem-solving approach to policing. It

Children play on the steps of a decaying Housing and Urban Development (HUD) property. Disorder such as this can be corrected by collaborative problem-solving strategies.

begins with an explanation of the change in focus on individual incidents or symptoms to a focus on problems or causes. Next efficiency and effectiveness are described, followed by an explanation of the importance of addressing substantive problems. Then the four-stage SARA model for problem solving is examined, including a look at problem analysis. This is followed by a discussion on making ethical decisions using the DOC model and using mediation as a problem-solving tool. Then problem solving and crime-specific planning are discussed as well as crime analysis. This is followed by a discussion of how technology is used for problem solving, including explanations of crime mapping, Geographic Information Systems and geographic profiling. Next common mistakes in problem solving are examined, as well as the role of creativity in problem-solving efforts. The chapter concludes with a look at problem solving at work, describing several promising practices from the field.

From Incidents to Problems

During the past quarter century, law enforcement agencies around the country have combined the operational strategies of community-oriented policing and problem solving to address crime and quality-of-life issues. Frazier (2000, p.11), a former director of the Office of Community Oriented Policing Services, asserts: "Police need to act as problem solvers and peacemakers in their communities. Police and citizens must work together if we are to develop long-term solutions to crime, and if we are to enhance trust between police and the communities they serve."

Community policing or variations of it that rely on problem solving are known by several names, including community-oriented policing and problem solving (COPPS), neighborhood-oriented policing (NOP), problem-oriented policing (POP), and community-based policing. Eck and Spelman (1987) define **problem-oriented policing** as "a departmental-wide strategy aimed at solving persistent community problems. Police identify, analyze and respond to the underlying circumstances that create incidents." No matter what the approach is called, all use a problem-solving approach to crime and disorder. Throughout this text, references to community policing infer that problem solving is involved.

Many practitioners equate community policing and problem solving. As Wilson and Kelling (1989, p.49) note: "Community-oriented policing means changing the daily work of the police to include investigating problems as well as incidents. It means defining as a problem whatever a significant body of public opinion regards as a threat to community order. It means working with the good guys, and not just against the bad guys." Wilson and Kelling suggest that community policing requires the police mission to be redefined "to help the police become accustomed to fixing broken windows as well as arresting window-breakers."

Goldstein (1990, p.20), who is credited with originating problem-oriented policing (POP) and coined the term, was among the first to criticize the professional model of policing as being incident driven: "In the vast majority of police departments, the telephone, more than any policy decision by the community or by management, continues to dictate how police resources will be used." The primary work unit in the professional model is the **incident**, that is, an isolated event that requires a police response. The institution of 911 has greatly increased the demand for police services and the public's expectation that the police will respond quickly.

As Rahtz (2001, p.57) explains: "The emphasis on solving problems is what separates our two styles of policing [traditional policing and community policing]. Reactive Jack's day is dictated by the radio. Anyone in the community who picks up the phone and dials 911 has more control over Jack than his supervisor does. Jack's workday is not informed by any serious analysis of the problems on his beat. Instead, he runs willy-nilly where the radio calls lead. He handles the calls as quickly as possible, and in the time between radio runs he cruises about with little purpose waiting for the next dispatch. For a lot of cops, that is the sum total of police work. For beat officers tired of the merry-go-round of reactive policing, for cops looking for a more intelligent approach to police work, community policing emphasizing problem solving will be a godsend."

Goldstein (p.33) also asserts: "Most policing is limited to ameliorating the overt, offensive symptoms of a problem." He suggests that police are more productive if they respond to incidents as symptoms of underlying community problems. He (p.66) defines a problem as "a cluster of similar, related, or recurring incidents rather than a single incident, a substantive community concern, and a unit of police business." Once the problems in a community are identified, police efforts can focus on addressing the possible causes of such problems.

Problem-solving policing requires police to group incidents and, thereby, identify underlying causes of problems in the community.

Although problem solving may be the ideal, law enforcement cannot ignore specific incidents. When calls come in, most police departments respond as soon as possible. Problem solving has a dual focus. First, it requires that incidents be linked to problems. Second, time devoted to "preventive" patrol must be spent proactively, determining community problems and their underlying causes.

A problem-solving approach relies heavily on citizen involvement and partnerships. An analogy can be drawn between a physician and a patient. The physician can examine the patient, take the patient's history and prescribe a treatment based on the patient's symptoms. To recover, however, the patient must be honest and thorough in describing the symptoms and must follow the prescribed treatment. Further, in medicine as in policing, the best approach is to prevent the illness in the first place.

Regardless of whether police officers respond to incidents, seek symptoms of problems or both, the public can help or hinder their efforts. Police and community members must discuss and agree to any community involvement program before it is adopted. At times well-meaning individuals and community groups, acting unilaterally, can actually interfere with a police effort and cause unnecessary destruction, injury and even death.

The dual themes of this book are the manner in which police can form effective partnerships with the community to address the issues of crime and disorder and the necessity of a problem-solving approach to such issues. Like any response, the problem-solving process will not always result in success. In fact, mistakes should be expected and seen as learning opportunities. If no mistakes are made, then little problem solving is taking place.

Community Policing Compared to Problem-Oriented Policing

While Goldstein suggests community involvement is a positive development, his problem-oriented policing or POP relies mostly on police participants. In addition, Goldstein's model emphasizes problem solving over partnerships. The differences between community policing and problem-oriented policing are summarized in Table 4.1.

A problem-solving approach to policing was developed partially in response to concerns for efficiency and effectiveness.

Table 4.1 Selected Comparisons between Problem-Oriented Policing and Community Policing Principles

Principle	*Problem-Oriented Policing*	*Community Policing*
Primary emphasis	Substantive social problems within police mandate	Engaging the community in the policing process
When police and community collaborate	Determined on a problem by problem basis	Always or nearly always
Emphasis on problem analysis	Highest priority given to thorough analysis	Encouraged, but less important than community collaboration
Preference for responses	Strong preference that alternatives to criminal law enforcement be explored	Preference for collaborative response with community
Role for police in organizing and mobilizing community	Advocated only if warranted within the context of the specific problem being addressed	Emphasizes strong role for police
Importance of geographic decentralization of police and continuity of officer assignment to community	Preferred, but not essential	Essential
Degree to which police share decision-making authority with community	Strongly encourages input from community while preserving ultimate decision-making authority to police	Emphasizes sharing decision-making authority with community
Emphasis on officers' skills	Emphasizes intellectual and analytical skills	Emphasizes interpersonal skills
View of the role or mandate of police	Encourages broad, but not unlimited role for police, stresses limited capacities of police and guards against creating unrealistic expectations of police	Encourages expansive role for police to achieve ambitious social objectives

SOURCE: Michael S. Scott. *Problem-Oriented Policing: Reflections on the First 20 Years.* Washington, DC: U.S. Department of Justice, Office of Community Oriented Policing Services, 2000, p.99.

Being Efficient and Effective

Wilson and Kelling (p.46) illustrate the consequences when emphasis is placed on efficiency:

> The police know from experience what research by Glenn Pierce, in Boston, and Lawrence Sherman, in Minneapolis, has established: fewer than 10 percent of the addresses from which the police receive calls account for more than 60 percent of those calls. If each call is treated as a separate incident with neither a history nor a future, then each dispute will be handled by police officers anxious to pacify the complainants and get back on patrol as quickly as possible. . . .
>
> A study of domestic homicides in Kansas City showed that in eight out of ten cases the police had been called to the incident address at least once before; in half the cases they had been called five times or more.

Efficiency involves minimizing waste, expense or unnecessary effort. Efficiency is doing things right. The police in the preceding studies were very efficient, responding promptly and dealing with the problem, usually to the citizen's satisfaction. But were they effective? And if they are not effective, efficiency does not really pay off. Making the same efficient responses to the same location is *not* really efficient. The response needs to be effective as well.

Effectiveness has to do with producing the desired result or goal. Effectiveness is doing the right thing. Ideally, both efficiency and effectiveness are present in policing. There can be effectiveness without efficiency, but there cannot be efficiency without effectiveness because any effort that does not achieve the desired goal is wasted.

Police, along with other emergency services, face an inherent contradiction between effectiveness and efficiency. To have the capacity to respond to an emergency quickly, staffing levels must be sufficient to have personnel available to respond at all times. To have that capacity, however, requires a number of personnel with substantial slack time. Without slack time, all personnel may be busy when emergencies occur, reducing response effectiveness. Unfortunately, too often police departments have emphasized efficiency, for example, rapid response to calls, number of citations issued and the like, rather than what will produce the desired outcomes of the department.

Across the country, most police departments respond in a timely manner to every call for service. Just one example of this policy illustrates how efficiency can overshadow effectiveness. For years, a convenience store across the street from a high school had been a magnet for high school students during the three lunch periods at the open campus school. The store complained of disturbances, thefts and intimidation of customers. Other businesses complained about "spill-over" from the gatherings which affected their businesses. The grocery store experienced shoplifting; the dry cleaners had students smoking in the back of their building; and they all complained about drug sales at the bus stop at that intersection. Nearby residential neighbors complained about cigarette butts and empty soda cans littering their yards after lunch each day. Everyone disliked the loud music played on car stereos throughout the lunch periods. Every day one or more people called the police department to complain. And every day the police department dispatched one or two squad cars. Often the squads reported everything was quiet when they arrived. Lunchtime had ended, and the students had returned to school. Or if there was still a problem, the students scattered when they saw the police, and no action was necessary. Nearly every school day for years, these same calls came into the police department. The police response was polite and quick. By police department standards, their response was efficient. By neighborhood standards, the police response was completely ineffective.

Efficiency, doing things right, has been the traditional emphasis in law enforcement. Effectiveness, doing the right things, is the emphasis in community policing, but it should also produce an increase in efficiency, proactively solving problems rather than simply reacting to them.

A focus on substantive problems (effectiveness) rather than on the smooth functioning of the organization (efficiency) is a radical change and difficult for some departments to make. Those departments that have made the shift in focus have achieved excellent results.

Addressing Substantive Problems

Traditionally police have responded to incidents, handled them as effectively as possible and then moved on to the next call. This fragmented approach to policing conceals patterns of incidents that may be symptomatic of deeper problems. Goldstein (p.33) contends: "The first step in problem-oriented policing is to move beyond just handling incidents. It calls for recognizing that incidents are often merely overt symptoms of problems."

The first step in problem solving is to group incidents as problems.

The basic elements in a problem-solving approach combine steps a police department can take and theoretical assumptions to make the steps work. Many departments have developed problem-solving approaches that incorporate these basic elements. One of the best known problem-solving approaches is the SARA model.

The SARA Model: A Four-Stage Problem-Solving Process

Eck and Spelman describe the four-stage problem-solving process used in the Newport News Police Department known as the SARA model.

The four stages of the SARA problem-solving model are scanning, analysis, response and assessment.

Scanning refers to identifying recurring problems and prioritizing them to select one problem to address. The problems should be of concern to the public as well as the police. At this stage broad goals may be set.

Analysis examines the identified problem's causes, scope and effects. It includes determining how often the problem occurs, how long it has been occurring as well as conditions that appear to create the problem. Analysis also should include potential resources and partners who might assist in understanding and addressing the problem.

Response is acting to alleviate the problem, that is, selecting the alternative solution or solutions to try. This may include finding out what other communities with similar problems have tried and with what success as well as looking at whether any research on the problem exists. Focus groups might be used to brainstorm possible interventions. Experts might be enlisted. Several alternatives might be ranked and prioritized according to difficulty, expense and the like. At this point goals are usually refined and the interventions are implemented.

Assessment refers to evaluating the effectiveness of the intervention. Was the problem solved? If not, why? Assessment should include both qualitative and quantitative data. **Qualitative data** examines the excellence (quality) of the response; that is, how satisfied were the officers and the citizens? This is most frequently determined by surveys, focus groups or tracking complaints and compliments. **Quantitative data** examines the amount of change (quantity) as a result of the response. This is most frequently measured by pre/post data.

The SARA model of problem solving stresses that there are no failures, only responses that do not provide the desired goal. When a response does not give the desired results, the partners involved in problem solving can examine the results and try a different response. Other communities might benefit from what was learned.

Scanning and Analysis

Scanning and analysis are integrally related. The sources for analyzing a community's problems provide the basis for analysis. Table 4.2 illustrates potential sources of information for identifying problems obtained through scanning. Comprehensively analyzing a problem is critical to the success of a problem-solving effort. Effective, tailor-made responses cannot be developed unless you know what is causing the problem (*Problem-Solving Tips,* 2002, p.11).

This step in the SARA model is often skipped for a variety of reasons. Sometimes it is because at first the nature of the problem seems obvious or because there is pressure to solve the problem immediately. Taking the time for analysis may be seen as too time consuming without producing tangible results, especially when responding to calls seems to preclude this type of activity. But if not done, there is a chance of addressing a nonexistent problem or of applying ineffective solutions.

Problem-Solving Tips (p.12) suggests: "The first step in analysis is to determine what information is needed. This should be a broad inquiry, uninhibited by past perspectives; questions should be asked whether or not answers can be obtained. The openness and persistent probing associated with such an inquiry are not unlike the approach that a seasoned and highly regarded detective would take to solve a puzzling crime: reaching out in all directions, digging deeply, asking the right questions." This document also presents a way to envision crime in a community: "Generally,

Table 4.2 Potential Sources of Information for Identifying Problems

Crime Analysis Unit—Time trends and patterns (time of day, day of week, monthly, seasonal, and other cyclical events), and patterns of similar events (offender descriptions, victim characteristics, locations, physical settings and other circumstances).

Patrol—Recurring calls, bad areas, active offenders, victim types, complaints from citizens.

Investigations—Recurring crimes, active offenders, victim difficulties, complaints from citizens.

Crime Prevention—Physical conditions, potential victims, complaints from citizens.

Vice—Drug dealing, illegal alcohol sales, gambling, prostitution, organized crime.

Communications—Call types, repeat calls from same location, temporal peaks in calls for service.

Chief's Office—Letters and calls from citizens, concerns of elected officials, concerns from city manager's office.

Other Law Enforcement Agencies—Multi-jurisdictional concerns.

Elected Officials—Concerns and complaints.

Local Government Agencies—Plans that could influence crimes, common difficulties, complaints from citizens.

Schools—Juvenile concerns, vandalism, employee safety.

Community Leaders—Problems of constituents.

Business Groups—Problems of commerce and development.

Neighborhood Watch—Local problems regarding disorder, crime and other complaints.

Newspapers and Other News Media—Indications of problems not detected from other sources, problems in other jurisdictions that could occur in any city.

Community Surveys—Problems of citizens in general.

SOURCE: John E. Eck and William Spelman. *Problem Solving: Problem-Oriented Policing in Newport News.* Washington, DC: Police Executive Research Forum, 1987, p.46. © 1987 Police Executive Research Forum. Reprinted with permission by PERF.

three elements are required to constitute a crime in the community: an offender, a victim and a crime scene or location." This crime triangle is illustrated in Figure 4.1.

Problem solvers are advised to discover as much about all three sides of the triangle as it relates to the problem by asking: Who? What? When? Where? How? Why? and Why not? about each side.

"Recent research has shown that a small number of victims account for a large amount of crime incidents. Researchers in England found that victims of burglary, domestic violence and other crimes are likely to be revictimized very soon after the first victimization—often within a month or two. Effective interventions targeted at repeat victims can significantly reduce crime."

"According to one study of residential burglary in the Huddersfield Division of the West Yorkshire Police in England, victims were four times more likely than nonvictims to be victimized again, and most repeat burglaries occurred within six weeks of the first. Consequently, the Huddersfield Division developed a tailored, three-tiered response to repeat burglary victims, based on the number of times their homes had been burglarized. According to initial reports, residential burglary has been reduced more than 20 percent since the project began, and they have experienced no displacement" (*Problem-Solving Tips,* p.14).

Displacement is the theory that successful implementation of a crime-reduction initiative does not really prevent crime. Instead it just moves the crime to the next

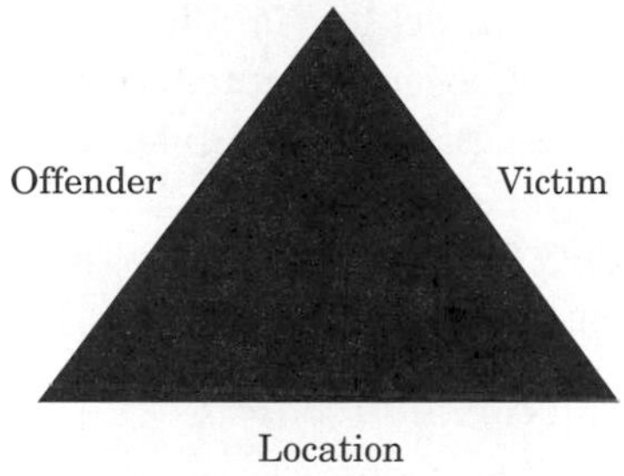

Figure 4.1 The Crime Triangle

SOURCE: *Problem-Solving Tips: A Guide to Reducing Crime and Disorder through Problem-Solving Partnerships.* Washington, DC: Office of Community Oriented Policing Services, June 2002, p.13. (NCJ 196527)

block, neighborhood or city. Police databases are not designed to track repeat victims, so police in the West Yorkshire project had some difficulty tracking repeat victims.

A Problem Analysis Guide To assist in problem analysis, the Newport News Police Department developed a problem analysis guide that lists topic headings police should consider in assessing problems.

Problem analysis considers the individuals involved, the incidents and the responses.

Their problem analysis guide highlights the complex interaction of individuals, incidents and responses occurring within a social context and a physical setting. The problems Newport News Police identified and how they approached them are discussed later in the chapter. Problem-solving experts Goldstein, Eck and Spelman suggest that effective problem solving involves the following steps:

- Adopt a proactive stance.
- Focus on problems of concern to the public.
- Group incidents as problems.
- Focus on substantive problems as the heart of policing.
- Encourage a broad and uninhibited search for solutions.
- Capture and critique the current response.
- Make full use of the data in police files and the experience of police personnel.
- Avoid using overly broad labels in grouping incidents so separate problems can be identified.
- Seek effectiveness as the ultimate goal.
- Use systematic inquiry.
- Acknowledge the limits of the criminal justice system as a response to problems.
- Identify multiple interests in any one problem and weigh them when analyzing the value of different responses.
- Be committed to taking some risks in responding to problems.
- Strengthen the decision-making processes and increase accountability.
- Evaluate results of newly implemented responses.

As Bynum (2001, p.2) contends: "Problem solving is based on the belief that patterns and trends can be discovered that reflect the causes of the problem. Analysis is the key to detecting these patterns and planning an effective response." However, according to the *PSP National Evaluation Final Report* (2000, p.42): "The National Assessment of the COPS PSP program indicated that analysis was the weakest phase of the problem solving process." Bynum (p.12) lists five principles of analysis:

1. Analysis is based on common sense.
2. There is no one way to do analysis.
3. Individual problems require individual analysis.
4. Analysis requires creativity and innovation.
5. Analysis does not need to be complex.

Bynum (p.15) suggests: "In most cases, simple frequencies of events, percentages of various categories and tables showing how characteristics relate to each other (e.g., type of burglary by time of day) are sufficient for an adequate analysis. The analysis should focus on how to best characterize the problem and what characteristics are most frequently associated with the problem. The purpose is to discover points of intervention for responses, not to prove causations." Bynum identifies the following as impediments to conducting analysis:

- Emphasis on rapid response
- Lack of institutional and organizational support for long-term responses
- Requirements for nontraditional police activities
- Perception that all the information needed has been collected
- Tendency to want to do something about it now
- Hunches and/or experience driving disparate response selection
- Perception that specialized knowledge is necessary
- Perception that analysis requires too much time or resources
- Perception that analysis is irrelevant to the action that needs to be taken
- Perception that once done, analysis can never be revisited

When identifying problems, it is important to be aware of the magnet phenomenon.

The **magnet phenomenon** occurs when a phone number or address is associated with a crime simply because it was a convenient number or address to use.

A magnet telephone is one that is available when no other telephones are, for example, a telephone in a convenience store that is open all night and on weekends. Victims of or witnesses to a crime in the area may use that telephone to report the crime, even though the store was not the scene of the crime. Similarly, a magnet address is one that is easy for people to give, for example, a high school or a theater. High numbers of calls from one location can give skewed results as the assumption is often made, for record-keeping purposes, that the location of the call is also the location of the incident.

When specific crimes are identified during the first stage of problem solving, crime-specific planning may be appropriate. Before looking at crime-specific planning, however, consider how to assess whether the interventions are effective.

Assessing Responses to Problems

According to Eck (2002, p.6): "You begin planning for an evaluation when you take on a problem. The evaluation builds throughout the SARA process, culminates during the assessment and provides findings that help you determine if you should revisit earlier stages to improve the response." Figure 4.2 illustrates the problem-solving process and evaluation.

Eck (p.10) describes two types of evaluations to conduct: **Process evaluation** determines if the response was implemented as planned, and **impact evaluation** determines if the problem declined. Table 4.3 provides guidance in interpreting the results of process and impact evaluation.

Eck (p.27) suggests several nontraditional measures that will indicate if a problem has been affected by the interventions:

- Reduced instances of repeat victimization
- Decreases in related crimes or incidents
- Neighborhood indicators: increased profits for legitimate businesses in target area; increased use of area/increased (or reduced) foot and vehicular traffic; increased property values; improved neighborhood appearance; increased occupancy in problem buildings; less loitering; fewer abandoned cars; less truancy
- Increased citizen satisfaction regarding the handling of the problem, which can be determined through surveys, interviews, focus groups, electronic bulletin boards and the like
- Reduced citizen fear related to the problem

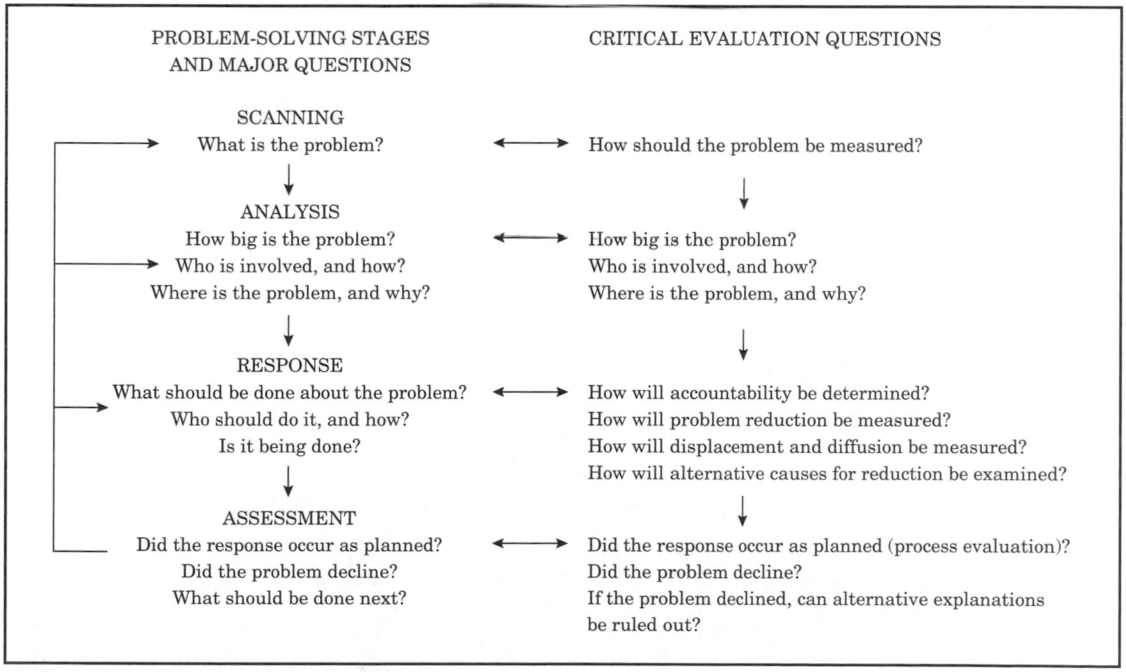

Figure 4.2 The Problem-Solving Process and Evaluation

SOURCE: John E. Eck. *Assessing Responses to Problems: An Introductory Guide for Police Problem-Solvers.* Washington, DC: Office of Community Oriented Policing Services, 2002, p.6.

Table 4.3 Interpreting Results of Process and Impact Evaluations

		Process Evaluation Results	
		Response implemented as planned, or nearly so	Response not implemented, or implemented in a radically different manner than planned
Impact Evaluation Results	Problem declined	A. Evidence that the response caused the decline	C. Suggests that other factors may have caused the decline, or that the response was accidentally effective
	Problem did not decline	B. Evidence that the response was ineffective, and that a different response should be tried	D. Little is learned. Perhaps if the response had been implemented as planned, the problem would have declined, but this is speculative

SOURCE: John E. Eck. *Assessing Responses to Problems: An Introductory Guide for Police Problem-Solvers.* Washington, DC: Office of Community Oriented Policing Services, 2002, p.10.

The SARA Model in Action

The Herman Goldstein Award for Excellence in Problem-Oriented Policing was established in 1993, honoring Professor Herman Goldstein for conceiving and developing the theory of problem-oriented policing. This award is given to innovative, effective POP projects that have demonstrated measurable success in reducing specific crime, disorder or public safety problems.

The 1998 award winner was *Operation Cease Fire,* Boston Police Department (adapted from Brito and Allan, 1999, pp.328–339). This exemplary model, although five years old, is included because it has had a tremendous impact on police departments across the country, being replicated and adapted nationwide.

Scanning In 1987 Boston had 22 victims of youth homicide. In 1990 that figure had risen to 73 victims—a 230 percent increase. Responding to six or seven shootings every night, police were overwhelmed. For many of Boston's youths, the city had become a dangerous, even deadly, place, which led to the formation of a gun project working group.

The working group's line-level personnel were convinced the gun violence problem was a gang problem because most victims and offenders were gang members and because the worst offenders in the cycle of fear, gun acquisition and gun use were gang members. Another part of the problem identified was that many of the youths involved were not "bad" or inherently dangerous but were participating because gang membership had become a means of self-protection.

Analysis The Harvard team framed the relevant issues in gun market terms. Gun trafficking and other means of illegal firearm acquisition represented the supply side, whereas fear and other factors potentially driving illicit gun acquisition and use represented the demand side. Research techniques included geographic mapping of youth homicides, gun market analysis using BPD/ATF gun recovery and tracing data, gathering of criminal histories of youth homicide victims and offenders and collection of hospital emergency room data. Key findings of this research included:

- Most youth gun and knife homicides and woundings occurred in three specific neighborhoods.
- Of the 1,550 firearms recovered from youths, 52.1 percent were semiautomatic pistols.
- Trace analysis revealed that 34 percent of traceable firearms recovered from youths were first sold at retail establishments in Massachusetts.
- Of all traceable guns recovered from youths, 26 percent were less than two years old and, thus, almost certainly trafficked rather than stolen.
- Nearly 20 percent of all guns recovered from youths had obliterated serial numbers, suggesting they were relatively new "trafficked" guns.
- Of the 155 youth gun and knife homicide victims, 75 percent had been arraigned for at least one offense in Massachusetts courts.
- Boston had roughly 61 gangs with 1,300 members in the three high-risk neighborhoods previously identified. Although this represented less than 3 percent of the youths ages 14 to 24 in these neighborhoods, these gangs were responsible for at least 60 percent of Boston's youth homicides.

Response The working group framed two main responses into a program called "Cease Fire." The first response was to mount a direct law enforcement attack on illicit gun trafficking by (1) using trace information to identify gun traffickers and (2) systematically debriefing gang offenders facing serious charges for violent, drug and other crimes.

The second, and perhaps more important, response involved creating a powerful deterrent to gang-related violence by making clear to youths that future violence would most certainly result in overwhelming crackdowns and "costs" imposed on the gang. Such "costs" would extend to the whole gang, not just the shooter, and might include cash-flow problems caused by street-drug market disruption, arrests from outstanding warrants, the humiliation of strict probation enforcement and possibly severe sanctions brought by federal involvement. Because of their familiarity with local gangs, the working group was usually able to link a particular act of violence to a certain gang relatively quickly and dispense sanctions swiftly. Operation Cease Fire transformed the police response to violence, turning uncertain, slow and often mild responses into ones that were certain, rapid and of whatever severity the working group deemed appropriate.

Assessment In the project's first two years, youth homicides dropped roughly 70 percent. Between 50 and 60 percent of the residents in the three identified high-risk neighborhoods felt satisfied the BPD was doing all it could to reduce area crime, with more than 33 percent of those residents reporting a great deal of confidence in the BPD's ability to prevent crime (up from an average 10 percent in 1995). Citywide, 76 percent of residents felt safe out alone in their neighborhoods at night (compared with 55 percent in 1995). Perhaps the most noteworthy result was that

88 percent of residents said they would be willing to work with each other and police to reduce and prevent crime. It is noteworthy that Operation Cease Fire not only achieved its goal, but it also did so ethically.

Making Ethical Decisions

Romano et al. (2000, p.98) suggest that SARA needs an additional component to address ethics and moral decision making. To this end, Facing History and Ourselves (FHAO), a national educational and training organization whose mission is to engage students in examining racism, prejudice and anti-Semitism, developed a framework for addressing ethical and moral issues called the DOC model.

The **DOC model** (dilemmas-options-consequences) challenges officers to carefully consider their decisions and the short- and long-term consequences of those decisions. The goal is to fuse problem solving and morality.

Romano et al. (p.99) suggest that if officers are facing a dilemma and a decision that feels wrong, they should ask themselves questions such as: What feels wrong? Is there a moral or ethical threat to me or someone else? Will I, or someone in the community, be affected or hurt physically or emotionally or be treated disrespectfully? Such questions prompt officers to think about how others feel and how they may or may not be affected by the actions officers take.

After the dilemma is identified, an action is needed, leading to the options phase and questions such as: What are my options? Am I considering all options? Am I being open minded and creative? Do my options rely on only me, or could I use a resource or someone's help? Whose?

For each choice, officers must assess the consequences by asking: What happens because of my choice? What if I do nothing? Who is affected by what I do? How? Will I protect myself? Will I protect the quality of life and dignity of others? Will I preserve my moral and ethical integrity? What are the short-term effects? The long-term effects?

In addition to considering the ethics involved in problem solving, community policing officers often find they must rely on their skills in mediation as well.

Mediation as a Problem-Solving Tool

Research shows that many calls for service involve landlord/tenant disputes, loud parties, rowdy teens, traffic complaints and even domestic calls, not requiring law enforcement intervention. But police traditionally use enforcement strategies such as rapid response and random patrol to address these problems.

Mediation, sometimes called alternative dispute resolution (ADR), is shared problem solving by parties in dispute guided by a neutral person. In many instances the mediator might be a police officer. Changing roles from law enforcer authority to a partner in conflict resolution requires different skills than many officers are accustomed to using. If a police officer is the mediator, mediation may provide a short-term solution, but this is often the result of the perceived coercive power of the mediating officer (resolve this, or else . . .).

As Cooper (2000, p.10) notes: "When departments use mediation to resolve conflicts in their communities, they empower residents to take responsibility for their actions and to resolve their own problems, not just in arguments with their neighbors but in other areas of their lives, as well." The Boston Police Web site (www.ci.boston.ma.us/police/) describes the department's community mediation program as an alternative to court proceedings. It is a process of talking and listening to one another to settle disputes. The parties make their own decisions whether to accept or reject a solution. Mediation is strictly confidential. Exceptions to confidentiality include the final agreement reached and any criminal activity revealed, including abuse or neglect.

Problem-Solving Policing and Crime-Specific Planning

To maintain effective police–community partnerships, police must also fulfill their crime-fighting role. Police can approach this role with many of the problem-solving skills just discussed, using crime-specific planning, a more precise strategy than problem-oriented policing in that it considers underlying problems categorized by type of offense. **Crime-specific planning** involves reviewing the following factors:

- *The offense:* Seriousness, frequency of occurrence, susceptibility to control, whether a crime of opportunity or calculation, the modus operandi and any violent characteristics present
- *The target:* Property taken or damaged, when attacked, how attacked, where located, number of potential targets in area, accessibility, transportation patterns surrounding the target
- *Impact:* On the community, public concern, drain on resources of the criminal justice system
- *Response:* Of the victim, the community, the criminal justice system

Traditionally, crime-specific planning involved only the first two factors. The last two factors have been added as a result of the community policing philosophy.

Crime-specific planning uses the principles of problem solving to focus on identified crime problems.

A careful analysis of these factors provides the basis for problem solving and deriving alternatives for approaching each specific crime problem.

Crime Analysis

According to Wideman (2000, p.59): "Crime analysis is the systematic gathering, evaluation, and analysis of information on individuals and/or activities suspected of being, or known to be, criminal in nature." As Wernicke and Stallo (2000, p.56) point out: "An increasing number of agencies, large and small, are establishing crime analysis units."

Assistance is available to agencies developing crime analysis units from the International Association of Crime Analysts (IACA), a group "dedicated to advocacy for professional standards, to providing practical educational opportunities and to the creation of an international network for the standardization of analytic techniques" (Wernicke and Stallo, p.57). The group's Web site is www.iaca.net.

Also of assistance to crime analysis is computer software that provides probability assessments. As Miles (2000, p.102) notes, software is available that lets investigators quantify and combine judgments to assess the probability that evidence proves guilt or innocence, simplifying the task and eliminating the guesswork. By mathematically evaluating circumstantial evidence, investigators can come to more reliable conclusions that will lead to sounder verdicts. Further assistance in crime analysis and problem solving is available from technological advances made in crime mapping and in geographic profiling.

Using Technology for Problem Solving

Technology has become an indispensable tool for law enforcement. In fact: "Some say the computer is changing policing today the way the two-way radio changed policing in the 1940s" (Wartell and Greenhalgh, 2000, p.1). Computers can greatly assist departments using the SARA model for problem solving. In the scanning phase, crime analysis can use information from the Records Management System (RMS) to identify problems. Computer Aided Dispatch (CAD) can identify locations getting repeat calls for police service. Likewise, databases, charts, graphs and spreadsheets can identify similarities in incidents indicating a need for problem solving. Basic analysis can also be done with computerized data, including CompStat, crime mapping and Geographic Information Systems (GIS).

CompStat

"CompStat, short for 'computer statistics' or 'comparison statistics,' is a multifaceted system for managing police operations with a proven track record in several major metropolitan police departments tracing its roots back to 1994 in the New York City Police Department" (Schick, 2004, p.17).

Wiley and Smith (2003, p.47) provide a brief history: "The most prevalent quality-of-life complaints in New York's Time Square were noise, panhandlers, peep shows and squeegee boys. The police department's CompStat program required officers to address these quality-of-life matters and others—graffiti, litter, broken windows, abandoned cars and buildings and a host of other seemingly minor violations of city codes. In the process of solving these problems, officers found that the neighborhood improved in surprising ways and more serious crimes became less frequent. The lesson is that if we ignore our neighborhoods because they seem less than desirable, then the problem will become worse. This is known as the broken window theory, and it has been the heart and soul of community-oriented policing for many years."

McDonald (2004, p.37), likewise, notes how CompStat can enhance community policing efforts: "CompStat, when applied correctly and effectively, strengthens community policing. Communities are critical resources for information, for the development of solutions to issues and crime problems, and for behaviors that will help reduce opportunities for perpetrators. CompStat will provide accountability for community policing activities, will ensure that all community activities have direction and application to solving problems, and will reinforce the need for commanders to complete their strategies by involving the community in their problem solving."

Crime Mapping—Geographic Information Systems

As Rogers (2000, p.36) notes: "Crime analysis and crime mapping technology are changing the way law enforcement does business."

Crime mapping changes the focus from the criminal to the location of crimes—the **hot spots** where most crimes occur.

Aragon (2000, p.8) presents several facts that support use of crime mapping and attention to hot spots:

- Two-thirds of all crime occurs indoors, not visible to the police.
- Most serious crimes are perpetrated within a short time frame; for example, the average armed robbery takes approximately 90 seconds.
- Patrol officers intercept less than 1 percent of street crimes.
- The same 10 percent of locations within a jurisdiction generate approximately 65 percent of that jurisdiction's total calls for service.

Aragon concludes:

> Law enforcement is behind the power curve and must work on strategies for preventing incidents from occurring in the first place. The analogy I find highly applicable . . . is this: less successful agencies "shoot where the target was"; run-of-the-mill agencies "shoot where the target is"; successful agencies "shoot where the target is going."

The National Institute of Justice has released *Mapping Crime: Principle and Practice,* a research guide designed to help police understand crime data analysis through crime mapping and designed for agencies just starting to use GIS. It is available on the Web at www.ncjrs.org/nij/mapping/for.html. Warden and Shaw (2000, pp.81–86) describe how mapping helped predict a residential break-in pattern in Edmonton, Alberta, Canada (adapted and reprinted by permission).

Problem Identification In November 1998, Constable Jerry Shaw (the crime analysis section's crime mapping specialist) observed break-and-enter crime clusters within a specific area of the North Division. Tactical crime hot spot maps were created and forwarded to the division's criminal investigation section staff sergeant.

The geographic area in question was primarily an older residential area where the crime clusters were self-evident and had, compared to previous crime maps of the same area, revealed a marked increase in activity.

Problem Solving Crime mapping showed where the suspects operated and the evolving pattern of their movement. Time/date sequencing of 240 break-ins in the hot spot area revealed these were daytime break-and-enters. The method of entry also was similar in each case: Either a window next to the door lock was broken, or the door itself was pried open. A comparison of method of entry for each incident tied the suspects to specific break-ins. The preceding analyses were collected in a Microsoft Excel spreadsheet to show time/date/location and method of entry.

A Predictive Tool Based on the cluster movement over time and space, Constable Shaw was able to predict the approximate area in which the suspects would next operate, providing investigators a geographic starting point for surveillance team placement.

Results The combination of investigative work, crime maps, tactical analysis and pattern prediction enabled investigators to set up surveillance in the area of highest probability. Two suspects were soon apprehended while engaged in a residential break-in and were taken into custody.

The investigation, supported by the tactical analysis, conclusively linked the two suspects to more than 123 residential break-ins, of which 77 were cleared by victims identifying their stolen property; 27 were cleared by "recent possession," i.e., pawned property; and the remaining 43 were cleared on the basis of the similar fact analysis.

More than $500,000 worth of property was stolen in these break-ins. Property valued at $70,000 was recovered. The two accused pled guilty; each was sentenced to nearly eight years in prison.

LaVigne and Wartell (2000, p.ix) note: "'Data-driven decision-making' has become a catch phrase to define the intelligent use of information and statistics to guide policy and practice. . . . Agencies are increasingly investing in Geographic Information Systems (GIS) as one of their primary analytical tools. . . . GIS can be used to predict the likely time and location of a serial offender's next crime, determine the optimal locations for checkpoints in construction site theft and direct police resources to achieve the greatest possible impact on gun violence."

Some departments post information gathered from crime mapping on their Web sites, a practice that has sparked heated debate. As Wartell (2000, p.52) notes, real-estate agents are concerned about the effects such data have on housing prices. Although most departments' maps are not detailed enough to show exact addresses, the concern for privacy is still an issue. However, Wartell (p.55) also contends: "Making crime maps and data easily available can increase public awareness and participation in keeping their communities crime-free. This can help to reduce the workload on department personnel and increase community policing potential." Crime mapping has evolved further into the relatively new science of geographic profiling.

Geographic Profiling

Geographic profiling, as Krish (n.d., p.1) explains, "helps to organize an abundance of information via geographical links in order to accelerate the apprehension process. . . . Geographic profiling enables crime officers and analysts to focus the investigation in a small area of the community, rather than on the whole metropolitan area, which means it cuts down on the amount of time and resources required for what can shape up to be a major investigation."

Nislow (2000, p.1) describes how geographic profiling works: "The computer calculates the probability of [a certain] point being the offender's home. . . . Those areas where it is least likely a suspect would live are colored a cool blue. Those areas where it is most likely are red." Nislow (p.10) suggests: "Geographic profiling can't solve a crime, but it can provide a focus, especially where there are too many suspects or too many tips."

Krish describes a similar, popular approach to geographic profiling, a psychological theory called **least-effort principle:**

> This concept proposes that criminals tend to commit acts of crimes within a comfort zone located near but not too close to their residence. With at least five or six incidents traceable back to the perpetrator, the search area for the criminal's residences is reduced by more than 90 percent. Key locations are weighted and then geocoded onto a map. The end process is known as a "jeopardy surface," a map that resembles a topographical map showing peaks and valleys color ramped to highlight the most likely area where the criminal resides.

Dr. Kim Russmo, a former police detective from Vancouver, Canada, first proposed the concept of geoprofiling (or geographic profiling) in his doctoral thesis while at British Columbia's Simon Fraser University. His concept was eventually packaged commercially by Environmental Criminology Research, Inc. into a software program called RIGEL and has been used by police agencies worldwide, including the FBI, ATF and Scotland Yard.

Geographic profiling can be used as the basis for several investigative strategies, including suspect and tip prioritization, address-based searches of police record systems, patrol saturation and surveillance, neighborhood canvasses and searches, DNA screening prioritization, Department of Motor Vehicle searches, postal/zip code prioritization and information request mail-outs. It is important to stress that geographic profiling does not solve cases, but rather provides a method for managing the large volume of information typically generated in major crime investigations. It should be regarded as one of several tools available to detectives and is best employed in conjunction with other police methods. Geographic crime patterns are clues that, when properly decoded, can be used to point in the offender's direction.

Geographic profiling has proven highly accurate in cases solved by the FBI, the Royal Canadian Mounted Police and several state police departments. It has been used to help investigators prioritize suspect lists, assign patrol saturation and plan stakeouts. Lewis (n.d., p.1) notes: "With no solid leads in their hunt for a sniper who has gunned down eight people in the Washington, DC, area, investigators have turned to a relatively new technological tool: geographic profiling. Barring a lucky break, the technology currently seems like the police's best chance to find the shooter." Whether that tool actually played a part in the apprehension of the two suspects in the shooting has not been established.

Geographic profiling (RIGEL) was used in an investigation of 35 cases of sexual assaults between July 1996 and January 2001 in Marl, Germany. Marl is a city of 30,000 located in an industrial area of the country. In 2000 the police in Marl asked for assistance from Detective Sergeant Neil Trainer, a geographic profiler from the United Kingdom. Trainer was able to pinpoint the suspect's likely residence to within 1.42 square kilometers. A DNA mass screening of suspects within that area then led to the perpetrator, who had until recently lived there with his mother.

Despite advances in technology, human intelligence and creativity are also still extremely important in problem solving. Consider next some of the most common mistakes that occur in problem solving.

Common Mistakes in Problem Solving

Bennett and Hess (2004, p.128) note: "Common mistakes in problem solving and decision making include spending too much energy on unimportant details, failing to resolve important issues, being secretive about true feelings, having a closed mind and not expressing ideas. . . . Inability to decide, putting decisions off to the last minute, failing to set deadlines, making decisions under pressure and using unreliable sources of information are other common errors in problem solving and decision making." Other mistakes commonly made during problem solving and decision making include making multiple decisions about the same problem, finding the right decision for the wrong problem (that is, dealing with symptoms rather than causes), failing to consider the costs, delaying a decision and making decisions while angry or excited.

Bennett and Hess (p.129) offer a checklist against which to evaluate decisions. Is the decision: consistent with the agency's mission, goals and objectives; a long-term solution; cost effective; legal; ethical; practical; and acceptable to those responsible for implementing it?

Problem Solving and Creativity

Several structured approaches to problem solving have been discussed. These approaches will be more effective if creativity is incorporated into the approach. Bynum (p.51) stresses: "The problem-solver is as much a craftsman as a technician. The craft of problem-solving requires creativity and the much-discussed ability to think outside the box. It means looking at problems and situations in new ways; involving individuals, groups and organizations in a collective effort to analyze and address community problems and using nontraditional approaches to solve these problems."

Creativity is a process of breaking old connections and discovering useful new connections. It is often synonymous with **innovation**. von Oech (1983, p.7) states: "Discovery consists of looking at the same thing as everyone else and thinking something different." However, effective problem solving can be sabotaged if you fall prey to mental locks or killer phrases.

Two barriers to creative problem solving are mental locks and killer phrases.

In problem solving, it is important to avoid **mental locks**, or ways of thinking that prevent creativity. Some examples of mental locks are: "That's not logical. Be practical. To err is wrong. Avoid risk taking. That's not my area. I'm not creative." Whereas mental locks are self-imposed obstacles to creative problem solving, killer phrases are used by others to deter creative solutions. **Killer phrases** are judgmental, critical statements; they are put-downs that stifle creativity. Some of the most common killer phrases are: "That's too radical. It's contrary to policy. That's not our area. We'll never get help. That's too much hassle. It just won't work. It's too impractical. It costs too much. We've never done it that way before. Get serious" (Buchholz and Roth, 1987, p.136).

Problem Solving at Work

The theoretical foundation of problem solving in Newport News was discussed earlier. During the problem-identification process, several problems became evident (Eck and Spelman, p.44). The Newport News police categorized the problems so they could be analyzed. The way the department addressed the problem of commercial burglaries illustrates the problem-solving approach. The patrol officers surveyed the area and found that some major streets had been barricaded due to a major highway-construction project. This resulted in limited vehicle traffic, limited police patrol at night and a large increase in nighttime burglaries. To alleviate these problems, patrol officers were instructed to leave their squads and patrol the area on foot at night. The officers also persuaded the merchants to clean up the piles of trash and debris that could easily conceal the burglars' activities. Table 4.4 illustrates the types of problems that might be addressed.

Besides dealing with the environment, Sgt. Quail, the officer in charge, also analyzed the specific problem (p.83):

> He collected offense reports of burglaries committed in the area. To help identify geographic patterns, he plotted them on a detailed spot map. To identify M.O. and repeat offender patterns, Quail recorded a description of the suspects, time of commission, type of property taken, and similar information on a specially

Table 4.4 Types of Problems

	Citywide	*Neighborhood*
Crime problems	Domestic homicides Gas station driveoffs Assaults on police officers	Personal robberies (Central business district) Commercial burglaries (Jefferson Avenue business district) Vacant buildings (Central business district) Residential burglaries (New Briarfield Apts) Residential burglaries (Glenn Gardens Apts) Larcenies (Beechmont Gardens Apts) Thefts from autos (Newport News Shipbuilding) Drug dealing (32d and Chestnut)
Disorder problems	Runaway-youths Driving under the influence Disturbances at convenience stores	Rowdy youths (Peninsula Skating Rink) Shot houses (Aqua Vista Apts) Disturbances (Marshall Avenue 7-Eleven) Dirt bikes (Newmarket Creek) Disturbances (Village Square Shopping Center)

SOURCE: John E. Eck and William Spelman. *Problem Solving: Problem-Oriented Policing in Newport News.* Washington, DC: Police Executive Research Forum, 1987, p.82.

designed form. Finally, he suspected that some of the offenders were using vacant apartments located above some of the businesses to conceal stolen property; he began to investigate this possibility.

These efforts resulted in the apprehension of several burglars and a decrease in the burglary rate. When the construction was completed and the barriers removed, the burglaries decreased further. Since construction is frequent, Sgt. Quail began to develop a policy and procedure statement so that police and city agencies could communicate better regarding construction projects, street closing and potential burglary problems.

Promising Practices from the Field

The COPS office Web site (www.cops.usdoj.gov) contains numerous examples of promising practices in problem solving. Two examples follow.

San Diego, CA—Prostitution A business strip was plagued with a prostitution problem. The initial police response was to attempt undercover arrests of "johns" and prostitutes. Although they were able to take hundreds of johns into custody, few prostitutes were arrested because they knew the undercover detectives on sight.

The police decided to take a problem-solving approach to improve results. In examining the problem, officers learned many of the prostitutes were transients who would stay in the area only while it was profitable. To diminish profitability, the police obtained a temporary restraining order (TRO) prohibiting the defendants (prostitutes) from flagging down motorists, loitering on corners or participating in other solicitation conduct within 100 yards of the plaintiffs (local business owners). Violation of the TRO meant an immediate five days in jail and a $1,000 fine.

One month after the TRO was obtained, the problem had been solved. Prostitutes abandoned the area, customers no longer cruised the business strip, and businesses reported increased revenues. The area has remained free of prostitution for over three years.

Mankato, MN—Minnesota Police Reclaimed Park for Use by Law-Abiding Citizens One area of a local park had become the gathering place for "Motorheads"—a group of car devotees—who would meet every day around noon to drink and socialize. Their parties would continue throughout the day and into the evening, so that by 10 P.M., the crowd had grown to between 300 and 400 people. Problems linked to the Motorhead parties included the harassing of other park users, assaults, public urination, public and juvenile drinking, suspected drug dealing and thousands of dollars in criminal property damage to the park. The initial police response included police park patrols, installation of floodlights in the area where the parties were occurring and the scheduling of many nonparty events at the park. None of these approaches, however, were effective.

Taking a problem-solving approach, officers spent several weeks observing and interacting with the partygoers. During this time, they learned the Motorheads liked the spot because it was next to a large parking lot, had two exits and, while being out of sight, still allowed them to see the police coming from a distance. Interviews with former park users revealed they had stopped visiting the park because they were intimidated by the partygoers. A community meeting was then held to solicit more information about the problem.

The officers partnered with the city parks director to develop a long-term solution to the problem. Aiming to lessen the appeal of the park to the partiers, park officials reduced the size of the large parking lot and restricted the flow of traffic to one way. Meanwhile, the officers had found an alternative site for the party group—an empty, highly visible downtown parking lot near the police department where activity could be easily monitored.

Once the Motorheads relocated downtown, young families and other former park attendees resumed use of the park. Even though some Motorhead-related problems continued downtown (juvenile drinking, drug sales, reckless driving), immediate targeted enforcement efforts by the police convinced the Motorheads to "clean up their act" or risk losing access to the downtown lot.

The International Association of Chiefs of Police's Community Policing Awards

The International Association of Chiefs of Police (IACP) began its award program in 1998. In 2002 it received 84 "excellent" nominations from six countries, including the United States. The awards are made in five categories based on the population of the department's jurisdiction. Throughout the remainder of this text case studies presenting award winners and runners up will be presented.

2002 IACP Community Policing Award Winner, Category—Agency Serving a Population of 50,001 to 100,000 Residents: Gastonia, NC Police Department

The police department identified the problem of three low-income troubled neighborhoods in Gastonia where fear of gangs, crime and drugs was high and where trust of the police was low.

A neighborhood enhancement team (NET) was formed within city government to address issues in the target neighborhoods. This partnership of city department heads and other key employees represented community development, code enforcement, the police department, parks and recreation, fire department, public information, solid waste, electrical and utilities departments, and the street department. Using records of problems, complaints and enforcement activities in the neighborhoods, NET selected one neighborhood in which to focus its resources and efforts. The objectives were:

- To bring all necessary resources of the city together to apply to crime, disorder and quality-of-life neighborhood issues.
- To develop a prioritized plan of action in partnership with the community.
- To engage in problem solving as a partnership.

To learn what concerns the residents had, NET surveyed 582 homes in the targeted area and distributed the results to the residents, along with information on how they could be involved. Their concerns were incorporated into the action plan. What followed was a cooperative effort between NET, the local neighborhood watch, a church and community members. Their combined efforts included code enforcement citations (49), prostitution-related arrests (60), other arrests of prostitutes and johns on more than 48 loitering, sex and drug charges, weapons and traffic charges (11), and improvements in trash pickups. They also demolished two houses, installed smoke detectors in 75 homes, trimmed 150 trees, repaired 100 street lights, improved playgrounds, held a community cleanup, and repaired water drainage and runoff problems. The neighborhood-watch group raised $10,000 for new playground equipment for the elementary school.

Evaluation of the initiative showed a 41.7 percent decrease in crime. Follow-up surveys showed that 90 percent of neighborhood residents were aware of the project and 74 percent believed it helped improve their neighborhood. Almost 95 percent would recommend this project for other neighborhoods. The NET published and distributed a newsletter to residents outlining the project results.

Summary

A problem-solving approach requires police to group incidents and, thereby, identify underlying causes of problems in the community. One concern of a problem-solving approach is differentiating between efficiency and effectiveness. Efficiency, doing things right, has been the traditional emphasis in law enforcement. Effectiveness, doing the right things, is the emphasis in community policing.

The first step in problem solving is to group incidents as problems. Four stages in the SARA model of problem solving are scanning, analysis, response and assessment. Problem analysis considers the individuals involved, the incidents and the responses. Such analysis should take into account the magnet phenomenon, which occurs when a phone number or address is associated with a crime simply because it was a convenient number or address to use.

The DOC model (dilemmas-options-consequences) challenges officers to carefully consider their decisions and the short- and long-term consequences of those decisions. The goal is to fuse problem solving and morality.

Crime-specific planning uses the principles of problem-solving policing to focus on identified crime problems. Crime mapping shifts the focus from the criminal to the location of crimes—the hot spots where most crimes occur. Both crime-specific planning and problem solving can be more effective if those working on the problem approach it creatively. Two barriers to creative problem solving are mental locks and killer phrases.

Discussion Questions

1. How do you approach problems? Do you use a systematic approach?
2. Do you think problem solving takes more time than the traditional approach to policing? Which is more effective? More efficient? More expensive?
3. Does your department use problem solving?
4. Does your law enforcement agency employ anyone to specifically conduct crime analysis?
5. What difficulties can you foresee for a department that uses problem-solving techniques?
6. How do problem solving and crime-specific planning differ?
7. Some officers have resisted the implementation of problem-solving strategies. Why might they be opposed to problem solving?
8. In what kinds of problems do you think a problem-solving approach would be most effective?

9. What is the relationship between community policing and a problem-solving approach to policing?
10. How might computers help police in their problem-solving efforts?

InfoTrac College Edition Assignments

- Use InfoTrac College Edition to help answer the Discussion Questions when applicable.
- Find an example of a police–community partnership that successfully used problem solving to deal with community issues. (You might also see the Community Policing Consortium at www.communitypolicing.org; the Police Executive Research Forum at www.PoliceForum.org/; or other community policing sites.)
- Research at least one of the following subjects: crime mapping, geographic profiling or problem-oriented policing. Take good notes and be prepared to share them in class.

Community Project

Select and research a chronic problem that exists in your community. Form a problem-solving team with classmates, assign appropriate roles (police, business owner, school official, residents, etc.) and, using the SARA problem-solving model, develop solutions. Be creative.

References

Aragon, Randall. "Community Policing: It's What's Up Front that Counts." *Law Enforcement News,* February 29, 2000, p.8.

Bennett, Wayne W. and Hess, Kären M. *Management & Supervision in Law Enforcement,* 4th ed. Belmont, CA: Wadsworth Publishing Company, 2004.

Brito, Corina Sole and Allan, Tracy, eds. *Problem-Oriented Policing,* Vol. 2. Washington, DC: Police Executive Research Forum, 1999.

Buchholz, Steve and Roth, Thomas. *Creating the High-Performance Team.* New York: John Wiley and Sons, 1987.

Bynum, Timothy S. *Using Analysis for Problem Solving: A Guidebook for Law Enforcement.* Washington, DC: Office of Community Oriented Policing Services, September 14, 2001.

Cooper, Christopher. "Training Patrol Officers to Mediate Disputes." *FBI Law Enforcement Bulletin,* February 2000, pp.7–10.

Eck, John E. *Assessing Responses to Problems: An Introductory Guide for Police Problem-Solvers.* Washington, DC: Office of Community Oriented Policing Services, 2002.

Eck, John E. and Spelman, William. *Problem-Solving: Problem-Oriented Policing in Newport News.* Washington, DC: The Police Executive Research Forum, 1987.

Frazier, Thomas C. "Community Policing Efforts Offer Hope for the Future." *The Police Chief,* August 2000, p.11.

Goldstein, Herman. *Problem-Oriented Policing.* New York: McGraw-Hill Publishing Company, 1990.

Krish, Karthik. "Application of GIS in Crime Analysis and Geographic Profiling." GIS Development Web site: www.gisdevelopment.net.

LaVigne, Nancy and Wartell, Julie. *Crime Mapping Case Studies,* Vol 2. Washington, DC: Police Executive Research Forum (PERF), 2000.

Lewis, Christina. "In the Search for a Killer: A High-Tech Tool." Court TV Web site: www.courttv.com.

McDonald, Phyllis P. "Implementing CompStat: Critical Points to Consider." *The Police Chief,* January 2004, pp.33–37.

Miles, Martin J. "Computer-Based Probability Assessments." *Law Enforcement Technology,* May 2000, pp.102–105.

Nislow, Jennifer. "Location, Location, Location: Geographic Profiling Helps Police Close in on Serial Criminals." *Law Enforcement News,* June 15, 2000, pp.1, 10.

Problem-Solving Tips: A Guide to Reducing Crime and Disorder through Problem-Solving Partnerships. Washington, DC: Office of Community Oriented Policing Services, June 2002.

PSP National Evaluation Final Report. Washington, DC: Police Executive Research Forum, 2000.

Rahtz, Howard. *Community-Oriented Policing: A Handbook for Beat Cops and Supervisors.* Monsey, NY: Criminal Justice Press, 2001.

Rogers, Donna. "Trends in Crime Analysis and Crime Mapping." *Law Enforcement Technology,* May 2000, pp.36–42.

Romano, Linda J.; McDevitt, Jack; Jones, Jimmie; and Johnson, William. "Combined Problem-Solving Models Incorporate Ethics Analysis." *The Police Chief,* August 2000, pp.98–102.

Schick, Walt. "CompStat in the Los Angeles Police Department." *The Police Chief,* January 2004, pp.17–23.

von Oech, Roger. *A Whack on the Side of the Head.* New York: Warner Books, 1983.

Warden, John and Shaw, Jerry. "Predicting a Residential Break-In Pattern." In *Crime Mapping Case Studies: Successes in the Field,* Vol. 2, edited by Nancy LaVigne and Julie Wartell. Washington, DC: Police Executive Research Forum, 2000, pp.81–87.

Wartell, Julie. "Putting Crime on the Map." *Police,* June 2000, pp.52–55.

Wartell, Julie and Greenhalgh, Fiona. "Using Technology for Problem Solving." *Problem Solving Quarterly,* Winter 2000, pp.1, 6–7.

Wernicke, Susan C. and Stallo, Mark A. "Steps toward Integrating Crime Analysis into Local Law Enforcement." *The Police Chief,* July 2000, pp.56–57.

Wideman, Dean A. "Multifunctional Aspects of Crime Analysis in the Investigation of Violent and Sexual Crimes." *The Police Chief,* July 2000, pp.59–63.

Wiley, Charles and Smith, Timothy. "The CAMStat Service Delivery Initiative." *The Police Chief,* November 2003, pp.47–48.

Wilson, James Q. and Kelling, George L. "Making Neighborhoods Safe." *The Atlantic Monthly,* February 1989, pp.46–52.

CHAPTER 5

Implementing Community Policing

There is nothing more difficult to plan, more uncertain of success, or more dangerous to manage than the establishment of a new order; because the innovator has for enemies all those who have derived advantage from the old order and finds but lukewarm defenders among those who stand to gain from the new one.

—Machiavelli

Do You Know?

- What basic changes are required in making the transition to community policing?
- What participatory leadership is?
- What a department's vision should include?
- Who should be included in a needs assessment?
- How law enforcement agencies have traditionally been organized?
- Which may be more important, targeting a "critical mass" of individuals or mobilizing the community at large?
- What a strategic plan includes?
- What the most important consideration in selecting strategies to implement community policing is?
- What POST-21 is?
- Whether training should be the spearhead of change?
- What the most important areas are to cover in training?
- What transition managers should anticipate and prepare for?
- What common pitfalls there are in making the transition to a community policing philosophy?
- What impediments to community policing may need to be overcome?
- When conducting evaluations, how failures should be viewed?

Can You Define?

change management
critical mass
decentralization
empowered
flat organization
participatory leadership
strategic planning
systems thinking
transition management
vision

Introduction

You have looked at the philosophy of community policing as well as at the key players—politicians, businesspeople, faith-based organizations, civic organizations, the schools, the community and the police. You have also considered a basic component of community policing—problem solving. The challenge is to move from theories about using problem-solving techniques and partnerships to actual implementation.

This chapter begins with a consideration of the basic nature of change, how it influences implementing community policing and the changes needed to successfully transition. This is followed by a discussion of how the community policing philosophy should be reflected in the management style as well as in the vision and mission statement and the possible impact on the entire police organization. Next is a look at needs assessment for both the department and community, including an in-depth examination of how police are typically organized and managed. Next is an explanation of strategic planning and ways to develop strategies. Then the importance of hiring, promoting and training is presented. Next are examples of how community policing has been implemented, including a discussion of the benefits that might be achieved. Anticipating and preparing for resistance is covered next, followed by pitfalls to avoid and impediments to overcome. The chapter concludes with ways to evaluate progress and a look at a new advocacy group for community policing.

An officer conducts a neighborhood survey to learn of residents' needs and concerns. A survey sends a clear message to community stakeholders that their opinions matter.

Change

It has been said that nothing is constant except change. Nonetheless, police administrators, supervisors and even line personnel frequently resist change in any form and prefer the status quo. But change is occurring and will continue to occur. Police departments can resist, or they can accept the challenge and capitalize on the benefits that may result. Issues requiring departments to change include technological advances, demographic changes, fiscal constraints, shifting values, the need to do more with less, heightened media coverage of police misconduct and citizen fear of crime, disorder, violence, gangs and terrorism.

Change takes time. Traditions die hard. Most police officers will find proposed changes to their culture extremely threatening. However, although the police culture is tremendously strong, remember that a huge ship can be turned by a small rudder. It just takes time and steadfast determination.

Greenberg and Flynn (2003, p.73) stress: "When preparing for change, a police leader should never underestimate the importance to the department of history and tradition. It is wise to take the pulse of officers, civilian employees and citizens with regard to a tradition before changing it."

Abshire and Paynter (2000, p.54) contend: "To do it well community policing should be viewed as a constant work in progress." They interviewed the chief of police of the San Diego Police Department who commented: "Success doesn't happen overnight. It's been 12 years and we're still identifying some areas where we can really improve and expand community policing through our department." Chief Bejarano also noted: "It [community policing] is not a project. It's not a program. It's a culture."

Goldstein (1992, pp.14–15) cites five concerns that have most strongly influenced the development of problem-oriented policing:

1. The police field is preoccupied with management, internal procedures and efficiency to the exclusion of appropriate concern for effectiveness in dealing with substantive problems.
2. The police devote most of their resources to responding to calls from citizens, reserving too small a percentage of their time and energy for acting on their own initiative to prevent or reduce community problems.
3. The community is a major resource with an enormous potential, largely untapped, for reducing the number and magnitude of problems that otherwise become the business of the police.
4. Within their agencies, police have readily available to them another huge resource: their rank-and-file officers, whose time and talent have not been used effectively.
5. Efforts to improve policing have often failed because they have not been adequately related to the overall dynamics and complexity of the police organization. Adjustments in policies and organizational structure are required to accommodate and support change.

It is also helpful to be familiar with the five categories of "adopters" to expect within any organization, as Figure 5.1 shows.

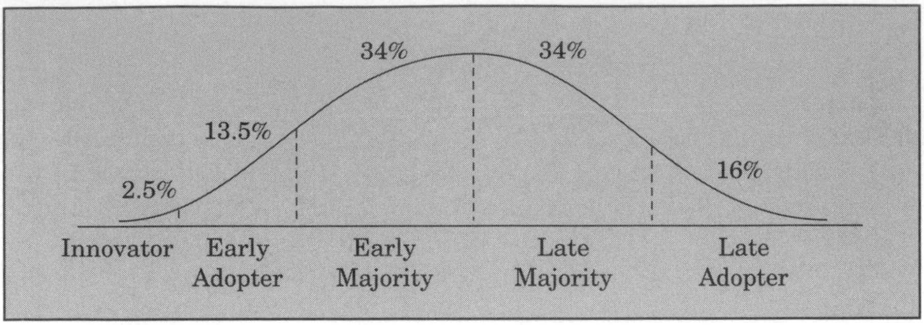

Figure 5.1 Change Takes Time

The innovators are risk takers. They embrace uncertainty and change. The early adopters are opinion leaders, the ones to whom others come for advice. The early majority accept new ideas slightly ahead of the majority. The late majority is more skeptical. They can be persuaded but usually require a great deal of peer pressure. The late adopters are the most difficult to convince. They tend to be suspicious of all innovations. Recognizing these individual characteristics may be helpful in developing strategies to "sell" community policing to the troops.

Some changes have already occurred within many departments that should make the transition to community policing easier, including better-educated police officers who are less inclined to accept orders unquestioningly, more diversity within the police ranks and a shift in incentives with intrinsic, personal-worth-type rewards becoming as important as extrinsic, monetary rewards. Other changes are needed to move from the traditional, reactive, incident-driven mode of policing to the proactive, problem-solving, collaborative mode typical of community policing.

Needed Changes

Some changes basic to implementing the community policing philosophy have already been briefly described in Chapter 2.

Community policing will require a change in management style, mission statement, departmental organization and the general approach to fighting crime.

How these changes fit into the transition from a philosophy to practice will become evident.

The Community Policing Consortium (CPC) (2000, p.1) suggests two kinds of management required for the transition to community policing, change management and transition management: "**Change management** is the development of an overall strategy which will review the present state of the organization, envision the future state of the organization and devise the means of moving from one to the other. **Transition management** is overseeing, controlling and leading that move from present state to future state."

Although the consortium uses the term *management*, it also recognizes the importance of *leadership* in this transition: "To embark wholeheartedly on the transition process first requires a leader who is open, willing to make change and provides support for those decisions with commitment and energy."

Table 5.1 Old and New Style Leadership Compared

Authoritarian Style	***Participatory Style***
Response to incidents	Problem solving
Individual effort and competitiveness	Teamwork
Professional expertise	Community orientation; ask customers what they want
Go by the "book"; decisions by emotion	Use data-based decision making
Tell subordinates	Ask and listen to employees
Boss as patriarch and order giver	Boss as coach and teacher
Maintain status quo	Create, innovate, experiment
Control and watch employees	Trust employees
Reliance on scientific investigation and technology rather than people	Reliance on skilled employees—a better resource than machines
When things go wrong, blame employees	Errors mean failed systems/processes—improve them
Organization is closed to outsiders	Organization is open

SOURCE: Wayne W. Bennett and Kären M. Hess. *Management and Supervision in Law Enforcement*, 4th edition. Belmont, CA: Wadsworth Thomson Learning, 2004, p.63. Reprinted by permission.

Management Styles

Yet another change is that community policing usually requires a different management style. The traditional autocratic style effective during the industrial age will not have the same effect in the twenty-first century. One viable alternative to the autocratic style of management is participatory leadership.

In **participatory leadership** each individual has a voice in decisions, but top management still has the ultimate decision-making authority.

What is important is that everyone has an opportunity to express their views on a given issue or problem. Bennett and Hess (2004, p.61) stress:

> Democratic or participative leadership has been evolving since the 1930s and 1940s. Democratic leadership does not mean that every decision is made only after discussion and a vote. It means rather that management welcomes employees' ideas and input. Employees are encouraged to be innovative. Management development of a strong sense of individual achievement and responsibility is a necessary ingredient of participative or consultative leadership.
>
> Democratic or participative managers are interested in their subordinates and their problems and welfare. Management still makes the final decision but takes into account the input from employees.

Table 5.1 summarizes the key concepts of and compares the authoritarian and participatory styles of management. The leader must also have a vision for the department and the community.

Creating a Vision and Mission Statement

Vision might be thought of as intelligent foresight. Examining the department's past for strengths and weaknesses, successes and failures is an important step in creating a vision for the future.

This vision should include the essential elements of the community policing philosophy: problem solving, empowerment, forming community partnerships and being proactive—making preventing crime as important as enforcing the law.

The vision for each department will be different. It must be tailored to reflect the personnel within the department and the community the department serves. Vision should be something everyone involved can buy into and feel a part of. This means involving leaders from within the department and the community from the beginning of the transition if possible. The Community Policing Consortium recommends that the entire workforce be directly involved in the envisioning and planning processes—at least having a cross section of the workforce representing all ranks or grades and incorporating sworn, unsworn and civilian personnel and their respective union representations.

Union support for community policing is absolutely necessary. Without it, or worse, with open opposition, the risk of failure is high. Union leadership has tremendous influence over its members who will likely follow union officials' lead. Unions are concerned about issues they perceive as affecting officers negatively, including the likelihood of permanent shifts and area assignments, concern that COP may negatively affect the union contract, the perceived increase of power and influence the community will have in department matters, the potential that citizen review boards may come about under community policing, the perceived softening of the police image, officer safety concerns and the concern of officers being held responsible for the crime that occurs in their assigned area.

Agencies with unions can take the opportunity to form partnerships within by inviting union leaders to participate in the process. Having been elected by their membership, they will have the advantage of not being seen as management's hand-selected few.

The Community Policing Consortium also recommends that those who have been identified as antagonistic to the change process be deliberately co-opted. They cannot be ignored because they will not go away. Actively seek ways to avert their antagonism.

Ramsey (2000, p.16) draws an interesting analogy between a successful transition to community policing and winning a 4-by-100-meter relay race: "In the relay race, the outcome depends not only on how fast the individual contestants run, but also on the smooth handoff of the baton from one runner to the next. It is the same in policing. Smooth handoffs get the best results. We are more likely to solve problems of crime and disorder when we share information, coordinate activities and involve everyone, smoothly and enthusiastically."

He takes the analogy one step further by asking the reader to imagine what would happen in a relay race if the runners were told after they passed the baton that they must leave the stadium because the outcome was not their concern. Noting that this would be "preposterous," he suggests that is exactly what is done in policing: "We forget that everyone—police officers and citizens—needs to feel a sense of ownership and achievement." This sense of ownership and achievement should start with the vision statement.

Once the vision is articulated, it should be translated into a mission statement as discussed in Chapter 2. The development of a mission statement is important for any organization, but it is critical in developing and implementing community policing. Its importance cannot be overstated. Again, the mission statement must be something everyone can buy into and feel a part of. Once the vision and mission statement have been articulated, the next step is to conduct a needs assessment.

Assessing Needs

A needs assessment should include not only the department but also the community of which it is a part.

Analyzing the Department

The traditional law enforcement organization design has been that of a pyramid-shaped hierarchy based on a military model, as Figure 5.2 depicts.

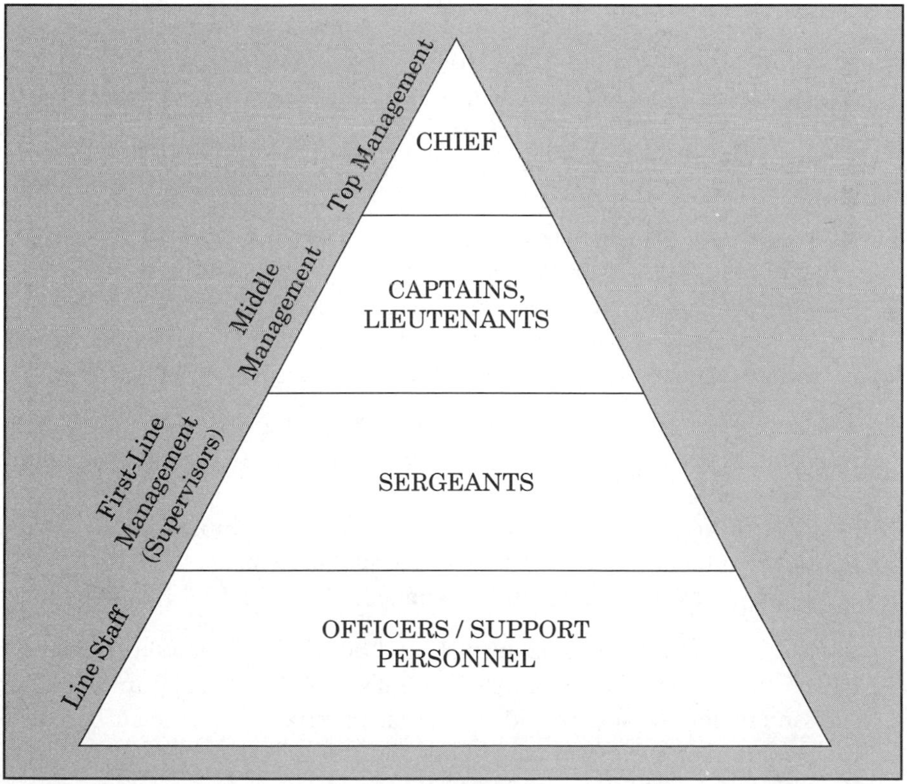

Figure 5.2 Typical Police Department Management Structure

Command officers and supervisors had complete authority over subordinates, and they had little tolerance for ideas originating at the bottom of the pyramid. Communication flowed downward through the bureaucratic chain of command. This bureaucratic organizational structure worked well for decades. Recently, however, it has been called into question, with many looking to corporate America as a more appropriate organizational model.

To remain competitive, business and industry are undergoing extensive changes in organization and management styles. Law enforcement agencies also face the need for change to meet the competition of private policing. According to Harr and Hess (2003, p.68): "Private security is the nation's primary protective resource today, outspending public law enforcement by more than 73 percent and employing nearly three times the workforce."

Law enforcement agencies must compete not only with private police but also for the college graduates now entering the workforce. In addition, like business, many departments are turning to a **flat organization**: fewer lieutenants and captains, fewer staff departments, fewer staff assistants, more sergeants and more patrol officers. Typical pyramid-organization charts will have the top pushed down and the sides expanded at the base.

Progressive businesses are restructuring top-heavy organizations, pushing authority and decision making as low as possible. Successful businesses concentrate on soliciting ideas from everyone in their organization about every aspect of their operation. This approach can be applied to policing, especially in small departments. If officer retention is to be maintained and loyalty and morale preserved and heightened, officers must be **empowered**, that is, given authority and enabled to make decisions.

Decentralization, Turner (2000, p.50) notes, generally refers to a department's organizational structure and operations: "It is an operating principle that encourages flattening of the organization and places decision-making authority and autonomy at the level where information is plentiful. In police organizations, this is usually at the level of the patrol officer, where officers interacting with the public need the freedom to exercise discretion within predetermined parameters."

In summary, departments who have successfully implemented community policing have made several organizational changes:

- The bureaucracy is flattened and decentralized.
- Roles of those in management positions change to leaders and mentors rather than managers and supervisors.
- Patrol officers are given new responsibilities and empowered to make decisions and problem solve with their community partners.
- Permanent shifts and areas are assigned.

The department's organization should be carefully analyzed to identify barriers within the agency likely to impede the community policing initiative. This needs assessment should also consider external constraints controlled by others outside the department such as finance and budgeting, hiring rules and state-mandated training programs.

One of the most important implementation needs, Mittleman (2000, p.51) stresses, is that "community policing must permeate the entire department from the top down. Line personnel must be given time away from calls for service to practice community policing."

Analyzing the Community

> There are many ways to identify a community's concerns. One approach is to interview neighborhood leaders such as clergy, the heads of business groups and school principals. Another way is to hold focus groups that bring together citizens—teenagers, single mothers, members of various ethnic groups—to discuss their neighborhood. These methods, however, only reach a small segment of the community. To build on this information and develop the most complete picture possible, many community justice planners use another tool: community surveys. . . .
>
> A survey sends a clear message to community stakeholders that their opinions matter. This is especially important in neighborhoods that are wary of government intervention and suspicious of outsiders. By conducting a survey, planners show that their project will be different: it will not be an unwanted government program. Rather, the project will be tailored to the community's needs and concerns (*Palk*, May 2003).

At the heart of the community policing philosophy is the recognition that the police can no longer go it alone—if they ever could. They must use the eyes, ears and voices of law-abiding citizens. A starting point is to analyze the community's demographics as described in Chapter 3. How much social capital is available for community policing efforts?

Correia (2000, p.54) suggests: "In communities with low levels of Putnam's social capital and high levels of COP activities, police officers may be perceived as facilitators who take responsibility for engaging citizens in alleviating complex social problems. On the other hand, in areas with high levels of Putnam's social capital and high levels of community policing, COP may be characterized as a partnership—that is a collaborative effort featuring citizens and police working together to develop and implement effective problem-solving activities to enhance quality of life." Correia further suggests that COP activity may be driven more by community factors than by factors internal to police organizations.

Police must develop a comprehensive picture of their community. They can do this by surveys and direct interaction with citizens. How community members respond when asked what problems they think the police should focus on and what solutions they would suggest can help the department meet the community's needs. Surveys ask for input from everyone instead of just the few citizens who are the most involved. According to Adam Mansky, coordinator of the Red Hook Community Justice Center (Brooklyn, New York): "There are about 15 or 20 leaders at every community meeting, but how do you reach beyond them to the average person on the street? A survey is the perfect tool for this. It offers some reassurance that community leaders are accurately representing the needs and interests of their constituents" (*Surveying Communities: A Resource for Community Justice Planners,* May 2003).

It would be enlightening to conduct a similar survey with police officers and their managers. Such shared information could go far in building trust among line officers, managers and citizens.

The Bureau of Justice Statistics (BJS) and the Office of Community Oriented Policing Services (COPS) have available for local law enforcement agencies a computer software package designed to help conduct public opinion surveys about how well the police are doing their jobs. The program can be downloaded from www.ojp.usdoj.gov/bjs. The project used the standard National Crime Victimization Survey (NCVS) questionnaire as the core data-collection instrument.

While conducting needs assessments, attention should be paid to who might be community leaders to enlist in the community policing initiative. According to Correia (p.56): "It appears that the number of participants actively engaged in a community policing program is not as important as the character of the individuals participating. A 'critical mass' of individuals with high levels of social engagement may be more effective in solving a community's problems than a large number of individuals with low levels of social cohesion." A critical mass in physics is the smallest amount of a fissionable material that will sustain a nuclear chain reaction. In the context of community policing efforts, a **critical mass** is the smallest number of citizens and organizations needed to support and sustain the community policing initiative. Correia (p.57) concludes:

> It may be more important for COP-oriented police agencies to target this "critical mass" of individuals than to try to mobilize the community at large.

Once the needs assessment has been conducted, the next step is to develop a blueprint, that is, to do some strategic planning.

Strategic Planning

Strategic planning is long-term, large-scale, future-oriented planning. It begins with the vision and mission statement already discussed. It is grounded in those statements and guided by the findings of the needs assessment. From here, specific goals and objectives and an accompanying implementation strategy and time line are developed. What looks like a straightforward process can turn extremely difficult as dilemmas arise and threaten the plan. Among the most predictable are the resistance to change and fear of the unknown that will be played out in the department and in the community. This resistance is also one of the most serious and difficult issues to be faced in a transition.

Switzer (2000, p.39) suggests: "To implement community-oriented policing successfully, it is important to have a strategic plan that identifies where the department stands in the implementation process, where the department would like to be, and most importantly, how the department intends to get there."

Because each community is unique, no template can be suggested. However, the key elements outlined in the vision and mission statement should be incorporated, as should a plan for addressing areas identified as weaknesses in the needs assessment.

As the plan is being developed it is important that those developing it engage in **systems thinking**. DeParis (2000, p.108) explains: "Systems thinking is a conceptual framework that recognizes the contribution of each component to the system; i.e., everything affects everything else." Planners must think in terms of the whole rather than the individual parts.

The strategic plan should include community partnerships and problem solving as well as any needed cultural and organizational changes in the department. It should include a realistic time line and a way to assess progress. It must also be tied to the department's budget.

Remember that the strategic plan is long range. Departments do not successfully implement community policing in a year or two. It takes time—years for most departments to fully implement it. Again, all interested parties should be allowed input into the strategic plan, and it should be realistic.

At the end of each year, progress toward accomplishing the vision, mission statement, goals and objectives should be measured. This may require a change in how performance has typically been assessed. Historically police have measured their failures—the number of crimes committed—and successes—the number of arrests made. Such statistics are relatively easy to gather and to analyze. Assessing the effectiveness of crime prevention efforts, however, is much more difficult. How does a department measure reduced fear of crime or satisfaction with the police service? Nonetheless, as the Community Policing Consortium notes: "What gets measured gets done."

In addition to having a realistic time line, the strategic plan must also be tied to the agency's budget. Without the resources to implement the activities outlined in the long-range plan, they are not likely to be accomplished. Again, the transition will take time and, in some instances, additional resources. The Community Policing Consortium cautions: "Don't get lost in the process":

> The plan can become an end in itself. The project manager, the planning group, draft papers, lengthy dialogue, revised drafts, additional papers, circulated memoranda, further discussion, establishing working groups or sub-committees—this is the stuff that bureaucracies are made of. Some people actually enjoy it. The strategic plan and the planning process are only a means to an end—delivering the future organization built on core values, agreed goals and an effective implementation process.

Strategic plans need not be elaborate. Small departments with limited resources might follow the example Kurz (2000, p.28) describes. His department implemented strategic planning in the small town of Durham, New Hampshire: "The

Durham strategic plan project consisted of three phases: a survey of citizen satisfaction with police services; a survey of police officer satisfaction with the department; and a one-day planning session attended by police officers and community leaders." The introduction to the 2000 strategic plan (p.34) states:

> The Durham Police Department 2000 Strategic Plan is designed to be an evolving document, constantly reviewed, updated, and brought into line with the desires of the community. It is the culmination of a series of exercises, all designed to ensure that the vision, mission, and objectives of the agency are successfully achieved. . . . An outgrowth of this process is the enhanced ability to effectively manage resources, provide accountability through measured results and adjust to change. Successful planning requires the fortitude to change course when opportunities and community demands arise. Ultimately, it is the planning process itself that keeps the agency focused on what it wishes to accomplish and the best route to get there.

Developing Strategies

Hundreds of strategies have been developed to implement community policing. Among the most common are use of foot, bike and horse patrol; block watches; newsletters; community surveys; citizen volunteer programs; storefronts; special task units; and educational programs. Another common strategy is to assign officers to permanent beats and teach them community organizing and problem-solving skills. Some communities help train landlords in how to keep their properties crime free. Many communities encourage the development of neighborhood organizations, and some have formed teams (partnerships); for example, code and safety violations might be corrected by a team consisting of police, code enforcers, fire officials and building code officers.

Other communities have turned to the Internet to connect with their citizens. In Los Angeles, for example: "Community leaders see the new Web site as a bridge to the public and an important repository for the latest news, facts and figures on the LAPD" (Malinowski et al., 2000, p.62). Between January and August of 2003, LAPDOnline averaged nearly 300,000 hits per day, up nearly 100,000 a day over 2002. They had a total in 2002 of more than 75,700,000 hits to their Web site. Naturally, smaller departments would not expect such impressive results, but even the smallest communities might find a computer expert to volunteer to set up and manage a Web site for the department.

"What works?" "Has somebody tried . . . ?" "What can we do about . . . ?" "Why can't we . . . ?" Such questions are being asked by communities nationwide as they tackle the challenges of reducing violence, drugs, other crimes and homeland security.

The most important consideration in selecting strategies to implement community policing is to ensure that the strategies fit a community's unique needs and resources.

Section III describes numerous strategies that have been used throughout the country as departments move toward community policing.

Hiring and Promoting

Recruiting and selecting personnel are among the most important considerations in successfully implementing the community policing philosophy. Officers for the twenty-first century working in a department that has made the transition to community policing will need attitudes and skills that are different from those used in the past. One assessment instrument supported by many community policing practitioners throughout the country is the "Police Officer Screening Test for the 21st Century" or "POST-21."

POST-21 is an add-on to an agency's existing application examination and selection process designed to identify applicants with traits and attitudes compatible with a community policing environment.

Harris and Kolkman (2000, p.64) explain that the test has three objectives: (1) to bring the hiring process to a more personal level by evaluating the applicants' "community" perspective, (2) to assist agencies in finding candidates who are "service-minded" as well as those with a traditional crime-fighting mindset and (3) to reduce costs by identifying candidates compatible with the community policing philosophy, reducing training costs after selection. The test consists of four parts (Harris and Kolkman, pp.64–65):

1. Evaluation of the applicant's "policing orientation," or whether a person has the ability and inclination to use a variety of policing strategies in working with the community
2. A series of questions to test flexibility in responses
3. Evaluation of realistic expectations of police officer duties
4. An essay section on problem-solving techniques

Whether an agency uses this specific instrument or not, the content is what should be considered when selecting—and promoting—officers. Are they community oriented? For example, do they volunteer in the community? Are they problem solvers? Good communicators?

The oral interview can be very helpful in selecting service-oriented officers. Goldstein believes police agencies that still hold tight to the traditional "crime fighting" model of policing will have difficulty transitioning to new ways of doing the job. He states: "Of all the changes required, redefining the role of rank-and-file police officers is the most important and has the greatest implications for the future of policing" (*Recruitment and Selection for Community Policing,* n.d.). According to Goldstein, the hiring of minority officers so that the department would more closely resemble the community it serves would enhance community problem-oriented policing. Skills needed by officers in a problem-oriented policing environment are:

- Creativity.
- Flexibility.
- Imagination.
- Intelligence.
- Ability to function independently.

- Problem-solving ability.
- Critical reasoning ability.
- Conflict mediation.
- Capacity to relate to others.
- Sensitivity to problems of urban life and community organization.
- Considers the chief task of the job to be relating to people.

Training

Training is critical for a successful transition to community policing. The Community Policing Consortium recommends that departments embark on a training program for all personnel at all levels to explain the change process and reduce fear and resistance. Training should also explore the community policing philosophy and the planning process and encourage all stakeholders to participate. The consortium advises, however:

"DON'T make training the spearhead of change."

The consortium says that many efforts have been made to place training at the leading edge of change in both the public and private sector. Much time and energy are expended in such efforts, but, no matter how effective the training, they will be neutralized if what is learned is at variance with practices and procedures occurring in the department. The consortium stresses: "Unless the culture, structure and management of the organization are in harmony with the training, then the impact of the latter will be minimized. . . . What is needed is the agreed vision, values, goals, and objectives to drive the organization and affect every aspect of policing—not expecting a training program to be a short cut to acceptance."

As the community policing philosophy takes hold in a department, officers will be more receptive to the training they will need to be effective community policing officers. Paoline et al. (2000, p.582) describe several areas in which training would be essential: "Training that enhances officers' capacity to perform community-policing functions—analyzing problems, working with community groups, developing and implementing responses that do not rely on the criminal law—could shape officers' outlooks on the police role and their attitudes toward the public."

Among the most important areas to include in training are communication skills, problem-solving skills and leadership skills.

Communication skills are the focus of Section II. Problem-solving skills were discussed in Chapter 4. The COPS office in conjunction with the Reno Police Department and the Police Executive Research Forum (PERF) have developed a model Police Training Officer (PTO) Program that incorporates contemporary adult educational methods and a version of problem-based learning (PBL). The fifteen-week program begins with a one-week integration period followed by four three-week phases: non-emergency incident response, emergency incident response, patrol activities and criminal investigation. A week between the second and third phase is devoted to mid-term evaluation. The last week is devoted to final evaluation. During each phase journals (not part of the evaluation) are kept and neighborhood portfolio exercises (NPE) are completed. The NPE is designed to give trainees a sense of the community as well as to develop community contacts. Each phase also includes weekly coaching and training as well as problem-based learning exercises. Table 5.2 presents the learning matrix for this program.

Table 5.2 The Learning Matrix

Core Competencies	*Phase A Non-Emergency Incident Response*	*Phase B Emergency Incident Response*	*Phase C Patrol Activities*	*Phase D Criminal Investigation*
Police vehicle operations	A1	B1	C1	D1
Conflict resolution	A2	B2	C2	D2
Use of force	A3	B3	C3	D3
Local procedures, policies, laws, organizational philosophies	A4	B4	C4	D4
Report writing	A5	B5	C5	D5
Leadership	A6	B6	C6	D6
Problem-solving skills	A7	B7	C7	D7
Community-specific problems	A8	B8	C8	D8
Cultural diversity and special needs groups	A9	B9	C9	D9
Legal authority	A10	B10	C10	D10
Individual rights	A11	B11	C11	D11
Officer safety	A12	B12	C12	D12
Communication skills	A13	B13	C13	D13
Ethics	A14	B14	C14	D14
Lifestyle stressors/ self-awareness/ self-regulation	A15	B15	C15	D15
Learning activities	Introduction of learning matrix	Use of learning matrix	Use of learning matrix	Use of learning matrix
	Daily journal entry	Daily journal entry	Daily journal entry	Daily journal entry
	Introduction of neighborhood portfolio exercise	Introduction of neighborhood portfolio exercise	Introduction of neighborhood portfolio exercise	Introduction of neighborhood portfolio exercise
Evaluation activities	Weekly coaching and training reports	Weekly coaching and training reports	Weekly coaching and training reports	Weekly coaching and training reports
	Problem-based learning exercise	Problem-based learning exercise	Problem-based learning exercise	Problem-based learning exercise

SOURCE: Washington, DC: Police Executive Research Forum and the COPS. Office, no date, p.22.

According to *PTO: An Overview and Introduction* (n.d., p.15): "The program has produced outstanding results. . . . New officers enter the field with problem-solving skills that are rarely seen at that career level. New officers also display remarkable leadership and a willingness to work as partners with the local community to fight crime and disorder."

Leadership skills that Mook and Dempsey (2000, p.115) identified include:

- The ability to motivate people to achieve goals, to set an example for positive behavior, and to adapt to and facilitate change
- Knowledge of the job and community as well as of diverse populations
- Willingness to assume responsibility and to accept responsibility for mistakes
- Skill in diplomacy; in communicating with individuals and group; in organizing and prioritizing time, resources and community meetings; and in conflict resolution
- Ability to adapt to and facilitate change
- Skill in organizing and prioritizing time, resources and community meetings

Other areas Mook and Dempsey (p.116) suggest should be included in training are time and stress management and ethics.

An Example of Implementing Community Policing

The transitional plan of Vancouver, Washington, provides an example of how one department planned to implement community policing.

What Is Vancouver Doing to Implement COPPS?

Enhancing Partnerships

Strategies

- Increase community ownership for personal safety and problem solving.
- Increase the trust and working relationship between the police and the community we serve.
- Enhance the use of volunteers and others in solving local problems.
- Police with a "citizen" perspective in mind.

Activities

1. Teams of citizens and employees will be formed to address many issues.
   (a) Precinct Advisory Teams.
   (b) Explorer Programs.
2. The Police Department will actively participate in community outreach activities such as:
   (a) Developing and implementing ongoing training classes for citizens.
   (b) Developing a community outreach plan that supports the diversity of the community.

3. Patrol officers assigned to specific patrol beats will be assigned responsibility as neighborhood liaisons.
4. Department Managers will be assigned to various ad hoc community groups as liaisons.
5. The Police Department will assign liaisons to other city departments, government agencies, social service agencies and private non-profit agencies.

Problem Solving

Strategies

- Provide officers with uninterrupted amounts of time for problem solving assignments and interaction with citizens.
- Provide officers with permanent territorial responsibility in order to facilitate communication and problem solving between the beat officer(s) and the citizens who live within a geographic area.
- Develop a method in which problem areas can be identified (chronic call locations) and problem solving can be initiated.

Activities

1. A differential response plan will be developed and implemented for alternative methods of handling specific calls.
2. The Department will develop and implement a staffing plan to include:
   (a) Police Service Technician.
   (b) Tactical information function.
   (c) Officer assignments to beats will be stabilized.
   (d) Tactical Squads at the precinct level.
3. Problem tracking methods will be implemented for identification, assessment and problem-solving purposes.
4. Partnerships will be formed with:
   (a) Code Enforcement.
   (b) Neighborhood Mediation.

Expansion of Crime Prevention

Strategies

- Empower citizens by providing resources and crime prevention training to them.
- Increase community ownership for personal safety and problem solving.
- Shift the Department from the traditional "reactive" style of policing to a style that addresses crime before it occurs.
- Develop crime prevention programs that meet the diverse needs of the community in regards to cultural issues, language barriers, modes of communication, etc.

Activities

1. The Department will assign to each precinct a Neighborhood Support Specialist.
2. Volunteers will be recruited by each precinct to help manage special programs:
   (a) Residential Crime Prevention
   (b) Commercial Crime Prevention
   (c) Youth Crime Prevention
   (d) Senior Crime Prevention
   (e) Personal Safety
   (f) Traffic Safety Support
3. The Department will develop information networks.
4. Work with other city departments to establish a Crime Prevention Through Environmental Design (CPTED) Program.

Decentralization and Despecialization

Strategies

- To enhance customer oriented access to the Police Department and to other services.
- To increase personal responsibility and accountability or problem solving in geographic areas of the city.
- To move appropriate levels of specialized police services to the control of Precinct Commanders.

Activities

1. The department will develop and implement a patrol redeployment plan that decentralizes the existing force.
2. The Department will expand services by:
   (a) Opening East Precinct.
   (b) Opening Central Precinct.
   (c) Remodel and open West Precinct.
   (d) Opening and staffing Citizen Contact Centers city-wide.
   (e) Offering Mobile Citizen Contact Centers.
3. The Department will decentralize/despecialize target functions such as:
   (a) Investigations.
   (b) Youth Services.
   (c) Crime Prevention.
4. Each precinct will be established as a Community Service Center by offering additional city services.

Organizational Development

Strategies

- To ensure that the organizational culture changes to support COPPS.
- To ensure that systems, structures and strategies are adapted to a COPPS environment.

Activities

1. The Department will revise its Mission/Vision/Values statements.
2. The Department will establish a new organizational structure.
3. A communication plan will be developed.
4. The Department will implement COPPS training.
5. The personnel system will be redesigned.
6. A new staffing plan will be established.
7. The press information policy will be revised.
8. A performance monitoring system will be developed and implemented.
9. An internal survey will be conducted.
10. The Department will conduct a community survey.
11. Precinct profiles will be completed.
12. Specific improvements will be made to the Department's information systems.

Lessons Learned from Team Policing

Walker (1993, pp.36–37) suggests that those implementing community policing should take some lessons from what was learned from the team policing programs instituted during the mid-1960s to mid-1970s. Both community policing and team policing had a neighborhood focus, decentralized decision making, community input and a new police role. But the basic goals of community policing differ radically from team policing, with community policing rejecting the crime-attack model in favor of an emphasis on order maintenance and quality-of-life problems. In addition, the team policing effort faced three major obstacles (pp.41–44):

1. Opposition from middle management—captains and lieutenants resented their loss of authority as greater responsibility was placed on sergeants and police officers.
2. Trial by peers—where it was a success, or reputed to be a success, there was resentment on the part of other officers, often as the result of unequal workloads.
3. Problems with dispatching technology—dispatching technology remained centralized, with team members spending as much as half their time outside their team area.

The most important lesson to be learned from team policing, according to Walker (p.44), was the problem associated with unclear definition of goals. He (p.54) notes:

> The problem of unclear goals is probably greater in community policing than in team policing. . . . Community policing . . . represents a radical role redefinition, eschewing crime control in favor of attention to problems that have traditionally been defined as not part of the police role. . . .

> Redefining the police role in such a radical fashion introduces a number of problems. The most important is socializing the various actors and publics into the new role. Resocializing police officers is a major change. . . . Equally difficult is the task of resocializing the public.

Doing the Little Things—A Shift in Policy Focus

Hoffmann (2000, p.54) offers a final piece of advice to those implementing community policing:

> The Broken-Windows theory contends that a broken window left unfixed is a sign that nobody cares and can lead to serious crime, abandonment of neighborhoods to criminals, and urban decay. "The policy corollary is that minor problems warrant serious attention, a premise that challenges reigning criminal justice practices," George L. Kelling said in a Department of Justice lecture series.

Benefits That Might Be Achieved

The benefits of implementing community policing are numerous, both to the department and to the community at large. Community policing brings police closer to the people, building relationships between police and community and among community members themselves. As police interaction with the community becomes more positive, productive partnerships are formed, and community and officer leadership skills are developed. Citizens see that problems have solutions, giving them courage to tackle other community issues. As citizens feel more empowered to get involved, prevention and detection of crime increases, leading to reduced fear of crime in the community and improved quality of life. Reduced levels of crime allow more police resources to be allocated to services that have the greatest impact on the quality of community life. Making effective use of the talents and resources available within communities further extends severely strained police resources. Community policing also provides real challenges for officers, making them more than "order takers and report writers," which leads to increased job satisfaction among officers.

Research conducted by Sherwood (2000, p.191) found that: "Officers from the department that was observed to be more advanced in implementing community policing reported significantly higher scores for skill variety, task identity, task significance and autonomy." Sherwood (p.209) reports: "Allowing officers to work regularly with neighborhood residents creates a natural work unit that will increase skill variety and task identity. Furthermore, by granting police officers the increased responsibility and authority to engage in proactive problem solving, managers enhance the vertical loading of the job and increase autonomy. Combining tasks into a more identifiable and complete piece of work to be performed by the officer also strengthens skill variety and task identity." Community policing also makes the police department *effective,* instead of only efficient, which leads to greater community satisfaction with police services.

Resistance to Community Policing

As the chapter-opening quote by Machiavelli suggests, establishing a new order can be difficult, even dangerous to manage:

> There is nothing more difficult to plan, more uncertain of success, or more dangerous to manage than the establishment of a new order; because the innovator has for enemies all those who have derived advantage from the old order and finds but lukewarm defenders among those who stand to gain from the new one. Such a lukewarm attitude grows partly out of fear of the adversaries, who have the law on their side, and partly from the incredulity of men in general, who actually have no faith in new things until they have been proved by experience.

Managers should anticipate and prepare for resistance to the community policing philosophy and the changes that accompany the transition.

Consider the following analogy: A professional truck driver does not drive his 50-ton trailer-truck the same way he drives a sports car. In the truck, he corners more slowly and avoids braking sharply; otherwise the trailer's momentum can overturn or jackknife the truck.

Police organizations also have considerable momentum. Resistance to change often can be around 25 percent of the department personnel. Resistance can be reduced by positive communication from the chief or head of the agency. Their resistance is caused in part by concerns about community policing, which may be somewhat allayed by changes in the communication process of the organization.

"This communications strategy should be geared towards overcoming resistance; increasing the readiness for change; preparing and equipping people for the change; and helping to reduce uncertainty and anxiety" (Community Policing Consortium).

Pitfalls to Avoid

Common pitfalls in making the transition to community policing include unrealistic expectations and focusing on short-term instead of long-term results; adopting a task force approach; resisting the move toward community empowerment; taking advantage of the position; and misrepresenting an inadequate program as legitimate in order to receive funding.

Reconciling Expectations and Results

One pitfall is the common expectation that implementing a new strategy such as community policing, highly touted as an effective method of crime reduction, will have immediate and measurable results. It may have immediate results—but not the ones citizens were expecting. Ironically, increased citizen vigilance and reporting, although a desirable and positive outcome of successful community policing, may initially indicate an *increase* in crime and lead to disappointment and widespread skepticism regarding the effectiveness of community policing. Such misunderstandings, generated by ambiguous promises, can sabotage a department's efforts to build the relationships with citizens necessary for community policing. Before making predictions and promises regarding the long-term benefits of community policing, make sure everyone understands the possible short-term outcomes.

Walker (p.51) cautions against another hazard of inflated expectations: "Community policing places a heavy burden of responsibility on rank-and-file officers to develop creative, neighborhood-specific programs. This is an enormous burden indeed and the unpleasant truth may be that it is unrealistic to expect that much creativity among the police rank and file."

The Specialized Unit Approach

Another pitfall is the inability of a department's management to gain the commitment of the entire organization. This often occurs when an agency adopts a specialized unit approach, isolating acceptance of the philosophy to those in the community policing unit. As one reviewer commented: "Marginalizing COPPS in a separate unit or single district is essentially to doom the initiative to failure." Isolation has nearly always happened when specialized units have been formed. The area of crime prevention in agencies has almost always been the responsibility of specialized units. This usually resulted in a shift in thinking of officers, that being that they felt preventing crime was the job of those few personnel assigned to the unit. It is not uncommon for an officer, when asked by a citizen how to prevent being burglarized, for example, to respond by telling the citizen to contact someone in the crime prevention unit.

There has also been a tendency for officers not assigned to specialized units to minimize the importance of such units, claiming that their own assignment was "real police work" and everything else was essentially not important. In some cases, officers assigned to special units became discounted and ignored by their colleagues as irrelevant and not part of the group.

Community Empowerment

Lansing, Michigan, has had a citywide neighborhood-watch program in effect for more than 20 years with 151 watches serving more than 11,500 households. As part of a department reorganization designed to make officers "more accessible to the citizens they serve and enhance communication and problem-solving potential," the police department began working to strengthen neighborhood-watch groups in the southern part of the city where they were less organized and active.

Problem-solving teams were formed which included a sergeant and officers from each shift as well as several watch coordinators from this part of the city. At team meetings, the sergeants explained the department reorganization to the coordinators and solicited feedback on the watch program and the department reorganization. The neighborhood-watch coordinators shared some of their concerns about the watch program. There was an information line, updated four times a week, with information on crimes occurring the previous day. Coordinators believed the information line was insufficient and not specific enough to be useful. After discussing how the information line could be improved, the teams developed an anonymous survey to gather information from the 91 coordinators in the southern part of the city.

The survey used a combination of Likert scales, dichotomous (yes/no) fill-in values and open-ended questions. Surveys were mailed with a cover letter explaining the purpose, with self-addressed stamped envelopes for returning them to the police department. The teams had a response rate of 63 percent of completed surveys. The data were analyzed and a committee of neighborhood-watch coordinators and a police sergeant reviewed the results and made recommendations for improving the program.

The survey revealed that nearly half of the respondents (48 percent) rated the performance of their team as "unknown." Figure 5.3 illustrates the correlation between the respondent's contact with a team member and his or her subsequent rating of the team's performance.

The results showed a correlation between a coordinator having contact with a team officer and the coordinator's positive feelings toward a team approach to problem solving. Conversely, a lack of communication between the police organization and the citizenry was shown to be a primary reason for a lack of support by watch coordinators.

The committee made creative and useful recommendations for improving the neighborhood-watch program. The suggestions are as follows:

- That neighborhood watch teams have a separate voice mailbox at the police department to provide specific crime information about each team area
- That coordinators attend the officers' monthly team meetings, which would enable them to discuss neighborhood problems with team members and improve communication with the officers
- That coordinators "ride along" with their team officers to get a better idea of what the officers do every day
- That the department start a neighborhood watch mentor program to assist in the development of new watches

As a result, the police department continues to involve coordinators in the decision-making process to continue improving communications between officers and citizens. According to Lansing Mayor David Hollister: "Decentralization of the police

Q I have personally met my team sergeant. Yes No

56% of "yes" respondents rated the team performance as excellent or good.
68% of "no" respondents rated the team performance as unknown.

Q The team approach to problem solving has been explained to me by a Lansing police officer. Yes No

50% of "yes" respondents rated team performance as excellent or good.
75% of "no" respondents rated team performance as unknown.

Figure 5.3 Correlation between Contact with a Team Member and Rating of Performance

department is not being done as an end in itself; it is being done to help foster open and honest communication between the police officers and the citizens they serve." This kind of open communication often leads to the identification and solving of problems.

Taking Advantage of Your Position

A COPS grants officer served as a school liaison officer at the local high school, working the day shift, Monday through Friday. A school administrator, concerned about a possible growing problem with gangs, asked the COPS officer to work some night shifts to determine which students were out roaming the streets at night. Instead of scheduling himself for the afternoon-to-evening shift, where his contact with roaming youths would be increased, he chose to work the midnight shift, selecting nights when that shift was at maximum staffing to minimize his chances of being assigned radio calls. He also scheduled himself to work the Thursday night/Friday morning shift to give himself a longer weekend, being able to get off duty early Friday morning. To make matters worse, he boasted of his scheme at the midnight shift roll call.

Unfortunately, this officer's scheme was very damaging because it created the perception that the community policing program was a way to get a soft assignment. Officers' work schedules must comply with their work requirements, and empowering officers to become creative problem solvers does not mean supervision is abandoned. Challenging officers to justify their actions can be a useful mechanism for helping them think through strategies and tactics, helping to revise faulty practices and end abuses of the position (*Community Policing Pages*, 2000).

Walker (p.48) concludes "If community policing has the potential for unleashing the untapped creativity of officers on the street, it also has the danger of allowing them to revert to the gross abuses of a previous era in policing."

Misrepresentation—Talking the Talk without Walking the Walk

Community Policing Pages reports:

> One department adopted community policing by forming a Neighborhood Patrol Unit. Their "community policing" tactics consist of serving warrants. An officer in the unit was candid enough to say ". . . we're just called a neighborhood unit so we could get the federal funding."

The strategy: If the title sounds like community policing, it will bring in new money. Unfortunately, according to *Community Policing Pages,* too many so-called community policing programs have no real community policing component, while others use only limited community policing techniques. This deception, however, undermines the chances for success of legitimate community policing efforts. *Community Policing Pages* urges: "True supporters of community policing need to expose this abuse. If they do not, these programs will be cited as evidence that community policing has failed when the funding cycle runs dry."

Impediments to Overcome

Sadd and Grinc (1996, pp.1–2) report on a National Institute of Justice survey of eight cities implementing innovative neighborhood-oriented policing (INOP). This study revealed the following:

- The major implementation challenges were resistance by police officers to community policing and the difficulty of involving other public agencies and organizing the community.
- Police officers generally did not understand community policing.

This survey (p.13) also looked at the "untested assumptions of community policing that residents really want closer contact with the police and want to work with them to reduce crime." Another implementation problem the survey identified (p.14) was the nature of the target neighborhoods: The economically disadvantaged urban areas that generally serve as testing grounds for community policing tend to be highly disorganized, characterized by poverty, unemployment, inadequate educational services, and high crime rates. In areas encumbered by such an array of problems it is often difficult to find well-organized community groups that are attempting to address quality-of-life issues. Polzin (1997) notes:

> The research [on community policing] reveals many obstacles to community policing design and implementation including:
>
> confusion over the definition and appropriate application of community policing; middle management indifference; lack of community support; perceptions of employee resistance; disagreements about resource allocation and personnel deployment; confusion or disagreement about changes in departmental systems and structures; clashes between "command-and-control" management styles and expanded decision making by line officers; and failure within the department to view employees as "internal customers."
>
> Interviews with several Michigan police department labor leaders revealed still other barriers:
>
> failure to integrate community policing with traditional police responsibilities; confusion about the differences between community policing and traditional police work leading to skepticism about the program and the department's leadership; lack of involvement in the initiative's design, implementation, and monitoring; performance measures incongruent with community policing goals; management assumptions that a "union buy-in" means "giving in" to management control; lack of team focus; failure to recognize accomplishments; perceptions that community policing is a management tool to circumvent the contract, particularly seniority provisions; preferential treatment for community police officers; and poor communication between the administration, middle management, and union.
>
> These barriers are neither unique to police departments nor insurmountable. Yet, if left unattended, they are likely to fester, causing discontent and cynicism, and undermining the department's leadership and the community policing concept.

Impediments to COP implementation include:

- Organizational impediments—resistance from middle management, line officers and unions; confusion about what COP is; problems in line-level accountability; officers' concern that COP is "soft" on crime; and lack of COP training
- Union impediments—resistance to change, fear of losing control to community, resistance to increased officer responsibility and accountablity, fear that COP will lead to civilian review boards
- Community impediments—community resistance, community's concern that COP is "soft" on crime, civil service rules, pressure to demonstrate COP reduces crime and lack of support from local government
- Transition impediments—balancing increased foot patrol activities while maintaining emergency response time

Evaluating Progress

As the Community Policing Consortium warns, without specifying desired outcomes as part of the strategic plan, the community policing initiative could be reduced to another series of community relations exercises rather than the anticipated cultural, organizational and structural change achieved through community policing in partnership and problem solving. Recall from Chapter 4 that the SARA model of problem solving shows that there are no failures, only responses that do not provide the desired goal. Remember also from Chapter 4 the mental lock: "To err is wrong." Avoid this thinking trap by understanding risk taking is a necessary part of progress, and erring is wrong only if you fail to learn from your "mistake." Edison is quoted as saying he did not fail 25,000 times to make a storage battery. He simply knew 25,000 ways *not* to make one.

Evaluating progress can take many forms. It should have been built into the strategic plan in concrete form. Which goals and objectives have been met? Which have not? Why not? The evaluation might also a year later consist of conducting a second needs assessment of both the department and community and determine whether needs are being better met. It can be done through additional surveys and interviews assessing reduced fear of crime and improved confidence in police. Are citizens making fewer complaints regarding police service? Are officers filing fewer grievances?

When evaluating, failures should be as important as successes—sometimes more important—because a department learns from what doesn't work.

Evaluating effectiveness is difficult. Police have long been able to evaluate their efficiency by looking at police activity; what police do rather than what effect it had. It is far easier to look at numbers—crime reports filed, arrests made, tickets issued, drugs seized—than to measure how problems have been solved. Measuring effectiveness requires that "performance indicators need to be carefully thought through and some pioneering undertaken to establish realistic and meaningful measures. These indicators need to be responsive to community concerns and reflect the accomplishments of the community policing philosophy and strategies. They involve devising new output measures reflecting police capability to adapt, to consult, to mobilize, to diagnose, and to solve problems" (Community Policing Consortium).

Giving COP Implementation a Boost

To promote the community policing concept and recognize law enforcement executives who have strived to implement the COP philosophy, the American Association for the Advancement of Community-Oriented Policing (AAACOP or Triple A-Cop) was launched in May 2000. Composed of criminal justice theorists, academics and members of the policing community, Triple A-Cop is "a grassroots attempt to maintain community policing measures around the country" ("New Advocacy Group . . .," 2000, p.6). A major component of the group's effort is an awards ceremony named for the late Robert Trojanowicz, a pioneer in community policing, to honor individuals, police agencies and communities who have taken the concept to a higher level. Information on training courses, conferences and general COP information is available online at www.aaacop.org.

SUMMARY

The transition to community policing requires a change in mission statement, departmental organization, leadership style and the general approach to "fighting crime." A department's vision should include the essential elements of the community policing philosophy: problem solving, empowering everyone, forming community partnerships and being proactive—making preventing crime as important as enforcing the law. The vision is used to create a mission statement.

Once the vision and mission statement have been articulated, the next step is to conduct a needs assessment. A needs assessment should include not only the department but also the community of which it is a part. The traditional law enforcement organization design has been that of a pyramid-shaped hierarchy based on a military model. However, to implement community policing, the pyramid might be inverted. Another change might occur in leadership style, with a preference for participatory leadership, where each individual has a voice in decisions, but top management still has the ultimate decision-making authority.

While conducting needs assessments, the department should pay attention to potential community leaders to enlist in the community policing initiative. It may be more important for COP-oriented police agencies to target the "critical mass" of individuals—the smallest number of citizens and organizations needed to support and sustain the community policing initiative—than to try to mobilize the community at large.

A strategic plan should include community partnerships and problem solving as well as any needed cultural and organizational changes in the department. It should also include a realistic time line and ways to assess progress. It must also be tied to the department's budget. The most important consideration in selecting strategies to implement community policing is to ensure that the strategies fit the unique needs of the community.

Recruiting and selecting personnel are of great importance in the successful implementation of the community policing philosophy. POST-21 is an add-on to an agency's existing application examination and selection process designed to identify applicants with traits and attitudes compatible with a community policing environment. Training is also critical for a successful transition to community policing. However, do not make training the spearhead of change. Among the most important areas to include in training are communication skills, problem-solving skills and leadership skills.

Managers should anticipate and prepare for resistance to the community policing philosophy and the changes that accompany the transition. They should also be aware of and try to avoid the common pitfalls in making the transition to community policing, including unrealistic expectations and focusing on short-term instead of long-term results; adopting a task force approach; resisting the move toward community empowerment; taking advantage of the position; and misrepresenting an inadequate program as legitimate to receive funding.

Impediments to COP implementation include organizational impediments (resistance from middle management, line officers and unions; confusion about what COP is; problems in line-level accountability; officers' concern that COP is soft on crime; and lack of COP training), community impediments (community resistance, community's concern that COP is soft on crime, civil service rules, pressure to demonstrate COP reduces crime and lack of support from local government) and transition impediments (balancing increased foot patrol activities while maintaining emergency response time).

When evaluating, failures should be as important as successes—sometimes more important—because a department learns from what does not work.

Discussion Questions

1. What do you consider the greatest obstacles to implementing community policing?
2. If you had to prioritize the changes needed to convert to community policing, what would your priorities be?
3. Find out what your police department's mission statement is. If it is not community policing focused, how might it be revised?
4. How would you determine whether community policing efforts are working?
5. Why might citizens not want to become involved in community policing efforts?
6. Discuss the similarities between team policing and community policing and describe the most important lesson to be learned from team policing.
7. How would you go about assessing your community's needs regarding efforts to reduce crime and violence?
8. Are there conflicting groups within your "community"? Does one group have more political power than another?
9. Can you explain why some police officers oppose community policing?
10. Name at least three attributes that would indicate a job candidate might be a good fit for a department engaged in community policing.

InfoTrac College Edition Assignments

- Use InfoTrac College Edition to help answer the Discussion Questions as appropriate.
- Find and outline two articles that discuss strategic planning. Do they suggest the same approach? If not, how do they differ?
- Research and take notes on how an administrator can build support within the department and the community.
- Outline two articles on leadership, one from a law enforcement journal, one from a business journal. Give the complete cite for each. Compare the contents of the two articles, and be prepared to discuss your outlines in class.

Community Projects

1. Conduct a community survey of business owners or campus or neighborhood residents. Ask about:
   - Their fear of crime.
   - Their opinion of police services in the community.
   - What they think community policing means.
   - Whether they believe their police or sheriff's department practices community policing.
   - What they would direct the police to concentrate on.

2. Research the importance of mission statements to an organization. Collect some examples of mission statements. Ask employees of organizations if they know the mission statement of their organization. What are the implications of their knowing or not knowing their mission statement?

References

Abshire, Richard and Paynter, Ronnie L. "Putting the 'Community' in Community Policing." *Law Enforcement Technology,* October 2000, pp.50–58.

Bennett, Wayne W. and Hess, Kären M. *Management and Supervision in Law Enforcement,* 4th ed. Belmont, CA: Wadsworth Thomson Learning, 2004.

Community Policing Consortium. *The Police Organization in Transition* (Monograph), 2000. www.communitypolicing.org/pforgtrans/index.html

Community Policing Pages. Summer 2000. Edition, Vol. 6, No. 3. www.msnhomepages. talkcity.com/LibraryLawn/devere_woods/.

Correia, Mark E. *Citizen Involvement: How Community Factors Affect Progressive Policing.* Washington, DC: Police Executive Research Forum, 2000.

DeParis, Richard J. "How Contemporary Police Agencies Can Adapt to the Community Policing Mission." *The Police Chief,* August 2000, pp.108–114.

Goldstein, Herman. *The New Policing: Confronting Complexity.* Washington, DC: National Institute of Justice Research in Brief, December 1992.

Greenberg, Sheldon and Flynn, Edward A. "Leadership and Managing Change." In *Local Government Police Management.* Washington, DC: International City/County Management Association (ICMA), 2003, pp.67–88.

Harr, J. Scott and Hess, Kären M. *Seeking Employment in Criminal Justice and Related Fields,* 4th ed. Belmont, CA: Wadsworth Publishing Company, 2003.

Harris, Wesley and Kolkman, Aaron. "Selecting Community Oriented Officers." *Law and Order,* April 2000, pp.53–66.

Hoffmann, John. "How to Make Citizens Hate Community Policing." *Law and Order,* April 2000, pp.53–56.

Kurz, David L. "Strategic Planning and Police–Community Partnership in a Small Town." *The Police Chief,* December 2000, pp.28–36.

Malinowski, Sean W.; Kalish, David J.; and Parks, Bernard C. "From *Dragnet* to the Internet: One Police Department Extends Its Reach." *The Police Chief,* September 2000, pp.62–66.

Mittleman, Pete. "Community Policing: Building Community Trust Thinking Outside of the Box." *The Police Chief,* March 2000, pp.50–55.

Mook, Dennis and Dempsey, Tom. "University Partnership Educates Officers in Community Leadership." *The Police Chief,* August 2000, pp.115–116.

"New Advocacy Group to Boost Community Policing." *Law Enforcement News,* May 15/30, 2000.

Palk, Leslie. *Surveying Communities: A Resource for Community Justice Planners,* BJA Monograph, May 2003. (NCJ 197 109)

Paoline, Eugene A., III; Myers, Stephanie M.; and Worden, Robert E. "Police Culture, Individualism, and Community Policing: Evidence from Two Police Departments." *Justice Quarterly,* September 2000, pp.575–605.

Polzin, Michael J. *A Labor-Management Approach to Community Policing.* East Lansing, MI: Michigan State University, 1997.

PTO: An Overview and Introduction. Washington, DC: Police Executive Research Forum and the COPS Office, no date.

Ramsey, Charles H. "Organizational Change: Preparing a Police Department for Community Policing in the 21st Century." *The Police Chief,* March 2000, pp.16–25.

Recruitment and Selection for Community Policing (Monograph). Washington, DC: Community Policing Consortium, no date.

Sadd, Susan and Grinc, Randolph M. *Implementing Challenges in Community Policing: Innovative Neighborhood-Oriented Policing in Eight Cities.* Washington, DC: National Institute of Justice Research in Brief, February 1996.

Sherwood, Charles W. "Job Design, Community Policing, and Higher Education: A Tale of Two Cities." *Police Quarterly,* June 2000, pp.191–212.

Switzer, Merle. "In Search of Community-Oriented Policing." *The Police Chief,* March 2000, pp.38–41.

Turner, Yvonne C. "'Decentralizing' the Specialized Unit Function in Small Police Agencies." *The Police Chief,* February 2000, pp.50–51.

Walker, Samuel. "Does Anyone Remember Team Policing? Lessons of the Team Policing Experience for Community Policing." *American Journal of Police,* Vol. XII, 1993, pp.35–55.

Additional Resources

Community Policing Consortium	www.communitypolicing.org
COPS Office (Department of Justice)	www.usdoj.gov/cops
Justice Information Center	www.ncjrs.org
National Center for Community Policing	www.cj.msu.edu/~people/cp
Police Executive Research Forum	www.policeforum.org
Upper Midwest Community Policing Institute	www.umcpi.org

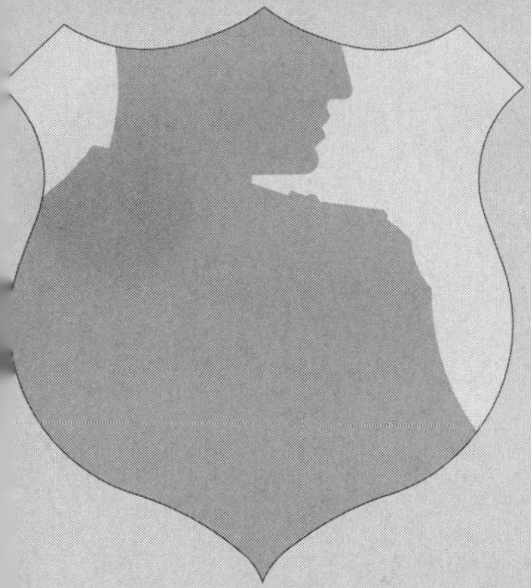

SECTION II

BUILDING RELATIONSHIPS AND TRUST

CHAPTERS IN THIS SECTION

With the basic background supplied in Section I, you are ready to look at the interaction occurring between the police and the public they serve and protect. At the most basic level, police–community relations begin with one-on-one interaction between an officer and a citizen.

The section begins with a discussion of the communication skills needed to interact effectively with citizens, including interacting effectively with the increasing diversity within the United States, as well as interacting effectively with victims and witnesses (Chapter 6). Next, building partnerships with key stakeholders and selling the concept of community policing, both internally and externally, is explored (Chapter 7). The section concludes with a look at building partnerships with the media and how the media can also collaborate in selling the concept (Chapter 8).

Although these crucial components of community policing are discussed separately, overlap often exists.

Chapter 6

Communicating Effectively—One on One

What we are communicates far more eloquently than anything we say or do. There are people we trust because we know their character. Whether they're eloquent or not, whether they have human-relations techniques or not, we trust them and work with them.

—Stephen R. Covey

Do You Know?

- What is critical to self-understanding?
- The difference between prejudice and discrimination?
- What the communication process consists of?
- What individual characteristics are important in the communication process?
- Why police officers may have more barriers to communication than other professionals and what these barriers consist of?
- What two human relations practices used in business might be adopted for improving police–community relations?
- What kinds of diversity are found in the United States?
- What racial profiling is?
- What disabilities police officers frequently encounter?
- What disabilities can mimic intoxication or a drug high?
- What the four civil criteria for detainment and commitment of mentally ill individuals are in most states?
- What youths with special needs police officers should be familiar with?
- What national organizations exist to help victims?
- What two types of programs have been established to help victims? What services are most commonly provided in each?
- What special populations have been targeted for additional needs if victimized?

Can You Define?

acculturation
ADA
Alzheimer's disease (AD)
assimilation
attention hyperactivity deficit disorder (AHDD)
bias
body language
communication
communication process
crack children
crisis behavior
cultural conflict

cultural pluralism
culture
deinstitutionalization
disability
discrimination
EBD
empathy
ethnocentrism
fetal alcohol syndrome (FAS)
hyphenated American
jargon
kinesics
learning disability
networking
nonverbal communication
posttraumatic stress disorder (PTSD)
poverty syndrome
prejudice
racial profiling
racism
stereotyping
sympathy
victim compensation programs
victim/witness assistance programs

Introduction

A woman executive at a shopping center discovered a minor theft of company property from her company car. The car had been parked outside a police office where several traffic officers took breaks between shifts. The office was not accessible to the public but had an identification sign on the locked door.

The woman knocked on the door and asked the sergeant who opened it who was responsible for watching the parking area. She also commented on the officers she could see sitting in the room and suggested they were not doing their jobs. The

Police stand guard between a group of anti-abortion protestors and a group of pro-choice protestors outside a clinic in Little Rock, Arkansas. Their presence maintains order.

officers in the room stopped talking with each other and turned their attention to the conversation at the office door.

The sergeant and the woman never got around to discussing the missing item. Instead he responded to her comments with questions. "What do you mean by that?" "What are you trying to say?" She left to tell her supervisor, refusing to file a police report. She soon returned, however, and encountered another officer just outside the office. Their conversation, later characterized as "heated" by witnesses, centered on the woman's suggestion that the officers should do more to prevent theft in the parking lot. She implied they were lazy and shirked their responsibilities.

At this point the woman asked to file a police report, and the officer asked her to enter the police office with him to do so. They entered the office, but when the officer suggested they enter a private office away from the hubbub of the break area, she refused to do so. She later said the officer intimidated her by slamming drawers, moving quickly and ordering her into the room. She feared being alone with him.

The officer's perception of the incident was entirely different. He commented that the woman had a "chip on her shoulder" and an "attitude." She was demanding and impossible to deal with.

After refusing to enter the office to file the report, the woman sat down on a chair in the break area. She was told to either go into the other room and file the report or leave. When she refused to do either, she was escorted from the office and left outside the locked doors. The woman filed a complaint against the police department.

With better communication, this problem and thousands like it could be avoided. Effective communication with the public is vital to good police–community relations. In fact, at the heart of police–community relations are one-on-one interactions between officers and citizens.

This chapter begins with a discussion of understanding yourself—a prerequisite for effective interpersonal relationships. This is followed by an explanation of understanding others and the nature of the interaction between police and citizens. Next the communication process is described, including nonverbal communication and body language, communication barriers and active listening. The general discussion of communication concludes with lessons learned from business.

Next the discussion turns to community policing in a diverse society, beginning with a description of the multicultural diversity in the United States, including racial and ethnic diversity. Next racism is discussed, including a look at racial disparity, followed by racial profiling and strategies to overcome barriers based on racial or ethnic diversity. This is followed by a brief discussion of religious diversity and socioeconomic diversity with a closer look at those in the lower socioeconomic class, the homeless and the powerful and privileged. The discussion of diversity concludes with a consideration of the challenges facing police in the twenty-first century as they strive to "serve and protect" an increasingly diverse society.

The third major area of discussion is one-on-one interaction with individuals with disabilities, including those with physical and mental disabilities and interacting with the elderly as well as with youths. The final major discussion focuses on communicating with victims of and witnesses to criminal acts.

Understanding One's Self

Officers who seek to build effective relationships with the citizens they serve first need to understand themselves and potential barriers to such relationships. They need to recognize their own level of self-esteem as well as the roles they play. Officers need to understand how their view of the world has been shaped and how it affects their interactions with others. For example, when one person kills another, is it an act of murder, an act of temporary insanity, an act of homicide, an accident or an act of heroism?

Prejudice, Bias, Stereotyping and Discrimination

It is important to recognize that no one can be completely objective. Everyone, consciously or unconsciously, has certain preferences and prejudices.

It is critical to self-understanding to recognize prejudices and stereotypes.

A **prejudice** is a negative judgment not based on fact; it is an irrational, preconceived negative opinion. Prejudices are often associated with a dislike of a particular group, race or religion. They represent overgeneralizations, a failure to consider individual characteristics.

Prejudices are also referred to as **bias**, a belief that inhibits objectivity. Taken to an extreme, a bias becomes hatred. It is important for law enforcement to understand bias and its extreme form—hate—in order to deal with the increase in bias and hate crimes. The manner in which police deal with hate crimes is discussed in Chapter 10. Prejudices or biases are the result of overgeneral classification or stereotyping.

Stereotyping assumes that all people within a specific group are the same; they lack individuality. Simply because a person is a member of a specific group, that person is thought to have certain characteristics. Common stereotypes associated with nationalities include the French being great lovers, the Italians being great cooks, the Scotch being thrifty and American Yankees being ingenious. Often the stereotype of Americans is very negative, as illustrated in the novel *The Ugly American.*

Many people stereotype police officers based on what they see on television—scenes showing cops in car chases and shootouts. Officers are not shown standing on the street corner in late January directing traffic after an accident or being tended to at the medical center because they were bitten on the arm by a hooker who resisted arrest.

Police officers may also stereotype those with whom they come in contact. In the traditional mode of policing, officers spend a considerable amount of time dealing with criminals and their victims. Some officers may begin to categorize certain types of individuals as perpetrators. Police officers focus so much attention on crime, they may develop a distorted view of who the "bad guys" are. Generalizing from a few to the many is a serious problem for many police. It is a very natural tendency to stereotype people but one that can be fatal to effective police–community relations.

Prejudices may lead to **discrimination,** showing a preference in treating individuals or groups or failing to treat equals equally, especially illegally unequal treatment based on race, religion, sex or age. Some male traffic officers, for example, are known to issue warnings to females who violate traffic laws and to issue tickets to males for the same violation. It is often alleged that members of minority groups receive rougher treatment from police officers than a Caucasian would receive, as discussed in Chapter 7.

Prejudice is an attitude; discrimination is a behavior.

This difference between attitude and overt behavior was summed up by an English judge in his comments to nine youths convicted of race rioting: "Think what you like . . . But once you translate your dark thoughts into savage acts, the law will punish you, and protect your victim."

Understanding Others

Understanding others is particularly important in police work. Understanding others does not, however, mean that you sympathize with them or even that you agree with them. Ciaramicoli (2000, p.9) defines empathy as "the capacity to accurately perceive and respond to another person's thoughts and feelings. . . . Empathy is unquestionably the most important capacity for a successful personal and professional life." **Sympathy** is an involuntary sharing of another person's feelings of fear, grief or anger. **Empathy** is an active process involving trying to *understand* another person's feelings.

The Communication Process

Communication is basically the transfer of information from one person to another. Fulton (2000, p.130) stresses the importance of effective communication: "Communication at any level is an inexact art. But misunderstood communication can have grave consequences in the 'life and death' world of police work." Depending on the situation, the communication process involves four or five components.

The **communication process** involves a sender, a message, a channel, a receiver and sometimes feedback.

Communication involves transferring thoughts from one person's mind to another's. The people involved, how well the message parallels the sender's thoughts and the channel used will all affect the communication.

The sender encodes the message in words—spoken or written—and then transmits the message by telephone, fax, letter, in person or in some other way. The receiver decodes the message. The receiver may then provide the sender with some kind of feedback that indicates the message has been received. Many factors will influence the message.

Important individual characteristics in communication include age, education, gender, values, emotional involvement, self-esteem and language skills.

Imagine, by way of illustration, that people see the world through tinted glasses. The tint represents their particular worldview. If the sender of a message sees the world through yellow glasses and the receiver of the message sees the world through red glasses, the message received will be a mixture of the worldviews of both and will result in a different color—orange.

A Rutgers University study found law enforcement involves about 97 percent verbal interaction and only 3 percent physical interaction (Scott, 2000, p.54). This finding underscores the importance of effective officer communication. According to Dr. George Thompson, an English-professor-turned-police-officer, the most dangerous weapon today's police officer carries is not the firearm but the "cocked tongue." He claims when we react to a situation, the situation controls us, but when we respond, we control the situation (Scott, p.54). To help officers respond more effectively, Thompson developed a system of verbalization tactics called Verbal Judo. As Scott (p.54) explains, the main theme of Verbal Judo is generating voluntary compliance through verbal persuasion and maintaining what Thompson calls "professional face." The three goals of Verbal Judo are officer safety, enhanced professionalism and reduced vicarious liability.

Not all communication is verbal. For officers to communicate effectively, they must also understand nonverbal communication.

Nonverbal Communication and Body Language

Nonverbal communication includes everything other than the actual words spoken in a message such as tone, pitch and pacing. **Body language** refers to messages conveyed by how a person moves. To test the power of body language, consider what the following say about a person.

Walking—fast, slow, stomping
Posture—rigid, relaxed
Eye contact—direct, indirect, shifting
Gestures—nod, shrug, finger point
Physical spacing—close, distant

The nonverbal communication of police officers was discussed in Chapter 2. Officers communicate with the public most obviously through the uniform they wear, the way they wear it and the equipment they carry. Other forms of body language are equally important. How officers stand, how they look at those to whom they are talking, whether they smile or frown—all convey a message.

Eye contact is a powerful nonverbal communication tool. Eye contact inspires trust and shows confidence, even if it is merely the illusion of confidence. It can buy you time if you are caught off guard and need to form a response. Eye contact quietly keeps control while deftly wielding power.

Usually police officers want to convey the impression that they "know their way around." However, this may actually interfere with effective communication. For example, consider the person who asks directions about how to find a certain store in Boston. If the person is from Boston, the directions given are likely to be brief, with obvious landmarks omitted. If the person is from out of town, however, the directions are likely to be much more detailed. When interviewing a truthful witness, police officers may want to modify their body language and soften up their language, in a sense pretending to be from out of town. A relaxed manner may result in more in-depth communication and better understanding.

Reading the Nonverbal Messages and Body Language of Others In addition to understanding nonverbal messages, many police officers develop an ability to interpret body language, also called **kinesics,** to such an extent that they can tell when a person is lying or about to become aggressive or flee. This is what some call a "sixth sense," and it alerts officers when something is not as it appears or when someone is suspicious, untruthful, afraid or hesitant.

Criminals are often apprehended because an officer thought they looked suspicious or because something did not feel right about a traffic stop or other contact. Many law enforcement officers develop an uncanny ability to spot stolen cars in traffic based on a driver's movements, actions and driving maneuvers. Officers also learn to read their own hunches. Acting on a hunch can save lives. Police officers can tell story after story of nagging and intuitive feelings that they acted on.

Barriers to Communication

Police officers may have more barriers to communication because of the image they convey, their position of authority and the nature of their work. Common barriers include prejudices and stereotypes, lack of time, use of police jargon, lack of feedback and a failure to listen.

Prejudices and stereotypes can greatly interfere with communication. Preconceived ideas about a person's truthfulness or "worth" can result in strained relationships with individuals and little or no interchange of ideas. The very language used to refer to others can interfere with communication. For example, would you rather be called a victim or a survivor? A cripple or a person with a disability?

Lack of time is another barrier to effective communication. Police officers and members of the public are busy. Often neither want to take the time to communicate fully and to establish high empathy. Bad timing can also interfere with communication. Police officers frequently are interrupted by calls for service and need to cut short conversations with others.

The use of **jargon,** the technical language of a profession, is another barrier to communication. Law enforcement has its own special terminology, for example, alleged perpetrator, modus operandi and complainant. Officers should avoid using such terms when talking with the public.

Lack of feedback can also reduce effective communication. I know that you believe that you understand what you think I said, but I am not sure you realize that what you heard is not what I meant.

A failure to listen is one of the most common and most serious barriers to effective communication. Our educational system concentrates on the communication skills of reading and writing. Some time is devoted to speaking, but little or no time is devoted to listening. It is simply assumed that everyone knows how to listen.

Active Listening

When speakers realize officers listen to and evaluate what they say carefully, they generally make sure their output is factual and accurate and that their responses are appropriate under the circumstances.

Officers can use several techniques to improve listening effectiveness, including the following: actively working at listening, concentrating, looking for the main points, listening between the lines, noticing body language, keeping an open mind and emotions in check, not drawing conclusions or interrupting, offering encouragement and periodically clarifying what is being said.

Lessons from Business

Changes in technology and in our society have had a profound effect on business. Many businesses have changed their basic approach toward their employees as well as toward their customers. Businesses recognize the importance of service and of good customer relations.

Law enforcement might adopt two practices used successfully in business: networking and being service oriented.

Networking

Personal networks are connections individuals have with others in their lives. Consciously establishing such networks has become popular in the business world, with networking a popular buzzword. **Networking** is building and maintaining professional relationships for mutual benefit.

Just as police officers need to communicate with the people in their jurisdiction, they also need to communicate with the institutions and agencies in the area including churches, schools and business associations such as the Lions, Rotary and Kiwanis; social service agencies; storefront organizations and shelters; hospitals, clinics and emergency care providers; city inspectors and licensors; courts and corrections personnel; politicians and members of advisory councils; and special-interest groups such as MADD. Networks including law enforcement agencies and human services agencies can yield substantial benefits not only for the agencies involved but also for individuals who need help.

As suggested earlier, community policing creates a partnership between the police and groups of concerned individuals to address specific community problems. Those involved in the problem may also be part of its solution.

A Service Orientation: The Citizen as Customer

A customer is one who buys goods and services. Indeed, it is the citizens of a community who pay for the services provided by law enforcement. This dates back to the early days in this country when citizens were expected to take their turn serving as watchmen and decided they would rather pay someone to do that job.

Police officers do not traditionally think of the members of their community as customers. Many officers think of criminals as their customers and the public as those who should just stay out of the way. Some officers consider the time they spend dealing with law-abiding citizens as wasted time that could be better spent on "real" police work.

Law enforcement, like business, might benefit by emphasizing the value of customer service. They must also keep in mind the unfortunate ripple effect of poor customer satisfaction: Customers who have bad experiences want to tell everyone about it, whereas customers who have positive experiences, perhaps because good service is expected and taken for granted, will maybe tell one or two people. In a very real sense, citizens are the customers of law enforcement agencies.

Suggestions for treating citizens as customers might include making customer service a top priority, going beyond fulfilling a customer's basic needs, and being user friendly, for example, providing a business card with a phone number and e-mail address and a Web site with frequently asked questions and answers.

How something is said can also make a big difference in citizen satisfaction. For example, saying, "That's not my job" is not going to enhance the police department's image; but saying, "Officer Kraft usually handles that but isn't available right now. I will find someone else to help you" leaves a positive impression. Likewise, an officer who says, "No, we cannot do that for you" is not going to satisfy the citizen, but saying, "Let me see what I can do" will come across as helpful, even if the request ultimately cannot be fulfilled.

In addition to external customers are important internal customers—for example, detectives, patrol, records and dispatch. Customer service is not just how the police work with the public; it is also how they help each other.

The organization must train the people who interact directly with customers, and then it must empower them. That is, it must give them the authority, responsibility and incentives to recognize, care about and attend to customer needs. Empowering the bottom of the organizational pyramid can be threatening, especially to middle-level managers, who may view such empowerment as an erosion of their own authority. Empowerment of all members of an organization is absolutely essential to good service. Employees close to the customer are the first to know about problems and are in the best position to determine what can be done to satisfy the customer.

Law enforcement agencies, like many successful businesses, would benefit from having an empowered workforce. It is vital to community policing to give patrol officers the authority and training necessary to make good decisions and to reward them when they do so.

Diversity: An Overview

Police officers and their agencies can accomplish much by working in partnership with citizens to implement the American vision of diverse and tolerant communities that offer freedom, safety and dignity for all (International Association of Chiefs of Police).

Cherry (2000, p.8) asserts: "As America has become more racially, religiously and ethnically diverse, the call for police departments to reflect and partner with these burgeoning groups has become more insistent." Dealing effectively with diversity is important to community policing because community outreach, communications, trust and activism are all necessary to community partnerships, and none of these can be achieved without accepting—indeed, embracing—diversity.

Skogan et al. (2002, p.1) stress: "The influx of immigrants and the corresponding changes in the racial and ethnic composition of the nation's population have placed significant demands on the infrastructure of the nation's public service sector, particularly the criminal justice system." They (p.3) report that Hispanic and Asian groups—younger and with larger families—are projected to account for more than half of the nation's population growth over the next 50 years: Recall that the U.S. Census Bureau projects that by 2050 the non-Hispanic whites will constitute a bare majority at 52 percent.

Culture is a collection of artifacts, tools, ways of living, values and language common to a group of people, all passed from one generation to the next. Diversity is most obvious and sometimes most problematic when different "ways of living" coexist in the same community.

As discussed, language (an element of culture) shapes how people view the world. The culture itself also provides a framework or worldview, a cultural window through which events are interpreted. **Ethnocentrism** is the preference for one's own way of life over all others.

People are naturally attracted to others who are similar to themselves. If we surround ourselves with others similar to us, we minimize uncertainty regarding how people will respond to us and maximize the likelihood we will be in agreement. Minimizing uncertainty motivates people because uncertainty is uncomfortable. Ethnocentricity and segregation are consequences of our desire to avoid uncertainty.

Several different cultures came to the New World and established the United States. In fact, everyone who was not a Native American or Mexican American was a "boat person." The sociological literature on ethnic and racial diversity has three theories on the consequences of two or more cultures inhabiting the same geographic area: assimilation, cultural pluralism and cultural conflict. These are not mutually exclusive and may occur at the same time, creating problems for the transition to community policing. **Assimilation** theorists suggest that our society takes in or assimilates various cultures in what is commonly referred to as a "melting pot."

Assimilation, also referred to as **acculturation**, was, indeed, what happened among the early colonists. Initially the colonists came from various countries with different religions. They settled in specific geographic areas and maintained their original culture, for example, the Pennsylvania Dutch.

Over time, the triple forces of continued immigration, urbanization and industrialization turned the United States into a "melting pot" with diverse cultures from the various colonies merging. The melting pot was accomplished relatively painlessly because of the many similarities among the colonists. They looked quite similar physically, they valued religion and "morality," most valued hard work and, perhaps most important, there was plenty of land for everyone. The "homogenization" of the United States was fairly well accomplished by the mid-1800s. The formerly distinct cultures blended into what became known as the American culture, a white, male-dominated culture of European origin.

Unfortunately, the colonists excluded the Native Americans. Like animals, they were herded onto reservations. Native Americans have only recently begun to enter into the mainstream of American life. Some Native Americans no longer want to be assimilated—they seek to maintain their culture and heritage. The same is true of many African Americans. Consequently, cultural diversity will continue to exist in the United States. Assimilation does not always occur.

An alternative to assimilation is for diverse cultures to peacefully coexist. **Cultural pluralism** suggests many melting pots. Some groups are comfortable in one pot; other groups are comfortable in another. One example of cultural pluralism is the Native American. The American Indians are a nation of over 450 recognized tribes and bands in this country, with populations ranging from less than 100 to more than 100,000. Prior to colonization of the United States, the Indian tribes had distinct territories, languages and cultures. Later, as the settlers took their lands, they joined together in self-defense. Today, Native Americans are often referred to as a single entity, although the individual tribes still maintain their unique identities.

Cultural pluralism is particularly noticeable when new immigrants arrive in the United States. Usually, instead of attempting to assimilate into the mainstream of the United States, immigrants seek out others from their homeland, resulting in Chinatowns, Little Italys, Little Havanas, Little Greeces and, most recently, Hmong and Somali communities. This has resulted in what is sometimes referred to as the **hyphenated American**: the Italian-American, the Polish-American, the African-American, the Asian-American and so forth.

Cultural pluralism rests on the assumption that diverse cultures can coexist and prosper; but peaceful coexistence is not always the reality. The **cultural conflict** theory suggests that diverse cultures that share the same territory will compete with and attempt to exploit one another. Such cultural conflict was common between the early settlers and the Native American tribes. Conflict was also common between the white immigrants and the more than 6 million slaves imported from Africa between 1619 and 1860. The hostile treatment of Japanese Americans during World War II was also rooted in cultural conflict. Following Japan's attack on Pearl Harbor, many U.S. citizens saw Japanese Americans as a national threat. Over 110,000 Japanese, the great majority of whom were American-born citizens, were forced by the government to sell their homes and businesses and then placed in internment camps.

Cultural conflict can currently be seen in growing tensions between specific ethnic groups as they compete for the limited remaining resources available. In Minnesota, for example, only Native Americans are allowed to harvest wild rice or to spear fish. The Mille Lacs band of Chippewa has sued the state of Minnesota, claiming treaty rights allow them to fish outside their reservation without state regulation. Native Americans are also lobbying to be allowed to take motorboats into the wilderness area to enhance their guide business.

Organizations working for women's rights, gray power and gay power make it clear that the United States is, indeed, a culturally pluralistic nation. Assimilation, cultural pluralism and cultural conflicts coexist and are all realities in the United States, presenting a formidable challenge for those who must maintain the "public peace." Much of this cultural diversity can be categorized more specifically as racial or ethnic diversity.

It is important for police officers to be aware of other cultural differences that may hinder communication. For example, in some Asian cultures, only the oldest family member will deal with the police on behalf of the entire family. In the last few years many immigrants have come from Southeast Asia. Often victims of discrimination and crime, they tend to not seek police assistance or report crimes. Many, in fact, especially the elderly, fear the police. Compounding this communication problem is the fact that many immigrants from Asian and other Third World nations often mistrust U.S. banks and keep their money and other valuables at home. The cultural backgrounds of these people leave them extremely vulnerable to scams, burglaries and robberies, but even after they are victimized, they still hesitate to talk to the police.

Racism

For the community policing philosophy to become a reality, racism, wherever it exists, must be recognized and dealt with. **Racism** is a belief that a human population having a distinct genetically transmitted characteristic is inferior. It also refers to discrimination or prejudice based on race. The racist idea that some groups (races) are somehow genetically superior to others has no scientific basis.

The issue of racism as it relates to community policing is multifaceted and extremely charged. Furthermore, racism flows in both directions between the police and the citizens within the communities they serve. Holmes (2000, p.343) acknowledges: "Many minority citizens distrust the criminal justice system, just as many criminal justice agents distrust them. Nowhere is that tension more apparent than in the relation between minorities and the police." Some officers make the critical mistake of trying to achieve rapport by using terminology they hear members of a minority group using among themselves.

Racial Disparity

The connections between race, class and perceived police discrimination and misconduct have been the focus of much research. *The Public Image of the Police,* a study by the International Association of Chiefs of Police and the Administration of Justice Program, George Mason University, October 2001, found the following:

- At the end of the 20th century, a majority of the American public perceived racial profiling to be a widespread practice and a problem.

- Across nearly all indicators of the public image of the police, racial minorities consistently showed lower assessments of police than did whites. These race effects appear to be particularly enduring for citizens' assessments of police fairness and use of force.
- A more positive general image of the police is associated with the following characteristics of the public:
  - Being older. National samples of high school seniors consistently rate the job police (generally) are doing as substantially lower than do national samples of older persons.
  - Being of higher wealth or socioeconomic status.
  - Living in suburban (as opposed to urban) areas.
  - Being white (as opposed to black).
  - Having positive attitudes about one's own neighborhood.

Public Perceptions of Policing Processes

- A substantial majority of the public express positive attitudes about the fairness of the police, but a significant portion rate them as "only fair or poor."
- Blacks, younger people, singles and low-income respondents tend to offer less positive evaluations of police fairness. The difference is particularly striking between blacks and whites.
- Racial disparities in assessments of police fairness may be caused in part by indirect exposure to unfair treatment by receiving secondhand accounts from others in their neighborhood.
- Almost one in five respondents fear that the police will stop and arrest them when they are completely innocent.
- Approximately one in ten respondents in a national survey reported that they had been stopped by police because of their racial or ethnic background.
- Blacks were seven times more likely to report this than whites.
- Most vehicle operators stopped by police felt that they had been stopped legitimately, but there were significant differences by race and gender.
- Men and blacks were less likely to feel that their stops were legitimate.
- Most vehicle operators who are searched by police feel that the search was not legitimate.
- Blacks were substantially more likely to view the search as illegitimate than whites.
- In 1999, 59 percent of the American public perceived racial profiling by the police as "widespread," and in 2000, 75 percent viewed it as a problem in the United States.
- Blacks were much more likely than whites to perceive that racial profiling by police was widespread.
- The citizen's race was a significant influence on the citizen's assessment of the quality of the police process.
- Hispanics, and especially blacks, evaluated police less favorably on the use of force, fairness, friendliness and promptness.
- For citizens who have had contact with the police within the previous two years, when the level of satisfaction with that contact was taken into account, race was

no longer a significant influence on citizens' assessments of police friendliness and promptness. However, race remained a significant influence on assessments of use of force and fairness.

- Trust in the motives of legal authorities, such as the police, had more impact on police legitimacy than the citizen's view of the fairness or favorability of the outcome for that person. This was uniform across racial and ethnic groups.
- Citizens' assessments of police competence and fairness were both significant predictors of the public's general confidence in and support for the police, but the fairness assessment was by far the more powerful of the two predictors. This held for both whites and racial minorities.

A survey by the Police Foundation also found race to be a divisive issue for American police, with black and nonblack (white and other minority) police officers in strong disagreement about the significance of a citizen's race in how they are treated by police. Weisburd et al. (2000) report: "Black and nonblack officers had significantly different views about the effect of a citizen's race and socioeconomic status on the likelihood of police abuse of authority and about the effect of community policing on the potential for abuse." In comparing black officers' views about police abuse with those of white and other minority officers, Weisburd et al. found:

> A small minority of white officers in the sample believed that police treat white citizens better than they treat black or other minority citizens in similar situations, while the majority of black police officers held this view. Similar differences existed between black and other officers' views on the likelihood of police using force against minorities and poor citizens. In addition, the survey found that black officers had a more positive view of community policing's ability to control the abuse of police authority. The magnitude of these race-based differences in opinion suggests a large gap between black police officers and other officers in the sample.

When asked whether police officers are more likely to use physical force against blacks and other minorities than against whites in similar situations, only 5.1 percent of white officers agreed that such unequal treatment occurs. However, 57.1 percent of the black officers surveyed thought officers were more likely to use physical force against blacks and other minorities than against whites in similar situations. Furthermore, the attitudes of "other minority" officers were more similar to those of white police officers than to those of black officers, with 12.4 percent of other minority officers agreeing with the statement concerning unequal treatment. Weisburd et al. conclude these findings "seem to corroborate the view that there is a racial divide between whites and blacks in American society—a divide so pronounced that even the apparently strong culture of policing does not transcend it."

Racial disparity is an unfortunate reality of the criminal justice system for both juveniles and adults. A report by the National Council on Crime and Delinquency (NCCD) states: "While 'Equal Justice Under Law' is the foundation of our legal system, and is carved on the front of the U.S. Supreme Court, the juvenile justice system is anything but equal. Throughout the system, minority youths—especially

African American youths—receive different and harsher treatment" ("Race Disparity Seen . . . ," 2000, p.7). The same report (p.6) notes: "Black youths are overrepresented at every decision point in the juvenile justice system, beginning with a police officer's decision about whether to arrest a youth, send him back to his parents, or simply give him a warning, and ending with the most severe outcome possible, prosecution as an adult and incarceration in an adult prison."

Data from the FBI, the Bureau of Justice Statistics and the Office of Juvenile Justice and Delinquency Prevention (OJJDP) indicate that minority youths face accumulating disadvantages as they move through the juvenile justice system. For example, even though blacks constitute only 15 percent of all youths under age 18, they make up 26 percent of juvenile arrestees, 31 percent of the cases referred to juvenile court, 46 percent of the cases that juvenile courts waive to adult court and 58 percent of the youths sent to adult prisons (p.7).

Some argue that crime policy has become a substitute for public policy, with politicians inappropriately using the criminal justice system to deal with difficult economic, social and family problems. A study on sentencing disparity by Spohn and Holleran (2000, p.281) examined four offender characteristics—race/ethnicity, gender, age and employment status—and how they interact to affect sentencing decisions. Their study found:

> The four offender characteristics interact to produce harsher sentences for certain types of offenders. Young black and Hispanic males face greater odds of incarceration than middle-aged white males, and unemployed black and Hispanic males are substantially more likely to be sentenced to prison than employed white males. Thus, our results suggest that offenders characterized as "young black male" pay a punishment penalty.

Prior to the September 11, 2001 attacks on the World Trade Center and the Pentagon, the practice of racial profiling was being denounced by one police chief after another, across the country. Suddenly the debate was renewed, as they tried to decide if racial profiling was not only necessary but also the only sensible thing to do in view of the threat to our country and our people. With the heightened threat of more terrorist attacks, Arab or Middle Eastern–looking people began reporting they had been singled out for stops, questioning, searches or arrest, based solely on their appearance.

The contention that police single out subjects based solely on the color of their skin frequently leads to allegations of racial profiling, a serious concern for any department engaged in such a practice and for the credibility of the police profession as a whole.

Racial Profiling

In some areas of the country, it seems motorists of certain racial or ethnic groups are being stopped more frequently by police, oftentimes, the drivers claim, for no apparent reason. Such an event may be called DWB (driving while black), DWA (driving while Asian) or DWM (driving while Mexican). Regardless of the acronym used, the event signals an unethical and illegal practice called **racial profiling**, the process of using certain racial characteristics, such as skin color, as indicators of criminal activity.

Margolis et al. (2000, p.18) note that racial profiling has been the subject of litigation, legislation and politics, stating: "The issue of racial profiling is one of the most important issues facing law enforcement today. Racial profiling is a national focal point of the wider concerns about race relations in law enforcement." Wexler (2000, p.2) submits: "Issues like racial profiling are a manifestation of larger issues of effective communication, trust, respect, sensitivity and accountability."

In a Gallup poll, a random sample of Americans responded to the following statement and question: "It has been reported that some police officers stop motorists of certain racial or ethnic groups because the officers believe that these groups are more likely than others to commit certain types of crimes. Do you believe that this practice, known as 'racial profiling,' is widespread?" Kurlander (2000, p.148) reports: "The poll . . . showed that six out of every 10 Americans, over the age of 18, believe the practice is widespread. Seventy-six percent of black Americans replied that they believe the practice to be commonplace, 56 percent of the whites polled agreed, and even more importantly, more than 80 percent of both races disapproved of the practice."

The International Association of Chiefs of Police (IACP) also disapproves, recommending zero tolerance for officers who commit racial profiling and the removal of such officers from positions of authority. Cohen et al. (2000, p.15) assert: "Racial profiling is inconsistent with the basic freedoms and rights afforded in our democracy. It erodes the foundation of trust between communities and public authorities. Worst of all, it inflames racial and ethnic strife and undermines America's progress toward color-blind justice."

Olson (2000, p.2) concurs: "The stopping of any person solely because of the color of his skin is contrary to the law of our land, and intolerable."

Racial profiling is a form of discrimination and singles out people of racial or ethnic groups because of a belief that these groups are more likely than others to commit certain types of crimes. Race-based enforcement is illegal.

Profiling has been described as more of an art than an exact science. Scoville (2000, p.16) states: "While other types of profiling—such as the psychological profiling of serial killers and serial rapists practiced by the FBI—have been recognized and accepted as forensically viable, racial profiling stands alone as a vocational pariah. Its practice is often deemed tantamount to racism, and allegations of its use can stigmatize officers and whole departments."

However, Kurlander (p.150) notes: "Profiles of common characteristics shared by the perpetrators of certain crimes have been used since the 1970s." In questioning whether officers should be allowed to take appearance into account when "sizing up" a subject, Scoville (p.23) asks: "What is law enforcement's mission? Do we want aggressive law enforcement when it comes to [crime]? Or are we expected to take a hands-off approach because of the possibility of offending sensibilities of certain racial groups?"

Addressing the Issue Several recommendations have been proposed to help law enforcement address and overcome the problem of racial profiling. Wexler (p.2) contends: "The issue of racial profiling is a challenge for many departments, but . . . it's [also] an important opportunity to reposition the department's relationship with the community it serves."

An example of such repositioning is found in Chicago ("Strengthening Relations between . . . ," 2000, p.1), where race relations improved after the police superintendent sponsored a daylong, closed-door meeting involving leaders from the city's minority community and police representatives from every rank in the department. To examine the practices and policies potentially responsible for the increasing tension between the police and members of some of Chicago's minority communities, the superintendent decided to go right to the source and "ask the customer" (p.4):

> "I wanted a candid assessment of where we are with respect to police/community relations, and that's just what I got," [the superintendent] said. "In my 32 years as a police officer in this city, I never heard such honest, heartfelt, and forthright dialogue." . . .
>
> The community leaders freely expressed their concerns about the relationship between police and their communities. They also recognized the difficulties and complexities faced by police. In the end, their insights challenged the police to take a hard look at the way some department members interact with the community they serve.

Cohen et al. (p.12) stress: "Profiling uses race as a proxy for criminal intent or culpability because police often lack specific information about specific individuals. Modern information systems and strong police–community interaction that fosters the exchange of information will ensure that police make decisions based on facts and data instead of race."

They further contend: "What we need is the right kind of targeting, based on better information about lawbreakers and closer cooperation between the police and the community." To achieve this, Cohen et al. suggest replacing racial profiling with tools to help the police make better judgments, deploy resources more strategically and recruit citizens in reclaiming control of their neighborhoods. They also advocate focusing on hot spots and high-risk offenders.

The IACP Highway Safety Committee ("Policies Help Gain Public Trust," 2000, p.24) stresses:

> From the standpoint of professional law enforcers, there are two overarching reasons why we must ensure that racial and ethnic profiling is not substituted for reasonable suspicion in traffic stops and other law enforcement activities. First and foremost, it is the right thing to do. The Constitution must always come first in law enforcement. The ends do not necessarily justify the means, and we cannot take shortcuts with civil liberties. Second, law enforcement needs the public's trust in order to be successful in our mission. This includes the trust of people of all races, ethnic groups, religions and political beliefs.

How many incidents involve minority subjects, and what percentage of the total does this comprise? Zingraff et al. (2000, p.1) state: "The research literature lacks a consensus on the issue of the extensiveness of discrimination in police stops, searches and arrests." To help present a more complete picture, many agencies now require the collection of additional racial data about drivers and passengers involved in traffic stops: "Civil rights groups and others have called for such data collection in order to determine whether police use 'racial profiles' in making traffic stops. As of midyear 1999, 32 state highway patrol agencies collected racial data on drivers who received traffic citations. . . . Twenty-three required officers to note the race of the driver, and nine required data for all of the vehicle's occupants" ("Many State Police Agencies . . .," 2000, p.5).

A retired police lieutenant notes the paradox of this new requirement: "'Tis ironic that in order to prove we're color-blind, we now have to keep stats of the race of the people we search so we can disprove allegations of bias" (Scoville, p.18). Another police officer indicates a built-in flaw in the effort, citing officer discretion as a variable that can lead to reverse bias:

> I can tell you what it already has done in the two cities I am aware of (San Diego and San Jose) that are undertaking a study of the issue. They are making decisions based upon race, and not upon good policing. For instance, one officer I am aware of has decided to cite all white drivers he stops (instead of cutting them a break sometimes) so as to skew numbers higher for actual cites for whites (Scoville, p.20).

Kurlander (p.153) comments: "Whether agencies are forced to collect the data by legislation, litigation, or do so voluntarily, the fact remains that this is an issue that will not go away. Prudent law enforcement executives will take action to detect officers who are engaged in race-based enforcement and correct that behavior. Those that do not will be at risk for litigation."

Margolis et al. (pp.22–23) offer several ways for agencies to minimize their risk of racial profiling charges, including hands-on instructive and corrective supervision, enforceable policies against discriminatory law enforcement, proper and ongoing officer training and aggressive action in handling allegations of racial profiling. They (p.23) conclude: "If racial profiling exists in a department, it must be zealously, but fairly, abolished. If the problem does not exist, a department must stand firm."

Strategies to Overcome Barriers Based on Racial and Ethnic Diversity

Various strategies have been proposed to help agencies attack bias and overcome racial or ethnic barriers between the police and community. Some are very general, whereas others are quite specific.

One of the first steps to take is implementing a zero tolerance policy for bias within police ranks and publicizing that philosophy. One police chief explains (Paynter, 2000, p.63): "With the advent and implementation of community policing, it's important that the police profession be viewed as the guardians of the Constitution and human and civil rights." Paynter (p.66) asserts: "A police officer doesn't represent himself or herself, he/she represents every individual in the community. Biased attitudes among police officers violate every tenet of good policing, and tend to reinforce the isolation of the victims and the groups they represent."

Another strategy is to develop an outreach effort to diverse communities to reduce victimization by teaching them practical crime prevention techniques. A critical part of this effort involves training and education for both police and citizens, as well as the formation of key partnerships between law enforcement and community groups.

Police must often rely on the services of translators, interpreters, community liaisons, religious leaders and other trusted members of an ethnic community to develop an effective crime prevention program for ethnic groups. Schools can also assist by including crime prevention techniques in classroom instruction and special ESL classes.

Yet another strategy is to create formal programs and policies to support the assimilation and needs of recent immigrant groups. *350 Tested Strategies . . .*, (1995, p.27) lists key components of this strategy as the "recognition of recent immigrants' needs for information, services, and other support to help in their transition to life in American society; cooperation with community groups in surveying the needs of immigrant residents; policies and programs that ensure access to services needed by the immigrants; cultural awareness and language training for relevant local government employees; community-based transition assistance services to help educate new residents about communication and language skills, banking and managing family budgets, employment, conflict resolution, and crime reporting; victim and witness services in the language(s) of the immigrant community; and neighborhood-based services to help ensure access by residents in need."

Before considering more issues surrounding cultural differences and the challenges posed to community policing, consider two other forms of diversity in the United States, religious diversity and socioeconomic diversity.

Religious Diversity

Many of those who came to America did so to escape religious persecution. The colonists' desire for religious freedom is evident in our Bill of Rights. The First Amendment protects, among other freedoms, freedom of religion. The First Amendment was drafted and adopted to protect the segregated turfs of different religious communities in the early colonies: Congregationalism in New England, Quakerism in Pennsylvania and Catholicism in Maryland. Over the years, these distinctions have become much less important, with "Christians" becoming a sort of religious melting pot for people of quite similar religious beliefs. However, religious tension still exists between many Christians (the majority) and those of Jewish faith (the minority). Anti-Semitism is a problem in some communities and may result in hate crimes, as discussed shortly.

Religious diversity continues to increase, presenting unique challenges to community policing efforts aimed at enhancing citizens' levels of trust, communication and activism. Cults may pose special challenges to community policing efforts because they zealously advocate beliefs that are unorthodox or counterculture, deviating significantly from what mainstream society considers normal or acceptable. Szubin et al. (2000, p.16) observe:

> There is a common tendency to view "cults" with a combination of mistrust and fear. Much of this hostility derives from widespread misconceptions about the nature of "cults," founded upon popular stereotypes and simple ignorance. While such misconceptions are unfortunate in the general populace, they may be dangerous when harbored by law enforcement officers charged with dealing with these groups and ensuring the safety of both "cult" members and the general public.

In Oregon a group lobbied for an exception to the general drug laws to make it legal for Native Americans to smoke peyote during their rituals. In this case, the Supreme Court ruled that such an exception need not be granted. Smoking peyote was illegal across the board; the Native Americans were not a special group that had been singled out.

Socioeconomic Diversity

Even the casual observer recognizes that social and economic class factors create diversity in the United States. Sociologists typically divide individuals within the United States into three basic classes. The three basic socioeconomic classes, based primarily on income and education, are the lower, middle and upper classes. These basic classes may be further subdivided. As noted, the middle class is shrinking, and the gap between the rich and the poor has become wider, resulting in tension.

The Lower Socioeconomic Class Poor people have more frequent contact with the criminal justice system because they are on the streets and highly visible. A poor person who drives an old car will get a repair ticket, whereas a wealthier person is more likely to drive a newer car not requiring repairs. In addition, the repair ticket issued to the poor person is likely to be a much greater hardship for that person than a similar ticket would be to someone in the middle or upper classes.

Certain races and ethnic groups are frequently equated with poverty and crime in an interaction described as the poverty syndrome. The **poverty syndrome** includes inadequate housing, inadequate education, inadequate jobs and a resentment of those who control the social system.

One hazard associated with poverty, often resulting in inadequate or substandard housing is the increased possibility of lead exposure, a serious threat to children's well-being. The Centers for Disease Control (CDC) (2000) report: "Lead poisoning is entirely preventable. However, nearly 1 million children living in the United States have lead levels in their blood that are high enough to cause irreversible damage to their health."

The Homeless Police need to balance the needs of the homeless with protecting the public from interference with its rights. Because in many cases homelessness is a temporary condition, and people who are homeless one month may not be the following month. It is difficult to accurately measure the number of homeless on any given day.

The police must interact with the population of homeless people sleeping on our nation's streets, including women and children, alcoholics and drug addicts, the retarded and the mentally ill. Carrying their worldly goods and camping everywhere from laundry rooms to train and bus stations, the homeless pose a challenge for the police who must look after their safety while attempting to minimize their public presence. Many homeless are also alcoholics and drug abusers. National data reveal 38 percent of the homeless abuse alcohol and 26 percent abuse drugs (Klein, 2000, p.42).

The needs of the homeless are as varied as the people who comprise the homeless population. Besides needing the obvious—a place to live and an income to support themselves—other needs include better nutrition, medical care, clothing, chemical addiction treatment and, especially for children, an education.

For some children, the mental and physical stress of being homeless spawns a host of other difficulties. According to the National Alliance for the Mentally Ill (NAMI), nearly 25 percent of homeless people in the United States are children, few of whom escape emotional, behavioral and academic problems. Furthermore, few receive help for such problems. In one study, more than a third (37 percent) of the homeless children had depression scores high enough to warrant a psychiatric evaluation, and 28 percent were in the borderline range for serious behavioral problems.

The homeless also face safety issues and are more often the victims of crime than the perpetrators and have no phone from which to call 911. According to Klein (p.42), common problems of homeless people include:

- Lack of food—20 percent eat one meal a day or less, and 40 percent had gone one or more days in the previous month without anything to eat because they could not afford food.
- Health problems—26 percent have acute infectious conditions such as pneumonia or tuberculosis; 46 percent have chronic health conditions such as arthritis, diabetes or cancer; and 55 percent have no medical insurance.
- Victimization—38 percent have had money or possessions stolen directly from them, and 41 percent have had money or possessions stolen when they were not present.

Although being homeless is not a crime, the activities of some homeless people do violate laws and local ordinances. Such activities include public drunkenness, public urination and defecation, loitering, trespassing, panhandling, littering, disorderly conduct or more serious offenses such as vandalism, theft and assault.

Sampson and Scott (2000, p.113) note even when the homeless obey the law, citizens feel that street-living and panhandling degrade a community's image. The average citizen is uncomfortable around and may feel threatened by those who are homeless. Whether motivated by guilt or fear, they want the homeless people "removed," and they look to the police for solutions to a problem that society has thus far been unable to resolve. In New York City, for example, the mayor called on the police to help clean up the city and sweep out the homeless, a practice not uncommon across the county. As Fabyankovic (2000, p.113) states: "According to Out of Sight—Out of Mind? a report published by the National Law Center on Homelessness and Poverty, police in half of the 50 largest U.S. cities have engaged in sweeps in the past two years."

In those communities where sleeping on the streets is illegal, what begins as a social problem becomes a criminal justice problem, and the officer on the beat is expected to enforce the law. However, in some areas of the country the constitutionality of such notices is being contested in court. For example, in *Pottinger v. City of Miami* (1992), a U.S. district court judge found the city's practice of conducting bum sweeps, making minor arrests of transients, and confiscating and destroying the property of the homeless was a violation of their constitutional rights. The central question in this case was whether the government can lock you up for being outside when you have no place to go.

Many have criticized laws that, in effect, criminalize homelessness, stating such legislation ignores the underlying reasons why people live on the streets and can even cause the problem to "spread." Fabyankovic (p.115) contends: "Politicians are often more concerned with the so-called 'quality of life' issues than solving the homeless dilemmas. Ordinances that prohibit panhandling and sleeping in public places usually force many homeless people to become transient, moving from one jurisdiction to another rather than tackling a solution to the problem."

As with other diversity issues, training for officers can be a valuable step toward improving relations with a community's homeless population. Taking a lesson from the Miami case, the Fort Lauderdale (Florida) Police Department has implemented a two-hour training session known as "Homelessness 101," in which every staff member explores the causes of homelessness and strategic responses to the problem. The assistant chief states: "We have a policy, we have a special report for homeless contacts, we have the training, and we encourage our officers, particularly in the downtown and along the River Walk, to make proactive contact with the homeless to assure ourselves that they're aware of the available social services" ("Ft. Lauderdale Learns . . .," 2000, p.1).

The police chief (p.14) also believes that educating officers about the causes of homelessness has effected a cultural change in the department and eliminated the narrow-minded notion that all homeless people are lazy bums who do not want to work and just cause problems for everyone else: "I learned myself about the issue of homelessness and learned how enforcement alone is not effective if you're going to have a long-term change with homeless people." Hibbert (2000, p.47) adds that the Fort Lauderdale Homeless Outreach Program has taught officers to view the homeless as people who are in trouble instead of people who are trouble.

Unfortunately, many departments do not provide the means, training or tools necessary for officers to successfully reach out to the community's homeless. In a recent survey of police, 30 percent of the respondents stated they had "no policies specifically relating to incidents involving street people and are not informed of available shelters and services. Some 96 percent mentioned they wanted a formal program or unit to address these unique needs" (Fabyankovic, p.113). However, in jurisdictions where police are educated and empowered to address the issue of homelessness, their intervention can benefit both the homeless and the neighborhood. A New York City police officer, Fran Kimkowski, developed an innovative approach to the homeless problem for a group of homeless men in the Long Island City section of Queens, New York. Assigned to calm the fears of residents when the

Salvation Army opened a shelter for homeless veterans in the neighborhood, Kimkowski wanted to show the residents that the homeless men could and would contribute to the community if given a chance. She organized V-Cops, a group of homeless veterans who volunteer to help prevent crime in the neighborhoods.

V-Cops use foot patrols to deter, detect and report crimes to the police. They patrol local banks, particularly when people cash social security and welfare checks. The V-Cops program has many other components, including crime prevention presentations to organizations, talks to high school students and patrol of subways and "play streets" for neighborhood youths during the summer months. Furthermore, chemically dependent V-Cop members are required to participate in recovery programs for drug abuse or alcoholism. Consequently, beyond the obvious benefits to the community, the participating homeless veterans have an opportunity to make a contribution while regaining their self-esteem and getting their lives back on track.

The Powerful and Connected

At the opposite end of the socioeconomic scale are powerful, privileged and connected people. In the traditional role of crime fighter, the police seldom interact with the upper class, but when they must, problems can arise. However, in community policing the personal and financial resources of those in the public eye and upper socioeconomic level can be invaluable. A population's socioeconomic profile can reveal much about the balance of power within a community. A community's power structure may also be regarded in the context of its members' worldview.

Facing the Challenge

Keeping the peace, serving and protecting in a society as diverse as the United States presents an extreme challenge to police officers. To meet the challenge, police might consider the following guidelines.

- Each person is, first and foremost, an individual.
- Each group, whether racial, ethnic, religious or socioeconomic, consists of people who share certain values. Knowing what these values are can contribute greatly to effective police–community interactions.
- Each group can contribute to making the community safer.
- Communication skills are vital. Empathy, listening and overcoming language barriers are crucial to implementing the community policing philosophy.
- An awareness of personal prejudices and biases can guard against discrimination. An awareness of the language used to talk about different groups is extremely important.

The term *minorities,* for example, has subtle secondary if not caste status that implies the opposite of the majority, frequently polite code for "white." People of color also places distance between those so designated and Caucasians. Officers should consider the terms they use and how they might be perceived by those who are being labeled. Of course, in an emergency when officers need to communicate with each other rapidly, a descriptive term such as black or white is appropriate and, indeed, necessary to rapid response. It is important for officers to know when to use certain terminology.

A Cultural Diversity Value Statement

The Aurora (Illinois) Police Department's cultural diversity value statement is a model of what departments might strive for (reprinted by permission).

As professional police officers, we commit to:

- The fair and impartial treatment of all individuals, placing the highest emphasis on respect for fundamental human rights.
- Nurturing and protecting the individual dignity and worth of all persons with whom we come into contact.
- Understanding the differences of all people.
- Zero tolerance for racially, sexual, gender or religious biased behavior.
- Maintaining a welcoming environment of inclusion through which communication is open to all people whose problems become our priorities to resolve.

In addition to the racial, ethnic, religious and socioeconomic subcultures found in the United States, another subculture exists in the United States—those with physical and mental disabilities—populations that provide even more diversity and more challenge to community policing efforts.

Persons with Disabilities

According to Fuller (2000, p.84): "Many well-intentioned police officers have uncomfortable attitudes toward the disabled, often viewing them as individuals to be pitied or ignored. This attitude may originate from an uneasiness of being around people who are perceived to be 'different,' or simply from ignorance about disabilities in general."

Estimates of disability prevalence in the United States vary, but McNeil (2001) suggests that about 52.6 million people have some type of disability, 19.7 percent of the population, making those who are disabled the nation's biggest minority.

Understanding Physical and Mental Disabilities

A police officer asks a woman to perform some field sobriety tests and she cannot do so even though she is not under the influence of any drug, including alcohol. Another person ignores the direct order of a police officer to step back on the sidewalk. Yet another person approaches an officer and attempts to ask directions, but his speech is so slurred he is unintelligible. These common occurrences for police officers can often be misinterpreted. In each of the preceding instances, the individual interacting with the officer has a disability: a problem with balance, a hearing impairment and a speech disability. A **disability** is a physical or mental impairment that substantially limits one or more of a person's major life functions.

Greater recognition of this "minority" came on July 26, 1990 when then-President Bush signed into law the Americans with Disabilities Act (**ADA**), calling it "another Independence Day, one that is long overdue." Colbridge (2000b, p.28) states: "For purposes of the ADA, disability means having a physical or mental impairment that substantially limits one or more major life activities, having a record of such an impairment, or being regarded as having such an impairment."

The ADA guarantees that persons with disabilities will have equal access to any public facilities available to persons without disabilities. Colbridge (2000a, p.26) states the ADA also deals with broad issues concerning discrimination against those with disabilities in the areas of education, transportation, communications, recreation, institutionalization, health services and voting. The ADA does not, however, grant special liberty to individuals with disabilities in matters of law, nor does it dictate the police must take a "hands off" approach toward people with disabilities engaged in criminal conduct. As Litchford (2000, p.15) notes: "The courts have held that the ADA does not prohibit officers from taking enforcement action, including the use of force, necessary to protect officer or public safety."

Because the ADA guarantees access to government services, it helps build partnerships for community policing. Under the ADA, all brochures and printed material must be available in braille or on audiotape if requested. To include people with disabilities in community partnerships, the police must be able to communicate with them and should conduct their meetings in barrier-free places.

Many people in our communities have made treatment of those with disabilities a priority and are available and willing to work with law enforcement agencies to ensure that people with disabilities are treated respectfully and protected from those who would victimize them. The outcome of increased awareness and service in this area will not only make police officers' jobs easier when they encounter people with disabilities, but will also help reduce their fear and vulnerability. The focus on those with disabilities will make the community a better and safer place for everyone and help to build police–community relations.

Disabilities police officers frequently encounter include mobility impairment, vision impairment, hearing impairment, impairment as a result of epilepsy, and mental or emotional impairment.

The first three types of disabilities may hinder communication, but seldom pose a significant hinderance for community policing efforts. Likewise, those who have epilepsy do not pose a problem unless their symptoms are mistaken for intoxication. See Table 6.1.

An epileptic seizure may be mistaken for a drug- or alcohol-induced stupor because the person may have incoherent speech, glassy-eyed staring and aimless wandering.

Individuals with mental or emotional disabilities, in contrast to the preceding disabilities, pose a significant challenge to community policing efforts.

Mental Disabilities Historically society institutionalized the people who were mentally ill or mentally retarded. In the mid-1960s, however, treatment in the community replaced institutionalization. **Deinstitutionalization** refers to the release of thousands of mentally ill individuals into society to be cared for by family or a special network of support services.

Table 6.1 Epileptic Seizure or Drug/Alcohol Abuse

Complex Partial Seizure Symptoms	***Drug/Alcohol Abuse Symptoms***
■ Chewing, lip-smacking motions	not likely
■ Picking at clothes	not likely
■ Should regain consciousness in 30 seconds to 3 minutes, except in the rare case of a complex partial status (when seizure continues)	a drunk/high person will not recover in 3 minutes or less
■ No breath odor	a drunk will smell like alcohol
■ Possibly wearing an epilepsy ID bracelet/tag	not likely
Symptoms Common to Both	
■ Impaired consciousness	■ Incoherent speech
■ Glassy-eyed staring	■ Aimless wandering

SOURCE: *Epilepsy: A Positive I.D.* Epilepsy Education, University of Minnesota, 1991. Reprinted by permission.

This was the result of several factors including development of medications to control mental illness; research showing that institutionalized people did not receive adequate treatment and could do better in the community; federal programs to build and operate mental health centers; and patients' rights litigation and state legislation.

Community-based mental health service rests on the premise that people have the right not to be isolated from the community simply because they are mentally ill. This premise works only if a support system for them exists. Unfortunately, the network of support services has developed slowly. As a result, thousands of mentally ill people are on the street, homeless, and hundreds more are living with families ill-equipped to provide necessary care and assistance. In both situations, the mentally ill persons are likely to have encounters with the local police, usually as a result of some bizarre behavior rather than committing a crime.

As Strandberg (2000, p.90) notes: "States have closed mental health institutions across the country and pushed their patients out into the community, many times directly into the path of local law enforcement." He suggests: "Releasing the mentally ill has created a new problem for law enforcement that requires a new set of skills."

Mental Illness Mental illness should not be confused with crisis behavior. **Crisis behavior** results when a person who is not mentally ill has a temporary breakdown in coping skills. Anyone can suffer from a crisis. The mentally ill people police encounter frequently lack social support. They are difficult to manage and may have complications such as alcohol or drug abuse. Often people who feel threatened by the strange behavior of a mentally ill person may call the police to handle the problem.

Officers become involved with the mentally ill because the police have the only 24-hour-a-day, seven-day-a-week, mobile emergency response capacity, as well as the authority to detain, arrest and use force when needed. When police are called to manage mentally ill persons, the behaviors they most frequently encounter are bizarre, unusual or strange conduct; confused thoughts or action; aggressive actions;

destructive, assaultive, violent or suicidal behavior. Suicide is the 11th leading cause of death in the United States and the third leading cause of death among people age 15 to 24. An estimated 29,350 Americans committed suicide in 2000. For every "successful" suicide, an estimated eight to twenty-five attempts "fail."

One chief of police noted ("Congress Approves Grants . . .," 2000, p.3): "Our local police forces have become armed social workers. This is a mission that we are both ill-equipped and ill-trained to carry out. All too often, police officers confront the mentally ill equipped with little more than their verbal skills and the means to employ deadly force. The results are often disastrous."

Police in one city shot and killed a suspect who had just robbed a gas station. The suspect turned out to be a mentally disturbed female whom they had dealt with often over the past year. After robbing the gas station, she ordered the clerk to call 911 and stayed there until he did. The confrontation and subsequent shooting seemed orchestrated, forced by the woman who was depressed and suicidal. She claimed to have a gun, threatened to shoot the officers and advanced toward one with an object in her hand. The object turned out to be a comb. This is a tragic situation where a suicidal person arranges to die at the hands of the police.

The four civil criteria for detainment and commitment of mentally ill individuals in most states are (1) mental illness, (2) dangerous to self or others, (3) gravely disabled and (4) in need of treatment.

Another challenging and frequently misunderstood mental disability that police encounter is mental retardation, often, and incorrectly, equated with mental illness.

Mental Retardation Mental retardation is the nation's fourth ranking disabling condition, affecting 3 percent of the U.S. population. Mental retardation means that normal intellectual development fails to occur. Unlike mental illness, mental retardation is permanent. It is diagnosed when three criteria exist: (1) significant subaverage general intellectual functioning (as measured by IQ tests), (2) resulting in, or associated with, defects or impairments in adaptive behavior, such as personal independence and social responsibility, (3) with onset by age 18.

The mentally retarded are usually aware of their condition and may be adept at concealing it. Thus, it may be more difficult to recognize mental retardation than mental illness. Communication problems, interaction problems, inability to perform tasks and personal history can help officers make this determination. In addition to those who have mental illnesses or mental retardation, police officers may interact with people who have extreme emotional problems, including suicidal behavior.

Disabled individuals are also frequently victims of crime and in some instances are perpetrators of crime.

Lawbeakers with Disabilities One of six prison inmates is severely mentally ill. This is three times the number of mentally ill individuals in prison than in mental institutions (Human Rights Watch, 2003). It is natural to assume that disabled individuals are victims, not victimizers. However, this is not always true. Physically and mentally disabled people can also violate the law.

Of course, an individual's behavior will be limited by his or her physical or mental ability, and officers can expect a wide range in the severity of crimes committed by offenders with disabilities. However, the popular contention that mentally disabled people are unstable and therefore prone to more serious and violent offenses is unsupported by data: "The misconception that people with mental retardation usually commit serious crimes is unwarranted. . . . Research finds that people with mental retardation commit less serious crimes, such as misdemeanors and public disturbances" (Davis, 2000). Police departments across the country have begun training officers in dealing with the mentally ill, in hopes of reducing the number of injuries and deaths that occur each year when police and the mentally ill interact.

The U.S. Department of Justice, Bureau of Justice Statistics compiles statistics about "justifiable homicides by police (in the report, all killings by police are called justifiable homicides). The report analyzes justifiable homicides based on race, gender and age of the person killed. . . . In contrast, there is no official count of the number of persons with severe and persistent mental illness (SPMI) who are shot by police each year. And despite an unfortunate wealth of such tragic incidents, no national organization of any type keeps track of them."

The Treatment Advocacy Center has begun tracking some of these by conducting newspaper research. Although in 2002, they found 52 mentally ill persons injured or killed by police, this does not represent all such events because not all newspapers appear in their search and not all coverage of police shootings mention the mental illness of the victim. They also found incidents of 25 officers injured or killed by mentally ill persons. The Treatment Advocacy Center is a national, nonprofit organization that works to eliminate legal and clinical barriers to treatment for millions of Americans with severe brain disorders.

Adapting law enforcement duties and services to accommodate the millions of disabled U.S. citizens will not only help accomplish law enforcement's objectives more efficiently and safely but will also help provide the services all citizens need and deserve. When that happens, excellent police–community relations are a likely by-product.

The Elderly

Older, retired people are one of the fastest growing segments of our population. The U.S. Census Bureau estimates retired people will comprise more than 25 percent of the total population by 2025. During their careers, police officers have extensive contact with senior citizens. Police contact with older people rarely involves criminal activity; such contact usually arises from their vulnerability and the effects of the aging process.

Forst (2000, p.125) suggests: "Police officers, like other professionals, may have difficulty understanding the needs of older citizens. This alienation is compounded by the fact that patrol officers are typically young and fit. . . . They may find it difficult to empathize with or relate to the physical and emotional challenges of the aged. Police organizations must be sensitized to aging issues in order that they may deliver the best possible service to the elderly."

The elderly tend to admire and respect authority, and they are often grateful for any help the police may offer. Older people are usually in contact with the police if they become victims of crime, are involved in an automobile accident or are stopped for a traffic violation. Some elderly people suffer from Alzheimer's disease, a progressive, irreversible disease of the brain that adversely affects behavior. Many elderly people have other serious medical problems for which they may require emergency medical assistance. Older people may also have one or more of the disabilities just discussed. In fact, more than half of the U.S. population over age 65 is disabled in some way (Fuller, p.84).

Alzheimer's disease (AD) is a progressive, irreversible and incurable brain disease affecting 4 million elderly Americans. Pronounced "altz'-hi-merz," it afflicts people of all social, economic and racial groups.

Officers should know the symptoms, the most classic of which is gradual loss of memory. Other symptoms include impaired judgment, disorientation, personality change, decline in ability to perform routine tasks, behavior change, difficulty in learning, loss of language skills and a decline in intellectual function. A number of behavior patterns common to AD patients may bring them to the attention of police officers.

Alzheimer's victims may wander or become lost, engage in inappropriate sexual behavior, lose impulse control, shoplift, falsely accuse others, appear intoxicated, drive erratically and become victims of crime.

Many symptoms of intoxication and AD are identical: confusion and disorientation; problems with short-term memory, language, sight and coordination; combativeness and extreme reactions; and loss of contact with reality.

AD victims are often physically able to drive a car long after the time when their memory, judgment and problem-solving ability make it safe. Drivers who have Alzheimer's can drive erratically; "lose" their car and report it stolen; leave the scene of an accident because they actually forget it happened; and wander in the car because they are lost or have forgotten their destination. Sometimes drivers with AD are found several hundred miles from home.

People afflicted with AD may also become victims of crime because they are easy prey for con artists, robbers and muggers. Also, police may become aware of AD patients as a result of legal actions such as evictions, repossessions and termination of utility service due to the patients' forgetfulness or inability to make payments.

The Helmsley Alzheimer's Alert Program, started in 1991, provides information on missing patients to public safety agencies. When a person with AD is reported missing, the Alzheimer's Association sends an alert and identifying information to a fax service that transmits simultaneously to hundreds of locations, including police, hospital emergency rooms and shelters. When the patient is found, another fax is sent to inform the agencies that the search is over.

Just as the elderly may pose communication challenges, youths may also present challenges, particularly those with special needs.

Our Nation's Youths

A frequently overlooked segment of the population important to community policing implementation is youths. Because youths lack economic and political power, their problems and concerns may not receive the attention they deserve. But our nation's future depends on the values they form—they are the future decision makers of our country. As you read this part of the chapter, do not become discouraged about the future of our youths. Most young people (95 % according to FBI statistics) have not been in trouble with the law. Almost certainly, some of these juveniles were arrested multiple times, pushing the actual percentage of youths who have been arrested even lower.

The overwhelming majority of "good kids" should not be forgotten in community policing efforts. They can be valuable as partners in problem solving and, if provided opportunities to become active in areas of interest to them, will most likely continue to be good citizens. The following discussion, however, focuses on those youths with whom law enforcement most often interacts.

Youths with Special Needs and the Police

Police officers may have to deal with children who have very special needs.

> Children with special needs include those who are emotionally/behaviorally disturbed, who have learning disabilities, who have an attention deficit disorder or who have behavior problems resulting from prenatal exposure to drugs, including alcohol, or to HIV.

One group of young people police will encounter are emotionally/behaviorally disturbed children, often referred to as **EBD.** Usually EBD youths exhibit one or more of the following behavioral patterns: severely aggressive or impulsive behavior; severely withdrawn or anxious behavior such as pervasive unhappiness, depression or wide mood swings; or severely disordered thought processes reflected in unusual behavior patterns, atypical communication styles and distorted interpersonal relationships.

Parents and teachers in some communities have expressed concerns that children labeled as EBD have fewer coping skills to deal with police contacts than other children and may be traumatized by such contacts. A large percentage of children who are suspects in crimes are EBD and that condition is one cause of their unlawful behavior. It is impossible, however, to arrange for an EBD specialist to be present at all police contacts because a majority of contacts are unplanned events that occur on the street.

Attention deficit hyperactivity disorder (ADHD) is one of the most common disruptive behavior disorders in youths, with an estimated 5 to 10 percent of all children having it. Occurring four times more often in boys than girls, ADHD is characterized by heightened motor activity (fidgeting and squirming), short attention span, distractibility, impulsiveness and lack of self-control. Children with ADHD may do poorly in school and have low self-esteem. Although the condition often disappears by adulthood, by then former ADHD children may have other behavior problems including drug abuse, alcoholism or personality disorders.

Other children may present special challenges because of some form of **learning disability**, which the Association for Children with Learning Disabilities (ACLD) (p.4) defines as "one or more significant deficits in the essential learning processes." Essential learning processes are those involved in understanding or using spoken or written language and do not include learning problems that result from visual, hearing or motor handicaps, mental retardation or emotional disturbance.

The ACLD (p.3) identifies the most frequently displayed symptoms of learning disabilities as short attention span; poor memory; difficulty following directions; disorganization; inadequate ability to discriminate between and among letters, numerals or sounds; poor reading ability; eye-hand coordination problems; and difficulties with sequencing. Such children are often discipline problems, are labeled "underachievers" and are at great risk of becoming dropouts.

Although learning disabilities are usually discussed in an educational context, the ACLD (p.8) notes: "The consequences are rarely confined to school or work." Characteristics that may bring a learning disabled youth into conflict with the law include responding inappropriately to a situation, saying one thing and meaning another, forgetting easily, acting impulsively, needing immediate gratification and feeling overly frustrated, which results in disruptive behavior. Those who interact with such children need to be patient and communicate effectively. Youths with learning disabilities look like their peers. Inwardly, however, most are very frustrated, have experienced failure after failure and have extremely low self-esteem.

Prenatal exposure to drugs or HIV can also cause serious problems. The term **crack children** is sometimes used to refer to children exposed to cocaine while in the womb. They may exhibit social, emotional and cognitive problems. Drug-damaged children may also have poor coordination, low tolerance levels and poor memory. Police officers should be aware of these symptoms and recognize that they reflect a condition over which the youth has limited or no control.

Another pressing problem is that of **fetal alcohol syndrome (FAS)**, the leading known cause of mental retardation in the western world. FAS effects include impulsivity, inability to predict consequences or to use appropriate judgment in daily life, poor communication skills, high levels of activity and distractibility in small children and frustration and depression in adolescents.

Yet another group of at-risk children who present special problems to law enforcement are children prenatally exposed to HIV. Such children may have mental retardation, language delays, gross- and fine-motor skill deficits, and reduced flexibility and muscle strength.

Children with special needs are likely to be in contact with the police, and many may become status offenders. Others may become more serious offenders. Many youths with special needs are also likely to join gangs, as discussed in Chapter 10. A final population presenting communiction challenges are victims of and witnesses to criminal acts.

Victims and Witnesses

If you haven't been there, you don't know the feelings of emptiness and fear and how it changes your life. I was in a state of shock. I walked around in a daze for weeks. I wasn't functioning. No one really understood how I felt.

—Sherry Price, rape victim.

In his proclamation of National Crime Victims' Rights Week (April 22, 1991), President George H. Bush stated: "In the Nation's ongoing fight against crime, statistics tell only part of the story. More than a violation of the law, every crime is a violation of the rights, property, person, or trust of another human being. Thus, behind every tally of offenses ranging from misdemeanors to aggravated felonies are innocent victims—individuals and families who must be recognized in the administration of justice."

Results of Being Victimized

Lurigio and Mechanic (2000, p.26) observe: "Victimization can destroy people's basic trust of the world, challenge their assumptions about personal safety and security, and disrupt their abilities to function at work, school, and home."

Victims of crime may suffer physical injury, financial and property losses, emotional distress and psychological trauma. Some suffer from **posttraumatic stress disorder (PTSD)**, a persistent reexperiencing of a traumatic event through intrusive memories, dreams and a variety of anxiety-related symptoms.

Nonreporting of Victimization

Victims and witnesses are a major source of common crime information known to law enforcement. Many victims feel it is their civic duty to report victimization and hope doing so will bring offenders to justice. Others report crimes simply because they want to recover their property or file an insurance claim. In the absence of such motivators, however, a large percentage of robberies, aggravated assaults, burglaries and rapes go unreported to the police. Victims may consider the matter private, feel ashamed or believe the police will be unable to do anything.

In 2000 about half the violent crimes—rape, sexual assault, robbery, and simple and aggravated assault—committed against persons age 12 or older were reported to the police. About a third of both property crimes—burglary, motor vehicle theft, and property theft—and pocket pickings or purse snatchings were also reported (Hart and Rennison, 2003). When crime is underreported the police do not know there is a problem or may think it is only a minor problem. They do not have a true picture of the situation, which makes it difficult to problem-solve effectively.

Some victims and witnesses fear threats or retaliation from the offender(s). Many victims of violent crimes are warned by their attackers that going to the police will result in dire consequences for either the victims themselves or people they care about.

One reason gangs flourish is that they operate through intimidation, both inside and outside of court. Police must often deal with courtroom intimidation. Sometimes the court is packed with gang members who give threatening looks and suggestive signals to witnesses. Some departments counter this tactic by taking classes of police cadets into the courtroom. Confronted with this law enforcement presence, gang members usually give up and leave. It is important for law enforcement to encourage the reporting of crime by reassuring victims and witnesses they will be protected against threats, intimidation or reprisals by the victimizers.

Assisting Victims

Society has made progress in assisting victims of crime. In 1981 then-President Ronald Reagan proclaimed National Victims of Crime Week, putting the full weight and influence of his office behind the victims' movement. Since then, a variety of organizations and programs have been created to help victims receive the assistance they need.

Organizations Providing help to crime victims originated as a grassroots effort in the 1960s and 1970s to help battered women and victims of sexual assault.

Organizations dedicated to helping victims include the National Organization for Victim Assistance (NOVA), founded in 1976; the Office for Victims of Crime (OVC), founded in 1984; and the National Victim Center, founded in 1985.

Other victim organizations have been formed including Mothers against Drunk Driving, Students against Drunk Driving, Parents of Murdered Children, the National Organization of Victim Assistance and Victims for Victims. In addition, victim compensation laws and victim advocacy and protection programs attempt to address what is widely perceived as the system's protection of the accused's rights to the victim's detriment.

Programs Implemented Numerous programs also have been implemented to help victims deal with the financial and emotional fallout of victimization.

The two main types of programs provided for victims are victim compensation programs and victim/witness assistance programs.

- **Victim compensation programs** help crime victims cope with crime-related expenses such as medical costs, mental health counseling, lost wages and funeral or burial costs.
- **Victim/witness assistance programs** provide services such as crisis support, peer support, referrals to counseling, advocacy within the justice system and, in some cases, emergency shelter.

Crime victim compensation programs have been established in every state. Programs are based on identified needs of victims and witnesses. The most frequent services provided by victim/witness programs are summarized in Table 6.2. In addition to the formation of victims' organizations and programs, progress has also been made in formalizing the rights of victims.

Victims' Bill of Rights Victims and witnesses have two basic rights: the right to obtain certain information from the criminal justice system and the right to be treated humanely by the system. Most victims' bills of rights include both informational and participatory rights. They commonly require the victim to be informed

Table 6.2 Victim-Witness Program Services

Emergency Services	*Claims Assistance*
Medical care	Insurance claims aid
Shelter or food	Restitution assistance
Security repair	Compensation assistance
Financial assistance	Witness fee assistance
On-scene comfort	
Counseling	***Court-Related Services***
24-hour hotline	Witness reception
Crisis intervention	Court orientation
Follow-up counseling	Notification
Mediation	Witness alert
Advocacy and Support Services	Transportation
Personal advocacy	Child care
Employer intervention	Escort to court
Landlord intervention	Victim impact reports
Property return	***Systemwide Services***
Intimidation protection	Public education
Legal/paralegal counsel	Legislative advocacy
Referral	Training

SOURCE: Peter Finn and Beverly Lee. *Establishing and Expanding Victim Witness Assistance Programs.* Washington: National Institute of Justice, 1988. Reprinted by permission.

about available financial aid and social services, as well as the whereabouts of the accused; advised of case status and scheduling; protected from harassment and intimidation; provided with separate waiting areas during the trial; and a speedy disposition of the case and return of property held as evidence.

Goven (2000, p.17) notes the applicability of such strategies to community policing efforts: "Law enforcement plays a compelling and vital role in the treatment of victims of crime. . . . These hands-on strategies for innovation in police-based victim services provide an excellent opportunity for police to establish cross-disciplinary ties with victim assistance agencies and residents of their communities."

Police officers can also help victims by letting them know their rights, including the right to become active in the case processing and to prepare a victim impact statement (VIS). They might also tell victims what services are available.

Some departments are using innovative approaches to reach out to victims and maintain lines of communication. For example, in some lower income communities where few residents can afford telephone service, cellular phone links have been established to help crime victims reach the police. Cell phones have no lines to cut and can be preprogrammed with 911 and the general information number of the police department while locking out all other calling capability. An example of how communications are maintained with prior victims is seen in Jefferson County, Kentucky, where the Victim Information and Notification Everyday (VINE™) system automatically alerts victims with a telephone call when an inmate is released from custody. VINE could serve as a national model for using technology.

Agencies That Can Assist

The following types of agencies should be included in a victim/witness assistance referral network: community groups, day care centers, domestic violence programs, food stamp distribution centers, job counseling and training programs, mental health care programs, physical health care programs, private sector allies, private and community emergency organizations, rape crisis centers, unemployment services, victim assistance or advocacy organizations, victim compensation boards, volunteer groups and welfare agencies.

The Direction of Victims' Rights and Services in the Twenty-first Century

New Directions from the Field: Victims' Rights and Services for the 21st Century (1998) is a comprehensive report and compilation of more than 250 recommendations targeted to nearly every profession that comes in contact with crime victims—from justice practitioners, to victim service, health care, mental health, legal, educational, faith, news media and business communities. The result of a collaborative effort of more than 1,000 individuals in a broad spectrum of occupations, *New Directions* encourages professionals who deal with crime victims to redouble their efforts to enhance the rights and services afforded to such victims. According to *New Directions* (p.xxi):

> In the last two decades, many promising practices in victim services have been developed across the nation. These innovative programs use a multidisciplinary or team approach to respond to the needs of diverse crime victims; maximize technology to deliver high-quality services to victims more quickly and effectively; and utilize community police, prosecutor, court, and corrections programs.

Examples of "promising practices" that are transforming victim services include (pp.xxi–xxiii) children's advocacy centers; community criminal justice partnerships; crisis response teams; technologies to benefit crime victims (such as VINE); community police, prosecutors and court programs; initiatives of allied professionals (such as partnerships between criminal justice agencies, schools, the medical and mental health community, religious communities and the business community); comprehensive victim service centers; and specialized programs for diverse crime victims (including disabled victims and victims of gang violence).

SUMMARY

Effective police–community relations depend on an understanding of oneself and of others. Critical to self-understanding is recognizing prejudices and stereotypes. Prejudice is an attitude; discrimination is a behavior.

The quality of police–community relations depends largely on the communication process. The process involves a sender, a message, a channel, a receiver and sometimes feedback. Important individual characteristics in communication include age, education, gender, values, emotional involvement, self-esteem and language skills. Police officers may have more barriers to communication because of the image they convey, their position of authority and the nature of their work. Other common communication barriers include prejudices and stereotypes, time, use of jargon, lack of feedback and failure to listen. Law enforcement might benefit by adopting two practices used successfully in business: networking and seeking customer satisfaction, that is, being service oriented.

One challenge facing our increasingly diverse society is racism, a belief that a human population having a distinct genetically transmitted characteristic is inferior. It also refers to discrimination or prejudice based on race. The contention that racism exists among officers has led to allegations of racial profiling, a serious concern for any department engaged in such a practice and for the credibility of the police profession as a whole. Racial profiling is a form of discrimination and singles out people of racial or ethnic groups because of a belief that these groups are more likely than others to commit certain types of crimes. Race-based enforcement is illegal.

Disabilities police officers frequently encounter include mobility impairment, vision impairment, hearing impairment, impairment as a result of epilepsy, and mental or emotional impairment. An epileptic seizure may be mistaken for a drug- or alcohol-induced stupor because the person may exhibit incoherent speech, glassy-eyed staring and aimless wandering. Officers may also encounter mentally disabled individuals, some of whom may need institutionalization. The four civil criteria for detainment and commitment of mentally ill people are mental illness, dangerousness, being gravely disabled and being in need of (mental health) treatment.

Another population the police encounter daily is the elderly, people age 65 and older, who may be victims of Alzheimer's disease (AD). Police contact with AD patients is likely because Alzheimer's victims may wander or become lost, engage in inappropriate sexual behavior, lose impulse control, shoplift, falsely accuse others, appear intoxicated, drive erratically and become victims of crime. Many of the symptoms of intoxication and Alzheimer's are identical: confusion and disorientation; problems with short-term memory, language, sight and coordination; combativeness; and in extreme reaction cases, loss of contact with reality.

A frequently overlooked segment of the population that is important to community policing implementation is youths. Children with special needs include those who are emotionally/behaviorally disturbed, have learning disabilities, have an attention deficit hyperactivity disorder or have behavior problems resulting from prenatal exposure to drugs, including alcohol, or to HIV.

The two main types of programs provided for victims are (1) victim compensation programs that help crime victims cope with crime-related expenses such as medical costs, mental health counseling, lost wages and funeral or burial costs; and (2) victim/witness assistance programs that provide services such as crisis support, peer support, referrals to counseling, advocacy within the justice system and, in some cases, emergency shelter. "Special" crime victims who require additional services include immigrants, people with disabilities and elderly victims of crime or abuse.

Discussion Questions

1. In what ways might a person become a victim and need assistance from the police?
2. What role do euphemisms ("soft" words) play in communication?
3. In what ways might the general public be perceived as "customers" of a police department? What implications does this have?
4. How diverse is your community?
5. Have you ever tried to communicate with someone who does not speak English? What was it like?
6. How would you define the American culture?
7. Would you favor eliminating the word *minority* when talking about diversity? If so, what term would you use instead?
8. Do you consider yourself "culturally literate"? Why or why not?
9. Have you encountered instances of racism? Explain.
10. Which type of disability do you feel would pose the greatest challenge for effective community policing? Why?

InfoTrac College Edition Assignments

- Use InfoTrac College Edition to help answer the Discussion Questions as appropriate.
- Research at least one of the following subjects and write a brief (three to four page) report of your findings: discrimination, jargon, listening, nonverbal communication, prejudices or stereotypes. Be prepared to share your report with the class.
- Research and report on at least one of the following subjects: cultural conflict, hate crime, homelessness, racial profiling or racism.
- Research how mental retardation affects the likelihood of criminal activity, conviction, incarceration and rehabilitation. What systemic changes, if any, would you recommend based on your research?
- Research what police services are available for the mentally ill in your area.

Community Project

What are the criteria for institutionalization in your state? How do they compare to other states—are they more or less restrictive?

References

Association for Children with Learning Disabilities. "Taking the First Step to Solving Learning Problems." Pittsburgh: Association for Children with Learning Disabilities (no date).

Centers for Disease Control. "CDC's Lead Poisoning Prevention Program." October 27, 2000. www.cdc.gov/nceh/lead/factsheets

Cherry, Mike. "Cultural Diversity: Reaching Out to the Communities within the Community." *Community Policing Exchange,* January/February 2000, p.8.

Ciaramicoli, Arthur. "The Amazing Power of Empathy: It's in All of Us . . . How to Bring It Out." *Bottom Line: Personal,* September 15, 2000, p.9.

Cohen, John D.; Lennon, Janet J.; and Wasserman, Robert. "Eliminating Racial Profiling—A 'Third Way.' " *Law Enforcement News,* March 31, 2000, pp.12, 15.

Colbridge, Thomas D. "The Americans with Disabilities Act." *FBI Law Enforcement Bulletin,* September 2000a, pp.26–31.

Colbridge, Thomas D. "Defining Disability under the Americans with Disabilities Act." *FBI Law Enforcement Bulletin,* October 2000b, pp.28–32.

"Congress Approves Grants for Mental Health Courts." *Criminal Justice Newsletter,* October 24, 2000, pp.2–3.

Davis, Leigh Ann. "People with Mental Retardation in the Criminal Justice System." 2000. http://thearc.org/

Fabyankovic, Janet. "Alternatives to Homeless Criminalization." *Law and Order,* August 2000, pp.113–115.

Forst, Linda S. "Working with the Aged." *Law and Order,* October 2000, pp.125–128.

"Ft. Lauderdale Learns a Lesson from Miami in Dealing with the Homeless." *Law Enforcement News,* March 31, 2000, pp.1, 14.

Fuller, John. "Cultural Diversity? Don't Forget the Disabled!" *Law and Order,* November 2000, pp.84–85.

Fulton, Roger. "On the Road to Good Communications." *Law Enforcement Technology,* September 2000, p.130.

Goven, Patricia. "Law Enforcement Takes Action for Victims: IACP Summit Recommendations Released." *The Police Chief,* June 2000, pp.14–24.

Hart, Timothy C. and Rennison, Callie. *Reporting Crime to the Police, 1992–2000,* Washington, DC: Bureau of Justice Statistics Special Report, March 2003.

Hibbert, Alison D. "Homeless Outreach Program." *The Police Chief,* May 2000, pp.44–47.

Holmes, Malcolm D. "Minority Threat and Police Brutality: Determinants of Civil Rights Criminal Complaints in U.S. Municipalities." *Criminology,* May 2000, pp.343–367.

Human Rights Watch, October 2003-10-22.

Klein, Sid. "Dealing with the Homeless and Improving Quality of Life." *The Police Chief,* May 2000, pp.34–43.

Kurlander, Neil. "Software to Track Traffic Stop Data." *Law Enforcement Technology,* July 2000, pp.148–153.

Litchford, Jody M. "ADA Decisions Provide Guidance for Enforcement Activities." *The Police Chief,* August 2000, pp.15–17.

Lurigio, Arthur J. and Mechanic, Mindy B. "The Importance of Being Responsive to Crime Victims." *Police,* October 2000, pp.22–28.

"Many State Police Agencies Requiring Racial Data Collection." *Criminal Justice Newsletter,* February 18, 2000, p.5.

Margolis, Jeremy; Watts, Darren; and Johnston, Iain. "Proactive Defense Strategies Can Minimize Risk." *The Police Chief,* July 2000, pp.18–23.

McNeil, John M. *Americans with Disabilities: Household Economic Studies, U.S. Bureau of the Census. Current Population Reports.* Washington, DC: U.S. Government Printing Office, 2001, pp.70–73.

National Alliance for the Mentally Ill. © 1996–2000. www.nami.org

National Institutes of Health. www.nih.gov

New Directions from the Field: Victims' Rights and Services for the 21st Century. Washington, DC: U.S. Department of Justice, Office for Victims of Crime, May 1998.

Olson, Robert K. "From the President." *Subject to Debate,* September 2000, p.2.

Paynter, Ronnie L. "Protecting All the People." *Law Enforcement Technology,* April 2000, pp.62–66.

"Policies Help Gain Public Trust: Guidance from the IACP Highway Safety Committee." *The Police Chief,* July 2000, pp.24–29.

"Race Disparity Seen throughout Juvenile Justice System." *Criminal Justice Newsletter,* April 25, 2000, pp.6–7.

Sampson, Rana and Scott, Michael S. *Tackling Crime and Other Public-Safety Problems: Case Studies in Problem-Solving.* Washington, DC: U.S. Department of Justice, Office of Community Oriented Policing Services, 2000.

Scott, Brian. "Verbal Judo: Talk Your Way through Confrontations." *Police,* August 2000, pp.54–56.

Scoville, Dean. "A View Askew: A Sideways Look at Racial Profiling." *Police,* August 2000, pp.16–23.

Skogan, Wesley G.; Steiner, Lynn; DuBois, Jill; Gudell, J. Erik; and Fagan, Aimee. *Community Policing and "The New Immigrants": Latinos in Chicago.* Northwestern University, Institute for Policy Research, July 2002. (NCJ 189908)

Spohn, Cassia and Holleran, David. "The Imprisonment Penalty Paid by Young, Unemployed Black and Hispanic Male Offenders." *Criminology,* February 2000, pp.281–306.

Strandberg, Keith. "De-Institutionalization." *Law Enforcement Technology,* October 2000, pp. 90–98.

"Strengthening Relations between Police and Minority Communities: Ensuring Accountability for Effective Policing in Chicago's Diverse Neighborhoods." *Subject to Debate,* June 2000, pp.1, 3–4.

Szubin, Adam; Jensen, Carl J.; and Gregg, Rod. "Interacting with 'Cults': A Policing Model." *FBI Law Enforcement Bulletin,* September 2000, pp.16–24.

350 Tested Strategies to Prevent Crime: A Resource for Municipal Agencies and Community Groups. Washington, DC: National Crime Prevention Council. 1995.

Weisburd, David; Greenspan, Rosann; Hamilton, Edwin E.; Williams, Hubert; and Bryant, Kellie A. *Police Attitudes toward Abuse of Authority: Findings from a National Study.* Washington, DC: National Institute of Justice Research in Brief, May 2000.

Wexler, Chuck. "F rom the Executive Director." *Subject to Debate,* June 2000, p.2.

Zingraff, Matthew T.; Smith, William R.; and Tomaskovic-Devey, Donald. "North Carolina Highway Traffic and Patrol Study: 'Driving while Black.'" *The Criminologist,* May/June 2000, pp.1, 3–4.

CHAPTER 7

Building Partnerships: The Glue of Community Policing

Problem-solving without partnerships risks overlooking the most pressing community concerns. Thus, the partnership between police and the communities they service is essential for implementing a successful program in community policing.

—Chief Darrel Stephens, Charlotte-Mecklenburg Police Department

DO YOU KNOW?

- Why police are asking the community to help them identify and prioritize crime concerns?
- What the core components of community partnerships are?
- What the four dimensions of trust are?
- Whether beats and shifts should be permanent?
- What kind of beats community policing officers should be assigned to? Why?
- What two factors most influence how individuals perceive police officers?
- What may impede a shared vision and common goals?
- In addition to commonalities, what must be recognized when forming partnerships?
- What the benefits of partnerships are?
- What the common criticisms of community policing are?
- How these common criticisms can be addressed?
- How some cities are diverting nonemergency calls from 911?
- What purposes are served by citizen police academies?
- What key collaborators may be overlooked in community policing efforts?
- What some benefits of using senior citizens as volunteers are?
- Why it can be more difficult to build partnerships in a lower income neighborhood?

CAN YOU DEFINE?

call management
call reduction
call stacking
collaboration
stakeholders
TRIAD
working in "silos"

Introduction

The COPS Office Web site states: "In community policing, citizens are viewed by the police as partners who share responsibility for identifying priorities and developing and implementing responses. In community policing, the term *partnerships* refers to the collaboration that takes place between police officers, community members, government agencies and other stakeholders. The police become an integral part of the community culture, and the community assists in defining future priorities and in allocating resources. The difference is substantial and encompasses basic goals and commitments."

Community partnership means adopting a policing perspective that exceeds the standard law enforcement emphasis. This broadened outlook recognizes the value of activities that contribute to the orderliness and well-being of a neighborhood (Community Policing Consortium Web site). As noted by Jurik et al. (2000, pp.293–294): "Community partnerships have surged in popularity during the past decade. . . . Crime prevention partnerships that join criminal justice agencies to work with business, university or other community members have been a prominent part of this trend. . . . Partnership models have been embraced by conservatives and liberals alike as avenues for crime prevention, community revitalization and citizen empowerment."

This chapter begins with a discussion of why partnerships are important in community policing and the core components making up successful partnerships. This

President Bush views a bomb-disposal robot while touring a citizen police academy in Knoxville, Tennessee, Such academies teach citizens about police operations and procedures.

is followed by a discussion of the benefits of partnerships as well as some criticisms that have been raised. Next is a look at how departments can make time for partnerships through call management and how citizens can become educated partners through citizen academies. Then some key partners are identified: criminal justice partners, including prosecutors, courts and corrections; government agencies; the private security sector; victims; and elderly volunteers. It then discusses community policing partnerships in diverse neighborhoods. The chapter concludes with a look at some effective partnerships in action.

Why Partnerships?

Community partnerships are crucial for police agencies serious about community policing. Community policing cannot succeed without them. Collaborations may be with businesses, schools, youths, residents, organizations and other government agencies, depending on the problem and who the stakeholders are.

Traditional policing expected the community members to remain in the background. Crime and disorder were viewed as police matters, best left to professionals. That meant most citizen–police interactions were *negative contacts.* After all, people do not call the police when things are going well. Their only opportunity to interact with officers was either when they were victims of crime or were involved in some other emergency situation or were the subject of some enforcement action, such as receiving traffic tickets.

Some people may question why the police would consult the public about setting police priorities and why they would ask them to work with them to solve neighborhood problems. Some feel that the police are paid to deal with crime and disorder and should not expect communities to take any responsibility or do their job for them. Others feel that until something is done about the "whole laundry list of community woes that social scientists tell us are the causes of crime (poverty, teen pregnancy, racism, homelessness, single-parent families, lousy schools, no jobs) the crime problem will never go away" (Rahtz, 2001, pp.35–36). To this Rahtz says: "They are flat-out wrong. Beat cops, working with the people in their neighborhoods, have proven that crime and community disorder can be reduced without waiting for the underlying problems to be solved. I am not saying that poverty, teen pregnancy, etc., are not important issues and do not deserve attention. But if we, as police officers and citizens, sit back in the belief that we are impotent in the face of crime until the problems are solved, we are doing a grave disservice to ourselves and our neighborhoods." Rahtz (p.35) calls partnerships "the glue of community policing."

Partnerships usually result in a more effective solution to a problem because of the shared responsibilities, resources and goals.

Partnerships are often referred to as collaboration. Rinehart et al. (2001, p.7) explain: "**Collaboration** occurs when a number of agencies and individuals make a commitment to work together and contribute resources to obtain a common, long-term goal." When it works correctly, a successful problem-solving collaboration that results in a workable solution tends to be a positive experience for everyone involved.

Rinehart et al. (p.7) suggest: "Not all law enforcement relationships must be collaborative, nor should they strive to be. Under some circumstances it may be appropriate for law enforcement personnel just to establish a good communication plan. Under other circumstances cooperation between two individuals may be sufficient. Perhaps coordination between two agencies to avoid duplication of effort is all that is required. Collaboration is, however, critical for many community policing endeavors." They (p.6) cite the following reasons for developing law enforcement–community partnerships:

- Accomplish what individuals alone cannot.
- Prevent duplicating individual or organizational efforts.
- Enhance the power of advocacy and resource development for the initiative.
- Create more public recognition and visibility for the community policing initiative.
- Provide a more systematic, comprehensive approach to addressing community- or school-based crime and disorder problems.
- Provide more opportunities for new community policing projects.

To accomplish these results, several components of a partnership or collaboration are necessary.

The Core Components of a Partnership or Collaboration

The core components of effective community partnerships are:

- Stakeholders with a vested interest in the collaboration.
- Trusting relationships among and between the partners.
- A shared vision and common goals for the collaboration.
- Expertise.
- Teamwork strategies.
- Open communication.
- Motivated partners.
- Means to implement and sustain the collaborative effort.
- An action plan (Rinehart et al., p.6).

Figure 7.1 illustrates these core components.

Stakeholders

"Without stakeholder involvement there is no chance for collaborative problem-solving or other community policing initiatives" (Rinehart et al., p.12). Partnerships are made up of **stakeholders**, those people who have an interest in what happens in a particular situation. For example, a project to reduce thefts from cars on a college campus could involve stakeholders from several groups: students, administrators, teachers, the maintenance department and police. Stakeholders will change depending on the problem the collaboration is solving, but when possible the collaboration should reflect the diversity of the community.

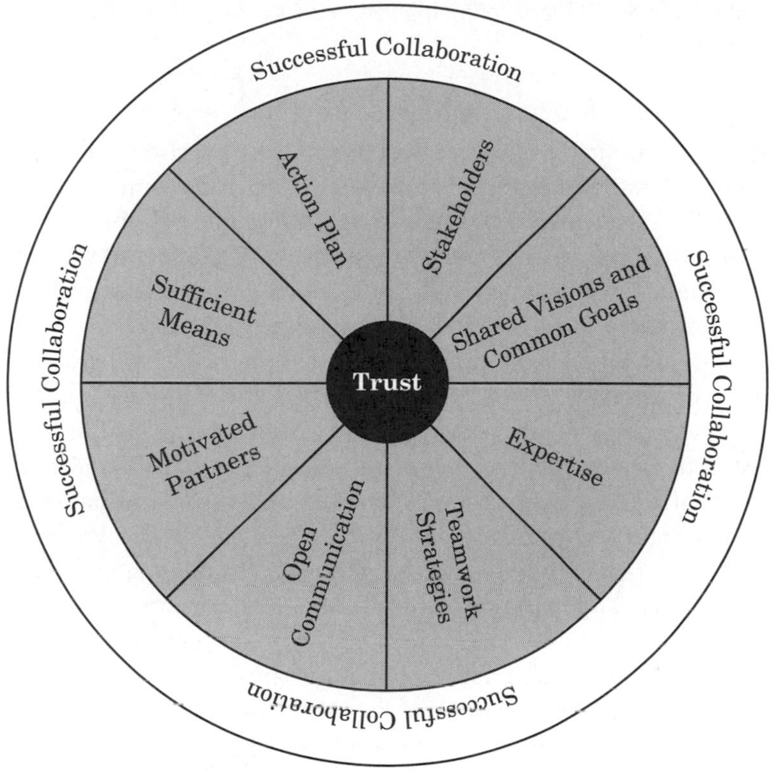

Figure 7.1 Core Components of a Successful Collaboration Partnership

SOURCE: Tammy A. Rinehart, Anna T. Laszlo and Gwen O. Briscoe. *Collaboration Toolkit: How to Build, Fix and Sustain Productive Partnerships.* Washington, DC: U.S. Department of Justice, Office of Community Oriented Policing Services, 2001, p.7.

Identifying Stakeholders Rinehart et al. (p.2) identify the following potential stakeholders: school administrators and other school personnel, school board members, business leaders, elected officials, neighborhood-watch/block clubs, youth organizations, community-based organizations, community activists, probation/parole/pretrial services, district attorney/state attorney general, trade organizations, faith community, social service organizations, federal law enforcement (FBI, DEA, ATF, INS, etc.) corrections, media and private foundations and other charitable organizations. They provide the following examples:

- In a school-based partnership to address a bullying problem, stakeholders may include parents, students, school administrators, teachers, school support personnel, school board members and school bus drivers.
- When addressing auto theft in one district of a city, stakeholders may include car dealerships, neighborhood-watch groups, victims and elected officials.
- While preparing a crisis management strategy in a school, stakeholders may include representatives of social services and rescue services, parents, students, school administrators, teachers, school board members, mental health professionals and the media.

To obtain stakeholders' participation, community expectations may need to be changed.

Active Community Involvement

Community policing relies on active community involvement. Community policing recognizes that community involvement gives new dimension to crime control activities. While police continue to handle crime fighting and law enforcement responsibilities, the police and community work together to modify conditions that can encourage criminal behavior. The resources available within communities allow for an expanded focus on crime prevention activities.

Patrol officers are the primary providers of police services and have the most extensive contact with community members. In community policing efforts, they will provide the bulk of the daily policing needs of the community and they will be assisted by immediate supervisors, other police units and appropriate government and social agencies. Upper level managers and command staff will be responsible for ensuring that the entire organization backs the efforts of patrol officers.

Effective community policing depends on optimizing positive contact between patrol officers and community members. Patrol cars are only one method of conveying police services. Police departments may supplement automobile patrols with foot, bicycle, scooter and horseback patrols, as well as adding mini-stations to bring police closer to the community. Regular community meetings and forums will afford police and community members an opportunity to air concerns and find ways to address them. Once the stakeholders are enlisted in partnerships, the key is to build trust among all collaborators.

Building Trust

"Without trust there will be hesitancy to work together as a team. People will hold back and be reluctant to share talents, time, and resources" (Rinehart et al., p.12). Establishing and maintaining mutual trust is a central goal of community policing and community partnership. Police recognize the need for cooperation with the community. In the fight against serious crime, police have encouraged community members to come forth with relevant information. In addition, police have spoken to neighborhood groups, participated in business and civic events, worked with social agencies and taken part in educational and recreational programs for school children.

Special units have provided a variety of crisis intervention services. So then how do the cooperative efforts of community policing differ from the actions that have taken place previously? These activities could include helping accident or crime victims, providing emergency medical services, helping resolve domestic and neighborhood conflicts (e.g., family violence, landlord–tenant disputes or racial harassment), working with residents and local businesses to improve neighborhood conditions, controlling automobile and pedestrian traffic, providing emergency social services and referrals to those at risk (e.g., adolescent runaways, the homeless, the intoxicated and the mentally ill), protecting the exercise of constitutional rights (e.g., guaranteeing a person's right to speak and protecting lawful assemblies from disruption) and providing a model of citizenship (helpfulness, respect for others, honesty and fairness). Although these are all services to the community, none are true partnerships, which require sharing of power and responsibility to identify and respond to problems.

Nonetheless, these services are important as they help develop trust between the police and the community. This trust will enable the police to gain greater access to valuable information from the community that could lead to the solution and prevention of crimes, will engender support for needed crime control measures and will provide an opportunity for officers to establish a working relationship with the community. The entire police organization must be involved in enlisting the cooperation of community members in promoting safety and security.

Hawdon et al. (2003, p.472) describe the dimensions of trust and suggest four questions that address the complexity of the issue of trust:

1. Priorities—Do the police share the residents' priorities and concerns?
2. Competency—Can they effectively control crime and accomplish the other requirements of their jobs?
3. Dependability—Are they dependable?
4. Respect—Do they treat residents with respect?

Four dimensions of trust are shared priorities, competency, dependability and respect.

Building trust will not happen overnight; it will require ongoing effort. But trust must be achieved before police can assess the needs of the community and construct the close ties that will engender community support. To build trust for an effective community partnership, police must treat people with respect and sensitivity. The use of unnecessary force and arrogance, aloofness or rudeness at any level of the agency will dampen the willingness of community members to ally themselves with the police. In addition, how officers have been traditionally assigned needs to be changed.

Changing Beat and Shift Assignments

Traditional shift and beat *rotation* work to the detriment of building partnerships.

Officers whose assignments continually change have no chance to develop the relationships and trust needed for community policing. Communities also do not have the opportunity to get to recognize and know officers who work in their neighborhoods.

According to the Community Policing Consortium: "Having officers periodically rotate among the shifts impedes their ability to identify problems. It also discourages creative solutions to impact the problems, because the officers end up rotating away from the problems. Thus, a sense of responsibility to identify and resolve problems is lost. Likewise, management cannot hold the officers accountable to deal with problems if the officers are frequently rotated from one shift to another."

The goal of community policing is to reduce crime and disorder by carefully examining the characteristics of problems in neighborhoods and then applying appropriate problem-solving remedies.

The community (beat) for which a patrol officer is given responsibility should be a small, well-defined geographical area.

Beats should be "configured in a manner that preserves, as much as possible, the unique geographical and social characteristics of neighborhoods while still allowing efficient service" (Community Policing Consortium Web site).

Officers who have permanent assignments become experts about their beat.

Beat officers know the community leaders, businesspeople, school personnel and students. They know the crime patterns and problems and have the best chance to develop partnerships for problem solving. Community members will become accustomed to seeing the permanent beat officers working in the community. The increased presence and permanence will help build mutual trust and reduce the fear of crime. Officers working long-term assignments on the same shift and beat will become familiar figures to community members and will become aware of the day-to-day workings of the community. This increased police presence is an initial move in establishing trust and serves to reduce fear of crime among community members, which, in turn, helps create neighborhood security. Fear must be reduced if community members are to participate actively in policing. People will not act if they feel that their actions will jeopardize their safety.

Police work proactively, often identifying and addressing issues before they become problems. They often collaborate with other agencies and community members to solve problems and identify potential trouble spots or situations and act on them instead of waiting for the radio calls that will surely come if the situation is ignored. They are able to respond to questions about crime in their area, for example, why burglaries or auto theft have increased in a particular time period and what is going to be done about it. Of course they still take all the enforcement action necessary and respond to calls as well. It is a far more challenging job and provides more job satisfaction because officers can see they are making a real difference. They are affecting a neighborhood, helping make it a safer and better place to live and work and are building trust.

Efforts at building trust need to be sustained over time. Mutual trust is required to access community needs and to develop the close relationship needed for collaboration between police and community members. As trust increases, citizens' perception of the police should also become more positive.

Citizen Perception of the Police in the Community As Schafer et al. (2003, p.441) stress: "Public service agencies such as the police must secure the support of the public if they are to provide efficient and effective services." And as Carter (2002) notes, there is a nexus between public perceptions of the police and their ability to achieve goals and objectives. In reviewing the literature, Schafer et al.

(p.443) conclude: "Most Americans are confident in, are satisfied with, and hold favorable impressions of their local police, although variations have been found based on respondent characteristics, neighborhood contexts, contact with police and the way in which research questions are worded." Consistent with other researchers, Schafer et al. state, whites were most satisfied with police, blacks less satisfied, and Hispanics somewhere in between. They also found that race and socioeconomic class were closely related and that socioeconomic class was more important than race. Schafer et al. (p.445) report: "Factors such as individuals' marital status and employment status and whether they own or rent their dwellings are of particular importance when evaluating perceptions from a community-policing perspective. All three variables reflect individuals' 'stakes' or 'investments' in their community. Those who have higher stakes may be more inclined to support community-policing efforts designed to improve their quality of life." Perhaps their most important finding is: "Although demographic factors matter, they are less important than being satisfied with police contacts" (p.462). They (p.463) conclude: "These findings . . . clearly demonstrate that the police can improve their standing with the public by making efforts to ensure the public is satisfied with their specific interactions with the police."

Researchers Relsig and Parks (2002) also studied what makes citizens satisfied with police. They report: "The biggest factor, according to new research, is people's perceptions about the quality of their lives—their sense of safety for example. . . . But the research also shows that the second biggest factor in shaping opinions is direct contact with officers—how police behave when they interact with residents."

The two factors most influencing citizens' perception of their police are personal contacts and perceptions of the quality of life in the community.

A Shared Vision and Common Goals

"Without a shared vision, there will be disorder. A shared vision brings focus to the team. A lack of agreed-upon focus allows team members to pursue conflicting agendas" (Rinehart et al., p.12). However, sometimes competing interests get in the way of successful problem solving.

Competing Interests Although the delivery of police services is organized by geographic area, a community may encompass widely diverse cultures, values and concerns, particularly in urban settings. A community consists of more than just the local government and the neighborhood residents. Churches, schools, hospitals, social groups, private and public agencies and those who work in the area are also vital members of the community. In addition, those who visit for cultural or recreational purposes or provide services to the area are also concerned with the safety and security of the neighborhood. Including these "communities of interest" in efforts to address problems of crime and disorder can expand the resource base of the community.

Concerns and priorities will vary within and among these communities of interest. Some communities of interest are long lasting and were formed around racial, ethnic, occupational lines or a common history, church or school. Others form and reform as new problems are identified and addressed. Interest groups within communities can be in opposition to one another—sometimes in violent opposition. Intracommunity disputes have been common in large urban centers, especially in times of changing demographics and population migrations.

These multiple and sometimes conflicting interests require patrol officers to function not only as preservers of law and order but also as skillful mediators.

Demands on police from one community of interest can sometimes clash with the rights of another community of interest. Such conflicting interests may impede establishing a common vision and shared goals.

For example, a community group may oppose certain police tactics used to crack down on gang activity, which the group believes may result in discriminatory arrest practices. The police must not only protect the rights of the protesting group, but also work with all community members involved to find a way to preserve neighborhood peace. For this process to be effective, community members must communicate their views and suggestions and back up the negotiating efforts of the police. In this way, the entire community participates in the mediation process and helps preserve order. The police must encourage a spirit of cooperation that balances the collective interests of all citizens with the personal rights of individuals.

When forming partnerships, conflicts within communities are as important to recognize as the commonalities.

Police must recognize the existence of both to build the cooperative bonds needed to maintain order, provide a sense of security and control crime. Police must build lasting relationships that encompass all elements of the community and center around the fundamental issues of public safety and quality of life. Again, the key to managing this difficult task is trust.

In addition, as researchers Jurik et al. (p.295) suggest: "We conceptualize *partnerships* as unique interorganizational niches from which to pursue innovation and change. The change agendas of partnerships may be progressive, reactionary or some combination of the two. Change goals may involve their own contradictions from the outset. We will suggest that partnerships in general, and criminal justice partnerships in particular, often entail contradictory goals aimed simultaneously at empowering and reinforcing domination."

Scott (2000, p.67) discusses the importance of understanding the multiple and competing interests at stake in problems. He (p.68) suggests that to begin, one should ask what are the *social* interests and what are the *government's* interests. He notes:

> There are often hidden commercial interests involved in many problems, as well as latent social prejudices and biases. These interests should at least be brought out in the open, where they can be considered. The careful probing of interests is among the most enlightening parts of the problem-solving process. Police officers who engage in this probing of interests begin to appreciate just how many different perspectives there may be regarding the same problem. The multiple and competing interests of the police themselves are often not well considered.

For example, some conventional responses to chronic problems, however ineffective, promote some police interests. In some jurisdictions, police officers rely heavily on either overtime or outside security employment for their incomes. Sometimes an alternative response to a problem has the potential to eliminate the need for the overtime or off-duty assignments, obviously presenting ethical challenges to the police.

The Remaining Core Components of Successful Collaboration and Partnerships

The remaining components, although vital, are only briefly described as they are either self-explanatory or have been discussed elsewhere in the text (Rinehart et al., p.12).

Expertise "Without expertise, there will be apprehension. It is frustrating to know what should be done but not to have the talent within the team to accomplish the goal."

Teamwork Strategies "Without teamwork (i.e., joint decision making, joint responsibility, and shared power), there will be fragmented action." Secretary of State Colin Powell has been quoted as saying, "The best method for overcoming obstacles is the team method."

Open Communication "Without open communication, there will be disorganized and uninformed partners. Information must be freely and regularly shared for a team to function collaboratively." This was the focus of Chapter 6.

Motivated Partners "Without motivators, there will be slow progress toward the goal. Motivators prevent apathy, keep the partners interested, and sustain involvement."

Means to Implement and Sustain the Collaborative Effort "Without sufficient means, there will be discouraged team members. If the project is larger than the resources available, it is easy for partners to fall into a 'what's the use?' frame of mind."

Action Plan "Without an action plan, there will be a lack of focus. An action plan is necessary to guide the team and serves as a means of accountability."

With this understanding of the core components of partnerships, how can stakeholders be convinced to participate in collaborations? One way is to point out the personal benefits they might attain.

The benefits of participating in a partnership include:

- A sense of accomplishment from bettering the community.
- Gaining recognition and respect.
- Meeting other community members.
- Learning new skills.
- Fulfilling an obligation to contribute (Rinehart et al., p.2).

Despite these benefits, partnerships have been criticized by some.

Criticisms of Partnerships

Criticism of the partnerships in community policing usually center on time and money.

Partnerships are time consuming and therefore cost money. Most police agencies do not have extra personnel available for community policing–type projects. Many departments are 911 driven. Officers respond to one call after another and have a difficult time keeping up with the demand for service. When would they have the time to meet with stakeholders and develop plans to solve problems?

Working as partners with the community may take time and cost more in the short run, but continuing to treat the symptoms without solving the problem has its own costs. It will mean responding again and again to the same calls, often involving the same people, and using temporary tactics to resolve the problem. One way many departments free up time for officers to problem-solve with community members is to manage the volume of 911 calls and to ultimately reduce the number of calls through call management or call reduction.

Making Time for Partnering and Problem Solving: Call Management or Call Reduction

In most departments, calls for service determine what police officers do from minute to minute on a shift. People call the police to report crime, ask for assistance, ask questions, get advice and many other often unrelated requests. Police departments try to respond as quickly as possible, and most have a policy of sending an officer when requested.

Departments might free up time for partnerships without expense through effective call management or call reduction.

When using **call management** or **call reduction**, departments look at which calls for service must have an officer(s) respond and, regardless of past practice, which do not. In call management, calls are prioritized based on the department's judgment about the emergency nature of the call (e.g., imminent harm to a person or a crime in progress), response time, need for backup and other local factors. Priority schemes vary across the country, but many have four or five levels. Table 7.1 presents a typical call priority scheme.

McEwen et al. (2003, p.50) stress: "In a police organization committed to community policing, the community should play a role in setting and reviewing police call priorities and response policies. The community has a vested interest in how quickly officers are dispatched, the extent to which police expedite through neighborhoods, the extent to which multiple units are dispatched or stay at the scene, whether calls are handled by alternative means and related issues."

Call management usually involves **call stacking**, a process involving a Computer Aided Dispatch system in which nonemergency, lower priority calls are ranked and held or "stacked" so the higher priorities are continually dispatched first. According to McEwen et al. (p.35): "The objective of call stacking is to reduce cross-beat dispatches

Table 7.1 Call Prioritizing Scheme

Priority	*Designation*	*Response*	*Numbers of Units*
1	Emergency	Immediate; lights and siren; exceed speed limit	2
2	Immediate	Immediate; lights and siren; maintain speed limit	2 if requested
3	Routine	Routine	1
4	Delayed	Delay up to one hour; routine	1
5	TRU	Delay up to two hours	TRU

SOURCE: Tom McEwen, Deborah Spencer, Russell Wolff, Julie Wartell and Barbara Webster. *Call Management in Community Policing: A Guidebook for Law Enforcement.* Washington DC: U.S. Department of Justice, Office of Community Oriented Policing Services, February 2003, p.50.

and allow the unit in the area of responsibility to handle as many calls in that area as possible. This has significant advantages for community policing, which in the majority of departments involves assigning patrol officers to specific geographic areas such as beats or neighborhoods. As officers spend more time in their beats, they gain opportunities to become familiar with conditions, problems and resources in those areas. Cross-beat dispatches reduce those opportunities by taking officers out of their assigned areas, as well as adding to the time required to respond to calls."

Using an officer to take telephone reports of nonemergency, low-priority calls is one change that has helped. Reports of minor thefts occurring days or even months in the past and made for insurance purposes are an example of incidents that could be handled completely by phone.

Similar results can be obtained by taking reports by appointment. If the reporting party is willing, appointments can be set up to have an officer take the report at a less busy time for the department and one convenient to the caller. Many people find this method agreeable. Certain kinds of reports can be made on an agency's Web page, by mail or fax. Figure 7.2 illustrates the type of intake and response common in call management.

Call management may also involve having civilians handle certain calls such as those not involving dangerous situations, suspects or follow-up; traffic accidents (no injury), traffic control, parking issues, and abandoned vehicles; vehicle lockouts; building checks; burglary, theft, lost and found property; vandalism and criminal mischief; runaways; paperwork relays and services; subpoena service and funeral escorts; animal complaints; bicycle stops and park patrol (McEwen et al., p.39). However, police unions may take issue with such an approach unless reserve officers were used.

Call management may also involve dealing with the 911 system, set up for emergency calls for assistance. As noted by McEwen et al. (p.7), however: "In one sense, 911 became too successful. It resulted in a dramatic increase in the number of nonemergency calls coming in to the police." Large numbers of callers use 911 to ask for information or to report nonemergency situations. Most agencies field hundreds or even thousands of phone calls a year from citizens seeking information, often unrelated to police services. Keeping the public informed in other ways such as on a Web site

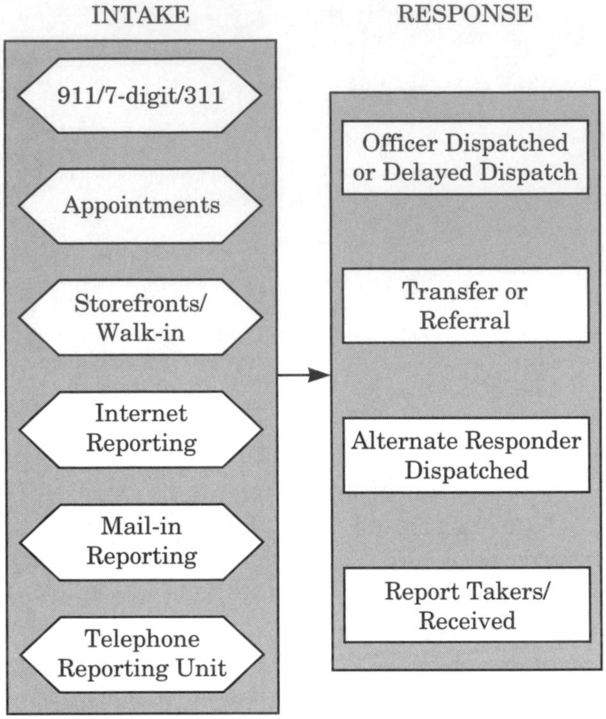

Figure 7.2 Call Management: Intake and Response

SOURCE: Tom McEwen, Deborah Spencer, Russell Wolff, Julie Wartell and Barbara Webster. *Call Management in Community Policing: A Guidebook for Law Enforcement.* Washington, DC: U.S. Department of Justice, Office of Community Oriented Policing Services, February 2003, p.12.

or through newspapers and newsletters with information about city policies, services, procedures and when and when not to call police can reduce the volume of calls.

People call the police for nonpolice matters for a variety of reasons: because they do not know who can help; because they believe the police know or should know the answers to all questions; because they know the phone number (911); and because, no matter what day of week or time of day it is, they know the phones will be answered. Every 911 call center fields calls asking why the electricity is out, what the weather conditions or driving conditions are, when the snow plows will start plowing, what time the shopping center opens, what time the neighborhood-watch meeting begins, what the driving directions are to a distant state, what the juvenile curfew hours are, where to pay a utility bill and why there is no stop sign or semaphore at a certain location. Calls reporting pot hole locations, complaining about raccoons, deer and other wildlife and even about noisy church bells are clogging 911 lines across the country.

Large cities have begun to implement 311 lines to divert nonemergency calls from 911.

Police nonemergency lines are nothing new but since the advent of 911, most callers use it for all calls to the police because they do not have to look up a nonemergency phone number. The hope is with an easy-to-remember number for nonemergency matters, people will reserve 911 for emergencies.

As McEwen et al. (p.22) note: "The primary reason most jurisdictions implement a 311 strategy is to reduce the number of nonemergency calls and information requests coming in to 911. Another goal of 311 is to quickly connect citizens with appropriate agencies to serve their needs. The 311 number also has the potential to benefit community policing in other ways.

- It can alert other agencies to citizen problems for which they, rather than the police, have mandates to assume primary responsibility.
- It eases the burden on police personnel who answer emergency calls.
- It can facilitate communication between community members and agencies by attempting to connect citizens with the right agency, department or person the first time.
- It can improve accountability for follow-up. Some 311 systems provide callers with a 'tracking number' so they can check on the status of their service request.
- It can promote coordination of city services. Regardless of which agency staffs the 311 line, planning the service and operating it effectively require significant police involvement."

In Dallas, where 311 is a city service, call takers noted that 311 reduced the number of times citizen callers were transferred when trying to reach various city departments. In addition, the 311 call takers felt they were knowledgeable and helpful regarding all city services, and that by knowing the bigger picture, they could deal with an extensive range of citizen problems.

All of these responses to freeing officer time require change from the traditional police response and may be met with resistance by communities and officers. The key is to continue to provide the best service possible and to explain the reasons for changes. "Research shows that the public will not insist on an immediate response to a nonemergency service request if the alternative response is both appropriate and performed as described" (Community Policing Consortium Web site). To see examples of 311 call management strategies, check the Web sites of the Las Vegas Metro Police Department (www.lvmpd.com/home/311call.htm); the San Diego Police Department (www.sdpd.org/311.html) or the Washington (DC) Metropolitan Police Department (www.mpdc.dc.gov/info/phone/311.shtm).

Calls for Service and Problem Solving

The data departments obtain using Computer Aided Dispatch can be valuable in problem-solving efforts. The data can help identify top problem locations, hot spots, repeat callers and help to predict emerging problem locations. Table 7.2 shows the percent of departments using problem-solving measures or planning to do so using call for service data.

In addition to call management, many departments are finding that they can improve citizens' participation in community policing and build trust through citizen police academies.

Table 7.2 Percent of Departments Using Problem-Solving Measures*

Measures	***Currently Doing***	***Plan to Do***	***No Plan to Do***
Identifying top problem locations	92	7	1
Reporting/analyzing frequency of call types	84	13	3
Conducting "hot spot" analysis	66	23	12
Identifying repeat callers	65	17	18
Capturing and using premise history	61	27	12
Predicting emerging problem locations/areas	58	32	10
Assessing problem-solving efforts through change in number of calls	50	29	22
Determining which officers are performing problem-solving efforts	44	30	26
Assessing problem-solving efforts through displacement	32	28	40

*Totals may not equal 100 percent due to rounding.

SOURCE: Tom McEwen, Deborah Spencer, Russell Wolff, Julie Wartell and Barbara Webster. *Call Management in Community Policing: A Guidebook for Law Enforcement.* Washington DC: U.S. Department of Justice, Office of Community Oriented Policing Services, February 2003, p.104.

Citizen Police Academies

Citizen police academies educate the public about the nature of police work and encourage their involvement in crime prevention and problem-solving efforts.

According to Bonello and Schafer (2002, p.19): "Citizen police academies (CPA), workshops for citizens about local crime and police operations, have become so popular in the United States that by 2002, 45% of police and sheriff's agencies were offering some type of CPA. Some even are designed especially for youths, senior citizens or immigrants." They note that the typical academy is held over 10 or 11 weeks, meeting one evening a week for three hours. CPAs are popular among community members too. Many agencies have waiting lists for admission to the next academy. Designed to give the participants a basic view of crime and policing in their community, many chiefs and sheriffs believe CPAs improve public relations and help build partnerships between the citizens and the police. Little research has been done on CPAs to learn what impact they are actually having.

Most academies include lectures, demonstrations, a ride-along with an officer and an opportunity for participants to try their hand at some police technical skills. For participants, the experience is a rare opportunity to get an insider's view of the police or sheriff's department. They learn about the challenges faced by police officers and the complex nature of the job and come to better understand police procedures. Does the experience change community attitudes or improve the relationship between the police and the community? Bonello and Schafer describe what has happened with the Citizen Police Academy in Lansing, Michigan.

The Lansing Police Department, which has had a CPA since the early 1990s, used a survey of all its CPA graduates to evaluate its program. Key findings are as follows:

- Participants increased their knowledge, by large percentages, of crime, safety, community policing and police activities.
- The number of participants who were motivated to volunteer to support police department programs increased modestly.
- Seventy-four percent of respondents changed their view of media reports about the police.
- All respondents had positive or very positive views of the police department. Five stated they had a negative view when they started the program. Four of those had a positive or very positive impression of the department upon completion of the academy. Seventy-seven percent stated they viewed the department differently after attending the academy and overwhelmingly, their views changed in a positive direction.
- Ninety-eight percent of the respondents told others of their experience.
- Ninety-four percent of the respondents were more likely to collaborate with the police to solve a problem.

The survey results indicated that the Lansing Police Department was meeting its goals with its CPA program. They decided the program would have even more impact if they recruited future participants in different segments of the community because, in Lansing, and elsewhere, typical participants in CPAs hold positive impressions of the police before they enroll in a CPA.

Candidates for CPA programs are screened before being accepted into most programs and anyone with a criminal history is usually automatically excluded. Some have suggested that CPAs might want to reconsider this practice in the case of very minor offenses or in cases where the offense(s) occurred many years ago. In Lansing's case, the survey results revealed that the department needed to capitalize on many graduates of CPAs' willingness to volunteer and collaborate with the department to solve neighborhood problems, yet there was only a modest increase in graduates being involved in these ways.

Bonnelo and Schafer (p.6) note: "The LPD has begun to take steps to recruit their detractors to join the CPA. Such efforts include providing CPA applications to those who contact internal affairs about minor complaints or misunderstandings which stem from a lack of knowledge about police procedures; encouraging leaders in minority communities to attend the academy; and discussing the CPA on a radio talk show that has a large minority audience. . . . For agencies hoping to strengthen community alliances, the challenge for the future is to begin including a broader range of the public in their citizen police academy programs. . . . Agencies need to improve relationships with those citizens who mistrust or feel alienated from their police, which is especially important if an agency hopes to succeed in carrying out community policing."

In addition to providing CPAs, police departments might identify some key collaborators and be certain they are included in community policing efforts.

Some Key Collaborators

Key collaborators who might be overlooked include prosecutors, courts, corrections, other government agencies, private security providers, victims, the elderly and even such groups as taxi drivers.

Prosecutors

As community policing evolves, new collaborations continue to emerge. Including the prosecutor as a partner is one collaboration gaining popularity and for good reason. Community members' concerns are often not murder or robbery but the types of things that contribute to neighborhood decline and fear of crime, such as abandoned buildings, heavy neighborhood traffic or street-drug dealing. These neighborhood stability issues are frequently addressed by police, but prosecutors tend to see them as low priority or not important. When prosecutors become involved as partners in community policing, they attend neighborhood meetings, ride with officers on their beats and get a completely different view of the kinds of things that devastate communities and that breed more crime and disorder. As Swope (2001, p.11) explains: "In addressing the level of fear, the quality of life and disorder, the police and the community at some point will have to employ law enforcement tools as a tactic. Along with the police, the community can identify the problems needing a law enforcement response and they can team up and collaborate in the application of such a response. But the police are only the gatekeepers, and the law enforcement effort really has no teeth without the support of the prosecutor."

According to Goldkamp et al. (2002, p.1): "Community prosecution initiatives put into practice the belief that crime problems are best prevented and solved when community members work with prosecutors and the police."

Key Dimensions

GoldenKamp et al. (pp.2–3) explain:

Like other community justice innovations, community prosecution strategies vary according to the needs and circumstances of each locality, but they share underlying features. Seven key dimensions characterize community prosecution initiatives. These dimensions are (1) the target problems, (2) the geographic target area, (3) the role of the community, 4) the content of the response to community problems, (5) organizational changes within the prosecutor's office, (6) case processing adaptations, and (7) interagency collaboration and partnerships relating to the initiative. Drawing on the 38 identified community prosecution programs, Table 7.3 illustrates the diversity of problems confronted by community prosecution and the variety of strategies programs use to address these problems.

Table 7.3 Key Dimensions of Community Prosecution Strategies

Key Dimensions	***Examples from the Sites***
1. Target Problems/Goals	Quality-of-life offenses. Drug crime. Gang violence. Violent crime. Juvenile crime. Truancy. Prostitution. Housing and environmental issues. Landlord/tenant issues. Failure of the justice system to address community needs. Community alienation from prosecutor and other justice agencies. Improved cooperation of victims/witnesses. Improved intelligence gathering for prosecution of serious cases.
2. Target Area	Urban/inner city. Rural/suburban. Business districts. Residential neighborhoods.
3. Role of the Community	Recipient of prosecutor services. Advisory. Core participants in problem solving. Core participants in implementation. Community justice panels. Sanctioning panels. Ad hoc. Targeted.
4. Content of Response to Community Problems	Facilitating community self-help. Crime prevention efforts. Prosecuting cases of interest to the community. Receiving noncriminal as well as complaints.
5. Organizational Adaptations/ Emphasis	Field offices staffed by attorneys. Field offices staffed by nonattorneys. Attorneys assigned to neighborhoods. Special unit or units. Officewide organization around community prosecution model.
6. Case Processing Adaptations	Vertical prosecution. Horizontal prosecution. Community prosecutors do not prosecute cases.
7. Interagency Collaboration/ Partnerships	Police. City attorney. Housing authority. Community court/other court. Other justice agencies (probation, pretrial services). Other social services agencies. Other regulatory agencies.

SOURCE: John S. GoldKamp, Cheryl Irons-Gaynn and Doris Weiland. "Community Prosecution Strategies: Measuring Impact." Washington, DC: Bureau of Justice Assistance Bulletin, November 2002, pp.2–3.

Mike Kuykendall, manager of the Community Prosecution Program American Prosecutors Research Institute, Alexandria, Virginia, contends: "[Community prosecution is] a grassroots effort by the local elected prosecutor to get their assistant prosecutors, citizens, local government resources, police and other stakeholders in the community involved in identifying low-level criminal offenses and neighborhood livability issues and engaging in long-term solutions to those offenses. The emphasis is not on arrest and prosecution, but on learning new ways to prevent crime from occurring. . . . That's the vision the federal government has embraced as have the majority of jurisdictions now practicing community prosecution. . . . We do on occasion see prosecutors who claim they're embracing community prosecution by putting lawyers in the field to do just drug prosecutions or other traditional prosecution, but that's not really community prosecution because that's not involving the community in solving problems that affect their neighborhood." The similarities to community policing are many and as you will see in the following project profile, work well in conjunction with community policing.

Portland Neighborhood D.A. Program (OR) (adapted from the Web site of Community Justice [www.communityjustice.org]) Like most prosecutors, Portland District Attorney Michael D. Schrunk came into office ready to do battle with the county's most heinous criminals. "I always thought if I took care of murders, rapes and robberies, I'd be a hero," Schrunk says. And then Schrunk learned that his constituents wanted him to pay as much attention to quality-of-life problems as he did to the serious crimes that make the papers. "I got out into the community and found out they wanted me to take care of the small things—speeding, someone urinating in a doorway, a one rock [cocaine] sale on a corner."

A community policing initiative was already working on these quality-of-life crimes, but Schrunk believed his office also had a role to play. "The police and community would hammer out good ideas and then they'd say, 'But can we do that? Is that legal?' And many great, slam-dunk strategies ended up on the floor because the police involved were not sure if it was legal and they'd never heard of anyone doing it before so they just said 'No' to be safe. It became apparent that community policing could be exponentially greater if we had a community prosecutor in place to provide on-going legal strategic advice to bring together both practical and legal solutions to these street behavior problems," says Pearson, who led Portland's foray into community prosecution as Multnomah County's first neighborhood D.A.

Schrunk launched the community prosecution program in downtown Portland's Lloyd District, where business leaders were worried that quality-of-life crimes were detracting from efforts to convert the area, which is about 10 by 15 blocks, into a major commercial center. The business group actually paid Pearson's salary, a fact that demonstrated its strong support for the project but also created a stir when a local newspaper called him a "hired gun" in a front-page headline. Critics quoted in the article suggested that this meant the D.A.'s office was for sale, and that the rich could "buy" the prosecutor's services.

But instead of a backlash against the newly launched Neighborhood D.A. Program, county residents rallied behind it. "The result of the article was that Mike [Schrunk] got calls from a lot of different people saying 'We want one, too.'" Since that moment of crisis in 1990 Schrunk has expanded the program to cover the entire county with seven neighborhood D.A.s paid for with mostly public money. (The $772,331 annual budget is funded through an array of sources, including the county, a federal block grant and the local public transportation agency. Other government sources, such as the police and the cities of Portland and Gresham, provide office space and legal assistants, and the downtown business group provides office space and the salary of a legal assistant.)

Pearson met frequently with stakeholders—the business leaders, store owners, residents and people who worked in the area—who told him again and again that they were most concerned and bothered by the low-level offenses that had given the district a seedy reputation: public drinking, prostitution, vandalism, public urination, littering and car thefts.

Pearson's first initiative in the Lloyd District focused on illegal camping in Sullivan's Gulch. The business community considered the large number of transients who called the gulch home a public nuisance and blamed them for a significant number of petty crimes in the area. Traditional enforcement—occasional arrests of outstanding troublemakers—was not working, and Pearson and the police agreed that it was not realistic to commit police resources to continually arrest those who violated the city's no-camping ordinance. Especially since jail space was at a premium, offenders would likely be back on the street within hours of their arrest, and sanctions, if any, would not be imposed for months or even years. "As a prosecutor, I knew that the traditional tools weren't going to work," Pearson explains.

Pearson pulled together citizens and police to tackle the problem. But before devising a strategy, he took stock of his resources. "For any strategy in my estimation to outlast a problem, you can't keep throwing money at it and expect the strategy to still be in place six months from now or two years from now. You take stock of the human resources that are already there. If you have one district officer and that's all you've got, you don't build a model on 15 officers working overtime; how long will that last? A week? A month?" Pearson says: "In this instance, the resources at hand included 12 committed volunteers from the business community, plus general police coverage of the area. There was also an annual, city-financed cleanup of the gulch. The city spent up to $40,000 every spring to clean the gulch, removing the garbage and debris that the transients had left behind over the past year."

Transients returned immediately following the cleanup. This time, however, Pearson had brightly colored "No Camping" signs posted in the gulch. On the back of the signs were shelter locations. The 12 community members were each assigned a particular section of the gulch to drive by two or three times a week. When they spotted illegal campsites, they notified Pearson who contacted the district patrol officer. The officer went to the campsites and asked the people to leave. Almost always, the transients were cooperative. "The whole issue was to tell people they can't be there, to send a strong consistent sensitive message: 'You can't be there.' It sounds too simple, I know," Pearson says.

Pearson drew in other city agencies to clean out brush, making it harder for campers to hide, and also installed bars under highway viaducts—another location where the transients had previously concealed themselves. Eventually the citizens on patrol began on their own to ask campers to leave—although they asked Pearson first if it was legal for them to do so. Pearson explained that it was well within the law for anyone to tell transients that they were violating a city ordinance by squatting on city property. Emboldened with their knowledge of the law, some of the volunteers even gave the transients garbage bags and asked them to clean up after themselves.

The volunteers' willingness to do the work saved police resources, reflecting what Pearson calls the community's "barn-raising mentality"—a do-it-yourself attitude that Pearson feels is essential for effective neighborhood problem solving. In short order, the problem of illegal camping in Sullivan's Gulch was solved and area stakeholders saw a decline in quality-of-life problems on their streets. "The City of Portland has never had to go down there and spend another nickel on a cleanup," Pearson proudly points out. Citizens have continued the patrols for the last nine years although the number of volunteers has dropped to about four. Still, "there's almost never anyone in the gulch anymore," Pearson says.

Schrunk says being a neighborhood D.A. "means getting in the community and trying to solve problems at the lowest possible level and when appropriate, making lightning strike—an indictment or filing a charge. They're looking for long-term systemic infrastructure solutions to problems that are causes of or breeding grounds for criminal conduct."

Community Courts

A recent alternative to the traditional courtroom is the community court. As Goldkamp et al. (2001, p.7) state: "Community courts differ in the kinds of problems they have been designed to address, including a wide range of low-level offenses, from public order violations, graffiti, nuisance crimes, prostitution and minor drug offenses to illegal vending and panhandling. . . . Depending on the highest priority problems and the locations selected by community court strategies, courts also differ in the specific types of offenders and/or cases they will prosecute." Goldkamp et al. (p.26) note: "An important feature of the Hartford court is the collaborative participation of state and city social service agencies. Although the city took the early lead in providing social services, an arrangement was negotiated whereby responsibility could be shared with state agencies. The resulting service delivery system is virtually seamless." Goldkamp et al. (p.27) note the special significance of the Hartford Police Department:

> Police cooperation in the enforcement of quality-of-life offenses and in working with the courts and neighborhoods to address community crime problems is essential to the community court strategy. . . . Individually certain community

service officers have developed constructive relationships with the community court, believing that the court offers an immediate and visible response to the quality-of-life offenses that are so disruptive to the community and a convenient way to process the most frequent types of complaints.

To these officers, issuing summonses makes processing offenders much easier than completing the paperwork required for a normal arrest that would be adjudicated in the traditional court, where little may happen to the offender for the efforts involved. They believe the risk of a community court arrest deters criminals from carrying guns or drugs because they fear being caught with these when arrested on a minor matter such as loitering. The officers also believe the community service sanction is a strong deterrent for the types of offenders targeted by the court. They have noted a particularly positive impact on open prostitution in some neighborhoods.

In May 2000, as part of a quality-of-life enforcement action supported by a BJA Local Law Enforcement Block Grant and conducted by the Community Response Division, police officials met with the community court team and community representatives to identify quality-of-life problems and high-priority target areas or "hotspots" in each neighborhood. Those priority areas have been reviewed periodically since then and have been the focus of enforcement activity. During that time, the community court has seen a steady growth in the number of cases it receives, leveling off near expected peak levels, particularly in the area of crimes identified by the residents and the court as vital for enforcement: public drinking and excessive noise.

The third component of the criminal justice system, corrections, also is an often overlooked partner in the community policing effort.

Community Corrections

As noted by Wrobleski and Hess (2003, p.445): "Community corrections includes any activities in the community aimed at helping offenders become law-abiding citizens and request a complicated interplay among judicial and correctional personnel from related public and private agencies, citizen volunteers and civic groups." According to Etter and Hammond (2001, p.114) community service work is often a part of offenders' sentences and plays a role in their rehabilitation.

One important partnership that has proven successful is that between a patrol officer and a probation officer in the same neighborhood. Probation officers who ride along with patrol officers can often spot probationeers violating a condition of their probation, and the officer can make an immediate arrest. Or the probation officer can talk with the offending probationeer, letting him or her know that the illegal activities will no longer go unnoticed.

Leitenberger et al. (2003, p.20) describe what they call a "perfect match" between community corrections and community policing in Richland County, Ohio, to enhance post-release control (PRC) or supervision of offenders who have completed their sentences. They explain: "Richland County formed a community corrections board composed of citizens and representatives from the court system, law enforcement agencies, local government organizations, social service agencies and victim services, to study current supervision and treatment methods and criminal offender profiles in Richland County to determine how best to safely and effectively supervise correctional clients in the community." This board recommended the partnering of the probation office, the sheriff's department, the police department and the regional state parole office. This partnership allowed the intensive supervision program (ISP) employing electronic monitoring bracelets that enabled any police or corrections officer equipped with a drive-by or hand-held unit to identify and closely monitor offenders. They (p.22) contend: "Statistics seem to support the assertion of Richland County authorities that unified supervision programs result in lower crime rates."

Other Government Agencies

Criminal justice agencies are not the only local government agencies responsible for responding to community problems. Partnering with other city and county departments and agencies is important to problem-solving success. Sometimes described as **working in "silos,"** local government agencies and departments have traditionally worked quite independently of each other. Under community policing, appropriate government departments and agencies are called on and recognized for their abilities to respond to and address crime and social disorder issues. Fire departments, building inspections, health departments, street departments, park and recreation and child welfare frequently are appropriate and necessary stakeholders in problem-solving initiatives.

State and federal agencies may also be of assistance, including the FBI, the DEA, the U.S. attorney in the region, the state's attorney, the state criminal investigative agency and the state highway department.

Private Security Providers

Samuels (2002, p.6) notes: "We are not the only protective force operating in towns and cities around the globe. Private-sector security represents a vast and vital resource, and we must strengthen our existing partnership with this profession. The events of September 11, the frequency and impact of public protests resulting in civil disobedience or criminal violations, and the fiscal and psychological consequences of Internet-related crime demonstrates a need for greater communication and cooperation."

Recognizing this need, the International Association of Chiefs of Police held a summit in early 2004 to discuss possible collaborations between public and private police around the issue of terrorism. Their goal is to develop a national strategy to build such partnerships between federal, state, tribal and local public sector police agencies and private security agencies. The focus of such partnerships will be terrorism prevention and response. The summit was supported by the Office of Community Oriented Policing Services (COPS). The summit also looked at the drawbacks to such collaboration and there are some significant ones. There are differences in the screening, hiring, training and policy between private security and public police officers.

Current estimates of public-sector policing strength by the Bureau of Justice Statistics indicate that there are 16,661 state, local and county law enforcement agencies in the United States, and they employ a total of 677,933 sworn officers. Studies on private security force staffing indicate there may be as many as 10,000 private security agencies employing slightly less than 2 million private security officers in the United States. Clearly, if these numbers are accurate, then private security officers are a vast potential resource that can assist law enforcement agencies in fulfilling their mission.

In addition, many retired police officials at the federal, state and local level migrate to post-retirement positions within private sector security. These officers, supervisors and executives are dispersed across the many security firms nationally. For example, one retired FBI agent, an expert in counterintelligence, now works for a detective agency specializing in employee background checks. A former director of a state police agency now runs the security division for a major bank.

Victims

Bringing Victims into Community Policing (2002, p.4) suggests: "Victims are stakeholders. Police usually treat victims as clients, with services being delivered to them. While victims of crime do need help, they are also key participants in the immediate response to the crime, the ongoing investigation of the incident and efforts to prevent a recurrence. By approaching victims as powerful and resourceful stakeholders, police can have a greater impact on crime and perceptions of community safety."

Bringing Victims into Community Policing notes: "Victim service organizations offer unique opportunities for partnerships. Victim service organizations (VSO) have unique knowledge and capabilities that could enhance efforts to investigate and prevent crime. Victims often give different kinds of crime-related information to counselors at VSOs than they would to a police officer. Still respecting the confidentiality of their clients, VSOs can identify patterns of crime as well as gaps and deficiencies in police services that police may not know of otherwise, participate in problem-solving activities, and help to prevent repeat victimization."

This same resource guide (p.5) states: "Partnership is key to preventing repeat victimization. There is an opportunity to transform society's response to crime by building collaborative relationships between victims of crime, the organizations that serve them and police. Because the time that officers can spend with victims is limited, police organizations should develop responses that include civilian employees and other non-police agencies and organizations. By breaking down organizational barriers and building strategic alliances, police can improve the response to victims without necessarily increasing their workload."

The Elderly

Elderly people fear crime, especially violent crime, and that fear causes many to remain in their homes. Police department crime prevention programs aimed specifically at the elderly can help immensely, and the elderly are usually enthusiastic about participating in a department's special efforts. Such programs can remind seniors to have their social security checks deposited directly in their bank, to not carry much cash or other valuables on their person and to let go of a purse if it is grabbed. Too many senior citizens have tried to hold on to their purses and been dragged along, suffering broken bones and other injuries.

To help the elderly avoid victimization, police might start a block or building watch, set up a daily telephone-contact program or enroll the elderly in Operation ID. These programs will help prevent crime and improve police–community relations among the elderly, as well as the rest of the community, by demonstrating the professional concern the police department has for its elderly citizens.

Police departments across the United States have developed many effective partnerships for older citizens. Such partnerships can easily be adapted to other communities and are successful because they can reduce victimization, reduce the fear of crime and improve police–community relations. Honolulu, for example, has a Senior Citizen Watch Program where organized senior citizen groups become the eyes and ears for the department.

Local law enforcement is also a vital element in the National Aging Services Network, a collaboration of federal, state and local agencies and services brought together under the Older Americans Act of 1965 and overseen by the Administration on Aging (AOA). The AOA works to heighten awareness among other federal agencies, organizations and the public about the valuable contributions older Americans make to the nation and alerts them to the needs of vulnerable older people. Figure 7.3 illustrates this network and helps officers identify resources available to address the needs and concerns of the elderly.

Older Volunteers with Law Enforcement Seniors make excellent volunteers. The AOA notes: "Older Americans represent a great reservoir of talent, experience, and knowledge which can and is being used to better their communities and the Nation." Older people tend to be dependable, experienced, stable, available, trainable, committed, skilled, conscientious and service oriented. In addition, older volunteers have fewer accidents, are more careful of equipment than younger volunteers, use good judgment, follow directions, like to avoid trouble, have good attendance records and tend to be team players.

Police departments across the country staff innovative programs with elderly citizens. Older volunteers are involved in neighborhood-watch clubs and anonymous reporting and court-watch programs and provide extensive benefits to both the police department and the community.

Benefits to a police department that uses senior volunteers may include improved service delivery, increased cost effectiveness, relief of sworn personnel for other duties, improved public image, enhanced understanding of police functions, provision of new

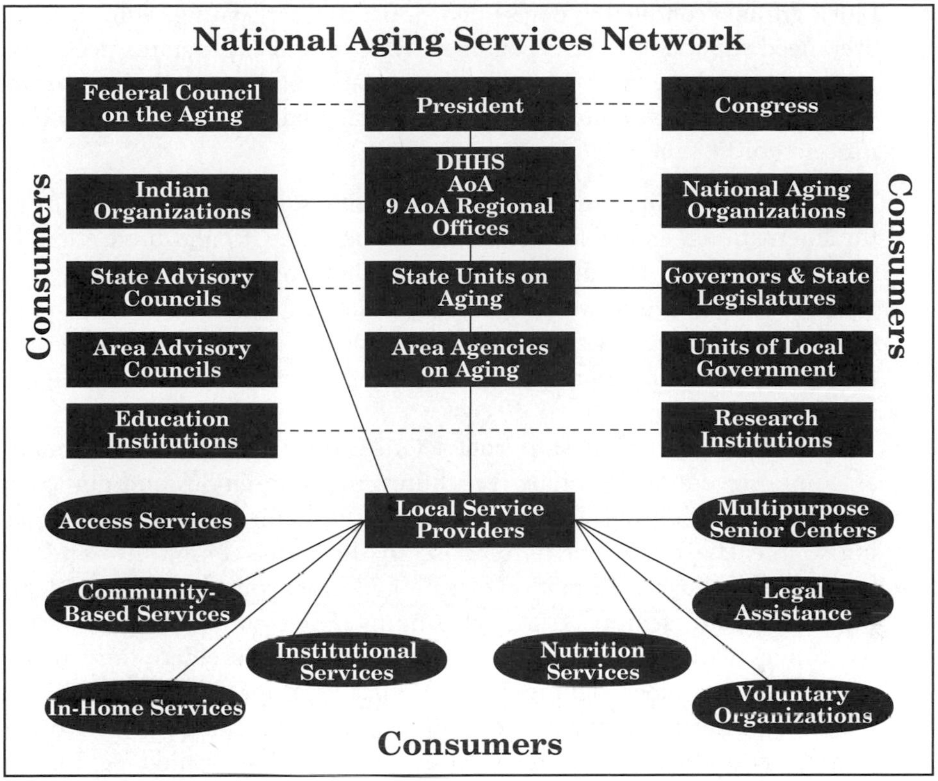

Figure 7.3 National Aging Services Network
SOURCE: AOA.

program opportunities, increased political support, restored community responsibility, reduced crime and increased property values.

In addition, volunteers may benefit from reduced fear of crime, use of their skills and expertise, the opportunity to help others, enrichment of their daily lives and a greater sense of belonging and worth. These benefits, compiled by the American Association of Retired Persons (AARP), are by no means exhaustive. Police-sponsored programs that use elderly volunteers have, however, raised some concerns.

Concerns about Using Seniors as Volunteers One frequently expressed concern is that volunteers may do police officers' duties, thereby affecting future departmental hiring decisions. Other concerns are that volunteers need to be supervised while working in the department or that they may come in contact with sensitive or confidential material.

Volunteer programs can be tailored to address most objections. Volunteers rarely perform actual police functions. They frequently work in programs the department could not otherwise afford to provide such as fingerprinting children, distributing literature, maintaining equipment, entering computer data, organizing block groups, conducting department tours and translating. Volunteers do, however, need supervision and recognition, and volunteer programs need a coordinator to handle those tasks. In some cases a staff member can act as coordinator, or, when an extensive volunteer program is anticipated, a department may enlist a volunteer coordinator.

TRIAD—A Coordinated Approach A joint resolution was adopted by the AARP, the International Association of Chiefs of Police (IACP) and the National Sheriffs' Association (NSA) to address criminal victimization of older people. The three organizations agreed to work together to design interjurisdictional approaches and partnerships to reduce victimization of older persons, assist those who have been victimized and generally enhance law enforcement services to older adults and the community.

This three-way partnership, called **TRIAD**, provides specific information such as crime prevention materials (brochures, program guides and audiovisual presentations on crime prevention and the elderly), policies, exemplary projects relating to the law enforcement response to the older community and successful projects involving the formation of senior advisory councils to advise departments on the needs of seniors. TRIAD also trains police about aging, communication techniques with elderly citizens, victimization of the elderly and management programs using older volunteers. TRIAD has been identified as a concrete example of community policing. Leadership is provided by an advisory group of older persons and those providing services to the elderly called Seniors and Law Enforcement Together (SALT). The organizational structure of SALT is illustrated in Figure 7.4.

Taxi Drivers

Haldar (2001, p.13) says New York City has 12,000 cabs on the streets all hours of the day and night, and almost half their time is spent cruising for fares. He estimates cab drivers in New York are eight times more likely than the average citizen to witness or be involved in crimes and emergencies. Haldar explains how the New York Police Department capitalizes on this partnership through "Cab Watch":

> Cab Watch broadens the city's reach in law enforcement without spending a dime of tax money. With the help of the New York Police Department, Cab Watch trains cab drivers to report incidents and accidents without putting themselves or others at risk. Then, it outfits the drivers with 911-direct wireless phones, which are donated by Sprint PCS. More than 40 professionals have volunteered to help Cab Watch with management, accounting, public relations and graphic design. . . .
>
> In the last two years, Cab Watch has expanded from a 50-driver pilot program to more than 1,700 drivers outfitted with wireless phones and ready to dial 911 on the spot. Drivers have alerted police to hundreds of incidents, helping to lead to the arrest of suspects in slayings, hit-and-runs, burglaries, assaults, even incidents of pick-pocketing. The cabbies' quick calls also have helped save lives in car accidents and building fires.

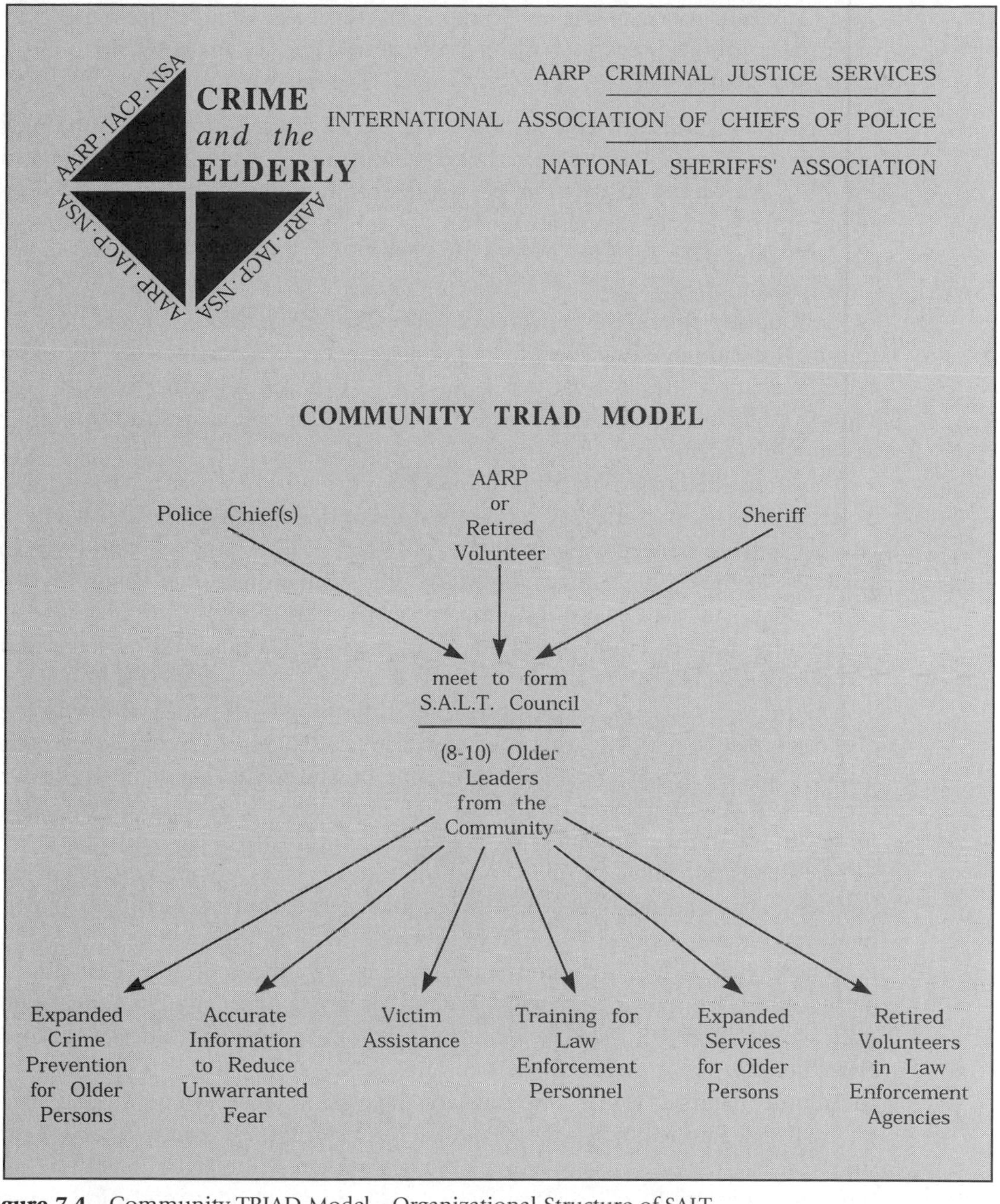

Figure 7.4 Community TRIAD Model—Organizational Structure of SALT

SOURCE: *Crime and the Elderly.* AARP Criminal Justice Services. Reprinted by permission.

Building Partnerships in a Variety of Neighborhoods

The effective mobilization of community support requires different approaches in different communities. Establishing trust and obtaining cooperation are often easier in middle-class and affluent communities than in poorer communities, where mistrust of police may have a long history.

Building partnerships in lower income neighborhoods may be more difficult because often there are fewer resources and less trust between the citizens and law enforcement.

Building bonds in some neighborhoods may involve supporting basic social institutions (e.g., families, churches, schools) that have been weakened by pervasive crime or disorder. The creation of viable communities is necessary if lasting alliances that nurture cooperative efforts are to be sustained. Under community policing, the police become both catalysts and facilitators in the development of these communities.

Community policing expands police efforts to prevent and control crime. The community is no longer viewed by police as a passive presence or a source of limited information, but as a partner in this effort. Community concerns with crime and disorder thus become the target of efforts by the police and the community working in tandem.

The close alliance forged with the community should neither be limited to an isolated incident or series of incidents nor confined to a specific time frame. The partnership between the police and the community must be enduring and balanced. It must break down the old concepts of professional versus civilian, expert versus novice and authority figure versus subordinate. The police and the community must be collaborators in the quest to encourage and preserve peace and prosperity.

The more conspicuous police presence of the long-term patrol officer in itself may encourage community response, but it is not sufficient. The entire police organization must vigorously enlist the cooperation of community residents in pursuing the goals of deterring crime and preserving order. Police personnel on every level must join in building a broad rapport with community members.

For the patrol officer, police–community partnership entails talking to local business owners to help identify their problems and concerns, visiting residents in their homes to offer advice on security and helping to organize and support neighborhood-watch groups and regular community meetings. For example, the patrol officer will canvass the neighborhood for information about a string of burglaries and then revisit those residents to inform them when the burglar is caught. The chief police executive will explain and discuss controversial police tactics so community members understand the necessity of these tactics for public and officer safety. The department management will consult community members about gang suppression tactics, and every level of the department will actively solicit the concerns and suggestions of community groups, residents, leaders and local government officials. In this police–community partnership, providing critical social services will be acknowledged as being inextricably linked to deterring crime, and problem solving will become a cooperative effort.

Successful Partnerships in Action

The following examples of successful partnerships range from very simple to award-winning programs.

Partnerships to Accommodate the Homeless

To address the challenges presented by homelessness, the police need to partner with many organizations, from detoxification facilities to children's shelters, from hospital crisis units to county social services. Police also need to move beyond the arrest-and-detain mentality and take on the role of educator and facilitator, making the homeless aware of available services and encouraging them to seek appropriate assistance. Fabyankovic (2000, p.113) notes: "As the national trend seems to hint toward criminalizing those who have no home, several cities have found productive approaches to deal with these concerns." An example of such an innovative effort is seen in Oregon (p.113).

> Until recently, many Oregon police officers regularly swept encampments of homeless people after giving occupants a 24-hour notice. Now, through a collaboration with JOIN: A Center for Involvement and the Oregon Department of Transportation, two Portland officers and two JOIN outreach workers identify low profile encampment areas. The police allow the homeless to remain in these encampments while the outreach workers find them shelters, housing and services as a smooth transition.

This project has improved relations between the city's police and its homeless residents, who now view the officers as helpful friends who are not harassing them. The plan is so successful that it is guaranteed funding in future years.

A More Complex Partnership

Rinehart et al. (p.8) provide the following example (quoted):

> ***Communication/Networking***
>
> Sheriff Smith meets Principal Gibson at a community meeting. Principal Gibson shares with Sheriff Smith that over the past several weeks some students have complained that in the student parking lot at Dogwood High School, trash has been dumped into the backs of pickup trucks, key marks have been scratched onto several cars, and textbooks and backpacks have been stolen from unlocked vehicles. Sheriff Smith shares with Principal Gibson that similar problems have been occurring in the neighborhood adjacent to Dogwood High School and in the parking lot of a pizza place one block away.
>
> ***Cooperation***
>
> Sheriff Smith asks Principal Gibson to call the department when another incident occurs so that a deputy can capture the incident in a report and take a look at the scene for any evidence of who committed the offense. Principal Gibson agrees to call.
>
> ***Coordination***
>
> To avoid duplication of efforts, Principal Gibson and Sheriff Smith also agree that a copy of the county incident report will be supplied to the school so that it may be kept in the school's incident records—in lieu of filing a second report with the same information. If a deputy cannot come to the school immediately,

Principal Gibson offers to capture the necessary information and obtain a statement and contact information from the witness or victim that reported the problem. He will then fax the information to the dispatcher. Sheriff Smith offers his appreciation.

Collaboration Forming

Several weeks later, after reviewing several incident reports from Dogwood High School involving vandalism and theft in the student parking lot, Sheriff Smith calls Principal Gibson to suggest that their organizations initiate a problem-solving project to address the ongoing pattern of vandalism and theft in the student parking lot and the surrounding area. Sheriff Smith and Principal Gibson assign Deputy Morgan and Coach Lee as the primary partners in the effort. Principal Gibson offers a classroom as a meeting facility, and Sheriff Smith assures Principal Gibson that his crime analysis division will provide data analysis support.

Successful Law Enforcement/Community Partnership in Action

Throughout the next six months, Deputy Morgan and Coach Lee bring other stakeholders into the partnership (e.g., the pizza shop manager, local block watch president, student victims, Project SAVE club members, school janitor and a social science teacher who agreed to write a report on the project and conduct an evaluation). They met to talk about the purpose of their partnership and the types of tasks (e.g., interviews with student and neighborhood victims, environmental analysis, review of police/school incident reports, mapping the location of the incidents, interviews with suspects, review of the student parking lot access and policies, review of school activity schedules, response development, fundraising and evaluation of the responses) and resources required for the problem-solving effort to succeed. They wrote their vision, tasks, timeline and resource needs down in an action plan, ensuring that every partner received a copy.

The partners met every two weeks (sometimes at school, sometimes at the pizza place, and a few times at a local park a few blocks from school) to exchange information, report on progress, determine whether other partners or stakeholders should be added, and to celebrate milestones achieved (e.g., interviews completed, fundraising success, responses implemented). At the end of six months, the partners had implemented responses that resulted in a number of positive changes. For instance, there was a reduction of theft from vehicles in the school parking lot and neighborhood, better foot and vehicle traffic flow through the parking lot and increased trash removal leading to improved appearance. In addition, a team of individuals who learned the value of teamwork were acknowledged in the school and the local paper, and were also awarded honors by the sheriff and principal for their efforts. The partners have decided to continue working together on other problem-solving projects in and around the school.

IACP Community Policing Award-Winning, Category—Agency Serving a Population of 100,001 to 250,000 Residents—Halton, Ontario, Regional Police Service

The Problem

For several years, the youthful patrons of the NRG nightclub in Halton were creating an enormous problem for the neighborhood and the police. Drawing from an area population of 8.8 million people in Ontario and New York, 1,200 to 1,800 young people were at the club on Saturday nights. NRG and the surrounding area were the scene of violent crimes, damage to property, parking complaints, trespassing, vehicle theft, gang activity, drug trafficking, underage drinking and social disorder. Off-duty officers working at the club were overwhelmed by the sheer numbers of patrons and problems. They required so much assistance from on-duty officers that department resources were being drained to the detriment of other areas of the city. Two riots at the club within 10 days resulted in 300 unruly patrons who caused injuries to other patrons, officers and the neighborhood.

The Solution

Aware that their reactive efforts to this point had no effect, the department built a collaborative partnership and, using the SARA model, tackled the problem with great success. With a goal of improving the quality of life and safety for the neighborhood, the police began working with an adjacent city, with local residents and business owners to get their input in identifying priorities that had to be addressed immediately. Their effort to close the club failed, and they moved on to developing other strategies.

Because the problem was so big, they built multiple partnerships, creating the NRG Team. Twenty-eight stakeholders developed a plan that police officers implemented every Saturday night. The implementation, which focused on the club and the surrounding neighborhood, was critiqued every week and changed as needed, based on the previous week's results. Strategies included:

- Extra lighting and gates installed on private property near the club.
- Restricted neighborhood parking.
- A highly visible command post van, positioned within 15 feet of the front door of NRG.
- Club security personnel checks of patrons' IDs.
- Close police monitoring of the parking lot.
- Recording of license numbers by volunteers to be checked the following day for intelligence information.
- Prohibiting of all gang clothing from the club.
- Monitoring of nearby plazas and shopping centers for activity and nearby restaurants closed between 2 A.M. and 4 A.M. to discourage groups from gathering.
- Having departing patrons pass multiple uniformed officers on the way to the parking lot.

Partners also participated in this initiative by attending strategy meetings, paying for related changes to their properties, initiating training for employees on drugs and alcohol service, handling violent patrons, preventing underage drinking, providing cleanup in the neighborhood and providing translators for police and patrons as needed.

Evaluation

Crime decreased 75 percent in and around NRG. A public survey of neighborhood residents revealed an increase in their satisfaction with police from an already high 88 percent to 94 percent after the problem at NRG was dealt with. Analysis also showed a 1,500 percent increase in enforcement over a five-year period. In addition, patrons reported feeling safer at NRG. Over the five-year period, there were only six complaints relating to use of force.

SUMMARY

Partnerships usually result in a more effective solution to a problem because there are shared responsibilities, resources and goals. The core components of effective community partnerships are (1) stakeholders with a vested interest in the collaboration, (2) trusting relationships among and between the partners, (3) a shared vision and common goals for the collaboration, (4) expertise, (5) teamwork strategies, (6) open communication, (7) motivated partners, (8) means to implement and sustain the collaborative effort and (9) an action plan (Rinehart et al., p.6).

Traditional shift and beat rotation work to the detriment of building partnerships. The community (beat) for which a patrol officer is given responsibility should be a small, well-defined geographical area. Officers who have permanent assignments become experts about their beat.

The two factors most influencing citizens' perception of their police are personal contacts and perceptions of the quality of life in the community. In addition, demands on police from one community of interest can sometimes clash with the rights of another community of interest. Such conflicting interests may impede establishing a common vision and shared goals. When forming partnerships, conflicts within communities are as important to recognize as the commonalities. The benefits of participating in a partnership include (1) a sense of accomplishment from bettering the community, (2) gaining recognition and respect, (3) meeting other community members, (4) learning new skills and (5) fulfilling an obligation to contribute (Rinehart et al., p.2).

Criticism of the partnerships in community policing usually center on time and money. Departments might free up time for partnerships without expense through effective call management or call reduction. Large cities have begun to implement 311 lines to divert nonemergency calls from 911.

Departments might also enhance partnerships by providing citizen police academies. Such programs educate the public about the nature of police work and encourage involvement in crime prevention and problem-solving efforts. In addition, key collaborators who might be overlooked include prosecutors, courts, corrections, other government agencies, private security providers, victims, the elderly and even such groups as taxi drivers. Benefits to a police department that uses senior volunteers may include improved service delivery, increased cost effectiveness, relief of sworn personnel for other duties, improved public image, enhanced understanding of police functions, provision of new program opportunities, increased political support, restored community responsibility, reduced crime and increased property values.

Building partnerships in lower income neighborhoods may be more difficult because often there are fewer resources and less trust between the citizens and law enforcement.

Discussion Questions

1. What are the most important factors that lead you to trust another person? To distrust someone?
2. Have you been involved in a community partnership? What was the partnership trying to accomplish and what accounted for its success or failure?
3. Discuss the pros and cons of using volunteers in a law enforcement agency.
4. Select a community problem you feel is important and describe the partners who might be involved in a collaboration to address the problem.
5. Why are permanent shift and area assignments for officers important in community policing?
6. Why is trust an issue between police and residents of low-income neighborhoods?
7. What are the main criticisms or arguments against having police involved in community policing partnerships?
8. What strategies can help free up time for officer involvement in partnerships?
9. Explain the difference between community courts and traditional courts.
10. Discuss the problem of homeless people in American cities. Should they be treated as criminals?

InfoTrac College Edition Assignments

- Use InfoTrac College Edition to answer the Discussion Questions as appropriate.
- Select one of the following articles to read, outline and be prepared to share with the class.
  - "Citizen Police Academies: Do They Just Entertain?" by Elizabeth M. Bonello and Joseph A. Schafer
  - "Community Mobilization: The Foundation for Community Policing" by Recjea; Stewart-Brown
  - "Community Corrections and Community Policing: A Perfect Match" by David Leitenberger et al.
- Read "Patterns of Exclusion; Sanitizing Space, Criminalizing Homelessness" by Randall Amster. Discuss the article in light of Portland, Oregon's, problem-solving initiative in Sullivan's Gulch, which was highlighted in this chapter. Did the Sullivan's Gulch project work and for whom?

Community Project

Research local police and sheriff's departments' use of volunteers. Find out why they use volunteers or why not.

References

Bonello, Elizabeth M. and Schafer, Joseph A. "Citizen Police Academies: Do They Just Entertain?" *FBI Law Enforcement Bulletin,* November 2002, p.19.

Bringing Victims into Community Policing. Washington, DC: Community Oriented Policing Services and the National Center for Victims of Crime, September 17, 2002.

Carter, D.I. *The Police and the Community,* 7th ed. Englewood Cliffs, NJ: Prentice Hall, 2002.

Community Policing Consortium. www.communitypolicing.org/chap4fw.html

Etter, Gregg W. and Hammond, Judy. "Community Service Work as Part of Offender Rehabilitation." *Corrections Today,* October 2001, pp.114–115, 125.

Fabyankovic, Janet. "Alternatives to Homeless Criminalization." *Law and Order,* August 2000, pp.113–115.

Goldkamp, John S.; Weiland, Doris; and Irons-Guynn, Cheryl. *Developing an Evaluation Plan for Community Courts: Assessing the Hartford Community Court Model.* Washington, DC: Bureau of Justice Statistics Monograph, Community Justice Series 4, July 2001. (NCJ 185689)

Goldkamp, John S.; Irons-Guynn,Charyl; and Weiland, Doris. "Community Prosecution Strategies: Measuring Impact." *Bureau of Justice Assistance Bulletin,* November 2002.

Haldar, Sujoy. "NYC Cabbies Extend Police Reach." *Community Links,* March 2001, p.13.

Hawdon, James E.; Ryan, John; and Griffin, Sean P. "Policing Tactics and Perceptions of Police Legitimacy." *Police Quarterly,* December 2003, pp.469–491.

Jurik, Nancy C.; Blumenthal, Joel; Smith, Brian; and Portillos, Edwardo L. "Organizational Cooptation or Social Change?" *Journal of Contemporary Criminal Justice,* August, 2000, pp.293–320.

Leitenberger, David; Semenyna, Pete; and Spelman, Jeffrey B. "Community Corrections and Community Policing: A Perfect Match." *FBI Law Enforcement Bulletin,* November 2003, pp.20–23.

McEwen, Tom; Spencer, Deborah; Wolff, Russell; Wartell, Julie; and Webster, Barbara. *Call Management and Community Policing: A Guidebook for Law Enforcement.* Washington, DC: Community Oriented Policing Services, February 2003.

Rahtz, Howard. *Community Policing: A Handbook for Beat Cops and Supervisors.* Monsey, NY: Criminal Justice Press, 2001.

Reisig, Michael D. and Parks, Roger B. *Satisfaction with Police—What Matters?* Washington, DC: National Institute of Justice Research for Practice and Community Oriented Policing Services, October 2002.

Rinehart, Tammy A.; Laszlo, Anna T.; and Briscoe, Gwen O. *Collaboration Toolkit to Build, Fix, and Sustain Productive Partnerships.* Washington, DC: U.S. Department of Justice, Office of Community Oriented Policing Services, 2001.

Samuels, Joseph, Jr. "The Challenge Before Us." *The Police Chief,* November 2002, pp.8–9.

Schafer, Joseph A.; Huebner, Beth M.; and Bynum, Timothy S. "Citizen Perceptions of Police Services: Race, Neighborhood Context and Community Policing." *Police Quarterly,* December 2003, pp.440–468.

Scott, Michael S. *Problem-Oriented Policing: Reflections on the First 20 Years.* Washington, DC: Community Oriented Policing Services, October 2000.

Swope, Ross E. "Community Prosecution: The Real Deal." *Law Enforcement News,* January 15/31, 2001, pp.11, 14.

Understanding Community Policing: A Framework for Action. Washington, DC: Community Policing Consortium Monograph, August 1994. (NCJ 148957)

Wrobleski, Henry M. and Hess, Kären M. *Introduction to Law Enforcement and Criminal Justice,* 7th ed. Belmont, CA: Wadsworth Publishing Company, 2003.

CHAPTER 8

Forming Partnerships with the Media

Police work is very much an "us-and-them" kind of thing. They are the beleaguered minority who are out there protecting the citizens from themselves, and the citizens are not smart enough to appreciate them. And the newsies are out there lying in wait, and the moment they screw up, we're there to jump their throats and tell the world.

—Kevin Diaz

Do You Know?

- What the common goal of the police and the media is?
- Why the police–media relationship can be called symbiotic?
- What amendment protects freedom of the press?
- What amendment guides the police in their relationship with the media?
- What a national survey concluded regarding the police–media relationship?
- What legitimate reasons for not giving information to the press are?
- How to enhance the safety of members of the media during explosive situations?
- Whether conflict between the police and the press must be dysfunctional?
- What five interview failures are?
- Whether it is ever appropriate or justifiable to lie to the media?
- In a police–media relationship survey, what factor was found to most affect the relationship?
- Why reporters may foul up stories? What implications this has for law enforcement?
- How officers can improve relations with the media?
- Why partnerships with the media are critical to the successful implementation of community policing?

Can You Define?

anticipatory benefit
geographical diffusion of benefit
marketing mix
misinformation synergy
news media echo effect
Pager Information Network (PIN)
perp walks
PIO triangle
public information officers (PIOs)
sound bites
symbiotic

Introduction

"Do not underestimate the importance of the media as a vital ingredient in the community oriented policing recipe. The media has a tremendous impact on the public's perception of crime and criminal justice" (Buice, 2001, p.59). The media can be a powerful ally or a formidable opponent in implementing the community policing philosophy. Positive publicity can enhance both the image and the efforts of a department. Conversely, negative publicity can be extremely damaging. Therefore, police agencies can and should make every effort to build positive working partnerships with the media.

The police and members of the media share the common goal of serving the public.

In addition to sharing a common goal, they also rely heavily on each other.

This chapter begins with a discussion of the mutual reliance of the police and the media and the inherent conflict between the guarantees of the First Amendment and the Sixth Amendment. This is followed by an examination of victims' privacy rights. Next is a discussion of the conflict between the media and the police, including the sources and the potential benefits of such conflict. General policies and protocols for media relations are presented, as well as recommendations on how to be professional when interviewed, whether police should ever lie to the media, the role of

Montgomery County, Maryland, Police Chief Charles Moose speaks to the media about the Beltway Sniper case in 2002. Effective communication with the media is vital to community policing.

public information officers and how departments commonly address photographing and videotaping at crime scenes. Then suggestions for improving media relations and specific strategies for developing positive relationships with the media are discussed. Next is a discussion of marketing community policing through the media. The chapter concludes with a discussion of how the media can help prevent crime.

Mutual Reliance of the Police and the Media

As Garner (2001, p.8) stresses: "In reality, police and the media need each other. The news business needs law enforcement and its leaders as perhaps the single, biggest source of the stories the public wants to hear and see. The police executive, on the other hand, needs the access to his or her citizenry the press can provide. The wise law enforcement executive will take advantage of that access to recognize the good work done by the frontline troops, enlist the public's support in backing a new program or crime prevention effort and get the community's help in solving a tough case."

Police departments and individual officers need the press. The press can shape public opinion, and most police agencies are concerned about their public image. Administrators know that crime and police activities are covered by the media regardless of whether the police provide reporters with information. Most police departments understand that the level of police cooperation will ultimately affect how the public views the police.

Van Blaricom (2001, p.52) notes: "If an atmosphere of mistrust and hostility has developed between the newsmakers and the news reporters, it will be reflected in how the news is reported. That is the nature of such a relationship. The solution to the status quo is to change the institutional attitudes. The police should start that potentially difficult process because they have the most to gain. The outcome can be more than worth the effort." According to Van Blaricom: "When critically examined, it is hard to imagine two professions whose practitioners have more similar personalities than police officers and news reporters. When either of them really wants to find out something, they will do everything within their power to learn the answer. And, the more difficult the search is made for them, the greater their competitive instincts become."

The police and the media share a **symbiotic** relationship; they are mutually dependent upon each other.

Toohey (2001, p.43) also underscores this relationship: "Law enforcement and the news media need one another. It may not always be a comfortable relationship, but is an essential one for both sides."

Rosenthal (2003, p.3) suggests that the media can be law enforcement's "single biggest force multiplier, and a genuine asset in time of need." According to Rosenthal: "Cops can truly win with the media, if they only had the will to win, and a little training on how to make that happen."

Understanding the relationship between the police and the media starts with being aware of what rights the media have, what their mission is and why law enforcement does not always appear in a positive light in the media.

The First Amendment and Freedom of the Press

The First Amendment to the U.S. Constitution states: "Congress shall make no law . . . abridging the freedom of speech or of the press." The free flow of information is a fundamental right in our society.

The First Amendment to the U.S. Constitution guarantees the public's right to know, that is, freedom of the press.

According to the Freedom Forum Online (2000): "Freedom of the press was specifically mentioned in the First Amendment because James Madison and other supporters of the Bill of Rights felt it was necessary to the health of a democratic society. . . . [They] believed a free press [could] counter government's tendency to misuse power and to restrict the free flow of information." In fact, our society deems the public's right to know so important that the media operate without censorship but are subject to legal action if they publish untruths.

Police beat reporters are often eager and aggressive in carrying out their duty to inform the public. Anxious to do well and to be the first with information, they gather and publicize police and crime news as much as they can. The police beat is a visibility beat, considered a prestigious assignment by many newspapers and television stations and is, therefore, sought by the experienced, aggressive reporters.

Coverage of crime events also draws increased viewership and readership, prompting many news organizations to give "top billing" to such stories. In fact, many media markets are unofficially guided by the axiom, "If it bleeds, it leads." Although keeping the public informed about situations affecting their personal and community's safety is an important and valuable service, the priority and emphasis placed on these stories often confuse the public about the true extent of crime and inflate the general level of fear people feel regarding their chances of personal victimization.

The Media and the Public's Fear of Crime

The public's rising fear of crime, despite reports the crime rate is decreasing, has led to much scrutiny of the media and their practices. Dorfman (2001, p.3) reports:

> The news media report crime, especially violent crime, out of proportion to its actual occurrence. Studies of newspapers and television identified three clear patterns. First, and most consistent over time, is that newspapers and television emphasize violent crime. Second, the more unusual the crime, the greater the chance it will be covered. Third, the rate of crime coverage increased while real crime rates dropped. While all media emphasize violence in their news, newspapers do it to a lesser degree than network television, which does it less than local TV news. There are fewer studies of Spanish language newspapers and television news broadcast in the US, but those that exist also demonstrate an emphasis on crime consistent with studies of English-language US news.

The recent media focus on violence in schools has also drawn widespread criticism. Lawrence (2000, p.1) notes: "Hundreds of newspaper and television stories have been done on incidents of school violence, in spite of the fact that school violence has not been increasing, and the fact that the number of youth killed or injured per day by other means far outnumbers those killed or injured at school."

Hiltbrand (2002) notes how reporting of the Washington, DC, sniper case was handled by the media: "Indeed, the most poignant images from the Beltway were of children sprinting from parents' cars into school, of people crouching behind their vehicles as they gassed up, as if living in a war zone. The fear factor was incredible."

According to some researchers, political leaders and law enforcement officials use the media to serve propaganda functions in the state's ideological machinery and to promote their "law-and-order" crime control agendas. They influence public perception of crime by filtering or screening the information provided to the media and, therefore, share responsibility with the media for the misleading depictions of crime and crime policy.

Such influence undermines the efforts of community policing by diminishing the importance of and need for partnerships between law enforcement and the community to effectively address crime. In addition to heavily influencing the public's perception of crime, the media also play a significant role in how the public views the criminal justice system, including law enforcement.

The Media's Impact on the Criminal Justice System

Acknowledging the power of the media to shape public perception, some have also speculated that the media, through their coverage of isolated, high-profile cases, can influence the operations of the criminal justice system and even the disposition of individual cases, a phenomenon called the **news media echo effect**. Much like a pebble thrown into a pond, the impact of a highly publicized case has a rippling effect that spreads throughout the judicial system and affects the entire process. That is, defendants in a similar crime category as one recently publicized may be treated differently within the criminal justice system from the way they would have been treated had such a high-profile case not preceded theirs.

Dorfman (pp.9–10) describes how media reporting has created a **misinformation synergy** resulting from three significant distortions in print and broadcast news.

> It is not just that African Americans are over represented as criminals and under-represented as victims, or that young people are over represented as criminals, or that violent crime itself is given undue coverage. It is that all three occur together, combining forces to produce a terribly unfair and inaccurate overall image of crime in America. Add to that a majority of readers and viewers who rarely have any personal experience with crime by Black youth, and a white adult population who must rely on the media to tell them about minority youth crime, and the result is a perfect recipe for a misinformed public and misguided power structure.

The media have been aided in their quest for newsworthy information through the passage of some legislation, including the Freedom of Information Act. This act, however, is a double-edged sword, also protecting certain information.

Freedom of Information Act

The Freedom of Information Act (FOIA) establishes the presumption that the records of the agencies and departments of the U.S. government are accessible to the people. The "need to know" standard has been replaced by a "right to know" standard, with the government having to justify keeping certain records secret. Exceptions include when the national security is involved, if an investigation's integrity might be compromised or when the privacy rights of individuals might be violated.

In addition, every state has a public records law that specifies what information a law enforcement agency must release, what information must not be released and what is discretionary. Such laws are enacted to protect the rights of citizens under suspicion of breaking the law, as guaranteed by the Sixth Amendment. Rosenthal (2002, p.34) states that officers know exactly what provisions of their state open records/freedom of information law apply to what records in their agency, the requirements of and provisions for handling requests made under the law and the like.

The Sixth Amendment, Suspects' Rights and Criminal Investigations

The Sixth Amendment of our Constitution establishes that "in all criminal prosecutions, the accused shall enjoy the right to a speedy and public trial, by an impartial jury of the state and district wherein the crime shall have been committed."

The Sixth Amendment guarantees suspects the right to a fair trial and protects defendants' rights.

In addition to ensuring these rights, police officers are also responsible for investigating the crimes that suspects are accused of committing. Law enforcement officers sometimes view reporters as an impediment to fulfilling their duties. Law enforcement officers often try to protect information they deem imperative to keep out of the media and may, therefore, be at odds with reporters. Such conflicts arise when police try to prevent public disclosure of information that may tip off a criminal of impending arrest, make prosecution of a particular crime impossible or compromise privacy rights or safety of a victim or witness. Reporters are anxious to do well on their assignments while officers try to avoid weakening their case and reprimands for being too open with the press. The parties' conflicting interests may result in antagonism.

Leaks

As Parrish (2003) points out: "Police officers need to be aware that they are not the only source of information and that a good reporter will often dig up nonpublic information." Of special concern are information leaks from within the department. Gary (2003, p.28) notes: "Inevitably, there are going to be at least a few unauthorized anonymous spokesperson in every high-profile case. At their worst, these leakers will put their own agendas ahead of the investigation." Sometimes leakers are showing off how much they know. But the results can be devastating in an investigation. Gary (pp.28–29) gives the following example that occurred in the DC area sniper crisis in 2003:

> A week after the sniper incidents began, police found a note presumably left by the killers, near the school where a 13-year-old boy had been shot. Written on a Tarot card known as the "death" card was: "Dear policeman. I am God." Hoping to coax more communication, Moose went on live national television to deliver a thinly veiled response, alluding to God in his statement. But by the next day the Tarot's card message had been leaked. Pundits and psychics had taken their own 15 minutes to comment on its significance. Moose was outraged."

Why? Because that leak sent a message to the shooters that law enforcement was not to be trusted.

Victim Privacy Rights

As mentioned, the FOIA protects the privacy rights of some people such as sex crime victims. However, amidst the shock and confusion that often occur immediately after a crime event, victims may easily be caught off guard by aggressive media personnel and may unwittingly put themselves or the investigation at risk by agreeing to an interview.

Herman (2000, p.3) notes: "While satisfying a public appetite for grim tidbits, reporters may ride roughshod over victims, oblivious to their need for privacy, dignity and even safety. The consequences for victims are often devastating. In the aftermath of murder, rape, assault, abduction or robbery, insensitivity and disrespect exacerbate trauma and even jeopardize victims' ability to cooperate with investigators." Herman describes how victims' might react:

> Victims react differently to crime, but few are prepared for an onslaught of media interest. Some victims welcome interaction with journalists. They find it fulfills important emotional and psychological needs or delivers other tangible benefits. It can restore a sense of control by increasing the likelihood of more accurate reporting, or can increase the pressure on law enforcement to pursue the investigation. Other victims want to maximize their privacy: they see their experience as personal and don't want public exposure. Others fear the press will distort the facts or their views. In fact, there are many risks to consider. Interviews can compromise criminal investigations. Publicity can increase intimidation or jeopardize a victim's physical safety. For many victims, media attention increases anger, anxiety and distress.

In addition, as Carmichael (2000, p.1) points out, in one case the personal safety of a witness to a homicide would have been jeopardized when the victim granted media interviews, revealing the existence of the witness who was previously unknown to the perpetrator. Carmichael notes: "Fortunately we learned of the situation in time to contact media and request that the interviews not be used, to which the media agreed. In still another case, the victim of one of a series of incidents in which money had been stolen jeopardized the investigation by giving certain details to a television reporter who had traced the victim down by going door to door. In all of these cases, the strong possibility exists that the problems might have been averted had the persons involved been advised that news media might be contacting them and where to turn to advice and help if that occurred."

Herman (p.3) suggests: "Police should encourage victims to see a victim advocate who can provide the information needed to decide what is in their own best interest. The role of advocates, in turn, is to highlight the options and support victims in their choices." In addition, the Office of Victims of Crime (OVC) has created a new online Directory of Crime Victim Services, which links crime victims and victim service providers to contact information for assistance 24/7. Searchable by location, type of victimization, agency type and available services, OVC's new online directory is becoming the best resource for finding crime victim assistance (www.ovc.ncjrs.org/findvictimservices).

To help victims and witnesses protect their own rights, as well as safeguard the criminal investigation, some departments have begun distributing media relations advisory cards. The Fairfax County (Virginia) Police Department (FCPD) is one such agency, as Rosenthal (2000d, p.21) notes:

> For several years, supervisors in the FCPD public information office and victim services section have tried to find some way of assisting victims and witnesses who've been involved in serious incidents that draw media attention. The goal has always been to ensure the public's right to know, while also protecting the rights of privacy and safety of victims and witnesses.
>
> An additional concern was law enforcement's legitimate need to temporarily withhold information when its release might jeopardize the successful conclusion of an investigation. . . .
>
> An incident involving the attempted forcible sodomization of a [5-year-old] boy . . . spurred FCPD to draft a victim/witness media information card. A reporter covering the story for a television station broadcast an interview with the boy's distraught mother—and even broadcast video of the little boy.

In response, the FCPD, led by former public information office director, Warren Carmichael, created a brief media advisory the size of a business card for officers to distribute to victims and witnesses of certain serious or sensitive cases. The card, available in English, Spanish, Korean, Vietnamese and Farsi, reads:

> News media may wish to interview you regarding this incident. You have the right to grant or refuse interviews. If you choose to give an interview, please call one of the numbers on the reverse side. You will be given advice important to protecting your rights and the investigation, but there is no legal requirement to contact police prior to an interview.

The back of the card gives the phone number for the public information office and the victim services section. Rosenthal (2000d, pp.21–22) also reports:

> In a further effort to balance the rights of all concerned, FCPD has developed guidelines for distribution of the cards. These state, in part:
>
> "These information cards are intended for distribution only in connection with serious or high profile cases, such as homicides, robberies, sex offenses and

> certain fatal accidents. The cards should only be presented in conjunction with the other victim services information normally provided. Any discussion about media interviews should . . . *always* [emphasize] that the decision to speak with the media is solely the individual's. Advising against interviews should be done only in cases where there are legitimate personal safety issues and/or extremely sensitive investigative issues."

Such cards, however, have caused concern among some journalists who contend the advisories will interfere with news gathering.

> Members of the Society of Professional Journalists [SPJ], a group that includes a broad range of media professionals, said the practice could have an impact on whether immigrants and those who do not know their rights decide to speak with reporters.
>
> "People who are told by police, 'Call us first before you talk to a reporter,' are going to listen and not talk," said . . . a member of the society's District of Columbia chapter ("The Right to Remain . . . ," 2000, p.1).

The president of the SPJ contends: "Accurate and timely information on crimes is important to any community. That means victims should not be deterred from talking to reporters." A *Washington Post* editorial clearly expresses a firm opposition to the advisory cards: "Precisely because police departments should not be the sole source of information, they should not be in the business of putting a damper on the willingness of people to share with fellow citizens valuable news about crime." But the FCPD and many other law enforcement agencies disagree (Rosenthal, 2000d, p.22). Carmichael argues: "We advise criminals of their rights. Why is it so out of line for us to advise victims and witnesses of their rights?"

Not surprisingly, these opposing perspectives generate substantial conflict between the media and the police, which can contaminate an agency's efforts to fulfill its community policing mission.

Conflict between the Media and the Police

The press and the police are two powerful forces in our society that depend on one another but are often hostile toward and mistrust each other. According to Chermak and Weiss (2001, p.i):

> Previous research has described the relationship between law enforcement and media organizations in many different ways, including "contentious," "symbiotic" and "parasitic." Situations certainly arise which strain police–media interactions. Media attention to a high-profile incident involving several members of a department or a story criticizing a police organization will affect a department's willingness to cooperate, provide access and divulge organizational information to the media. The survey [they conducted nationally on PIOs and media personnel] research presented here, however, concludes that the relationship is typically quite accommodating, cooperative and mutually supportive.

A national survey of law enforcement–media relations found them to be typically accommodating, cooperative and mutually supportive.

At the outset of one workshop that brought law enforcement and media personnel together to air grievances, discuss issues of common concern and generally get to know one another better so that the two groups could work more effectively together, participants were asked to list three adjectives they thought best described "the other side." Rosenthal (2000b, p.22) reports:

> The responses were very telling. While there were a few positives, the majority of the adjectives from both sides were negative.
>
> Law enforcement described the media as "demanding," "unethical," "uncaring," "biased," "arrogant," and "negative." The media participants described their police peers as "evasive," "uncooperative," "non-trusting," "self-important," "indifferent," and "withholding."

Another question posed to conference participants was: "What is the most important thing you think the 'other side' doesn't understand about you and your work that you want them to learn from this conference?" Again, Rosenthal (2000c, p.21) observes: "The written responses from each side were enlightening."

A major theme among media participants was their need to get information from law enforcement in a timely manner to keep the public informed. Their comments include:

> The public has the right to know. . . . The media are vital to keeping the public informed about what law enforcement does on its behalf. . . . Media is the connection between police and public. . . . We have deadlines. We wish they'd [police] respect them and try to help. . . . Sometimes we are under a major time crunch. . . . We're not trying to be difficult; that information, even a little, can help us in breaking news situations (Rosenthal, 2000c, p.21).

Police participants, of course, had their own slant on the issue of timely information release:

> There are times during an ongoing investigation that divulging information would jeopardize the case. We're not simply being evasive. . . . We can't publicly disclose all info or give opinions on issues. . . . Laws and guidelines that we must abide by prohibit us all too often from commenting on certain subjects, but the 'other side' [of the case] can and do, thus giving a very slanted view. . . . We are busy investigating, helping people, [and are] too busy to talk. . . . Police often do not know all of the story within the first minutes of the investigation. . . . We do not always have time for them [media]. . . . They need to learn patience with the gathering of information. . . . We are more concerned about doing our job than giving them a story (Rosenthal, 2000c, pp.21–22).

This last comment perhaps strikes the greatest nerve between the police and the media, for part of the community policing job is communicating with the public through the media, and the media are often in a position to help police reach vital sources of information about crime within the community. Nonetheless, conflict continues because significantly different perspectives exist between the police and the media concerning what the priorities should be for officers in "doing their jobs."

Differing Perspectives

Two articles reporting on how the media handled the 2002 Washington area sniper case shed light on the differing perspectives of the media and law enforcement. Excerpts from the first article, "Sniper Case Pulled Back Curtain on Media-Police Relations" (Hiltbrand), published by Knight-Ridder/Tribune News Service follow:

> The one constant—through three weeks of frayed nerves and blind alleys—was the underlying tension between the media and the police over who controlled the flow of information. Criticism was still flying even after arrests were made.
>
> "Here's what my desk was fuming about today," Jerry Nachman, MSNBC's executive editor and on-air commentator, said Thursday. "The license plate (on John Allen Mulhammad's car) was never released by the authorities. It was picked up by the press from the police scanners and, in a lightning-short time, led to a citizen spotting the vehicle and pointing the police to it." . . .
>
> "The media had information the police did not want them to broadcast, and the police had information they wanted broadcast in a very precise, controlled way," said Kathleen Hall Jamieson, dean of the University of Pennsylvania's Annenberg School for Communication and author of *The Press Effect*. Both those situations made the press very nervous. . . .
>
> "It turned into an intellectual and emotional taffy pull between the press and this particular police chief," Nachman said. "For all the strategic reasons he may have felt justified in being elusive, it was in variance with the way progressive law enforcement officials operate in America." . . .
>
> Information media analysts also initially questioned the information embargo.
>
> "Chief Moose was naïve to think he could demand media attention and at the same time dictate the story line," said Matthew T. Felling, director at the Center for Media and Public Affairs in Washington. "In a competitive news environment, that's just not going to happen.
>
> "But when he became aware he would not be able to control the press flow, he started to manipulate it. . . . The press corps had every reason to believe (the police) were fumbling in the dark, but apparently they had a direction they were following the whole time."
>
> Stonewalled by the task force, print and broadcast reporters cultivated other sources and continued to uncover news.

A different perspective is provided in "Handling the Media: The Lessons of Some Moose-Terpiece Theater" published in *Law Enforcement News* (Collins, 2002, p.9).

> The recent excellent performance of Montgomery County, MD Police Chief Charles Moose as a media spokesman in the Beltway Sniper case was a striking example of the importance of effective communication with the media. Moose's virtuoso effort in handling the media had three key components. First of all, the chief refused to engage in speculation, thereby defusing all of the "what if" scenarios posed by copy-hungry reporters. Second, he conducted media briefings on a regular basis. Although this high degree of access may go against the grain of some in law enforcement, it was an important bit of media relations and control in the sense of minimizing coverage based upon commentary by the army of "experts" that surface in the presence of such a major news event. Finally, this high degree of access enabled Chief Moose to advance his agenda and build public trust rather than have reporters engage in further and often damaging speculation as the case progressed.

Collins went on in his article to outline ways police departments can enhance media relations. Despite the difference in length of the excepts quoted, the difference in perspective is obvious. In addition to differences in perspective, there are other sources that may cause conflict.

Sources of Conflict

Conflict between the media and the police may arise from a variety of sources, but perhaps the most basic are competing objectives, contradictory approaches to dangerous situations and stereotyping.

Competing Objectives A fundamental source of conflict is the competing objectives of the press and the police. The First Amendment guarantee of freedom of the press is often incompatible with the Sixth Amendment guarantee of the right to a fair trial and protection of the defendant's rights. This leads to a basic conflict between the public's right to know and the individual's right to privacy and a fair trial.

Police may need to withhold information from the media until next of kin are notified, in the interest of public safety or to protect the integrity of an investigation.

To do their job, members of the media need information from the police. Press people say they have problems obtaining information they are entitled to because the police refuse to provide it. In some cases, reporters believe they have been singled out by the police for "punishment" in response to a negative story about the police. Reporters tell of police who restrict information, refuse requests for interviews, disregard reporters' deadlines, hang up the telephone on reporters, provide inaccurate information, play dumb or even blackball a particular reporter in retaliation for a story they did not like.

Indeed, some police agencies or officers who have had negative experiences with the media or believe they have been tricked into releasing information do react by becoming uncooperative, not giving information to which the press is entitled, playing favorites among reporters and even lying. However, this behavior only aggravates an already difficult relationship.

Motivated by a desire to protect their case and the privacy of those involved, police complain that the press is critical and biased against the police, that reporting is often inaccurate, that reporters lack sensitivity, especially toward victims, and that the press releases sensitive material and betrays the trust of officers.

One point of contention concerns "off the record" comments some public officials are inclined to make to reporters. Many have been unpleasantly surprised to be quoted in the next edition of the newspaper. Officers must learn to say only that which they can accept attribution for and are prepared to read or hear reported in the media. To speak to a reporter "off the record" does not guarantee the information will not be reported. It may, in fact, make it more likely to be reported.

In some cases, reporters promise to keep information "off the record" when they have no authority to do so. And while many media professionals do respect "off the record," they may misquote, which can cause significant problems and additional conflict.

Sometimes the media distort information received from the police department for a political purpose. For example, Houston had two newspapers—the *Houston Chronicle* and the *Houston Post*. The editors of the *Post* disliked the mayor and took every opportunity to twist police department information into damaging prose. In one instance, *Post* reporters had counted the number of dead body investigations listed in the Homicide Division log book to compare with published UCR statistics. Noting discrepancies, the *Post* eagerly printed "news" of the department's cover-up and tampering with statistics. The department, in turn, issued a report explaining why the dead body log differed from the UCR data (some deaths were determined to be from natural causes, suicides, etc.). The *Post*, however, refused to acknowledge the explanation and continued to repeat the accusations even after the discrepancies were justified. The department then restricted *Post* reporters' freedom to roam around, limiting their access to the Public Information Office. The *Post* eventually went out of business.

As discussed, the way the public views crime and the police depends in large part on what the media report. Although many police officers are keenly aware of the conflict between themselves and the media, they often do not understand how the need to withhold information contributes to the conflict and the resulting negative coverage or what they and their department can do to alleviate the problem. Officers must remember, however, that the media consist of businesses in fierce competition with each other for readers, listeners and viewers. What officers may consider sensationalism, reporters might consider the competitive edge.

Contradictory Approaches to Dangerous Situations Another source of conflict between law enforcement and the media is the danger members of the media may expose themselves to in getting a story and the police's obligation to protect them. As with that of the general public, the safety of the media at crime scenes, riots or potentially dangerous situations is important. While most reporters and photographers will not cross yellow police tape lines, many are willing to risk a degree of personal safety to get close to the action.

If a situation is unfolding and the police and the media are both on the scene, officers should not tell journalists to stay away—a red flag to most reporters.

Instead, officers, better trained at reading dangerous situations, should urge reporters and photographers to leave an area if they deem it unsafe and tell them why, not just shout, "Get out of here!"

Parrish, at the time a television news director whose crew was attacked during a riot, talked with police after the incident. The officers said they knew their first responsibility was to secure the area and calm things down, but they also felt responsible for the safety of the media, and it angered them that the media were "stupid" enough to be in the middle of the riot. The crew was told to leave and was doing so when attacked. But despite their alleged dislike of the media, the officers did not want to see the media crew hurt.

According to Parrish: "We were there and they [the rioters] were angry. They saw us more as the arm of the law than as an unbiased journalist." The reporter was left unable to walk for two months and eventually left the news business, burdened by stress. She said the assault changed her perspective and she began to identify with victims. "We'd cover crime and show the video on the news and not take into consideration the victim's family watching that. I'd feel grief. I'd go home and cry myself to sleep at night." She now frequently shows video footage of her attack and its aftermath to journalism students. "I like to let young wanna-be reporters see what they are up against" (*Covering Crime and Justice*).

To avoid similar scenarios, police should meet with local media representatives to discuss rules of safety so they might, together, develop a general policy. This should be done before an incident arises. It might boil down to deciding the media have the right to make decisions about their own well-being but that officers will issue warnings to try to ensure the safety of news crews.

To help ensure the safety of media personnel at explosive situations, police should meet with media representatives to explain the safety rules *before* an incident arises.

The issue of media crew safety, and whether the police are responsible for that safety, remains a big issue.

Another important issue, according to Parrish, is live media coverage of major incidents, such as hostage situations. Parrish notes that some agencies are signing "Live Coverage Agreements" that urge the media to refrain from airing live pictures of officers at a major incident or crime scene. Although they are voluntary, they have generally been followed. And the meetings and discussions that take place in setting up these agreements are invaluable in opening lines of communication between the police and the media.

Without such agreements, images of officers can be totally misleading. For example, in an officer-involved shooting in which a suspect is killed, the officers might be shown smiling and hugging one another. The public could mistakenly believe they were celebrating the suspect's death when, in fact, they were celebrating that they were alive.

Stereotyping Chapter 6 discussed the need for police to avoid stereotypes. Stereotyping is a dangerous habit and can greatly impede good working relationships between law enforcement and members of the media. Although it happens to both the police and the media, by each other as well as by the general public, it is important for officers and reporters to see each other as individuals. Both work under the U.S. Constitution and, thus, need to open the lines of effective communication and work together for the public good.

Understanding differences in personality can help build effective relationships between individual police officers and individual media personnel and greatly reduce the barriers between the two professions. There can and must be a trust factor for this to be effective. For example, a radio newscaster who has the trust of the police department can be given confidential information, knowing that he or she will not release it until given the go-ahead. This one-on-one relationship can be of value to law enforcement and to the media.

Dissolving stereotypic views of each other is a significant step toward changing a dysfunctional conflict between the police and the media into a healthy, beneficial conflict.

Benefits of Conflict

Conflict between the police and the media is necessary because each must remain objective and able to constructively criticize the other when needed.

Conflict need not be dysfunctional. In fact, healthy conflict between the media and the police is necessary and beneficial.

Conflict can stimulate people to grow and change. It can diffuse defensiveness if those in conflict recognize that their roles are, by definition, conflicting yet complementary. Better understanding of each other may lead to a cooperative effort to serve the public.

Most large law enforcement agencies recognize that a cooperative relationship with the media is to their benefit. Many have developed media policies that set forth for officers exactly what may and may not be released to the press, how information will be released and by whom.

General Policies and Protocol for Media Relations

Most agencies have developed written policies governing release of information to the press. These policies recognize the right of reporters to gather information and often direct officers to cooperate with the media.

Toohey (p.43) stresses: "No matter what the size of your agency, one of the most important steps you can take is to adopt a written policy for dealing with the media. . . . media guidelines should contain certain essential elements:

- What information can be released during an investigation
- What officers can say following an arrest
- What access the media will have to incident scenes
- Who will deal with the media on a day-to-day basis and during crises

You must also decide whether you are going to allow ride-alongs with patrol and investigative units, or whether you will release mug shots of suspects who are in custody. Specifying this information will help reduce confusion on your own staff about procedures, and it will also help the media.

Perhaps the most important policy regarding media relationship is stated by Tyler (2001, p.51): "Do not let your first meeting with the media occur only after there has been a major crisis." Buice (2001, p.58) echoes this sentiment a bit more graphically: "Just as the time to buy a fire truck is not on the way to the fire, the time to establish sound message management is not when the news hits the fan. Successful police chiefs and PIOs realize that effective message management is a journey, not a destination, and they understand that the journey is a long one."

Officers who encounter and release information to the media are expected to display the highest level of professionalism, for not only will their message be relayed to the public but so will their image and, by reflection, the image of their department. Consequently, many agencies have specific policies and protocol to guide officers during media interviews.

Parrish, one of the authors of the Model Media Policy of the IACP, says policies are important to guarantee consistency in the manner in which information is disseminated to media.

Being Professional When Interviewed

Parrish cautions that police often respond too quickly when they get a request for an interview, saying "yes" or "no" rather than buying some time and finding out just who will be doing the interviewing, what the subject(s) will be and what the deadline is. Parrish notes that the closer the deadline is, the more frantic and pushy journalists may become. Parrish also suggests that officers who are interviewed learn to speak in **sound bites.** Most television interviews run only 7 to 12 seconds. The most important information should be put up front.

Rosenthal (2003, p.3) says: "A sound bite has two essential elements. First, a sound bite must contain good, solid nuggets of information. . . . Don't ever speculate. Tell them only what you're sure you know. . . . It must be short. That's the second essential element of a good sound bite. . . . Sound bites. Good information stated briefly."

It has been said, "You don't argue with people who buy ink by the barrel." Officers should avoid using "no comment," and instead provide a truthful explanation of why they cannot respond, for as the director of media relations for one police department contends: "'No comment' implies that there is a story there that you are not telling" (Strandberg, 2000, p.93). To allay concerns over being misquoted, ask the reporter to provide a transcript of your quotes. Strandberg (p.93) notes: "In most cases, the media will not allow its sources to review the complete story before it is printed or aired, but many times they will provide quotes." Covello, who teaches media at Columbia University, suggests the five biggest interview failures (Buice, 2003a, p.26).

Five interview failures are (1) failing to take charge, (2) failing to anticipate questions, (3) failing to develop key messages, (4) failing to stick to the facts and (5) failing to keep calm.

The press knows that bad relations between the media and the police can result in limited access to police information. Cooperation and mutual trust benefit both the press and the police.

Lying to the Media

Lying to the press is always a bad idea. So is making promises that you cannot keep or misleading reporters. Such actions usually haunt the individual officer or the agency in the form of negative press or lack of media cooperation when the police need help. It is better to honor commitments to the media and be straightforward when information is to be released.

Agencies and officers who make a practice of deceiving the media are at great risk of losing public confidence, for as Rosenthal (2000a, p.17) notes: "For law enforcement to have effective public relations, it must build bridges of cooperation with the media. Three essential pillars of those bridges are mutual trust, mutual credibility, and mutual respect." However: "There are those extraordinary circumstances under which police may be justified in lying to the media." The following incident illustrates how police might be justified in lying to the media (details from Rosenthal, 2000a, pp.17–18).

> In the summer of 2000, Jimmy Gordon and his wife, Shirley, were going through a divorce, and he was taking it badly. One day while Shirley was at the home of friends, the Clarks, Jimmy got desperate and went looking for her, with a double-barreled 12-gauge shotgun and a handful of shells.
>
> At the Clarks, Jimmy forced his way into the house and demanded to see his wife. The Clarks managed to escape with one of their children, but four other children, ranging in age from 6 to 23, remained inside as hostages. Shirley Gordon was also in the house, hiding in a basement storage space. The Clarks called the police, and the tactical unit, including a negotiator, responded. So did the media.
>
> Unaware that she was hiding in the basement, Jimmy demanded to the police to talk to his wife. The Clarks told the police Shirley was still in the house, which elevated the tension surrounding the event because Jimmy had told the negotiator earlier that he planned to kill his wife and himself.
>
> In the meantime, all three local TV stations and a radio news station were interrupting normal programming with live broadcasts from the scene. In fact, Jimmy told police he, too, was watching reports of the event on the TV inside the house. Reporters were kept informed by Public Information Officer Sergeant Bruce Elrod, who had worked hard over the years to earn the trust and respect of the media. But they were pressing PIO Elrod for details. What was Jimmy Gordon demanding, and how did the police plan to handle the situation? Elrod found himself in a precarious position. He knew he could stall reporters for awhile but that, eventually, whatever he told the media would also reach Jimmy. So Elrod, after consulting with the tactical unit commander, made the tough decision to lie to the media.
>
> He told them Jimmy Gordon's demand was that he be allowed to talk to his wife (true); that she was not in the house (false); that the police didn't know

> where she was (false); and that authorities were looking for her (false). The message got through—negotiators and the news reports convinced Jimmy that his wife was nowhere to be found and that he was at a dead end. He began releasing his hostages, walked out of the house and surrendered, with no one getting hurt.
>
> As soon as Jimmy was in handcuffs, the first thing Elrod did was go back to the media and admit he'd been lying to them all afternoon. He stressed he'd never deceived the press during his four years as PIO, but that in this case, where Shirley Gordon's life, as well as those of the hostages, was at stake, he had no other option than to lie and that he hoped the media would understand.
>
> Afterward, a news director for one of the local stations agreed Elrod's decision was "perfectly justifiable in order to ensure the woman's safety. She was in clear danger. Lying does not come naturally to Elrod. I don't think there were any [negative] repercussions or hard feelings on the part of the media."

On the very rare occasions when it becomes necessary to lie to the media, it must be followed at the earliest opportunity with an explanation for the deception.

If lying to the media might save a life or protect the public safety, after the need to lie has passed, the department should explain why lying was necessary and, perhaps, apologize.

The nature of police business often requires the delicate handling and release (or retention) of information, and it is frequently difficult and time consuming, particularly for larger agencies, to keep all officers equally informed about which details of a case may be provided to the media. Consequently, many agencies now employ public information officers. Having a public information officer is among the suggestions for improving media relations made by Tyler (pp.48, 51): (1) build relationships, (2) establish a press policy for the agency, (3) establish a spokesperson for the agency and (4) accentuate the positive.

Public Information Officers

Some police departments feel comfortable allowing any member to talk to the media and provide information. Former Minneapolis chief of police, Tony Bouza, did not have press officers during his administration: "Every member of the department serves as a spokesperson. Reporters are free to call any member of the department and ask them any questions they want. And you will get an answer, regardless of the rank of the officer you speak to." Bouza was fond of saying that the Minneapolis Police Department had 714 public information officers. Journalists, however, often complain that although any officer could speak on behalf of the police department, the police usually release far less information than such an open policy permits.

Some departments discourage individual officers from talking to reporters and instead designate **public information officers (PIOs)** to disseminate all information to the media. As Arms (2001, p.10) explains: "The PIO is an ambassador for the agency he or she represents. Through the PIO, information is conveyed to the media with credibility, accurately and in a timely manner." PIOs are officers trained in public relations who try to consistently provide accurate information while controlling leaks of confidential or inaccurate details and managing controversial or negative situations to the department's benefit.

Gary (p.25) explains the fundamental duties of a PIO at a crime scene:

- Reassure the public the department is doing all it can to solve the crime.
- Ask the public for help.
- Find and correct any inaccuracies.
- Field media questions.
- Accommodate the press, but steer them clear of areas and behavior that may have an adverse effect on the investigation.

Chermak and Weiss's (2001) national survey of public information officers and media personnel found the following:

- Almost all of the agencies surveyed relied primarily on public information staff to disseminate information about the department, and the PIOs have considerable access to the major media outlets within a city. Media personnel also discussed how they depend primarily on access to the law enforcement agency to construct crime stories.
- Law enforcement and media personnel have a positive view of this relationship. The public information officers were generally satisfied with the presentation of policing in the news. Similarly, media personnel were satisfied with the amount and types of information provided, although there were some differences in satisfaction when comparing results across medium (newspaper versus television) and across organizational position (reporter versus manager).
- The burdens of responding to daily and frequent requests for crime incident information leaves very little time for public information officers to promote community policing initiatives. Most of the public information officer's time is spent providing information about specific crime incidents.
- Law enforcement agencies relegated the task of promoting community policing to different individuals in the department. Some agencies, for example, gave this responsibility to the public information officer. Others, however, have decentralized this function, relying on community policing staff to promote it. Finally, many departments coordinate public information and community policing staff to share the responsibility for promoting community policing.

Buice (2003b, p.32) suggests a "three-ingredient recipe for media relations similar to the crime triangle: the **PIO Triangle.** The three sides of the PIO Triangle are Action, Reaction and Impact. Those three components encompass (1) what happened, (2) what responders are doing and (3) how the public (or a portion of it) will be affected by both number 1 and number 2." Figure 8.1 illustrates the PIO triangle.

The PIO has a significant amount of responsibility. When PIOs properly carry out their responsibilities, they can improve police–media relations. As Staszak (2001, p.11) cautions: "The overwhelming search for news should warn law enforcement that the media will get their story one way or another. Cooperating with the

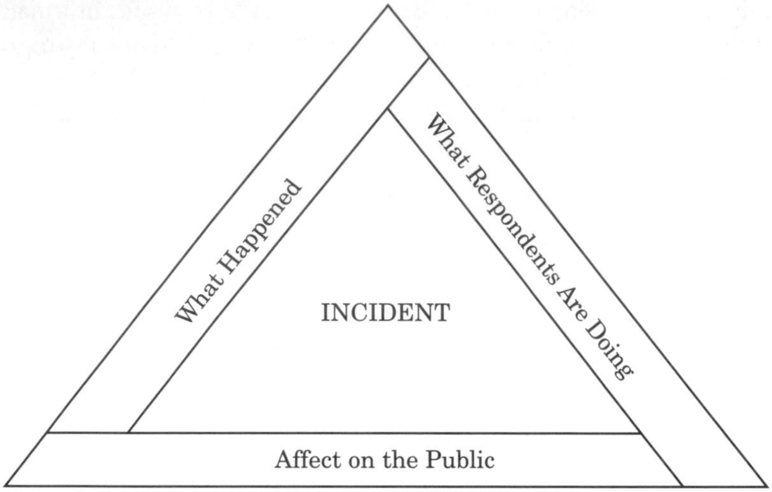

Figure 8.1 The PIO Triangle

media remains the most reasonable avenue for PIOs to take to advise the public of the department's position."

While talking with reporters is one thing, allowing the media to photograph or shoot video at crime scenes is something quite different because there are important Fourth Amendment constraints for police to consider. As a result, many departments have policies in place regarding the use of cameras at crime scenes.

Policies Regarding Photographing and Videotaping

They say a picture is worth a thousand words. Crawford (2000, p.26) recounts:

> The American public recently awoke to the news that INS agents had ended a standoff with the relatives of young Elian Gonzales by forcibly entering the relatives' Miami home under the authority of a federal search warrant and seizing the boy. Within hours of the operation, poignant pictures of the seizure appeared on televisions and front pages of newspapers across the country. Probably the most memorable photograph is one depicting a terrified young Elian, cowering in the arms of a man, as an armed INS agent reaches for him.

According to Crawford (p.26): "Americans have grown accustomed to detailed news coverage of law enforcement activities. The public's seemingly unquenchable interest in viewing the exploits of law enforcement officers has spawned the ever increasing media coverage of such events." Indeed, the popularity of television shows where camera crews ride along with officers as they patrol the community and respond to calls is evidence of the public's fascination with such activities. Crawford (p.27) also notes, however: "When the media is present to document law enforcement activities inside most private premises, they are there at the invitation of the officers. It is this invitation . . . that has given rise to a number of civil suits against law enforcement officers."

In *Wilson v. Layne* (1999), the U.S. Supreme Court confronted the issue of whether a media presence, at law enforcement's invitation, to document police activities conducted on private premises violated privacy rights protected by the Fourth Amendment. In this case, the police and accompanying journalists were seeking a fugitive but went to the wrong address, that of the fugitive's parents. Early one morning, Charles and Geraldine Wilson awoke to the sounds of someone forcibly entering their home. Moments later they encountered not only several armed police officers but also a photographer taking pictures and a reporter taking notes. When the officers learned of their mistake, they left, but the entire incident had been captured on film by the media. And although the photographs taken that day were never published, the Wilsons filed suit against the officers who had invited the media into their home.

The Court found that, although the officers had entered the residence under the lawful authority of a warrant, the media were not present for any purpose reasonably related to the execution of the warrant and, thus, the officers exceeded the authority of the warrant by inviting the media to take part. Furthermore, the Court ruled that, while law enforcement does possess a legitimate objective in publicizing its efforts to combat crime and minimize the likelihood of both police abuse and physical resistance of subjects, those objectives were not sufficient to outweigh the "right of residential privacy at the core of the Fourth Amendment."

Perp walks, another once-common police practice where suspects were paraded before the hungry eyes of the media, have also fallen on shaky legal ground. As Lunney (2002, p.6) notes: "This issue [the perp walk] was highlighted by the judgment of a civil trial judge in New York City . . . when he ruled that the perp walk was a violation of the constitutional rights of a burglary suspect who was led before TV cameras by the NYPD." Although the public likes to see the "bad guys" apprehended and facing trial, if the perp walk is conducted before the trial, what happens to a core principle of the criminal justice system that a defendant is innocent until proven guilty? According to Lunney (pp.6–7): "The Code of Ethics of the Society for Professional Journalists counsels its members to be cautious about naming criminal suspects before the formal filing of charges, and to balance a criminal suspect's fair trial rights to be informed." Lunney (p.7) concludes: "For the present, the perp walk is the prevailing custom, serving as both a moral statement and the visible evidence of the process of justice. For the police, it's nothing more than another duty to be carried out with dignity and decorum."

However, this nearly century-old tradition may not see much action in the twenty-first century. As with the media ride-alongs, courts have begun ruling that perp walks violate a suspect's right to privacy. Many jurisdictions have suspended the practice of perp walks, while others await rulings by the appellate courts.

Police departments also vary in whether they allow news cameras in or around crime scenes. Prohibiting cameras may give the impression that the police have something to hide. However, people not involved in an investigation must not be allowed to contaminate the crime scene.

Another problem with allowing cameras at crime or accident scenes is viewed not from the police perspective but from that of the victim or complainant, who might not want themselves, their family members or their home to be on someone's video, documentary or TV series. However, nobody has a right to expect privacy in a public place.

Police officers should also be aware of the news system called "file video" or "file photos," where pictures are kept indefinitely and can be reused at any time. For example, in one case a photographer arranged to go with a squad on a high-risk entry into a crack house. The police department let the reporter come along to get some video of how they were working to curb drug traffic in the city. The reporter did the story, and the police were pleased with the resulting public image. Two years later, one officer involved in the high-risk entry unit faced an indictment by a federal grand jury for police brutality. The reporter mentioned to his boss that they had video of this officer breaking into the home of some poor black citizens on the north side. The editors decided that was just what they needed for the story, and the video the police had at one time encouraged the media to take was used against the officer.

Understanding and Improving Relations with the Media

"Community policing depends on building relationships with the community, and public information is a major conduit through which we reach our community" (Skinner, quoted by Braunstein, 2001, p.62). Braunstein notes: "Good relations with the media are critical to police departments, but many police officers are more comfortable confronting armed suspects than facing reporters with television cameras." However, she (p.64) stresses: "As departments implement the community policing philosophy, working well with the media becomes increasingly important."

The national survey on police–media relations by Chermak and Weiss (2001) found: "Perhaps the most important factor influencing how the media viewed the quality of their relationship was accessibility to police data and police personnel. Media personnel indicated that the level of access to the police department determined their most effective relationships. When asked what made a relationship with a law enforcement agency adversarial, media personnel indicated that lack of access was the driving force."

A police–media relationship survey found that the factor most affecting this relationship was accessibility to police data and personnel.

Police need to understand that the media are facing some of the same challenges law enforcement is facing, especially cutbacks and being asked to do more with less. They also usually work under extreme time pressure and under the public eye. Seldom do reporters bungle a story intentionally. They are often uninformed about how their reporting may affect a case and are often also under extreme pressure to get the story submitted before a deadline.

Reporters may bungle a story due to ignorance, oversimplification or time constraints.

Reporters, particularly rookies or those new to the police beat, may be ignorant of law enforcement procedures and of Sixth Amendment requirements. Journalists must often fashion a complicated investigation or series of events into a paragraph-long news story or a 15- to 20-second story at the top of the hour. Furthermore, they commonly work under severe deadline pressure.

To improve police–media relations, the press should be informed of a department's policies and procedures regarding the media and crime scenes. Officers should avoid police jargon and technical terminology and respect reporters' deadlines by releasing information in a timely manner so the press has a chance to fully understand the situation.

Training is another way to improve relationships and enhance the media's understanding of what police work involves. The Lakewood (Colorado) Police Department, for example, invited the local newspaper and broadcast reporters to enroll in a citizens' police academy. The reporters were given laser guns and acted out different scenarios to demonstrate the difficult decisions police must make. Inviting members of the media to ride in squad cars is also an effective way to enhance the media's understanding of policing. (Recall, however, such invitations should not extend into citizens' private premises.) Conversely, police officers could benefit from learning more about the media and their mission and responsibilities. Officers must remember that reporting is a highly competitive business.

A good rapport with the media can also help the police department accomplish its mission, for improved media relations leads to improving community relations. As stated earlier, the media are often the primary link between the law and the citizenry. To reach the community, the victims of crime and possible witnesses, the police must first reach the media.

The media can also be of assistance in public education programs. For example, an agency in California wanted to increase the accuracy of citizens' reports of suspicious and criminal activities. They enlisted the aid of the local newspaper to run a public announcement about what to include in suspect and vehicle descriptions.

In Chicago, the police use the media in their crime prevention efforts. The Federal Communications Commission (FCC) requires all media to set aside airtime or publication space for community projects. This is another excellent avenue for law enforcement agencies to convey educational messages to the residents of their communities.

Other media possibilities include talk shows, in which an agency spokesperson can discuss a controversy or a trend. Sometimes the editor of a local newspaper or publication will permit an organization a regular column. Letters to the editors may be written in response to other letters sent in to the editorial page. Other ways to improve media relations include developing a relationship with the editorial boards and op-ed page editors of newspapers or television and not giving exclusive interviews to national correspondents, bypassing local reporters. Local reporters can help make or break an agency in the local news.

According to Staszak (pp.12–13): "In view of the media's reluctance to decrease the reporting of criminal matters, law enforcement must continue furnishing details of criminal activity, but it also must establish a strategy for soliciting community and media interest in nontraditional issues, such as proactive programs for a safer community. To garner media interest, law enforcement must become better at packaging their messages and making them more attractive."

When the relationship between the police and media is improved, effective and valuable partnerships can be forged for the benefit of the entire community, as well as the individual agencies involved. As Chermak and Weiss (2003, p.1) suggest: "In community policing, it's essential to gain citizen support and involvement. The news media can play a key role in this effort through their wide dissemination of information. The police know that most people form their impressions of crime and the justice system from newspapers, television and radio rather than from direct exposure (as crime victims, for example). For the police, the media convey their message to the public; for the media, the police are an indispensable information source."

Strategies for Developing Partnerships with the Media

Recall from Chapter 1 the definition of community policing: a philosophy that emphasizes working proactively with citizens to reduce fear, solve crime-related problems and prevent crime. It is a collaborative effort founded on close, mutually beneficial ties between the police and the people. There is no more effective or efficient way for law enforcement to forge a relationship with the community than to partner with the media. Community leaders, key elected officials, church leaders, school boards and parent teacher association members, philanthropists and local celebrities often maintain contact with media sources. These people could be brought together through a police–media partnership to sponsor or support crime prevention activities in the community.

Parrish suggests that one of the most effective ways for police and media to better understand each other is using a ride-along program:

> Police managers should spend a shift riding with a reporter or a photographer—not as part of a story but as a way to get to know the individual and better understand the job of a journalist. Reverse ride-alongs are also important with police managers accompanying a reporter or photographer on a story.
>
> Many police agencies allow the media to ride with officers for stories on topics such as DUI enforcement. The end result is that the public learns about police programs, and the media get to know officers as individuals.
>
> Recently, some agencies are inviting the media to "embed" with officers on high-profile events such as protests. Philadelphia P. D., Miami, P. D. and Sacramento P. D. are among the agencies who have tried this. The police often end up with pictures and video of arrests that can be used to show what really happened on the street. Many cases of police brutality went away when defendants saw the video.

Buice (2001, pp.59–60) contends: "The success of community oriented policing depends on partnerships built on trust and mutual respect, from which come open and honest communication. Knowledge is power, and sharing the knowledge through the media exponentially increases the power."

Such partnerships with the media are not entirely new. For example, the McGruff "Take a Bite Out of Crime" national media campaign and other crime prevention public service announcements have existed for decades. (Using the media in crime prevention efforts is discussed again in Chapter 12). However, local efforts to enjoin the media in the police effort to prevent crime have been lacking.

Sparks and Staszak (2000, p.22) suggest: "Because the media covers issues of public interest, prudent managers should realize the importance of proactively using the media as a tool to get their department's message out to the community."

An example of how technology can enhance police–media partnerships is seen in New York. Press information officers from the Albany Police Department, the New York State Police and other area law enforcement agencies as well as representatives from the media formed the Capital District Law Enforcement/Media Group. This group, representing 80 different agencies as well as print and electronic media, met bimonthly to discuss areas of mutual concern. One problem the group tackled was the need to get information to all the media rapidly. Most media personnel believed the practice of PIOs calling down through a media list was inequitable and also required a great deal of the PIOs' time. The group found a mutually acceptable solution to the problem: the **Pager Information Network (PIN)**. The PIO can make one phone call from anywhere—the department, home, cellular telephone or pay phone—and simultaneously notify all the media enrolled in the network.

Pagers can display full text messages and also have printing capability. They can be used to advise drivers of major traffic obstructions on highways and hazardous road conditions, to warn citizens of shams and cons, to announce newsworthy criminal events or arrests and to announce press conferences. The system is kept secure through the use of passwords and identification codes.

Jedic (2000, p.2) suggests: "Law enforcement agencies rushing to embrace new technology should not overlook the old technology that continues to be the most influential and accessible of all—television. More specifically, community-access cable television. With the boom of local-access channels throughout the nation, every police agency would benefit by contacting its cable operators for scheduling and program information. Most local-access channels are free."

In Cleveland the mayor obtained sponsorship of a local television and radio station to publicize the city's gun exchange, violence reduction and crime prevention initiatives. The television station not only helped to announce these very successful initiatives, it also operated the telephone banks for donations.

Law enforcement officials in San Antonio, Texas, invited prominent local media figures to participate in a city crime prevention commission. By involving the media in the panel's deliberations and programs, the department created a partnership that generated positive media coverage and provided free broadcast equipment and facilities for public service announcements and other programming.

The Utah Council for Crime Prevention also invited local media personnel to serve on the council's board, a collaboration resulting in locally produced television documentaries and public service announcements, as well as other activities raising public awareness of crime prevention throughout the state.

Rosenthal (2001, p.16) describes a strategy used by the Phoenix (Arizona) Police Department, developing a Police/Media Quick Reference Guide for reporters. This 12-page guide provides names, phone numbers and photos (so they can be recognized at incident scenes) of the department's PIOs, a detailed department phone directory, basic "freedom of information" guidance about what information can and cannot be released to the media, important unit radio call signs and the units' on-scene job responsibilities, the department's incident radio codes, a map showing boundaries of Phoenix's six precincts and details of the system for paging PIOs. Says Rosenthal: "It is a solid reference for reporters and answers many of the questions they would otherwise be calling in to headquarters to ask." Rosenthal also suggests other strategies they have used, including a police training academy for members of the media—the first of its kinds in the nation—less formal get-acquainted breakfast and lunch meetings between officers and reporters and a general attitude of accessibility to and cooperation with the media.

Buice (2002, p.16) suggests other strategies to partner with the media: "It's more important than ever that PIOs help journalists chart the course to correct conclusions and proper context. Giving reporters a chance to see the view from the other side can have a dramatic impact. A couple of years ago, after Chattanooga officers were involved in two deadly force incidents in less than a week, Chattanooga Police put reporters through a 'shoot/don't shoot' scenario using real firearms loaded with Simunition. Journalists who participated or observed admitted that it was an eye-opening experience and their subsequent news stories reflected that." He also notes: "Many agencies find that asking members of the media to go through Citizens Police Academies or even separate Media Academies can prevent potentially deadly blunders by reporters." He concludes: "In the big league media environment that law enforcement currently finds itself, we must remind ourselves that our ultimate obligation is to our citizens, not the reporters. As onerous as it may sometimes be, we must often go the extra mile to help the media paint an accurate picture."

Rosenthal (2001, pp.16–17) describes how reactive policing resulted in what could have been a media disaster and how a more proactive approach turned into a success.

> This past June a white male drove up to the drive-through window at a Largo fast food restaurant, told the startled server "All [racial slur] should be killed," and drove off. The staff called police, and the responding officer took basic information but filed no formal report. Within the next few nights the same individual repeated his drive-through slurs two more times, the last time adding a specific threat to kill the store manager. Employees called police after both incidents, and once again informational reports were filled out. Unfortunately, a different officer responded to each call, and none filed a formal report, so there was no investigative follow-up. The restaurant staff became frustrated with what they saw as police ineffectiveness in dealing with this harassment and went to the local newspaper.
>
> The *St. Petersburg Times* picked up the story, and asked Chief Aradi for his comment. Aradi could have stonewalled, run from the issue, told the *Times* to "go away" or give a "No comment." But the smart law enforcement leaders like Aradi know that's absolutely the wrong way to go when facing a potentially messy situation. So Aradi looked into the matter, found that in this case there could have been better communications within his department, and said so, on the record, in a statement to the *Times*. In its August 1 edition the *Times* headline

> read, "Police Admit Mistake in KFC Threats Case." Chief Aradi was quoted as saying, "We owe [the manager] an apology. . . . The Largo Police Department dropped the ball on this, but we have every intention of picking it up and running with it."
>
> It was a great quote and a great message. Even so, the story would have remained in the news had Aradi not followed through. His investigators quickly found and arrested 47-year-old James M. Donahue, the man believed responsible for the slurs and threats. They learned he had a long record of prior offenses and was on probation when these incidents occurred. Donahue admitted his actions, his probation was voided, and he is now back behind bars. . . .
>
> That would have been satisfaction enough, but the *Times* threw him a well-deserved bouquet. In an editorial on August 3, the *Times* wrote: "Aradi's straightforward approach to the problem is refreshing and seems to indicate that he wants to do things right." Aradi said, "You have to deal with the media quickly, responsibly and honestly. By accepting responsibility, apologizing and assuring we're going to move forward and do a better job, the matter died."

While these collaborations, and many others throughout the country, have generated a plethora of benefits for their respective communities, the strategy of developing partnerships with the media is not without obstacles. As Chermak and Weiss (2003, p.2) caution: "No matter how good the working relationship with the media might be, it cannot overcome the constraints PIOs face. They must spend more time handling media inquiries about crime than doing anything else, which leaves them little time to invest in marketing community policing and similar initiatives." Despite such constraints, police departments should take every opportunity to forge creative, supportive, respectful partnerships with the media.

As police departments adopt the community policing philosophy and implement its strategies, public support is vital. The media can play an important role in obtaining that support—or in losing it.

Chermak and Weiss not only studied the police–media relationship, but also identified strategies used by law enforcement agencies to market community policing initiatives to the public. Among their findings were the following:

- Although law enforcement agencies do not make significant efforts to promote community policing, news media are very accommodating when police request coverage for a community policing activity. However, media personnel indicated that law enforcement did a much better job in providing information about crime incidents than publicizing community policing.
- It is clear that media organizations have not been included as community policing partners, and police departments are not taking full advantage of their access to media organizations to promote community policing. It would seem to make sense for departments to use their access to reporters as an opportunity to generate publicity for these innovative strategies and encourage citizen cooperation. However, the efforts of law enforcement agencies to promote community policing have not translated into a significant amount of news coverage.

- Even when community policing is presented in the news, the coverage represents a limited view of this philosophy. There is very little discussion of the goals or history of community policing in these stories, and citizen involvement and cooperation is also not frequently mentioned. It would appear that the type of coverage that community policing gets in the news are efforts at public relations, but do not encourage the involvement of citizens in community policing.
- This research indicates that police departments are clearly missing an opportunity to promote community policing in the news. Indeed, community policing did not receive a significant amount of coverage even in areas where our survey results indicated that the police–media relationship was excellent. For example, we collected data on the sources used in community policing stories and the police were provided primary attribution in these stories. News media also responded that it was their view that the public was interested in these types of stories. Although police are involved in the production of these stories, the image of community policing received by the public in the news is very limited. It is also clear that in order to generate the type of publicity that might inform citizens about community policing, and ultimately encourage involvement, police departments will have to take a much more systematic approach towards publicizing community policing in the news.

In short, police departments need to *market* community policing.

Marketing Community Policing

The first recommendation of Chermak and Weiss is: "Law enforcement agencies should implement and devise broad marketing strategies to increase public awareness and involvement in community policing activities." Their other recommendations include:

- Law enforcement agencies will need to increase the amount of personnel and monetary resources to more effectively market community policing in the news and in the community.
- Media and community policing training curriculum will have to be broadened to include a discussion of more effective ways to market community policing.
- Research has to be conducted that can effectively evaluate whether implementing a broad marketing strategy is effective.

Fazzini (2003) stresses: "Police agencies easily can adapt the concepts of business marketing to help them reach their customers (citizens) and educate them about the many services they provide." He notes a reality long known in businesses regarding their customers: "Various research has indicated that satisfied people tell their stories of police contact to at least three other people, whereas dissatisfied individuals will tell, on average, ten others about a negative experience with the police."

Fazzini suggests: "Today, the single most significant marketing doctrine is the **marketing mix**, which encompasses all of the agency's tools that it uses to influence a market segment to accomplish its objectives (emphasis added)." Among the options available to police departments are positive media stories (free advertising), a Web site sharing department information, marketing alliances such as formation of a citizen police academy, a media academy, joining committees and participating in community groups, poster campaigns, public service announcements, addresses to community groups—all can help raise awareness of and interest in community policing.

Brewer (2002) provides an example of how his department marketed their highway safety campaign using five marketing strategies. First is advertising, known as the best way to reach the public. It comes in two forms: free (in the form of public interest articles) and paid. Second is creation of a police agency Web site. Third is partnerships with the local community to act as force multipliers and to increase the effectiveness of their enforcement strategy. Fourth is partnering with major sporting events to provide a creative forum to deliver highway safety information and promote enforcement. Fifth is a less conventional means to market highway safety, including company newsletters, telephone hold messages, T-shirt giveaways and school visits.

Marketing often goes beyond the media. Following are some creative marketing strategies described by Chermak and Weiss (2003, pp.4–5):

> Chicago mounted an innovative campaign intended to heighten awareness of community policing among its linguistically diverse citizens, using multimedia and multilingual information initiatives. Brochures, newsletters, billboards, television and radio ads, and information hotlines were some of the components. Partly as a result of the aggressive marketing, awareness increased, though not as much among Spanish-speaking Latinos.
>
> New Haven, Connecticut, has a widely acclaimed and award-winning community policing program whose outreach components include a public cable TV program aimed to increase awareness and access, a series of workshops for residents on various aspects of community policing, and production of a documentary film profiling the city's police and community policing.
>
> To reach out to the many Latino residents of Corcoran, California, the police department created Amigos de la Communidad, a Spanish-language citizen police academy. One outcome was the formation, by several academy graduates, of a Spanish-language unit in the department's volunteer community patrol.
>
> Creative ways to reach the community can also be borrowed from programs other than community policing. After recognizing that newspapers, fliers and radio spots were not enough to motivate people to attend community meetings, the New Britain, Connecticut, Weed and Seed site organized a street parade. The event was intended as a means to recruit people to participate in focus groups that would target specific neighborhood problems.

A comprehensive discussion of marketing techniques available to police departments is beyond the scope of this text. Numerous resources in this area are available. Marketing community policing is important in efforts to make neighborhoods safe and to prevent or reduce crime. Interestingly, publicity of policing efforts has been shown to also have a deterrent effect on crime.

Publicity as a Means to Prevent Crime

Johnson and Bowers (2003, p.497) report: "The effectiveness of crime reduction schemes may be significantly enhanced by publicity. . . . Carefully planned publicity campaigns may represent a powerful yet cost-effective tool in crime prevention." Their research suggests that publicizing crime prevention efforts increases the offenders' perceptions of the risks involved in perpetrating crime. In fact, publicizing such efforts before they go into effect can have an **anticipatory benefit,** that is, criminals may be deterred even before the efforts are implemented. According to their findings, the most frequently used publicity was newspaper articles (90 percent), followed by leaflets, letters and cards (62 percent). The strategies used by participants in their research are summarized in Table 8.1.

Their research (p.515) found that: "Of all the other variables analyzed, only the number of partner agencies involved in the implementation of the scheme, and publicity in terms of the number of press articles and radio interviews conducted, were significantly related to scheme success. In comparison to the other variables for which quarterly data were available, publicity was the most significant predictor of decreases in the burglary rate."

Table 8.1 Number of Schemes Undertaking Different Forms of Publicity

Publicity Type	*Specific Item*	*% of schemes (n)*
General publicity	Radio Interviews (local/national)	33% (7)
	Newspaper Articles (local/national)	90% (19)
	Television Appearances (local/national)	24% (5)
	Leaflets/letters/cards	62% (13)
	Posters	38% (8)
	Publicity directed at offenders (e.g., Christmas cards)	14% (3)
	Stickers (e.g., neighborhood watch or smartwater)	19% (4)
	Significant community meetings explaining the scheme	43% (9)
	Informal information or scheme to community offenders	14% (3)
Stand alone publicity campaigns		57% (12)
Surveys (including fear of crime, alleygating, target hardening)		33% (7)
Other (any other form of publicity)		43% (9)

SOURCE: Shane D. Johnson and Kate J. Bowers. "Opportunity Is in the Eye of the Beholder: The Role of Publicity in Crime Prevention." *Crime and Justice,* Vol. 2, No. 3, 2003, p.505. Reprinted by permission.

Another interesting finding of this research was that of a **geographical diffusion of benefit**. Properties immediately adjacent to the intervention also experienced a reduction in burglary. Johnson and Brewer (p.518) note: "To capitalize on this finding, we suggest that a cost-effective way of targeting resources may be to employ a kind of bull's-eye resource targeting approach, whereby a scheme area would be divided into concentric zones, and resources targeted into every other zone," as shown in Figure 8.2.

These researchers (p.519) also suggest that advertising may be more effective if done in bursts rather than over continuous periods and that the effects of advertising campaigns extend beyond the period during which they are active.

Past and present efforts to enlist the media in crime prevention and reduction efforts will be included throughout the next section of this text.

SUMMARY

One important group with which the police interact is the media. The police and the media, sharing the common goal of serving the public, have a symbiotic relationship; they are mutually dependent upon each other. However, the media are guided by the First Amendment to the U.S. Constitution, which guarantees the public's right to know, that is, freedom of the press, while the police are guided by the Sixth Amendment, which guarantees the right to a fair trial and protects the defendant's rights. The differing objectives of these amendments may lead to conflict between the media and the police. However, a national survey of law enforcement–media relations found them to be typically accommodating, cooperative and mutually supportive. Police may need to withhold information from the

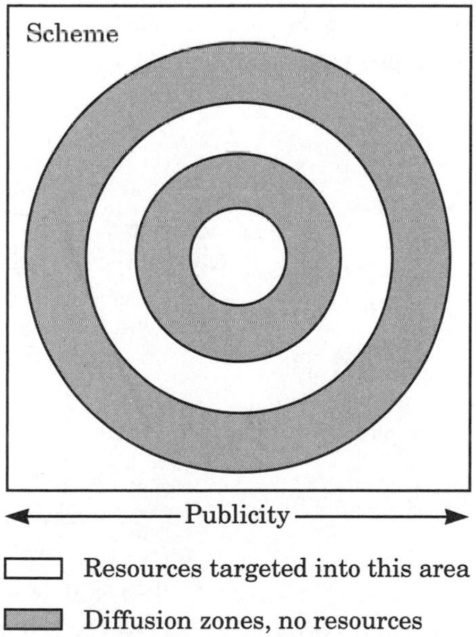

Figure 8.2 Bull's-Eye Resource Targeting Strategy and Publicity

SOURCE: Shane D. Johnson and Kate J. Bowers. "Opportunity Is in the Eye of the Beholder: The Role of Publicity in Crime Prevention." *Crime and Justice,* Vol. 2, No. 3, 2003, p.519. Reprinted by permission.

media until next of kin are notified, in the interest of public safety or to protect the integrity of an investigation.

Another source of conflict between the press and the police is the danger in which members of the press may place themselves when trying to obtain a story. To help ensure the safety of media personnel at explosive situations, police should meet with media representatives to explain the safety rules before an incident arises. Conflict between the police and the media need not be dysfunctional. In fact, healthy conflict between the media and the police is necessary and beneficial. Five interview failures are (1) failing to take charge, (2) failing to anticipate questions, (3) failing to develop key messages, (4) failing to stick to the facts and (5) failing to keep calm.

Lying to the press is always a bad idea, and it is better to be straightforward when disseminating information. However, there are occasional extraordinary circumstances when an exception to this rule exists. If some morally overriding reason, such as public safety, obliges an official to lie, then it also requires an explanation or apology for the deception later, after the crisis has passed.

A step toward improved media relations is to recognize why reporters may foul up a story. Reporters may bungle a story because of ignorance, oversimplification or time constraints. A police–media relationship survey found that the factor most affecting this relationship was accessibility to police data and personnel.

To improve police–media relations, inform the press of your department's policies and procedures regarding the media and crime scenes; simplify your information, avoiding police jargon and technical terminology; and respect reporters' deadlines by releasing information in a timely manner so the press has a chance to fully understand the situation.

Developing partnerships with the media is critical to the successful implementation of community policing because, as police departments adopt the community policing philosophy and implement its strategies, public support is vital. The media can play an important role in obtaining that support—or in losing it.

Discussion Questions

1. Why should the police never lie to the press?
2. Does your police department have a press information officer?
3. How fairly do you feel the media in your community report crime and violence? Collect three examples to support your position.
4. How fairly do you feel national media (radio, television, magazines, newspapers) cover crime and violence? Collect three examples to support your position.
5. What might make good topics for PIOs during crime prevention week?
6. Why is it important to remember that journalism is a for-profit business?
7. Do you feel the media are sometimes insensitive to victims and could also be part of the second injury of victimization? If so, can you give examples?
8. What media are available in your community to inform the public of police department operations?
9. Which media do you feel have the most impact on the public?
10. Which view of the media's handling of the Beltway sniper case do you find more accurate?

InfoTrac College Edition Assignments

- Use InfoTrac College Edition to help answer the Discussion Questions when appropriate.
- Find and outline one of the following articles:
  - "When Rights Collide" by Jane Kirtley,
  - "Media Trends and the Public Information Officer" by Dennis Staszak or

- "Focus on Police-Community Relations: Marketing Available Police Services: The MAPS Program" by Mark Fazzini.

■ Driven by TV ratings or newspaper sales, media news coverage has become almost completely crime reporting. Insensitivity toward victims, close-up photos of carnage, revelation of sensitive case facts or of suspects and often just plain poor taste have many Americans fed up with the media. Reporters have accompanied officers on arrest warrant services, ridden along with officers and photographed police work in progress. Research crime reporting ("police and the press") and discuss the pros and cons of the current sensational atmosphere around crime and the media and how it affects perceptions of the crime situation and fear of crime.

Community Projects

■ Examine a weeks' worth of local media crime reporting (newspaper and television). How often do crime stories lead? Do they appear sensationalized? Are crime stories overrepresented?

■ If possible, interview a local crime reporter and a police department representative about crime reporting in your city. How does the reporting relate to the level of crime?

References

Arms, Skip. "Working with the Media in the Case of the 'Texas 7.'" *Problem Solving Quarterly,* Spring 2001, pp.10–11.

Braunstein, Susan. "IACP's PIO Section: Helping Police Executives Meet Today's Media Challenges." *The Police Chief,* April 2001, pp.62–65.

Brewer, Rodney W. "Marketing Your Highway Safety Campaign." *The Police Chief,* July 2002, pp.30–31.

Buice, Ed. "Leadership Principles for Effective Message Management." *The Police Chief,* April 2001, pp.58–60.

Buice, Ed. "Going the Extra Mile with the Media." *Law and Order,* April 2002, p.16.

Buice, Ed. "Keys to Successful Media Interviews." *Law and Order,* September 2003a, p.26).

Buice, Ed. "The PIO Triangle." *Law and Order,* October 2003b, p.32).

Carmichael, Warren R. "Helping Crime Victims Deal with the News Media." *Subject to Debate,* December 2000, pp.1, 2.

Chermak, Steven and Weiss, Alexander. *Identifying Strategies to Market Police in the News.* Washington, DC: National Institute of Justice, 2001. (NCJ 194130)

Chermak, Steven and Weiss, Alexander. *Marketing Community Policing in the News: A Missed Opportunity?* Washington, DC: National Institute of Justice Research for Practice, July 2003. (NCJ 200473)

Collins, Patrick. Handling the Media: The Lessons of Some Moose-Terpiece Theater." *Law Enforcement News,* November 30, 2002, pp.9–12.

Covering Crime and Justice. www.justicejournalism.org/crimeguide

Crawford, Kimberly A. "Media Ride-Alongs: Fourth Amendment Constraints." *FBI Law Enforcement Bulletin,* July 2000, pp.26–31.

Dorfman, Lori. *Off Balance: Youth, Race & Crime in the News.* Washington, DC: Building Blocks for Youth, April 2001.

Fazzini, Mark. "Marketing Available Police Services: The MAPS Program." *FBI Law Enforcement Bulletin,* May 2003, pp.6–9.

Freedom Forum Online. www.freedomforum.org/press/resources/resources.asp

Garner, Gerald W. "Media Guidelines for the Law Enforcement Executive." *Subject to Debate,* October/November 2001, pp.8, 11.

Gary, Charles. "How To . . . Cope with the Press." *Police,* December 2003, pp.24–29.

Herman, Susan. "NCVC Provides Victims with Resources for Handling the Media." *Subject to Debate,* December 2000, p.3.

Hiltbrand, David. "Sniper Case Pulled Back Curtain on Media-Police Relations." Knight-Ridder/Tribune News Service, October 29, 2002.

Jedic, Thomas. "Rechannel Your Approach: Try Cable TV." *Community Policing Exchange,* November/December 2000, p.2.

Johnson, Shane D. and Bowers, Kate J. "Opportunity Is in the Eye of the Beholder: The Role of Publicity in Crime Prevention." *Crime and Justice,* Vol. 2, No.3, 2003, pp.497–524.

Lawrence, Richard. "School Violence, the Media, and the ACJS." *ACJS Today,* May/June 2000, pp.1, 4–6.

Lunney, Robert. "The Public Exposure of Persons in Custody Prior to Conviction." *Subject to Debate,* September 2002, pp.6–7.

Parrish, Penny, media relations instructor at the FBI Academy. Personal conversation, 2003.

"The Right to Remain Silent Takes on a New Meaning." *Law Enforcement News,* July/August 2000, p.1.

Rosenthal, Rick. "Don't Ever Lie to the Media, But . . ." *Law and Order,* September 2000a, pp.17–18.

Rosenthal, Rick. "Meeting with 'The Enemy.'" *Law and Order,* July 2000b, pp.22–24.

Rosenthal, Rick. "Messages from the Front Lines." *Law and Order,* August 2000c, pp.21–22.

Rosenthal, Rick. "Victims, Witnesses and the Media." *Law and Order,* March 2000d, pp.21–22.

Rosenthal, Rick. "More Winning Media Strategies." *Law and Order,* October 2001, pp.16–17.

Rosenthal, Rick. "Tactics of a Great PIO." *Law and Order,* February 2002, pp.32–34.

Rosenthal, Rick. "Training the Media." *ILEETA Digest,* October/December 2003, p.3.

Sparks, Ancil B. and Staszak, Dennis D. "Fine Tuning Your News Briefing." *FBI Law Enforcement Bulletin,* December 2000, pp.22–24.

Staszak, Dennis. "Media Trends and the Public Information Officer." *FBI Law Enforcement Bulletin,* March 2001, pp.10–13.

Strandberg, Keith W. "Back to Basics: Media Relations 101." *Law Enforcement Technology,* August 2000, pp.90–94.

Toohey, Bill. "Tips from the Trenches: Advice from a PIO." *The Police Chief,* April 2001, pp.43–46.

Tyler, Gary K. "Four Ways to Improve Your Media Relations." *The Police Chief,* April 2001, pp.48–51.

Van Blaricom, D. P. "The Media: Enemies or Allies?" *The Police Chief,* April 2001, pp.52–56.

Additional Resources

Pparrish@FBIacademy.edu

Radio Television News Director's Association, 1000 Connecticut Avenue NW, Suite 615, Washington, DC 20036; (202) 659-6510.

SECTION III

COMMUNITY POLICING IN THE FIELD: COLLABORATIVE EFFORTS

CHAPTERS IN THIS SECTION:

The Office of Community Oriented Policing Services (COPS) leads in the efforts to implement community policing throughout the country. The COPS Office defines community policing as "a policing philosophy that promotes and supports organizational strategies to address the causes and reduce the fear of crime and social disorder through problem-solving tactics and police–community partnerships."

The director of the COPS Office is Carl R. Peed, who was appointed on September 4, 2001, by Attorney General John Ashcroft. Director Reed was formerly the director of Virginia's Department of Juvenile Justice and prior to that, he served for 25 years with the Fairfax County Sheriff's Office, the last 10 years as sheriff.

Community policing focuses on crime and social disorder through the delivery of police services that include aspects of traditional law enforcement, as well as prevention, problem solving, community engagement and partnerships. The community policing model balances reactive responses to calls for service with proactive problem solving centered on the causes of crime and disorder. Community policing requires police and citizens to join together as partners in the course of both identifying and effectively addressing these issues.

As explained in the previous section, communities consist of individuals, organizations, businesses, agencies, the media, citizen groups, schools, churches and police departments. Effective interactions with the members of ethnic and cultural minorities, the disabled, the elderly, the young, crime victims and witnesses and the media are critical to developing projects and programs to meet a community's needs.

This section begins by describing early experiments in crime prevention and community policing strategies (Chapter 9). It then looks at efforts to address crime, disorder and fear concerns at the neighborhood level (Chapter 10). Next is a discussion of partnerships to involve youths and to make our schools safer (Chapter 11) and then a discussion of strategies to combat gang problems (Chapter 12). This is followed by strategies to combat the drug problem (Chapter 13) and strategies to combat violence and terrorism (Chapter 14). The section concludes with a look at what research reveals about the effectiveness of various strategies, including where efforts might be focused in the future (Chapter 15).

CHAPTER 9

Early Experiments in Crime Prevention and the Evolution of Community Policing Strategies

Don't be afraid to take a big step if one is indicated.
You can't cross a chasm in two small jumps.

—David Lloyd George, former prime minister of England

DO YOU KNOW?

- What the most commonly implemented crime prevention programs have traditionally been?
- What types of special crime watches have been used?
- What organizations have concentrated their efforts on community crime prevention?
- How volunteers are used in crime prevention?
- What traditional programs for youths have promoted positive police–community relations and enhanced crime prevention efforts?
- What a police–school liaison program is? What its dual goals are?
- What the most common strategies used in community policing have traditionally been?
- What was demonstrated in studies of community policing in Flint? Newark? Oakland? San Diego? Houston? Boston? Baltimore County?
- What was demonstrated in studies of community crime prevention programs in Seattle, Portland and Hartford?
- What the CPTED Commercial Demonstration Project in Portland found?
- What components of the criminal justice system can help reduce the crime problem?
- What court-based approaches have proven effective?
- What corrections-based approaches have proven effective?
- How successful the McGruff national campaign was?
- How successful crime prevention newsletters are?
- What are characteristics of several exemplary police–community strategies?
- What impediments might hinder implementing community policing?

Can You Define?

CPTED
cross-sectional analysis
DARE
empirical study
Guardian Angels
PAL
panel analysis
police–school liaison program
PSAs
qualitative evaluations
reciprocity
statistically significant

Introduction

Community involvement with and assistance in accomplishing the mission of law enforcement is becoming widely accepted. The change toward community involvement is illustrated in a change in the Portland Police Department's mission statement. The old mission statement proclaimed:

> The Bureau of Police is responsible for the preservation of the public peace, protection of the rights of persons and property, the prevention of crime, and the enforcement of all Federal laws, Oregon state statutes and city ordinances within the boundaries of the City of Portland.

The new mission, in contrast, is:

> To work with all citizens to preserve life, maintain human rights, protect property and promote individual responsibility and community commitment.

A typical backyard gathering on National Night Out. Police officers commonly visit such gatherings to connect with community members.

The change from traditional policing to community involvement does require many chiefs of police and their officers to take risks. Are the results of the shift toward community policing worth the risks? This chapter reviews experiments conducted across the country to answer this question.

Although this chapter may appear somewhat dated, it is a necessary addition to document efforts during the past decades to improve crime prevention strategies and to involve citizens in such efforts. Many lessons were learned from the experiments of this time period.

The chapter begins with a look at traditional approaches to crime prevention and other effective initiatives, including traditional programs for youths. Next is a description of empirical studies in crime prevention conducted in the 1970s and 1980s, followed by a discussion of how community policing efforts may be enhanced through partnerships with the other elements of the criminal justice system—namely, the courts and corrections. Use of the media in crime prevention is discussed as well as lessons learned from previous decades. The chapter concludes with a discussion of qualitative evaluations and salient program features, impediments to community policing and the important distinction of programs versus community policing.

Traditional Approaches to Crime Prevention

When crime prevention became popular in the late 1960s and early 1970s, many communities undertook similar types of programs. These programs have continued into the twenty-first century.

Among the most commonly implemented crime prevention programs have been street lighting projects, property marking projects, security survey projects, citizen patrol projects and crime reporting, neighborhood-watch or block projects.

Claims of success should be carefully examined. Critics often say that the evaluations are flawed. Indeed, research within communities is extremely difficult because:

- Measuring what did not happen is nearly impossible.
- Crime is usually underreported.
- A reduction in reported crime could be the result of the crime prevention program or because the responsible criminal or criminals left town, went to jail on some other charge, died and so on.
- Crime can be influenced by everything from seasonal and weather changes, school truancy rates and the flu, to road construction or even a change in a bus stop location. A drop in the crime rate does not necessarily mean a crime prevention program is working.

In addition, many of these programs are evaluated by people who have no training or experience in appropriate research methods; consequently, they sometimes produce flawed results.

Some also argue that crime is not prevented by programs like Neighborhood Watch but instead is displaced to neighborhoods where the residents are not as likely to report suspicious activity to the police. Even if this is true, such programs do raise community awareness and have a "chilling effect" on criminals who are inhibited by those who watch and call the police.

Use of crime data to evaluate crime prevention projects poses special problems. Crime data, obviously, are limited to reported crimes. Practitioners are aware of the dark side of crime, that is, the huge amount of crime that is unreported. When projects are instituted to enlist the community in preventing crime, the citizens' heightened awareness and involvement often results in an increase in reported crime, but this does not necessarily mean that crime itself has actually increased.

As you read this chapter, consider the difficulties in evaluating crime prevention projects or, indeed, any project involving many diverse individuals and problems.

Street Lighting Projects

Since ancient times, lighting has been one means to deter and detect crime. Street lighting projects aimed at crime prevention through environmental design (CPTED) are important elements in a community's crime suppression efforts. Most street lighting projects seek to not only improve the likelihood of deterring and detecting crime but also to improve the safety of law-abiding citizens. Available research indicates that street lighting does not decrease the incidence of crime in participating target areas but that it is useful to reduce citizens' fear of crime and increase their feelings of security.

Property Identification Projects

Often referred to as "Operation Identification" or "O-I" projects, property identification is aimed at deterring burglary and at returning property that is stolen when deterrence fails. Most property identification projects provide citizens with instructions, a marking tool and a unique number to be applied to all valuable items within a household. Stickers are provided to homeowners to display on windows and doors warning possible burglars that the residents have marked their valuables and they are on record with the police. In addition to its deterrent effect, the property identification program also helps police track the source of stolen goods and return stolen property to its rightful owners.

It is sometimes difficult to get people to participate in the program. In addition, although the burglary rate may drop for those enrolled in the program, it may not drop citywide. There is no evidence available to suggest a difference in the number of apprehended or convicted burglars in communities that do or do not participate in the program.

Crime Prevention Security Surveys

Crime prevention security surveys are also usually an integral part of projects that focus on the environmental design of facilities and on "target hardening" as a means to deter or prevent crime. As noted by Crowe (1992, p.22A):

> **CPTED** [Crime Prevention Through Environmental Design] is based on the theory that the proper design and effective use of the built environment can lead

> to a reduction in the incidence and fear of crime and an improvement in the quality of life. Years of experiments and field applications have demonstrated that CPTED works in all environments—that is, it applies to commercial, residential, transportation, recreational and institutional environments.
>
> It has worked on scales as small as a single room and as large as an entire community. [emphasis added]

Surveys used to determine the effectiveness of the existing environmental design are usually conducted by police officers specially trained in this area. They do comprehensive on-site inspection of homes, apartments and businesses. Of particular interest are doors, windows, locks, lighting and shrubbery that might be used to a burglar's advantage. The officer suggests specific ways to make a location more secure.

Citizen Patrol Projects

Many variations of citizen patrol exist in the United States. Some are directed at a specific problem such as crack houses and the sale of drugs in a neighborhood. Others are aimed at general crime prevention and enhanced citizen safety. Citizen patrols may operate throughout a community or may be located within a specific building or complex of buildings such as tenement houses.

The most successful patrols are affiliated with a larger community or neighborhood organization, sustain a working relationship with law enforcement and are flexible enough to engage in noncrime prevention activities when patrolling is patently unnecessary.

One hazard of citizen patrols is the possibility of vigilantism which has a long, often proud, history in the United States and, indeed, in the history of law enforcement and criminal justice. Now this hazard is quite serious because of the increase of readily available handguns in our country.

Probably the best known citizen patrol is the **Guardian Angels**, a group of private citizens who seek to deter crime and to provide a positive role model for young children. Greenberg (1991, p.42) notes: "The Angels wear bright red berets and T-shirts imprinted with a flapping wing and badge insignia. They carry a pad, pen, whistle and—sometimes—handcuffs. Although they carry no weapons, they do attempt to arrest felony suspects and hold them for the police."

A modern expansion of the Angels is the all-volunteer Internet Safety organization. Membership in this group unites more than 1,000 users from 32 countries who police the Internet through what they call Cyberspace Neighborhood Watch. Calling themselves CyberAngels, they focus on protecting children from online abuse by fighting child porn and advising online victims about hate mail.

Citizen Crime Reporting, Neighborhood or Block Programs

Citizen crime reporting programs (CCRPs) help to organize neighborhoods as mutual aid societies and as the eyes and ears of the police. Thousands of Neighborhood-Watch programs exist in the United States, and many describe them as the backbone of the nation's community crime prevention effort. Typically local residents hold meetings of such programs in their homes or apartments. During the meetings, neighbors get to know each other and what is normal activity for their neighborhood. They receive educational information about crime prevention from the local police department and are told how to contact the police if they see something suspicious. Signs are posted throughout the neighborhood warning possible offenders of the program. Often the programs provide safe houses for children to use if they encounter danger on their way to or from school.

Some programs work to enhance citizens' reporting capability. Whistlestop programs, for example, provide citizens with whistles, which they can blow if they are threatened or see something requiring police intervention. Anyone hearing the whistle is to immediately call the police. Whistlestop programs are the modern-day version of the "hue and cry." Other programs have implemented special hotlines whereby citizens can call a specific number with crime information and perhaps receive a monetary reward.

Table 9.1 illustrates the types of activities engaged in by Neighborhood-Watch programs and the relative popularity of each.

Very few of the programs concentrate on only the "Neighborhood Watch." Project Operation Identification and home security surveys are by far the most common activities of Neighborhood-Watch programs. Street lighting programs, crime tip hotlines and physical environmental concerns are also quite common.

Special Crime Watch Programs

In addition to the traditional types of crime watch programs commonly implemented throughout the country, some communities have developed more specialized types of crime watch programs.

Specialized crime watch programs include mobile crime watch, youth crime watch, business crime watch, realtor watch and carrier alert.

Honolulu's mobile crime watch enlists the aid of motorists who have CBs, car phones or cell phones. Volunteers attend a short orientation that trains them to observe and report suspicious activity. Participants also receive Mobile Watch decals for their vehicles. They are advised to call 911 if they hear screaming, gunshots, breaking glass or loud explosive noises or if they see someone breaking into a house or car, a car driven dangerously or erratically, a person on the ground apparently unconscious, anyone brandishing a gun or knife or an individual staggering or threatening others.

They are also trained to recognize and report other unusual behaviors such as children appearing lost; anyone being forced into a vehicle; cars cruising erratically and repetitively near schools, parks and playgrounds; a person running and carrying something valuable; parked, occupied vehicles at unusual hours near potential robbery sites; heavier than normal traffic in and out of a house or commercial establishment; someone going door-to-door or passing through backyards; and persons loitering around schools, parks or secluded areas or in the neighborhood.

Table 9.1 Activities Engaged in by Neighborhood Watch Programs (Based on Program Survey Responses)

Activity	*Number*	*Percent*
Neighborhood Watch Only	49	8.9
Crime Prevention Specific		
Project Operation Identification	425	80.6
Home security surveys	357	67.9
Street lighting improvement	183	34.7
Block parenting	144	27.3
Organized surveillance	66	12.0
Traffic alteration	37	7.0
Emergency telephones	24	4.6
Project Whistle Stop	18	3.4
Specialized informal surveillance	18	3.4
Escort service	12	2.3
Hired guards	11	2.1
Environmental design	7	1.3
Lock provision/installation	4	0.7
Self-defense/rape prevention	3	0.5
Crime Related		
Crime tip hotline	197	37.5
Victim witness assistance	101	19.2
Court watch	17	3.2
Telephone chain	7	1.3
Child fingerprinting	2	0.4
Community Oriented		
Physical environmental concerns	201	38.1
Insurance premium deduction survey	20	3.6
Quality of life	9	1.6
Medical emergency	4	0.7

SOURCE: James Garofalo and Maureen McLeod. *Improving the Use and Effectiveness of Neighborhood Watch Programs.* Washington, DC: U.S. Department of Justice, National Institute of Justice Research in Action Series, April 1988. p.2.

Pace (1992) describes three other specialized watch programs implemented by the Miami-Dade Metro Police Department.

Youth Crime Watch: Elementary and secondary students are trained in crime prevention and in observing and reporting incidents in their schools.

Business Crime Watch: A general meeting of all businesses is held to conduct crime prevention and crime watch training.

Realtor Watch: Realtors throughout the county are trained to crime watch during their working hours in the neighborhoods and commercial areas in which they are selling.

Another specialized type of crime watch is the Carrier Alert program, initiated by the U.S. Postal Service. Mail carriers are asked to become aware of elderly citizens or citizens with special needs on their routes, to look out for them and to report any lack of activity or suspicious activity at their homes to the police.

Most successful community-based programs that focus on crime prevention or safety issues have a close partnership with law enforcement. The community and law enforcement have vital components to offer the other, making cooperation between the two highly desirable. It is difficult to imagine, for instance, an effective community-based crime watch program without input or cooperation from the local police agency. Crime watch programs are built on the premise of mutual aid—citizens and police working together.

Other Efforts to Enhance Crime Prevention

Continuing the community crime prevention momentum generated during the 1960s and 1970s, new programs were initiated during the 1980s and 1990s to encourage citizens to play an active role in reducing crime in their own neighborhoods. These initiatives have included National Night Out; the creation of organizations focused on crime prevention, such as Crime Stoppers and MADD; and the expanded use of volunteers.

National Night Out

National Night Out (NNO) is a program that originated in 1984 in Tempe, Arizona. Held annually on the first Tuesday of August, this nationwide program encourages residents to turn on their porch lights, go outside and meet their neighbors. Neighborhood-Watch programs are encouraged to plan a party or event during National Night Out.

Since 1984, when 2.5 million people in 23 states gathered for the first NNO, the event has grown significantly. In 2003 an estimated 33 million people in nearly 10,100 communities located in all 50 states and a large number of U.S. territories, Canadian cities and U.S. military bases around the world gathered with police officers and administrators to celebrate the event with block parties, safety fairs, youth events, cookouts and parades.

Organizations Focused on Crime Prevention

Among the most visible organizations focused on crime are citizen crime prevention associations, Crime Stoppers and MADD.

Citizen Crime Prevention Associations The many activities undertaken by citizen crime prevention associations include paying for crime tips; funding for police–crime prevention programs; supporting police canine programs; raising community awareness through crime prevention seminars, newsletters, cable TV shows and booths; providing teddy bears for kids; raising money through sources such as business contributions, membership fees, charitable gambling and sales of alarms, mace and "Call Police" signs (usually sold as a service to a community, not to raise any substantial money); and funding specific programs such as rewards to community members who call the hotline with crime information.

Crime Stoppers Crime Stoppers is a nonprofit program involving citizens, the media and the police. Local programs offer anonymity and cash rewards to people who furnish police information that leads to the arrest and indictment of felony offenders. Each program is governed by a local board of directors made up of citizens from a cross section of the community, the businesses of the community and law enforcement. The reward money comes from tax-deductible donations and grants from local businesses, foundations and individuals.

When a crime-related call is received by Crime Stoppers, it is logged in with the date, time and a summary of the information given by the caller. Callers are given code numbers to be used on all subsequent calls by the same person regarding that particular case. Each week, one unsolved crime is selected for special treatment by the media. Over 850 programs throughout the United States, Canada, Australia, England and West Africa are members of Crime Stoppers International.

Mothers Against Drunk Driving (MADD) Mothers Against Drunk Driving is a nonprofit, grassroots organization with over 400 chapters nationwide. Its membership is open to anyone: victims, concerned citizens, law enforcement, safety workers and health professionals. As noted in their literature: "The mission of Mothers Against Drunk Driving is to stop drunk driving and to support victims of this violent crime."

MADD was founded in California in 1980 after Candy Lightner's 13-year-old daughter was killed by a hit-and-run driver. The driver had been out of jail on bail for only two days for another hit-and-run drunk driving crash. He had three previous drunk driving arrests and two convictions; but he was allowed to plea-bargain to vehicular manslaughter. His two-year prison sentence was spent not in prison but in a work camp and later a halfway house. MADD differentiates between accidents and crashes:

> Those injured and killed in drunk driving collisions are not "accident victims." The crash caused by an impaired driver is a violent crime. Drunk driving involves two choices: to drink AND to drive. The thousands of deaths and injuries caused each year by impaired driving can be prevented . . . they are not "accidental." ("Help Keep Families Together," n.d., p.2)

MADD seeks to raise public awareness through community programs such as Operation Prom/Graduation, their poster/essay contest, their "Tie One on for Safety" Project Red Ribbon campaign and a Designated Driver program. Their national newsletter, MADD in Action, is sent to members and supporters. MADD also promotes legislation to strengthen existing laws and adopt new ones. In addition, MADD provides victim services. Annual candlelight vigils are held nationwide to allow victims to share their grief with others who have suffered loss due to drunk driving.

Using Volunteers

Many police departments make extensive use of volunteers.

Volunteers may serve as reserve officers, auxiliary patrol, community service officers or on an as-needed basis.

Reserve officers, auxiliary patrol or community service officers (CSOs) usually wear uniforms and badges but are unarmed. However, in some departments, reserve officers are armed and receive the same training as sworn officers. They are trained to perform specific functions that assist the uniformed patrol officers. They may be used to patrol watching for suspicious activity, to direct traffic, to conduct interviews with victims of and witnesses to crimes and to provide crime prevention education at neighborhood watch meetings, civic groups, churches and schools.

CSOs may work with youths to prevent delinquency, refer citizen complaints to the appropriate agency and investigate minor thefts. They are usually heavily involved in public relations activities as well. Some CSOs are paid, but much less than police officers. Many departments ask professionals such as physicians, teachers and ministers to volunteer their services, sometimes as expert witnesses.

Often volunteers perform office functions in police departments, such as conducting tours or answering telephone messages. They might also provide assistance to police at crime prevention programs and Neighborhood-Watch meetings. Many departments use the AARP volunteer program, capitalizing on the experience and free time of the elderly citizens of the community.

Volunteers provide a communication link between the citizens and the police department. They can help establish the credibility of the department's public relations and educational efforts. Volunteers provide additional sources of information and perspectives.

Using volunteers may, however, cause certain problems. In fact, some police officers feel volunteers are more trouble than they are worth. Among the reasons commonly given for not using volunteers are that they sometimes lack sensitivity to minorities; some citizens seek profit and gain for themselves and develop programs that are mere window dressing; some citizens lack qualifications and training; since volunteers receive no pay, they cannot be docked or penalized for poor performance; citizens lack awareness of the criminal justice system in general and specific agencies in particular; and the use of volunteers by some departments has led to the failure of the local communities and politicians to take responsibility for solving the larger social problem and/or the refusal to hire adequate numbers of personnel or pay better wages.

In addition, some police unions have reacted negatively to volunteers, sometimes viewed as competitors for police jobs. Reserve officers, in particular, tend to cause patrol officers to feel their jobs are threatened by those willing to do police jobs for free or at greatly reduced pay. Officers should know that programs using volunteers are those that could not otherwise exist due to lack of personnel and funding.

Traditional Programs for Youths

Youths have traditionally been included in police–community relations efforts and crime prevention initiatives in several ways.

Common programs aimed at youths include the McGruff "Take a Bite Out of Crime" campaign, police athletic leagues (PALs), Officer Friendly, police explorers, police–school liaison programs and the DARE program.

Other efforts have included school safety programs, bicycle safety programs and programs to fingerprint young children. In different localities, police have developed variations of many of these programs. (Chapter 12 is devoted entirely to projects and programs aimed at youths.)

The McGruff "Take a Bite Out of Crime" Program

The traditional McGruff as a crime prevention spokesperson program, for example, has expanded in some areas to include McGruff Houses, which are safe havens for young children. Another expansion is the McGruff crime dog robot developed by Robotronics. Operated by remote control, the robot winks, blinks, moves his hands and arms, tips and turns his head and has a two-way wireless voice system allowing the operator to talk and listen. The McGruff media campaign is discussed in greater detail later in this chapter.

Police Athletic Leagues

Police departments have also expanded upon the PAL program. The National Police Athletic League (**PAL**), now over 50 years old, was developed to provide opportunities for youths to interact with police officers in gyms or ballparks instead of in a juvenile detention hall.

The Portland (Oregon) Police Department adapted the PAL program to deal with escalating gang violence and street sale of drugs. As Austin and Braaten (1991, p.36) note, the goals of the Portland-area PAL were to reduce the incidence of juvenile crime, substance abuse and gang violence; provide positive alternative activities for boys and girls; guide boys and girls to make responsible decisions in life; and foster better understanding between youths and the police.

To accomplish their goals, the department undertook several activities, including a weeklong Sport Quickness Day Camp for 600 at-risk youths that kept them productively occupied for eight hours a day in boxing, wrestling, football, soccer, martial arts, basketball, racquetball, track and field, volleyball, and speed and quickness training. The department also organized events in which officers could participate with PAL youths, including a one-day fishing excursion, trips to Seattle Sea Hawks football games and scholarships to summer camps.

Officer Friendly

Officer Friendly programs are designed for elementary school children and generally include a police officer who goes into classes to discuss good citizenship, responsibility and general safety. The program uses coloring books and a special activity book that teachers can use with their regular social studies curriculum.

Police Explorers

The traditional police explorer program, an advanced unit of the Boy Scouts of America, also serves many communities. Explorers are typically trained in various aspects of police work such as fingerprinting, identification techniques, first aid and firearms safety. The minimum age for most programs is 15. Explorers usually have a three- to six-month probation with full membership contingent on completing training and meeting proficiency standards as well as acceptable personal conduct.

Explorer programs have two purposes: positive community relations and early recruitment for police departments. Some departments, in fact, make even greater use of their explorer programs. The Chandler (Arizona) Police Department, for example, used two 18-year-old explorers in a sting operation involving a bar and liquor store's employees who sold alcohol to minors.

Many programs for juveniles involve the schools, which have historically been charged with instilling discipline in the students who attend.

Police–School Liaison Programs

In 1958 Flint, Michigan, developed a highly publicized delinquency prevention program involving joint efforts of school authorities, parents, businesses, social agencies, the juvenile court and the police department. Known as a school liaison program, it became widely replicated across the country.

> A **police–school liaison program** places an officer in a school to work with school authorities, parents and students to prevent crime and antisocial behavior and to improve police–youth relationships.

The goals of most police–school liaison programs are to reduce crime incidents involving school-age youths, to suppress by enforcement of the law any illegal threats that endanger the children's educational environment and to improve the attitudes of school-age youths and the police toward one another.

According to Hess and Drowns (2004, p.235): "The techniques used by school [liaison] officers involve counseling children and their parents, referring them to social agencies to treat the root problems, referring them to drug and alcohol abuse agencies and being in daily contact in the school to check their progress. Often school [liaison] officers deal with pre-delinquent and early delinquent youths with whom law enforcement would not have been involved under traditional programs."

Police–school liaison officers do not get involved in school politics or in enforcing school regulations. The school administrators are involved in these matters.

> The joint goals of most police–school liaison programs are to prevent juvenile delinquency and to improve police–youth relations.

The police–school liaison programs can also do much to promote better relations among the police, school administrators and teachers. A number of organizations can focus attention on school–police relations and provide supportive programs both on the community and national levels, for example, the International Association of Chiefs of Police, the National Association of Secondary School Principals and the National Association of School Boards.

Drug use is often a target of police educational programs. Frequently, officers work with schools to develop and promote programs aimed at preventing drug and alcohol abuse, one of the most popular of which is DARE.

The DARE Program

The Drug Abuse Resistance Education (**DARE**) program was developed jointly by the Los Angeles Police Department and the Los Angeles Unified School District. This controversial program is aimed at elementary school children and seeks to teach them to "say no to drugs," to resist peer pressure and to find alternatives to drug use. The program uses a "self-esteem repair" approach.

The city of Ridgecrest, California, initiated a DARE program and wanted a public relations program to help promote it. Ridgecrest used cards similar to baseball cards, each featuring numerous officers in different settings.

DARE is not without its critics, however. It has met with a great deal of opposition in some communities, and the design of some of the research done on DARE is questionable. In addition, much of the research fails to support any long-term, positive results of the program. One study by the University of Kentucky found:

> While DARE produced some initial changes in the attitudes held by children about drug use, the effects were not long-lasting. The findings are nearly identical to those of a 1996 study that followed the progress of some 2,000 students five years after participating in the DARE program. . . .
>
> According to the findings, . . . DARE had no significant effect on either the students' use of drugs, cigarettes and alcohol or their expectancies about the substances. . . . [And] consistent with the findings of earlier research, the study said there appear to be "no reliable short-term, long-term, early adolescent or young adult positive outcomes associated with receiving DARE intervention." ("DARE Chief Raps . . .," 1999, p.1)

The founder and president of DARE America concedes the program is not a "magic bullet" but believes it is a valuable part of the big picture and is confident it helps reduce drug use. Nonetheless, many police departments who have used the DARE program for years are discontinuing its use—and this appears to be a growing trend. Perhaps the reason is that not enough emphasis is placed on what to say "yes" to.

During the 1980s many of these early strategies and programs were adopted by departments moving toward community policing. Also during this time, many departments began experimenting with a variety of community policing strategies. As evidenced by numerous studies, some strategies were successful; others were not.

Empirical Studies of Community Policing

An **empirical study** is based on observation or practical experience. Greene and Taylor (1991, pp.206–221) describe studies of community policing in major cities throughout the country, including Flint, Newark, Oakland, San Diego, Houston, Boston and Baltimore County.

The most common strategies traditionally used in community policing were foot patrol, newsletters and community organizing.

Flint, Michigan

The classic Neighborhood Foot Patrol Program of Flint, Michigan, was conducted from January 1979 to January 1982. It focused on 14 experimental neighborhoods to which 22 police officers and 3 supervisors were assigned. The officers were given great discretion in what they could do while on foot patrol, but communication with citizens was a primary objective.

The Flint Neighborhood Foot Patrol Program appeared to decrease crime, increase general citizen satisfaction with the foot patrol program, reduce citizens' fear of crime and create a positive perception of the foot patrol officers.

Mastrofski (1992) explains that the Flint study tried to document what police did on foot patrol and how that differed from motorized patrol. He (p.24) notes:

> Looking at the department's daily report forms, the researchers found that foot officers reported many more self-initiated activities—such as home and business visits and security checks—than police in cars. Officers on foot averaged much higher levels of productivity across most of the standard performance measures: arrests, investigations, stopping of suspicious persons, parking citations, and value of recovered property. The only category in which motor patrol officers clearly outproduced their foot patrol counterparts was in providing miscellaneous services to citizens.

According to citizen surveys (Trojanowicz, 1986, pp.165–167), 64 percent were satisfied with the project and 68 percent felt safer. When asked to compare foot patrol and motorized patrol officers, citizens rated the foot patrol officers higher by large margins on four of the six areas: preventing crime, encouraging citizen self-protection, working with juveniles and following up on complaints. Motorized patrol officers were rated superior only in responding to complaints. In addition, in the foot patrol neighborhoods' crime rates were down markedly, and calls for service were down more than 40 percent.

No statistical tests were done, however, and results across the 14 neighborhoods varied greatly. Therefore, the results should be interpreted with caution. In addition, problems were encountered in the Flint Foot Patrol Program. For example, because the program was loosely structured, some officers were not accountable, and their job performance was poor. Nonetheless, according to Skolnick and Bayley (1986, p.216):

> Foot patrol . . . appears from our observations and other studies to generate four meritorious effects. (1) Since there is a concerned human presence on the street, foot patrol is more adaptable to street happenings, and thus may prevent crime before it begins. (2) Foot patrol officers may make arrests, but they are also around to give warnings either directly or indirectly, merely through their presence. (3) Properly carried out, foot patrol generates goodwill in the neighborhood, which has the derivative consequence of making other crime prevention

tactics more effective. This effectiveness in turn tends to raise citizen morale and reduce their fear of crime. (4) Foot patrol seems to raise officer morale.

Newark 1

The original Newark Foot Patrol Experiment was done between 1978 and 1979 and addressed the issues of untended property and untended behavior. This experiment used 12 patrol beats. Eight of the beats, identified as using foot patrol, were divided into pairs, matched by the number of residential and nonresidential units in each. One beat in each pair dropped foot patrol. An additional four beats that had not previously used foot patrol added foot patrol officers. As in the Flint experiment, officers had great flexibility in their job responsibilities while on foot patrol.

In the first Newark Foot Patrol Experiment, residents reported positive results, while business owners reported negative results.

In areas where foot patrol was added, residents reported a decrease in the severity of crime and evaluated police performance more positively. Business owners, however, believed that street disorder and publicly visible crime increased and reported that the neighborhood had become worse. Pate (1986, p.155) summarizes the results of the first experiment.

> The addition of intensive foot patrol coverage to relatively short (8–16 block) commercial/residential strips during five evenings per week over a one-year period can have considerable effects on the perceptions of residents concerning disorder problems, crime problems, the likelihood of crime, safety, and police service. Such additional patrol, however, appears to have no significant effect on victimization, recorded crime, or the likelihood of reporting a crime.
>
> The elimination of foot patrol after years of maintenance, however, appears to produce few notable negative effects. Similarly, the retention of foot patrol does not prove to have notable beneficial effects.

Newark 2

A second foot patrol experiment was conducted in Newark in 1983 and 1984. This experiment used three neighborhoods and a control group (which received no "treatment").

The second Newark Foot Patrol Experiment included a coordinated foot patrol, a cleanup campaign and distribution of a newsletter. Only the coordinated foot patrol was perceived to reduce perception of property crime and improve assessments of the police.

The cleanup effort and newsletter programs did not affect any of the outcome measures studied, nor did they reduce crime rates. Nonetheless, the Police Foundation (1981, p.118) notes: "If vulnerable and weak people feel safe as a result of specific police activity and if that feeling improves the quality of their life, that is terribly important."

Oakland

In 1983 Oakland assigned 28 officers to foot patrol in Oakland's central business district. In addition, a Report Incidents Directly program was established whereby local businesspeople could talk directly to the patrol officers about any matters that concerned them. Mounted patrol and small vehicle patrols were also used.

The Oakland program, using foot patrol, mounted patrol, small vehicle patrol and a Report Incidents Directly program, resulted in a substantial drop in the rate of crime against individuals and their property.

The crime rate dropped in the Oakland treatment area more than citywide declines, but again, no statistical tests were reported for this experiment.

San Diego

San Diego conducted a community profile project from 1973 to 1974 designed to improve police–community interactions. Twenty-four patrol officers and three supervisors were given 60 hours of community orientation training. The performance of these officers was compared with 24 other patrol officers who did not receive the training.

The San Diego Community Profile Project provided patrol officers with extensive community-orientation training. These officers became more service oriented, increased their nonlaw enforcement contacts with citizens and had a more positive attitude toward police–community relations.

The project did not consider the effect of community profiling on crime or on citizens' fear of crime.

Houston

Like the second Newark experiment, Houston conducted a fear-reduction experiment between 1983 and 1984, testing five strategies: a victim recontact program following victimization, a community newsletter, a citizen contact patrol program, a police storefront office and a program aimed to organize the community's interest in crime prevention.

The victim recontact program and the newsletter of the Houston Fear-Reduction Project did not have positive results. The citizen contact patrol and the police storefront office did, however, result in decreases in perceptions of social disorder, fear of personal victimization and the level of personal and property crime.

The victim recontact program, in fact, backfired, with Hispanics and Asians experiencing an increase in fear. Contact was primarily with white homeowners rather than minority renters. As Skogan and Wycoff (1986, pp.182–183) note, the police storefront officers developed several programs, including monthly meetings, school programs, a fingerprinting program, a blood pressure program, a ride-along program, a park program and an anticrime newsletter. A comparison of these results to those achieved in the Newark experiment is made on pp.264, 265.

Boston

In 1983 Boston changed from predominantly two-officer motorized patrol to foot patrol and shifted the responsibilities of the foot patrol and motorized one-officer patrol to less serious crimes and noncrime service calls. The experiment studied 105 beats to determine whether high, medium, low, unstaffed or no change in foot patrol affected calls for service by priority.

The Boston Foot Patrol Project found no statistically significant relationship between changes in the level of foot patrol provided and number of calls for service or the seriousness of the calls.

Violent crimes were not affected by increased or decreased foot patrol staffing. After the department shifted to foot patrol, the number of street robberies dropped, but the number of commercial robberies rose.

Baltimore County

The Baltimore Citizen Oriented Police Enforcement (COPE) Project, started in 1981, focused on the reduction of citizens' fear of crime. This problem-oriented project focused on solving the community problems of fear and disorder that lead to crime. According to Taft (1986, p.10): "'Citizen Oriented Police Enforcement' officers would engage in intensive patrol, develop close contacts with citizens, conduct 'fear surveys' (door-to-door canvassing to identify concerns) and use any means within their power to quell fear."

Baltimore County's COPE Project reduced fear of crime by 10 percent and crime itself by 12 percent in target neighborhoods. It also reduced calls for service, increased citizen awareness of and satisfaction with the police, and improved police officer attitudes.

A study conducted in 1985 indicated that the COPE Project "passed its first statistical test with flying colors" (Taft, p.20). The results of the study are summarized in Figure 9.1.

Summary and Implications of the Experiments

Greene and Taylor (p.215) note that "there is not much consistency in findings across studies." Regarding fear of crime, Newark 1 observed a reduction; Newark 2 observed a reduction in the **panel analysis** (where the data were analyzed by individuals responding). It did not show a reduction in the **cross-sectional analysis** (where the data were analyzed by area rather than by individuals responding). The Houston study had the opposite results: a reduction in fear in the cross-sectional analysis but not in the panel analysis. In the Flint study, citizen perceptions of the seriousness of crime problems increased. In Baltimore County it declined slightly. The San Diego, Oakland and Boston programs did not consider fear of crime. Greene and Taylor (p.216) conclude: "Based on the problems associated with the evaluation of each of these programs, there is at present no consistent evidence that foot patrol reduces fear of crime."

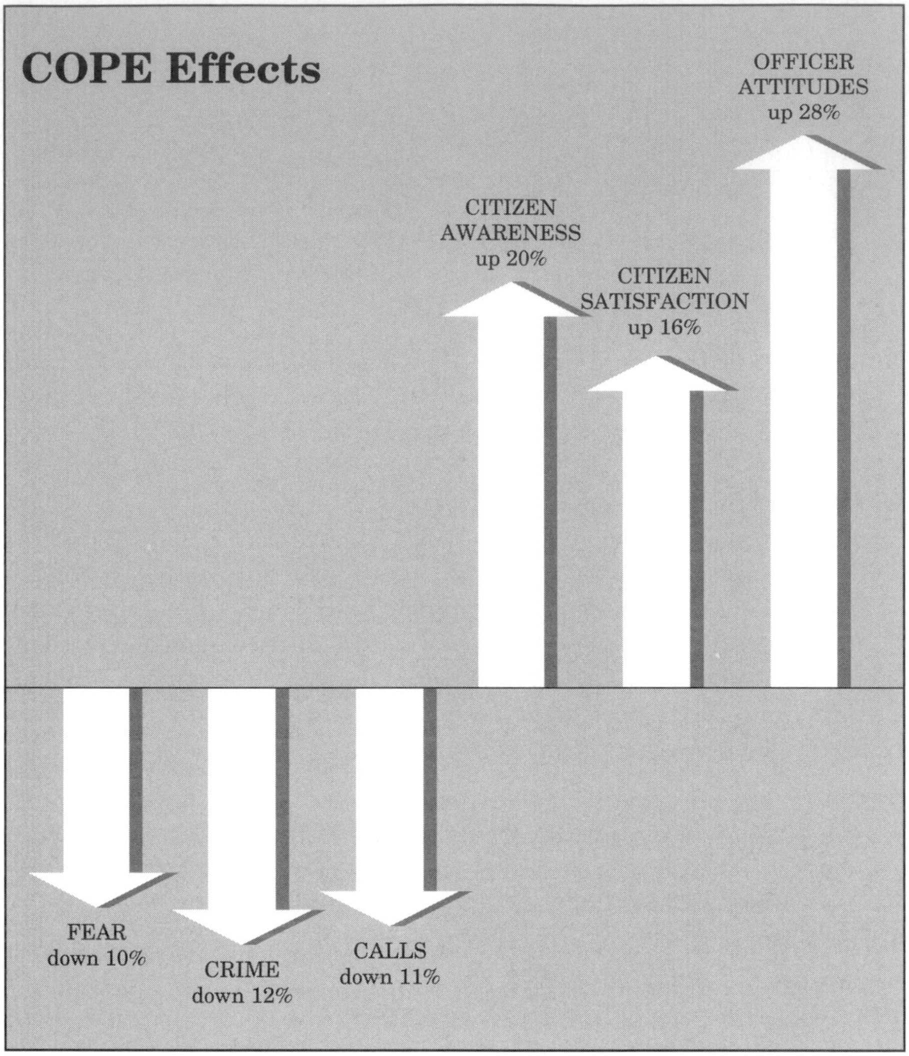

Figure 9.1 COPE Effects

SOURCE: Philip B. Taft, Jr. *Fighting Fear: The Baltimore County COPE Project.* © The Police Executive Research Forum, 20. Washington: 1986. Reprinted with permission of PERF.

Greene and Taylor also note inconsistent findings regarding crime rates. The Oakland study was the only one to demonstrate a reduction, but no statistical treatment was done. Again they (p.216) conclude: "Clearly, these studies do not point to decreases in crime or disorder as a consequence of community policing or foot patrol."

Greene and Taylor discuss several problems with the research designs of the eight studies of community policing and suggest ways to improve the designs. This is not the view taken by Wycoff (1991, p.103), however, who states that the fear-reduction studies conducted in Houston and Newark: "provide evidence of the efficacy of what the authors referred to as 'community-oriented' policing strategies for reducing citizen fear, improving citizens' attitudes toward their neighborhoods and toward the police and reducing crime."

Fear-Reduction Strategies Experiments Compared

Wycoff (pp.107–108) summarizes the seven strategies tested in the Newark and Houston experiments as follows:

> *Newsletters* (Houston and Newark). These were tested with and without crime statistics. They were police produced and provided residents of the test area with information about crime prevention steps they could take, the police department, and police programs in their area.
>
> *Victim recontact* (Houston). Patrol officers made telephone contact with victims to inform them of the status of their case, inquire whether they needed assistance, offer to send crime prevention information, and ask whether victims could provide additional information.
>
> *Police community station* (Houston). A neighborhood storefront operation was conducted by patrol officers. The station provided a variety of services for the area.
>
> *Citizen contact patrol* (Houston). Officers concentrated their patrol time within the target area where they made door-to-door contacts, introducing themselves to residents and businesspeople, and asking whether there were any neighborhood problems citizens wished brought to the attention of the police.
>
> *Community organizing* (Houston). Officers from the Community Services Division worked to organize block meetings attended by area patrol officers. They organized a neighborhood committee that met monthly with the district captain and developed special projects ("safe" houses for children, identifying property, and a cleanup campaign) for the area.
>
> *Signs of crime* (Newark). This program focused on social disorder and conducted "random intensified enforcement and order maintenance operations" (e.g., foot patrol to enforce laws and maintain order on sidewalks and street corners, radar checks, bus checks to enforce ordinances and order, enforcement of disorderly conduct laws to move groups off the street corners and road checks for DWI, improper licenses or stolen vehicles). Addressing physical deterioration involved an intensification of city services and the use of juvenile offenders to conduct cleanup work in the target areas.
>
> *Coordinated community policing* (Newark). This was the "kitchen sink" project that included a neighborhood community police center, a directed police–citizen contact program, a neighborhood police newsletter, intensified law enforcement and order maintenance and a neighborhood cleanup.

Two types of samples were used: (1) cross-sectional analysis that gave data for each area and (2) panel respondents who gave data for individuals. The results of the testing are summarized in Tables 9.2 and 9.3.

The checks in the tables indicate that the results were **statistically significant** at the .05 level. This measurement means that the results would occur by chance

Table 9.2 Effects of Fear-Reduction Programs (Cross-Sectional Results) (Area Results)

Programs	*Reduce Perceived Area Physical Deterioration*	*Reduce Perceived Area Social Disorder*	*Reduce Fear of Personal Victimization*	*Reduce Worry about Property Crime*	*Reduce Perceived Area Personal Crime*	*Reduce Perceived Area Property Crime*	*Improve Evaluation of Police*	*Increase Satisfaction with Area*
Houston Newsletters with and without Statistics	n.a.	n.a.						
Newark Newsletters with and without Statistics	n.a.	n.a.						
Houston Victim Recontact Program	n.a.	n.a.						
Houston Police Community Station	n.a.	✔	✔		✔	✔		
Houston Citizen Contact Patrol	n.a.	✔	✔		✔	✔		✔
Houston Community Organizing Response Team	n.a.	✔					✔	
Netwark "Signs of Crime" Program								
Netwark Coordinated Community Policing		✔		✔		✔	✔	

✔ = Desired goal achieved; significant at .05 level

n.a. = Not applicable

SOURCE: A. M. Pate, W. G. Skogan, M. A. Wycoff and L. W. Sherman. *Reducing the "Signs of Crime": The Newark Experience.* Washington, DC: The Police Foundation, 1986. © The Police Foundation. Reprinted by permission.

only five times in one hundred. This level is most frequently used in such studies. A statistically significant finding at the .01 level means the results would occur by chance only one time in one hundred.

The programs were least effective reducing concerns about property crime and most effective reducing perceived social disorder. According to the data provided by individuals, the Newark Coordinated Community Policing study met the greatest number of goals.

Other Crime Prevention Program Studies in the 1980s

Several communities conducted crime prevention studies in the 1980s. Studies in Seattle, Portland and Hartford focused on citizen efforts to prevent residential crime; the study in Portland also focused on preventing crime in and around commercial establishments. Two studies examined the media and crime prevention: the McGruff national media campaign and the effectiveness of anticrime newsletters.

According to Heinzelmann (1986, p.7): "In general, the results of these evaluations are favorable, indicating that community crime prevention programs can serve

Table 9.3 Effects of Fear-Reduction Programs (Panel Results) (Individual Results)

Programs	***Reduce Perceived Area Physical Deterioration***	***Reduce Perceived Area Social Disorder***	***Reduce Fear of Personal Victimization***	***Reduce Worry about Property Crime***	***Reduce Perceived Area Personal Crime***	***Reduce Perceived Area Property Crime***	***Improve Evaluation of Police***	***Increase Satisfaction with Area***
Houston Newsletters with and without Statistics	n.a.	n.a.						
Newark Newsletters with and without Statistics	n.a.	n.a.						
Houston Victim Recontact Program	n.a.	n.a.						
Houston Police Community Station	n.a.		✔		✔			
Houston Citizen Contact Patrol	n.a.	✔					✔	✔
Houston Community Organizing Response Team	n.a.	✔			✔	✔	✔	
Newark "Signs of Crime" Program								
Newark Coordinated Community Policing		✔	✔	✔		✔	✔	✔

✔ = Desired goal achieved; significant at .05 level

n.a. = Not applicable

SOURCE: A. M. Pate, W. G. Skogan, M. A. Wycoff and L. W. Sherman. *Reducing the "Signs of Crime": The Newark Experience* 28. Washington, DC. The Police Foundation, 1986. © The Police Foundation. Reprinted by permission.

to reduce crime and fear, and at the same time improve the quality of life and the economic viability of urban neighborhoods and commercial settings."

The Seattle Program

The Citywide Crime Prevention Program (CCPP) of Seattle, described by Lindsay and McGillis (1986, pp.46–67), focused on residential burglaries and included three primary police services: property identification, home security checks and organizing neighborhood block watch programs.

The Seattle Citywide Crime Prevention Program used property identification, home security checks and neighborhood block watches to significantly reduce the residential burglary rate as well as the number of burglary-in-progress calls.

Fleissner et al. (1992, p.9) note:

> When citizens and police in South Seattle banded together to fight crime, quarterly crime statistics showed dramatic improvements in the quality of life. Citizen

activity spread in the city's other three police precincts; now community policing is a going concern throughout Seattle—a citywide success.

According to Lindsay and McGillis (p.65), not only did the burglary rate drop significantly, "burglary-in-progress calls as a proportion of all burglary calls to police increased significantly in treated areas, and their quality was relatively high as measured by presentation of suspect information and the occurrence of subsequent arrests."

The Portland Program

Portland also instituted a burglary prevention program, described by Schneider (1986, pp.68–86), which included providing citizens with information about locks, alarms, outside lighting around entrances, removal or trimming of hedges and precautions to take while on vacation. The program also encouraged citizens to mark property with identification numbers. Door-to-door canvassing and a heavy emphasis on neighborhood rather than individual protection were important components of the program.

The Portland antiburglary program succeeded in reducing the burglary rate for those who participated.

As Schneider (p.84) notes: "In the high crime areas of Portland more than 20% of the homes could expect to be burglarized at least once a year. This was reduced to about 8% for participating households in those areas." Schneider (p.85) also points out a class bias in this study: "Those attending meetings, engraving their property, and displaying the decals tended to be in the higher socioeconomic groups."

The Hartford Experiment

The Hartford Experiment, described by Fowler and Mangione (1986, pp.87–108), used a three-pronged approach to reduce crime and the fear of crime: changing the physical environment, changing the delivery of police services and organizing the citizens to improve their neighborhoods. This experiment centered on the interdependence of citizens, the police and the environment. As Fowler and Mangione (p.89) note: "The approach focuses on the interaction between human behavior and the (physically) built environment. It was hypothesized that the proper design and effective use of the built environment can lead to a reduction in crime and fear."

The program was based on four previous research efforts. First was that of Jacobs (1961), which found that neighborhoods that were relatively crime free had a mix of commercial and residential properties, resulting in many people on the streets and a great opportunity for police surveillance. In addition, a community with such mixed use property tended to have residents who cared about the neighborhood and watched out for each other.

Angel (1968) described similar findings in his concept of "critical density," which states that if quite a few people are present on the most frequently used streets, they will serve as deterrents to burglary. In addition, Newman's classic work

(1972) suggests that crime can be reduced by redesigning buildings to increase the number of doorways and other spaces that could be easily observed. Finally, Repetto (1974), like Newman, found that opportunities for surveillance could reduce crime and, like Jacobs, that neighborhood cohesiveness could have the same result.

Based on this research, the Hartford Experiment focused on Asylum Hill, a residential area a few blocks from the central business district of Hartford that was rapidly deteriorating. It was found that due to the high rate of vehicle traffic, residents did not use their yards and felt no ties to the neighborhood. The physical design of the neighborhood was changed to restrict through traffic and visually define the boundaries of the neighborhood. Cul-de-sacs were built at a few critical intersections, and some streets were made one way.

A second change in the neighborhood involved patrol officer assignments. Instead of rotating assignments within a centralized department, Hartford began using a decentralized team of officers assigned permanently to the Asylum Hill area.

Finally, the Hartford Experiment helped organize the neighborhood, including the establishment of block watch programs, recreational programs for youths and improvements for a large neighborhood park.

As a result of these changes: "Residents used their neighborhood more, walked more often both during the day and evening hours, used the nearby park more often, and spent more days per week outside in front of their homes" (Fowler and Mangione, p.96).

The Hartford Experiment restructured the neighborhood's physical environment, changed the way patrol officers were assigned and organized the neighborhood in an effort to reduce crime and the fear of crime.

Fowler and Mangione (p.106) caution: "A crime control program such as this must be custom fit to a particular set of circumstances. What one would want to derive from the Hartford project is not a program design, but rather an approach to problem analysis and strategies to affect them."

The Portland Commercial Demonstration Project

The Crime Prevention through Environmental Design (CPTED) Commercial Demonstration Project implemented in Portland from 1974 to 1979, described by Lavrakas and Kushmuk (1986, pp.202–227), also built upon the research of Jacobs and Newman and the concept of "defensible space." The CPTED Project incorporated four major strategies: motivation reinforcement, activity support, surveillance and access control, as described in Figure 9.2.

The CPTED Project developed seven specific strategies (Lavrakas and Kushmuk, pp.206–207): (1) creation of a "Safe Streets for People" component, (2) creation of a residential activity center and miniplazas along Union Avenue Corridor (UAC), (3) general promotion of UAC, (4) improved transportation both into and out of UAC, (5) security services provided by a UAC security advisor, (6) increased law enforcement support throughout UAC and (7) development of a "Cash Off the Streets" program. The first two strategies of the CPTED Project involved redesigning

MOTIVATION REINFORCEMENT

Design and Construction: Design, build, and/or repair buildings and building sites to enhance security and improve quality.

Owner/Management Action: Encourage owners and managements to implement safeguards to make businesses and commerical property less vulnerable to crime.

Territorial Identity: Differentiate private areas from public spaces to discourage trespass by potential offenders.

Neighborhood Image: Develop positive image of the commercial area to encourage user and investor confidence and increase the economic vitality of the area.

ACTIVITY SUPPORT

Land Use: Establish policies to prevent ill-advised land and buildings uses that have negative impact.

User Protection: Implement safeguards to make shoppers less vulnerable to crime.

Social Interaction: Encourage interaction among businessmen, users, and residents of commercial neighborhoods to foster social cohesion and control.

Police/Community Relations: Improve police/community relations to involve citizens in cooperative efforts with police to prevent and report crime.

Community Awareness: Create community crime prevention awareness to aid in combating crime in commercial areas.

SURVEILLANCE

Surveillance Through Physical Design: Improve opportunities for surveillance by physical design mechanisms that serve to increase the risk of detection for offenders, enable evasive actions by potential victims, and facilitate intervention by police.

Mechanical Surveillance Devices: Provide businesses with security devices to detect and signal illegal entry attempts.

Private Security Services: Determine necessary and appropriate services to enhance commercial security.

Police Services: Improve police services in order to efficiently and effectively respond to crime problems and to enhance citizen cooperation in reporting crimes.

ACCESS CONTROL

Access Control: Provide secure barriers to prevent unauthorized access to building grounds, buildings, and/or restricted building interior areas.

Figure 9.2 Commercial Environment Objectives of CPTED

Note: The four key hypotheses are not mutually exclusive. Surveillance objectives also serve to control access; activity support involves surveillance; and motivation reinforcement provides support for the other three hypotheses.

SOURCE: H. Kaplan, K. O'Kane, P. J. Lavrakas, and S. Hoover. *CPTED Final Report on Commercial Demonstration in Portland, Oregon.* Arlington: Westinghouse Electric Corporation, 1978. © Westinghouse Electric Corporation. Reprinted by permission.

some streets, improving roads, adding street lighting and generally making the area more attractive.

The Portland CPTED Commercial Demonstration Project found that the most successful strategies were security services, organization and support of the business community and the street lighting program.

According to Lavrakas and Kushmuk (p.223): "Of moderate success were the economic development activities. Large-scale and comprehensive improvements in

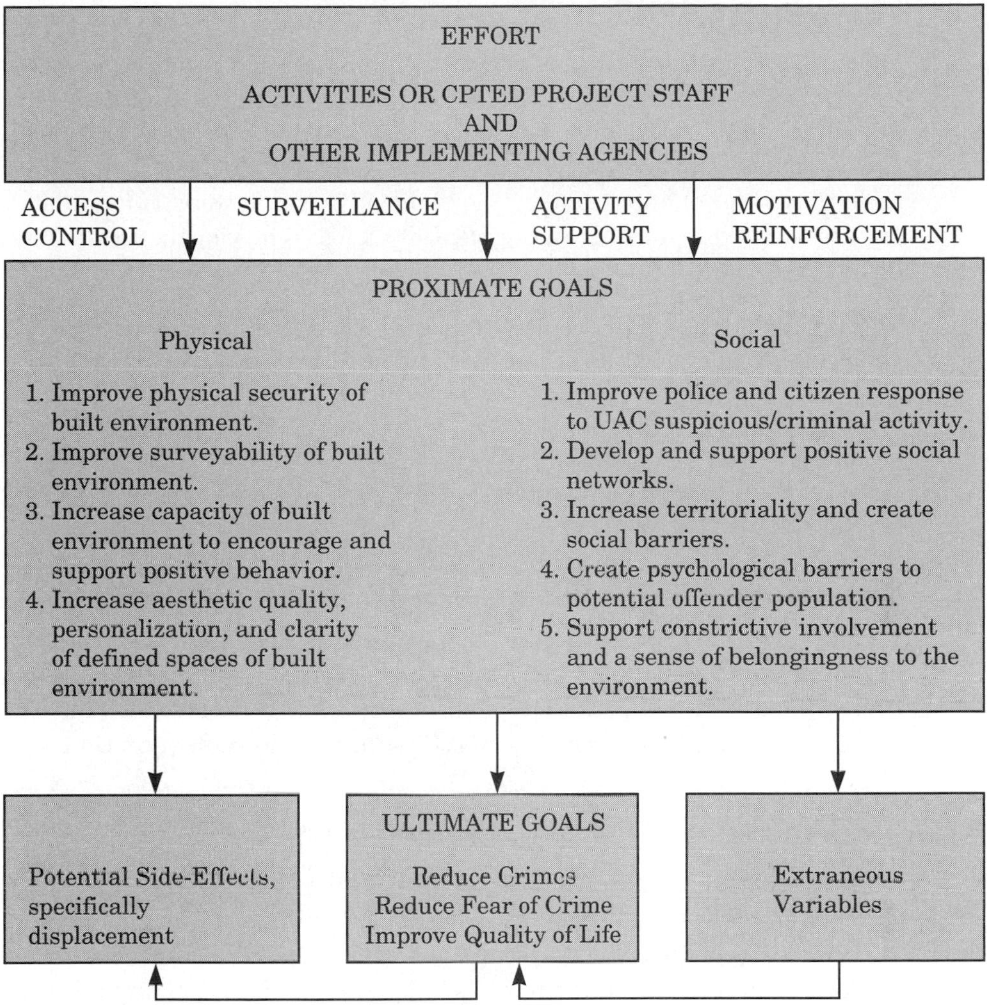

Figure 9.3 CPTED Evaluation Design

SOURCE: P. J. Lavrakas, J. Normoyle and J. Wagener. *CPTED Commercial Demonstration Evaluation Report.* Evanston: Westinghouse Electric Corporation, 1978. Reprinted by permission.

the physical environment (with the exception of the redesign of Union Avenue itself), promotional events, and residential social cohesion were judged to have achieved, at best, low levels of success." (See Figure 9.3.)

Lavrakas and Kushmuk (pp.223–224) suggest three important lessons learned from this project. First, it is essential to have a realistic time frame and strong political support. Second, the more groups involved, the more complicated and difficult the project will become. And third, changes in the social environment of a community are much more difficult to make than those in the physical environment.

Community Policing and the Criminal Justice System

The criminal justice system includes law enforcement, the courts and corrections. What happens in each component of the criminal justice system directly affects the other two components, and many of the trends that affect the criminal justice system as a whole directly affect the type of programs police departments should implement to improve community relations. Consequently, partnerships among the various entities within the criminal justice system are vital to achieving the community policing mission.

A coordinated effort among law enforcement, courts and corrections is required to effectively deal with the crime problem and to elicit the support of the community in doing so.

Effective efforts are those that partner various community institutions to address issues of housing, unemployment, illiteracy, lack of recreational opportunities for youths and other social problems.

Community Policing and the Courts

The way courts address the accused has a direct impact on the crime problem and on community policing efforts. The National Symposium identified two model court programs: the Albany (New York) Community Dispute Resolution Centers and the Madison (Wisconsin) Deferred Prosecution/First Offenders Unit.

Model court programs also involving the police include community dispute resolution centers and a deferred prosecution/first offenders unit.

Community Dispute Resolution Centers (Albany) The 32 dispute resolution centers were independent, community-based, nonprofit organizations contracted by the Unified Court System of the State of New York, Albany, to (1) provide dispute resolution resources for local communities, (2) prevent escalation of disputes, (3) relieve the courts of matters not requiring judicial intervention and (4) teach individuals to resolve their problems through mediation.

Police officers, probation officers, judges, district attorneys and legal aid offices could refer cases to a local dispute resolution center, or individuals could be self-referred. The mediation, conciliation or arbitration services were provided free. Mediation rather than law enforcement or court intervention was effective.

The Deferred Prosecution/First Offenders Unit (Madison) This program sought to prevent offenders' further involvements in crime by deferring prosecution on the condition that they satisfactorily complete appropriate treatment and rehabilitation programs. The program recognized the hazards of labeling individuals and the potential of treatment for first offenders who accept responsibility for their actions.

An offender's suitability for the program was based on several criteria: the nature of the offense, prior criminal record, admission of guilt, attitude, whether the offender was dangerous to self or community, likelihood of repeating the crime and whether the offender would benefit from the treatment process.

The program used a large network of social service agencies and public and private organizations. Because a "substantial portion" of program participants were shoplifters, the staff conducted a one-day Saturday workshop on retail theft. Another integral part of the program was voluntary community service, not as a means of punishment, but as a way to repay the community for the crime committed and to change the offender's behavior patterns. The program conserved police, prosecutorial, judicial and correctional resources. In addition, offenders' lives were minimally disrupted because they could continue to pursue their occupations and fulfill family obligations.

Community Policing and Corrections

Community-based corrections gained popularity in the 1990s but is still resisted by many neighborhoods. Sometimes referred to as intermediate sanctions, community corrections may take many forms including halfway houses, prerelease centers, transition centers, work furlough and community work centers, community treatment centers, restitution centers and a host of other innovative approaches to involving the community in efforts to reintegrate offenders into the community *without* danger to the citizens.

Residents may live either part time or full time at such centers, depending on the other conditions set forth by the court. Evans (1996, pp.124–125) notes: "Community corrections is effective and efficient when it works in partnership with local communities and other agencies interested in safer communities and justice."

Community corrections can be viewed as a part of the broader justice system and represents a growing interest in what many are referring to as community justice. According to Evans (p.125), community corrections can more effectively accomplish its goals and enhance public safety by fostering partnerships with law enforcement and the community at large by encouraging citizens to join in the challenge of creating safer communities and by recognizing the importance of positive relationships between the community and the offender.

The National Symposium identified one model corrections program, the Volunteers in Parole program of the State Bar of California in San Francisco.

The model corrections program Volunteers in Parole provided a support system for young parolees and eased their transition from incarceration to productive citizenship.

This program was designed to ease the caseload of parole officers, many of whom had caseloads of up to 150 parolees. As Sulton (1990, p.93) notes:

> Many of the individuals supervised are youthful offenders without family, friends, permanent housing, employment, or other resources. These teenagers and young adults are uneducated and illiterate, unmarried parents of small children, struggling with drug or alcohol dependency, stigmatized by lengthy criminal records, suspicious, fearful, and uncertain. They frequently commit new crimes or violate the conditions of their parole because adequate support systems are unavailable.

The program, modeled after the Big Brothers and Big Sisters programs, paired youthful parolees, ages 15 to 23, with attorneys who volunteer their time. Attorneys are used because, as Sulton (pp.93–94) notes, they: "(1) understand the legal system; (2) are familiar with community resources and have referral skills; (3) are experienced in dealing with bureaucracies; (4) are not intimidated by the sophistication of parolees; and (5) have an office where they can conveniently meet with parolees and privately discuss their concerns." In addition, attorneys have undergone a licensing procedure that should ensure they are of good moral character and will be able to answer the numerous questions parolees may have about the criminal justice system, governmental agencies, leases, contracts and other legal issues.

In addition to matching parolees with attorneys, the program conducts street law classes and informal lectures for the youthful parolees. Although no studies have been conducted on the effectiveness of the program, given the high cost of incarceration, according to Sulton (p.96): "Should only a small number of the matches result in a reduction of the number of youth being returned to detention facilities or prisons, the State of California probably saved millions of dollars by investing in this program."

Strategies Recommended by the National Crime Prevention Council

The National Crime Prevention Council (*350 Tested Strategies,* 1995) has suggested several strategies the criminal justice system, particularly courts and corrections, might use to prevent crime—most of which focus on juveniles.

Boot Camps Boot camps (pp.246–247) focus on physical conditioning, leadership and counseling in a military-type setting, diverting juvenile offenders from more expensive long-term detention while building life skills to help youths avoid criminal behavior when they return to the community. The council notes that juvenile justice system partnerships with correctional agencies, military resources and community-based programs increase the likelihood that discipline imparted during the program will continue through reintegration into the community. Support from local and state legislators is also important.

Restitution by Juvenile Offenders Restitution programs (pp.245–246) usually originate as a sentencing option imposed on nonviolent offenders. Court-ordered community service programs require juvenile offenders to work at jobs in public agencies or community organizations and contribute a portion of their stipend as payment for damages caused. Many restitution programs have expanded to include training in job skills, life skills and values. Some include academic enrichment and tutoring. Such programs are usually operated by juvenile courts. Key partnerships include public agencies, community organizations and private firms that make jobs available to youthful offenders. A potential obstacle is that community members may feel such programs are "soft" on youths.

In-School Probation In-school probation (pp.249–250) allows nonviolent offenders to remain connected to the educational setting, helps ensure discipline and improves compliance with behavioral standards through intensive supervision provided by a probation officer placed in the school. This officer helps address behavior standards, assists with academic difficulties and addresses absenteeism issues and discipline problems. Key partnerships include teachers, parents, substance abuse treatment, counseling and other services youths and their families need. A potential obstacle is that school staff and community leaders may feel students on probation should be expelled or put on long-term suspension to prevent them from disrupting the learning environment.

Diversion from Incarceration Diverting juvenile offenders (pp.250–251) into intensive monitoring and support programs in community settings provides communities with a less costly and more effective strategy for reducing recidivism. According to the council, juvenile diversion programs include an array of community-based services to support youthful offenders, prevent reoffending through supervision and promote academic and employment success. Successful programs require small caseloads for staff so they have time to develop partnerships with the youth, family members, counselors and others assisting the youth. Again a potential obstacle is that community members may feel such a strategy is inadequate punishment and may put the public at risk of additional victimization.

Combine Corrections with Treatment Juvenile offenders who are incarcerated should also be provided with treatment, (pp.243–244) opportunities for achievement and aftercare focused on reintegration into the community. The council (p.243) notes: "Programs that incorporate community reintegration emphasize partnerships with local employment programs; community-based, residential treatment facilities; and family support services—to increase the likelihood that the treatment's effects will last beyond the detention term." The most likely obstacle to this strategy is the cost.

In addition to partnering with the courts and corrections, collaborative efforts with the media (as discussed in Chapter 8) may enhance community policing strategies aimed at crime prevention.

Early Efforts Using the Media in Crime Prevention Efforts

Two different approaches to using the media have also been extensively studied: the "McGruff" media campaign and the use of police–community anticrime newsletters.

The "McGruff" National Media Campaign

McGruff, the crime dog, is to law enforcement what Smokey the Bear is to the National Forest Service. A press release from the National Crime Prevention Council describes the creation of McGruff and the campaign:

> The concept of a national public education campaign to teach Americans that they could prevent crime (and how to do so) was first conceived in 1978. The Department of Justice supported the plan, as did distinguished civic leaders and

> such organizations as the AFL-CIO, the International Association of Chiefs of Police, and the National Sheriffs' Association. The Advertising Council, Inc. agreed to support the campaign. Research and program development advisory groups helped formulate a strategy. . . . The first McGruff public service ads were developed in 1979 and premiered in February 1980. . . .
>
> The campaign's objectives were clear: (1) to change unwarranted feelings and attitudes about crime and the criminal justice system, (2) to generate an individual sense of responsibility for crime prevention, (3) to initiate individual action toward preventing crime, (4) to mobilize additional resources for crime prevention efforts and (5) to enhance existing crime prevention programs and projects conducted by national, state and local organizations.

This campaign, also known as the "Take a Bite Out of Crime" campaign, was aimed at promoting citizen involvement in crime prevention activities through public service announcements (**PSAs**). As O'Keefe (1986, p.259) notes: "Most said they thought the ads were effective in conveying the message, that they liked the McGruff character and that they felt the information in the ads was worth passing on to other people." In addition, people indicated they felt more confident about their own ability to protect themselves from crime. Most important, almost one-fourth of the people took preventive action after exposure to the PSA, particularly to improve their own household security and work with neighbors in cooperative efforts—the two main themes of the McGruff promotions.

The public favorably received the "McGruff" format and content, and the campaign had a sizeable impact on what people know and do about crime prevention.

Police–Community Anticrime Newsletters

Lavrakas (pp.269–291) reviewed the results of three studies on a relatively new crime prevention strategy at the time, the police–community anticrime newsletter. Included in the review were ALERT, the Evanston (Illinois) Police Department newsletter; the Community Policing Exchange newsletter of the Houston Police Department; and ACT I, the newsletter of the Newark Police Department.

One important finding of these three studies was that although readers were much more aware of crime, at a statistically significant level, their fear of crime did not increase. According to Lavrakas (p.286): "In each of the cities, results indicated that residents were overwhelmingly positive in their assessments of the newsletters, especially the versions that included crime statistics. Not only was exposure greater to the version with crime statistics, but it was rated as significantly more interesting and more informative."

Studies of three police–community anticrime newsletters found them to be highly effective, especially if crime statistics were included.

Lavrakas (pp.289–290) concluded that the three tests "suggest that such newsletters merit consideration elsewhere as one strategy in the arsenal in the fight against crime."

Lessons Learned

Yin (1986, pp.294–308) analyzed 11 research studies of community policing/crime prevention and suggests that they "point to the desirability of joint police–citizen initiatives in successful community crime prevention efforts" (p.304). Table 9.4 summarizes the research studies Yin analyzed and the results of each.

A key finding, according to Yin, is that any crime prevention strategy, taken singly, is likely to be ineffective. A second finding points to the importance of improving the police–community relationship. Yin (p.306) suggests that the results of these studies provide a general pattern and a major lesson about crime prevention: "Successful crime prevention efforts require joint activities by the residents and police and the presumed improvement of relationships between these groups."

Skolnick and Bayley (p.212) describe this as police–community **reciprocity**: "Police–community reciprocity means that police must genuinely feel, and genuinely communicate a feeling, that the public they are serving has something to contribute to the enterprise of policing." Both parties can benefit from working together. In addition to these relatively formal evaluations, other less quantitative evaluations have been conducted.

Qualitative Evaluations and Salient Program Features

Qualitative evaluations are more descriptive and less statistical. One large-scale qualitative evaluation, undertaken by the National Symposium on Community Institutions and Inner-City Crime Project, sought to identify model programs for reduction of inner-city crime. According to Sulton (p.8) almost 3,500 national organizations, criminal justice scholars and federal, state and local government agencies were asked to recommend outstanding local programs. This resulted in the identification of approximately 1,300 programs. Each was sent a request for detailed information, and 350 (27 percent) responded. From these, 18 were selected for site visits.

Sulton (p.10) notes that although each program was unique, they shared some common characteristics.

Eighteen model programs shared the following characteristics. The program:

- Focused on causes of crime.
- Built on community strengths.
- Incorporated natural support systems.
- Had an identifiable group of clients.
- Targeted those who were less affluent.
- Had clearly stated goals and well-defined procedures.
- Had sufficient resources.
- Had a strong leader.

Sulton (p.10) observes that many of the problems focus on specific social problems of inner-city residents "identified as correlates with, if not causes of, inner-city

Table 9.4 Summary of Eleven Evaluation Studies

Description of Intervention	Study Author(s)	Intervention Sites and Period	Types of Crime Addressed	Type of Outcomes Examined	Nature of Outcomes	Analytical Criteria Used in Test Outcomes
Hartford Project: physical redesign, police redeployment, and community organizing	Fowler & Mangione	Hartford, Connect cut 1973–1979	residential	informal social control; burglary and robbery victimization rates; fear of crime	crime reduction when whole intervention in place	statistical significance
Crime Newsletters: distribution of community newsletters in target neighborhoods	Lavrakas	Evanston, Illinois, 1981 Houston, Texas, 1983 Newark, New Jersey, 1983	residential	awareness of newsletter; perceived crime problem; fear of crime	positive changes at one of three sites	statistical significance
Portland Project: physical redesign, police assistance, and business organizing	Lavrakas & Kushmuk	Portland, Oregon 1974–1980	commercial	reported burglaries; fear of crime; quality of life	burglary reduction	statistical significance
Seattle Community Crime Prevention Program: block watch, security inspections, and property engraving	Lindsay & McGillis	Seattle, Washington 1974–1975	residential	burglary victimization rate	burglary reduction	statistical significance
McGruff National Media Campaign: information used in mass media and pamphlets	O'Keefe	Nationwide campaign, 1979	residential	awareness of announcements; reported learning; reported preventive actions	reported learning and actions increase	data in supplemental report
Netwark Foot Patrol: foot patrols from 4.P.M. to midnight	Pate	Newark, New Jersey 1973–1979	residential	reported crime victimization rates; perceived crime, safety, and satisfaction with police	no crime reduction; changed perceptions	statistical significance

Description of Intervention	***Study Author(s)***	***Intervention Sites and Period***	***Types of Crime Addressed***	***Type of Outcomes Examined***	***Nature of Outcomes***	***Analytical Criteria Used in Test Outcomes***
Urban Crime Prevention Program: block watches and related neighborhood meetings	Rosenbanum, et al.	Chicago, Illinois 1983–1984	residential	victimization rates; perceived crime; fear of crime; perceived efficacy; social disorder; physical deterioration	crime reduction at only one of four sites; increases at others	statistical significance
Portland Anti-Burglary Program: street lighting, property engraving, and community education	Schneider	Portland, Oregon 1973–1974	residential	reported burglaries; victimization rates	burglary reduction	statistical significance
Commercial Security Field Test: security surveys undertaken by business proprietors	Tien & Cahn	Denver, Colorado, 1981 Long Beach, California, 1981 St. Louis, Missouri, 1981	residential	burglary victimization rates; fear of crime	burglary reduction at one of three sites	statistical significance
Neighborhood Foot Patrol: foot patrol and community organizing	Trojanowicz	Flint, Michigan 1979–1982	residential	reported crime; satisfaction with police	crime reduction; increase in satisfaction	descriptive data only
Storefront Police Office: location of storefront office, staffed by police, in local neighborhood	Wycoff & Skogan	Houston, Texas 1983–1984	residential	fear of crime; perceived crime, safety, and satisfaction with police	fear reduction: improved perceptions	statistical significance

SOURCE: "Community Crime Prevention, A Synthesis of Eleven Evaluations." In *Community Crime Prevention: Does It Work?* 297–99, edited by Dennis P. Rosenbaum. Beverly Hills: Sage Publications, 1986.

crime, such as emotional or family instability, lack of education, absence of vocational skills, unemployment, drug and alcohol abuse, juvenile gangs and sexual abuse and exploitation." The programs have a clear focus, a clear audience and a clear idea of how to proceed.

On a much smaller scale, but equally instructive, is the Newport News Police Department's reliance on data to identify a problem and to evaluate a solution (adapted from Guyot, 1992, p.321).

> Local hunters and other gun owners held target practice at an excavation pit. Officer Hendrickson found that between April and September one year, the department had been called 45 times to chase away shooters and that the problem had existed for at least 15 years. Most of the calls had come from a couple whose nearby home was bullet-riddled and who thought the police were doing a good job because each time they chased away the shooters.
>
> Officer Hendrickson interviewed shooters and learned that most were soldiers from nearby Ft. Eustis; many others were sent to the pit by gun shop owners. The officer also determined the pit was close enough to a highway to make any firearms discharge there illegal. Deciding to use education backed by legal sanctions, he first photographed the damage and other evidence, which he used to persuade a judge to give anyone convicted once of illegal shooting a suspended sentence and a small fine; a second offense would result in confiscation of the weapon and a jail sentence. The officer obtained from the property owners permission to arrest on their property and the same from the C & O Railroad for shooters crossing the tracks to reach the pit. He also wrote a pamphlet defining the problem and the department's intended enforcement action, and distributed it to the military base and all area gun shops. Finally, he had "no parking—tow zone" signs erected on the shoulder where most shooters parked.
>
> The results were simple. Officers issued 35 summonses to shooters in September, 15 in October, and the last on November 12. The pit soon became so overgrown that it was uninviting for target practice.

Success in the preceding incident and others might indicate that community policing and problem-solving policing would be readily accepted by law enforcement officials and the communities they serve. Such acceptance is not, however, always the case because of several impediments.

Impediments to Community Policing Revisited

Recall from Chapter 5 the challenges facing implementation of community policing as described by Sadd and Grinc (1996, pp.1–2):

- Resistance by police officers
- Difficulty involving other agencies and organizing the community
- Reluctance of average citizens to participate, either because of fear or cynicism

Resistance to change is common, especially in a tradition-oriented profession such as law enforcement. Sadd and Grinc (p.8) suggest: "Community policing is a fight for 'hearts and minds' of patrol officers and the public . . . involving a shift in the culture of policing." Skolnick and Bayley (pp.225–226) describe six impediments to implementing innovative community-oriented policing.

Impediments to implementing innovative community-oriented policing include:

- The powerful pull of tradition.
- Substantial segments of the public not wanting the police to change.
- Unions that continue to be skeptical of innovation.
- The high cost of innovation.
- Lack of vision on the part of police executives.
- Police departments' inability to evaluate their own effectiveness.

A challenge noted by Sadd and Grinc is that projects were usually established as special units that some saw as elite: "The perception of elitism is ironic because community policing is meant to close the gap between patrol and special units and to empower and value the rank-and-file patrol officer as the most important agent for police work."

Another substantial impediment is how to respond to calls for service. A potential conflict exists between responding to calls for service and community policing efforts because calls for service use much of the time needed for problem identification and resolution efforts. The unpredictability of calls for service presents management problems for agencies wanting to implement community policing strategies. Departments must set their priorities and determine how to balance calls for service (reactive) with a problem-oriented approach (proactive). As stressed throughout this text, the one-on-one interaction between police officers and the citizens they serve is critical.

Cost versus Benefit

Some simple services that police departments might provide for the community cost little and require limited personnel. For example, relatively inexpensive efforts to enhance community safety through crime prevention might include conducting monthly meetings, meeting with school administrators, conducting fingerprinting programs and blood pressure programs, participating in athletic contests, publishing newsletters and providing ride-alongs. Other services, however, may be relatively expensive and require many officers.

Whatever the cost to implement, community policing appears to offer a realistic approach to reducing violence, crime and the drug problem. The remaining chapters discuss several approaches to community policing and problem solving to address these issues.

A Final Note: The Important Distinction Between Programs and Community Policing

It must be stressed that programs identified throughout this chapter are not community policing, although community policing may incorporate the use of these and other strategies. Too many police officials think that because they have a Neighborhood-Watch program or a ride-along program, they are doing community policing. In fact, some police chiefs and sheriffs state with pride that they are deeply involved in community policing because they have a DARE program. Community policing is an overriding philosophy that affects every aspect of police operations; it is not a single program or even a hundred programs. Such programs, particularly in isolation, are more community relations or even public relations, not community policing.

SUMMARY

Crime prevention became popular in the late 1960s and early 1970s, with many communities taking an active role. Among the most commonly implemented crime prevention programs have been street lighting projects, property marking projects, security survey projects, citizen patrol projects, and crime reporting and Neighborhood-Watch or block projects. Specialized crime watch programs include mobile crime watch, youth crime watch, business crime watch, realtor watch and carrier alert.

Continuing the community crime prevention momentum generated during the 1960s and 1970s, new programs and organizations were initiated during the 1980s and 1990s to encourage citizens to play an active role in reducing crime in their own neighborhoods. Among the most visible organizations focused on crime are citizen crime prevention associations, Crime Stoppers and MADD. Many police departments also expanded their use of volunteers, who may serve as reserve officers, auxiliary patrol, community service officers or on an as-needed basis.

Youths, who had traditionally been included in police–community relations efforts and crime prevention initiatives, were also addressed through programs including the McGruff "Take a Bite Out of Crime" campaign, police athletic leagues (PALs), Officer Friendly, police explorers, police–school liaison programs and the DARE program. Many programs for juveniles involve the schools, which historically have been charged with instilling discipline in their students. For example, police–school liaison programs place an officer into a school to work with school authorities, parents and students, to prevent crime and antisocial behavior and to improve police–youth relationships. The joint goals of most police–school liaison programs are to prevent juvenile delinquency and to improve police–youth relations.

The most common components of community policing experiments have been foot patrol, newsletters and community organizing. Several empirical studies in the 1980s assessed the effectiveness of community policing efforts. The Flint Neighborhood Foot Patrol Program appeared to produce a decrease in crime, an increase in general citizen satisfaction with the foot patrol program, a decline in the public's fear of crime and a positive perception of the foot patrol officers.

In the first Newark Foot Patrol Experiment, residents reported positive results, while business owners reported negative results. The second Newark Foot Patrol Experiment used coordinated foot patrol, a cleanup campaign and distribution of a newsletter. Only the coordinated foot patrol reduced the perception of property crime and improved assessments of the police.

The Oakland program, using foot patrol, mounted patrol, small vehicle patrol and a Report Incidents Directly program, resulted in a substantial drop in the rate of crime against persons and their property. The San Diego Community Profile Project provided patrol officers with extensive community orientation training. These officers became more service oriented, increased their nonlaw enforcement contacts with citizens and had a more positive attitude toward police–community relations.

The Houston Fear-Reduction Project did not achieve desired results from the victim recontact program or the newsletter. Citizen contact patrol and the police storefront operation did, however, result in decreases in the public's perception of social disorder, fear of personal victimization and the level of personal and property crime.

The Boston Foot Patrol Project found no statistically significant relationship between changes in the level of foot patrol provided and number of calls for service or the seriousness of the calls. Baltimore County's COPE Project reduced fear of crime by 10 percent and crime itself by 12 percent in target neighborhoods. It also reduced calls for service, increased citizen awareness of and satisfaction with the police, and improved police officer attitudes.

Other studies have reviewed the effectiveness of community crime prevention efforts. The Seattle Citywide Crime Prevention Program, using property identification, home security checks and neighborhood block watches, significantly reduced the residential burglary rate as well as the number of burglary-in-progress calls. The Portland antiburglary program also succeeded in reducing the burglary rate for the participants. The Hartford Experiment restructured the physical environment, changed how patrol officers were assigned and organized the neighborhood in an effort to reduce crime and the fear of crime.

The Portland CPTED Commercial Demonstration Project found that the most successful strategies were security services, organization and support of the business community and the street lighting program.

The criminal justice system includes law enforcement, the courts and corrections. What happens in each component of the criminal justice system directly affects the other two components. Consequently, a coordinated effort among law enforcement, courts and corrections is required to effectively deal with the crime problem and to elicit the support of the community in doing so. Model court programs include a community dispute resolution center and a deferred prosecution/first offenders unit. The model corrections program Volunteers in Parole provides a support system for young parolees and eases their transition from incarceration to productive citizenship.

The effectiveness of the media in assisting crime prevention efforts is another evaluation focus. The public has favorably received the "McGruff" format and content. The "McGruff" campaign has had a sizeable impact on what the public knows and does about crime prevention. Studies of three police–community anticrime newsletters found them to be highly effective, especially if they included crime statistics.

Some general conclusions can be drawn from the preceding studies, including the finding that successful crime prevention efforts require joint activities by the residents and police and the presumed improvement of relationships between these groups.

Eighteen model programs identified by the National Symposium on Community Institutions and Inner-City Crime Project shared the following characteristics: The programs (1) were focused on causes of crime, (2) built on community strengths, (3) incorporated natural support systems, (4) had an identifiable group of clients, (5) targeted those who were less affluent, (6) had clearly stated goals and well-defined procedures, (7) had sufficient resources and (8) had a strong leader.

The implementation of community policing must be weighed against several impediments including the powerful pull of tradition, substantial segments of the public who do not want the police to change, the skepticism of unions with regard to innovation, the cost of innovation, lack of vision on the part of police executives and the incapacity of police departments to evaluate their own effectiveness.

Discussion Questions

1. Why is it difficult to conduct research on the effectiveness of community policing?
2. Which studies do you think have the most value for policing in the next few years? Which studies have the most promise?
3. Why would a police department want to reduce fear of crime rather than crime itself?
4. Which of the fear-reduction strategies do you believe holds the most promise?
5. What do you think are the most reasonable aspects of the crime prevention through environmental design (CPTED) approach?
6. Do you think that victims who ignored the CPTED approach to crime prevention are culpable?
7. Has your police department conducted any research on community policing or crime prevention efforts? If so, what were the results?
8. Does your police department have its own McGruff costume or robot? If so, how does the department use him?
9. What do you think are the most important questions regarding police–community relations that should be researched in the next few years?
10. How much of a police department's budget should be devoted to research? Which areas should be of highest priority?

InfoTrac College Edition Assignments

- Use InfoTrac College Edition to help answer the Discussion Questions as appropriate.
- Research and outline at least one of the following subjects: citizen crime reporting, DARE, National Night Out, police athletic leagues.

Community Projects

- In what police–community relations programs does your police department participate?
- What changes have been made in your police department in the past five years?
- Does your department permit ride-alongs? If so, who can participate?

References

Angel, S. *Discouraging Crime through City Planning.* Berkeley: University of California Press, 1968.

Austin, Dave and Braaten, Jane. "Turning Lives Around: Portland Youth Find a New PAL." *The Police Chief,* May 1991, pp.36–38.

Crowe, Timothy D. "The Secure Store: A Clean, Well-Lighted Place." *Security Management,* March 1992, pp.22A–24A.

"DARE Chief Raps 'Bogus Research' as New Study Questions Anti-Drug Program's Long-Term Impact." *Law Enforcement News,* September 30, 1999, pp.1, 10.

Evans, Donald G. "Defining Community Corrections." *Corrections Today,* October 1996, pp.124–145.

Fleissner, Dan; Fedan, Nicholas; and Klinger, David. "Community Policing in Seattle: A Model Partnership between Citizens and Police." *National Institute of Justice Journal,* August 1992, pp.9–18.

Fowler, Floyd J., Jr. and Mangione, Thomas W. "A Three-Pronged Effort to Reduce Crime and Fear of Crime: The Hartford Experiment." In *Community Crime Prevention: Does It Work?* edited by Dennis P. Rosenbaum. Beverly Hills: Sage Publications, 1986, pp.87–108.

Greenberg, Martin Alan. "Volunteer Police: The People's Choice for Safer Communities." *The Police Chief,* May 1991, pp.42–44.

Greene, Jack R. and Taylor, Ralph B. "Community-Based Policing and Foot Patrol: Issues of Theory and Evaluation." In *Community Policing: Rhetoric or Reality,* edited by Jack R. Greene and Stephen D. Mastrofski. New York: Praeger Publishers, 1991, pp.195–223.

Guyot, Dorothy. "Problem-Oriented Policing Shines in the Stats." In *Source Book: Community-Oriented Policing: An Alternative Strategy,* edited by Bernard L. Garmire. Washington, DC: ICMA, May 1992, pp.317–321.

Heinzelmann, Fred. "Foreword." *Community Crime Prevention: Does It Work?* edited by Dennis P. Rosenbaum. Newbury Park: Sage Publications, 1986, pp.7–8.

"Help Keep Families Together." Irving, TX: MADD, no date.

Hess, Kären and Drowns, Robert W. *Juvenile Justice*, 4th ed. Belmont, CA: Wadsworth Publishing Company, 2004.

Jacobs, J. *The Death and Life of Great American Cities.* New York: Vintage, 1961.

Lavrakas, Paul J. "Evaluating Police–Community Anticrime Newsletters: The Evanston, Houston, and Newark Field Studies." In *Community Crime Prevention: Does It Work?* edited by Dennis P. Rosenbaum. Beverly Hills: Sage Publications, 1986, pp.269–291.

Lavrakas, Paul J. and Kushmuk, James W. "Evaluating Crime Prevention through Environmental Design: The Portland Commercial Demonstration Project." In *Community Crime Prevention: Does It Work?* edited by Dennis P. Rosenbaum. Beverly Hills: Sage Publications, 1986, pp.202–227.

Lindsay, Betsy and McGillis, Daniel. "Citywide Community Crime Prevention: An Assessment of the Seattle Program." In *Community Crime Prevention: Does It Work?* edited by Dennis P. Rosenbaum. Beverly Hills: Sage Publications, 1986, pp.46–67.

Mastrofski, Stephen D. "What Does Community Policing Mean for Daily Police Work?" *National Institute of Justice Journal*, August 1992, pp.23–27.

Newman, O. *Defensible Space: Crime Prevention through Urban Design.* New York: Macmillan, 1972.

O'Keefe, Garrett J. "The 'McGruff' National Media Campaign: Its Public Impact and Future Implications." In *Community Crime Prevention: Does It Work?* edited by Dennis P. Rosenbaum. Beverly Hills: Sage Publications, 1986, pp.252–268.

Pace, Denny F. "Community Policing Defined." *Law and Order*, August 1992, pp. 46, 56–58.

Pate, Anthony M. "Experimenting with Foot Patrol: The Newark Experience." In *Community Crime Prevention: Does It Work?* edited by Dennis P. Rosenbaum. Beverly Hills: Sage Publications, 1986, pp.137–156.

Police Foundation. *The Newark Foot Patrol Experiment.* Washington, DC: The Police Foundation, 1981.

Repetto, T.A. *Residential Crime.* Cambridge: Ballinger, 1974.

Sadd, Susan and Grinc, Randolph M. *Implementation Challenges in Community Policing.* Washington, DC: National Institute of Justice Research in Brief, February 1996.

Schneider, Anne L. "Neighborhood-Based Antiburglary Strategies: An Analysis of Public and Private Benefits from the Portland Program." In *Community Crime Prevention: Does It Work?* edited by Dennis P. Rosenbaum. Beverly Hills: Sage Publications, 1986, pp. 68–86.

Skogan, Wesley G. and Wycoff, Mary Ann. "Storefront Police Offices: The Houston Field Test." In *Community Crime Prevention: Does It Work?* edited by Dennis P. Rosenbaum. Beverly Hills: Sage Publications, 1986, pp.179–199.

Skolnick, Jerome H. and Bayley, David H. *The New Blue Line: Innovation in Six American Cities.* New York: The Free Press, 1986.

Sulton, Anne Thomas. *Inner-City Crime Control: Can Community Institutions Contribute?* Washington, DC: The Police Foundation, 1990.

Taft, Philip B., Jr. *Fighting Fear: The Baltimore County C.O.P.E. Project.* Washington, DC: Police Executive Research Forum, 1986.

350 Tested Strategies to Prevent Crime: A Resource for Municipal Agencies and Community Groups. Washington, DC: National Crime Prevention Council, 1995.

Trojanowicz, Robert C. "Evaluating a Neighborhood Foot Patrol Program: The Flint, Michigan, Project." In *Community Crime Prevention: Does It Work?* edited by Dennis P. Rosenbaum. Beverly Hills: Sage Publications, 1986, pp.157–178.

Wycoff, Mary Ann. "The Benefits of Community Policing: Evidence and Conjecture." In *Community Policing: Rhetoric or Reality*, edited by Jack R. Greene and Stephen D. Mastrofski. New York: Praeger Publishers, 1991, pp.103–120.

Yin, Robert K. "Community Crime Prevention: A Synthesis of Eleven Evaluations." In *Community Crime Prevention: Does It Work?* edited by Dennis P. Rosenbaum. Beverly Hills: Sage Publications, 1986, pp.294–308.

Additional Resources

Many organizations offer expertise in building partnerships and provide a variety of publications, training and services that can strengthen local efforts. A sampling follows.[1]

[1]Every interest organization has a Web page on the Internet, including several federal agencies. A search using the words *community policing* or *crime prevention* will yield a tremendous amount of current information.

Bureau of Justice Assistance Clearinghouse, Box 6000, Rockville, MD 20850; (800) 688-4252.

Center for Community Change, 1000 Wisconsin Ave. NW, Washington, DC 20007; (202) 342-0519.

Citizens Committee for New York City, 305 7th Ave., 15th Floor, New York, NY 10001; (212) 989-0909.

Community Policing Consortium, 1726 M St. NW, Suite 801, Washington, DC 20006; (202) 833-3305 or (800) 833-3085.

National Center for Community Policing, School of Criminal Justice, Michigan State University, East Lansing, MI 48824; (517) 355-2322.

National Crime Prevention Council, 1700 K St. NW, 2nd Floor, Washington, DC 20006-3817; (202) 466-6272.

National Training and Information Center, 810 North Milwaukee Ave., Chicago, IL 60622-4103; (312) 243-3035.

Police Executive Research Forum, 2300 M St. NW, Suite 910, Washington, DC 20006; (202) 466-7820.

Chapter 10

Safe Neighborhoods and Communities: From Traffic Problems to Crime

In the last analysis, the most promising and so the most important method of dealing with crime is by preventing it—by ameliorating the conditions of life that drive people to commit crime and that undermine the restraining rules and institutions erected by society against anti-social conduct.

—President's Commission on Law Enforcement and Administration of Justice, 1967

Do You Know?

- What synergism is and how it relates to crime prevention efforts?
- What role crime prevention plays in community policing?
- What is usually at the top of the list of neighborhood concerns and what behaviors are involved?
- What responses can address the problem of speeding in residential areas?
- What the defining characteristics of Safe Communities are?
- How community policing has addressed citizen fear of crime?
- What three federal initiatives can assist communities in implementing community policing?
- What the Weed and Seed program does?
- What the three primary components of CPTED are?
- On what five principles CPTED is based?
- How CPTED directly supports community policing?
- What two side effects of place-focused opportunity blocking may be?
- What the risk factor prevention paradigm is?
- What partnerships have been implemented to prevent or reduce crime and disorder?
- What strategies might help to prevent burglaries of single-family residences? Burglary of retail establishments? Shoplifting? Robbery at ATMs? Assaults in and around bars? Street prostitution? Thefts of and from vehicles?
- What the two primary messages of most auto theft programs are?

CAN YOU DEFINE?

cocoon neighborhood watch
contagion
diffusion
infrastructure
opportunity blocking
place
protective factor
risk factor
risk factor prevention paradigm
road humps
synergism
target hardening
traffic calming

Introduction

Community policing stresses using partnerships and problem solving to address making neighborhoods and communities safer, including looking at concerns related to traffic, at neighborhood disorder, at crime and at the fear of crime. Many Americans, including many police, believe traffic problems and crime prevention

A police officer checks a child-restraint seat for correct installation. Programs around the country emphasize the use of safe car seats for children.

are solely the responsibility of law enforcement. When crime surges in a community, the usual public response is to demand the hiring of more officers. Citizens often believe that a visible police presence will deter and reduce crime, even though most studies indicate this is not the case. For example, the classic study, *Kansas City Preventive Patrol Experiment,* found overwhelming evidence that decreasing or increasing routine preventive patrol within the range tested had no effect on crime, citizen fear of crime, community attitudes toward the police on the delivery of police services, police response time or traffic accidents. In 1975 the FBI's *Uniform Crime Reports* noted:

> Criminal justice professionals readily and repeatedly admit that, in the absence of citizen assistance, neither more manpower, nor improved technology, nor additional money will enable law enforcement to shoulder the monumental burden of combating crime in America.

The advent of community policing and partnerships are often credited with the decrease in crime. Other reasons for the decline in the crime rate are suggested in the study "To Establish Justice, To Insure Domestic Tranquility." This report suggests that economic good times, not get-tough criminal justice policies, are the primary reason for the "dizzying drop in the nation's crime rate over the past seven years" ("Good News, Bad News . . .," 2000, p.1).

To whatever factors one attributes the decreasing crime rate, the broad nature of policing in the 1990s highlighted the critical contributions citizens, community agencies and organizations can make to combat crime. For communities to thrive, citizens need to have a sense of neighborhood and to work together as a team. The resulting synergism can accomplish much more than isolated individual efforts.

Synergism occurs when individuals channel their energies toward a common purpose and accomplish together what they could not accomplish alone.

The technical definition of synergism is "the simultaneous actions of separate entities which together have greater total effect than the sum of their individual efforts." A precision marching band and a national basketball championship team are examples of synergism. Although there may be some outstanding solos and a few spectacular individual "dunks," it is the total team effort that produces the results.

The police and the citizens they serve must realize that their combined efforts are greater than the sum of their individual efforts on behalf of the community. When police take a problem-solving approach to community concerns and include the community, what they are doing often falls under "crime prevention."

Crime prevention is a large part, in fact a cornerstone, of community policing.

Community policing and crime prevention are, however, distinct entities. Further, crime is usually not the greatest concern of a neighborhood—traffic-related problems are of greater concern because they affect all citizens daily.

This chapter begins with a discussion of the traffic concerns of neighborhoods and how community policing partnerships have addressed these concerns. This is followed by a discussion of how community policing addresses disorder concerns and citizen fear of crime. Next is a discussion of the national focus on community policing and crime prevention and the assistance offered by COPS, the Community Policing Consortium and the Weed and Seed program. Next is a description of CPTED and a discussion of the importance of place and of the risk factor prevention paradigm. The discussion then turns to descriptions of partnerships and strategies to prevent or reduce crime and disorder and use of advances in technology to fight crime. Next, specific strategies are described to prevent burglaries of single-family residences, in public housing and in retail establishments; shoplifting; robberies at ATMs; assaults in and around bars; street prostitution; and thefts of and from vehicles. The chapter concludes with examples of partnerships to prevent crime.

Conspicuously absent from this chapter are discussions of domestic violence. Domestic violence is most certainly a crime, but the discussion of community policing and domestic violence is placed later in the text (Chapter 14) where violence is discussed in depth.

Traffic Enforcement and Safety

Sweeney (2003, p.43) reports: "Police chiefs who have surveyed members of their communities to find out what they consider the most serious problems in their neighborhoods know that traffic problems are at the top of the list."

Traffic problems top the list of concerns of most neighborhoods and communities. Concerns include corridor safety, speeding in residential areas, street racing, red light running, impaired drivers, elderly drivers and nonuse of seat belts.

Sweeney notes: "This rating has been found in quiet residential communities and crime-ridden inner cities alike. Citizens want to see police on the street, and they don't want to see them ignoring traffic violations. Traffic enforcement is not at odds with community policing; in fact, it helps police satisfy important objectives of community-oriented policing services—namely, increasing the visibility of officers and improving the quality of life for every member of the community."

Miller (2002) describes how a problem stretch of road in southern Maine was addressed by community policing, beginning with bringing in identified major stakeholders along the corridor for discussions. These discussions resulted in a three-pronged approach: enforcement, education and engineering. Meetings among MDOT, police and town representatives resulted in both short- and long-term solutions. Miller (p.26) cites Chief Deputy Ouellette's belief "that incorporating the major stakeholders' concerns has been paramount to the nascent program's success. 'The people see that we're working together, and they have the satisfaction of knowing that something is being done.' . . . The general consensus—and the numbers—indicate that even for traffic enforcement, community policing takes just a little and goes a long way."

Canby (2002, p.5) notes an "urgent need" for partnerships between public safety agencies and transportation: "New operational partnerships between public safety and transportation agencies are urgently needed to improve the operational efficiency and effectiveness of both our transportation and public safety systems. By sharing technology, information and incident management protocols, transportation and public safety agencies can improve emergency response and alleviate incident-related traffic congestion." Such partnerships are vital to corridor safety programs.

Corridor Safety Programs

Helmick et al. (2001, p.32) describe a U.S. Department of Transportation initiative bringing together public safety and transportation to shape the Intelligent Transportation System (ITS) Public Safety Program. ITS technologies include roadside emergency call boxes, closed circuit television and mayday devices (such as General Motor's OnStar) to better detect, respond to and manage incidents on the nation's highways. According to Helmick et al.: "Corridor safety projects involve community leaders, state and local law enforcement and transportation departments, emergency service providers, public and private transportation safety organizations and other stakeholders interested in improving safety." They (p.35) conclude: "It is easy to pay lip service to the importance of traffic safety, but improving traffic safety takes real commitment. And ITS and corridor safety programs show that a multidisciplinary, collaborative approach to traffic safety can save lives and prevent injuries." Another common traffic concern is speeding in residential areas.

Speeding in Residential Areas

Scott (2001c, p.1) suggests that speeding in residential areas causes five basic types of harm: (1) It makes citizens fear for children's safety; (2) it makes pedestrians and bicyclists fear for their safety; (3) it increases the risk of vehicle crashes; (4) it increases the seriousness of injuries to other drivers, passengers, pedestrians and bicyclists struck by a vehicle; and (5) it increases noise from engine acceleration and tire friction. He (pp.9–19) suggests several responses to residential speeding.

Engineering responses to speeding include using traffic calming, posting warning signs and signals, conducting antispeeding public awareness campaigns, informing complainants about actual speeds and providing realistic driver training (Scott, pp.9–15).

"**Traffic calming** describes a wide range of road and environment design changes that either make it more difficult for a vehicle to speed or make drivers believe they should slow down for safety" (Scott, pp.10–11). Among the most common traffic calming measures are (Scott, pp.10–11):

- Narrowing the road.
- Putting bends and curves in the road.
- Installing **road humps** (short, narrow raised portions of the road that can be crossed safely only at lower speeds—more appropriate in parking lots than on roads that emergency vehicles might travel).
- Building traffic circles and roundabouts.
- Installing gateways to residential neighborhoods.
- Permitting parking on both sides of residential streets.

- Timing traffic signals for vehicles traveling the desired speed.
- Erecting mid-block barriers that create two cul-de-sacs.
- Adding mid-block build-outs (sidewalk area extensions into the road).

Enforcement responses include (1) enforcing speeding laws, (2) enforcing speeding laws with speed cameras—photo radar, (3) using speed display boards, (4) arresting the worst offenders and (5) having citizen volunteers monitor speeding (Scott, pp.15–19).

Such aggressive enforcement of speed limits may seem to run counter to community policing efforts to establish rapport with citizens. However, as researchers Chermak et al. (2001, p.365) report: "Overall the findings suggest that citizens strongly support aggressive traffic enforcement practices and that the implementation of such strategies does not reduce their support."

Scott (pp.9–19) stresses that responses to speeding must be tailored to local circumstances: "Regardless of which responses you prefer, it is strongly recommended that you consult with affected citizens and transportation authorities before implementing the responses."

Scott (pp.20–22) also describes responses with limited effectiveness: (1) reducing speed limits, (2) increasing fines and penalties, (3) erecting stop signs and (4) installing speed bumps. Many citizens believe these responses will make drivers slow down and press the police and city officials to implement them. However, such responses have limited effectiveness, especially erecting stop signs. What often happens is that drivers speed up mid-block after a stop sign to make up for lost time, keeping average speeds high and increasing acceleration noise. Closely related to the problem of speeding in residential areas is the problem of street racing.

Street Racing

Lowery (2003, p.51) describes how the Kent (Washington) Police Department addressed the concern: "The department partnered with state and local law enforcement agencies, private property owners, local businesses and the insurance industry to develop a high-profile enforcement action plan known as Curb Racing and Achieve Safer Highways, or CRASH." Street racers gravitate to business and industrial areas normally vacant at night. Police identify these areas and work with private property owners to limit access to their properties to increase the level of security and make the location less attractive to racers. Installing gates and fences and repositioning equipment to block entry can help. Police also enter into trespass agreements with property owners giving police authority to act as the owner's agent and arrest any cars found illegally on their property. CRASH has met with much success in addressing this citizen concern.

Red Light Running

The Federal Highway Administration (FHWA) and Insurance Institute for Highway Safety (IIHS) estimate that red light running causes as many as 218,000 crashes that result in about 880 deaths and 181,000 injuries. Automated red light cameras are being used in many jurisdictions to address the problem of red light running. Helmick (2003, p.49) describes how public education and community involvement are crucial to the acceptance of such a program:

> A multifaceted public awareness and education program is of paramount importance in jurisdictions using photo enforcement. These programs should begin prior to the deployment of red light cameras and should continue throughout the life of the photo enforcement programs. . . . The formation of groups committed to preventing red light running is also effective in reducing red light running in a community.
>
> In Phoenix, Arizona, a group of parents formed a group named the Red Means Stop Coalition after their sons and daughters were hit by red light runners. Since it was founded in 1999, the group has worked alongside local police departments, the governor's highway safety office and local corporations to elevate the issue of red light running prevention in the press and among elected and public officials. . . . Similar traffic safety groups across the United States complement the efforts of law enforcement officials by informing the public of the red light running problem and focusing on driver behavior changes.

Impaired Drivers

Bolton (2003, p.162) describes how the Lake Charles (Louisiana) Police Department enlisted community help to reduce impaired driving:

> Citizens participate in two separate task force activities. The first, a program called Operation Extra Eyes, relies on citizen volunteers to augment the department's work to detect alcohol violations and apprehend violators. The volunteers are graduates of the department and its procedures. They also receive additional training to prepare them for the operation. . . . On the street, two volunteers are assigned to an enforcement team of several officers. The volunteers, working from their personal vehicles, watch motorists for signs of impaired driving and report their observations to the enforcement team using a two-way radio issued by the department. . . . Another task force program calls on students from Students Against Drunk Driving (SADD) to help police officers with the paperwork associated with impaired driving arrests. . . . The students have no contact with arrestees. Having the students available to handle some of this detail work saves officers about 20 minutes per arrest. . . . The students also help distribute traffic safety literature and work on related projects when they're not helping with arrest forms.

The department has seen a 77 percent increase in impaired driving arrests since instituting these two task forces.

Impaired Elderly Drivers Farrow (2003, p.51) describes the Older Californians Traffic Safety (OCTS) Task Force, noting that the task force brings together the state departments of aging, motor vehicles, health services, consumer affairs, transportation, social services, rehabilitation, insurance and various law enforcement agencies including the California Police Chiefs Association, Sacramento County Sheriff's Department, California State Sheriffs Association and the California Commission on Peace Officer Standards and Training. Also included are doctors, therapists, nurses, private organizations concerned with senior safety and mobility, Safety Center Incorporated, the American Society on Aging, the AARP, the Alzheimer's Association and the Congress of California Seniors. The task force is administered by the California Highway Patrol and seeks innovative ways to help seniors remain behind the wheel as long as safe, to identify seniors who are driving impaired and to help those identified transition to a nondriving lifestyle.

Nonuse of Seat Belts

The National Highway Traffic Safety Administration (NHTSA) estimates that more than 14,000 lives are saved by safety belts each year with another 300 lives saved by appropriate child restraints. Sixty percent of passenger vehicle occupants killed in traffic crashes were unrestrained (Cahill, 2003, p.62). Enforcement is one key to seat belt use. According to Runge (2003, p.13): "As a result of the May 2002 Click It or Ticket campaign, seat belt use increased an average of nearly 9 percentage points in states using the full implementation model." Enforcement, however, is not enough.

Partnerships are crucial in efforts to get drivers and passengers to buckle up. McMahon (2000, p.37) notes that partnerships are an essential component of statewide success: "It was clear that changing the potentially deadly habits of tens of thousands of New York motorists required the cooperation of many agencies and organizations. The success of *Buckle Up New York* hinged on key partnerships as well as interagency and interdisciplinary cooperation." More than 400 police departments participated in the program along with the National Safety Council (NSC) and its Air Bag and Seat Belt Safety Campaign. The National Highway Traffic Safety Administration and the New York State Governor's Traffic Safety Committee secured federal funding and provided professional support. The campaign also sought buy-in from nontraditional sources such as several at-risk groups including parents of child passengers, minority communities and elderly populations. The New York State Police developed public service announcements using NASCAR drivers as role models. The Cable Television and Telecommunications Association of New York State and its members provided targeted dissemination of these announcements across the state.

According to McMahon: "As the program has grown in visibility, new partners have emerged and forged important partnerships founded upon common concerns. These partners include New York's medical community. The New York State Association of Family Physicians . . . is spreading the message through more than 1,100 doctor's offices. The state police and the governor's traffic safety committee are providing free brochures, posters and other educational materials to family physicians." The campaign also has enlisted the support of partners from the private sector including Wal-Mart stores, Macy's local supermarkets, Daimler Chrysler and General Motors.

McMahon (p.39) reports that the results of the campaign were immediate and profound with 183,000 citations being issued for safety restraint violations. The effect of enforcement efforts was that safety restraint use went from 75 percent in the fall of 1998 to 85 percent in January 2000.

Casstevens and Rizzo (2001, p.41) describe their Red, White and Blue Team concept for child passenger safety: "The colors signify the team concept—red for fire service; white for medical service, health care, and volunteer organizations such as Safe Kids, citizen police and fire academies, and civic groups; and blue for law enforcement. . . . Once a month the team hosts a child seat checkup event." According to Casstevens and Rizzo (p.43): "We have a combined 40 years in law enforcement, and we have never seen a program that has as great a chance to positively impact a child's life as a program in which a child seat technician inspects a child seat. With our experience showing a 90 percent misuse rate of child restraint systems in different parts of the country, this represents an opportunity to save someone's life. There is no better public service."

Tampa, Florida, also has a program aimed at children, Buckle Up Kids, that uses a car seat checkpoint and partnerships. Weiss and Davis (2002, p.155) describe this program: "To make the program successful, the TPD partners with the Hillsborough County Sheriff's Office and AAA Auto Club South; the agencies share certified technicians at checkpoints. Other assistance is provided by the TPD's Civilian Volunteers Assisting Police (CVAP)." They report that community parents also help and that Tampa Junior League purchased $1,000 in needed supplies. The National Highway Safety Team provided unlimited safety literature. In addition, State Farm Insurance donated seats to the program and joined in conducting checkpoints. Weiss and Davis (pp.155–156) stress: "The key to the future of this program is forming partnerships; it could not work without technicians, business partners and community assistance."

Brewer (2002, p.31) describes some innovative partnerships that departments have used to market their seat belt campaigns: "Partnerships in the community can act as force multipliers to enhance the effectiveness of an agency's marketing and enforcement strategy. The Kentucky State Police, for instance, teamed with the Kroger grocery chain to put a seat belt message on every plastic grocery bag that would be used in our state for the month of June." Brewer also suggests partnering with sports teams and major sporting events to promote traffic safety.

Safe Communities

Mineta (2001, p.3) in a *Report to Congress* notes: "The Safe Community concept as adopted and refined by the U.S. Department of Transportation addresses all injuries, with traffic safety positioned within this overall context. . . . Motor vehicle injuries are the leading cause of all injury deaths, the principal cause of on-the-job fatalities and the third largest cause (trailing heart attacks and cancer) of all deaths in the United States."

The defining characteristics of Safe Communities are:

- Data from multiple sources.
- Expanded partnerships.
- Citizen involvement.
- An integrated and comprehensive injury control system.

Mineta (pp.3–4) reports: "Expanded partnerships are not only a defining characteristic of safe community programs, but an important benefit. Community Traffic Safety Programs have built coalitions of law enforcement, local government, schools, courts, businesses, health agencies, and community and advocacy groups for many years. Safe community programs continue to work with these groups, but expand the partnership base to actively involve the medical, acute care (trauma and hospital-based systems) and rehabilitation communities. These groups, which have traditionally been focused on *treating* injuries, are now being engaged as partners in *preventing* injuries."

In addition to traffic concerns, citizens are often more concerned about minor offenses (disorder) than they are about crime and violence in their communities.

Addressing Disorder Concerns

According to Katz et al. (2001, pp.825–826): "Over the past two decades, police agencies across the nation have been adopting a variety of community policing strategies, including several that focus on the aggressive enforcement of disorder offenses. These aggressive strategies are popularly known as 'zero-tolerance,' 'order-maintenance' and 'quality-of-life' policing." They note that addressing disorder dates back to Wilson and Kelling's broken window theory that if social and physical disorder in a community are not addressed, more serious forms of disorder and eventually increased levels of crime, will follow. Katz et al.'s research found that zero tolerance policies significantly reduced disorder problems, but had limited or no effect on major crimes.

Scheider et al. (2003, pp.372–373) describe several conditions that indicate the level of neighborhood disorder: abandoned cars and/or buildings, rundown/neglected buildings, poor lighting, overgrown shrubs/trees, trash, empty lots, illegal public drinking/public drug use, public drug sales, vandalism or graffiti, prostitution, panhandling/begging/loitering, hanging out, truancy/youths skipping school and transient/homeless sleeping on benches or streets. In some instances these conditions are not illegal but concern citizens and reflect that they do not take pride in their neighborhood.

Problem-oriented policing is often used in addressing disorder problems. When Rojek (2003, p.502) studied the characteristics of Goldstein award winners for excellence in problem-oriented policing, he found that the most common primary problem was neighborhoods with concentrated crime and disorder. Related problems included drug activity, high level of Part I crime(s), gang activity, vandalism, nuisance problems, transients, problem liquor establishments, abandoned houses, public intoxication, prostitution and traffic congestion. The most common responses were crime prevention through environmental design (discussed shortly), community mobilization and targeted enforcement efforts.

Smith (2001, p.60) notes: "Community disorder programs geared toward addressing minor offenses in hopes that the more major crimes will be positively affected have received a great deal of positive publicity, suggesting that zero-tolerance programs may effectively reduce crime. However, the body of research on these programs has also failed to produce a scientific consensus on their effectiveness."

Research again appears to indicate that enforcement efforts alone are not enough. Partnerships are needed.

Weiss and Dresser (2001, p.117) describe how St. Petersburg, Florida's "seedy decline" was reversed by cleaning up the city, adding lighting and working with landlords to screen tenants, returning it to a center for arts, culture, sports and entertainment.

Neighborhood and business district improvements such as cleaning up trash, landscaping and planting flowers can serve as a focus for community organizing and help residents take pride in their neighborhoods. Key partnerships in beautification projects include police departments, public works staff, the business community and residents. These partnerships can also be expanded to help fight crime and to reduce the fear of crime.

Reducing the Fear of Crime

A major goal of community policing is to reduce the fear of crime in communities so that citizens will be willing to join together to prevent crime. Scheider et al. (pp.380–381) stress: "An unreasonably high level of fear of crime concerns both police and residents because it reduces quality of life and neighborhood cohesion and in doing so can increase crime. Exaggerated levels of fear of crime can cause residents to unnecessarily reduce neighborhood activities and enjoyment of their surroundings and can cause them to isolate themselves from their communities, which can subsequently increase social disorder and ultimately result in increased crime."

Scheider et al. studied the relationship between citizen perceptions of community policing and fear of crime. They (p.365) note: "Throughout the history of American policing, police have focused on three primary and interrelated functions: crime control, order maintenance and service provision. . . . Community policing shifts the focus of police by placing an equal emphasis on all three activities and, in addition, asks police to work with citizens in efforts to increase overall quality of life. Thus, the model moves away from police-dominated crime control through reactive responses to calls for service and moves toward proactive problem solving centered on the causes of crime and disorder and on fostering partnerships between the police and the community. . . . This expansion of the role of police to include quality of life issues and partnerships with citizens has increasingly brought fear of crime under the purview of police professionalism." Scheider et al. (p.366) describe efforts to deal with citizen fear of crime.

"Community policing efforts to deal with citizen fear have been varied. They have included foot and vehicle patrol in high-crime neighborhoods, community meetings, citizen patrol, neighborhood cleanup programs, opening neighborhood substations and citizen awareness campaigns."

Zhao et al. (2002) reviewed 50 quasi-experimental studies on the relationship between community policing and reducing fear of crime. They identified 31 that found fear of crime decreased, 18 that found no change and 1 that reported an increase in fear of crime. Their review also indicated that mere increase in police presence was not as effective as proactive and/or community policing strategies in reducing fear. Scheider et al. (p.381) conclusions are also of interest:

> This study finds that increased citizen perceptions of community policing do not directly result in reductions in fear of crime. However, community policing was found to have a strong positive effect on crime prevention behaviors on the part of citizens and on satisfaction with police. Although satisfaction was related to decreased levels of fear (although no causal order could be determined), crime prevention behaviors either had no effect or increased fear of crime.
>
> It appears that community policing efforts need to go beyond the distribution of crime and crime prevention information if they hope to directly reduce fear of crime, at least in the short term. Police may need to work on developing ongoing working relationships with residents to help alleviate community problems and to increase quality of life. Perhaps it is more likely that these types of long-term problem-solving partnerships will increase feelings of resident safety to a greater extent than will the mere distribution of crime prevention information.
>
> Police should work to strike a balance between increasing awareness of crime and crime prevention behaviors with feelings of fear. Although in some areas increasing levels of fear may be warranted, in many others it may not be a desirable outcome. Police should work closely with community members and assess their levels of fear prior to engaging in efforts designed to affect their fear of crime. Where the police hope to achieve the goal of fear reduction through community policing, it may be incumbent on them to focus on increasing citizen satisfaction with police and working closely with citizens on solving local crime problems and perhaps somewhat less on informing them about crime and crime prevention techniques.

National Emphasis on Community Policing and Crime Prevention

Three federal initiatives to assist communities in implementing community policing are the COPS Office, the Community Policing Consortium and the Weed and Seed program.

The Office of Community Oriented Policing Services

The Violent Crime Control and Law Enforcement Act of 1994 authorized $8.8 billion over six years for grants to local police agencies to add 100,000 officers and promote community policing. To implement this law, Attorney General Janet Reno created the Office of Community Oriented Policing Services (COPS) in the Department of Justice.

Although originally the COPS Office was destined to go out of business after six years, its success at increasing the numbers of police officers across the country and in raising awareness of community policing has resulted in Congress extending the life of the agency for several more years. According to the COPS Web site:

> The COPS Office was created as a result of the Violent Crime Control and Law Enforcement Act of 1994. As a component of the Justice Department, the mission

of the COPS Office is to advance community policing in jurisdictions of all sizes across the country. Community policing represents a shift from more traditional law enforcement in that it focuses on prevention of crime and the fear of crime on a very local basis. Community policing puts law enforcement professionals on the streets and assigns them a beat, so they can build mutually beneficial relationships with the people they serve. By earning the trust of the members of their communities and making those individuals stakeholders in their own safety, community policing makes law enforcement safer and more efficient, and makes America safer.

What We Do

COPS provides grants to tribal, state and local law enforcement agencies to hire and train community policing professionals, acquire and deploy cutting-edge crime-fighting technologies, and develop and test innovative policing strategies. COPS-funded training helps advance community policing at all levels of law enforcement—from line officers to law enforcement executives—as well as others in the criminal justice field. Because community policing is by definition inclusive, COPS training also reaches state and local government leaders and the citizens they serve. This broad range of programs helps COPS offer agencies support in virtually every aspect of law enforcement, and it's making America safer, one neighborhood at a time.

COPS has helped nearly 12,950 jurisdictions through 27 different grant programs since 1994. In September 2002, COPS had provided funding for 116,573 community policing professionals across the country.

The Community Policing Consortium

Another organization that provides assistance is the Community Policing Consortium, a partnership of five police organizations: the International Association of Chiefs of Police (IACP), the National Organization of Black Law Enforcement Executives (NOBLE), the National Sheriffs' Association (NSA), the Police Executive Research Forum (PERF) and the Police Foundation (PF). The consortium is funded and administered by COPS within the Department of Justice. They provide training throughout the United States, especially to agencies that receive COPS grants. The training materials emphasize community policing from a local perspective, community partnerships, problem solving, strategic planning and assessment. Their quick-read periodicals, *The Community Policing Exchange, Sheriff Times* and the *Information Access Guide,* relate real-life experiences of community policing practitioners across the country.

The Weed and Seed Program

A third federal initiative is the Weed and Seed program. Launched in 1991 with three sites, it has since grown to include 200 sites nationwide. The program strategically links concentrated, enhanced law enforcement efforts to identify, arrest and prosecute violent offenders, drug traffickers and other criminals operating in the target areas and community policing (weeding) with human services—including after-school, weekend and summer youth activities; adult literacy classes; and parental counseling—and neighborhood revitalization efforts to prevent and deter further crime (seeding).

The Weed and Seed program seeks to identify, arrest and prosecute offenders (weed) while simultaneously working with citizens to improve quality of life (seed).

The National Institute of Justice (NIJ) conducted a national evaluation of the program by selecting eight sites representing different aspects of Weed and Seed (Dunworth and Mills, 1999). The evaluation found:

- Preexisting community features—such as the strength of the social and institutional **infrastructure** (an established network of community-based organizations and community leaders), the severity of crime problems, geographical advantages favoring economic development, and transience of the community population—may make the program easier or more difficult to operate effectively.
- The mix of weeding and seeding activities and the sequencing of these components—including early seeding, sustained weeding, high-level task forces combined with community policing and an active prosecutorial role—represent important factors in gaining community support for the program.
- Greater success occurred when sites concentrated their program resources on smaller population groups, especially if they could also channel other public funds and leverage private funds.
- Active, constructive leadership of key individuals represented a less tangible ingredient in the more successful programs.
- Implementation strategies that relied on bottom-up, participatory decision-making approaches, especially when combined with efforts to build capacity and partnership among local organizations, proved the most effective.

Branson (2000, p.82) reports on a 40 percent reduction in crime in less than two years accomplished by the Weed and Seed program in Honolulu, stating: "The key is community input." She (p.85) notes: "The presence of uniformed police who fraternize readily with the residents is one of the main factors in the continued success of the Weed and Seed concept."

An approach to combating crime and disorder that also focuses on the environment but in a much more literal sense, is the crime prevention through environmental design (CPTED) approach being used in many community policing efforts.

Crime Prevention through Environmental Design

CPTED, introduced in Chapter 9, has been a strategy for dealing with crime for decades and has had some proven successes.

CPTED has three major components: target hardening, changes to the physical environment and community building.

Target hardening refers to making potential objectives of criminals more difficult to obtain. The three main devices used for target hardening are improved locks, alarm systems and security cameras. Most people do not object to locks and alarm systems properly used, but some have "Big Brother" concerns about surveillance cameras. Gorovici (2000, p.36) notes: "Most of us have become accustomed to video monitoring in banks, at ATMs, in convenience stores, in large parking areas and other locations. In recent years, video monitoring has expanded into other public areas—city centers, schools, transportation hubs, housing projects—and the evidence so far suggests this crime-fighting tool has tremendous potential. In the U.S. today, there are more than one million cameras in use for security monitoring."

What can be done to make such surveillance acceptable to the majority of citizens? Gorovici (p.38) says: "Create partnerships. From the beginning, strive to form a wide coalition of partnership that includes law enforcement, government bodies, neighborhood groups, businesses, retail associations and individual citizens. The more wide-ranging the partnership, the more sources of funding, expertise and potential support."

Changes in the physical environment often include lighting. Increasing lighting has been a means of increasing security for centuries. Phillips (p.10) contends: "Although there is a strong indication that increased lighting decreases the fear of crime, there is no statistically significant evidence that street lighting affects the actual level of crime." Other changes usually involve removing items that give potential offenders the ability to hide, for example dense vegetation, high shrubs, walls and fences.

Community building, the third element of CPTED, can have the greatest impact on how individuals perceive the livability of their neighborhood. Community building seeks to increase residents' sense of ownership of the neighborhood and of who does and does not belong there. Community building techniques can include social events such as fairs or neighborhood beautification projects. Files (1999, p.42) outlines five principles underlying CPTED.

Five principles underlying CPTED are territoriality, natural surveillance, access control, activity support and maintenance of the environment.

Territoriality establishes ownership and sends a clear message of who does and does not belong there. *Natural surveillance* allows potential victims a clear view of surroundings and inhibits crime. *Access control* delineates boundaries and where people do and do not belong. *Activity support* involves programming activities that promote proper site use and discourages nonlegitimate use. *Maintenance of the environment* provides both physical maintenance and continuing education of the public, increasing awareness of surroundings.

By emphasizing the systematic analysis of crime in a particular location, CPTED directly supports community policing by providing crime prevention strategies tailored to solve specific problems.

The Importance of Place

Eck (no date) contends: "Most places have no crimes and most crime is highly concentrated in and around a relatively small number of places. If we can prevent crime at these high crime places, then we might be able to reduce total crime." His definition of **place** is quite specific: "A place is a very small area reserved for a narrow range of functions, often controlled by a single owner and separated from the surrounding area." This concept of place is similar to the hot spots discussed earlier.

Eck suggests that **opportunity blocking**, changes to make crime more difficult, risky, less rewarding or less excusable, is one of the oldest forms of crime prevention. Opportunity blocking at places may have a greater direct effect on offenders than other crime prevention strategies, he contends. Eck notes two side effects from place-focused opportunity blocking efforts.

Two side effects of place-focused opportunity blocking efforts are displacement of crime and diffusion of prevention benefits.

Displacement, offenders simply changing the location of their crimes, has been discussed as a potential negative of prevention efforts. However, concern about displacement may cause a benefit of prevention efforts to be overlooked, that is, diffusion. **Diffusion** of prevention benefits occurs when criminals believe that the opportunity blocking of one type of criminal activity is also aimed at other types of criminal activity. For example, when magnetic tags were put in books in a university library, book theft declined, as did the theft of audiotapes and videotapes, which were not tagged. According to Eck: "Diffusion is the flip side of the coin of crime contagion. **Contagion** suggests that when offenders notice one criminal opportunity they often detect similar opportunities they have previously overlooked. Crime then spreads. The broken window theory is an example of a contagion theory. Thus under some circumstances offenders may be uncertain about the scope of prevention efforts and avoid both the blocked opportunities and similar unblocked opportunities. When this occurs, prevention may spread."

The Risk Factor Prevention Paradigm

The **risk factor prevention paradigm** seeks to identify key risk factors for offending and then implement prevention methods designed to counteract them.

According to Farrington (2000, p.3): "By definition, a **risk factor** predicts an increased probability of later offending." The paradigm also includes a **protective factor**—which is not as easily defined. Some believe a protective factor is just the opposite end of the scale from a risk factor. Others believe this may not be true. In some instances a variable might be a protective factor but not a risk factor. For example, if high income predicts a low risk of delinquency, while medium and low income predict a fairly constant average risk, income could be regarded as a protective factor but not a risk factor (pp.8–9). This is important because when conducting research, it is necessary to investigate risk and protective factors in a way that allows them to be independent.

The risk factor prevention paradigm is highly relevant to community policing efforts as Farrington (p.1) explains: "This paradigm has fostered linkages between explanation and prevention, between fundamental and applied research, and between scholars, practitioners, and policy makers."

Partnerships to Prevent or Reduce Crime and Disorder

Partnerships to prevent or reduce crime and disorder include business anticrime groups, local government–community crime prevention coalitions, community coalitions, cooperation with grassroots organizations and working with landlords and residents in public housing, using advances in technology and celebrating community successes.

The National Crime Prevention Council (*350 Tested Strategies to Prevent Crime,* 1995) describes some of these partnerships.

Business Anticrime Groups

Business Watch groups can deter, detect and report crime in business and commercial districts. They can participate in Operation Identification. This strategy helps reduce many kinds of crimes in and around businesses, including shoplifting, theft, burglaries, drug dealing and vandalism. Police can provide education and training on robbery and burglary prevention as well as other forms of self-protection. A potential obstacle is that business owners may not feel they can significantly reduce crime by such efforts (pp.16–17).

Local Government–Community Crime Prevention Coalitions

A comprehensive local crime prevention plan developed through a coalition of community groups, local government agencies and other sectors has a good chance of success. This strategy can protect against all types of crimes. Key components include support of key political leaders and law enforcement officials, a commitment to a process open to all sectors of the community, a vision shared by all participants, specific goals and objectives and evaluation. A potential obstacle is that community members may hesitate to participate, fearing their input would not be valued.

This strategy was implemented by the mayors of the seven largest cities in Texas, who formed Mayors United on Safety, Crime and Law Enforcement (MUSCLE). With the support of the Bureau of Justice Assistance, the seven cities initiated local government–grassroots crime prevention planning projects. Of the plan's 56 objectives, 55 were implemented within two years, including the following: obtaining a $10 million increase in funding for youth recreation programs, establishing a late-night curfew for teenagers, initiating a locally developed gang-prevention effort highlighted by a public education campaign, establishing youth leadership development programs at area schools, implementing school-based conflict resolution programs, expanding community policing, establishing a business crime commission, garnering corporate support for mentoring programs and coordinating a weeklong focus on prayer for violence prevention by area religious leaders. Since the plan was implemented, youth victimization by crime during curfew hours has declined significantly, and overall crime has dropped each year (pp.35–36).

Community Coalitions

According to the NCPC: "Mobilizing community coalitions for neighborhood revitalization through resident partnership with government will reduce crime and drug trafficking and improve the quality of life." Key partnerships include residents, parent groups, block watches, businesses, schools, and civic and service organizations. The strategy involves (1) a grassroots approach to local citizen empowerment, (2) citizen identification of priority issues for action, (3) a partnership among residents and community organizations and local government and (4) development of strategies that residents and government officials can use to achieve their specific goals. Activities include rallies and marches, youth recreation programs, parent–teen workshops, citizen crime patrols, media involvement and intensive application of city services in targeted neighborhoods.

Key components can include drug-free school zones, drug abuse prevention curricula in schools, parent education and counseling groups, after-school programs and activities for youths, drug-free home and apartment lease clauses, identification of and action against drug "hot spots," allocation of community resources for rehabilitating drug abusers, youth employment and training programs, neighborhood beautification and revitalization and community rallies against drugs (pp.21–22, 37).

Cooperation with Grassroots Organizations

The NCPC contends: "When law enforcement supports the community-building efforts of an existing organization, the community benefits from a stronger network built on citizen concern and law enforcement expertise." One such grassroots organization found in many communities is Mothers Against Drunk Driving (MADD). Other groups might include the Parent Teacher Association (PTA) and local civic groups. In one instance, residents of a Waterloo, Iowa, neighborhood enlisted the support of police to close down bars that had been selling alcohol to minors. They transformed one abandoned bar into a recreation center for area youths (pp.117–118).

Working with Landlords and Residents of Public Housing

The NCPC describes 18 specific approaches to work with landlords and/or residents of public housing to deter crime and disorder (and drug dealing, discussed in Chapter 11): access control, cleanup projects, closed circuit television, crime prevention and awareness training, drug abuse prevention, enforcement of trespass law, enhanced outdoor lighting, eviction, fencing, partnerships with law enforcement, pay phone restrictions, police-in-residence programs, resident initiative groups, security headquarters, tenant screening, undercover street-level drug purchases, voluntary resident patrols and youth leadership development (p.379).

Using Advances in Technology to Fight Crime

Advances in technology, including cellular phones, fax machines, e-mail and video cameras, can be used effectively in crime prevention efforts. Whisenant and Panther (2000, p.8) describe how the Arlington County (Virginia) Police Department uses Crimereports.com, a Web-based service that allows police departments to send crime alerts, reports, statistics, pictures and other notices to members of the community via e-mail. A similar service used in the Seminole County (Florida) Sheriff's Office is described by Olson and Robinson (2000, pp.1–2). eLert is an electronic alert subscriber list that sends information via e-mail to subscribers about sex offenders, sexual predators or registered felons who have moved into the neighborhood. It offers crime alerts about traveling criminals, people with active warrants or others about whom the sheriff's office believes the public should be aware. Having considered general crime prevention partnerships and strategies, consider how partnerships and problem solving can address specific concerns related to crime and disorder.

Preventing Burglary of Single-Family Houses

Weisel (2002, pp.6–13) suggests the questions to be asked regarding the local problem of single housing burglary. A clear description is needed of the premises, the victims, the offenders if known, the specific incidents, locations and times. Weisel (pp.26–39) describes several crime prevention responses that might be taken.

Single-family burglaries might be prevented by installing burglar alarms; installing closed-circuit television (CCTV); target hardening locks, windows and doors; marking property, increasing occupancy indicators; improving visibility; and implementing Neighborhood Watch (NW).

According to Weisel (pp.39–40) increasing sanctions and providing generic crime prevention advice is usually ineffective: "Most people are never victims of burglary, and generic crime prevention advice is usually adopted by those who need it the least." It is better to concentrate efforts on houses at higher risk, especially those that have been previously burglarized. Burglars usually select their targets based on several factors, says Weisel (pp.5–13).

- Familiarity with the target and convenience of the location—houses near a ready pool of offenders, e.g., shopping centers, sports arenas, transit stations; near major thoroughfares; on the outskirts of neighborhoods; and near burglarized houses
- Occupancy—houses vacant for extended periods; routinely vacant during the day; houses of new residents; and houses without dogs
- Visibility or surveillability—houses with cover, that are secluded, with poor lighting, on corners, or with concealing architectural designs
- Accessibility—houses easily entered through side or back doors and windows or next to alleys
- Vulnerability—houses with weakened entry points, few or no security devices and residents careless about security
- Potential rewards—houses displaying signs of wealth

Preventing Burglary in Public Housing

Eck notes: "Public housing complexes have become notorious for high crime rates in the United States." He suggests that restricting pedestrian access and movement is key to reducing burglary in such places. A second strategy is target hardening by providing locks and improved security to access points. A third approach is to make burglary targets unattractive to offenders. Like Weisel, Eck suggests that focusing on residences with previous burglaries is effective, as is focusing on residences surrounding burgled dwellings. Focusing on only those living around at-risk places rather than an entire neighborhood is called **cocoon neighborhood watch**.

Preventing Burglary of Retail Establishments

According to Clarke (2002c, p.3), most retail burglars are young men who commit a variety of predatory crimes and who may have drug or alcohol abuse habits. A small number of retail burglars are highly prolific. In addition, most retail burglaries occur at night or on weekends when stores are closed. As with other crimes, problem-solving approaches to prevention involve asking the right questions about the offenses, the offenders and the targets, including locations and times. Clarke offers several possible responses to retail burglaries (pp.19–27).

Burglary of retail establishments might be prevented by targeting repeat offenders and repeatedly burgled stores; disrupting markets for stolen goods; establishing business/shop watch programs; upgrading external security and installing burglar alarms; safeguarding cash and valuable stock; locking escape routes; using CPTED measures; improving street lighting and installing CCTV; and promoting business improvement districts (BIDs).

Clarke (p.27) notes: "Many U.S. cities have designated BIDs formed by coalitions of local businesspeople. The objective is to promote investment in declining business areas. . . . Initiatives may include improvements in street lighting, installation of public CCTV systems, regular cleaning of graffiti and repair of vandalism, dedicated patrols by police and security guards and formation of a force of 'city guards' to provide a street presence and assist visitors or tourists." Another measure found to be effective in convenience stores is to require that two clerks be on duty at all times.

Preventing Shoplifting

Clarke (2002a) also discussed approaches to preventing shoplifting. He (p.5) notes: "Perhaps the principal factor determining a store's shoplifting rate is the type of goods sold." He (p.6) suggests that the acronym CRAVED captures the essential attributes of "hot products": They are concealable, removable, available, valuable, enjoyable and disposable." Clarke notes that police can do little on their own to prevent shoplifting and must persuade retailers to act in partnership with them.

Shoplifting might be prevented by improving store layout and displays, upgrading security, establishing early warning systems (notify one another about shoplifters), banning known shoplifters, installing and monitoring CCTV, using electronic article surveillance (EAS) and attaching ink tags to merchandise.

Electronic article surveillance uses a tag attached to merchandise and exit gates that detect the tags that have not been removed or deactivated, sounding an alarm. Ink tags, rather than sounding an alarm if not removed, ruin the merchandise to which they are attached when the offender tries to remove them.

Clarke (p.19) suggests: "Effective prevention often depends on well-rounded strategies encompassing good retailing practices, appropriate staffing, carefully articulated shoplifting policies and selective technology use. . . . Many depend on retailers' actions, but police may also have to collaborate with others in the community, including loss prevention specialists, business associations and court officials."

Preventing Robberies at Automated Teller Machines

ATMs were first introduced in the late 1960s in the United States and now can be found almost everywhere. Bank customers have traded safety for convenience (Scott, 2001d, p.1). According to Scott (2001d, p.2), the overall rate of ATM-related crime is between one per 1 million and one per 3.5 million transactions. Scott (p.4) presents the following general conclusions about ATM robbery. Most are committed by a lone offender—using some type of weapon—against a lone victim. Most occur at night, with the highest risk between midnight and 4 A.M. Most involve robbing people of cash after they have made a withdrawal. Robberies are somewhat more likely to occur at walk-up ATMs than at drive-through ATMs. About 15 percent of victims are injured. The average loss is between $100 and $200. Scott (pp.15–24) suggests specific responses to reduce ATM robberies.

ATM robberies might be reduced by altering lighting, landscaping and location; installing mirrors on ATMs; installing ATMs in police stations; providing ATM users with safety tips; installing CCTV; installing devices to allow victims to summon police during a robbery; and setting daily cash withdrawal limits.

Preventing Assaults in and around Bars

Factors contributing to aggression and violence in bars are described by Scott (2001a, pp.2–7), with the drinking of alcohol the most obvious factor. Other factors include the type of establishment (dance clubs have higher levels of reported violence), concentration of bars, aggressive bouncers, a high proportion of young male strangers, price discounting of drinks, refusal of service to intoxicated patrons, lack of comfort and crowding, competitive situations, low ratio of staff to patrons, lack of good entertainment, unattractive décor and dim lighting, tolerance for disorderly conduct, availability of weapons, and low levels of police enforcement and regulation.

Questions to ask about a local problem with assaults in and around bars include the incident characteristics including locations and times, victims, offenders, management practices, and regulation and enforcement practices. Scott (pp.15–24) outlines several strategies for preventing assaults in and around bars.

Assaults in and around bars might be reduced by discouraging price discounting, providing reduced alcohol or nonalcohol beverages, encouraging food service with alcohol service, reducing the concentration or number of bars, training staff to handle intoxicated patrons, relaxing or staggering bar closing times, controlling bar entrances and exits, reducing potential weapons and other sources of injury, and banning known troublemakers from bars.

Scott (pp.15–16) recommends enlisting community support for addressing the problem: "Broad-based coalitions that incorporate the interests of the community, the bars and the government are recommended. A number of communities . . . have organized 'bar watch' or 'pub watch' programs. These programs incorporate the interests of bar owners, community members and government regulators, including the police. The key is to keep all parties motivated and actively involved for extended periods of time." Scott (p.24) suggests that using extra police patrol in and around bars and marketing responsible consumption and service practices have limited effectiveness. He contends: "Heavy police involvement through patrols and enforcement is not essential if there is sufficient community, peer and regulatory pressure on licensees to manage bars responsibly."

Preventing Street Prostitution

A community may be concerned about street prostitution for a number of reasons, including moral concerns, public health concerns, personal safety concerns, economic concerns, civil rights concerns and spillover effect concerns (Scott, 2001b, pp.1–3). Spillover effects include the link between street prostitution and street drug markets; prostitution may provide profits for organized crime; prostitutes create parking and traffic problems where they congregate; and prostitution attracts strangers and criminals to a neighborhood (Scott, p.3).

Scott suggests that among the critical questions to be asked are how concerned the police department is about street prostitution and how concerned the community is. Who is particularly concerned and why? Is the prostitution linked to drugs? Scott (pp.21–28) provides several responses to prevent prostitution.

Prostitution might be prevented by identifying and targeting the worst offenders, imposing curfews on prostitutes, exposing clients to publicity, notifying those with influence over clients' conduct, helping prostitutes to quit, distributing information about known dangerous clients to prostitutes, closing streets and alleys, diverting traffic or regulating parking, warning property owners about use of their premises for prostitution, securing abandoned buildings and enhancing lighting.

Responses with limited effectiveness according to Scott (pp.29–30) include conducting sweeps, harassing and intimidating prostitutes, establishing formal or informal red light districts where street prostitution is tolerated, and legalization and decriminalization of prostitution.

The Des Moines (Iowa) Police Department encourages citizens to send "Dear John" letters to registered owners of vehicles involved in prostitution. Citizens are told they can obtain the owner's name, address, make, year and color of a vehicle by taking its license number to the Iowa Department of Transportation. The information is free. Citizens are also given a sample letter (see Figure 10.1) to send to the registered owner. In addition, citizens are instructed to send copies of the letter to the county attorney and to the vice squad. The Sunset Park, New York, neighborhood used this strategy, which resulted in more than 700 arrests and longer jail terms for prostitution (*350 Tested Strategies,* p.118).

Date: ____________________

____

____

____

____

Mr. and/or Mrs. ____:

Your ______________________________ was seen picking up a
(DESCRIPTION OF VEHICLE)

prostitute in the vicinity of ______________________________ in
(AREA)

Des Moines on ____________________, at approximately________.
(DATE) (TIME)

We hope you realize that by participating in such behavior you risk criminal prosecution, as well as exposing yourself — and possibly your family — to public humiliation and a host of diseases including the deadly AIDS virus.

Prostitution is unacceptable and it will not be tolerated any more in our neighborhood. A detailed description of your vehicle, complete with the license number, has been circulated to area residents.

Sincerely,

North Side Neighbors

cc: James Smith
Polk County Attorney

Vice Squad
Des Moines Police Department

Figure 10.1 Sample "Dear John" Letter

SOURCE: Des Moines Police. *Drugs: A Municipal Approach. A Community Handbook*, p. 15. Reprinted by permission.

Preventing Theft of and from Vehicles

According to Clarke (2002b) "Thefts *of* cars are much more often reported to the police due to insurance requirements, the potentially greater loss and the fact that police might help find stolen cars that are later abandoned. However, theft *from* cars is the larger category, constituting about 85 percent of all car-related thefts." Thefts from parking facilities is a concern that community policing can address. Clarke (pp.17–23) lists several recommended responses to prevent thefts of and from vehicles.

Thefts of and from vehicles might be prevented by hiring parking attendants, improving surveillance at deck and lot entrances/exits, hiring dedicated security patrols, installing and monitoring CCTV, improving the lighting, securing the perimeter, installing entrance barriers and electronic access, and arresting and prosecuting persistent offenders.

Many police departments furnish citizens with information on how to prevent auto theft. Information may be provided in the form of pamphlets, newspaper stories, PSAs on television or speeches made to civic organizations.

The two main messages of anticar theft programs are to not leave the keys in the car ignition and to lock the car.

These messages are conveyed in a variety of ways from stickers to put on dashboards to posters warning that leaving keys in the ignition is a violation of the law if the car is parked on public property. In addition, leaving one's keys in the ignition is an invitation to theft, could become a contributing cause of some innocent person's injury or death and could raise the owner's insurance rates.

New York City has developed a voluntary antiauto theft program that enlists the aid of motorists. The Combat Auto Theft (CAT) program allows the police to stop any car marked with a special decal between 1 A.M. and 5 A.M. Car owners sign a consent form affirming that they do not normally drive between 1 A.M. and 5 A.M., the peak auto theft hours. Those who participate in the program waive their rights to search and seizure protection.

Clarke (pp.23–25) describes programs with limited effectiveness: conducting lock-your-car campaigns, warning offenders, promoting car alarms and other "bolt-on" security devices, using decoy vehicles and redirecting joyriders' interest in cars.

Partnerships in Action against Crime and Disorder

Partnerships across the country are working on reducing crime and disorder, some focusing on one specific area, others taking more comprehensive approaches.

Norfolk, Virginia, cut homicides by more than 10 percent and has reduced overall crime rates citywide by 26 percent and in some neighborhoods by as much as 40 percent. A good share of the credit goes to Police Assisted Community Enforcement (PACE), a crime prevention initiative that works neighborhood by neighborhood in conjunction with teams of social, health and family services agencies (the Family Assistance Services Team, or FAST) and public works and environmental agencies (Neighborhood Environmental Assistance Teams, or NEAT) to cut through red tape and help residents reclaim their neighborhoods (NCPC).

The Minnesota Crime Prevention Association enlisted the support of families, public officials and 45 statewide and local organizations, including schools and churches, to wage a campaign against youth violence. Actions ranged from encouraging children and parents to turn off violent television shows to providing classroom training in violence prevention (NCPC).

In Trenton, New Jersey, a partnership of schools, parents, city leaders and others led to a Safe Haven program in which the schools in the neighborhood became multipurpose centers after school hours for youth activities including sports, crafts and tutoring. Children have flocked to the centers as a positive alternative to being at home alone after school or being at risk on the streets (NCPC).

Crime near a college campus in Columbus, Ohio, became an opportunity for a partnership formed by the City of Columbus, the State of Ohio, Ohio State University, the Franklin County Sheriff and the Columbus Police. The Community Crime Patrol puts two-person, radio-equipped teams of observers into the neighborhoods near the campus during potential high-crime hours. A number of these paid, part-time observers are college students interested in careers in law enforcement (NCPC).

In Danville, Virginia, a partnership approach to working with public housing residents resulted in a 53 percent reduction in calls about fights, a 50 percent reduction in domestic violence calls and a 9 percent reduction in disturbance calls. The Virginia Crime Prevention Association worked with the Danville Housing Authority to bring public housing residents, local law enforcement, social services and other public agencies together into an effective, problem-solving group. Residents were at the heart of the group, identifying problems that were causing high rates of aggravated assault in the community and working to provide remedies such as positive alternatives for youths, social services and counseling for adults and children. Residents developed a code of conduct for the community, spelling out expectations for the behavior of those who live there (NCPC).

Boston's Neighborhood Justice Network, in partnership with the Council of Elders, the Jewish Memorial Hospital, the Boston Police Department, the Department of Public Health and the Commission on Affairs of the Elderly, created a program to help reduce violence and other crimes against older people. It provides basic personal and home crime prevention education, assistance in dealing with city agencies, training in nonconfrontational tactics to avert street crime and other helpful services that reduce both victimization and fear among the city's older residents (NCPC).

The Fort Myers (Florida) Police Department has implemented a successful Weed and Seed program, experiencing a 41 percent increase in drug arrests in 1999 (Winton, 2000, p.12). The seeding component of the program has also flourished with social service organizations providing residents with specialized programs that reached more than 42,000 families and children in 1999.

Maryland began a "Hot Spots Communities" initiative in 35 sites statewide. The effort identifies high-crime areas and seeks to systematically help neighborhoods reduce crime. As Wooten and Schulten (2000, p.7) note: "At the core of the initiative are probation and police teams that follow the Community Probation–Community Police Team (CP-CPT) process." This process, sometimes called Operation Spotlight, develops high-performance teams from agencies that traditionally have never worked closely together. It is based on three premises: (1) the problems of high-risk offenders are too numerous and complex for probation and police officers; (2) well-trained teams are more effective than individuals acting alone; and (3) knowledge is power. One team in South Cumberland reduced its crime rate by 21 percent, compared to the countywide drop in crime of only 4 percent.

These are just a few of a wide range of programs designed by community groups that are changing the quality of life in small towns and large cities, in neighborhoods and housing complexes, in schools and on playgrounds. These groups have proved that there is strength in numbers and that partnerships can provide the community basis for correcting the problems and conditions that can lead to crime. They achieved success because they developed the skills to work together effectively.

Gastonia (North Carolina) Police Department Award Winner

International Association of Chiefs of Police finalist in the category of agencies serving a population of 50,001 to 100,000 residents report from IACP, 2002 Community Policing Awards.

The Problem

Although suffering from the decline of the textile industry, Gastonia, North Carolina, has strong manufacturing, shopping and service industries that serve the city's economic base. The problem-solving project in Gastonia addressed three low-income, crime-plagued neighborhoods where the residents, who had a low-trust level of the police, were living in fear.

The Solution

Beginning in 1990, the police department opened substations in the three neighborhoods to rid the area of gangs and drug dealers. Working with apartment managers, they created legal agreements to keep away troublemakers and to prevent those evicted from the apartments from renting in other complexes in Gastonia. The substations and the work done in these neighborhoods resulted in the reduction of crime and in the number of police calls as well as increasing the residents' trust level for the police department. The substations also became a resource for connecting residents with the wide variety of services in the community.

Bolstered by the success of the substations, the police and the city government gradually changed their approach to policing and to community problem solving and became committed to a philosophy involving three basic principles:

1. Be accessible to citizens.
2. Develop partnerships to share responsibility for crime and disorder.
3. Solve problems.

The next tactic was to use a city transit bus as a mobile substation to revitalize the city's Neighborhood-Watch program. As a result the program grew from three to seventy watch programs. The Gastonia Community Watch Association (GCWA) was formed as a way to improve communications between the watch groups.

In 2000–2001, a neighborhood enhancement team (NET) was formed to look for new ways to address quality-of-life issues in the city's neighborhoods. The NET membership included several city department heads and others from community development, code enforcement, the police department, parks and recreation department, the fire department, public information, solid waste, electrical and utilities department and the street department. The Westside Community Watch area was selected by NET as the area needing immediate attention. NET's objectives were:

- To create a team that had the ability to bring all the city's resources together.
- To develop priorities and a plan of action in partnership with the community.
- To solve problems through a team effort that could perpetuate the improvements through the joint efforts of the empowered residents with city resources.

NET conducted a door-to-door survey of the 582 homes of the Westside area. The survey revealed the following community concerns.

- Crime and prostitution.
- Lack of playgrounds or parks.
- Unkept property and environment.
- Unpredictable garbage pickup.
- Streetlights and tree concerns.
- Fire hazards.
- Lack of sidewalks and needed road repairs.
- Inadequate water and drainage systems.

The actual results of the partnership between the neighborhood and NET revealed that:

- Sixty people were arrested on prostitution-related charges, and 11 others were charged with weapons or traffic violations.
- Two houses were demolished.
- Forty-nine code and environmental enforcement citations were issued.
- The fire department visited more than 500 homes and installed 75 smoke detectors, free of charge.
- Trash collection schedule issues were corrected, and a community cleanup was held.
- The electrical department trimmed 150 trees and repaired 100 lights in the area.
- Efforts began to improve playground/recreational opportunities.
- Water drainage and water runoff problems were corrected.
- A local community watch raised $10,000 for playground equipment for the neighborhood elementary school, and the parks and recreation department installed a quarter-mile walking track at the school.

Evaluation

Crime decreased in the targeted area by 41.7 percent. Residents expressed their satisfaction with the prostitution arrests and, in fact, gave a standing ovation to the police department at a Westside Community Watch meeting. A follow-up survey indicated:

- Ninety percent of those surveyed were familiar with the NET/Westside project.
- Seventy-four percent believed the project helped to improve the neighborhood.

- Ninety-five percent would recommend a NET/Community Watch project in other neighborhoods.
- Ninety-six percent said they are good neighbors and take action to help their neighborhood.

NET sent a newsletter to all residents in the area, outlining the NET/Westside Community Watch accomplishments and urging the residents to continue their involvement in building a strong neighborhood. Acknowledging accomplishments is always important.

Summary

Synergism occurs when individuals channel their energies toward a common purpose and accomplish together what they could not accomplish alone. It can greatly enhance community policing efforts to prevent or reduce crime and disorder. Crime prevention is a large part, and in fact a cornerstone, of community policing.

Traffic problems top the list of concerns of most neighborhoods and communities. Concerns include corridor safety, speeding in residential areas, street racing, red light running, impaired drivers, elderly drivers and nonuse of seat belts. Engineering responses to speeding include using traffic calming, posting warning signs and signals, conducting antispeeding public awareness campaigns, informing complainants about actual speeds and providing realistic driver training. Enforcement responses to speeding include (1) enforcing speeding laws, (2) enforcing speeding laws with speed cameras—photo radar, (3) using speed display boards, (4) arresting the worst offenders and (5) having citizen volunteers monitor speeding. The defining characteristics of Safe Communities are (1) data from multiple sources, (2) expanded partnerships, (3) citizen involvement and (4) an integrated and comprehensive injury control system.

Community policing efforts to deal with citizen fear have been varied. They include foot and vehicle patrol in high-crime neighborhoods, community meetings, citizen patrol, neighborhood cleanup programs, opening neighborhood substations and citizen awareness campaigns.

Three federal initiatives to assist communities in implementing community policing are the Community Oriented Policing Services (COPS) Office, the Community Policing Consortium and the Weed and Seed program. The Weed and Seed program seeks to identify, arrest and prosecute offenders (weed) while simultaneously working with citizens to improve quality of life (seed).

One frequently used strategy is crime prevention through environmental design. CPTED has three major components: target hardening, changes to the physical environment and community building. Five principles underlying CPTED are territoriality, natural surveillance, access control, activity support and maintenance of the environment. By emphasizing the systematic analysis of crime in a particular location, CPTED directly supports community policing by providing crime prevention strategies tailored to solve specific problems. Another approach to crime prevention is focusing on place. Two side effects of place-focused opportunity blocking efforts are displacement of crime and diffusion of prevention benefits.

The risk factor prevention paradigm seeks to identify key risk factors for offending and then implement prevention methods designed to counteract them. It is useful in identifying strategies that might be effective for a specific community. Partnerships to prevent or reduce crime and disorder include business anticrime groups, local government–community crime prevention coalitions, community coalitions, cooperation with grassroots organizations, and working with landlords and residents of public housing.

Single-family burglaries might be prevented by installing burglar alarms; installing closed-circuit television (CCTV); target hardening locks, windows and doors; marking property; increasing occupancy indicators; improving visibility; and implementing Neighborhood Watch (NW).

Burglary of retail establishments might be prevented by targeting repeat offenders and repeatedly burgled stores; disrupting markets for stolen goods; establishing business/shop watch programs; upgrading external security and installing burglar alarms; safeguarding cash and valuable stock; locking escape routes; using CPTED measures; improving street lighting and installing CCTV; and promoting business improvement districts (BIDs).

Shoplifting might be prevented by improving store layout and displays, upgrading security, establishing early warning systems (notify one another about shoplifters), banning known shoplifters, installing and monitoring CCTV, using electronic article surveillance (EAS) and attaching ink tags to merchandise.

ATM robberies might be reduced by altering lighting, landscaping and location; installing mirrors on ATMs; installing ATMs in police stations; providing ATM users with safety tips; installing CCTV; installing devices to allow victims to summon police during a robbery; and setting daily cash withdrawal limits.

Assaults in and around bars might be reduced by discouraging price discounting, providing reduced alcohol or nonalcohol beverages, encouraging food service with alcohol service, reducing the concentration or number of bars, training staff to handle intoxicated patrons, relaxing or staggering bar closing times, controlling bar entrances and exits, reducing potential weapons and other sources of injury, and banning known troublemakers from bars.

Thefts of and from vehicles might be prevented by hiring parking attendants, improving surveillance at deck and lot entrances/exits, hiring dedicated security patrols, installing and monitoring CCTV, improving the lighting, securing the perimeter, installing entrance barriers and electronic access, and arresting and prosecuting persistent offenders. The two main messages of anticar theft programs are (1) do not leave the keys in the ignition and (2) lock the car.

Discussion Questions

1. What examples of synergy have you been a part of or witnessed?
2. What crime prevention programs are in your community? Have you participated in any of them?
3. Which of the programs discussed in this chapter seem most exemplary to you? Why?
4. What steps might be taken to repair a community's "broken windows" and protect against having them broken again?
5. Explain how "lease enforcement" reduces criminal activity in public housing.
6. Name and explain the five principles underlying CPTED.
7. Since taxes pay for police to combat crime, why should citizens get involved?
8. To what do you attribute the dramatic decline in crime: community policing, the economy, the dramatic rise in the prison population, the increased number of police officers or some other reason?
9. How has technology helped prevent crime?
10. Which do you feel merits the most attention from community policing, concerns about disorder, fear of crime or crime itself?

InfoTrac College Edition Assignments

- Use InfoTrac College Edition to help answer the Discussion Questions as appropriate.
- One of the most effective and least expensive security initiatives is to design and build safety from crime and fear of crime into a structure. Research CPTED and discuss how the following can affect crime and/or fear of crime: smell and sound, parking garages, maintenance, color, mix of activities, restrooms, signage, vehicle–pedestrian conflicts, loitering and "hanging out."

Community Projects

- Do you have any "broken windows" in your community? If so, how would you characterize them? What might be done to mend them?
- Conduct a survey of a portion of your institution's campus and determine whether any of the CPTED principles might make that portion of campus safer.

References

Bolton, Joel. "Task Force Enlists Community Help to Reduce Impaired Driving." *The Police Chief,* April 2003, p.162.

Branson, Helen Kitchen. "Weed and Seed in Honolulu: The Key Is Community Input." *Law and Order,* September 2000, pp.82–86.

Brewer, Rodney W. "Marketing Your Highway Safety Campaign." *The Police Chief,* July 2002, pp.30–31.

Cahill, Patricia. "November Safety Belt Mobilization: Show Some Restraint." *The Police Chief,* November 2003, p.62.

Canby, Anne. "The Urgent Need for Operational Partnerships between Transportation and Public Safety Agencies." *Subject to Debate,* June 2002, pp.1, 5.

Casstevens, Steven and Rizzo, Paul. "Approaching Child Passenger Safety from a Team Concept." *The Police Chief,* July 2001, pp.39–43.

Chermak, Steven; McGarrell, Edmund F.; and Weiss, Alexander. "Citizens' Perceptions of Aggressive Traffic Enforcement Strategies." *Justice Quarterly,* June 2001, pp.365–391.

Clarke, Ronald V. *Shoplifting.* Washington, DC: Office of Community Oriented Policing Services, Problem-Oriented Guides for Police Series No. 11, January 24, 2002a.

Clarke, Ronald V. *Thefts of and from Cars in Parking Facilities.* Washington, DC: Office of Community Oriented Policing Services, Problem-Oriented Guides for Police Series No. 10, January 24, 2002b.

Clarke, Ronald V. *Burglary of Retail Establishments.* Washington, DC: Office of Community Oriented Policing Services, Problem-Oriented Guides for Police Series No. 15, March 13, 2002c.

Dunworth, Terence and Mills, Gregory. *National Evaluation of Weed and Seed.* Washington, DC: National Institute of Justice, 1999. (NCJ 175685)

Eck, John E. "Preventing Crime at Places." In *Preventing Crime: What Works, What Doesn't, What's Promising: A Report to the United States Congress,* edited by Lawrence W. Sherman, Denise Gottfredson, Doris MacKenzie, John Eck, Peter Reuter and Shawn Bushway. www.ncjrs.org/works/index.htm

Farrington, David P. "Explaining and Preventing Crime: The Globalization of Knowledge—The American Society of Criminology 1999 Presidential Address." *Criminology*, February 2000, pp.1–24.

Farrow, Joe. "Senior Safety on the Road." *The Police Chief*, July 2003, pp.50–52.

Files, L. Burke. "Crime Fighting by Design." *Police*, October 1999, pp.52–56.

"Good News, Bad News: An Update of Landmark 1969 Violence Report." *Law Enforcement News*, January 15/31, 2000, pp.1, 10.

Gorovici, Eli. "10 Recommendations for Responsible Implementation of CCTA in the Fight to Reduce Crime." *Security Technology & Design*, January 2000, pp.36–40.

Helmick, D. O. "CHP Addresses Two Highway Safety Problems: Running Red Lights and Senior Citizen Driving Safety." *The Police Chief*, July 2003, pp.44–50.

Helmick, D. O.; Keller, John; Nannini, Robert; and Huffaker, Alice. "Corridor Safety Programs: A Collaborative Approach to Traffic Safety." *The Police Chief*, July 2001, pp.32–35.

Katz, Charles M.; Webb, Vincent J.; and Schaefer, David R. "An Assessment of the Impact of Quality-of-Life Policing on Crime and Disorder." *Justice Quarterly*, December 2001, pp.825–876.

Lowery, Patrick J. "Curb Illegal Street Racing." *The Police Chief*, September 2003, pp.51–54.

McMahon, James W. "New York State Takes the Next Step in Saving Lives through Occupant Restraint Enforcement." *The Police Chief*, July 2000, pp.34–39.

Miller, Christa. "Community Oriented Traffic Policing: Maine Police Seek to Reduce Traffic Crashes in the Long Term." *Law Enforcement Technology*, October 2002, pp.22–26.

Mineta, Norman Y. *Safe Communities, 1999: Report to Congress*. Washington, DC: U.S. Department of Transportation, May 2001. (DOT HS 809258)

Olson, Steve and Robinson, Pete. "Technology Brings Policing to Higher Level—and Closer to Community Level." *Community Policing Exchange*, Spring 2000, pp.1–2.

Phillips, Eric. *Crime Prevention through Environmental Design in the Bancroft Neighborhood*. http://freenet.msp.mn.us/org/npcr/reports/npcr1034/npcr1034.html

Rojek, "A Decade of Excellence in Problem-Oriented Policing: Characteristics of the Goldstein Award Winners." *Police Quarterly*, December 2003, pp.492–515.

Runge, Jeffrey W. "Law Enforcement Call to Action to Reduce Traffic Crashes." *The Police Chief*, April 2003, p.13.

Scheider, Matthew C.; Rowell, Tawandra; and Bezdikian, Veh. "The Impact of Citizen Perceptions of Community Policing on Fear of Crime: Findings from Twelve Cities." *Police Quarterly*, December 2003, pp.363–386.

Scott, Michael S. *Assaults in and around Bars*. Washington, DC: Office of Community Oriented Policing Services, Problem-Oriented Guides for Police Series No. 1, July 30, 2001a.

Scott, Michael S. *Street Prostitution*. Washington, DC: Office of Community Oriented Policing Services, Problem-Oriented Guides for Police Series No. 2, August 6, 2001b.

Scott, Michael S. *Speeding in Residential Areas*. Washington, DC: Office of Community Oriented Policing Services, Problem-Oriented Guides for Police Series No. 3, August 14, 2001c.

Scott, Michael S. *Robbery at Automated Teller Machines*. Washington, DC: Office of Community Oriented Policing Services, Problem-Oriented Guides for Police Series No. 8, September 14, 2001d.

Smith, Michael R. "Police-Led Crackdowns and Cleanups: An Evaluation of a Crime Control Initiative in Richmond, Virginia." *Crime and Delinquency*, 2001, p.60.

Sweeney, Earl M. "Traffic Stops: Neglect them at Your Peril." *The Police Chief*, July 2003, pp.38–43.

350 Tested Strategies to Prevent Crime: A Resource for Municipal Agencies and Community Groups. Washington, DC: National Crime Prevention Council, 1995.

Weisel, Deborah Lamm. *Burglary of Single-Family Houses*. Washington, DC: Office of Community Oriented Policing Services, Problem-Oriented Guides for Police Series No. 18, July 25, 2002.

Weiss, Jim and Davis, Mickey. "Buckle Up Kids: Tampa's Car Seat Checkpoint." *Law and Order*, September 2002, pp.152–157.

Weiss, Jim and Dresser, Mary. "Cleaning Up the City." *Law and Order*, June 2001, pp.117–118.

Whisenant, Greg and Panther, Tom. "For All Eyes to See: Community in the Know on Neighborhood Crime." *Community Policing Exchange*, Spring 2000, p.8.

Winton, Kara. "Fort Myers, Florida: A Case Study in Successful Community Policing." *The Law Enforcement Trainer,* March/April 2000, pp.10–12, 32–33.

Wooten, Harold B. and Schulten, Sue. "Community Teams Take a Case-by-Case Approach." *Community Policing Exchange,* September/October 2000, pp.1, 8.

Zhao, J.; Scheider, M.; and Thurman, Q. "The Effect of Police Presence on Public Fear Reduction and Satisfaction: A Review of the Literature." *The Justice Professional,* Vol. 15, 2002, pp.273–299.

CHAPTER 11

Community Policing and Drugs

Research has long shown that the abuse of alcohol, tobacco, and illicit drugs is the single most serious health problem in the United States, straining the health care system, burdening the economy, and contributing to the health problems and death of millions of Americans every year. Today, substance abuse causes more deaths, illnesses, and disabilities than any other preventable health condition.

—Nels Ericson

DO YOU KNOW?

- Whether crime and drugs are linked?
- What the key to reducing drug abuse is?
- What the first initiative to reduce drug-related crime and violence proposed by the original National Drug Control Strategy is?
- What strategies have been implemented to combat the drug problem in neighborhoods?
- What the mission of the National Drug Intelligence Center is?
- What new corps of police professionals might be needed to combat the drug problem?
- What Lead On America is?
- What federal grant programs aimed specifically at the drug problem are available?
- What type of drug market poses the greatest threat in apartment complexes?
- What conditions make apartment complexes susceptible to drug dealing?
- What strategies for getting impaired drivers off the street are supported?
- What Freeway Watch does?
- What a survey of over 2,000 residents living near college campuses found?
- What the three prongs in the 3 in 1 Prevention Program are?
- What strategies can discourage irresponsible marketing of alcohol?
- What two general approaches to address rave parties are?
- If crime, drugs and the American Dream are related?
- How the conservative and liberal crime control strategies differ?

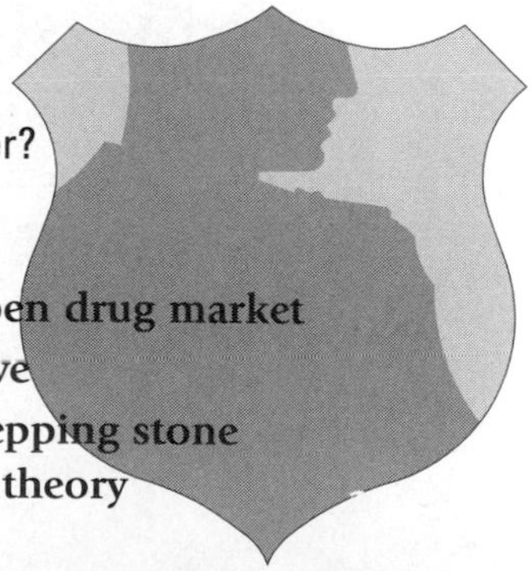

CAN YOU DEFINE?

binge drinking
closed drug market
conservative crime control
gateway theory
liberal crime control
open drug market
rave
stepping stone theory

Introduction

The correlation between drugs and crime is well established. Approximately three-fourths of prison inmates and over half of those in jails or on probation are substance abusers. Drug users often commit crimes to support their habit. Drug dealers fight territorial wars over the drug market, making neighborhoods hazardous. The research of Weisburd and Mazerolle (2000, p.331) shows that drug hot spots are more likely to experience crime and disorder problems as compared with nondrug hot spots: "The findings support a spatial link between street-level drug hot spot activity, disorder and serious crime."

Crime and drugs are clearly linked.

Any efforts to reduce the drug problem are likely to also lessen crime and disorder in a neighborhood and community. Walters (2002, p.1), director of the Office of National Drug Control Policy, says: "More than any other group of Americans, our nation's law enforcement officers understand how drug use frays the fabric of our communities. From the rural Midwest to our densely populated coasts, drug use is consistently connected with society's vilest ills: prostitution, child abuse, organized crime, gang violence, murder and corruption. Every day, law enforcement officers across America risk their lives as they invest time and resources attempting to thwart the violence and depravity wrought by drugs."

A DARE officer teaches elementary school children about the importance of avoiding alcohol and illegal drugs. This well-known program has yet to be proven effective.

This chapter begins with a discussion of the "war on drugs" and National Drug Control Strategy. This is followed by strategies for stopping drug use before it starts, including a discussion of the DARE program. Next is a description of strategies for dealing with a drug problem and the federal grants available to help partnerships combat this problem. Then the issues involved in addressing drug dealing in privately owned apartment complexes are examined. This is followed by a discussion of collaborative efforts to combat drug dealing and an example of a comprehensive, coordinated community approach. Next, problems associated with alcohol are described including getting the impaired driver off the streets and the problem of underage drinking. The chapter concludes by examining the relationship between crime, drugs and the American dream and providing another example of a successful problem-solving partnership in action.

The "War on Drugs"

In 1914 the Harrison Act made buying, selling or using certain drugs illegal. McNamara (2000, p.8) believes that since then we have had one drug war after another. He says the current war began in 1972 when President Nixon coined the phrase. That year the federal budget for the drug war was roughly $101 million. In 2000 the budget was $17.8 billion. To explain how drastic this increase is, McNamara says: "In 1972, the average monthly Social Security check was $177. If those benefits had increased at the same rate the drug war spending had increased, the average Social Security check today would be $30,444 a month. The average weekly salary of $144 would be $19,000 a week, and if you had a mortgage [payment] of $408 a month in 1972 and it had increased at the same rate, your mortgage [payment] today would be over $60,000 a month."

Even with all this money, many people believe we are losing the war. Oliver (2000, p.9), for example, says: "Our nation's premier drug-war strategy of more police, more interdiction, and more incarceration is failing. . . . Our rigid anti-drug strategy and our punitive prohibition efforts are failing." Oliver suggests: "Former Secretary of State George Schultz said recently that any real and lasting change that occurs in a democratic society is done through education and persuasion and not through coercion and force. Perhaps it's time to heed his sage advice and search for alternative approaches to our current drug-control strategies that will be more effective, fair, and humane in reducing drug usage and drug dependency; that will emphasize treatment, prevention, and education; and that will rely on our social and health systems more than on our criminal justice systems."

Lock et al. (2002, p.380) report: "Since the early 1980s, federal control expenditures have soared in response to six presidential administrations' commitment to the 'war on drugs.' During this period, spending on criminal justice programs grew from 30 percent of the total drug control budget to 52 percent, whereas the share devoted to drug treatment programs declined from 31 percent to 18 percent." These researchers surveyed residents of the five largest U.S. metropolitan areas and found that respondents generally were favorable toward spending on the drug problem, but did not support the way the war on drugs is being conducted. Support for criminal justice approaches to drug control lagged "significantly" behind support for prevention and treatment strategies. Fortunately, this is the attitude revealed in the National Drug Control Strategy.

The National Drug Control Strategy

The original National Drug Control Strategy (NDCS), a 10-year plan published in 1998, stated (p.4):

The key to reducing drug abuse is prevention coupled with treatment.

The National Drug Control Strategy, 1998 (p.35) acknowledges: "Our police forces continue to be the first line of defense against criminals. Men and women in uniform exhibit supreme dedication and face risks on a daily basis while confronting violent crime, much of it induced by drugs." The document then suggests: "The more we can link law enforcement with local residents in positive ways that create trusting relationships, the more secure our communities will be. . . . The strength of the COPS program is its emphasis on long-term, innovative approaches to community-based problems. This program reinforces efforts that are already reducing the incidence of drug-related crime in America."

The first initiative to reduce drug-related crime and violence is community policing.

In February 2002 President Bush unveiled his National Drug Control Strategy, which seeks to reduce use of illegal drugs by 10 percent over two years and 25 percent over five years. In his announcement President Bush stated: "We've got a problem in this country: Too many people use drugs. This is an individual tragedy, and, as a result, it is a social crisis" ("Bush Goal . . .," 2002, p.A7). President Bush also acknowledged: "We understand we can't [achieve our goals] alone here in Washington. That's why we recognize the true strength of the country is our people. And we know there are thousands of parents, thousands of educators, thousands of community activists, and law enforcement officials, all anxious to come together to achieve this strategy" (Walters, p.9). The strategy is based on three core principles:

1. *Stopping drug use before it starts: education and community action.* In homes, schools, places of worship, the workplace, and civic and social organizations, Americans must set norms that reaffirm the values of responsibility and good citizenship while dismissing the notion that drug use is consistent with individual freedom. The National Drug Control Strategy ties national leadership with community-level action to help recreate the formula that helped America succeed against drugs in the past.
2. *Healing America's drug users: getting treatment resources where they are needed.* Getting people into treatment will require the creation of a new climate of "compassionate coercion," which begins with family, friends, employers and the community. Compassionate coercion also uses the criminal justice system to get people into treatment.

3. *Disrupting the market: attacking the economic basis of the drug trade.* Domestically, attacking the economic basis of the drug trade involves the cooperative, combined efforts of federal, state and local law enforcement.

The first core principle, stopping drug use before it starts, stresses education and benefits from community policing efforts.

Stopping Drug Use before it Starts

"Keeping children on the right path is easier when drugs fail to surface in their lives," says Garrett (2003, p.8). She notes: "Enforcement and interdiction help keep drugs out of our children's hands, but are not the entire answer." According to Parsons: "We can't totally arrest our way out of the problem. The long-term solution to this problem is education and reaching kids at an early age" (Garrett, p. 8).

Making the Grade: A Guide to School Drug Prevention Programs (1999) reviewed 49 drug prevention programs and found that only 10 had been rigorously evaluated, and of those 10 only a few showed favorable results. Probably the most evaluated program is DARE, but most long-term studies of the program do not support its effectiveness.

The DARE Program

The DARE (Drug Awareness Resistance Education) pro-gram was developed in Los Angeles in 1983 and is now taught in over 10,000 communities nationwide, 75 to 80 percent of school districts and internationally in 54 countries (Mertens, 2003, p.25). According to Mertens (p.24): "DARE officers arm the country's children with weapons of knowledge and confidence to 'just say no' [to drugs]." Braiker (2003) says of the program:

> The most widespread school anti-drug program in the country is now taught in 80 percent of school districts nationwide and by some estimates enjoys upwards of $700 million in federal aid. . . .
>
> DARE, which puts police officers into elementary school classrooms to warn kids about the dangers of drugs, is a proponent of the **gateway** or **stepping stone theory** [emphasis added]. The program teaches that milder illicit drugs—like marijuana—lead directly to experimentation with and an addiction to hard drugs like crack cocaine and heroin. . . .
>
> The National Academy of Sciences says there's no scientific basis for the stepping-stone or gateway theory. . . .
>
> And another thing is that it can be appropriate to use police officers in classrooms to teach about public safety. But why are we using police officers to teach about drugs? Why is there reason to believe that police officers know anything about drugs? If you think about it, either they've never used drugs themselves or if they have they can't talk about it. Beyond that you would think it makes sense to have somebody that has some background in health, but why are we having a police officer who deals with public safety issues

teaching this? I think that's the fundamental flaw of DARE: it's the inappropriate use of police officers. . . .

When you start talking with teenagers you have to substitute "just say n-o" with "just say k-n-o-w."

A January report on DARE by the government's General Accounting Office concluded that the program has had 'no statistically significant long-term effect on preventing differences' in their 'attitudes toward illicit drug use' compared to children who had not been exposed to the program. In 2001 the U.S. Surgeon General categorized it as an 'Ineffective Program.'

Mertens (p.24) would disagree: "DARE is not just about drug prevention. Or officers. Or even community service. It's about kids. And most importantly, building relationships. DARE is a community in itself—one devoted to making a difference in the lives of children." In addition, based on the shortcomings of the DARE program revealed by extensive research, the curriculum has been completely revised thanks to a $15 million research grant given to the University of Akron by the Robert Wood Johnson Foundation, the largest health philanthropy in the world. As Mertens (p.31) explains: "The main difference in the programs is the focus on group learning and role-playing. An emphasis has been placed on the DARE instructor to act as a facilitator, rather than a lecturer." The new curriculum is undergoing extensive evaluation, but the results are not yet available. Another approach to drug education uses a reality-based approach.

A Reality-Based Approach to Drug Education

Rosenbaum's (1999) program, *Safety First,* stresses a reality-based approach to drug education. She (p.1) notes that: "Despite expenditures of more than $2.1 billion on prevention this year, government surveys indicate that many teenagers experiment with drugs." She believes the reason is that drug education is flawed in assuming that *drug use* is the same as *drug abuse.* Many programs use the terms interchangeably, but teenagers know there is a difference. The gateway theory, a drug education mainstay, argues that using marijuana leads to using "harder" drugs, but there is no evidence of this. Again, teenagers believe they are being told "untruths." Says Rosenbaum (p.9): "The consistent mis-characterization of marijuana may be the Achilles Heel of conventional approaches to drug education because these false messages are inconsistent with students' actual observations and experience."

The Safety First reality-based alternative rests on three assumptions: (1) Teenagers can make responsible decisions if given honest, science-based drug education; (2) total abstinence may not be a realistic alternative for all teenagers; and (3) use of mind-altering substances does not necessarily constitute abuse. Rosenbaum (p.14) concludes: "Reality-based drug education will equip students with information they trust, the basis for making responsible decisions." When educational efforts fail, other strategies come into play.

Strategies for Dealing with the Drug Problem

Dealing with the drug problem requires the collaborative efforts of the police, public housing authorities, other agencies and, most important, the residents themselves.

Strategies to deal with the drug problem include improving the physical environment, removing offenders, reducing the demand for drugs, improving intelligence, using police drug-control specialists, forming "meth" collaborations and empowering residents.

Although residents living in private dwellings can do much to reduce or prevent crime, efforts that have the most effect are usually aimed specifically at public housing in inner-city neighborhoods.

Improving the Physical Environment Improving indoor and exterior lighting has been successfully used in some projects. Cleanup efforts in trash-strewn lots, which provide easy hiding places for drugs, have also been successful. Some housing projects have developed identification cards for their residents so that outsiders can be readily observed. Others have limited access by limiting the number of entrances and exits. CPTED, as described in Chapter 10, is clearly applicable here. Many communities accomplish improvements in the physical environment through Weed and Seed programs.

Removing Offenders Increased efforts at *enforcing laws* against dealing drugs and *increasing prosecution* are also deterrents to drug dealers. Sometimes the housing authority makes an apartment available to the local police department in which to set up an office. This visible police presence can be a strong deterrent. It can also provide residents with a feeling of security as well as concrete evidence that the city is working on the problem.

Some housing agencies, residents and police departments have worked to create drug-free zones (DFZs) similar to those used around schools. Patrol efforts are concentrated in DFZs, and arrests for drug dealing carry increased penalties. Other cities, such as Fort Lauderdale, Tampa and Louisville, have targeted small geographic areas.

Some departments are using *technology* to aid in arresting drug dealers. For example, officers use a miniature video camera that is capable of filming participants in a drug transaction and recording their voices without the participants' awareness of what is occurring (Meyers, 2000a, p.3).

Asset seizures of drug dealers are also frequently used by police. Police departments use federal or state forfeiture laws that allow them to seize property and assets of drug dealers, including drugs, cars, boats, airplanes, mobile homes, land and cash—a type of financial death sentence. Asset seizures not only punish the offenders but also send a strong message to the youths of the community who may be quite impressed with the material possessions that drug dealers flaunt.

Police may also use *lease enforcement.* Beginning in April 1989, the Department of Housing and Urban Development (HUD) has required that leases include an explicit provision permitting eviction if any member of a household engages in drug-related criminal activity.

Finally police have found that simply *making drug dealing inconvenient* may be an effective deterrent. San Diego police, for example, discovered that drug dealers were using public phones on certain street corners. The police worked with the phone company to fix the phones so that they could be used only for outgoing calls, thereby stopping outsiders from calling in orders for drugs.

Reducing the Demand Another approach to the drug problem is to focus on those who use drugs. Some police departments have used *sting operations* during which undercover police agents sell drugs and then arrest those who buy them. These operations have sometimes been criticized as unethical or even an illegal form of entrapment. Police must exercise extreme care if they use such operations as a strategy to reduce the drug problem.

Educating users may be a more fruitful and perhaps more ethical approach to the drug problem. School programs can help youths resist peer pressure to experiment with drugs. *Providing diversions or alternatives* to finding acceptance or excitement through drug use may also help. Providing community recreational programs, improving ball fields and parks, installing a basketball court or sponsoring athletic contests are all important additions to a community in its fight against drugs.

Providing treatment and rehabilitation for drug users is sometimes also an effective strategy. Often residents are not aware of the existence of such treatment facilities. In many communities, however, such facilities do not exist.

Improving Intelligence If police can enlist citizens to provide information about drug dealing to the police, much can be accomplished. Most residents in public housing know where drug deals are made. Many also believe, however, that the police either do not care or are actually corrupt because they arrest few dealers. When dealers are arrested, they are often back on the street within hours. Residents should be educated about the difficulties of prosecuting drug dealers and the need for evidence.

Some departments conduct *community surveys* in low-income neighborhoods to learn about how residents view the drug problem. Some departments have established tip lines where residents can provide information anonymously.

Improved reporting can be accomplished in a number of ways. Police can also improve the information they receive about problems in other ways. Intelligence can be increased by unusual procedures. Police have been known to interview arrestees to obtain inside information on how certain criminal activities are conducted. In some agencies, arrestees have been interviewed in jail with a jail debriefing form. This kind of information is useful as police continue to document the link between drugs and criminal activity.

Housing personnel are often the closest to drug problems in public housing. These housing personnel can be trained to identify drugs or drug dealing behaviors, and cooperate with police in following up on complaints.

Intelligence information can also be improved by facilitating the communication between narcotics investigators and patrol officers. For example, in Atlanta, a narcotics supervisor recognized that patrol and narcotics had historically used a different radio frequency and were unable to communicate. The problem was quickly corrected.

One important aid in improving intelligence is the National Drug Intelligence Center (NDIC), established in 1993 as a component of the U.S. Department of Justice. Strong (2001, p.55) explains the mission of the NDIC.

The mission of the National Drug Intelligence Center is to provide the nation's law enforcement personnel and policymakers with strategic domestic drug intelligence for their use in establishing law enforcement priorities and formulating drug control policy.

Strong notes: "The NDIC relies on information from all levels of law enforcement, especially the local level," and local law enforcement relies on citizen input for much of its information.

Using Drug Control Specialists Greenberg (2001, p.9) suggests: "The problem of substance abuse, including alcohol, is enormous. An entirely new corps of police professional is needed to serve as 'drug control specialists.' " According to Greenberg: "The use of auxiliaries would appear to be a natural type of community policing strategy for reducing crime associated with drug abuse. . . . Units of auxiliary police could be assigned to such functions as:

- Providing antidrug presentations to children and their parents.
- Serving as role models for at-risk youths.
- Playing an active role in crisis intervention and recreational programs to divert youths from drug activity.
- Sponsoring community forums to share concerns about local drug problems.
- Energizing participants in Neighborhood-Watch groups by planning and implementing programs.
- Establishing and operating boys' and girls' clubs.
- Working closely with alternative school programs, clubs and other after-school activities.
- Staffing storefront police substations.
- Instructing and organizing citizen and youth police academies.
- Serving as departmental liaisons to civilian anticrime patrols and contract security personnel.
- Helping to educate store owners and tavern employees about the misuse of false identity cards.
- Serving as volunteer court and probation officers to assist in the work of night drug courts."

A new corps of police professionals might serve as drug control specialists.

Greenberg contends: "The recruitment of drug control police specialists could help communities achieve such goals as reducing personal harm for addicts, family members and bystanders; furthering overall safety; providing care for those who need it; diverting cases out of the criminal justice system through effective problem solving; and enhancing and promoting interventions involving informal mechanisms of social control." Greenberg also notes: "These new specialists would possess all of the powers of regular police officers and receive all of the appropriate training.

This is essential not only because of the violence associated with drug trafficking, but because 60 percent of the people who use heroin and cocaine are already involved in the criminal justice system."

Greenberg (p.10) concludes: "The start of a new millennium should offer new hope for old problems. . . . The new strategy, combined with existing demand-reduction approaches, may help to bring an end to the seemingly hopeless year-in, year-out criminal approach that has dominated this issue for more than 80 years."

Forming "Meth" Collaborations Scott (2002b, p.1) observes that when dealing with clandestine drug labs police agencies cannot be expected to know everything about hazardous materials, occupational safety, environmental protection and child protection: "They must collaborate with fire officials, hazardous materials experts, chemists, public health officials, social service providers and environmental protection officials."

Empowering Residents Many police agencies have focused on the broader needs of residents of low-income housing. In Tulsa, for example, officers believed that limited job opportunities were a problem for youths living in public housing. The officers now steer youths into Job Corps, a training and job service program that is an alternative to the traditional high school. Residents can also be empowered in other ways, for example, by forming associations or holding rallies.

In 2001 a Snohomish County (Washington) deputy introduced Tina Hagget and Susan York to each other. Both lived in neighborhoods plagued by car prowling, speeding and frenzied traffic associated with drug dealing. The women compared notes and realized the same cars were operating in both neighborhoods, about five miles apart. They agreed to partner with law enforcement to stop the drug market in their neighborhood. They learned deputies' names and schedules and contacted them with information, limiting the need to repeatedly explain the problem. As Sinnema (2003, p.10) notes: "With the help of the deputies, the women learned what to report to police: license plates and times of increased foot and car traffic at the suspected drug houses. The reports from Hagget and York helped law enforcement obtain search warrants." Soon Hagget and York became the unofficial community link between Snohomish County deputies and other neighborhoods struggling against drug crime, sharing their stories, giving advice on what to report to their local authorities, saving deputies hours of explanations to angry, frustrated residents. According to Sinnema (p.11): "Most people believe that a single 911 call should lead to arrests and elimination of drugs in their neighborhoods."

In January 2002 the women attended a Meth Summit sponsored by Snohomish County and volunteered with 10 other citizens and police officers to work on a law enforcement task force exploring options to reduce drug activity in their communities. The result of the task force was Lead On America.

Lead On America is a citizen coalition that helps instruct and mobilize communities to partner with law enforcement throughout the country to combat drug problems.

The group has published a guide that includes an activity log in which residents can describe suspicious vehicles and visitors to the suspect drug house, as well as the signs of a drug house. Figure 11.1 illustrates a portion of the log.

Neighborhood Activity Log

Never place yourself in any danger trying to gather information. Always call 911 if there is any reason to believe you or someone else is in danger or that there is an in-progress crime being committed.

Date	Start Time	Activity Description	License Number	Vehicle Description	# of Persons	Name or Description of Each Person	End Time	Other	Initial
/ /	: ☐AM ☐PM						: ☐AM ☐PM		
/ /	: ☐AM ☐PM						: ☐AM ☐PM		
/ /	: ☐AM ☐PM						: ☐AM ☐PM		

Figure 11.1 Neighborhood Activity Log

SOURCE: Cindi Sinnema. "Residents Learn Ways to Best Serve Sheriff's Office in Fight against Meth." *Community Links*, May 2003, p.12. Reprinted by permission.

According to Sinnema (p.12): "The tactics are working. The drug dealers in Hagget and York's neighborhoods have been relocated to much smaller quarters with bars on the windows. . . . The criminal justice system was able to work when the necessary information was delivered to officers by educated residents. . . . The primary summer neighborhood retail market has changed from drug dealers pushing methamphetamines to colorful, musical trucks distributing ice cream and smiles."

Available Grants to Assist in Implementing Selected Strategies

Federal assistance specifically aimed at the drug problem is available through the Weed and Seed program and the Drug-Free Communities program.

Weed and Seed Funding

As Simpson (2002, p.217) explains: "Coordinated by the Executive Office for Weed and Seed (EOWS) in Washington, DC, the Weed and Seed strategy provides federal funds—up to $250,000 per year for three years—to communities who wish to weed out criminal elements [including drug dealers] and seed in programs and agencies whose mission it is to enhance the quality of life for the community." Simpson notes: "Weed and Seed is a process and requires problem identification, planning, implementation and evaluation . . . The process is lengthy, manpower intensive and well worth the effort in the end."

Drug-Free Community Funding

The Drug-Free Communities Act of 1997 is "a catalyst for increased citizen participation in efforts to reduce substance use among youths, and it provides community antidrug coalitions with much-needed funds to carry out their important missions" (Simonson, 2001, p.1). The Drug-Free Communities Support Program is directed by the White House Office of National Drug Control Policy (ONDCP) in partnership with the Office of Juvenile Justice and Delinquency Prevention (OJJDP). According to Simonson: "This antidrug program provides grants of up to $100,000 to community coalitions that mobilize their communities to prevent youth alcohol, tobacco, illicit drug and inhalant abuse. The grants support coalitions of youths; parents; media; law enforcement; school officials; faith-based organizations; fraternal organizations; state, local and tribal government agencies; healthcare professionals; and other community representatives."

Simpson describes the two major goals of the Drug-Free Communities Support Program: (1) to reduce substance abuse among youths and, over time, adults, by addressing the factors in a community that increase the risk of substance abuse and enhancing factors that reduce that risk and (2) to establish and strengthen community collaboration—including their working with federal, state, local and tribal governments and private, nonprofit agencies—to support local coalition efforts to prevent and reduce substance abuse among youths.

He (pp.1–2) also outlines the program's four other objectives: (1) to catalyze citizen and organization participation and collaboration in community efforts to reduce substance abuse among youths, (2) to enhance community efforts to promote and deliver effective substance abuse prevention strategies to multiple sectors of the community, (3) to assess the effectiveness of community initiatives that focus on reducing substance abuse among youths and (4) to provide information about effective substance abuse reduction initiatives for youths that can be replicated in other communities. One frequent target of community policing efforts at reducing drug dealing is privately owned apartment complexes.

Addressing Drug Dealing in Privately Owned Apartment Complexes

Apartment complexes can harbor open or closed drug markets. In an **open drug market**, dealers sell to all potential customers, eliminating only those suspected of being police or some other threat. In a **closed drug market**, dealers sell only to people they know or who are vouched for by other buyers.

In apartment complexes open drug markets pose a greater threat than closed drug markets.

According to Sampson (2001, p.3): "Open markets in apartment complexes are much more susceptible to drive-by shootings, customers who care little about the property, and customers who use drugs on the property. In comparison, closed-market dealers are generally averse to attracting attention to their operation, so they often keep their customers' behavior in line."

Sampson (pp.4–7) describes what is known about open drug markets. Most are outdoors and, therefore, less secure. Dealers usually sell small amounts of drugs to each buyer and are vulnerable to market disruption and intervention approaches. They attract buyers who want to obtain drugs quickly.

Dealers may specialize in one drug or offer a variety of drugs. These stranger-to-stranger sales usually operate near where people congregate, near major streets or busy places such as shopping centers, office buildings, recreation areas, schools and the like. This not only maximizes customer traffic, but the activities of law-abiding community members also mask the drug dealing.

Open markets operating on apartment complex grounds allow dealers to see if police are coming and escape into the security of a specific apartment. Such markets can operate only if there is no meaningful intervention by the owner or property manager. Dealers are vulnerable to undercover police officers and informants, alert and active property management and community intervention (such as identifying where dealers hide stash). Traffic management techniques such as altering the direction of the street, creating a cul-de-sac or limiting the number of escape routes raise buyers' risk level.

Sampson (pp.7–10) also describes what is known about closed drug markets. These markets are likely to be indoors, with dealers supplying larger quantities of drugs, but only to friends and acquaintances. They can easily store scales and packaging supplies inside an apartment. Dealers may specialize in one drug or offer a variety. Because they rely on word of mouth, they do not need to locate in well-trafficked areas. These dealers are vulnerable to robbers who know the dealers cannot rely on police to intercede. Seldom are apartment owners or managers working with the dealers; therefore they should be willing partners in addressing the problem. Police intervention in closed markets requires specific knowledge of buyers, the seller and the product to pass the initial scrutiny to enter. Such information may be obtained from informants or nearby residents. Practices that may increase the vulnerability of closed markets include frequent property owner inspections of each apartment, strict lease conditions, explicit house rules and immediate follow-through on eviction if drug dealing is established.

Conditions Making Apartment Complexes Susceptible to Drug Dealing

Sampson (pp.3–4) describes several conditions that make privately owned apartment complexes in low-income, high-crime neighborhoods susceptible to open-market drug dealing.

> Conditions making apartment complexes susceptible to drug dealing include tenants and nearby residents with drug histories, easy access, absentee owners and/or inadequate or untrained property managers and limited natural surveillance of the property.

Tenants and Nearby Residents with Drug Histories Chronic users often live near their markets so they can readily buy drugs. This helps sustain the market. Also, drug markets in low-income neighborhoods can provide a source of part- or full-time employment, and apartment complexes can be ripe recruiting grounds due to a high population of poorly paid, underemployed or unemployed tenants.

Easy Access Open drug markets in apartment complexes typically operate near main streets. Other factors that appear to facilitate open markets are ease of parking (or stopping) for buyers and access to apartment complex grounds.

Absentee Owners and/or Inadequate or Untrained Property Managers Property owners often do not live in their apartment complexes, and in the case of smaller complexes and those encumbered by debt, they may not employ on-site managers, reducing the risk that visitors will be stopped, questioned or prevented from entering the property. In large apartment complexes, tenants, police and property managers do not always know who belongs at the complex and who does not. This makes it easy for people to come and go unquestioned and for drug traffic to appear as just another part of the routine activity.

Limited Natural Surveillance of Property Buyers are often safeguarded from police surveillance because they purchase drugs on private property, sometimes behind the security of fences or shrubs, or inside an apartment.

Enlisting Property Owners' Help in Closing a Drug Market

Sampson (pp.18–19) asserts: "Drug dealing in apartment complexes exacts high costs. . . . Most apartment complexes where drug dealing occurs experience many other problems as well, including high tenant turnover and vacancy rates; vandalism or squatting in vacant apartments; increased calls to police; increased police presence on the property; poor reputation of the complex and the property management among neighbors, police and local realtors; lower property values for the complex and for surrounding properties; fear among law-abiding tenants (including fear of retribution); apathy among law-abiding tenants if they perceive the property owner as ignoring or encouraging the market; ceding of common space by law-abiding tenants to those engaged in crime; isolation of law-abiding tenants who stay indoors when dealing (and crimes associated with dealing) are more prevalent; and illicit gun possession by those (sometimes juveniles) seeking to protect themselves against dealers." The presence of drug-dealing tenants in an apartment complex sometimes attracts other criminals as tenants because the drug dealing can mask their activities or provide them with a ready market for their activities. The property owner might incur these typical financial costs:

$500	Average cost if drug dealer simply stops paying rent for one month
$50	Dispossessor warrant
$25	Writ of Possession
$250	Loss of rent due to tenant turnover
$150	Labor costs of a painter
$100	Paint costs
$100	General cleaning of apartment
$40	Carpet cleaning
$1,215	Cost to property owner (if there is no damage to the apartment)

Law enforcement officers might consider using these costs to engage the property owner in tackling the problem.

Collaborative Efforts to Combat the Drug Problem

Just as one of the underlying causes of violence in this country is believed to be the ready availability of guns, another cause commonly acknowledged is the ready availability of drugs. Scoville (2000, p.8) graphically notes: "Stopping the flow of drugs in this country is a lot like having bailing duty on the Titanic." Nonetheless, communities across the country are rallying to stop that flow.

In Minneapolis, Minnesota, police and property owners are using black and gold "No trespassing" signs in inner-city neighborhoods. The signs are part of a new program intended to improve residents' security and deter street-level drug dealing by telling officers that they can enter the properties to question loiterers without a call from the property owner. This expands the power of the police greatly and removes from landlords the sometimes threatening responsibility of signing a citizen's arrest form before the police can act.

In another area of the city, a group called HOPE (Homes on Portland Enterprise) marched with their children near known crack houses, carrying signs and demanding that the dealers leave the neighborhood. Lacking money and no political clout, these citizens are determined to live in a safe neighborhood.

The city of St. Paul also enlisted the aid of residents to forge an alliance to fight drug dealers. The program, called FORCE (Focusing Our Resources on Community Empowerment), centered on getting longtime residents to permit narcotics officers to use their homes to monitor drug sales in the neighborhood. The FORCE team worked with a network of block club leaders to target drug dealers and to force the removal of, or improvements to, ramshackle drug houses. Ramsey County provided child protection services for youths found in drug houses.

Another grassroots effort has taken place in Price, Utah, a community of 10,000 people. The family services, school district, police and mental health professionals have established a volunteer interagency committee known as SODAA (Stop Our Drug and Alcohol Abuse). This committee coordinates prevention and education programs and strives to eliminate duplication of efforts. The committee developed and promoted a Substance Abuse Awareness Sabbath. They developed a five-page informational fact sheet, which they then distributed to the 44 churches in town. They asked each church to distribute a copy to every adult member and to spend part of their Sabbath on substance abuse awareness. The local newspaper also dedicated an entire page to the campaign, recognizing every church that participated.

Another very successful crime prevention program was developed in Wilson, North Carolina. Their program, "Operation Broken Window," was rooted in the broken window philosophy discussed earlier. The 500 block in Wilson was their "broken window," an open-air drug market widely known as a place where drugs could be easily bought. Undercover police operations had been unsuccessful in reducing the problem. The Wilson Police Department turned to problem-oriented policing as a possible solution. The department formulated a four-pronged attack: undercover operations, increased uniform police presence with more officers and a satellite police station in the target area, two K-9 units assigned to drug interdiction at the local bus station and attention to social and environmental conditions. They identified conditions that facilitated drug sales in the target area; cut grass; removed trash; and installed, repaired or replaced street lights. They inspected buildings for code violations and notified owners to correct the problems. They also boarded up abandoned buildings frequented by drug users. Operation Broken Window was a success. The drug dealers left, and crime rates went down.

In Honolulu a Weed and Seed program has been implemented in which the problem they most wanted to eliminate was drug dealing, which was occurring on the streets in broad daylight. Branson (2000, p.83) describes how the Housing and Community Development Corporation of Hawaii made available a two-bedroom unit to house a center, a safe haven where sports and recreation equipment, as well as donated computers, were available for people to use under supervision. To assist drug users and pushers arrested in the Weed part of the program, the state encouraged minor offenders to participate in drug treatment while on probation. As part of the seeding, adults tutor children in their homework and school subjects after school. A Head Start Early Childhood Center class also has begun.

In Rialto, California, a successful Operation Clean Sweep was conducted. The department used the SARA model to identify the problem. Their first step was to develop a target list of drug hot spots and dealers. Meetings were held with patrol officers, detectives and Neighborhood-Watch groups, which provided valuable, up-to-the-minute insight into activity on the street. Meyers (2000b, p.23) contends: "The community's involvement via these methods proved critically important. Neighborhood residents often know even more information than the best beat officers do; they can provide important intelligence."

This project used small video cameras to tape-record dozens of transactions made by undercover officers in unmarked patrol cars. The drug dealers "sauntered away" after completing their deals, not realizing the drugs they had sold would be taken to the crime lab for evidentiary analysis. The project also involved establishing liaisons with the district attorney and other agencies. Knowing the project would need a multiagency effort to "sweep" those involved in the 89 separate videotaped hand-to-hand narcotics buys, an arrest plan was made including 15 other agencies. For three days these agencies as well as the California Highway Patrol helped serve arrest warrants. According to Meyers (p.24):

> Operation Clean Sweep resulted in the arrest and prosecution of more than 100 felons. . . . The department recovered significant amounts of drugs, weapons, cash, and stolen property and also discovered a clandestine methamphetamine laboratory. Based on the evidence obtained during the roundup, the department obtained 12 additional search warrants, with the follow-up investigations yielding even more contraband. Several offenders—including a serial rapist who recently had been released from prison—face three-strike enhancements and long prison sentences.

Comprehensive, Coordinated Community Approaches

The Des Moines (Iowa) Police Department has a community involvement handbook, developed jointly by the police department, the United Way and over 35 neighborhood groups. The handbook serves as a source of information as well as a guide for action. It is intended to help neighborhood groups become active and start making a difference. Called the "municipal approach," the program has four "prongs": community involvement, enforcement, prevention/education and treatment. Portions of the handbook have been translated into Spanish, Vietnamese, Cambodian and Laotian. The handbook covers topics such as when to call the police; improving street lighting and residential security lighting; removing trash and litter; cutting down shrubbery; working with landlords and businesses in the area; boarding up abandoned houses; forming neighborhood associations; conducting neighborhood block walks, rallies and marches; occupying parks and streets; and writing newsletters.

The handbook contains an extensive list of suspicious activity and common indicators of residential drug trafficking that could be of much help to communities seeking to tackle this problem. (See Figure 11.2.)

This practical guide might serve as a model for other police departments that wish to involve the community in the fight not only against drugs but also against crime and violence.

Groups that can benefit from a partnership with law enforcement include home/school organizations such as parent–teacher associations; neighborhood

1. A high volume of foot and/or vehicle traffic to and from a residence at late or unusual hours.
2. Periodic visitors who stay at the residence for very brief periods of time.
3. Alterations of property by the tenants, including the following:
   a. Covering windows and patio doors with materials other than curtains or drapes;
   b. Barricading windows or doors;
   c. Placing dead bolt locks on interior doors; and
   d. Disconnecting fire alarms.
4. Consistent payment of rent and security deposits with U.S. currency, especially small denominations of cash. (Large amounts of 20 dollar bills are commonly seized from drug dealers.)
5. The presence of drug paraphernalia in or around the residence, including, but not limited to, glass pipes, syringes, propane torches, paper or tinfoil bundles, folded shiny-slick paper (snow seals), large quantities of plastic baggies, scales, money wrappers and small glass vials.
6. The presence of unusual odors coming from the interior of the residence, especially the odor of pungent chemical substances and/or burning materials.
7. The presence of firearms, other than sporting firearms, including fully automatic weapons, assault weapons, sawed off shotguns, machine pistols, handguns and related ammunition and holsters.
8. The presence of tenant's possessions and furnishings which are inconsistent with the known income level of the tenant. This would include, but is not limited to, the following:
   a. New and/or expensive vehicles;
   b. Expensive jewelry and clothing; and
   c. Expensive household furnishings, stereo systems and other large entertainment systems.
9. Tenants who are overly nervous and apprehensive about the landlord visiting the residence.

Any of the indicators, by itself, may not be reason to suspect drug trafficking. However, when combined with other indicators, they may be reason to suspect drug trafficking. If you suspect drug trafficking in your neighborhood, please contact the police department at 555–5555.

Figure 11.2 Suspicious Activity and Common Indicators of Residential Drug Trafficking
SOURCE: Des Moines Police. *Drugs: A Municipal Approach, A Community Handbook,* p. 26. Reprinted by permission.

associations; tenants' groups; fraternal, social and veterans' groups; community service clubs (such as Lions, Kiwanis, Jaycees, Rotary); religiously affiliated groups; and associations of homeowners, merchants or taxpayers.

A Drug Problem in New York City

The following description is from the COPS Web site.

> The Clinton Hill neighborhood had tremendous assets: landmark-worthy brownstone houses, an attractive park, nearby commercial strips and a hardworking, racially diverse population. A local college added a dependable stream of young consumers to the community's economy. Public signs and well-tended gardens indicated the existence of many block associations and of other civic activism.
>
> The residents' commitment to the community was strong, despite the abandoned and poorly kept rental buildings and high levels of car thefts and break-ins, muggings and drug activity. As drug dealing increased along a commercial corridor, resident anger at apparent police inaction grew. It took a tragedy to catalyze change.

A local convenience-store owner was murdered in his store, and neighborhood block leaders organized a mass meeting to find out what the police were doing. Unfortunately, residents did not think the police were prepared, and the meeting went poorly. As patrol officers stood in the back of the meeting hall, a yelling match ensued between residents and police department spokespeople. Relations between the two groups were at their worst.

Block leaders reached out to the Neighborhood Anti-crime Center of the Citizens Committee for New York City, due to its reputation for helping citizens and police get together to take back their neighborhoods. The Citizens Committee dedicated a staff organizer's time to helping the community go through a collaborative problem-solving process. A problem-analysis meeting was scheduled.

Block leaders prepared for the meeting by discreetly inviting a small, core group of concerned residents and identifying specific problem locations, offensive conditions and past efforts to solve the problems. Due to the rancor between residents and police, residents were urged to conduct this first meeting with limited police presence, so that issues could be aired and strategies developed to improve relations.

The meeting itself was the first positive outcome. Residents invited a couple of trusted community-oriented patrol officers, who helped to discern the nature of the problem. The meeting revealed that there were multiple privately owned, and a few city-owned, problem properties housing drug operations and/or addicts. One multi-family structure was identified as a major drug-dealing center, impervious to enforcement action for over two decades. It was a fortified drug house. However, much necessary information remained unknown.

The Citizens Committee trained the residents to conduct property research (identifying landlords), and then linked them up with key guardians: the district attorney's narcotics eviction unit; legal technical assistance; the city's housing agency representative, who could work on drug-infested property; and trusted police narcotics investigators, who had good information about specific locations. The Citizens Committee also designed an inside-building survey form, and introduced the resident leaders to a Muslim patrol organization, which was invited to visit problem locations in an effort to get more accurate information about the narcotics trade and landlord–tenant issues.

The resident leaders asked these guardians to join them in a collaborative planning meeting, which the Citizens Committee organizer facilitated. The pieces of the puzzle were now assembled, revealing that the police had never been able to get into the significant locations, especially the fortified one, because the landlords either colluded with the dealers or were unresponsive to police department contacts. A combined enforcement and legal strategy was hatched, and subsequent meetings kept everyone informed and on target with follow-up.

The block leaders committed to continued outreach and pressure on those landlords, such as the city itself, who were poorly managing their buildings but not allied with the dealers. And residents continued to provide information.

District Attorney Charles Hynes' office committed to pressing civil charges against landlords if they failed to secure their property appropriately after notification of problems and/or criminal activity. In addition, the community activists recruited a law firm (pro bono) to discuss whether, if criminal enforcement did not pan out, bringing a civil lawsuit for money damages was the best approach—similar to the Oakland Drug Abatement Institute strategy.

As a direct result of the collaborative analysis and meetings, the police received help from other city code-enforcement agencies to execute a new warrant at the most egregious location. Coordination continued between all parties after the search warrant revealed how extensive the drug-dealing operation was at the vacant, privately owned building.

Community members and police attended a housing court hearing and alerted the judge that the landlord's track record of failing to maintain the building warranted a case disposition that would serve community interests. The Clinton Hills neighborhood won. The judge legally bound the landlord to secure the property and maintain it crime-free, and authorized the police to have keys to the premises and check up on the landlord.

The landlord agreed to comply in court, but failed to do so. Residents, the police, and the district attorney took the landlord back to court, where the judge ruled against the landlord and granted the police permanent access to the premises for safety inspections. Illegal activity has never resumed at this vacant, and formerly fortified, building.

The community sought to build on this victory to publicize the value of working with the police and others, and to encourage efforts to clean up remaining problem locations. A media event was organized, celebrating everyone's hard work. The first court win proved to be just the beginning, as more buildings were successfully targeted, and block leaders and police communicated more openly and consistently.

Editors' note: The Neighborhood Anti-crime Center of the Citizens Committee for New York City builds community capacity to tackle neighborhood crime problems. In this case, they helped the community collect information from the police, residents and government agencies, and helped the community through a civil-court process. Closing the property made a huge difference in building the community's capacity to take on other problem buildings. This project offers insight into the citizen's perspective on neighborhood crime problems. Citizens sometimes think that if a highly visible crime problem exists in the neighborhood, the police must be allowing it to grow and fester. They may misconstrue police inability to solve a crime problem as collusion in it. This distrust in police must be addressed and worked through for collaborative work between the community and the police to proceed. Oftentimes, in the initial meeting between the community and the police concerning a particular problem, time must be devoted to airing and discussing the community's distrust.

SOURCE: Narrative prepared by Felice Kirby of the Citizens Committee for New York City, submitted to Rana Kirby as part of an NIJ-sponsored problem-solving project, and reprinted—with minor editorial changes—with Kirby's permission

A drug posing additional major challenges to community policing efforts is alcohol. The problem of impaired drivers was introduced briefly in Chapter 10. The following section addresses the problem in greater depth.

Getting Impaired Drivers Off the Street

Bolton (2001, p.73) contends: "There is broad public support for getting impaired drivers off our streets and highways. In one study, 97 percent of respondents see impaired driving as a major threat to their safety or the safety of their families. Saturation patrols and checkpoints are favored as two means of attacking the problem, and more severe penalties for violators are also supported."

Saturation patrols, checkpoints and more severe penalties for violators are supported as means to get impaired drivers off the street.

According to Greene (2003, p.5): "While many conclusions can be drawn from an analysis of sobriety checkpoints and saturation patrols, both serve a significant purpose and, used together, can be effective in reducing the number of impaired drivers. . . . It is proven that saturation efforts will bring more DUI arrests than sobriety checkpoints. If that represents an agency's goal and it has the resources, then it should use saturation patrols. If an agency's goal weighs heavier on the educational side, it should use sobriety checkpoints." Greene (p.2) stresses: "The key aspect in both sobriety checkpoints and saturation patrols rests with public awareness."

Law enforcement efforts to get alcohol-impaired drivers off the road can be greatly enhanced by citizen assistance. Peterson (2002, p.18) describes a program called Freeway Watch.

Freeway Watch encourages people to call 911 toll free to report drunk drivers.

Peterson says of Freeway Watch: "It is a neighborhood watch on wheels. Citizens with cell phones are partnering with law enforcement to increase community safety."

Other partnerships can also enhance efforts to get impaired drivers off the street. Bolton suggests that some such efforts are specific law enforcement responsibilities. Some involve legislative action or fall within the realm of the judicial system or the media. Others involve the community and its leadership and traffic safety organizations. He notes: "A partnership of the law enforcement, judicial, legislative and medical disciplines would be a major step forward in this battle [against impaired drivers]. Adding political and community leadership would increase the possibilities of success. Involving the news media would get a strong benefit as well."

Underage Alcohol Use

Monitoring the Future, an annual survey of approximately 45,000 eighth, tenth and twelfth graders, reports student use of alcohol and other drugs. Conducted by the University of Michigan and funded by the National Institute on Drug Abuse, the study shows that all categories of alcohol use for high school seniors have declined since 1982. These categories include lifetime use, yearly use, monthly use and **binge drinking** (five or more drinks in a row during the previous two weeks). While self-reported use in every one of these categories has increased since 1993, there was a slight decrease in 2000.

- Self-reported monthly alcohol use by high school seniors increased from 48.6 percent in 1993 to 50 percent in 2000. Binge drinking increased from 27.5 percent to 30 percent.
- By comparison, the percentage of fatalities that were alcohol related for 17- and 18-year-olds decreased from 37.7 percent in 1993 to 34.4 percent in 2000. For 17- and 18-year-olds, the number of alcohol-related fatalities increased from 838 to 841, or 2.7 percent.
- In 2000 more high school seniors disapproved of having five or more drinks once or twice each weekend, a level higher than during any year since 1995.

According to Geier (2003, p.100): "It is estimated that in the United States there are over 10 million people between the ages of 12 and 20 who drink on a regular basis. . . . The total costs to the nation are near $53 billion."

Wechsler et al. (2002, p.203) report on the 2001 Harvard School of Public Health College Alcohol Study. This study surveyed students in 119 four-year colleges in 38 states that had participated in the study in 1993, 1997 and 1999. More than 10,000 students participated. In 2001 approximately two in five (44.4 percent) college students reported binge drinking, almost the same as rates in the same three surveys (p.203). The problems related to alcohol use remained steady or increased slightly over the eight years of the study as shown in Table 11.1.

A study by the Task Force on College Drinking, commissioned by the National Institute on Alcohol Abuse and Alcoholism (*Changing the Culture of Campus Drinking*, 2002, p.1), found: "Drinking on college campuses is more pervasive and destructive than many people realize." The task force reported: "Alcohol consumption is linked to at least 1,400 student deaths and 500,000 unintentional injuries annually." In addition: "Alcohol consumption by college students is associated with drinking and driving, diminished academic performance, and medical and legal problems. Nondrinking students, as well as members of the surrounding community, also may experience alcohol-related consequences such as increased rates of crime, traffic crashes, rapes and assaults, and property damage."

Harvard researchers have found: "No longer just a problem on college campuses, binge-drinking by students—and the fallout from it—is spreading out to surrounding communities where behaviors such as public urination and vandalism are affecting residents' quality of life" ("There Goes the Neighborhood . . .," 2002, p.5).

A survey of more than 2,000 households nationwide found that those living near college campuses were more likely to experience the secondhand effects of alcohol, such as vomiting, drunkenness, noise and other disturbances.

Hearings before the U.S. Senate on Governmental Affairs

In testimony before the U.S. Senate Committee on Governmental Affairs, Hearing on College Drinking Prevention, Hingson (2002) described the key findings of his study "Magnitude of Alcohol-Related Mortality and Morbidity among U.S. College Students Ages 18-24," published in the *Journal of Studies on Alcohol* in April 2002. He estimated based on the information contained in his data sources that in 1998 there

Table 11.1 Alcohol-Related Problems among Students Who Drank Alcohol, 1993, 1997, 1999 and 2001

	Prevalence in %				Change over time		
					2001 vs 1993		
Alcohol-related problem	*1993*[a]	*1997*[b]	*1999*[c]	*2001*[d]	*OR*	*95% CI*	*Test for linear time trend* p
Miss a class	26.9	31.1	29.9	29.5	1.14	1.06, 1.23***	<.0001
Get behind in school work	20.5	24.1	24.1	21.6	1.07	0.99, 1.16	.0004
Do something you regret	32.1	37.0	36.1	35.0	1.13	1.06, 1.21***	<.0001
Forget where you were or what you did	24.7	27.4	27.1	26.8	1.12	1.03, 1.21**	.0005
Argue with friends	19.6	24.0	22.5	22.9	1.22	1.13, 1.31***	<.0001
Engage in unplanned sexual activities	19.2	23.3	21.6	21.3	1.14	1.06, 1.24***	.0002
Not use protection when you had sex	9.8	11.2	10.3	10.4	1.07	0.97, 1.19	.1840
Damage property	9.3	11.7	10.8	10.7	1.16	1.04, 1.30**	.0031
Get into trouble with the campus or local police	4.6	6.4	5.8	6.5	1.43	1.25, 1.65***	<.0001
Get hurt or injured	9.3	12.0	12.4	12.8	1.42	1.29, 1.57***	<.0001
Require medical treatment for an overdose	0.5	0.6	0.6	0.8	1.76	1.07, 2.91*	.0334
Drove after drinking	26.6	29.5	28.8	29.0	1.12	1.04, 1.21**	.0010
Have ≥ 5 different alcohol-related problems	16.6	20.8	19.9	20.3	1.28	1.27, 1.39***	<.0001

Note: Analysis limited to only those who drank alcohol in the past year. % is the prevalence of those who had the problem one or more times since the beginning of the school year; OR = odds ratio; CI = confidence interval.
[a]n = 12.708. [b]n = 11.506. [c]n = 10.825. [d]n = 8.783.
*p<.05; **p<.01; ***p<.001.

SOURCE: Wechsler et al. "Trends in College Binge Drinking during a Period of Increased Prevention Efforts." *Journal of American College Health,* March 2002, p.210.

were approximately 1,400 alcohol-related unintentional injury deaths among U.S. college students of which 1,100 were alcohol-related traffic deaths.

In addition, in the past year 2.1 million drove under the influence of alcohol, 500,000 were injured because of drinking, 400,000 had unprotected sex because of drinking and 100,000 had sexual intercourse when they were so intoxicated they were unable to give consent.

Further, the drinking college students not only put their own health at risk: Over 60,000 college students were hit or assaulted by another drinking college student, and 70,000 were a victim of a sexual assault or date rape by another drinking college student.

In addition to individual counseling approaches that have been demonstrated in numerous experimental studies to reduce alcohol problems, environmental changes can also reduce the alcohol-related death toll in this age group. These include:

- Enforcement of the legal drinking age of 21, and laws making it illegal to drive after any drinking if one is under 21 (the law in every state).
- Administrative license revocation (the law in 40 states).
- Lowering the legal blood-alcohol limit to .08% (the law in 32 states).
- Mandatory screening and treatment of persons convicted of driving under the influence of alcohol (the law in 23 states).
- Primary enforcement of safety belt laws (the law in 18 states).
- Increasing the price of alcohol and reducing the numbers of liquor outlets near colleges.

Hingson stressed: "We need colleges and their surrounding communities to work together in comprehensive partnerships to address this problem. If campuses crack down but surrounding communities are lax, the problem will be pushed out into the community. Conversely, tougher policies and enforcement by communities if not also pursued by colleges will only drive the problem back onto campuses. Finally, if students are involved as one of the partners in this process they will be less likely to regard these restrictions as authoritarian and paternalistic and more will be willing to comply with them."

Also testifying before the committee was Goldman (2002) who presented the findings of the Task Force of which he was a part:

> Although I hear and read the numbers reported by Dr Hingson on a regular basis, I am struck each time when I consider the shattered lives, shattered dreams, and the potential left unfulfilled. . . . Alcohol is tightly interwoven into the social fabric of college life, bringing with it enormous social, economic and personal consequences for our children—consequences, we are learning, that are probably more extensive than any of us imagined. . . . I cannot emphasize enough that it is a culture—*our* culture, which we face. . . . These circumstances cannot be dismissed, therefore, as simply a "rite of passage" or an inevitable part of college life. . . .

For presidents and their staff, the Task Force offers two very useful recommendations:

- First, the Task Force recommends an overarching framework for organizing alcohol prevention and intervention programs. The purpose of this organization, which is called the "3 in 1 Framework," is to create a comprehensive program that focuses simultaneously on multiple levels — individuals, the student population as a whole, and the surrounding community. Individual programs can be presented one-to-one, or in small groups, and are labor and time intensive, but may be best for individuals already experiencing difficulties. Reaching the student population as a whole involves media campaigns, and thoughtful creation and enforcement of rules. At the community level, all interested parties must be joined in an effort to modify the community attitudes and circumstances that unwittingly support these activities.

But each of these approaches must be used *in concert;* problems are likely to arise in any domain not included in the plan.

- Second, the Task Force recommends specific strategies that may be used within each of these levels. Strategies should be tailored to the unique needs and characteristics of each school.

The "3 in 1 Prevention Program" to curb college drinking has an individual prong, a general student body prong and a community prong.

Strategies to Combat Underage Drinking

Last Call for High-Risk Bar Promotions that Target College Students (Erenberg and Hacker, no date) describes how responsible hospitality councils (RHCs) have addressed the problem of underage drinking.

> The Lincoln/Lancaster County (Nebraska) Responsible Hospitality Council (RHC) includes representatives from the University of Nebraska, the Lincoln Council on Alcoholism and Drugs, the Lincoln Package Beverage Association, the Police Department, the Mayor's Office, the City Council, Mothers Against Drunk Driving, the Health Department, insurance companies, alcoholic beverage distributors, bars and other area businesses. In addition to offering server and manager training and service guidelines, the RHC sponsors community forums that bring together businesses, university representatives, students and community members to discuss ways to prevent alcohol-related problems and improve the quality of life in the downtown area.

In its first two years the RHC challenged several irresponsible bar marketing practices. One bar had developed a promotion in which patrons who consumed a "Gumbay Smash" (a gallon jug containing approximately 11 drinks) within one hour would have their names engraved in a brick at the bar. To qualify, patrons had to keep the drink in their system (no bathroom breaks or vomiting) and leave the premises immediately afterward. When an employee from another bar was hospitalized after taking the challenge, that bar owner contacted the RHC. The council held several meetings even discussing the development of laws restricting high-risk promotions. Those meetings provided an opportunity for other bar owners to "really come down hard" on the owner of the bar that offered the promotion. Ultimately, the group shamed the owner into discontinuing the special. After this success, the RHC sent letters to all area bars and restaurants discouraging irresponsible promotions.

Community and peer pressure as well as threats of additional regulation can be used to discourage irresponsible marketing of alcohol.

The RHC also sponsored a community forum to discuss Lincoln's long-standing tradition, the "birthday bar crawl." Students celebrating their 21st birthday travel to dozens of bars, receiving free drinks. By the end of the crawl problems arose such as drunken crawlers starting fights, damaging property, vomiting and passing out. Despite these problem, bar owners feared they would lose business if they stopped serving free drinks to birthday celebrants.

The RHC called a community forum to discuss the problems associated with the "birthday bar crawl," including downtown cleanup, law enforcement, alcohol poisoning, residence hall noise and vandalism and liability for bars. The forum included students to ensure that they would support recommended changes. Following negotiations, 37 bars pledged to stop offering free drinks and instead to offer nonalcoholic incentives to recognize birthdays, such as coupons for discounts on compact discs.

The end to the birthday bar crawls was enthusiastically supported by city government, the university and the press. The positive media attention to bars that adopted responsible business practices added an incentive for bars to cooperate. Erenberg and Hacker stress: "Successful partnerships use media events to recognize responsible bar owners and highlight positive changes. They hold recognition dinners and awards ceremonies to promote establishments committed to responsible marketing practices. Those events encourage continued cooperation, attract new members and raise public awareness of alcohol-related issues."

Educating Students about the Effects of Alcohol

"On the Right Track: DUI Awareness Training" (2002) describes how the Tampa Police Department formed a partnership with the Mendez Foundation to buy simulation equipment to produce an innovative DUI awareness program that area students look forward to and learn from using.

The simulator is the same as that used to train law enforcement officers. The driver's seat is real and can be adjusted, and students must use seat belts. The headlights must be turned on manually, and the CD player as well as all the console lights function. Three students in the session sit as passengers on a bench behind the driver, learning from each other whether driving or not and adding to the realism. It also helps them to grasp what can happen if they are riding with a driver who is impaired. The instructor can change the way the vehicle handles and sounds by using a computer.

GE engineers created the components necessary to turn the vehicle into a DUI simulator—the first exclusively high school–based DUI awareness driving simulator in the United States. When changed to its DUI mode, the steering and brake responses become sluggish. These slowed responses can be set for five different levels of intoxication, from .08 up to .22, although for the high school simulations the lowest level is used to show kids that even after a few drinks their driving will be impaired. The students also put on fatal vision glasses—goggles that look like those used in a workshop but that distort their vision slightly in much the same way as alcohol does (blurred vision and poor depth perception).

When asked how they think they drove when impaired, most students think they did well. Then they watch an instant replay in real time from the view of someone following the car in a helicopter. They are generally surprised at how poorly they did, and this is reinforced by reminding them that most people who drive impaired think they do just fine. It also makes them take responsibility for their actions because there is no one else to blame. Students can try the simulator only once to avoid having them think they can drive under the influence because they have had the experience. In addition, having only the one chance helps reinforce the idea that one chance is all they may have.

Alcohol is often involved in another major problem facing community policing, rave parties where alcohol and other drugs are in abundance.

Rave Parties

A **rave** is a dance party with fast-paced electronic music, light shows and use of a wide variety of drugs and alcohol both to enhance users' sensory perceptions and increase their energy levels. According to a COPS press release announcing the publication of *Rave Parties* ("COPS Office Helps Law Enforcement Respond to Rave Parties, 2002): "Raves present a unique challenge for law enforcement. Strict enforcement of the law—as many communities that find themselves beset with raves demand—can alienate the community's youths from law enforcement. To ignore raves, however, puts that youth population at risk of dangers ranging from drug overdoses to driving under the influence of controlled substances. This guide can help law enforcement professionals use community policing strategies to address this growing problem." According to COPS Director Reed: "The safety of the community and the participants must be protected, but without building walls between youths and police. This guide will help law enforcement address this very difficult situation."

Strategies to Address a Rave Problem In *Rave Parties,* Scott (2002a,) describes two general approaches to addressing rave party problems. One is *prohibition*—strictly enforcing all drug laws and banning raves (either directly or through intensive regulation). The other is *harm reduction*—acknowledging that some illegal drug use and raves are inevitable, and trying to minimize the harms that can occur to drug users and ravers.

The two general approaches to addressing rave party problems are prohibition and harm reduction.

Many jurisdictions blend enforcement with harm reduction approaches.

Whatever approach is adopted should be coherent and consistent. For example, if harm reduction is emphasized, it would be inconsistent to then use rave operators' adoption of harm reduction strategies, such as hiring private emergency medical staff, stocking bottled water or establishing rest areas ("chill out" areas), as evidence that they are condoning and promoting illicit drug use. Conversely, if a strict drug prohibition approach is used, it would be inconsistent to permit, for example, anonymous drug testing at raves.

Local public and political attitudes, as well as police policies regarding similar problems, will influence the general stance an agency takes. Says Scott (p.20): "It is important to consider how the public, and the various communities within it, will perceive the police response to rave party problems, particularly as that response is compared with police responses to similar problems. In some communities, the police have been criticized for taking a different stance on enforcement at raves, which are predominantly attended by white youths, than they have been perceived to take at events that are predominantly attended by minority youths."

In addition, Scott (p.20) points out: "To some extent, police and other regulators are forced to choose between the lesser of the harms arising from raves held in licensed venues and those held in unlicensed, clandestine venues. (This has some similarities to the public policy choices governing indoor vs. outdoor prostitution.) Shutting down all rave clubs would probably move raves and their associated problems back to outdoor, unlicensed and clandestine locations. Perhaps the biggest drawback to moving raves to indoor licensed venues is that it increasingly makes alcohol more available to ravers, increasing the medical risks from combining alcohol and rave-related drugs."

Before leaving the subject of community policing and drugs, it is appropriate to revisit a previous discussion of the American Dream.

Crime, Drugs and the American Dream

Crime, drugs and the American Dream are integrally related. In fact a drug problem may be the result of the American Dream for many people.

Messner and Rosenfeld (2001, p.ix) draw a very distinct correlation between crime and the American Dream: "The American Dream contributes to crime directly by encouraging people to employ illegal means to achieve goals that are culturally approved. It also exerts an indirect effect on crime through its interconnections with the institutional balance of power in society." They suggest that:

> **Conservative crime control** policies are draped explicitly in the metaphors of war. We have declared war on crime and on drugs, which are presumed to promote crime. Criminals, according to this view, have taken the streets, blocks, and sometimes entire neighborhoods from law-abiding citizens. The function of crime control policy is to recapture the streets from criminals to make them safe for the rest of us (p.92). . . .
>
> In contrast to conservative crackdowns on criminals, the **liberal crime control** approach emphasizes correctional policies and broader social reforms intended to expand opportunities for those "locked out" of the American Dream (p.96).

The conservative camp traditionally wages war on crime and drugs; the liberal camp wages war on poverty and inequality of opportunity.

These competing interests need to be considered in any strategies used to combat the drug problem in a given neighborhood or community. Messner and Rosenfeld (p.101) suggest that what is needed is crime reduction through social reorganization: "Crime reductions would follow from policies and social changes that vitalize families, schools and the political system, thereby enhancing the 'drawing power' of the distinctive goals associated with institutions and strengthening their capacity to exercise social control."

A Problem-Solving Partnership in Action—New Rochelle (New York) Police Department

IACP Community Policing Award Winner—Problem-Solving Partnership in Action: Drugs, Crime & Fear (From the IACP Web site)

Category—Agency Serving a Population of 50,001 to 100,000 Residents

The Problem

The New Rochelle Police Department and the community it serves identified a six-block area as the location in the city with the most recurring problems. This area, comprised mostly of municipal housing buildings, is centrally located in New Rochelle, the seventh largest city in New York. Drug dealing, shootings, assaults and robberies were prevalent in this area, and a consequence of this problem was not only fear amongst the residents but also increased calls for service for the police.

Compounding police–community interaction was a pervasive distrust of the police, who were perceived as insensitive and lacking in understanding of the needs of the community. The city of New Rochelle, always ethnically diverse, has experienced population increases in blacks and Hispanics. With these increases have come racial tensions as the composition of neighborhoods has altered, increased problems for the police in addressing these tensions, and more complex police–community relations issues. The Robert Hartley Housing Complex was no exception to these problems.

The Solution

In response to these tensions, local clergy and community leaders, in partnership with the department, created a group named, "Citizens for a Better New Rochelle." The group's mission was to facilitate a mutually respectful relationship between the police and community through open lines of communication and cooperation. This group consists of members from the department, clergy, NAACP, New Rochelle Municipal Housing Authority, Youth Bureau, City Council, United Tenants Council, Community Action Program and private citizens. With "Citizens for a Better New Rochelle" already in place as one key component, a multifaceted response plan called "The Robert Hartley Housing Complex Project" was formulated to deal with the area's problems. The objectives of this project can be summarized into five categories:

- Continual improvement of services to the community
- Strengthening of police relations and promotion of community participation
- Effective use of resources
- Enhancement of communications within and cooperation among agencies
- Development of creative and innovative approaches that promote quality and excellence in law enforcement

The project included the following:

- Training for a Neighborhood-Watch patrol
- Assignment of housing officers to patrol the area on foot

- Assignment of beat officers to patrol the area on foot and bicycle
- Assignment of critical incident unit officers to park and walk patrol during hours of past criminal activity
- Establishment of Community/Police Liaison Office to provide local residents with an immediate bridge to the department
- Involvement of the department's community resources coordinator to provide crisis intervention services to residents.

The Community/Police Liaison Office had a threefold purpose: (1) to improve mutual respect between the police and the community, (2) to improve the lines of communication between the police and the community (3) and to gain a greater degree of trust between the police and the community. Community organizations and private corporations donated all office space, telephone, carpeting and furniture. Citizens appear at the liaison office to report crimes and to request information on issues, such as domestic violence, quality-of-life enforcement and the civilian complaint process.

Because the community has more access to the police officers on a person-to-person basis, many barriers and tensions mentioned earlier have been broken down. Increased intelligence because of the greater trust has resulted in a safer neighborhood and fewer misunderstandings regarding police services. Gang-related issues have been dealt with by inviting the parents who have had children shot, killed or sentenced to prison to the liaison office to provide counseling and prevent future acts of violence by engaging in a proactive process of early intervention.

The department has addressed several quality-of-life issues after determining that these violations often contribute to some of the fear among residents in the Robert Hartley Housing Complex area. One of the residents' problems involved groups loitering on a particular corner, blocking pedestrians from entering a store, acting disorderly and creating additional calls for service for the police. The Neighborhood-Watch patrol began engaging in conversation with these groups and conveyed to them the community's displeasure with their conduct. In a short time, the loitering groups were dispersed. Another concern was drug activity in the Robert Hartley Housing buildings.

Due to limitations placed on the police because of ambiguous/poor signage in these buildings, as well as the absence of the definition of "public place" in the New Rochelle city code, police were often powerless to enforce trespassing statutes in these buildings. As a result of efforts from the "Citizens for a Better New Rochelle," a comprehensive definition of "public place," which now includes public housing property, was incorporated into the city code. In addition, a list was created to identify and ban those individuals who regularly disrupted the peace of the community through criminal behavior, loitering and drinking alcohol in public. These individuals were served an official notice advising them that they were no longer legally entitled to enter municipal housing authority property. This process now allowed the police to make an instant arrest of a banned individual, thereby eliminating the presence of the individual who negatively affected the quality of life in the community.

Evaluation

The Robert Hartley Housing Complex Project has been evaluated using several different methods. The department's records management system has been used for comparison statistics on crimes, calls for service, arrests and city code violations. Serious crimes (Part 1 crimes) have decreased 33 percent from 1999–2001 in the Robert Hartley Housing Complex area. Calls for service to the police have decreased 17 percent from 1999–2001. Arrests have increased by 38 percent from 1999–2001, and city code summonses have increased 45 percent from 1999–2001. Additionally, according to the FBI Uniform Crime Reports, New Rochelle was the fifth safest city of its size during the year 2000.

Intangibles such as trust and a perception of safety can be measured through neighborhood surveys at community meetings and during informal contacts between the police and the community. All of these continue to demonstrate that the police have gained the trust of the residents in the Robert Hartley Housing Complex area, and the residents feel safer. The Criminal Investigations Division closed 11 percent more cases in the Robert Hartley Housing Complex area, mostly due to more information provided because of greater cooperation between the police and the community.

In conclusion, it is important to remember for any community policing journey that the police and community are taking a TRIP: T is for training of all department members in problem-solving tactics and skills; R is for the necessary relationship between the police and the community; I is for intelligence in identifying the recurring problems; and P is for problem solving by the police and the community.

SUMMARY

Crime and drugs are clearly linked. The key to reducing drug abuse is prevention coupled with treatment. The first initiative to reduce drug-related crime and violence is community policing. Strategies to deal with the drug problem include improving the physical environment, removing offenders, reducing the demand for drugs, improving intelligence and empowering residents.

The mission of the National Drug Intelligence Center is to provide the nation's law enforcement personnel and policymakers with strategic domestic drug intelligence for their use in establishing law enforcement priorities and formulating drug control policy. In addition, a new corps of police professionals might serve as drug control specialists. Yet another source of assistance is Lead On America, a citizen coalition that helps instruct and mobilize communities to partner with law enforcement throughout the country.

Federal assistance specifically aimed at the drug problem is available through the Weed and Seed program and the Drug-Free Communities program. In apartment complexes, open drug markets pose a greater threat than closed drug markets. Conditions making apartment complexes susceptible to drug dealing include tenants and nearby residents with drug histories, easy access, absentee owners and/or inadequate or untrained property managers and limited natural surveillance of the property.

Problems presented by abuse of alcohol also present a challenge to community policing. Saturation patrols, checkpoints and more severe penalties for violators are supported as means to get impaired drivers off the street. Freeway Watch encourages people to call 911 toll free to report drunk drivers.

A survey of more than 2,000 households nationwide found that those living near college campuses were more likely to experience the secondhand effects of alcohol, such as vomiting, drunkenness, noise and other disturbances. The "3 in 1 Prevention Program" to curb college drinking has an individual prong, a general student body prong and a community prong. Community and peer pressure as well as threats of additional regulation can be used to discourage irresponsible marketing of alcohol. The two general approaches to addressing rave party problems are prohibition and harm reduction.

Crime, drugs and the American Dream are related, and, in fact, the drug problem may be the result of the American Dream for many people. How to approach the drug problem is often political. The conservative camp traditionally wages war on crime and drugs; the liberal camp wages war on poverty and inequality of opportunity.

Discussion Questions

1. What do you see as the relationship between drugs and the American Dream?
2. What programs in your community are directed at the drug problem?? Have you participated in any of them?
3. Which of the programs discussed in this chapter seem most exemplary to you? Why?
4. Explain how lease enforcement reduces criminal activity in public housing.
5. Explain why some rave party strategies used by police have been criticized as racist.
6. Did you receive DARE training as a child? What were your impressions? Do you believe it had any effect on your attitudes and actions regarding drugs?
7. Explain the strategy behind improving the physical environment of a neighborhood or apartment complex. What does that have to do with illegal drug activity?
8. What are the three core principles of the National Drug Control Strategy? Which do you believe to be the most effective? The least?
9. Explain the differing goals of saturation patrols and sobriety checkpoints. Which of those goals seems best to get drunk drivers off the roads? Which costs more for the policing agency and why?
10. What bar marketing promotions are you aware of that encourage irresponsible drinking?

InfoTrac College Edition Assignments

- Use InfoTrac College Edition to help answer the Discussion Questions as appropriate.
- Select one of the following assignments to complete:
  - Read and outline "Battling DUI: A Comparative Analysis of Checkpoints and Saturation Patrols" by Jeffrey W. Greene.
  - Read and outline two articles that address the pros and cons of zero tolerance policies.

Community Projects

- Research what colleges or universities in your area have programs addressing student alcohol use and misuse. Are they effective?
- Conduct a survey on your campus of student drinking behaviors. Include binge drinking and drinking and driving.

References

Bolton, Joel. "Getting the Impaired Driver off the Street." *The Police Chief,* November 2001, p.73.

Braiker, Brian. "Just Say Know." *Newsweek,* April 15, 2003.

Branson, Helen Kitchen. "Weed and Seed in Honolulu: The Key Is Community Input." *Law and Order,* September 2000, pp. 82–86.

"Bush Goal: Cut Drug Abuse 25% in Five Years." Associated Press, as reported in the (Minneapolis/St. Paul) *Star Tribune,* February 13, 2002, p.A7.

Changing the Culture of Campus Drinking. Bethesda, MD: National Institute on Alcohol Abuse and Alcoholism: Alcohol Alert, October 2002.

"COPS Office Helps Law Enforcement Respond to Rave Parties." Washington, DC: Office of Community Oriented Policing Services Press Release, September 12, 2002.

Erenberg, Debra F. and Hacker, George A. *Last Call for High-Risk Bar Promotions that Target College Students.* Center for Science in the Public Interest.

Garrett, Ronnie. "D.A.R.E.—Helping Parents Help their Kids." *Law Enforcement Technology,* October 2003, p.8.

Geier, Michael. "Party Patrol: A New Approach to Underage Drinking Enforcement." *Law and Order,* March 2003, pp.96–103.

Goldman, Mark. Testimony before the U.S. Senate Committee on Governmental Affairs, Hearing on College Drinking Prevention, May 15, 2002.

Greenberg, Martin A. "A Drug Strategy for the New Millennium." *Law Enforcement News,* September 28, 2001, pp.9–10.

Greene, Jeffrey W. "Battling DUI: A Comparative Analysis of Checkpoints and Saturation Patrols." *FBI Law Enforcement Bulletin,* January 2003, pp.1–6.

Hingson, Ralph. Testimony before the Committee on Governmental Affairs, U.S. Senate, "Magnitude of Alcohol-Related Mortality and Morbidity among U.S. College Students Ages 18–24 and Strategies for Prevention," May 15, 2002.

Lock, Eric D.; Timberlake, Jeffrey M.; and Rasinski, Kenneth A. "Battle Fatigue: Is Public Support Waning for 'War'-Centered Drug Control Strategies?" *Crime & Delinquency,* July 2002, pp.380–398.

Making the Grade: A Guide to School Drug Prevention Programs. Washington, DC: Drug Strategies, 1999.

McNamara, Joseph D. "The Hidden Cost of the Drug War: Police Integrity Pays the Price." *Law Enforcement News,* January 15/31, 2000, pp. 8–9.

Mertens, Jennifer. "Prevailing in Prevention and Protection." *Law Enforcement Technology,* October 2003, pp.24–32.

Messner, Steven F. and Rosenfeld, Richard. *Crime and the American Dream,* 3rd ed. Belmont, CA: Wadsworth Thomson Learning, 2001.

Meyers, Michael. "Creative Use of Technology and Partnerships Shuts Down Drug Dealers." *Community Policing Exchange,* Spring 2000a, p.3.

Meyers, Michael. "Operation Clean Sweep: Curbing Street-Level Drug Trafficking." *FBI Law Enforcement Bulletin,* May 2000b, pp.22–24.

Monitoring the Future. National Highway Traffic Safety Administration Web site www.nhtsa.dot.gov/

The National Drug Control Strategy, 1998. A Ten Year Plan. Washington, DC: Office of National Drug Control Policy, 1998.

Oliver, Jerry. "The Drug War Is Exacting a Terrible Price." *Law Enforcement News,* October 15, 2000, p.9.

"On the Right Track: DUI Awareness Training." *Law and Order,* September 2002.

Peterson, Suzanne Farr. "Freeway Watch: Call 911 to Zap Drunk Drivers." *Community Links,* March 2002, p.18.

Rosenbaum, Marsha. *Safety First: A Reality-Based Approach to Teens, Drugs, and Drug Education.* New York: The Lindesmith Center, 1999.

Sampson, Rana. *Drug Dealing in Privately Owned Apartment Complexes.* Washington, DC: Office of Community Oriented Policing Services, Problem-Oriented Guides for Police Series No. 4, August 13, 2001.

Scott, Michael S. *Rave Parties.* Washington, DC: Office of Community Oriented Policing Services, Problem-Oriented Guides for Police Series No. 14, April 29, 2002a.

Scott, Michael S. *Clandestine Drug Labs.* Washington, DC: Office of Community Oriented Policing Services, Problem-Oriented Guides for Police Series No. 16, April 29, 2002b.

Scoville, Dean. "The War on Drugs: Where Are We?" *Police,* December 2000, p.8.

Simonson, James M. *The Drug-Free Communities Support Program.* Washington, DC: OJJDP Fact Sheet #08, April 2001. (FS 200108)

Simpson, Kenneth. "Smokey Mountain Weed and Seed." *Law and Order,* September 2002, pp.217–231.

Sinnema, Cindi. "Residents Learn Ways to Best Serve Sheriff's Office in Fight Against Meth." *Community Links,* May 2003, pp.10–12.

Strong, Ronald L. "The National Drug Intelligence Center: Assessing the Drug Threat." *The Police Chief,* May 2001, pp.55–60.

"There Goes the Neighborhood: Binge Drinking Problems Spill Over from College Campuses." *Law Enforcement News,* July/August 2002, p.5.

Walters, John P. "Local Law Enforcement's Role in the National Drug Control Strategy." *Subject to Debate,* Police Executive Research Forum, March 2002, pp.1, 3, 8–9.

Wechsler, Henry; Lee, Jae Eun; Kuo, Meichun; Seibring, Mark; Nelson, Toben F.; and Lee, Hang. "Trends in College Binge Drinking during a Period of Increased Prevention Efforts: Findings from 4 Harvard School of Public Health College Alcohol Study Surveys: 1991-2001." *Journal of American College Health,* March 2002, pp.203–217.

Weisburd, David and Mazerolle, Lorraine Green. "Crime and Disorder in Drug Hot Spots: Implications for Theory and Practice in Policing." *Police Quarterly,* September 2000, pp.331–349.

CHAPTER 12

Bringing Youths into Community Policing

Children are likely to live up to what you believe of them.

—Lady Bird Johnson

Do You Know?

- What important group is often overlooked when implementing the community policing philosophy?
- How negative attitudes toward the police can be changed?
- What the youth development strategy involves?
- What the developmental asset approach to children involves?
- What youth-focused community policing involves?
- What many consider to be the cornerstone of the community?
- How schools should be viewed?
- Why it is important to build students' sense of community in school?
- At minimum, what links the school should have with the community?
- What the school safety pyramid rests on and what its components are?
- What is bullying more accurately termed?
- How bullying has been viewed and the result?
- What the "tell or tattle" dilemma is?
- How threats might be classified?
- What the FBI's four-prong threat assessment consists of?
- What most violent students do before they commit acts of violence?
- What two highly successful programs to build safe schools are?
- What the seven prongs in effective school security are?
- Whether zero tolerance is an effective deterrent to nonconforming behavior?
- What the three "Ps" for dealing with school violence are?
- What the top security strategy at all grade levels was in 2000?
- What the 8% problem refers to?

CAN YOU DEFINE?

- bullying
- conditional threat
- developmental assets
- direct threat
- 8% problem
- indirect threat
- leakage
- peer child abuse
- psychopath
- school-associated violent death
- sociopath
- tattling
- veiled threat
- zero tolerance

Introduction

The vast majority of today's youths are "good kids" who may occasionally get into trouble. If community policing is to succeed, it is imperative that this important segment of the community not be forgotten. If youths can come to feel a part of their community and their school early on, many future problems might be eliminated. Unfortunately, the violence so prevalent within our society has found its way into our schools, as the bloody school shootings in the past few years have dramatically shown. In addition, many youths turn to gangs for the support and feelings of self-worth they cannot find at home or school, as discussed in the next chapter.

This chapter begins with a discussion of the importance of involving youths in community policing and some strategies for building positive relationships between law enforcement and youths as well as some strategies aimed at engaging them in community policing efforts. Then the importance of involving parents in community

© Will Hart/PhotoEdit

Some schools hire personnel to assist with security and safety in their buildings. According to the National School Board Association, 65 percent of urban school districts use security personnel.

policing efforts to prevent youth delinquency and violence is discussed. Next the role of the school in promoting healthy growth and development is described, followed by the problems of crime, bullying, violence and school shootings in our schools. This is followed by a discussion of after school programs, creating safe schools, crisis planning and the importance of early intervention. The chapter concludes with an example of problem-solving partnerships with the school.

Youths and Community Policing

Williams (1999, p.150) notes that much research has been done on citizen perceptions and satisfaction with community policing but that an important segment of citizens has been overlooked and left out of this process—children and teenagers.

Children and teenagers are an important segment of the community often overlooked when implementing the community policing philosophy.

Williams used focus group interviewing to collect information about the perceptions and attitudes of East Athens, Georgia, citizens ages 6 to 18. The questions concerned issues of (1) community problems, (2) trust or satisfaction with police services, (3) knowledge of the ideals of community policing and (4) empowerment.

From these focus groups, four themes emerged (p.160). The first theme was infrequent, impersonal and negative interactions with police. Negative experiences that participants, their family members or friends had with the police were a key factor in all focus group discussions. One youth said: "One day we were walking to the store at about nine o'clock that night and the police stopped us. And when they got out of the car, we took off running. They stopped us for no reason. I wasn't fixing to stay around and get locked up, so I took off running." This general perception reinforces the contention that personal contact with police is a more significant factor than demographic variables.

A second theme was lack of knowledge of or familiarity with police or community policing. Except for one male child and one female teenager, all participants were reluctant to establish any rapport with community policing officers. When asked specifically about the community policing concept, few participants understood it. Nor did they understand the idea of partnerships.

A third theme was a perception of lack of respect for the East Athens community and its inhabitants by police officers. This perception surfaced in four complaints: slow response time, lack of timely intervention, alleged officer harassment and the perception that officers did not care about the community.

The fourth theme was community passivity as opposed to community apathy. Participants generally expressed little interest in helping officers solve community problems, often because of their fear of violent retribution: "I may know what happened, but I ain't giving away no names. . . . 'cause I ain't got nothing to do with it . . . 'cause the person could come back and get you . . . they did my sister like that." Williams (p.168) concludes:

> Passivity can undermine any community policing initiative. This study sheds light on the underpinnings of community passivity among East Athens teenagers and children. Their interactions with police tended to be infrequent, impersonal and

> negative. Consequently, they were not personally familiar with police officers and vice versa. This combination seems to explain their lack of respect toward all police. When combined with the real and ever present fear of nonrandom violence or retribution from within the neighborhood, it might be rational for children and teenagers to be passive toward officers assigned to community policing.

Although the study focused on just one small area of one community, it brings out the importance of considering youths as an important part of community policing efforts. It also draws attention to the sometimes negative perceptions of police held by youths, often because of having only negative contacts with them.

Another study by Jones-Brown (2000, p.209) of 125 high school African American males regarding attitudes toward police found: "A majority of the males report experiencing the police as a repressive rather than facilitative agent in their own lives and in the lives of their friends and relatives."

To counteract negative perceptions of police held by children and youths, many departments have programs aimed at fostering positive relations with them.

Building Personal Relationships

Departments across the country have developed programs to allow youngsters and police officers to get to know and understand each other better. The Denver Police Department, for example, has a program called "Brown Baggin' with the Blues" in which children have lunch with police officers.

The Kops 'n' Kids program, endorsed by the International Association of Chiefs of Police (IACP), brings together children and officers to have fun rather than to deliver antidrug or anticrime speeches. Officers come with their motorcycles and their K-9s for demonstrations; they share lunch; they form running clubs; they do whatever helps present police as positive role models and build trust with the children.

The Greeley (Colorado) Police Department has a similar program, "Adopt-an-Officer," in which police officers volunteer to be "adopted" by fourth- and fifth-grade students. They share meals, write letters, exchange cards and visit the police station. The LaGrange Park (Illinois) Police Department's Adopt-a-Cop Program calls on each participating elementary grade school level to "adopt" an officer who serves as their liaison for the entire school year (McCollum, 2000).

The Las Vegas Metropolitan Police Department's "Shop with a Cop" is designed to make the Christmas season happy for abused, neglected and disadvantaged children. Sporting badges rather than beards and driving squad cars rather than sleighs, these police officers are still like Santa to dozens of underprivileged Las Vegas youngsters. Over 100 officers each take an underprivileged child on a shopping spree at the local K-Mart. Each child has $75 to spend, the money contributed by local businesses.

Connecting Youths and the Community

Kanable (2000, pp.100–101) describes the Kid Watch program being implemented by the Los Angeles (California) Police Department Southwest Division: "Initially we were really concerned about recommending safe corridors for the kids to walk to and from school. . . . We concentrated on developing safe zones where we know there are less traffic accidents, less robberies and less gang activities." The department then turned to the community to watch over children as they went to and from school. Says Kanable (p.101): "Today there are 730 volunteers displaying yellow Kid Watch decals in windows of their homes, businesses, churches and nonprofit agencies and watching the kids as they go to and from school." Kanable (p.104) points out: "The bad guys know the volunteers are working overtime, and they avoid the area. . . . Another benefit of Kid Watch is a stronger neighborhood. We have noticed that when the community is focused on the safety of the children, the color of their skin is not too important." In addition to attending to the safety of children, it is important to actually involve them in efforts to keep them safe.

Community policing strategies to engage youths involve ensuring that the majority of "good kids" are supported and involved in community policing efforts and that problems of school crime and violence are addressed.

The Youth Development Approach

The youth development approach was designed by the U.S. Department of Health and Human Services over two decades ago.

The youth development strategy suggests that communities first explore what they want for young people, rather than what behaviors they would like to prevent among youths. More important, it involves young people in rebuilding communities.

The focus is on the positive rather than the negative; on the great majority of "good kids" rather than the minority who are delinquents, violent or gang members. "By identifying what they want for young people, they can then develop a plan to provide the range of services and opportunities necessary to enable young people to move through adolescence to healthy, productive adulthood."

By involving young people in developing services and opportunities, communities can draw on youths' unique talents and perspectives, building on their strengths and giving them a sense of community and of hope for the future.

The Developmental Asset Approach

Gersh (2000, p.SS15) describes "The Asset Approach: Giving Kids What They Need to Succeed" developed by the Search Institute, Minneapolis. The Search Institute promotes establishing 40 ideals, experiences and qualities—**developmental assets**—that "help young people make wise decisions, choose positive paths, and grow up competent, caring and responsible." These 40 developmental assets are grouped into eight categories.

The developmental asset approach promotes (1) support, (2) empowerment, (3) boundaries and expectations, (4) constructive use of time, (5) commitment to learning, (6) positive values, (7) social competence and (8) positive identity to help youngsters succeed in school and in life.

Gersh suggests that parents, guardians, grandparents, teachers, coaches, friends, youth workers, employers, volunteers and others can all help children in the community to build these assets. He notes: "A survey of 100,000 youths in grades 6–12 found that the more assets a young person possesses, the less likely they are to engage in problem alcohol use, illicit drug use, sexual activity and violence. In addition, increasing numbers of assets correlate with increased success in school, value of diversity, maintenance of good health and delay of gratification."

Recognizing Risk Factors

Although recognizing assets is crucial, communities that seek to include youths in their community policing efforts also must recognize the risk factors that have been identified, not only within the community, but also in the family, the school and the individual. These risk factors are summarized in Table 12.1

Youth-Focused Community Policing

Youth-Focused Community Policing (YFCP) is a collaborative effort of the Office of Juvenile Justice and Delinquency Prevention (OJJDP), the Office of Community Oriented Policing Services and the Community Relations Service.

Table 12.1 Communities that Care®

	Adolescent Problem Behaviors				
Risk Factors	***Substance Abuse***	***Delinquency***	***Teen Pregnancy***	***School Drop-Out***	***Violence***
Community					
Availability of drugs	•				•
Availability of firearms		•			•
Community laws and norms favorable toward drug use, firearms and crime	•	•			•
Media portrayals of violence					•
Transitions and mobility	•	•			•
Low neighborhood attachment and community disorganization	•	•		•	
Extreme economic deprivation	•	•	•	•	•
Family					
Family history of the problem behavior	•	•	•	•	•
Family management problems	•	•	•	•	•
Family conflict	•	•	•	•	•
Favorable parental attitudes and involvement in the problem behavior	•	•			•
School					
Academic failure beginning in late elementary school	•	•	•	•	•
Lack of commitment to school	•	•	•	•	•
Peer and Individual					
Early and persistent antisocial behavior	•	•	•	•	•
Rebelliousness	•	•		•	
Friends who engage in the problem behavior	•	•	•	•	•
Gang involvement	•	•			•
Favorable attitudes toward the problem behavior	•	•	•	•	
Early initiation of the problem behavior	•	•	•	•	•
Constitutional factors	•	•			•

Youth-Focused Community Policing is a U.S. Department of Justice initiative instrumental in establishing law enforcement–community partnerships to focus on prevention, intervention and enforcement.

YFCP emphasizes locally driven responses to locally based problems and has been implemented in eight communities: Boston, Chicago, Houston, Los Angeles, Kansas City (Kansas), Mount Bayou (Mississippi), Oakland and Rio Grande (Texas).

The Five Promises

America's Promise was founded after the April 1997 Presidents' Summit for America's Future attended by Presidents Clinton, Bush, Carter and Ford with First Lady Nancy Reagan representing her husband. Colin Powell was the founding chairman of the alliance which has grown to more than 400 national partner organizations and 400 local initiatives.

The alliance focuses on five promises: (1) caring adults, (2) safe places, (3) healthy start, (4) marketable skills and (5) opportunities to serve. America's Promise believes these factors can significantly improve a young person's chances of becoming a successful adult. A Five Promises Checklist identifies age-appropriate actions for each promise along with service providers who can address the action ("The Five Promises Checklist: . . .," (2003, p.5). Their Web site is www.americaspromise.org.

A Partnership to Prevent Juvenile Delinquency

An alliance in Livermore, California, has Horizons Family Counseling operating out of the police department. The program began in 1973 when the city received a grant for a juvenile delinquency program. When it was learned that the activities funded by the program were not having any effect on youthful offenders, the state Office of Criminal Justice Planning asked the Livermore Police Department to oversee the program. The focus of the program became high-risk youths who were running away, truant or beyond parental control, with Horizons brought in to provide counseling.

As Soto (2000, p.8) notes: "Horizons understood from the start that the whole family needed to be involved in the counseling to have any effect on a youth's internal environment." Police became concerned that counselors were giving up too early on families who resisted coming in for counseling. Their frustration led to creating a diversion program where first-time youthful offenders arrested for minor offenses may have the arrest erased if the family attends three family therapy sessions. This incentive created the chance to consider the arrest within the context of family dynamics.

This diversion program made police and Horizons more interdependent than ever and set the stage for the partnership's next evolution. In 1995 the police department and Horizons shared quarters in a new facility. Horizons has a separate public entrance, but inner doors permit regular interface with law enforcement. According to the Livermore police chief: "Horizons is a tremendous asset. Other departments have to travel miles to get services. Horizons fits perfectly within the community policing mold of reaching out, helping parents, working with kids and supporting alternatives in enforcement" (Soto, p.8).

Involving Youths in Violence Prevention

Partnerships should include youths at all levels of activity, with their roles considered as important as that of adults. A potential obstacle is the attitude of some adult policymakers and leaders that youths are the source of the community's violence problems rather than part of the solution. Forums where youths can present their views can help overcome this bias.

This strategy was applied in Teens on Target, a peer education program established by Youth Alive in partnership with Oakland, California's Unified School District and Pediatric Spinal Injury Service. Established after two high school students were shot by peers, the program trains high-risk students to advocate violence prevention by educating and mentoring their peers and younger children on gun violence, drugs and family conflict. The youths arrange trips to local hospital emergency rooms to give their peers a firsthand look at the impact of violence on victims.

The Importance of Parental Involvement

Findings released by the OJJDP suggest that violent acts of delinquency are less likely to be committed by youths who have adult supervision after school than by those who are unsupervised one or more days a week. Even more important than actual adult supervision is whether parents even know where their children are after school.

The family is viewed by many as the cornerstone of the community.

A report by the Bipartisan Working Group on Youth Violence ("Youth Violence Task Force . . .," 2000, p.4) says: "Parents are in the best position to teach children that hostility is not a means of problem-solving, and that actions have consequences."

Adams (2000, p.SS21) also stresses: "Community involvement starts with parents. . . . Students whose families are involved in their growth both inside and outside of school are more likely to experience school success and less likely to become involved in antisocial activities."

The Reno (Nevada) Police Department has also stressed the importance of families in their "Kid's Korner" program, which focuses on forging new ties with families living on the fringe of the city in the city's temporary housing—weekly hotels. Described as a "knock and talk" program by the Bureau of Justice Statistics, the bureau says: "'Kid's Korner,' with its emphasis on building positive relationships between law enforcement officers and the residents they serve, is an example of community policing at its finest" ("Cops Fight Crime . . .," 2000, p.10).

The Importance of Schools

A school should be viewed as a community, not as an institution.

The Child Development Project (CDP) is a comprehensive, whole-school improvement program developed by the Developmental Studies Center in Oakland,

California. This project fosters children's cognitive, ethical and social growth by providing all students with engaging, challenging learning opportunities and creating a strong sense of community among students, teachers and parents.

Research suggests that students' academic motivation, commitment to democratic values and resistance to problem behaviors depend on their experience of the school as a community.

CDP research suggests that increases in children's sense of community are linked to their later development of intrinsic academic motivation, concern for others, democratic values, skill and inclination to resolve conflicts equitably, intrinsic prosocial motivation, enjoyment of helping others learn, inclusive attitudes toward outgroups and positive interpersonal behavior in class. In addition to building a sense of community within the school, schools should also partner with the community of which they are a part.

At minimum schools need to link with parents and with local law enforcement departments to teach students about the dangers of crime.

Students whose families are involved in their growth both inside and outside of school are more likely to experience school success and less likely to become involved in antisocial activities. Adams (p.SS21) suggests that school staff, students and families should be involved in the development, discussion and implementation of fair rules. In addition, law enforcement can be brought into the school to get to know students and through select police–school programs can help students become mentors, peacekeepers and problem solvers.

School Teams

Some schools have developed teams to watch for signs of trouble and to step in to prevent problems. Butte County's Safe Schools teams are one example. These teams are a partnership of the Chico (California) Police Department, which assigns a full-time youth services officer to each school in the program; the Butte County Probation Department, which redefined its caseloads to correspond to specific schools; and the Chico Unified School District, which provides office space and equipment and integrates its referral services with those of the police and probation department. As noted by Harberts (2000, p.6): "Having probation and police officers on campus has resulted in swift and appropriate intervention with juveniles who attend the schools or frequent the campus. Because of the improved coordination among the agencies involved, matters that once took 30 days moving through the system now take 30 minutes."

The officers monitor the behavior of all students but focus on those on probation. They conduct safety checks, perform searches and enforce curfew and attendance policies. The team also makes a point of supporting youths working hard to "stay on track" by attending sporting events, graduations and other activities in which youths are taking part.

Another way the team is proactive is in forging relationships with gang members, their peers and others "in the know." Students alert team members when they think something is "going down." Harberts concludes: "Many teenagers, it should be remembered, are impulsive by nature. In order to impact behaviors, swift intervention must closely follow a negative choice. But we must also respect the fact that the behavior we are seeing might be more a family problem and less a criminal problem. We can keep it that way if we intervene successfully, and soon enough."

The School Safety Pyramid

The school safety pyramid, illustrated in Figure 12.1, was developed by the Center for the Prevention of School Violence. It shows the importance of the community concept in school safety, with the community providing the base.

> The school safety pyramid rests on the community and has as its components school resource officers, law-related education, conflict management and peer mediation, Students Against Violence in Education (SAVE), teen/student court, and physical design and technology.

School resource officers (SROs) are the next level, functioning as an integral connection between the school and the community. Dorn (2001, p.31) contends: "A

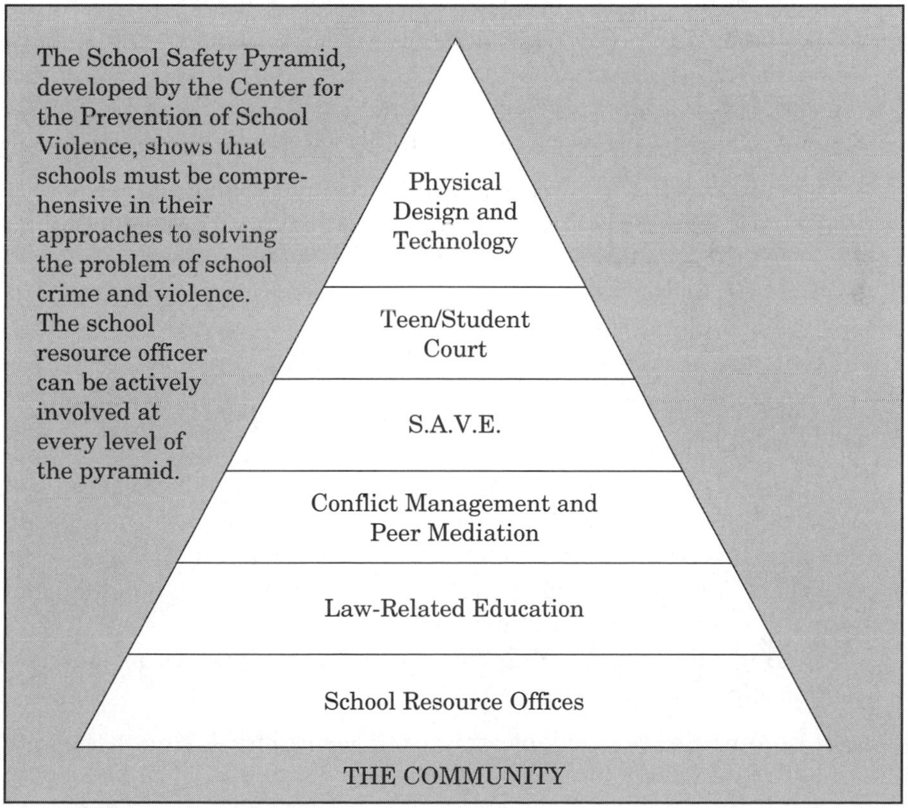
The School Safety Pyramid, developed by the Center for the Prevention of School Violence, shows that schools must be comprehensive in their approaches to solving the problem of school crime and violence. The school resource officer can be actively involved at every level of the pyramid.
Physical Design and Technology
Teen/Student Court
S.A.V.E.
Conflict Management and Peer Mediation
Law-Related Education
School Resource Offices
THE COMMUNITY

Figure 12.1 The School Safety Pyramid

SOURCE: Ronnie L. Paynter. "Policing the Schools." *Law Enforcement Technology,* October 1999, p.35. Reprinted by permission of the Center for the Prevention of School Violence.

school without a law enforcement partnership is as outdated as a school without electricity." Lavarello (2000, p.6) notes: "The fact remains that school-based policing programs are now one of the, if not THE, fastest growing areas of law enforcement." In a teaching capacity, an SRO can educate students about their legal rights and responsibilities. They can also assist in efforts to teach conflict management and peer mediation skills. Having a SAVE group can help build respect between students and SROs, who can directly affect the amount of crime in a school.

The COPS Office has awarded over $715 million to more that 2,600 law enforcement agencies to fund more than 6,000 school resource officers through their COPS in Schools (CIS) Program. In addition, COPS has dedicated approximately $21 million to training COPS-funded SROs and the school administrator in the partnering school(s) or school district(s) to work more collaboratively through the CIS Program (*Cops in Schools*: . . ., 2003, p.1).

Crime in Our Schools

Indicators of School Crime and Safety 2002 (DeVoe et al. 2002) presents data on crime and safety in schools from the perspectives of students, teachers, principals and the general population. Information was gathered from several sources, including the National Crime Victimization Survey (1992–2000), the School Crime Supplement to the National Crime Victimization Survey (1995, 1999 and 2001), the Youth Risk Behavior Survey (1993, 1995, 1997, 1999 and 2001), the Fast Response Survey System: Principal/School Disciplinarian Survey on School Violence (1997) and the School and Staffing Survey (1999–2000). Highlights include the following:

- Crime in schools continues to decline. Violent victimization rates for students varied from a high of 59 violent victimizations per 1,000 students in 1993 to a low of 26 per 1,000 students in 2000.
- The percentage of students who said they were victims of crime at school, both violent and property crimes, decreased from 10 percent of all students in 1995 to 6 percent in 2001.

Mendel (2000, pp.30–31) dispels some myths about juvenile crime, including that juvenile crime is not getting worse nor is it getting younger. In addition, the projected rise in youth population does not doom America to increasing juvenile crime. Mendel (p.65) cautions: "Attempting to reduce crime by focusing only on law enforcement and corrections is like providing expensive ambulances at the bottom of a cliff to pick up the youngsters who fall off, rather than building a fence at the top of the cliff to keep them from falling in the first place."

Among the "critical action steps to reduce juvenile crime, several focus on partnerships:

- Coordinate services among agencies—juvenile justice, education, mental health and child welfare that share responsibility for troubled youths.
- Implement effective school-based prevention models.
- Mobilize the entire community to plan and implement comprehensive youth crime prevention strategies that involve families, schools and neighborhoods."

In addition to strategies aimed at reducing school crime, schools also need to be aware of the potential for school violence and take steps to deal with it should it occur. Frequently school violence is linked to bullying.

Bullying in Schools

Bullying—name calling, fistfights, purposeful ostracism, extortion, character assassination, repeated physical attacks and sexual harassment—has been a common behavior in schools since they first opened their doors. According to Hamit (2000, p.89): "Bullying has always been one of the less pleasant features of growing up, usually excused as part of social maturation." Ericson (2001, p.1), likewise, states: "Bullying has long been considered an inevitable and, in some ways, uncontrollable part of growing up." Its occurrence is often taken lightly, referred to as "Kids will be kids."

Bullying is more accurately termed **peer child abuse**.

Unlike the common belief that bullies are social misfits or outcasts, psychologist Dorothy Espelage, an assistant professor of educational psychology at the University of Illinois at Urbana-Champaign, says "the typical bully is a popular kid, usually male, often an athlete, who knows how to butter up adults even as he persecutes his peers" ("Schoolroom Torment," 2001, p.91). As for his victims, Espelage says "taunting, teasing and coercion can leave victims depressed, anxious, even suicidal and inclined to do to someone else what has been done to them." In addition, the victims of bullies can suffer social isolation, loneliness, low self-esteem and poor academic achievement.

Olweus (2003, pp.14–15), an expert in bullying behavior, describes two kinds of bullying victims, the more common being the passive or submissive victim (80 to 85 percent of victims) and the provocative victim, also called *bully-victims* or *aggressive victims,* whose behavior may elicit negative reactions from a large part of the class. Figure 12.2 illustrates the bullying circle.

Bullying is greatly unreported for many reasons. Most children and adults view reporting as tattling. Other reasons for underreporting include feelings of shame, fear of retaliation and kids' belief that adults will not intervene even if they report the bullying. In that belief, they are often right.

"We've passed bullying off as a rite of passage and created schools where violence works," says Dorothy Espelage.

Adult Responsibility

"Bullying adversely affects practically every student in a school, whether he or she is a victim or a witness of a bullying incident. But many school staff members fail to address the problem because they are misinformed about the nature and extent of bullying behavior and believe they are already doing all they can to prevent it" (Cooper and Snell, 2003).

One often overlooked form of bullying is harassment. Woods (2002, p.20) reports: "Students say that sexual harassment often occurs right in front of educators,

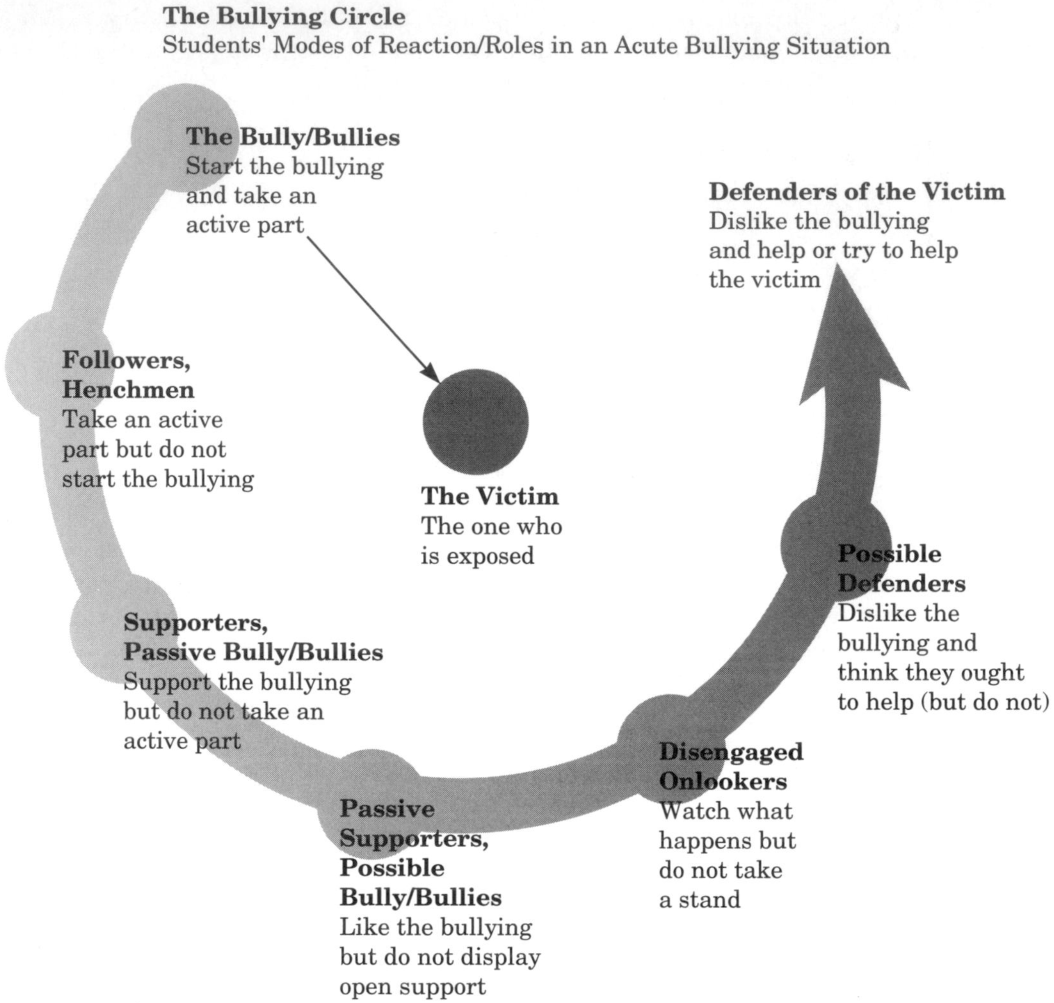
The Bullying Circle
Students' Modes of Reaction/Roles in an Acute Bullying Situation
The Bully/Bullies
Start the bullying and take an active part
Defenders of the Victim
Dislike the bullying and help or try to help the victim
Followers, Henchmen
Take an active part but do not start the bullying
The Victim
The one who is exposed
Possible Defenders
Dislike the bullying and think they ought to help (but do not)
Supporters, Passive Bully/Bullies
Support the bullying but do not take an active part
Disengaged Onlookers
Watch what happens but do not take a stand
Passive Supporters, Possible Bully/Bullies
Like the bullying but do not display open support

Figure 12.2 The Bullying Circle

SOURCE: Dan Olweus. "A Profile of Bullying at School." *Educational Leadership*, March 2003, p.14. Reprinted by permission.

and affects their lives emotionally and academically." Woods (p.22) notes: "Teachers and administrators are present in the public places where harassment occurs, yet victims—and harassers—know that, all too often, harassment is not punished." Wessler (2003, p.40) stresses: "Teachers who refuse to tolerate verbal harassment can create havens of safety and respect." Garbarino and deLara (2003, p.18) also stress: "Adults in middle and high schools must protect students from verbal harassment and emotional violence." They (p.210) contend: "If adults do not provide the intervention students need, then students will take matters into their own hands."

Strategies to Mediate Bullying

Strategies to mediate bullying include clear rules against such behavior applied consistently with appropriate sanctions for violation of the rules, a buddy system to pair younger students with older students, peer mediation and close monitoring of cafeterias, playgrounds and "hot spots" where bullying is likely to occur away from direct adult supervision.

The "tell or tattle" dilemma occurs when students hesitate to tell anyone that they are being bullied because it is seen as tattling—something they have been taught not to do.

A Johnson Institute program gives teachers step-by-step guidelines on how to teach students the difference between telling and tattling. Children, teenagers and adults need to learn that **tattling** is something done to get someone in trouble, but telling or reporting is done to keep someone safe.

Dr. Olweus, University of Bergen in Norway, has developed a program to prevent bullying that is used throughout the world. A basic tenet is intervention by teachers when they see bullying behavior. Olweus recommends seven strategies: (1) adult supervision at recess, (2) strict enforcement of clear rules for student behavior, (3) consistent, nonphysical punishment of students who misbehave, (4) assistance to bullying victims that helps them to assert themselves, (5) parental encouragement that helps students develop and maintain friendships, (6) clear and positive communication between parents and school officials and (7) clear and swift reaction to persistent physical or verbal bullying. Schools that implemented the program found a 40 to 50 percent reduction rate in bullying behavior within the first two years ("Protecting Kids . . .," 2000, p.7).

Sampson (2002, pp.20–23) suggests specific responses to reduce bullying in schools: using the "whole-school" approach, increasing student reporting of bullying, developing activities in less-supervised areas, reducing the amount of time students can spend less supervised, monitoring areas where bullying can be experienced (e.g., bathrooms), assigning bullies to a particular location or to particular chores during release time, posting classroom signs prohibiting bullying and listing the consequences for it, providing teachers with effective classroom management training and having high-level school administrators inform late-enrolling students about the school's bullying policy.

Sampson (pp.22–23) also describes responses that have been found to have limited effectiveness: training students in conflict mediation and peer mediation, adopting a zero tolerance policy, providing group therapy for bullies and encouraging victims to simply "stand up" to bullies.

A Case Study

In 1998 the police department in a small Washington town (Oak Harbor) noted an increase in the severity of injuries and in the number of weapons violations at the high school of 1,800 students. At the same time, school administrators reported an increase in bullying and harassment, and several students raised the issue with the Associated Student Body. In addition, Citizens Against Domestic and Sexual Abuse, a victim services agency, had seen an increase in the number of young people accessing its services. The police department secured a COPS School-Based Partnership grant of $135,800 and joined the school and the agency to study the problem.

Smith-LaBombard (2001, pp.9–10) describes the situation at Washington High School. Surveys including questions about students' experiences at the high school revealed that 35 percent of the respondents said they had felt harassed, bullied or intimidated at some time; 15 percent said they were physically assaulted. However, only 20 percent of the students who said they were physically assaulted had reported the assault to school authorities.

Among those who did report, 66 percent were not satisfied with the handling of their complaints, stating that nothing was done, offenders were given too many chances, or administrators did not take the report seriously. The high rate of dissatisfaction might explain in part the low rate of reports.

Nearly nine in ten students (89 percent) reported engaging in some type of bullying behavior—laughing at others, teasing or name calling. However, only 18 percent of parents surveyed thought that their child would act as a bully. In addition, 96 percent of students and 87 percent of faculty/staff reported witnessing bullying-type behavior. Students listed athletes as the most flagrant bullies and harassers. Next were the "popular" students.

"The high school in Oak Harbor, Washington, squelched the bullies," says Smith-LaBombard (p.9). They gathered data on the bullies, studied the data, devised a five-prong attack, and then attacked, especially in the lunchroom, which the surveys identified as the center for bullying and harassment. She reports: "Bullying, harassment, and intimidation decreased in reaction to:

- Increased staff presence in the lunchroom.
- Surveillance video cameras in the lunchroom.
- Students identified as harassers required to attend a Harassment Awareness Training class.
- A Big Brothers/Big Sisters mentoring program that pairs high school and middle school students to help prevent bullying among freshmen.
- Workshops, focusing on athletes, with students, school staff, victim services advocates, and police officers. (Parents, local counselors, and other community members concerned about bullying also attended.)"

An analysis of police reports and school disciplinary action for the 2000–2001 school year compared with the two previous years showed a decrease in the numbers of fights and confrontations. According to Smith-LaBombard: "The school's effort to 'catch abuse low in order to prevent abuse high' appears to be effective. (The slogan means that students report oral assaults and that school officials discipline the culprits to prevent the physical assaults.)" A follow-up survey showed 42 percent of students and 28 percent of faculty at the school for the last two years noticed changes in the numbers or types of bullying, harassment and intimidation as well as the school's quicker response to such behavior.

In addition, 22 percent of students and 65 percent of faculty believed an increased use of unmonitored surveillance cameras increased feelings of safety on campus. Some students complained, however, that video camera surveillance intruded on their privacy. School officials viewed the video only in response to complaints in the area under surveillance.

School Violence

Pearl, Mississippi; West Paducah, Kentucky; Jonesboro, Arkansas; Fayetteville, Tennessee; Springfield, Oregon; Richmond, Virginia; Littleton, Colorado; Conyers, Georgia; Santee, California—these cities house schools that come to mind when school violence is mentioned. And they were shocking instances of violence in our country's schools. But they are just the tip of the iceberg. Hall (2000, p.6) reports that an estimated 100,000 to 250,000 guns are carried to schools every day in this country, and since 1992 there have been 250 deaths at public schools.

Highlights from *Indicators of School Crime and Safety 2002* (DeVoe et al.) include the following:

- Crime in schools continues to decline. Violent victimization rates for students varied from a high of 59 violent victimizations per 1,000 students in 1993 to a low of 26 per 1,000 students in 2000.
- The percentage of students who said they were victims of crime at school, both violent and property crimes, decreased from 10 percent of all students in 1995 to 6 percent in 2001.
- In 1993, 1995, 1997, 1999, and 2001 between 7 and 9 percent of students reported being threatened or injured in the previous 12 months with a weapon such as a gun, knife, or club on school property.
- From July 1, 1992 through June 30, 1999 there were 358 school-associated violent deaths[1] in the United States, including 255 deaths of school-age children (ages 5 to 19). In each survey year, school-age children were at least 70 times more likely to be murdered away from school than they were to be murdered at school. In the most recent school year for which data are available, from July 1, 1998 to June 30, 1999, there were 47 school-associated violent deaths. Thirty-eight of these violent deaths were homicides, six were suicides, a law enforcement officer in the line of duty killed two, and one was unintentional.
- There was no consistent pattern of increase or decrease in the number of homicides or suicides of school-age children at school between July 1, 1992 and June 30, 1999.
- Of the 358 total school-associated violent deaths that occurred between July 1, 1992 and June 30, 1999, 218 were homicides of school-age children and 37 were suicides of school-age children. Away from school, during the same period, there were a total of 22,323 homicides of children ages 5 to 19. During the 1993 to 1999 calendar years, there were 14,813 suicides of children in this age group away from school.
- In the most recent year, from July 1, 1998 through June 30, 1999, 33 of the 38 school-associated homicides were of school-age children. During this same time frame, there were 2,358 homicides of children ages 5 to 19 away from school.

[1]A **school-associated violent death** is a homicide, suicide, legal intervention, or unintentional firearm-related death in which the fatal injury occurred on the campus of a functioning elementary or secondary school in the United States, while the victim was on the way to or from regular sessions at such a school, or while the victim was attending or traveling to or from an official school-sponsored event. Victims include nonstudents as well as students and staff members.

- Four of the six school-associated suicides, which occurred from July 1, 1998 to June 30, 1999, were of school-age children. Away from school, there were 1,855 suicides of children ages 5 to 19 during the 1999 calendar year.
- In the 2002–2003 school year, 16 school-related violent deaths occurred: 6 suicides, 4 stabbings, 3 shootings, 2 murder-suicides and 1 "other" (Trump).

Early Warning Signs of Impending Violent Behavior

Early warning signs of impending violent behavior include being a victim of violence, feelings of being picked on and persecuted, low school interest and poor academic performance, uncontrolled anger, intimidating and bullying behaviors, a history of discipline problems, drug and alcohol use and affiliation with gangs (*Early Warning, Timely Response,* 1998, pp.8–10). This same publication (p.11) describes signs of imminent violent behavior: serious physical fighting with peers or family members, severe destruction of property, severe rage for seemingly minor reasons, detailed threats of lethal violence, possession and/or use of firearms and other weapons, other self-injurious behaviors or threats of suicide.

Piazza (2001, p.68) states: "In the shadow of the school shootings that capture the country's attention lies a larger but less visible group of victims. . . . These victims are the youngsters whose anger, frustration, and loss of self-esteem results in violence directed not at others but at themselves. Suicide is bullying's quiet little secret. It's one kid at a time, so it doesn't catch our attention." Among the school-associated violent deaths that receive the most publicity are those involving school shootings.

School Shooters

"I hate being laughed at. But they won't laugh after they're scraping parts of their parents, sisters, brothers and friends from the wall of my hate." Piazza explains that these words were written in the journal of 15-year-old Kip Kinkel before he killed both parents and then moved into his Springfield, Oregon, high school and shot more than two dozen students, two fatally.

A study by the FBI's National Center for the Analysis of Violent Crime (NCAVC), *The School Shooter: A Threat Assessment Perspective* (O'Toole, 2000, p.5), notes: "All threats are not created equal." This study (p.7) describes four categories of threats.

Threats may be classified as direct, indirect, veiled and conditional.

"A **direct threat** identifies a specific act against a specific target and is delivered in a straightforward, clear and explicit manner: 'I am going to place a bomb in the school's gym.' An **indirect threat** tends to be vague, unclear and ambiguous. The plan, the intended victim, the motivation and other aspects of the threat are masked or equivocal: 'If I wanted to, I could kill everyone at this school!' . . . A **veiled threat** is one that strongly implies but does not explicitly threaten violence. 'We would be better off without you around anymore' clearly hints at a possible violent act, but leaves it to the potential victim to interpret the message and give a definite meaning to the threat. A **conditional threat** is the type of threat often seen in extortion cases. It warns that a violent act will happen unless certain demands or terms are met: 'If you don't pay me one million dollars, I will place a bomb in the school (p. 7).'"

The study (p.26) stresses: "It is especially important that a school not deal with threats by simply kicking the problem out the door. Expelling or suspending a student for making a threat must not be a substitute for careful threat assessment and a considered, consistent policy of intervention. Disciplinary action alone, unaccompanied by any effort to evaluate the threat or the student's intent, may actually exacerbate the danger—for example, if a student feels unfairly or arbitrarily treated and becomes even angrier and more bent on carrying out a violent act."

The study (p.10) describes an innovative model designed to assess someone who has made a threat and evaluate the likelihood that the threat will actually be carried out.

The FBI's four-prong assessment evaluates four major areas making up the "totality of the circumstances": (1) personality of the student, (2) family dynamics, (3) school dynamics and the student's role in those dynamics and (4) social dynamics.

Personality Traits and Behaviors The first behavior listed being associated with violence was *leakage*: **Leakage** occurs when a student intentionally or unintentionally reveals clues to feelings, thoughts, fantasies, attitudes or intentions that may signal an impending violent act. These clues can take the forms of subtle threats, boasts, innuendos, predictions or ultimatums. They may be spoken or conveyed in stories, diary entries, essays, poems, letters, songs, drawings, doodles, tattoos or videos. . . . Leakage can be a cry for help, a sign of inner conflict, or boasts that may look empty but actually express a serious threat. Leakage is considered to be one of the most important clues that may precede an adolescent's violent act.

Most violent students "leak" their feelings and intentions in the weeks and months before committing the violent act. Such messages should never be ignored.

Wattendorf (2002, p.11) notes: "In 75 percent of the 37 shooting incidents studied, school shooters disclosed their plans in advance to classmates." Further, *The School Shooter: A Threat Assessment Perspective* states: "Children who commit violent acts in school typically do not have a moment at which they 'snap' from nonviolence into violence, but rather evolve gradually toward violence, with signposts along the way." The report stresses: "The task for law enforcement agencies and school officials is to learn how to interpret the 'leakage,' and accurately assess whether a particular student poses a real threat to others or is merely 'having a bad day or blowing off steam.' "

An extensive list of other personality traits and behaviors is presented (pp.17–21): low tolerance for frustration, poor coping skills, lack of resiliency, failed love relationship, "injustice collector," signs of depression, narcissism (self-centered), alienation, dehumanizes others, lack of empathy, exaggerated sense of entitlement, attitude of superiority, exaggerated or pathological need for attention, externalizes blame, masks low self-esteem, anger management problems, intolerance, inappropriate humor, manipulative, distrustful, closed social group, change of behavior, rigid and opinionated, unusual interest in sensational violence, fascination with violence-filled entertainment, negative role models, behavior appears relevant to carrying out a threat.

The report (p.15) stresses: "It should be strongly emphasized that this list is not intended as a checklist to predict future violent behavior by a student who has not acted violently or threatened violence. Rather, the list should be considered only *after* a student has made some type of threat and an assessment has been developed using the four-pronged model." It also cautions: "No one or two traits or characteristics should be considered in isolation or given more weight than the others. . . . Behavior is an expression of personality, but one bad day may not reflect a student's real personality or usual behavior patterns."

In addition, as Piazza (p.68) reports: "A study by the Secret Service National Threat Assessment center that looked at 37 school shootings found that in more than two-thirds of the attacks, the attackers felt persecuted, bullied, threatened, attacked or injured by others."

Family Dynamics Factors associated with the family and violent behavior include a turbulent parent–child relationship, acceptance of pathological behavior, access to weapons, lack of intimacy, student "rules the roost" and there are no limits or monitoring of television and the Internet (pp.21–22).

School Dynamics According to *The School Shooter* (p.22): "If an act of violence occurs at a school, the school becomes the scene of the crime. As in any violent crime, it is necessary to understand what it is about the school which might have influenced the student's decision to offend there rather than someplace else. . . . from the *student's perspective.* Factors to consider include the student's attachment to school, tolerance for disrespectful behavior, inequitable discipline, inflexible culture, pecking order among students, code of silence and unsupervised computer access."

Social Dynamics "Social dynamics," according to O'Toole (p.13), "are patterns of behavior, thinking, beliefs, customs, traditions, and roles that exist in the larger community where students live." Factors to consider include easy, unmonitored access to media, entertainment and technology; peer groups; drugs and alcohol; outside interests and the copycat effect (pp.23–24). The study (p.24) reports that copycat behavior is common and that everyone in the school should be more vigilant in noting disturbing student behavior in the days, weeks and even months following a heavily publicized incident somewhere else in the country.

The Young Rampage Killer—Court TV (Reprinted by permission)

In April 2000, marking the first anniversary of the Columbine tragedy, *The New York Times* published a series about violence that was based on one hundred cases of American rampage killers from the past fifty years. They noted that the incident in Littleton, Colorado was one of thirteen for the year 1999. . . .

Of the 100 cases, nineteen were teenagers, and they showed a pattern that set them apart from the adults:

- While adults tended to act alone, kids often acted with the support of their peers. In some instances, those kids were helped by other kids who drove them to school, showed them how to use a gun, helped them get a firearm, or simply came to watch. There were times when these students were actually goaded into doing it. Quite often the killers boasted about what they were planning and even encouraged friends to be a witness.

- Kids may try to collaborate and get others involved, and some of them kill together, as was the case in Jonesboro and Littleton.
- They will often boast of their plans.
- While mental health problems are common, fewer kids than adults commit suicide.
- The youngest killers are less emotionally detached than older ones.

In forty cases of school violence in the past twenty years, the Secret Service's National Threat Assessment found that teenagers often told someone before they did the deed. Most of these kids were white and they preferred (and somehow acquired) semiautomatics. Almost half had shown some evidence of mental disturbance, including delusions and hallucinations.

School officials want to know if there are any clear signs to watch for and to tell parents about. They know they must be especially careful because any action they take has the potential of landing them in court. The problem is that few school psychologists have received training on this issue, so they're not sure what to do or what to look for. As with all dangerousness assessments, the most telling factor in what a child might do is what a child has already done. In other words, a history of violent actions or words is the best indicator of future violence potential.

- Any pattern of behavior that persists over time tends to intensify. This does not necessarily mean that a bully will become a school killer, but it means that kids who develop an obsession with weapons or violent games, and who tend to threaten violence are more likely to eventually act out than those who don't. Some of the behaviors to be especially concerned about include an increase in lying, blaming others, avoiding responsibility, avoiding effort to achieve goals, using deception or force or intimidation to control others, showing lack of empathy for others, exploiting others' weaknesses engaging in petty crimes like theft or damage to property. Other behaviors are getting involved in gang behavior, having a pattern of overreacting, having a history of criminal acts without a motive, experiencing continual family discord, having a history of criminality in the family, having a history of running away from home, showing a pattern of anger and being depressed or withdrawn. Yet other behaviors include showing inconsistencies, such as a sudden uncharacteristic interest in guns; developing an intense dislike of school; complaining about classmates treating him or her badly; having excessive television or videogame habits—three or more hours a day; carrying weapons like a knife; complaining of feeling lonely and showing intense resentment.

Violent children are sometimes divided into two categories: sociopaths and psychopaths. A **sociopath** is usually a bully—outgoing and manipulative, instigating fights. The sociopath is a type of violent leader. A **psychopath**, in contrast, tends to be a loner like the "Trench Coat Mafia" kids. Psychopaths tend to be socially inept.

After School Programs

After school programs are often touted as one means to keep youths out of trouble and to help them succeed in school. A Justice-Based After-School (JBAS) Program has been developed and is being piloted by the COPS Office. According to this office: "Without supervision between the hours of 2 and 10 P.M., children are more likely to be victimized and to engage in risk-taking behavior" (*Justice-Based After-School Program* (2002, p.1). This program encourages law enforcement officers to work in partnership with community organizations, especially in high-crime neighborhoods, to develop a preventive approach to juvenile crime and victimization. In Minneapolis, Minnesota, for example, COPS funds have been used to expand an existing Police Athletic League (PAL) Project in one school and to start programs in two other schools.

Research on whether such programs are effective is mixed. Perkins-Gough (2003, p.88) notes: "Two recent reports [on after school programs] come to dramatically different conclusions." *When Schools Stay Open Late: The National Evaluation of the 21st Century Community Learning Centers Programs* found that participation in federally funded after-school programs had little effect on academic performance. Another report by Miller (no date) found differently. After looking at evidence from research studies from a broad range of after-school programs, Miller concludes: Many studies over the past two decades point to the links between after-school program participation and educational success." With school resources becoming more limited, the debate over whether to provide after-school programs is likely to continue.

Creating Safe Schools

Argon and Anderson (2000, p.C6) note: "Media attention to random schoolyard violence has toned down considerably lately, suggesting that we as a society are becoming either numb to the problem or tired of hearing about it. But no one suggests that the problem is going away." "School violence is not just a school problem, it's a community problem. The entire community needs to get involved in these issues to make schools safer for everyone" (Paynter, 2000, p.72).

Grassie (2000, p.89) suggests: "The best defense against all forms of school threats and risks is a fully integrated school security program that carefully and effectively blends a wide variety of proven risk reduction strategies into a flexible, responsive school security program." Pollack and Sundermann (2001, p.13) stress: "We now understand that safe schools require broad-based efforts on the part of the entire community, including educators, students, parents, law enforcement agencies, businesses and faith-based organizations." Figure 12.3 illustrates the strategic process in designing a safe school.

Two highly successful programs to help build safe schools are *Student Crime Stoppers* and *PeaceBuilders.®*

Student Crime Stoppers, like the adult program, offers youths tools to stand up against crime and violence without reprisal or peer pressure through an anonymous TIPS line to get the information to those who can stop the crime or violence. Those

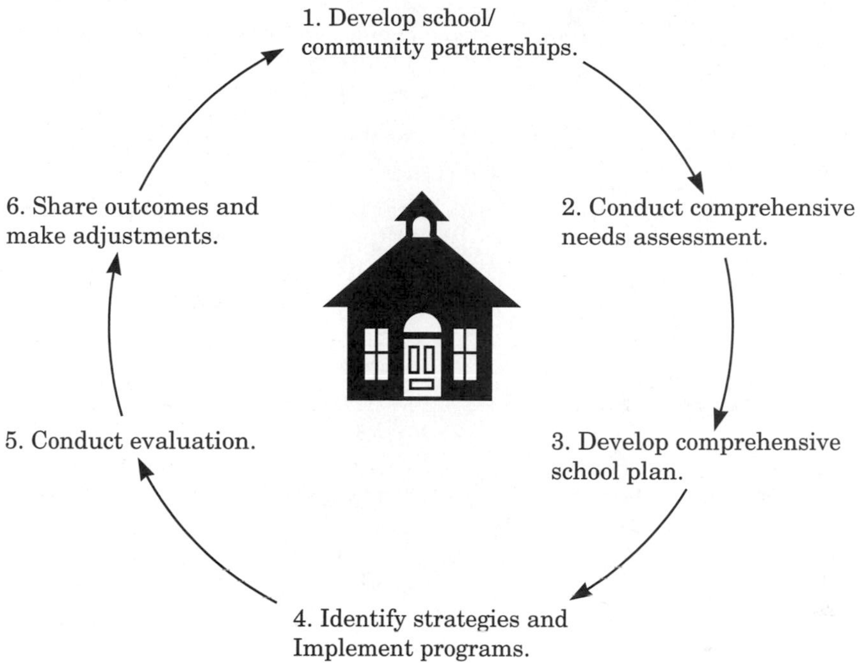

Figure 12.3 Strategic Process in Designing a Safe School

SOURCE: Ira Pollack and Carlos Sundermann. "Creating Safe Schools: A Comprehensive Approach." *Juvenile Justice,* June 2001, p.15.

with information about solving crimes on school property or at school events can qualify for cash awards up to $100. According to Aryani et al. (2001, p.1): "The implementation of a Scholastic Crime Stoppers program . . . constitutes one of the best and least expensive crime prevention strategies."

PeaceBuilders® is a long-term, community-based, violence reduction or prevention program designed to help create an environment that reduces violence and establishes more peaceful ways of behaving, living and working in families, schools, organizations and communities. Schools may send up to four people to attend a two-and-one-half-day training session to become site trainers. These site trainers then provide four-hour PeaceBuilders® Staff Implementation Workshops at their schools or in their own district. Up to 60 people may attend this workshop.

Safe schools depend not only on programs such as these but also on a comprehensive approach to safety.

A seven-pronged approach is needed for effective school security: (1) school/law enforcement/community partnerships, (2) education about nonviolence, (3) problem-solving training, (4) mediation and anger-management training, (5) clear policies on accepted behavior with consequences for nonconformity, (6) security procedures and technology and (7) crisis planning.

School/Law Enforcement/Community Partnerships

The differences between traditional policing in the schools and community policing in the schools parallel those in the community, as summarized in Table 12.2

Table 12.2 Comparison between Traditional and Community Policing in Schools

Traditional Policing in Schools	***Community Policing in Schools***
Reactive response to 911 calls	Law enforcement officer assigned to the school "community"
Incident driven	Problem oriented
Minimal school–law enforcement interaction, often characterized by a "us vs. them" mentality	Ongoing school–law enforcement partnership to address problems of concern to educators, students, and parents
Police role limited to law enforcement	Police role extended beyond law enforcement to include prevention and early intervention activities
Police viewed as source of the solution	Educators, students, and parents are active partners in developing solutions
Educators and law enforcement officers reluctant to share information	Partners value information sharing as an important problem-solving tool
Criminal incidents subject to inadequate response; criminal consequences imposed only when incidents reported to police	Consistent responses to incidents is ensured—administrative *and* criminal, as appropriate
Law enforcement presence viewed as indicator of failure	Law enforcement presence viewed as taking a positive, proactive step to create orderly, safe, and secure schools
Police effectiveness measured by arrest rates, response times, calls for service etc.	Policing effectiveness measured by the absence of crime and disorder

SOURCE: Anne J. Atkinson *Fostering School–Law Enforcement Partnerships.* Naperville, IL: Northwest Regional Educational Laboratory, September 2002, p.7. Reprinted by permission.

The IACP has published a *Guide for Preventing and Responding to School Violence,* which includes as one topic developing partnerships with schools. One of the oldest and most commonly used partnerships is assigning police officers to schools—the school resource officer (SRO). Atkinson (2002, pp.10–11) describes characteristics of effective schools and how school–law enforcement partnerships contribute, as shown in Table 12.3.

Bilchik (2000, p.57) stresses: "To foster safety in schools, the entire community must get involved. Some of the most promising prevention and intervention strategies involve administrators, teachers, families, students, law enforcement officers, juvenile justice practitioners and community members, working together to establish a crisis response plan as well as a long-term strategy to form positive relationships with all children and families."

Schuiteman (2000, p.77) reports on the initial evaluation of 57 Department of Criminal Justice Services (DCJS) grants supporting 63 SROs in 44 localities. The initial evaluation findings are that: "SROs report success in reducing violence, preventing conflict and improving school security."

Mattson (2000) describes the Phoenix "Wake Up" program, which resulted from the Phoenix Police Department's meeting with the community, school and business leaders to approach the problem of youth crime and violence. Together they identified the two biggest problems facing the area's youths as limited money and lack of things to do. Another problem was a lack of positive role models. Their solution: "Wake Up!"

Table 12.3 Characteristics of Effective Schools and How School–Law Enforcement Partnerships Contribute

Effective Schools Alone	***Effective Schools with Partnership***
Safe and Orderly Environment	
A safe and orderly environment is often referred to as "the number-one correlate of effective schools." In such schools there is an orderly, purposeful, atmosphere free from the threat of physical harm. School climate is not oppressive but is conducive to teaching and learning. Teachers and students interact in a positive, cooperative manner.	SROs bring to the school setting the expertise of a public safety specialist. They provide an immediate response to life-threatening situations, ensure that laws are enforced when illegal activities occur, and work collaboratively with schools to resolve problems that threaten the safety of schools. Their presence has a deterrent effect on illegal and disruptive behavior and communicates that the school and larger community have made school safety a priority.
High Expectations for Success	
In the effective school, there is a climate of expectation in which staff members believe and demonstrate that all students can master the essential content and school skills, and also believe that they have the capability to help all students achieve that mastery.	SROs reinforce clear expectations for appropriate behavior through enforcement of laws, law-related education, and involvement of students in crime prevention activities.
Clear School Mission	
In the effective school, there is a clearly articulated school mission through which the staff shares an understanding of and commitment to instructional goals, priorities, assessment procedures, and accountability.	The school–law enforcement partnership helps schools to focus on their central mission—educating—by reducing the amount of time the staff must spend on disciplinary matters.
Instructional Leadership	
In an effective school, the principal and other staff members take an active role in instructional leadership with the principal becoming a "leader of leaders" (rather than a leader of followers), functioning as a coach or partner.	When crime and other disruptive behaviors are reduced, school leaders can focus more effectively on their central instructional leadership role.
Frequent Monitoring of Student Progress	
In the effective school, student academic progress is measured frequently using a variety of assessment procedures. The assessment results are used to improve individual student performance and the instructional program.	The school–law enforcement partnership uses data on crime and discipline to assess and improve school safety.
Opportunity to Learn and Student Time on Task	
In the effective school, teachers allocate a significant amount of classroom time to instruction in the essential skills.	Opportunity to learn and student time on task are increased when disruptive behavior is reduced.
Home–School Relations	
Effective schools have formed partnerships with parents who are given the opportunity to play important roles in the school. These schools have built trust and communicated with parents who understand and support the school's basic mission.	Partnership, characterized by trust and communication, is a central component of community policing. Law enforcement adds a public safety specialist to home–school partnerships.

SOURCE: Anne J. Atkinson. *Fostering School–Law Enforcement Partnerships.* Naperville, IL: Northwest Regional Educational Laboratory, September 2002, pp.10–11. Reprinted by permission.

formally known as the Community Efforts to Abate Street Violence. The program placed Wake Up! clubs in the schools and had police officers teach students to make better choices in their lives. The clubs also taught positive life lessons such as communication, teamwork, self-confidence, leadership and respect. All seventh- and eighth-grade students were invited to join the clubs, which met for an hour each week at school. About once a month, each club had a community service project, making them feel a part of the community and encouraging them to make it better.

After one year, data were obtained from over 242 individuals from a pool of over 1,500 participants. School referrals were given to 144 nonclub students and 25 club students (whose referrals were for less serious offenses such as gum chewing). The incidence of truancy for club members was half that of the general population. Six students were arrested during the year, none of whom were club members. In the Wake Up! school, the crimes-against-person rate was 40 percent lower than that at the control school. The crimes-against-property rate in the club school was 70 percent lower than that at the control school. Testing of academic achievement also showed positive results. In the basic battery sections, the control school showed no change; the club school showed a 0.4 grade-level increase. On reading, the control school showed a 0.3 grade-level increase; the club school a 1.0 grade-level increase.

The Miami "Do the Right Thing" program, described by Makholm (2000), recognizes and rewards young people for good deeds. This program reinforces socially desirable behavior among youths, demonstrates that good kids are newsworthy and enhances the relationship between underprivileged youths, police officers, police departments and area businesses.

Education about Nonviolence Many school systems have successfully relied on counselors, nurses and other specialists to supplement teachers' efforts to teach nonviolence, giving students a sense of a supportive network of adults available to help them resolve problems nonviolently.

Problem-Solving Training Problem-solving training was discussed in Chapter 4.

Mediation and Anger Management Training When a dispute occurs on school grounds, the involved parties seek out a teacher or the program's adult coordinator. The coordinator assigns peer mediators to intervene and attempt to resolve the dispute peacefully through the parties' mutual agreement and commitment to a contract with set standards for conduct. Such mediation may substitute for detention or suspension of youths involved in fights, verbal threats or intimidation of others on school grounds.

Potential obstacles to this strategy include lack of funds for staff to train students and faculty and coordinate mediator assignments. In addition, convincing students that violence can be prevented can be difficult.

Clear Policies on Accepted Behavior with Consequences for Nonconformity Clear policies should be established for tardiness, absenteeism/class cutting, physical conflicts among students, student tobacco use, verbal abuse of teachers, drug use, vandalism of school property, alcohol use, robbery or theft, gangs, racial tensions, possession of weapons, physical abuse of teachers and sale of drugs on school grounds.

Rich et al. (2003) describe a National Institute of Justice funded software program, *School COP*, that allows SROs to record extensive data about student misconduct and crime more quickly than writing it down. It ensures consistency in the information recorded and simplifies reporting. Records regarding each student's disciplinary and criminal history can be easily retrieved. Information about incidents can be graphically displayed and can help identify hot spots.

Consequences for unacceptable behavior vary from detention to suspension to expulsion. Many schools have adopted **zero tolerance** toward possession of guns, drugs or alcohol in schools; that is, no matter what the underlying circumstances, a student bringing a weapon, drugs or alcohol to school will be suspended or expelled.

According to *School Security Roundtable 2000* (p.SS12), a zero tolerance policy was the second most common strategy used for school security at the elementary, middle and high school levels. One of the central components of zero tolerance is school expulsion. They (p.382) contend: "Zero tolerance strategies have begun to turn our schools into supplemental law enforcement agencies, but they have demonstrated little return despite a decade of hype."

No data suggest that zero tolerance policies reduce school violence. Such policies result in sometimes unreasonable suspensions and expulsions.

Hyman and Snook (2000, p.491) assert: "Many believe that safe and orderly schools require automatic punishments based on zero tolerance policies. The routine and unquestioning acceptance of these policies is not only undermining and distorting students' understanding and belief in constitutional rights; there is also the simple fact that such policies do not work." They suggest: "In contrast to toxic schools, schools that encourage participatory democracy are characterized by a climate in which students and staff members understand the need to respect one another's rights."

Holloway (2002, p.84) cites a government study that found more than three-quarters of all schools reported having zero tolerance policies. He suggests: "Policies that rely solely on suspending and expelling students do not remedy student misbehavior." In fact, says Holloway (p.85): "Any intervention for changing children's behavior that is simple is simple-minded, and those that substitute formulas for decisions made by people who understand the circumstances are dangerous."

An example is a young boy who was suspended from school for violating the three-cut policy by missing his family living class. Investigation revealed he waited outside his apartment to intercept his crack cocaine–addicted mother's government check (which she would cash and use to buy drugs). He took the check to the bank where the manager gave him cash, which he put into envelopes: one to pay the rent, another for food, another utilities and so on. By the time he got the bills paid, he was late for school. Was suspension really warranted? Hamit (p.90) also describes unfortunate results of zero tolerance policies:

> Zero tolerance for drugs in schools has led to incidents where female students have been expelled or suspended for giving Motrin for menstrual cramps. This is hardly crack cocaine, and if the women involved were of age, it would be perfectly legal.

Zero tolerance for weapons has led to incidents where a child has been expelled for bringing to school a kitchen knife intended only to cut a chicken sandwich.

Security Procedures and Technology "U.S. public schools are not designed as fortresses," says Bridges (2000, p.22). "However, by using basic crime prevention techniques and precautionary measures, communities can help create safer schools." A U.S. Department of Education survey of public schools (Grassie, p.89) reports that 96 percent required visitors to sign in upon entering the school building, 80 percent had a closed campus policy that prohibited most students from leaving the campus for lunch, 53 percent controlled access to their school buildings, 24 percent controlled access to their school grounds, 19 percent conducted drug sweeps, 4 percent of public elementary schools required students to wear uniforms during the school year, 4 percent performed random metal detector checks on students and 1 percent used metal detectors daily.

A National School Board Association survey of 720 school districts throughout the United States found that 39 percent of urban school districts use metal detectors, 75 percent use locker searches and 65 percent use security personnel (Welsh et al., 2000, p.243). Some schools require students to use backpacks and book carriers made of clear material to allow visibility of their contents.

The National Law Enforcement and Corrections Technology Center–Southeast Region (NLECTC-SE) and the IACP joined forces to bring together a group of law enforcement and education practitioners to discuss school safety technology. As Nettles (2001, p.14) explains: "The group recommended devising a way to facilitate the secure and timely sharing of information between the police, courts and schools regarding potentially dangerous events and individuals. . . . Currently, the major challenge is overcoming the natural reluctance to share juvenile records based on past prohibitions." In addition to finding ways to share timely information are the initiatives being tested to enhance safety in the school. Others include a personal distress device for school personnel, simulation technologies for school safety training, an assessment of the applicability of less-than-lethal weapons for schools and nonintrusive drug detection.

Sanchez (2003, pp.19–20) suggests the following technologies available to make schools safer: remote surveillance, global positioning system, intelligent surveillance, virtual tours, cellular telephones, biometrics and advanced weapons detection systems.

The COPS Secure Our Schools (SOS) initiative provides funds to help cover the cost of security measures such as metal detectors, locks and lighting as well as security assessments and training (*Secure Our Schools Initiative,* 2003).

Crisis Planning

Another aspect of proactively making schools safer includes having a contingency plan should a crisis occur, including violence by insiders or outsiders. The plan should be carefully thought out based on the unique characteristics of the specific school. It should be made known to and practiced by staff and students. Hoang (2000, p.107) suggests three "Ps" when dealing with school violence.

The three "Ps" for dealing with violence are prevention, planning and practice.

Hoang suggests that a key element in planning is a tactical survey whose results should be contained in a tactical survey packet. Among the elements to be included are a general area road map, a neighborhood area road map, an aerial photograph, a floor plan of the school, blueprints/schematics, a property diagram and exterior photographs.

Schmitt (2000, p.139) reports: "Some plans are simple, some so complex they require a notebook to hold them" Schmitt questions the wisdom of this approach, saying a simpler response plan would be more effective. Maps of the buildings and likely escape routes should be known.

Lockdowns

One strategy being used to reduce school violence is a lockdown. As Guy (2001, pp.7–8) explains: "During a lockdown students must remain in their classroom or attend an assembly until the lockdown is over. K-9 units trained to detect explosives and drugs conduct a systematic search of the school. In the classrooms, officers explain about 'amnesty time,' which allows students to turn over illegal narcotics, unlawful prescription medications, inhalants, knives or firearms in their possession without fear of prosecution. Students also are given the opportunity to list such items in their cars and lockers. To provide some degree of anonymity, teachers and officers leave the classrooms for several minutes while students put their lists and illegal items in an amnesty box." Some students complain that their constitutional rights are being violated, but to date the procedure has not been legally challenged.

School Mock Disaster Exercises

Minetti and Caplan (2000, pp.12–19) describe how the Hampton (Virginia) Police Department uses staged exercises to test the emergency response to acts of school violence: "The drills gauged the response capabilities of all the department's systems and units." They also illustrated the department's ability to work with fire departments and other police departments, SWAT teams, hostage negotiators, role players, emergency fire and medical personnel and school personnel.

The Benton County (Indiana) Sheriff's Department uses multijurisdictional mock school shootings as part of its crisis planning and practice. As Rosenbarger (2001, p.31) explains, the drill involves tactical teams from four different sheriff's departments, patrol officers from more than a dozen police and sheriff's departments, negotiators from the state police, EMS from three locations, emergency management, paramedics and a moulage team from the regional medical center, electronic and print media from three counties and a MedEvac helicopter. According to Rosenbarger: "The drill also involved school administrators, including the superintendent and several principals; school support staff; school teachers; concerned parents; and lots of junior and senior high students. In all, over 100 people participated in the drill."

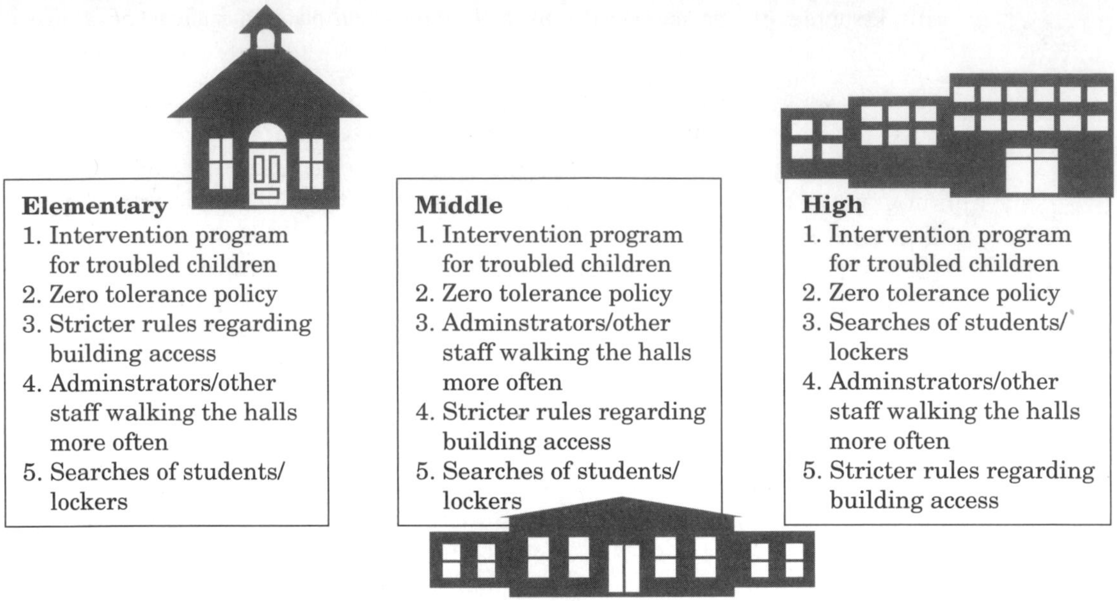
Elementary
1. Intervention program for troubled children
2. Zero tolerance policy
3. Stricter rules regarding building access
4. Adminstrators/other staff walking the halls more often
5. Searches of students/ lockers
Middle
1. Intervention program for troubled children
2. Zero tolerance policy
3. Adminstrators/other staff walking the halls more often
4. Stricter rules regarding building access
5. Searches of students/ lockers
High
1. Intervention program for troubled children
2. Zero tolerance policy
3. Searches of students/ lockers
4. Adminstrators/other staff walking the halls more often
5. Stricter rules regarding building access

Figure 12.4 Top Security Strategies by Type of School

SOURCE: *School Security Roundtable* Supplement to *Access Control & Security Systems Integration,* October 2000, p.SS12. Reprinted by permission.

Figure 12.4 presents the top security strategies by type of school. Whichever combination of strategies is selected to promote safe schools and communities, Figure 12.4 shows that early intervention with at-risk children and youths is important.

Early Intervention

Pederson (2000, p.66) notes: "Changing the paths of at-risk youth requires early intervention." This is reinforced by the statement of the Bipartisan Working Group on Youth Violence ("Youth Violence Task Force . . .," p.4): "Despite the range of issues, there were several recurring themes that spanned the breadth of the discussion. The first theme is that prevention and early intervention programs are essential to reducing youth violence."

The top security strategy for elementary, middle and high school in 2000 was intervention programs for troubled children (*School Security Roundtable,* p.SS12).

One such program is the Huntington Park, California, J.A.R. (Juveniles at Risk) Program, which combines the concepts of juvenile referral, parenting, "Scared Straight" approach, community services, counseling and schools (Luna et al., 2000). Targeted are at-risk youths: gang members, taggers, habitual truants and recalcitrant juveniles. Arrested juveniles are referred to the program, which includes mandatory completion of a number of community service hours. Mandatory participation of the family includes mothers, fathers and siblings. The program has six components:

- Pre-Intake—each juvenile and his or her parent(s) reports to the police department for an interview with the project coordinator.

- Intake Night—guest speakers graphically describe the harsh realities of confinement in the county and state prisons. The cadre of police officers is introduced and their roles explained.
- Day "Zero" Saturday—each youth is inspected, given a uniform and searched for weapons and contraband.
- Bootcamp—(weeks 1–5) emphasizes self-discipline, respect, integrity, leadership and teamwork. The majority of participants are strong willed and energetic. Staff tries to redirect this energy toward becoming productive and responsible individuals.
- Weeks 6–16—training focuses on education. Military recruiters speak to participants. Participants also participate in graffiti removal, trash cleanup and other community involvement projects.
- Graduation Day—a new direction and chance at success characterizes graduation day.

The 8% Problem/Solution

Schumacher and Kurz (2000) studied juvenile offenders in Orange County, California. They found—the good news—that 70 percent of juveniles referred to juvenile court never returned. Another 22 percent came back only once or twice within three years. However, a small group—8 percent—appeared four or more times within three years and committed more than half of all repeat juvenile crimes. They were incarcerated an average of 20 months over the three years at a cost of $44,000 per offender.

As the researchers examined their data to identify the 8 percent of chronic offenders, the factor that stood out almost immediately was age—57 percent were 15 or younger when they were first adjudicated. They also found these youths were four times as likely to become chronic offenders as youths first adjudicated at age 16 or above.

The **8% problem** refers to the fact that 8 percent of youthful offenders commit more than half of all repeat offenses and over half of them are under 15 years of age when they first offend.

Schumacher and Kurz stressed: "There will never be enough money, people or programs to solve all the problems faced by each youth in our society. In the fight against juvenile crime, we must focus our efforts on the group with the greatest potential to burden and victimize society and the ones most likely to fail in life. This group cries out for our attention."

Mendel (2001, pp.30–31) describes the core elements of the 8 percent solution devised by Orange County:

- All-day academic and youth development programming
- Family involvement and counseling
- Focus on substance abuse

Mendel (p.31) reports: "Initial results from this evaluation indicate that the program is significantly reducing the offending behavior of extreme-risk youths."

Problem-Solving Partnership in Action: School Impact Project—Dorchester High School by the Boston Police Department

Jordan and Gunaratne (2002, pp.4–7) describe the problem-solving partnership in Dorchester High School. (Abridged and reprinted by permission.)

> The Boston Police Department, led by supervisors and officers in the department's Schools Unit, collaborated with faculty, teachers, students and other stakeholders to develop a systematic approach to restore order and safety in the city's most troubled schools.

Scanning

The scan showed the incidents to be typically gang- and drug-related, with students being stabbed and shot at, in and out of school. School Safety Police Officers, a non-BPD patrol force hired by Boston Public Schools, were also being seriously attacked. The violent incidents led to calls by community leaders to shut down Dorchester High. The level of fear among the students was extremely high, exacerbated by the breakdown in basic order.

Analysis

An Intervention Team was convened whose members were identified by Boston Police and School Administrators as being the primary stakeholders in the school. This team, in additon to the school administration, consisted of representatives from the Boston Public School Police Unit, BPS School Safety officers, Boston Municipal Police and MBTA Police; Dorchester High School Faculty; probation officers; Department of Youth Services; Boston Street Workers Program; local faith-based organization members; Suffolk County District Attorney's Office; and Youth Service Providers Network (Boston police social workers).

The Intervention Team began by analyzing the incidents and underlying problems at the school. The results were 38 recovered weapons, 28 false fire alarms, 13 robberies and 25 assault and battery.

A major problem identified by the Intervention Team was a total lack of adherence to school rules. The Intervention Team found that Dorchester High had a strict code of conduct that had been completely disregarded over the previous few years. The Team then decided that the project would ultimately aim to restore the rules of the school and enforce the entire code of conduct, and thereby regain control to maintain a safe environment for learning. The appearance of the school and the tardiness of students also had to be turned around to show a respect for the school and its rules.

As far as academic achievement was concerned, Dorchester High was faring poorly. Only 1 percent of 11th graders at Dorchester High were found to be proficient on citywide grade level math tests.

Response

To create a safe environment, police presence was increased to ensure safety of students and staff. Metal detectors were also installed. A Boston Police K-9 unit conducted random certified sweeps of the school for drugs. School administrators also conducted random locker searches. A dress code was also instituted, disallowing the wearing of certain colors perceived to be gang-affiliated.

Immediate consequences included identification of problem students and their immediate expulsion. Suffolk County District Attorney's Office established a School Violence Prosecutor as well as a Juvenile Rapid Indictment Prosecutor to ensure fast track prosecution for students who engaged in violence. In addition, Dorchester Court Probation assigned several probation officers to the initiative.

Prevention activity included outreach and service provision to students at school. A clergy group, Boston Ten Point Coalition, instituted afterschool programs for at-risk youths. The Boston Police program, Youth Service Providers Network, a network of social workers in police districts, assigned a full-time supervisory-level social worker to partner with the Headmaster in providing service referrals and counseling.

The Boston Streetworkers program worked with at-risk youths on the streets and coordinated with the various agencies that had committed resources to the school. Home visits were also provided as well as building maintenance. "Along the lines of George Kelling's 'Broken Windows' Theory, the buildings were cleaned."

Assessment

The results of the initiative became apparent very soon after the intervention strategies were put in place. Over the following weeks the school saw dramatic results. The total number of incidents at the school dropped from 104 four months prior to implementation to just 14 incidents four months after the initiative—an 86.5 percent decrease in incidents.

Interview-style discussions with students and teachers overwhelming showed a reduction of fear. They reported feeling safer and their levels of fear decreased significantly. Students also felt better about being at school.

The other significant measure of success was the relationship established between the schools and Boston Police. Prior to this intervention, there was a reluctance on the part of the schools to utilize official police intervention. With the current existing relationship, any violence that occurs will draw immediate and coordinated responses, not only from police but also from community organizations. The Boston Police, from its past successes can bring to the table myriad partners, both from the community and other law enforcement agencies who are instrumental to successful intervention.

The overall success of the initiative can be summed up through a statement by the Superintendent of Schools: "Safety is no longer a concern at Dorchester High."

SUMMARY

Children and teenagers are an important segment of the community often overlooked when implementing the community policing philosophy. To counteract negative perceptions of police held by children and youths, many departments have programs aimed at fostering positive relations with them. The youth development strategy suggests that communities first explore what they want for young people, rather than what behaviors they would like to prevent among youths. More important, it involves young people in rebuilding communities.

The developmental asset approach promotes (1) support, (2) empowerment, (3) boundaries and expectations, (4) constructive use of time, (5) commitment to learning, (6) positive values, (7) social competence and (8) positive identity to help youngsters succeed in school and in life. Youth-Focused Community Policing is a U.S. Department of Justice initiative instrumental in establishing law enforcement partnerships to focus on prevention, intervention and enforcement.

The family is viewed by many as the cornerstone of the community and should be included in community policing efforts focused on youths. Likewise, a school should be viewed as a community, not as an institution. Research suggests that students' academic motivation, commitment to democratic values and resistance to problem behaviors all depend on their experience of the school as a community. At a minimum, schools need to link with parents and with local law enforcement departments to teach students about the dangers of crime.

The school safety pyramid rests on the community and has as its components school resource officers, law-related education, conflict management and peer mediation, SAVE (Students Against Violence in Education), teen/student court, and physical design and technology. A precursor to school violence is bullying. Bullying is more accurately termed *peer child abuse.* "We've passed bullying off as a rite of passage and created schools where violence works." The "tell or tattle" dilemma occurs when a student hesitates to tell anyone that he or she is being bullied because it is seen as tattling—something they have been taught not to do.

Threats may be classified as direct, indirect, veiled and conditional. The FBI's four-prong assessment evaluates four major areas making up the "totality of the circumstances": (1) personality of the student, (2) family dynamics, (3) school dynamics and the student's role in those dynamics and (4) social dynamics. A threat against school safety that has gained national attention is school shootings.

Two highly successful programs to build safe schools are Student Crime Stoppers and PeaceBuilders.® In addition, a seven-pronged approach is needed for effective school security: (1) school/law enforcement/community partnerships, (2) education about violence, (3) problem-solving training, (4) mediation and anger-management training, (5) clear policies on accepted behavior with consequences for noncomformity, (6) security procedures and technology and (7) crisis planning.

One of the most popular strategies to promote safe schools is a zero tolerance policy against violence, guns and drugs in school. However, virtually no data suggest that zero tolerance policies reduce school violence. Such policies result in sometimes unreasonable suspensions and expulsions. The three "Ps" for dealing with violence are prevention, planning and practice.

The top security strategy for elementary, middle and high schools in 2000 was intervention programs for troubled children. The 8% problem refers to the fact that 8 percent of youthful offenders commit more than half of all repeat offenses and over half of them are under 15 years of age when they first offend.

Discussion Questions

1. Which of the programs for youths do you feel are the most effective?
2. Why do school administrators not consider drugs a security or crime problem?
3. What major differences in philosophy often exist between school administrators and police?
4. On which age group do you think police–school programs should focus? Why?
5. Was violence a problem in the high school you attended? If yes, what was the major problem?
6. What are the advantages and disadvantages of expelling disruptive students from school?
7. Is zero tolerance for violence, drugs and weapons in school a workable policy? Why or why not?
8. How did you feel about the police when you were a child? Did that attitude change as you grew older? Why or why not and, if so, how?
9. Is bullying a serious problem? Did bullying occur in your school?
10. What risk factors for delinquent behavior do you think are most important?

InfoTrac College Edition Assignments

- Use InfoTrac College Edition to help answer the Discussion Questions as appropriate.
- Research either bullying or school violence. Outline your findings and be prepared to share them with the class.
- Read and outline "Scholastic Crime Stoppers: A Cost-Benefit Perspective" by Giant Abutalebi Aryani, Carl L. Sabrook and Terry D. Garrett.

Community Project

- What programs for youths are available in your community? Your school system?

References

Adams, Carey. "Community Involvement: A Partnership between Schools and the Community." *School Security Roundtable Supplement,* October 2000, p.SS21.

Argon, Joe and Anderson, Larry. "School Security by the Numbers." *School Security 2000: A Special Supplement to Access Control & Security Systems Integration,* May 2000, pp.C-6 to C-12.

Aryani, Giant Abutalebi; Sabrook, Carl L.; and Garrett, Terry D. "Scholastic Crime Stoppers: A Cost-Benefit Perspective." *FBI Law Enforcement Bulletin,* September 2001, pp.1–8.

Atkinson, Anne J. *Fostering School-Law Enforcement Partnerships.* Naperville, IL: Northwest Regional Educational Laboratory, September 2002.

Bilchik, Shay. "Collaboration among Federal Agencies Equals School Safety." *Corrections Today,* February 2000, pp.56–58.

Bridges, Dennis. "Safeguarding Our Schools." *FBI Law Enforcement Bulletin,* September 2000, pp.22–25.

Cooper, Doug and Snell, Jennie. "Bullying—Not Just a Kid Thing." *Educational Leadership,* March 2003, pp.22–25.

"Cops Fight Crime by Investing in Kids." *Law Enforcement News,* September 15, 2000, p.10.

Cops in Schools: The COPS Commitment to School Safety. COPS Fact Sheet. Washington, DC: Office of Community Oriented Policing Services, April 8, 2003.

DeVoe, Jill F.; Ruddy, Sally A.; Miller, Amanda K.; Planty, Mike; Peter, Katharin; Kaufman, Phillip; Snyder, Thomas D.; Duhart, Detis T.; and Rand, Michael R. *Indicators of School Crime and Safety: 2002.* Washington, DC: U.S. Department of Justice, November 2002. (NCJ 196753) Online: www.ojp.usdoj.gov/bjs/

Dorn, Michael. "Preventing School Weapons Assaults: The Nuts and Bolts of Stopping the Violence before it Happens." *Police,* May 2001, pp.30–35.

Early Warning, Timely Response: A Guide to Safe Schools. Washington, DC: U.S. Department of Education, April 1998.

Ericson, Nels. *Addressing the Problem of Juvenile Bullying.* Washington, DC: OJJDP Fact Sheet #27, June 2001. (FS 200127)

"The Five Promises Checklist: Helping Communities Help Youths." *OJJDP News @ a Glance,* September/October 2003, p.5. Web site www.americaspromise.org

Garbarino, James and deLara, Ellen. "Words Can Hurt Forever." *Educational Leadership,* March 2003, pp.18–21.

Gersh, David. "Asset Approach Helps Children Succeed." *School Security Roundup Supplement,* October 2000, p.SS15.

Grassie, Richard P. "Indulging Contemporary Risks: Road Rage and School Violence." *Security Technology & Design,* January 2000, pp.88–90.

Guide for Preventing and Responding to School Violence. www.theiacp.org

Guy, Joe D. "Lock Down." *Community Links,* September 2001, pp.7–9.

Hall, Dennis. "School Safety Panel Message: Hike the Profile of Officers." *Police,* January 2000, p.6.

Hamit, Francis. "The Problem with Kids Today." *Security Technology & Design,* April 2000, pp.89–90.

Harberts, Helen. "School Team Watches for Signs of Trouble, Steps in to Prevent Problems." *Community Policing Exchange,* September/October 2000, p.6.

Hoang, Francis Q. "Preplanning for School Violence." *Law and Order,* December 2000, pp.107–109.

Holloway, John H. "The Dilemma of Zero Tolerance." *Educational Leadership,* December/January 2002, pp.84–85.

Hyman, Irwin A. and Snook, Pamela A. "Dangerous Schools and What You Can Do about Them." *Phi Delta Kappan,* March 2000, pp.489–501.

Jones-Brown, Delores D. "Debunking the Myth of Officer Friendly." *Journal of Contemporary Criminal Justice,* May 2000, pp.209–229.

Jordan, Jim and Gunaratne, Hemali. "School Impact Project 2000—Dorchester High School by the Boston Police Department." *Problem Solving Quarterly,* Spring 2002, pp.4–7.

Justice Based After-School Program. COPS Fact Sheet. Washington, DC: Office of Community Oriented Policing Services, October 2002.

Kanable, Rebecca. "Neighbors Take Watch for the Children." *Law Enforcement Technology,* October 2000, pp.100–104.

Lavarello, Curtis. "School Based Policing: Specialized Training Will Ease Liability." *The Law Enforcement Trainer,* November/December 2000, pp.6–8.

Luna, Antonio; Hernandez, George; Winn, Rae; and Etienne, Stephen. "Juveniles at Risk Program." *Law and Order,* July 2000, pp.93–96.

Makholm, John A. "'Do the Right Thing: A Prescription for the Future.'" *Police,* December 2000, pp.30–32.

Mattson, Sean A. "Phoenix Police's 'Wake Up!' Program Proves Effective Crime Prevention Tool." *The Police Chief,* November 2000, pp.78–80.

McCollum, Daniel. "Adopt-a-Cop Program: An Opportunity to Interact with Schools." *Law and Order,* July 2000, p.130.

Mendel, Richard D. *Less Hype, More Help: Reducing Juvenile Crime, What Works—and What Doesn't.* Washington, DC: American Youth Policy Forum, 2000.

Mendel, Richard D. *Less Cost, More Safety: Guiding Lights for Reform in Juvenile Justice,* Washington, DC: American Youth Policy Forum, 2001.

Miller, Beth M. *Critical Hours: After-School Programs and Educational Success.* Nellie Mae Education Foundation. www.nmefdn.org/CriticalHours.htm

Minetti, P.G. and Caplan, Kelli. "School Mock Disaster Exercises." *The Police Chief,* April 2000, pp.12–19.

Nettles, William. "Partnership Explores School Safety Technology." *The Police Chief,* May 2001, pp.14–26.

Olweus, Dan. "A Profile of Bullying at School." *Educational Leadership,* March 2003, pp.12–17.

O'Toole, Mary Ellen. *The School Shooter: A Threat Assessment Perspective.* Washington, DC: Federal Bureau of Investigation, 2000. www.fbi.gov

Paynter, Ronnie L. "Back-to-School Security." *Law Enforcement Technology,* September 2000, pp.72–79.

Pederson, Dorothy. "Big Crimes, Little Culprits." *Law Enforcement Technology,* October 2000, pp.66–78.

Perkins-Gough, Deborah. "Do After-School Programs Help Students Succeed?" *Educational Leadership,* September 2003, p.88.

Piazza, Peter. "Scourge of the Schoolyard." *Security Management,* November 2001, pp.68–73.

Pollack, Ira and Sundermann, Carlos. "Creating Safe Schools: A Comprehensive Approach." *Juvenile Justice,* June 2001, pp.13–20.

"Protecting Kids from the Internet and More." *Law Enforcement News,* October 15, 2000, p.7.

Rich, Tom; Finn, Peter; and Ward, Shawn. *Guide to Using School COP to Address Student Discipline and Crime Problems.* Washington, DC: Office of Community Oriented Policing Services, July 8, 2003.

Rosenbarger, Matt. "Multi-Jurisdictional Mock School Shooting." *Law and Order,* December 2001, pp.30–36.

Sampson, Rana. *Bullying in Schools.* Washington, DC: Office of Community Oriented Policing Services, Problem-Oriented Guides for Police Series No. 12, March 22, 2002.

Sanchez, Tom. "Hi-Tech Crisis Plans: Tools for School Safety." *The Police Chief,* April 2003, pp.18–20.

Schmitt, Sheila. "Unlocking the Lockdown Mentality: Officers Teach Alternatives in School-Shooting Situations." *Law and Order,* June 2000, pp.139–144.

School Security Roundtable 2000. Special Supplement to *Access Control & Security Systems Integration,* October 2000.

"Schoolroom Torment." *People,* February 5, 2001, pp.91–92.

Schuiteman, John G. "Early Returns Positive for Virginia's Model SRO Program." *The Police Chief,* November 2000, pp.74–77.

Schumacher, M. and Kurz, G. A. *The 8% Solution: Preventing Serious, Repeat Juvenile Crime.* Thousand Oaks, CA: Sage Publications, 2000.

Secure Our Schools Initiative. COPS Fact Sheet. Washington, DC: Office of Community Oriented Policing, April 24, 2003.

Smith-LaBombard. "Bullies Find No Refuge in Oak Harbor." *Community Links,* September 2001, pp.2–10.

Soto, Ileana. "An Alliance Based on Interface and Interdependence." *Community Policing Exchange,* September/October 2000, p.8.

Trump, Kenneth S. *School-Related Deaths, School Shootings and School Violence Incidents, 2002–2003 School Year.* Cleveland, OH: National School Safety and Security Services, no date.

Wattendorf, George E. "School Threat Decisions Demonstrate Support for Early Action." *The Police Chief,* March 2002, pp.11–12.

Welsh, Wayne N.; Stokes, Robert; and Greene, Jack R. "A Macro-Level Model of School Disorder." *Journal of Research in Crime and Delinquency,* August 2000, pp.53–83.

Wessler, Stephen L. "It's Hard to Learn When You're Scared." *Educational Leadership,* September, 2003, pp.40–43.

When Schools Stay Open Late: The National Evaluation of the 21st Century Community Learning Centers Program, Washington, DC: U.S. Department of Education. www.ed.gov/pubs/21cent/firstyear

Williams, Brian N. "Perceptions of Children and Teenagers on Community Policing: Implications for Law Enforcement Leadership, Training, and Citizen Evaluations." *Police Quarterly,* June 1999, pp.150–173.

Woods, Jacqueline. "Hostile Hallways." *Educational Leadership,* December 2001/January 2002, pp.20–23.

The Young Rampage Killers, CourtTV.com. www.crimelibrary.com/serial_killers/weird/kids1/killer_6html?sect=19

"Youth Violence Task Force Says Early Intervention Is Key." *Criminal Justice Newsletter,* March 2000, pp.4–5.

CHAPTER 13

The Challenge of Gangs: Controlling Their Destructive Force

Gangs are the master predators of the urban landscape. Their ability to instill fear into the people of a community knows no bounds. They will kill indiscriminately to make their point. This fear percolates through the community.

—Wesley D. McBride

Do You Know?

- How prevalent gangs are?
- What needs are served by gangs?
- What implications for preventing youths from joining gangs are suggested by the Seattle study?
- What the GREAT program is? The GRIP program?
- What indicators of gang activity are?
- What indicators of gang membership are?
- What strategies have been used to address the gang problem? Which has been found to be most effective?
- What OJJDP initiatives are available to help communities address a gang problem?
- What National Youth Gang Center publications are available to help communities address a gang problem?
- What strategies are currently being used to address the gang problem?
- What additional strategies the National Crime Prevention Council recommends?
- Why a community might be ambivalent toward gangs?

Can You Define?

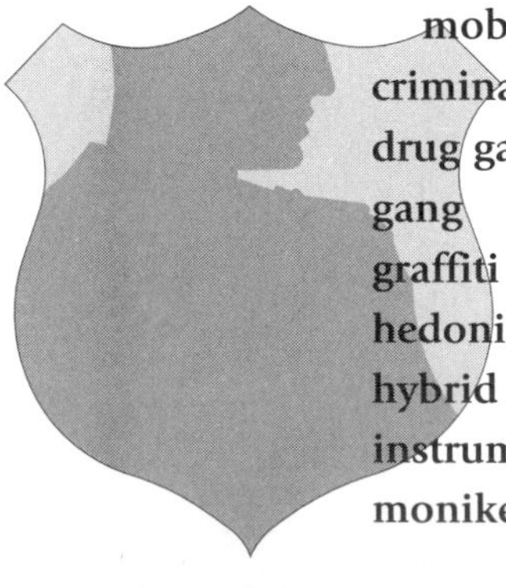

community mobilization
criminal gang
drug gang
gang
graffiti
hedonistic/social gang
hybrid gang
instrumental gang
moniker
organizational development (change)
organized/corporate gang
party gang
predatory gang
pulling levers
representing
scavenger gang
serious delinquent gang
social intervention
social opportunities
street gang
suppression
territorial gang
turf
youth gang

Introduction

In testimony before a Senate committee in October 2003 McBride, president of the California Gang Investigators Association, urged that the United States focus on reducing gang violence because Los Angeles County gangs, numbering more than 1,100 with a membership of nearly 100,000, have spread across the country: "These gangs began migrating across this country in the mid-1980s and have established their presence in nearly every state of the union. They freely cross state lines transporting firearms and narcotics, but possibly what may be even more important is that they bring their street-gang mentality with them, a mentality that depends on inane gang violence to establish their rule. The most important weapon in the gang's arsenal is fear. . . . After a time, physical threats are not needed; the threat is unspoken but part of the community culture" ("California Law Enforcement . . .," 2003, p.5).

The importance of the community in approaching the gang problem is stressed by Howell (2000, p.5): "Police should not be expected to assume sole responsibility for youth gang problems. Broad-based community collaboration is essential for long term success."

Three teens paint over a graffiti-covered wall as part of a neighborhood cleanup project. Such efforts show the neighborhood cares about its appearance and safety.

This chapter begins with a discussion of understanding gangs and gang members, including definitions of gangs, the types of gangs that exist, the demographics of gangs, their subculture and activities. Next is a look at why youths join gangs and how this might be prevented. This is followed by a discussion of recognizing the presence of gangs and identifying gang members. Then the typical police response is described followed by specific strategies to engage the community in addressing the problem. The chapter ends with examples of alternatives to gangs and other problem-solving partnerships in action.

Understanding Gangs and Gang Members

Valdez (2000a, p.32) stresses: "Understanding the culture of street gangs has become essential for most of us in the criminal justice profession. Street gangs and the associated crime has impacted the police, the courts, corrections and most importantly the quality of life for many Americans. The violence that accompanies some gang crime has cost Americans millions of dollars. The reality of the impact can be seen today because the presence of street gangs has been reported in all 50 states."

An estimated 850,000 gang members are active in nearly 31,000 gangs nationwide.

Gangs have spread through our country like a plague and now exist in every community—rural, suburban and inner city—in every metropolitan area. Some analogize the gang problem to a societal cancer, where street gangs prey upon the community like a malignant growth, eating away at its host until only a wasted shell remains. They use harassment, intimidation, extortion and fear to control their territory. Daily, countless news stories depict the tragedy of gang violence. The following document only the tip of the problem.

- A gang fight at a crowded park results in a seven-year-old girl being shot in the head while picnicking with her family.
- Shotgun blasts from a passing car, intended for a rival gang member, strike a child.
- A shoot-out between rival gangs kills a high school athlete as he jogged around the school track.

Egley and Major (2003, p.1) state: "All cities with a population of 250,000 or more reported gang activity in 2001, as did 85 percent of cities with a population between 100,000 and 249,900; 65 percent of cities with a population between 50,000 and 99,999; 44 percent of cities with a population between 25,000 and 49,999; and 20 percent of cities with a population between 2,500 and 24,999." Based on results of the 2001 National Youth Gang Survey, nearly 3,000 jurisdictions across the United States experienced gang activity in 2001. Of cities with a population of 25,000 or more, 42 percent reported an increase in the number of gang members and 45 percent reported an increase in the number of gangs. Of cities with a population of 100,000 or more, 56 percent reported either an increase or no significant change in the number of gang members. More than two-thirds (69 percent) of the jurisdictions reported that gang members returning from confinement considerably affected their jurisdictions' gang problem in 2001. A large proportion of these jurisdictions reported that returning members noticeably contributed to an increase in violent crime (63 percent of respondents) and drug trafficking (68 percent) by local gangs.

Survey recipients were asked to report information only for youth gangs, defined as "a group of youths or young adults in your jurisdiction that you or other responsible persons in your agency or community are willing to identify or classify as a 'gang.'" How gangs are defined significantly influences how great a gang problem a given community is facing.

Gangs Defined

Gangs have been defined as "any ongoing organization, association, or group of three or more persons, whether formal or informal, having as one of its primary activities the commission of one or more of the criminal acts . . ., which has a common name or common identifying sign or symbol, whose members individually or collectively engage in or have engaged in a pattern of criminal gang activity" (California Penal Code Section 186.22[f]). A **gang** is an organized group of people existing for some time with a special interest in using violence to achieve status. Gangs are identified by a name, **turf** (territory) concerns, symbols, special dress and colors. A gang is recognized by both its own members and by others.

A **street gang** is a group of people whose allegiance is based on social needs and who engage in acts injurious to the public. Members of street gangs engage in an organized, continuous course of criminality, either individually or collectively, creating an atmosphere of fear and intimidation in a community. Most local law enforcement agencies prefer the term *street gang* because it includes juveniles and adults and designates the location of the gang and most of its criminal behavior. For criminal justice policy purposes, a **youth gang** is a subgroup of a street gang. It may refer to a juvenile clique within a gang.

Esbensen et al. (2001a, p.105) discuss the varying definitions of what constitutes a gang, ranging from the least restrictive definition, which includes all youths who claim gang membership at some time, to the most restrictive definition, which includes only those youths who are current core gang members and who indicate that their gang has some degree of organizational structure and is involved in illegal activities. Esbensen et al. suggest that the definition used "greatly affects the perceived magnitude of the gang problem" (p.124).

Langston (2003, p.7) stresses: "A key issue in combating youth gangs is providing a uniform definition for them, distinguishing them from troublesome youth groups and adult criminal organizations." He reports: "A review of published books, articles and law enforcement policies revealed that no uniform definition used openly articulates what constitutes a gang-involved crime. Rather, considerable differences existed in what the law enforcement profession considers as gang-related or gang-motivated crime. Such variations in definitions and reporting characteristics can lead to inaccurate and unreliable gang-related crime statistics, which, in turn, can distort any national estimate of the gang problem and the extent of gang-related crime."

Langston (p.7) stresses: "The definition problem is not trivial. How to define a youth gang is one of the most contentious issues in the field of youth crime.

Policymakers, law enforcement personnel, social service agencies, researchers and other groups have not been able to reach consensus on this issue over the past 25 years, and current efforts to reach this goal have thus far met with only limited success. There is little disagreement among those who study or deal with gangs that the availability and widespread use of a uniform definition would be extremely useful for a variety of important purposes, but few are willing to relinquish and replace the definitions that have become established within their agencies and are intimately related to agency operations. Herein lies the issue that can lead to vagueness, conflict and denial, without a uniform gang-involved crime definition."

Langston (pp.8–9) suggests that law enforcement use the term *criminal gang* and offers the following definition: "**Criminal gang**: A group of people following a common code of conduct, having common beliefs and identifiers, existing in a semi-structured organization or hierarchy and attempting to accomplish their goals through criminal activity."

Types of Gangs

Although gangs are often classified by racial or ethnic composition, it is usually more helpful to classify them by their behavior. Shelden et al. (2001, pp.37–38) report that various studies by different researchers nationwide have identified several major types of gangs:

- **Hedonistic/social gang**—only moderate drug use and offending; involved mainly in using drugs and having a good time; little involvement in crime, especially violent crime
- **Party gang**—commonly called "party crew"; relatively high use and sale of drugs, but only one major form of delinquency—vandalism; may contain both genders or may be one gender; many have no specific dress style, but some dress in stylized clothing worn by street gang members, such as baseball caps and oversize clothing; some have tattoos and use hand signs; their flexible turf is called the "party scene"; crews compete over who throws the biggest party, with alcohol, marijuana, nitrous oxide, sex and music critical party elements
- **Instrumental gang**—main criminal activity is property crimes (most use drugs and alcohol but seldom sell drugs)
- **Predatory gang**—heavily involved in serious crimes (e.g., robberies and muggings) and the abuse of addictive drugs such as crack cocaine; may engage in selling drugs but not in organized fashion
- **Scavenger gang**—loosely organized group described as "urban survivors"; prey on the weak in inner cities; engage in rather petty crimes but sometimes violence, often just for fun; members have no greater bond than their impulsiveness and the need to belong; have no goals and are low achievers; often illiterate, with poor school performance
- **Serious delinquent gang**—heavy involvement in both serious and minor crimes, but much lower involvement in drug use and drug sales than party gangs
- **Territorial gang**—associated with a specific area or turf and, as a result, get involved in conflicts with other gangs over their respective turfs

- **Organized/corporate gang**—heavy involvement in all kinds of crime; heavy use and sale of drugs; may resemble major corporations, with separate divisions handling sales, marketing, discipline, and so on; discipline is strict, and promotion is based on merit
- **Drug gang**—smaller than other gangs; much more cohesive; focused on the drug business; strong, centralized leadership, with market-defined roles

The preceding types of gangs other than drug gangs might also be classified as street gangs. Table 13.1 illustrates the major differences between street gangs and drug gangs.

As Shelden et al. (p.157) point out: "Girls' involvement in gangs has never been as frequent as that of their male counterparts. When they have been involved, it has usually been as so-called auxiliaries to male gangs." Females are used by gangs in a variety of ways, often because they arouse less suspicion than male adults. Females may serve as lookouts for crimes in progress, conceal stolen property or tools used to commit crimes, carry weapons for males who do not want to be caught with them, carry information in and out of prison, and provide sexual favors (they are often drug dependent and physically abused).

Shelden et al. report: "There is a general consensus in the research literature that girls become involved in gang life for generally the same reasons as their male counterparts—namely, to meet basic human needs, such as belonging, self-esteem, protection, and a feeling of being a member of a family. The backgrounds of these young women are about the same as those of male gang members—poverty, single-parent families, minority status and so on."

They also note: "The case studies of girl gang members in many different parts of the country reveal the common circumstances in their lives. The crimes that they

Table 13.1 Common Differences between Street Gangs and Drug Gangs

Characteristic	***Street Gangs***	***Drug Gangs***
Crime focus	Versatile ("cafeteria-style")	Drug business exclusively
Structure	Larger organizations	Smaller organizations
Level of cohesion	Less cohesive	More cohesive
Leadership	Looser	More centralized
Roles	Ill-defined	Market-defined
Nature of loyalty	Code of loyalty	Requirement of loyalty
Territories	Residential	Sales market
Degree of drug selling	Members may sell	Members do sell
Rivalries	Intergang	Competition controlled
Age of members	Younger on average, but wider age range	Older on average, but narrower age range

SOURCE: From *The American Street Gang* by Malcolm Klein © 1995 by Oxford University Press, Inc. Used by permission of Oxford University Press, Inc.

commit are for the most part attempts to survive in an environment that has never given them much of a chance in life. Most face the hardships that correspond to three major barriers: being a member of the underclass, being a woman and being a minority. The gang, while not a total solution, seems to them a reasonable solution to their collective problems."

Gangs use children to commit shoplifting, burglaries, armed robberies and drug sales in schools. Their youthful appearance is an advantage because they often do not arouse suspicion. Furthermore, if they're caught, the juvenile justice system deals more leniently with them than with adults.

Demographics—Profile of Gang Members

The typical age range of gang members is 12 to 24, with an average age of about 17 or 18. Although younger members are becoming more common, it is the older membership that has increased the most. Gangs are overwhelmingly male organizations; the male–female ratio is approximately 9 to 1. However, the proportion of female gang members, while small, may be increasing.

The ethnic/racial makeup of gangs has also changed over the past few decades from predominantly white gangs to the majority of gangs now being African American, Hispanic and Asian. Some Native American gangs also exist in certain parts of the country. The racial makeup of gangs seems to correlate with the racial makeup of our society at or near the poverty level. A typical gang member is usually poor, a school dropout, unemployed and in trouble with the police.

Howell et al. (2002, p.1) note that modern-day youth gangs have proliferated in less traditional areas—smaller cities, towns, suburbs and even rural communities. They also report that gangs in jurisdictions with later onset of gang problems tend to have younger members and a larger proportion of white and black members than their counterparts in jurisdictions with earlier onset of gang problems. In addition: "Modern-day gangs are also less involved in violent crimes and drug trafficking than their predecessors."

Starbuck et al. (2001, p.1) also find differences between modern gangs and more traditional gangs and describe, in particular, the hybrid gang: "**Hybrid gang** culture is characterized by mixed racial and ethnic participation within a single gang, participation in multiple gangs by a single individual, vague rules and codes of conduct for gang members, use of symbols and colors from multiple—even rival—gangs, collaboration by rival gangs in criminal activities and the merger of smaller gangs into larger ones. Thus, hybrid gang customs are clearly distinguished from the practices of their predecessors." Starbuck et al. (p.6) note: "Although hybrid gangs are not new to the United States, they clearly have flourished in the past decade. . . . It is very important for law enforcement agencies to recognize the diverse gang culture of hybrid gangs, to approach them without any preconceived notions, and to concentrate on their gang-related criminal activity rather than on their presumed affiliations with traditional gangs. Every community—regardless of the presence or absence of hybrid gangs—should conduct a thorough assessment of its unique gang problem before devising strategies for combating it."

Howell (pp.49–50) describes some stereotypes that no longer fit modern youth gangs:

- The seemingly intractable connection of gangs, drugs and violence is not as strong among youth gangs as suggested by traditional stereotypes.
- It is not as difficult for adolescents to resist gang pressures as commonly believed.
- Gang members (especially marginal members) typically can leave the gang without serious consequences.
- At least in emerging gang areas, most adolescents do not remain in a gang for long periods of time, suggesting that members can be drawn away from gangs with attractive alternatives.
- Contemporary legends about gangs, especially initiation rites, are without scientific basis.
- Modern youth gangs are based less on territory than gangs of the past.
- Many members of modern adolescent gangs are "good kids" from respectable families with college-educated parents.
- White gang members are more prevalent than in the past.
- Females are more prevalent than previously reported.
- About one-third of all youth gangs have a significant mixture of racial and ethnic groups.

The Gang Subculture

A gang member's lifestyle is narrow and limited primarily to the gang and its activities. Members develop fierce loyalty to their respective gang and become locked into the gang's lifestyle, values, attitudes and behavior, making it very difficult for a member to later break away from a gang.

Shelden et al. (p.76) state: "An important part of the gang subculture . . . is the belief and value system . . . [which] includes honor, respect, pride (in oneself and in one's neighborhood), reputation, recognition, and self-esteem." They (p.77) identify friendship, manliness and hedonism as other important values, noting that among gang members: "A sense of wildness and locura (craziness) are often admired as ideal characteristics."

Gang members are commonly antisocial, aggressive and hostile, rebelling against society and getting support from the gang for feelings of anger and frustration: "Gangs offer a distillation of the dark side of adolescent rebellion. . . . Their revolt is total; it confronts and confounds adult authority on every level—sex, work, power, love, education, language, dress, music, drugs, alcohol, crime, violence" (Shelden et al., p.77).

A gang member may receive a new identity by taking on a nickname, or **moniker**, which others in the gang world would recognize. Monikers affirm a youth's commitment to gang life and may become their sole identity, the only way they see themselves and the only name they go by. They may no longer acknowledge their birth name, rejecting any previous identity or life outside the realm of the gang.

Gang Activities

Gangs have different characteristics based on the activities in which they engage. Some gangs are violent; others focus on crime commission with violence as a by-product. The same is true with a gang's relationship to drugs. Some focus on the drug business; others engage in business to meet their own drug needs.

Weisel (2002, p.35) conducted a national survey of police departments and found that specific gang types tended to favor certain types of crime: "Entrepreneurial gangs were reported to have the highest involvement in motor vehicle theft and theft in general, whereas violent gangs had the highest involvement in assault, intimidation, graffiti and vandalism. As expected, drug-dealing gangs were the most involved in selling crack, powder cocaine, marijuana and other drugs." Table 13.2 summarizes Weisel's findings regarding criminal activity.

Table 13.2 Criminal Activity, by Gang Type

Crime	*Percent of Police Who Report That Violent Gangs Commit the Offense Very Often or Often (n = 223)*	*Percent of Police Who Report That Drug-Dealing Gangs Commit the Offense Very Often or Often (n = 148)*	*Percent of Police Who Report That Entrepreneurial Gangs Commit the Offense Very Often or Often (n = 75)*
Motor vehicle theft	25	25	44
Arson	1	1	1
Assault	87	69	57
Burglary	36	25	37
Drive-by shooting	42	49	32
Crack sale	55	80	39
Powder cocaine sale	23	46	29
Marijuana sale	35	54	33
Other drug sale	17	26	25
Graffiti	67	50	38
Home invasion	10	11	27
Intimidation	81	72	74
Rape	7	4	8
Robbery	33	30	36
Shooting	37	41	38
Theft	49	37	52
Vandalism	57	38	37

NOTE: Reflects aggregation of police estimates of participation in criminal activity by a gang of that type in the jurisdiction.

SOURCE: Deborah Lamm Weisel. "The Evolution of Street Gangs: An Examination of Form and Variation." In *Responding to Gangs: Evaluation and Research*. Washington, DC: National Institute of Justice, July 2002, p.36. (NCJ 190351)

Why Youths Join Gangs

Domash (2001, p.49) explains: "Why children join gangs is a complicated combination of social, political, family, education and community factors." Experts writing in this area give strikingly similar reasons, but often with differing emphasis.

Gangs: A Community Response (2003) notes that vulnerable children seek love, protection and peer acceptance. If youths lack parental guidance and support or opportunities for positive involvement with their peers, they may turn to a gang to meet these needs. It notes: "The loyalties, love and dedication normally found in traditional nuclear families are transferred to the gang family. Members can develop intense bonds with other members and feel a need to protect them. Many times, problems at home act as a cohesive factor for gang members."

Gangs: A Community Response cites other reasons for joining a gang: excitement, physical protection, peer pressure, family tradition, perceived financial gain, an avenue to gain "respect," being wanted and valued by a group, being feared by others, getting girl friends, gaining notoriety or out of boredom.

Rowell (2000, p.35) presents a similar list of reasons: "Gangs grow because the gang provides kids with basic human needs. These include the need for security, love, friendship, acceptance, food, shelter, discipline, belonging, status, respect, identification, power and money."

Zatz and Portillos (2000, p.389) observe: "Historically, gangs have been important neighborhood institutions offering disenchanted, disadvantaged youth a means of coping with the isolation, alienation, and poverty they experience every day. . . . The youths identify strongly with their neighborhoods, consider themselves to be integral parts of their barrios, and view their gangs as neighborhood institutions. They see themselves as protectors of their neighborhoods, at least against intrusion by rival gangs."

They (p.396) further note how gangs were, and are, composed of brothers, sisters, cousins and neighbors, giving members a sense of community and a place where they belong: "Kicked out of school, assumed to be troublemakers, looking tough and feeling scared, these young people are well aware that their options in life are very much constrained by poverty, racial discrimination, cultural stereotyping, and inadequate education."

An estimated 80 percent of gang members are illiterate. Finding it almost impossible to get a job, they may turn to gangs as a way to earn a living through drug trafficking, illegal weapons sales, robbery and theft, and as a way to earn respect. As gang expert Valdez (2000b, p.55) cautions: "Today, most street gangs base 'respect' on fear. The more you fear me the more you respect me. The traditional rules of not involving innocent women and children in gang warfare are gone. For lack of a better way to say it, the 'gang ethic' has changed."

Youths seeking protection, security, status, an identity, a sense of belonging and economic security can fulfill all of these needs through gang membership.

Gangs often fulfill survival functions for youths in low-income, socially isolated ghetto or barrio communities and in transitional areas with newly settled populations.

Shelden et al.'s text on gangs devotes an entire chapter to inequality in American society and concludes: "Unemployment, poverty and general despair lead young people to seek out economic opportunities in the growing illegal marketplace, often done within the context of gangs" (p.191).

However, as Allender (2001, p.4) points out: "Not all street gangs exist to sell drugs or commit criminal acts. Instead, young people normally seek gang involvement for some combination of the following five reasons:

1. *Structure*. Youths want to organize their lives but lack the maturity to do so on their own. The gang provides rules to live by and a code of conduct.
2. *Nurturing*. Gang members frequently talk of how they love one another. This remains true even among the most hardened street gangs. These young people are trying to fill a void in their lives by substituting the gang for the traditional family.
3. *Sense of belonging*. Because humans require social interaction, some young people find that the gang fulfills the need to be accepted as an important part of a group.
4. *Economic opportunity*. Gang members motivated by this consideration alone probably would become involved in criminal activity anyway. Finding it hard to draw away from the lifestyle, but due to a lack of loyalty for the group, they often will provide authorities with information in exchange for some personal benefit.
5. *Excitement*. This often represents a motivation for suburban and affluent youths. Gangs composed of these types of individuals usually have very fluid membership, with associates joining and leaving to be replaced by others with a passing interest."

Knowing why youths join gangs is an important step in preventing them from doing so.

Preventing Gang Membership

Common sense suggests that preventing a gang problem in the first place is preferable to finding strategies to deal with such a problem after it surfaces. Research has identified risk factors associated with gang membership.

Early Precursors of Gang Membership

A study of Seattle youths, the Seattle Social Development Project (SSDP), identified childhood risk factors that predict whether a youth is likely to join a gang and the duration of the membership. Hill et al. (2001, p.3) report: "Youths join gangs as a result of antisocial influences in neighborhoods, antisocial tendencies in families and peers, failure to perform well in school and early initiation of individual problem behaviors. All of these factors distinguish youths who join gangs from those who do not. . . . Youths who were the most behaviorally and socially maladjusted in childhood were most likely to be gang members for several years." Table 13.3 summarizes the predictors of joining and remaining in a gang.

Table 13.3 Childhood Predictors of Joining and Remaining in a Gang, SSDP Sample

Risk Factor	Odds Ratio*
Neighborhood	
Availability of marijuana	3.6
Neighborhood youth in trouble	3.0
Low neighborhood attachment	1.5
Family	
Family structure†	
One parent only	2.4
One parent plus other adults	3.0
Parental attitudes favoring violence	2.3
Low bonding with parents	ns‡
Low household income	2.1
Sibling antisocial behavior	1.9
Poor family management	1.7
School	
Learning disabled	3.6
Low academic achievement	3.1
Low school attachment	2.0
Low commitment	1.8
Low academic aspirations	1.6
Peer group	
Association with friends who engage in problem behaviors§	2.0 (2.3)
Individual	
Low religious service attendance	ns‡
Early marijuana use	3.7
Early violence§	3.1 (2.4)
Antisocial beliefs	2.0
Early drinking	1.6
Externalizing behaviors§	2.6 (2.6)
Poor refusal skills	1.8

*Odds of joining a gang between the ages of 13 and 18 for youths who scored in the worst quartile on each factor at ages 10 to 12 (fifth and sixth grades), compared with all other youths in the sample. For example, the odds ratio for availability of marijuana is 3.6. This means that youths from neighborhoods where marijuana was most available were 3.6 times more likely to join a gang compared with other youths.

†Compared with two-parents households.

‡ns = not a significant predictor.

§These factors also distinguished sustained gang membership (i.e., more than 1 year) from transient membership (1 year or less). For each factor, the number in parentheses indicates the odds of being a sustained gang member (compared with the odds of being a transient member) for youths at risk on that factor.

SOURCE: Karl G. Hill, Christina Lui and J. David Hawkins. *Early Precursors of Gang Membership: A Study of Seattle Youths*. Washington, DC: OJJDP Justice Bulletin, December 2001, p.4.

Implications for Prevention

Findings from the SSDP study (p.4) have three implications for efforts to prevent youths from joining gangs.

Prevention efforts should (1) begin early, (2) target youths exposed to multiple risk factors and (3) address all facets of youths' lives (Seattle study).

Prevention Efforts Should Begin Early "Although the SSDP study found that the peak age for joining a gang was 15, this does not mean that prevention efforts should be aimed at 14-year-olds. The risk factors that predicted gang membership in this study were measured when the participants were ages 10 to 12 (fifth and sixth grades)—well before the peak age for joining a gang. Prevention efforts can target these risk factors during the late elementary grades."

Prevention Efforts Should Target Youths Exposed to Multiple Risk Factors The more risk factors present in a youth's environment, the higher his or her odds are of joining a gang. Compared with youths who experienced none or only 1 of the 21 risk factors, youths who experienced 7 or more were 13 times more likely to join a gang.

Prevention Efforts Should Address All Facets of Youths' Lives Efforts to prevent youths from becoming gang members must address the different aspects of their lives. No single solution or "magic bullet" will prevent youths from joining gangs. Hill et al. (p.4) suggest: "Although the thought of combating the 21 predictors of gang membership discussed here may seem daunting, anyone—a parent, brother, sister, teacher, friend, or member of the community—can find ways to reduce the chances that a youth will become a gang member. If these efforts are coordinated, the reduction of risk for gang membership will be even greater. . . . Prevention efforts should start early, focus on youths with multiple risk factors and take a comprehensive approach that addresses multiple influences."

According to Howell (p.54): "Preventing children and adolescents from joining gangs may be the most cost-effective solution, but little is known about how to do this. Providing alternatives for potential or current gang members appears to hold promise, particularly if gang conflicts are mediated at the same time. An anti-gang curriculum, especially if combined with after-school or anti-bullying programs, may be effective." One such program aimed at preventing gang membership is the Gang Resistance Education and Training (GREAT) program.

The GREAT Program

GREAT is a nationally used program with some proven success.

The Gang Resistance Education and Training (GREAT) program is aimed at stopping gang membership.

The GREAT program is a proactive approach to deter violence before it begins. The program builds a foundation focused on teaching children the life skills they need to avoid violence and gang membership. A study supported by the NIJ documented the benefits of the program in a cross-sectional evaluation. The study showed that students who graduated from the GREAT course showed lower levels of delinquency, impulsive behavior, risk-taking behavior and approval of violence. The study also found that students demonstrated higher levels of self-esteem, parental attachment, commitment to positive peers, antigang attitudes, perceived educational opportunities and positive school environments.

Esbensen et al. (2001b) conducted a study of several thousand students from six cities nationwide, comparing students who participated in the GREAT program with those who did not. They found that, over time, GREAT students showed more prosocial *attitudinal* changes than did non-GREAT students. However, they found no significant differences in *behavioral* outcomes of gang membership, delinquency or drug use. Based on these consistent but modest preventive effects, the researches conclude that law enforcement officers can be effective deliverers of prevention curricula in schools.

Another prevention program with some proven effectiveness is the Gang Resistance Is Paramount (GRIP) program.

The GRIP Program

The Gang Resistance Is Paramount (GRIP) program seeks to prevent youths from joining gangs through education.

The GRIP program was developed by the city of Paramount, California, after it recognized in the early 1980s that it had a severe gang problem and that its efforts to dismantle established gangs had little success. They decided the key to approaching their problem was prevention.

The program teaches second-, fifth-, and ninth-grade students about gangs and territory, gangs and vandalism, peer pressure, drugs, alcohol, gangs and family, self-esteem, gang violence, gangs and the police and alternatives to gang membership. A University of Southern California (USC) research team evaluated 20 years of experience with GRIP and found a number of positive trends: "There has been a significant decrease in the activity of major gangs, gang members and the ratio of gang members to residents in Paramount since 1982." A survey of 735 ninth-grade students found that those who had experienced the GRIP program were less likely to report involvement with gang activity than nonparticipating students, were more likely to have negative perceptions of gang activities and were more likely to believe that drugs and alcohol are a big part of gang life ("California Law Enforcement . . .," p.5).

When prevention efforts fail, it is important that communities recognize the presence of a gang or gangs in their neighborhoods and take steps to address the problem.

Recognizing the Presence of Gangs (or a Gang Problem)

According to Fraser (2001, p.11): "The presence of gangs may be seen everywhere. Gang members do not represent an invisible empire. They thrive on recognition and are constantly seeking ways to make their presence known or felt. They only go unseen when law enforcement personnel, as well as educators and parents, fail to recognize the signs of gang activity and an individual's involvement."

Within the school, gangs can thrive on anonymity, denial and lack of awareness by school personnel. The gang member whose notebook graffiti goes unaddressed today may likely be involved in initiations, assaults and drug sales in school in the near future.

The condition that makes the school environment most ripe for gang activity is *denial*. The most common initial response to gangs in almost all communities and schools is denial because public officials are more focused on image concerns for their organizations while they should be focusing on dealing with the problem. The longer they deny, the more entrenched the problem becomes and in the end, the worse their image will be. Even when school and community officials come out of denial and acknowledge a gang presence, they tend to downplay it and do a "qualified admittance" of the problem. They acknowledge it when they cannot deny it any longer, but even then they tend to downplay it and underestimate the extent of the problem. The only people those who play this political game fool in the long run is themselves. The longer they deny and downplay the problem, the worse it becomes, and the bigger gang problem—and image problem—they will face in the end.

The flip side of the issue is that the problem in a school or community should not be *overstated*, putting people in unnecessary fear or giving the gangs more credit and status. The majority of students in a given school are not in a gang and do not want gang activity in their schools. The problem, though, is that a small number of gang members, along with their associates outside the school, can account for a significant amount of violence in a short time if their activities go unaddressed. As Howell (p.53) observes: "Both denial of gang problems and overreaction to them are detrimental to the development of effective community responses to gangs. Denial that gang problems exist precludes early intervention efforts. Overreaction in the form of excessive police force and publicizing of gangs may inadvertently serve to increase a gang's cohesion, facilitate its expansion and lead to more crimes."

School officials and community leaders can prevent such occurrences—or at least reduce the risks and impact of those that do occur—by training their staff on gang identification, behavior, prevention and intervention strategies, and related school security issues. As Domash (2000, p.30) stresses: "The first step in dealing with gangs is the acknowledgement of their presence in the community." Table 13.4 shows the criteria used by some departments for identifying the existence of gangs.

Indicators of gang activity include graffiti, drive-by shootings, intimidation assaults, murders and the open sale of drugs.

Once a community recognizes a gang problem, the next step is to identify the gang members.

Identifying Gang Members

Often people think of "colors" or tattoos as indicating membership in a gang. However, as the National School Safety and Security Services suggests, gang membership indicators can be quite subtle, particularly as awareness increases among

Table 13.4 Criteria for Defining Gangs

Criteria Used	*Large Cities* (Percent)*	*Smaller Cities* (Percent)*
Use of symbols	93	100
Violent behavior	81	84
Group organization	81	88
Territory	74	88
Leadership	59	78
Recurrent interaction	56	60

*Of the cities surveyed 70 (89 percent) of the large cities and 25 (58 percent) of the smaller cities indicated the criteria used to define gangs.

SOURCE: G. David Curry et al. *Gang Crime and Law Enforcement Recordkeeping.* Washington, DC: National Institute of Justice Research in Brief, August 1994, p.7. Data from NIJ Gang Survey.

school officials, law enforcement, parents and other adults. Depending on the specific gang activity in a specific school or community, gang identifiers may include:

- *Colors:* obvious or subtle colors of clothing, a particular clothing brand, jewelry or haircuts (but not necessarily the traditional perception of colors as only bandannas)
- *Tattoos:* symbols on arms, chest or elsewhere on the body
- *Lit (gang literature):* gang signs, symbols, poems, prayers, procedures, etc., in notebooks or other documents
- *Initiations:* suspicious bruises, wounds or injuries resulting from a "jumping in" type initiation
- *Hand signs:* unusual hand signals or handshakes
- *Behavior:* sudden changes in behavior or secret meetings and many other methods

In addition, gang allegiance can be indicated by **representing**, a manner of dress that uses an imaginary line drawn vertically through the body. Anything to the left of the line represents "dress left" and vice versa. An example of right dress would be a hat cocked to the right side, right pants leg rolled up, a bandanna in gang colors tied around the right arm, one glove worn on the right hand, right-side pocket turned inside out and sometimes dyed gang colors, shoes or laces of the right shoe in gang colors, belt buckle worn loose on the right side, earrings worn in the right ear and two fingernails on the right hand painted in gang colors.

Indicators of gang membership include colors, tattoos, hand signs and behavior.

One or several of these identifiers may indicate gang affiliation. It is important to remember, however, that identifiers help recognize gang affiliation, but a focus on behavior is especially important.

According to Howell (p.27): "Determining a particular individual's gang involvement is as difficult as identifying true youth gangs. In many instances, a youth may associate occasionally with a gang, participate episodically in the activities of a gang or desire gang membership without actually being a member. Likewise, many youths leave gangs by drifting out, gradually dissociating themselves. Because severe criminal sanctions can be applied to gang membership in certain jurisdictions, a valid determination is important." The following criteria (any one of which qualifies the individual) might be used to determine whether a youth is a gang member.

- The individual admits membership in a gang (i.e., self-reported).
- A law enforcement agency or reliable informant identifies an individual as a gang member.
- An informant of previously untested reliability identifies an individual as a gang member, and this information is corroborated by an independent source.
- The individual resides in or frequents a particular gang's area and adopts its style of dress, use of hand signs, symbols or tattoos; maintains ongoing relationships with known gang members; and has been arrested several times in the company of identified gang members for offenses consistent with usual gang activity.

- There is reasonable suspicion that the individual is involved in a gang-related criminal activity or enterprise.

Because self-report is frequently used as the means to identify gang members, Esbensen et al. (2001a) studied the validity of the traditional self-nominating techniques for identifying gang members. (Recall the earlier discussion of the importance of how a gang is defined.) Esbensen et al. (2001a) found that estimates of the proportion of youths involved in gangs ranged from 2 to 17 percent, depending on the definitions used. Their research demonstrated that traditional self-nomination techniques for identifying gang members appear to be valid. They also found that former gang members had more prosocial attitudes and behaviors than active members and that programs designed to draw youths away from gang association (such as GREAT) are worth pursuing.

The Police Response

Typically, police chiefs in cities where gangs have recently arrived are slow to recognize the threat. If police chiefs deny a gang problem, despite mounting evidence, the gang problem often becomes unmanageable. On the other hand, if police publicly acknowledge the existence of gangs, this places the police administrator in a Catch-22. Publicly acknowledging gangs validates them and provides notoriety.

An important task in most police departments is gathering information or intelligence on gangs and their members.

Intelligence Gathering

Intelligence is knowing what gangs are out there, where they are, the names of the individual gang members and their gang affiliation, where they have been seen and who they have been seen with.

Howell (p.53) recommends: "Each city's gang program should be supported by a gang information system that provides sound and current crime incident data that can be linked to gang members and used to enhance police and other agency interventions. At a minimum, law enforcement agencies must ensure that gang crimes are coded separately from nongang crimes so that these events can be tracked, studied and analyzed to support more efficient and effective anti-gang strategies."

A computerized Gang Intelligence System (GANGIS), including comprehensive gang profile data such as monikers and vehicle information, can be an effective crime-fighting tool.

Table 13.5 describes the methods used for gathering gang information and their frequency of use.

National networks of gang intelligence databases can greatly enhance a department's effort to understand and respond to gang activities in their jurisdiction. The Regional Information Sharing System (RISS) network links six regional intelligence databases, including a gang database, RISS-GANGS. Another computer technology used for tracking gangs is the General Reporting, Evaluation and Tracking (GREAT) system—a combination hot sheet, mug book and file cabinet. This system is not to

Table 13.5 Methods Used for Gathering Information on Gangs, Ranked by "Often Used" Category

	Never Used	*Sometimes Used*	*Often Used*
Internal contacts with patrol officers and detectives	1	22	64
Internal departmental records and computerized files	4	22	62
Review of offense reports	2	25	60
Interviews with gang members	5	26	56
Obtain information from other local police agencies	1	35	51
Surveillance activities	6	37	44
Use of unpaid informants	2	44	42
Obtain information from other criminal justice agencies	3	43	42
Obtain information from other governmental agencies	3	47	37
Provision of information by schools	2	50	35
Reports from state agencies	11	63	14
Use of paid informants	28	46	13
Reports from federal agencies	16	62	9
Obtain information from private organizations	27	51	9
Infiltration of police officers into gangs or related groups	75	11	2

SOURCE: James W. Stevens. "Youth Gangs' Dimensions." *The Encyclopedia of Police Science* 2nd ed., edited by William G. Bailey. New York Garland, 1995, p.832. Reprinted by permission.

be confused with the GREAT program used in schools to teach children about resisting gangs, discussed earlier in the chapter.

Katz et al. (2000, pp.413–414) note that in the past 15 years, the number of specialized gang units has increased dramatically, with the majority of the units established to gather intelligence on gangs, gang members and gang-related activities. Information in the tracking systems usually includes a gang member's legal name, street name (moniker), address, criminal record, gang affiliation, photographs and vehicle information. Their research found that intelligence lists may be more helpful to the police than originally believed. Katz et al. (pp.415–416) cite four uses for gang information systems, with the first and most important being that documenting gang members and sharing the information with other criminal justice agencies will lead to greater clearance rates, higher conviction rates and longer prison sentences.

Second, such systems will allow police agencies to more effectively and efficiently suppress gang-related activity as well as to gain a greater understanding of gang organizational structures, leadership, rituals and cultural beliefs.

Third, gang information systems are important for allocation of department resources: "Gang intelligence can be used by law enforcement agencies to respond to denial about a community's gang problem and can be used to demonstrate the seriousness of a community's gang problem" (p.415).

Finally, gang information systems are useful in selecting suppression strategies and tactics as well as other strategies to address a gang problem.

Evolution of Strategies for Dealing with the Gang Problem

The Office of Juvenile Justice and Delinquency Prevention (OJJDP) reports a distinct difference in the approach used in the 1950s and 1960s compared to that used in more recent years. In the 1950s and 1960s law enforcement used a social services approach toward gangs. During more recent years the focus has been on suppression. Neither approach is clearly superior. Some communities have adopted a comprehensive approach combining social services intervention and suppression strategies.

According to the OJJDP, law enforcement has used five strategies to address the gang problem: suppression, social intervention, social opportunities, community mobilization and organizational development or change.

Suppression includes tactics such as prevention, arrest, imprisonment, supervision and surveillance. **Social intervention** includes crisis intervention, treatment for youths and their families, outreach and referral to social services. **Social opportunities** include providing basic or remedial education, training, work incentives and jobs for gang members. **Community mobilization** includes improved communication and joint policy and program development among justice, community-based and grassroots organizations. **Organizational development** or **change** includes special police units and special youth agency crisis programs.

Community mobilization was found to be the most effective strategy to address the gang problem (OJJDP).

According to Howell (p.5):

> Communities that begin with suppression as their main response generally discover later that cooperation and collaboration between public and private community agencies and citizens are necessary for an effective solution. Considerable advantage accrues from involving the entire community from the onset, beginning with a comprehensive and systematic assessment of the presumed youth gang problem. Key community leaders must mobilize the resources of the entire community, guided by a consensus on definitions, program targets and interrelated strategies. Comprehensive programs that incorporate prevention, intervention and enforcement components are most likely to be effective.

Suppression—The Traditional Response

Howell (p.53) reports: "Law enforcement agents view suppression tactics (e.g., street sweeps, intensified surveillance, hotspot targeting and caravanning), crime prevention activities, and community collaboration—in that order—as most effective in preventing and controlling gang crime. Targeting specific gang crimes, locations, gangs and gang members appears to be the most effective suppression tactic;

therefore, police increasingly adhere to the mantra: 'Investigate the crime; not the culture.'" Table 13.6 describes the frequency of use of specific law enforcement strategies and their perceived effectiveness.

To enhance suppression efforts, many departments have established gang units or task forces.

Gang Units

Katz (2001, p.37) suggests that the gang unit was created as a consequence of pressures placed on the police department from various powerful elements within the community. He reports on a survey conducted by the Law Enforcement and Management Administrative Statistics (LEMAS) that found among large agencies with 100 or more sworn officers, special gang units existed in 56 percent of all municipal police departments, 50 percent of all sheriff's departments, 43 percent of all county police agencies and 20 percent of all state law enforcement agencies. Based on these figures, approximately 360 police gang units are operating in the United States.

Valdez (2000b, p.54) suggests broadening the focus of a gang unit into what he calls a "full-service gang unit: 'To combat the gang problem, use the components of prevention, suppression and intervention." This concept is illustrated in Figure 13.1.

The *suppression component* involves a collaboration between police, probation and prosecution, targeting the most active gang members and leaders. The *intervention*

Table 13.6 Law Enforcement Strategies and Perceived Effectiveness*

Strategy	Used (Percent)	Judged Effective If Used (Percent)
Some or a lot of use		
Targeting entry points	14	17
Gang laws	40	19
Selected violations	76	42
Out-of-state information exchange	53	16
In-state information exchange	90	17
In-city information exchange	55	18
Federal agency operational coordination	40	16
State agency operational coordination	50	13
Local agency operational coordination	78	16
Community collaboration	64	54
Any use		
Street sweeps	40	62
Other suppression tactics	44	63
Crime prevention activities	15	56

*Percentage of cities n = 211. The number of cities responding to each question varied slightly.

SOURCE: James C. Howell. *Youth Gang Programs and Strategies.* Washington, DC: OJJDP, August 2000, p.46. (NCJ 171154)

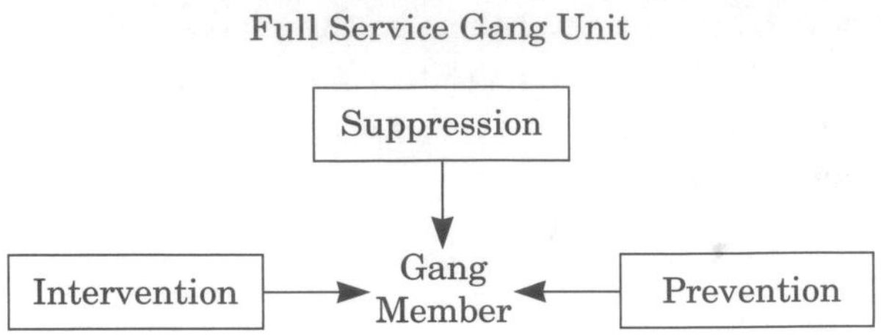

Figure 13.1 Full-Service Gang Unit

SOURCE: Al Valdez. "Putting Full-Service Gang Units to Work." *Police,* July 2000, p.54. Reprinted by permission.

component would help gang members who want to get out of the gang and help them immediately. They might be referred to a community program, given the chance to finish high school or obtain a GED, have tattoos removed or find employment. The *prevention component* would give young children the tools to handle the pressures involved in living in a gang neighborhood or attending a school with a gang problem.

Domash (2004, p.18) recommends partnering with corrections to combat a gang problem: "One major player in the game of combating gangs is corrections. Keeping tabs on incarcerated gang members can give hints as to what's going on in the outside world and can even help to curb convicts' influence on the streets. . . . Just because a person is incarcerated doesn't mean he's not recruiting. . . . Being locked up is just a temporary bump in the road for someone who's determined to make a career out of criminal activity."

A Collaborative Gang Initiative

Domash (2000, pp.23–24) notes: "The complexity of today's gangs suggests the need for a comprehensive, multifaceted effort that targets the reasons youths join gangs. Such an effort may involve three programmatic approaches: develop strategies to discourage gang membership; provide avenues for youths to drop out of gangs; and empower communities to solve problems associated with gangs through collaboration with law enforcement, parents, schools, youths, businesses, religious and social service organizations, local government officials and other community groups in a comprehensive, systematic approach." Figure 13.2 illustrates the comprehensive approach taken by Nassau County.

Community Policing and Gangs: Assistance from the OJJDP

Marble (2000, p.39) describes how the OJJDP can help communities with the gang problem: "OJJDP has developed a comprehensive, coordinated response to youth gang problems. The response encompasses a wide range of programs and projects, including research, prevention, intervention, suppression and information sharing."

OJJDP initiatives to help communities address the gang problem include the Comprehensive Gang Model, the National Youth Gang Center, the Rural Gang Initiative and Gang Prevention through Targeted Outreach.

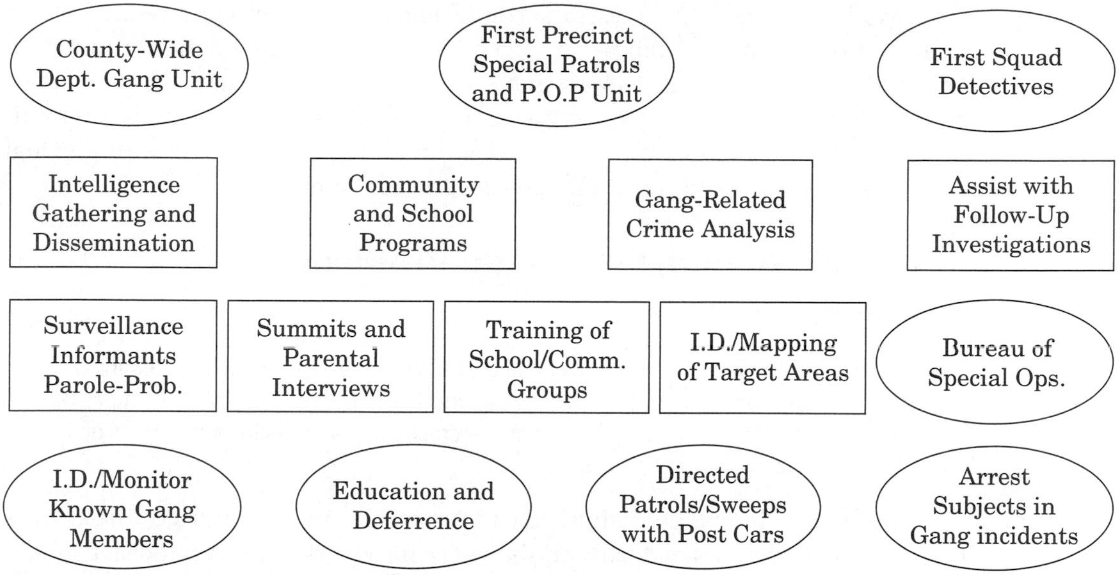

Figure 13.2 Nassau County's 1st Precinct Gang Initiative: Primary Functions

SOURCE: Shelly Feuer Domesh. "Youth Gangs in America: A National Problem Evading Easy Solutions." *Police*, June 2000, p.23. Reprinted by permission.

The *Comprehensive Gang Model* includes five strategies: mobilizing communities, providing youth opportunities, suppressing gang violence, providing social interventions and street outreach, and facilitating organizational change and development. The *National Youth Gang Center*, in Tallahassee, Florida, is a "one-stop shop" for information about gangs and effective responses to them.

The *Rural Gang Initiative* funds adaptation of the Comprehensive Gang Model at four rural sites and funds evaluation, training and technical assistance for these efforts. The *Gang Prevention through Targeted Outreach* enables local boys' and girls' clubs to prevent youths from entering gangs, intervene with gang members early in their involvement and divert youths from gang life into more constructive activities. In addition, the OJJDP provides publications, funding opportunities, training and technical assistance.

Community Policing and Gangs: Assistance from the National Youth Gang Center

The National Youth Gang Center has developed a protocol for assessing a gang problem as well as a planning guide to assist communities in addressing a gang problem.

The National Youth Gang Center (2001a) has developed a protocol that communities can use in assessing their gang problem. The protocol is applicable to communities of all sizes and characteristics.

The National Youth Gang Center (2001b) has also developed a planning guide to assist communities in developing a plan to implement the OJJDP's Comprehensive

Gang Model. The model addresses the youth gang problem through five interrelated strategies: community mobilization; social intervention, including street outreach; provision of opportunities; suppression/social control; and organizational change and development. According to Howell et al. (p.7): "Based on research and community experience, the model is multifaceted and multilayered and involves individual youths, families, the gang structure, agencies and the community."

Strategies to Address a Gang Problem and Gang Violence

Current strategies to address the gang problem include behavior codes, obtaining civil injunctions, establishing drug-free zones (DFZs) around schools, implementing conflict prevention strategies, applying community pressure, graffiti removal programs and pulling levers.

Behavior codes should be established and firmly, consistently enforced. These codes may include dress codes and bans on showing gang colors or using hand signals. On the positive side, schools should promote and reward friendliness and cooperation.

Another way to address the gang problem is through *civil injunctions.* This strategy was used by the Redondo Beach (California) Police Department in an award-winning experiment. The department got an injunction against the gang members who had essentially taken over a city park. The department sued them and won. The injunction resulted from a partnership between the community and the police department and exemplifies an innovative, proactive approach to ensuring public safety. The injunction restricted the following actions.

- Possessing, or remaining in the company of anyone with dangerous weapons, including clubs, bats, knives, screwdrivers, BB guns and so on
- Entering private property of another without prior written permission of the owner
- Intimidating, provoking, threatening, confronting, challenging or carrying out any acts of retaliation
- Forbidding a gang member under 18 years of age to be in a public place after 8:00 P.M. unless going to a legitimate business, meeting or an entertainment activity
- Disallowing gang members to associate or congregate in groups of three or more in the park or within 10 yards of the outside fence surrounding the park

The constitutionality of such an approach needs to be considered by any community wishing to implement this innovative strategy.

Drug-free zones (DFZs) around schools is another commonly used strategy. This may include rewiring any pay phones so that only outgoing calls can be made.

Conflict prevention strategies are also important to address the problem of gangs. Teachers should be trained to recognize and deal with gang members in nonconfrontational ways. Staff should identify all known gang members and try to build self-esteem and promote academic success for all students, including gang members.

Community pressure is also needed to effectively reduce and prevent gang activity. Parents and the general public should be made aware of gangs operating in the community, as well as of popular heavy metal and punk bands that may be having a negative influence on youths. They should be encouraged to apply pressure to television and radio stations and to book and video stores to ban material that promotes use of alcohol, drugs, promiscuity, devil worship or violence. This may raise constitutionality or censorship issues, but as long as it is private citizens who apply the pressure, it should not present a problem.

Graffiti removal programs should be put in place that call for the prompt removal of graffiti anywhere it appears. **Graffiti** is not only unattractive but also enables gang members to advertise their turf and authority. In some instances photographs of the graffiti may aid certain police investigations. School officials should give to the police remaining paint cans and paint brushes that might be used as evidence. As an alternative to graffiti, students might be encouraged to design and paint murals in locations where graffiti is most likely to occur.

Pulling levers refers to a multiagency law enforcement team imposing all available sanctions (**pulling levers**) on gang members who violate established standards for behavior.

Graffiti Removal Programs

Piraino (2002, p.23) asserts: "Graffiti vandalism is a quality-of-life issue. Globally, graffiti has an estimated annual cost of $30 billion." He describes the Northwest Block Watch Coalition, a partnership established in Phoenix, Arizona, in 1994 to reduce graffiti vandalism. The coalition developed a graffiti hotline for citizens to anonymously report graffiti vandals. The program offers a reward up to $250 for information. The hotline has responded to over 28,694 calls that generated 1,487 cases. Of these, 764 resulted in arrests.

Says Piraino (p.24): "The coalition was founded on creating partnerships and developing pro-active programs. With this in mind the coalition approaches businesses that could provide specialized equipment to aid in the fight against graffiti vandalism. ITT Industries Night Vision, ESRI Inc., Eastman Kodak, Hewlett-Packard, Motorola, Giant Industries, Southwest Gas, Wells Fargo Foundation, America West Airlines and Grote Industries are among local and national corporations that all answered the call to partner with the Northwest Block Watch Coalition. A donated truck and paint spray equipment aid in the removal of the graffiti." A different approach was taken in Seattle.

The Seattle Graffiti Prevention Project Vuong (2003) describes how Seattle tackled a graffiti problem on buildings that line a busy bus lane near Seattle's sports stadiums.

> The corridor once was littered with syringes and condoms, overrun by transient camps. It was an unlikely blank canvas for the many youths who would later gather to paint and connect with their community. That is, until Mike Peringer entered the picture. More than seven years ago, he saw the potential and tirelessly

pursued a project that united at-risk teenagers and merchants in a war against the Sodo district's rampant graffiti.

ArtWorks not only has created the Sodo Urban Art Corridor, it has enhanced construction sites, schools and parks around the city as well. Kids who participate don't just paint pictures—they develop team and leadership skills and find promising futures. "They can walk out there feeling they've accomplished something," said Peringer.

In fall 1995, ArtWorks began as a program under the Sodo Business Association, of which Peringer is president. He led efforts to form the association more than two years earlier to connect area businesses and present them as one voice before government. The group wanted to improve public safety and clean up lots and buildings. Singled out for attention was the corridor along Fifth Avenue South between Royal Brougham Way and Spokane Street, where 50,000 bus commuters pass through daily. It was a graffiti-plagued, trash-strewn eyesore. "All these folks come in and out of the city through all this mess," Peringer recalled. "This is the first thing they see."

Armed with a $15,000 grant from Seattle Public Utilities, volunteers went to work, removing graffiti left by "taggers" and hauling away some 300 tons of trash. But the job wasn't done.

Peringer was urged to apply for a matching grant from the city to help create art for the bordering buildings. ArtWorks received $80,000 the first year and produced more than a dozen murals. In summer 1996, 700 youngsters participated in the program, the majority at-risk or disadvantaged youth. Many came from unhappy homes and were ordered to participate by a judge.

"A lot of them are frustrated artists who are tagging," Peringer said. "When these kids were working on these murals and stuff, they didn't reoffend." They not only instill pride in the young artists, but also command respect from taggers. They bring the community together, Peringer said, recalling one mural worked on by an unlikely alliance of elementary school children, gang members and senior citizens.

Though initially a summer program, Peringer sought to keep the kids out of trouble year-round by securing donated indoor space so they could paint panels that would be installed later.

Pulling Levers in Boston

As noted, pulling levers refers to a multiagency law enforcement team imposing all available sanctions on gang members who violate established standards for behavior. This strategy was used in Boston with a small group of youths with extensive involvement in the justice system who accounted for a majority of youth homicides. Their pulling levers program, *Operation Cease Fire,* was initiated by a multiagency law enforcement team convening a series of meetings with the chronic gang offenders where law enforcement communicated new standards for behavior. Violence will no longer be tolerated. When the standards were violated, the multiagency law enforcement team responded by imposing all available sanctions. Since Boston implemented the strategy in 1996, youth homicides have fallen by two-thirds (Kennedy et al., 2001).

According to researchers Braga et al. (2001, p.195): "Our impact evaluation suggests that the Ceasefire intervention was associated with significant reductions in youth homicide victimization, shots-fired calls for service and gun assault incidents in Boston. A comparative analysis of youth homicide trends in Boston relative to youth homicide trends in other major U.S. and New England cities also supports a unique program effect associated with the Ceasefire intervention."

Other Strategies Recommended by the National Crime Prevention Council

The National Crime Prevention Council has recommended using state laws and ordinances to combat gangs, using multiagency gang interdiction teams, preventing gangs through community intervention with high-risk youths, providing positive alternatives to gang activity and setting up information networks on gang activity.

A review of nearly 100 studies of gangs summarizes what is known about youth gangs and offers suggestions about how to design prevention programs. *Preventing Adolescent Gang Involvement* (Esbensen, 2000) reports that most gang members were already committing crimes before joining a gang, but youths' delinquency rates increase dramatically after joining a gang. The report recommends that, because of this, gang prevention campaigns should not be limited to programs that target existing gangs trying to shut them down. Gang prevention efforts should include programs aimed at the entire population of adolescents. In fact, gang-suppression programs targeting youths who are already involved with gangs "have shown little promise," and some have had the unintended result of "increasing gang cohesion."

Task Forces

Another collaborative approach to addressing the gang problem is to form a task force, either regionally or statewide. Lesce (2000) describes how New Mexico established such a task force to coordinate information regarding gangs statewide. To date, 48 law enforcement agencies are involved. The task force is funded by a federal grant derived from drug money administered by the Bureau of Justice Assistance and allocated for drug enforcement. Exchanging information helps identify habitual offenders and has allowed the district attorney's office to identify, arrest and prosecute senior gang members. It has also enabled identifying and classifying the various types of gangs in the state.

Although most individuals involved in programs for youths see gangs as a negative influence, there may be a positive side to gangs on which to build relationships leading to a rechanneling of gang members' energies.

The Gang's Place within the Community

Despite a gang's desire for autonomy and rejection of outside authority, a relationship must still be maintained with the neighborhood and larger community. The OJJDP notes four factors that motivate gangs to make concerted efforts to establish ties with the community: (1) the gang's need for a "safe haven" and a place to exist;

(2) the need for a recruitment pool from which to draw its membership; (3) the community's ability to provide important information such as details concerning other gang activity within the city; and (4) psychological reasons. Regarding this final factor, the OJJDP explains: "A bonding occurs between the gang and the community that builds a social adhesive that often takes a significant amount of time to completely dissolve."

These bonds may present a challenge to the dissipation and eradication of local gang activity and can hinder law enforcement's efforts to rally a community against the presence of such gangs.

According to the OJJDP: "Community ambivalence toward gangs exists because many of the gang members are children of residents, the gangs often provide protection for residents, residents identify with gangs because of their own or relatives' prior involvement, and the gangs in some instances have become community institutions."

Recall that Zatz and Portillos (p.389) reported: "Historically, gangs have been important neighborhood institutions offering disenchanted, disadvantaged youths a means of coping with the isolation, alienation, and poverty they experience every day." They (p.396) believe: "The gang was, and is, composed of brothers, sisters, cousins, and neighbors. The gang gives them a sense of community, a place where they belong. Kicked out of school, assumed to be troublemakers, looking tough and feeling scared, these young people are well aware that their options in life are very much constrained by poverty, racial discrimination, cultural stereotyping, and inadequate education."

Zatz and Portillos (p.389) also note: "Regardless of what other neighborhood residents may think of them, the youths identify strongly with their neighborhoods, consider themselves to be integral parts of their barrios, and view their gangs as neighborhood institutions. They see themselves as protectors of their neighborhoods, at least against intrusion by rival gangs." This would imply that, at least for Hispanic gang members, a sense of community might be there to build on.

A Community Approach to a Gang Problem

Shelden et al. (p.223) explain: "The community approach, as the name suggests, reaches out to include a broad spectrum of individuals, groups and organizations. The community itself makes it clear that certain unhealthy behaviors are unacceptable and will not be tolerated. This approach takes advantage of existing community resources in the broadest sense and pools them to develop a community-wide strategy. The mobilization process involves four specific steps: (1) involving key community leaders, (2) forming a community board or task force, (3) conducting a community risk and resource assessment and (4) planning the program and deciding on evaluation methods."

Howell (p.53) stresses: "Community responses to gangs must begin with a thorough assessment of the specific characteristics of the gangs themselves, crimes they commit, other problems they present and localities they affect. To conduct a thorough assessment, communities should look at community perceptions and available data. Data from law enforcement sources such as local gang and general crime data are critical. Other data should be collected from probation officers, schools, community-based youth agencies, prosecutors and community residents."

Providing Alternatives to Gangs

Many gang experts stress the need to provide alternatives for youths who may be drawn to a gang or who may already be in a gang but are becoming disenchanted. Following are several examples of successful programs offering alternatives to gangs, many involving parents and building a sense of family.

The following material is adapted from the Web site of St. Edwards University, Austin, Texas (www.stedwards.edu/educ/eanes/ganghome.html).

Austin, Texas, Youth Options

Michael Price of Youth Options, part of East Austin–based RAYS program that helps improve the quality of the community, says the public needs to understand that gangs are a problem of the community that are not just going to go away without education and hard work. Gang members, especially gang leaders, have tremendous leadership ability that could do wonders for the community if it could be used constructively.

Price's office is located at the Alternative Learning Center (ALC), a school where students with discipline problems are sent from middle and high schools around Austin. Price works with many gang members who come through the ALC to build their self-esteem and educate them about the problems with gang rivalry.

He takes the youths on field trips, involves them in extracurricular activities such as basketball and ropes, and takes them camping. Rival gang members learn that they can get along through these activities. Price also meets with parents to talk about their problems with the youths and stresses that parents need to be more aware of what is going on in their youths' lives. Communication in families is important to helping stop gangs.

Austin, Texas, Roving Leader Program

The Roving Leader program is a nonprofit organization sponsored by the Austin–Travis County Mental Health–Mental Retardation Center. The program targets youths between the ages of 9 and 19 at risk of gang involvement or juvenile delinquency. The program provides groups on school campuses around Austin as well as after school and evening programs.

The goal of the program is to make students aware of the importance of finishing high school, build self-esteem, motivate and encourage goal setting and responsibility. The program offers youth and parent support groups, tutoring, cooking classes and recreation. Youths can get support 24 hours a day. Cindy Martinez, the program's supervisor, has helped many youths break out of gang life and start setting goals for their future. Even youths with families involved in gangs were able to change their lifestyle with the program's support. "Most of them just need to know that somebody cares for them and is concerned about their future," she says.

Dallas, Texas, Nuestro Centro, "Our Center"

The Nuestro Center program is a gang and drug intervention program for Dallas youths that offers counseling, parenting classes, tutoring, educational field trips, and high school and college courses. The program uses a holistic approach to therapy by utilizing a network of support services and incorporating every system that affects youths in the therapy.

The group counseling is modeled after AA (Alcohol Annoymous) groups. It focuses on five basic character-building areas. It allows youths an avenue to identify their problems, positive peer pressure and interaction and an alternative to gangs by fulfilling some of the youths' basic needs. Individual counseling teaches youths self-responsibility, honesty, decision-making skills and goal setting. Family counseling works to strengthen the family unit, increase communication between parent and youth, increase parenting skills and involve the family in the rehabilitation process.

The program also assigns one volunteer mentor per youth for a year. Once a week the youth and the mentor meet. The goals of the mentor program are to provide a strong support system, allow the youth to identify with a positive role model and identify problems not apparent in groups. Role model speakers also give presentations every week on topics such as barriers to reaching goals, career opportunities, AIDS and sex education, drugs, educational opportunities, and work and life skills. Parenting courses help to teach parents of at-risk youths positive and effective parenting skills and to increase communication between parent and child.

Through special arrangements with a local community college, youths are accepted provisionally as college students. They are also provided with remedial courses in English and math over the summer. Nuestro Centro also provides SAT and GED preparation programs to set students on the right track academically and give them hope for the future.

Pierce County, Washington, Safe Streets Campaign

Safe Streets is a community resource that helps individuals, families, communities and organizations to develop strategies to reduce gang violence and drug use. Programs for youths include the *Interagency Gang Task Force* that unites the schools, the health department, the sheriff and police departments, the prosecuting attorney's office and a children's commission to identify gang-involved youths and prevent the cycle of youth violence.

Youth Consortium is a partnership of 23 youth-serving organizations that meets once a month to network, plan and implement programs that address the specific needs of youths. *Joining with Schools* provides "Power Tour" assemblies where 5,000 students ages 12 to 18 are asked by role-mentoring adults to examine their power in the choices they make daily. *After school sports programs* include additional opportunities in conflict resolution, self-discipline, team building and intercultural understanding.

Urban League Academy of Arts Project provides youths with enriched arts and mathematics experiences as well as public recognition for achievements. *Positive Alternatives* is a youth-directed group that addresses alcohol and drug use, physical abuse, gang activity and dysfunctional families. *YMCA Late Night* gives troubled youths a safe alternative to the streets and offers many fun, educational opportunities. *Employment* helps get youths job training where they can get paid and build their skills at the same time. *Community Outreach* offers parenting classes and advice on how to deal with gang-involved children.

A Five-Pronged Approach to Gang Reduction

In introducing the OJJDP's new program to support community anti-gang efforts, Attorney General Ashcroft stated:

> We must focus on the immediate priority of safeguarding the public, while at the same time attacking the underlying causes that attract young people to gangs in the first place. We must work to offer our youths a viable alternative to gangs by providing opportunities for success as productive citizens, and we must also prepare those young people who have been held in confinement to return to their communities—not to their gangs ("New Program Supports Community Anti-Gang Efforts," 2003, p.1). The OJJDP's Gang Reduction Program (GRP) uses a five pronged approach:
>
> 1. *Primary prevention* targets the entire population in high-crime, high-risk communities. The key component is a one-stop resource center that makes services accessible and visible to community members. Services include prenatal and infant care, after-school activities, truancy and dropout prevention, and job programs.
> 2. *Secondary prevention* identifies young children (ages 7 to 14) at high risk and, drawing on the resources of schools, community-based organizations and faith-based groups, intervenes with appropriate services before early problem behaviors turn into serious delinquency and gang involvement.
> 3. *Intervention* targets active gang members, close associates and gang members returning from confinement and involve aggressive outreach and recruitment activity. Support services for gang-involved youths and their families help youths make positive choices.
> 4. *Suppression* focuses on identifying the most dangerous and influential gang members and removing them from the community
> 5. *Reentry* targets serious offenders who are returning to the community after confinement and provides appropriate services and monitoring. Of particular interest are "displaced" gang members who may cause conflict by attempting to reassert their former gang roles.

The program is being pilot tested in Los Angeles, California; Miami, Florida; Milwaukee, Wisconsin; and Richmond, Virginia.

Problem-Solving Partnerships to Address a Gang Problem in Action

McGarrell and Chermak (2003, pp.77–99) describe how problem-solving partnerships were used to reduce gang- and drug-related violence in Indianapolis. The following is an adaptation of their description, reprinted with permission:

> Indianapolis is a city with just over 800,000 residents in a metropolitan area of approximately 1.5 million people. It has traditionally ranked in the midrange among the nation's larger cities in terms of crime generally and violent crime in particular. Of the 45 cities included in the initial National Youth Gang Survey conducted in the late 1980s, Indianapolis was identified as one of 24 cities with an emerging gang problem.
>
> A Metropolitan Gang Task Force (MGTS) was created in 1987 to coordinate the law enforcement response to the gang problem. In 1996 Indianapolis was selected to participate in the Anti-Gang Initiative (AGI) of the U.S. Department of Justice, Office of Community Oriented Policing Services (COPS). One key element of the AGI was training all officers about gangs and gang identification. An apparent by-product of the training was that gang intelligence increased as officers became much more likely to complete gang contact sheets. One consequence of this activity was that by 1997 the number of confirmed gang sets increased from 80 to 198 and the number of confirmed gang members increased from 1,746 to 2,422, a 40 percent increase.
>
> In December 1997 criminal justice and city officials met to form the Indianapolis Violence Reduction Partnership (IVRP). The group's first step was to form a working group of criminal justice officials including representatives from the Bureau of Alcohol, Tobacco and Firearms; Federal Bureau of Investigation; Indiana Department of Corrections; Indiana State Police; Indianapolis Office of the Mayor; Indianapolis Police Department; Marion County Prosecutor's Office; Marion County Sheriff's Department; Marion Superior Court—Criminal Division and Juvenile Division; Marion Superior Court Probation—Adult and Juvenile Services Divisions; U.S. Drug Enforcement Administration; and the U.S. Marshal's Service.
>
> This multiagency structure was intended to serve two key goals: (1) to share information and (2) to bring expanded resources to the problem. The group also agreed to use a systematic problem-solving process. The initial analysis of homicides used existing information systems (police, incident reports, GIS crime mapping, court records). The analysis found that roughly two-thirds of homicide victims and 72 percent of suspects were African Americans and the majority were males.
>
> The official reports indicated that very few homicides involved either gangs (for example, one in 1998) or drugs (six in 1997, seven in 1998). Yet discussions with investigators and line-level officers indicated that they believed that gangs and drugs were involved in many if not most homicides. This was the direct result of the restrictive recording rules the homicide unit used. Incidents involving

known gang members or drug users/traffickers would be classified as gang or drug related only if it was clear that the gang or drug involvement was the motive for the homicide.

To obtain better information about the homicides, the IVRP brought together officials with street-level intelligence on homicide and violence to participate in a review of every homicide incident occurring in 1997 and 1998. The IVRP group adopted the terminology "groups of known, chronic offenders" to reflect the lack of a consensual definition of a gang and the reality that much gang activity in Indianapolis is of a relatively loose structure. That is, many of the groups of known, chronic offenders that law enforcement encounters are not part of a well-structured nationally or regionally organized gang but rather reflect local cliques or crews of offenders who are well known to law enforcement. Many of these groups have names and colors, but their membership is fluid, and many are not territorial. With this definition in mind, the incident review revealed that 58 percent of the homicides in 1997 and 61 percent of those in 1998 involved suspects or victims who were described as being part of a group of known, chronic offenders. In addition, over half the homicides had some type of drug connection. And the preceding are likely to be conservative estimates.

Now that the problem was identified, the IVRP held a series of meetings to develop a strategic plan that would focus interventions on the various factors identified in the city's homicides. Table 13.7 summarizes the key interventions.

The strategies fell into two categories with some overlap. A first set of strategies focused on tightening the criminal justice system to concentrate on violent, chronic offenders. The second category was based on the "lever pulling" (LP) concept developed in Boston's Operation Cease Fire. Lever pulling is based on several key principals: (1) to increase the perception among high risk individuals that they were likely to face criminal sanctions if they continued to be involved in violence (a "stick"), (2) to make these high-risk individuals aware of and have access to legitimate opportunities and services (a "carrot"), (3) to provide the message concerning the preceding two principals directly to the high-risk individuals and (4) to ensure that the criminal justice system followed through on the threat of sanctions when violence occurred and that services and opportunities were made available as an alternative to criminal opportunities.

From October 1998 through the early summer of 1999 nine meetings involving approximately 160 probationers and parolees were held to deliver the message. Preliminary evaluation data showed a reduction in violence following the crackdown, suggesting at least the need for further experimentation in the focused-deterrence strategy.

Finally, it will be important to assess whether the impact observed immediately following implementation of the interventions was temporary or lasting. Although crackdowns have been shown to generate short-term effects, the more fundamental question is whether crackdowns combined with linkages to services and community-building initiatives can generate long-term reductions in violent crime. In Indianapolis, the working group has attempted to build strong links to community organizations and community members to initiate the types of

Table 13.7 Key Interventions of the Indianapolis Violence Reduction Partnership (IVRP)

Problem (Target)	*Strategic Intervention*	*Nature of Intervention*	*Gang/Group Focus?*
Young men with extensive criminal records	Chronic violent offender program (VIPER)	System tightening—increase arrest and prosecution of most serious and chronic violent offenders	Not initially; over time began to focus on chronic violent offenders involved in groups/gangs
	Probation, parole, law enforcement field teams, U.S. marshal warrant service	System tightening—increase accountability	
	Lever-pulling meetings	Warn high-risk offenders to increase perception of sanctions for violence and link to legitimate services and opportunities	
	Faith-based groups intervening with youths	Increase legitimate opportunities; discourage participation in drug and violent activity	Street outreach, including former gang members in prevention efforts
	Covert investigations of drug-selling gangs	Gang suppression	Yes
Use of firearms in violent crime	Joint firearms unit	System tightening—increase prosecution of offenders using firearms and illegal possession	No
Areas with high levels of violent crime	Directed police patrol	Focused deterrence in these areas	No
	Probation, parole, law enforcement field teams; U.S. marshal warrant service	System tightening—increase accountability	Over time began to include group/gang members as a response to violent incidents
	Weed and seed	Increased police presence and community involvement in high-crime neighborhoods	Indirectly through prevention efforts aimed at youth

SOURCE: Edmund F. McGarrell and Steven Chermak. "Problem Solving to Reduce Gang and Drug-Related Violence in Indianapolis." In *Policing Gangs and Youth Violence* by Scott H. Decker. Belmont, CA: Wadsworth Publishing Company, 2003, p.87. Reprinted by permission.

broader changes that will be needed to achieve long-term and sustained impact on serious violent crime problems. Most of the energy devoted to the problem-solving effort has focused on identifying the nature of the homicide problem and developing suppression strategies to reduce violence. If such strategies are not linked to a commitment to changing the offender and the community, such an approach is unlikely to have a long-term impact on crime—or gangs.

SUMMARY

An estimated 850,000 gang members are active in nearly 31,000 gangs nationwide. Youths seeking protection, security, status, an identity and a sense of belonging can fulfill all of these needs through gang membership.

Prevention efforts should (1) begin early, (2) target youths exposed to multiple risk factors and (3) address all facets of youths' lives (Seattle study). The GREAT (Gang Resistance Education and Training) program is aimed at preventing youths from joining gangs. The GRIP (Gang Resistance Is Paramount) program also seeks to prevent youths from joining gangs through education.

Indicators of gang activity include graffiti, drive-by shootings, intimidation assaults, murders and the open sale of drugs. Indicators of gang membership include colors, tattoos, hand signs and behavior.

A computerized Gang Intelligence System (GANGIS), including comprehensive gang profile data such as monikers and vehicle information, can be an effective crime-fighting tool.

According to the OJJDP, law enforcement has used five strategies to address the gang problem: suppression, social intervention, social opportunities, community mobilization and organizational development or change. Community mobilization was found to be the most effective strategy to address the gang problem.

OJJDP initiatives to help communities address the gang problem include the Comprehensive Gang Model, the National Youth Gang Center, the Rural Gang Initiative and Gang Prevention through Targeted Outreach. Current strategies to address the gang problem include behavior codes, graffiti removal programs, drug-free zones (DFZs) around schools, conflict prevention strategies, pulling levers, obtaining civil injunctions and community involvement. The National Youth Gang Center has developed a protocol for assessing a gang problem as well as a planning guide to assist communities in addressing a gang problem.

The National Crime Prevention Council recommends using state laws and ordinances to combat gangs, using multiagency gang interdiction teams, preventing gangs through community intervention with high-risk youths, providing positive alternatives to gang activity and setting up information networks on gang activity. According to the OJJDP: "Community ambivalence toward gangs exists because many of the gang members are children of residents, the gangs often provide protection for residents, residents identify with gangs because of their own or relatives' prior involvement, and the gang in some instances have become community institutions."

Discussion Questions

1. What do you think are the main reasons individuals join gangs?
2. How does a street gang member differ from other juvenile delinquents?
3. What are the advantages and disadvantages of expelling disruptive gang members from school?
4. Were gangs present in your high school? How did you know? If they were, did they present a threat?
5. Are there efforts in your community to combat the gang problem?
6. Why is a uniform definition of gangs important for the law enforcement profession and what has prevented it from happening?
7. Why do schools and policing agencies sometimes deny or downplay the presence of gangs?
8. Explain the consequences of denying the existence of gangs.
9. In your opinion, is it possible to prevent youngsters from joining gangs?
10. Explain community ambivalence toward gangs.

InfoTrac College Edition Assignments

- Use InfoTrac College Edition to help answer the Discussion Questions as appropriate.
- Injunctions against gangs have been a highly successful strategy in some cities and states. Research the controversy surrounding the

constitutionality of using injunctions in this way. Be prepared to share your findings with the class.

- The city of Boston, using community policing strategies, won an Innovations in American Government Award for its Operation Cease Fire. Research this much-replicated program and explain why it was considered innovative and how it affected gang violence and teenage deaths by handguns.
- Select one of the following articles to read and outline.
  - "The Gangs Behind Bars" by Tiffany Davis
  - "Preventing Street Gang Violence" by Allen L. Hixon
  - "Gangs in Middle America: Are They a Threat?" by David M. Allender

Community Projects

- Go to the Web site of GangsOrUs (www.gangsorus.com) and outline the information given for gangs in your state.
- Research what strategies are used in your community to address the gang problem.

References

Allender, David M. "Gangs in Middle America: Are They a Threat?" *FBI Law Enforcement Bulletin,* December 2001, pp.1–9.

Braga, Anthony A.; Kennedy, David M.; Waring, Elin J.; and Piehl, Anne Morrison. "Problem-Oriented Policing, Deterrence and Youth Violence: An Evaluation of Boston's Operation Ceasefire." *Journal of Research in Crime and Delinquency,* August 2001, pp.195–225.

"California Law Enforcement Praises School Anti-Gang Program." *Criminal Justice Newsletter,* November 2, 2003, pp.4–5.

Domash, Shelly Feuer. "Youth Gangs: A National Problem Evading Easy Solutions." *Police,* June 2000, pp.22–30.

Domash, Shelly Feuer. "Stolen Dreams: When Kids Get Sucked into Gang Life and Don't Know How to Get Out." *Police,* June 2001, pp.46–51.

Domash, Shelly Feuer. "How to Crack Down on Gangs." *Police,* January 2004, pp. 16–22.

Egley, Arlen, Jr. and Major, Aline K. *Highlights of the 2001 National Youth Gang Survey.* Washington, DC: OJJDP Fact Sheet #01, April 2003. (FS 200301)

Esbensen, Finn-Aage. *Preventing Adolescent Gang Involvement.* Washington, DC: Juvenile Justice Clearinghouse, 2000. (NCJ-182210)

Esbensen, Finn-Aage; Winfree, L. Thomas, Jr.; He, Ni; and Taylor, Terrance J. "Youth Gangs and Definitional Issues: When Is a Gang a Gang, and Why Does It Matter?" *Crime & Delinquency,* January 2001a, pp.105–130.

Esbensen, Finn-Aage; Osgood, D. Wayne; Taylor, Terrance J.; Peterson, Dana; and Freng, Adrienne. "How Great Is G.R.E.A.T.? Results from a Longitudinal Quasi-Experimental Design." *Criminology and Public Policy,* November 2001b, pp.87–118.

Fraser, William J. "Getting the Drop on Street Gangs and Terrorists." *Law Enforcement News,* November 30, 2001, pp.11, 14.

Gangs: A Community Response. California Attorney General's Office, Crime and Violence Prevention Center, June 2003.

Hill, Karl G; Lui, Christina; and Hawkins, J. David. *Early Precursors of Gang Membership: A Study of Seattle Youths.* Washington, DC: OJJDP Juvenile Justice Bulletin, December 2001. (NCJ 190106)

Howell, James C. *Youth Gang Programs and Strategies: Summary.* Washington, DC: Office of Juvenile Justice and Delinquency Prevention, August 2000. (NCJ 171154)

Howell, James C.; Egley, Arlen, Jr.; and Gleason, Debra K. *Modern-Day Youth Gangs.* Washington, DC: OJJDP Juvenile Justice Bulletin, June 2002. (NCJ 191524)

Katz, Charles M. "The Establishment of a Police Gang Unit: An Examination of Organizational and Environmental Factors." *Criminology,* February 2001, pp.37–73.

Katz, Charles M.; Webb, Vincent J.; and Schaefer, David R. "The Validity of Police Gang Intelligence Lists: Examining Differences in Delinquency between Documented Gang Members and Nondocumented Delinquent Youths." *Police Quarterly,* December 2000, pp.413–437.

Kennedy, David M.; Braga, Anthony A.; and Piehl, Anne M. "Developing and Implementing Operation Ceasefire." In *Reducing Gun Violence: The Boston Gun Project's Operation Ceasefire.* Washington, DC: National Institute of Justice, September 2001, pp.1–53. (NCJ 188741)

Langston, Mike. "Addressing the Need for a Uniform Definition of Gang-Involved Crime." *FBI Law Enforcement Bulletin,* February 2003, pp.7–11.

Lesce, Tony. "New Mexico Gang Task Force: Coping with a Growing Problem." *Law and Order,* October 2000, pp.211–214.

Marble, Lynn. "The Youth Gang Problem: Fed Resources Are There to Assist." *Police,* June 2000, pp.38–41.

McGarrell, Edmund F. and Chermak, Steven. "Problem Solving to Reduce Gang and Drug-Related Violence in Indianapolis." In *Policing Gangs and Youth Violence,* edited by Scott H. Decker. Belmont, CA: Wadsworth Publishing Company, 2003, pp.77–101.

National Youth Gang Center. *Assessing Your Community's Youth Gang Problem.* Washington, DC: Office of Juvenile Justice and Delinquency Prevention, 2001a.

National Youth Gang Center. *Planning for Implementation of the OJJDP Comprehensive Gang Model.* Washington, DC: Office of Juvenile Justice and Delinquency Prevention, 2001b.

"New Program Supports Community Anti-Gang Efforts." *OJJDP News @ a Glance,* September/October 2003, pp.1–2.

Piraino, Anthony. "The Northwest Block Watch Coalition: Winning the War on Graffiti." *Law and Order,* April 2002, pp.22–26.

Rowell, James D. "Kids' Needs and the Attraction of Gangs." *Police,* June 2000, p.35.

Shelden, Randall G.; Tracy, Sharon K.; and Brown, William B. *Youth Gangs in American Society,* 2nd ed. Belmont, CA: Wadsworth, 2001.

Starbuck, David; Howell, James C.; and Lindquist, Donna J. *Hybrid and Other Modern Gangs.* Washington, DC: OJJDP Juvenile Justice Bulletin, December 2001. (NCJ 189916)

Valdez, Al. "Trying to Work Gangs? It's All About History, Infrastructure, and, Today, Even the Internet." *Police,* June 2000a, pp.32–37.

Valdez, Al. "Put Full-Service Gang Units to Work." *Police,* July 2000b, pp.54–55.

Vuong, Mary. "Jefferson Award Winner: Finding Creating Solution to Blight." *Seattle Post-Intelligence Reporter,* March 6, 2003.

Weisel, Deborah Lamm. "The Evolution of Street Gangs: An Examination of Form and Variation." In *Responding to Gangs: Evaluation and Research,* edited by Winifred L. Reed and Scott H. Decker, Washington, DC: National Institute of Justice, July 2002. (NCJ 190351)

Zatz, Marjorie S. and Portillos, Edwardo L. "Voices from the Barrio: Chicano Gangs, Families, and Communities." *Criminology,* May 2000, pp.369–401.

Additional Resources

Following are gang Web sites recommended for study.

Gangs and Security Threat Group Awareness: www.dc.state.fl.us/pub/gangs/index.html

This Florida Department of Corrections Web site contains information, photographs and descriptions on a wide variety of gang types, including Chicago and Los Angeles-based gangs, prison gangs, nation sets and supremacy groups.

GangsorUs: www.gangsorus.com

This site offers a broad range of information, including a state-by-state listing of all available gang laws, gang identities and behaviors applicable to all areas of the United States as well as links to other sites that provide information to law enforcement, parents and teachers.

Southeastern Connecticut Gang Activities Group (SEGAG): www.segag.org

This coalition of law enforcement and criminal justice agencies from southeastern Connecticut and New England provides information on warning signs that parents and teachers often observe first, along with a large number of resources and other working groups that are part of nationwide efforts to contain gang violence.

CHAPTER 14

Understanding and Preventing Violence and Terrorism

Violence is one of the most pressing social problems and important public health issues in American society.

—National Crime Prevention Council (NCPC)

Do You Know?

- What causes violence?
- What a problem-solving approach to preventing violence must attempt to do?
- What developing effective violence prevention tactics will require?
- What three strategies are suggested for general violence prevention?
- How hate can be classified?
- How to describe the majority of hate crimes?
- What the three phases in the gun violence continuum are?
- What strategy for each phase is suggested by the National Crime Prevention Council?
- Who the OJJDP has identified as potential partners in efforts to combat gun violence?
- How partner abuse differs from violent crime?
- Whether animal abuse is linked to domestic violence?
- What cultural diversity issue must be addressed when forming partnerships to prevent domestic abuse?
- What three risks face children in violent homes?
- What the CD-CP model emphasizes?
- How many people are victims of violent crime at work each year?
- What common motivations behind workplace violence are?
- What characteristics are common to workplace violence and school violence?
- What common elements in definitions of terrorism are?
- How the FBI classifies terrorism?
- What keys to combating terrorism are?
- What dual challenges in combating violence community policing is facing?

Can You Define?

bias crime
bias incident
cycle of violence
gun interdiction
hate crime
interoperability
macrosocial
microsocial
negative emotionality
process mapping
psychosocial
straw purchasers
terrorism

Introduction

Our nation was born in the violence of the Revolutionary War, and the union remained intact after a bloody Civil War that pitted brother against brother. Since then America has been willing to fight for freedom. It also cherishes the peace and freedom at home, however, that others fought to secure. But violence continues to exist, as shown in Figure 14.1.

In the United States, the estimated volume of violent crime reported to law enforcement decreased 0.9 percent in 2002, with 1.4 million estimated offenses. Five- and 10-year trend data revealed the estimated number of violent crimes was 7.0 percent lower than the 1998 number and 25.9 percent less than the 1993 number. The rate for violent crime, an estimated 494.6 offenses per 100,000 in population, decreased 2.0 percent when compared to the 2001 rate. The National Crime Victimization Survey (NCVS, 2002) also reports that violent crime has been declining since 1994 and in 2002 fell to its lowest level ever recorded. The most current information on rates of criminal victimization from the NCVS, the FBI

Community members hold an anti-violence sign addressing several issues. Citizens are key stakeholders in violence prevention partnerships.

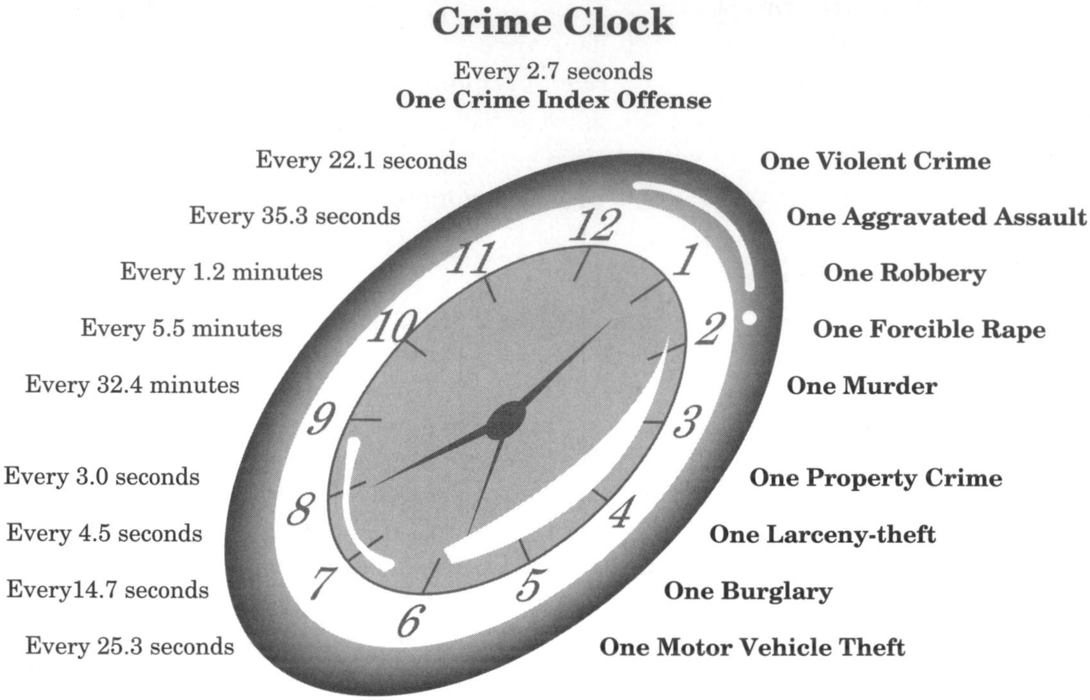

Figure 14.1 2002 Crime Clock

SOURCE: *Crime in the United States 2002*. Washington, DC: Federal Bureau of Investigation, October 27, 2003, p. 6.

and other sources is available on the Bureau of Justice Statistics (BJS) Web site at www.ojp.usdoj/gov/bjs/

Violence occurs on our streets as road rage, in our schools and workplaces as shooting sprees and behind closed doors as domestic abuse. It permeates and weakens our social fabric. This chapter begins with a discussion of the causes of violence and general guidelines on its prevention. Next is a discussion of bias or hate crimes. This is followed by an examination of gun violence, which is often manifested in other types of violence as well. Next domestic violence is examined, including spousal abuse and child abuse, followed by a discussion of workplace violence. The chapter concludes with an examination of terrorism, both domestic and international and a final look at a problem-solving partnership in action.

Causes of Violence

The causes of violence are as difficult to pinpoint as the causes of crime. Many suggest that the ready availability and lethal nature of guns, especially handguns, is a major factor. But in the colonial days every household had guns—survival depended on it. Yet children did not shoot each other in their one-room schoolhouses. Nonetheless, the gun factor must be considered.

Another major cause of violence is desensitization to violence. Violence permeates our television programs and movies, our video games and DVDs. Violence on our streets is graphically portrayed by the media.

Table 14.1 Matrix for Organizing Risk Factors for Violent Behavior

Units of Observation and Explanation	***Proximity to Violent Events and Their Consequences*** — ***Predisposing***	***Situational***	***Activating***
SOCIAL			
Macrosocial	– Concentration of poverty – Opportunity structures – Decline of social capital – Oppositional cultures – Sex role socialization	– Physical structures – Routine activities – Access: weapons, emergency medical services	– Catalytic social event
Microsocial	– Community organizations – Illegal markets – Gangs – Family disorganization – Pre-existing structures	– Proximity of responsible monitors – Participants' social relationships – Bystanders' activities – Temporary communication impairments – Weapons: carrying, displaying	– Participants' communication exchange
INDIVIDUAL			
Psychosocial	– Temperament – Learned social responses – Perceptions of rewards/ penalties for violence – Violent deviant sexual preferences – Social, communication skills – Self-identification in social hierarchy	– Accumulated emotion – Alcohol/drug consumption – Sexual arousal – Premeditation	– Impulse – Opportunity recognition
Biological	– Neurobehavioral* traits – Genetically mediated traits – Chronic use of psychoactive substances or exposure to neurotoxins	– Transient neurobehavioral* states – Acute effects of psycho-active substances	– Sensory signal processing errors

*Includes neuroanatomical, neurophysiological, neurochemical, and neuroendocrine. "Traits" describe capacity as determined by status at birth, trauma, and aging processes such as puberty. "States" describe temporary conditions associated with emotions, external stressors, etc.

Adapted from Albert J. Reiss, Jr. and Jeffrey A. Roth, eds. *Understanding and Preventing Violence,* Washington, DC: National Academy Press, 1993, p.297.

SOURCE: Jeffrey A. Roth. *Understanding and Preventing Violence.* Washington, DC: National Institute of Justice Research in Brief, p.7.

Causes of violence may include ready availability of guns, drugs and alcohol; a desensitization to violence; disintegration of the family and community; social and economic deprivation; and increased numbers of children growing up in violent families.

Table 14.1 presents risk factors for violent behavior in a matrix illustrating the complexity of social and individual factors that may cause violence. Notice the presence of weapons in both the **macrosocial** (big picture) and **microsocial** (smaller picture) situations. The macrosocial environment includes the amount of social capital available as discussed in previous chapters as well as existing diversity, including economic diversity. The microsocial environment focuses on smaller units such as the family. **Psychosocial** factors refer to individual psychological characteristics such as temperament and self-identity.

A problem-solving approach to preventing violence must attempt to identify the underlying causes of specific violent situations that threaten a community before solutions can be devised.

Those at Risk for Violence

Research by Lauritsen and White (2001, p.37) shows that non-Latino black, non-Latino white and Latino males and females in the United States experience significantly different levels of stranger and nonstranger violence and that these forms of nonlethal violence are more pronounced in areas with high levels of socioeconomic disadvantage. They (p.43) report: "Generally speaking, males report higher rates of violent victimization than do females, and whites have levels that are lower than those of other ethnic and racial groups. However, several new patterns are revealed. First, the risk for violence among males is highest for Latinos, followed by blacks and then whites."

Lauritsen and White (p.37) recommend: "The results suggest that victimization resources should be geographically targeted at places with high levels of poverty and single-parent families, and that the most stable institutions within these communities be drawn upon to deliver information about victimization prevention and services."

Preventing Violence

Developing effective prevention tactics will require long-term collaborations between criminal justice and juvenile justice practitioners and other social service agencies. It also requires involvement of the entire community of which these agencies are a part.

Prevention should include strategies directed toward children and their caregivers, especially those children who are at risk of becoming delinquent, as well as at areas with high levels of poverty and single-parent families. Efforts should also be directed at situations or locations where violent events cluster, such as illegal drug markets, certain places where alcohol and firearms are readily available, and physical locations conducive to crime.

Strategies for general violence prevention include public dialogue and community mediation, corporate support for antiviolence projects and addressing violence as a public health problem.

Key partnerships in a *public dialogue* and *community mediation* strategy include schools, police, probation agencies, area courts, community organizations and individual citizens, including youths. In addition community newspapers and grassroots word-of-mouth networks help publicize the community dialogue and mediation services. A potential obstacle to the service is that it may be difficult to finance. This obstacle might be overcome by another strategy, corporate sponsorship.

Corporate support for antiviolence projects encourages corporations to contribute to or implement antiviolence campaigns using their products, services and resources.

On their own and in partnership with local, state and national organizations, corporations can promote antiviolence messages and products. For example, Allstate Insurance Company served as a major corporate sponsor for a 5K "Race against Violence: America's #1 Challenge." The proceeds from registrations for the race, held in 10 major cities, went to local boys' and girls' clubs and the National Citizens' Crime Prevention Campaign (NCCPC). Another year the proceeds from the race went to Big Brothers and Big Sisters and the NCCPC. A potential obstacle to this strategy is that overreliance on corporate support can leave a program vulnerable to corporate managers' decisions.

A third strategy is to *address violence as a public health problem.* A successful public health campaign against violence requires violence prevention curricula, community partnerships, public awareness involving the mass media, and clinical education and training. Community groups, the clergy, business leaders, schools and parents can all contribute to a network of services. In addition, physicians, nurses and other health care providers can be trained in violence prevention techniques, including counseling and teaching patients anger management.

The Boston City Department of Health and Hospitals initiated the Boston Violence Prevention Project in 1982 to prevent youth violence. It began in high school classrooms with lessons presenting violence statistics and addressing ways to avert violence and expanded into a comprehensive effort to reach the entire community. This nationally known program also incorporates education and training for youth-serving agencies and has trained thousands of people and hundreds of agencies. The program also spurred development of the "Friends for Life, Friends Don't Let Friends Fight" media campaign and "Increase the Peace" weeks.

Potter and Krider (2000) describe a course developed by the Centers for Disease Control and Prevention called "Teaching about Violence Prevention: A Bridge between Public Health and Criminal Justice Education." The course overviews the public health approach to the prevention of violence and related injuries and compares it to the traditional approach taken by criminal justice. If courses such as this proliferate, they will better prepare future law enforcement officers and public health officials to effectively apply community policing strategies aimed at preventing violence.

Chapter 3 discussed the concept of community and its social capital. Some researchers suggest that communities with limited social capital will be a harder "sell" for community policing efforts. Others suggest that communities consisting largely of minority members will be a harder "sell." However, a study released in 1999 by the National Institute of Justice (NIJ) suggests differently ("We're Not Gonna Take It," 1999, p.1). This study, "Attitudes toward Crime, Police, and the Law: Individual and Neighborhood Differences," examined racial and ethnic differences in attitudes toward social deviance in 343 urban communities in Chicago. It found significantly lower levels of tolerance for antisocial behavior among black and Latino residents than among white residents.

NIJ Director Jeremy Travis says: "The data support a framework for community policing that is both tough on crime, but even tougher on police departments with regard to building stronger relationships within the community." Travis (p.10) suggests: "Law enforcement could use the constructive forces already present in the community to help develop strong local support for the legitimacy and need for police activities." In addition, Travis notes: "In the context of community policing there is a second bottom line after reducing crime—community support. It is a great asset for law enforcement to recognize that there will be strong support in disadvantaged communities, not necessarily because residents like police tactics, but because there is strong support for social norms."

Unfortunately, social norms are not always the same from one community to another, and the results can be manifested in hate crimes.

Bias or Hate Crimes

Many people feel threatened by simply coming in contact with those who are culturally different. No other nation is as culturally diverse as the United States, thrusting people of different customs, languages, lifestyles and beliefs together and hoping they can coexist peacefully. Unfortunately, this does not always happen, and severe tension can result between cultural groups when their members are poorly informed and suspicious of cultures and lifestyles outside their own. What people do not understand, they tend to fear, and what they fear, they tend to hate.

Hate can be classified into two categories: rational and irrational.

As Schafer and Navarro (2003, p.1) explain: "Unjust acts inspire rational hate. Hatred of a person based on race, religion, sexual orientation, ethnicity or national origin constitutes irrational hate." The International Association of Chiefs of Police (IACP), in its publication *Responding to Hate Crimes: A Police Officer's Guide to Investigation and Prevention* (1999), answers the question, "What is a hate crime?" A **hate** or **bias crime** is a criminal offense committed against a person, property or society that is motivated, in whole or in part, by an offender's bias against an individual's or group's race, religion, ethnic/national origin, gender, age, disability or sexual orientation.

Bias crimes include any act, or attempted act, to cause physical injury, emotional suffering or property damage through intimidation, harassment, racial or ethnic slurs and bigoted epithets, vandalism, force or the threat of force. The majority of hate crimes are against the person, including assault (the most common), harassment, menacing/reckless endangerment and robbery. Crimes against property include vandalism/criminal mischief (most common), arson/cross burning and burglary.

As discussed, cultural tension commonly occurs in this country due to an intolerance of racial and ethnic diversity. Although many would like to believe the intense racial hatred and slaughter of minorities is a relatively distant part of our nation's history and that we've come a long way from the "lynching era" of the late 1800s and early 1900s, events in the 1990s indicate otherwise.

- In 1998, James Byrd, Jr., a black man, was hitchhiking home when a truck pulled up. Byrd was kidnapped, taken to a wooden area, beaten to unconsciousness, chained to the back of the truck, and then dragged for several miles. His head and right arm were torn from his body during the dragging. His assailants were three white men with links to racist groups.

- Also in 1998, openly gay college student Matthew Shepard was beaten with a pistol and then tied to a fence on the edge of town and left to die.

According to the UCR Program in 2002, 7,462 hate crimes were reported involving 8,832 separate offenses, 9,222 victims and 7,314 known offenders. Of the total number of bias crimes reported, 48.8 percent were motivated by racial bias, 19.1 percent by religious bias, 16.7 percent by sexual-orientation bias, 14.8 percent by an ethnicity/national origin bias and 0.6 percent by disability bias. Crimes against persons accounted for 67.5 percent of reported hate crime. Intimidation continued to be the most frequently reported hate crime against individuals, accounting for 52.1 percent of all crimes against persons.

The majority of hate crimes are motivated by racial bias, are crimes against persons and use intimidation.

Destruction/damage/vandalism was the most frequently reported hate crime against property and accounted for 83.1 percent of the total hate crimes against property (*Crime in the United States,* 2002).

Bouman (2003, p.23) contends: "Hate/bias crimes destroy communities, as well as hoard resources from law enforcement agencies." Several states have passed mandatory reporting laws that require police departments to keep statistics on the occurrence of bias and hate crimes. In 1990 the Federal Hate Crime Statistics Act was passed, mandating the justice department to secure data on crimes related to religion, race, sexual orientation or ethnicity. While the laws vary considerably, the most common elements include (1) enhanced penalties for common-law crimes against persons or property motivated by bias based on race, ethnicity, religion, gender or sexual orientation; (2) criminal penalties for vandalism of religious institutions; and (3) collection of data on bias crimes. Currently, 40 of the 50 states, the District of Columbia and the federal government have passed penalty-enhancement hate crime laws (Vogel, 2000, p.3).

Paynter (2000, p.53) asserts: "Law enforcement must be prepared to deal with hate incidents and hate crimes. Incidents can be simplified to anything that's hateful in nature, and crimes are defined as those incidents that are prosecutable under the law." The law, however, can also be a complicating factor in handling hate incidents. The First Amendment protects freedom of speech and people's right to peaceably assemble. According to Wessler and Moss (2001, p.19): "The use of bigoted and prejudiced language does not in itself violate hate crime laws. This type of behavior is frequently classified as a **bias incident**. However, hate crime laws apply when words threaten violence. Similarly, hate crime laws apply when bias-motivated graffiti damages or destroys property."

Police must not simply turn a blind eye to activities such as the distribution of hate literature or the holding of hate assemblies, no matter how "peaceful," within their community, because such hate incidents may be precursors to hate crimes. The

IACP has defined a hate crime continuum (see Figure 14.2) showing what can happen if a community ignores "minor" incidents, allowing them to grow into a major and potentially deadly situation.

Hate literature can lead to hate tattoos, hate symbols and hate gatherings, which can lead to disturbing the peace, threats and vandalism, which may escalate into assault and other violations of civil rights, arson and even murder (Paynter, pp.52–53). In fact, an appropriate analogy is given in the likening of racism to carbon monoxide—it may be silent, you may not see or hear it, but uncontrolled, it can kill.

For this reason, officers must get out and talk with citizens to find out what is going on in their communities. Officers must address all hate-based events, whether major or minor. An IACP staffer (Paynter, p.53) contends: "If it's the police department's job to work closely with the community and make sure citizens feel safe, then it doesn't matter if it's a crime or an incident. Because if people are afraid, they're afraid, and you'd better tell them there's a way for them not to be afraid anymore." And as one police chief asserts (Paynter, p.58): "Hate crimes can be tackled through a combination of presence, partnership, prevention and outreach to the community. That's true community policing."

Nonetheless, police officers should recognize when crimes might be the result of bigotry and seek the causes for a particular incident. The IACP has compiled a list of key hate crime indicators to help officers determine whether an incident was motivated by bias and therefore a hate crime (Paynter, p.56). Officers should consider the perceptions of the victim(s) and witnesses about the crime; the perpetrator's comments, gestures or written statements that reflect bias, including graffiti and other symbols; any differences between the perpetrator and the victim, whether

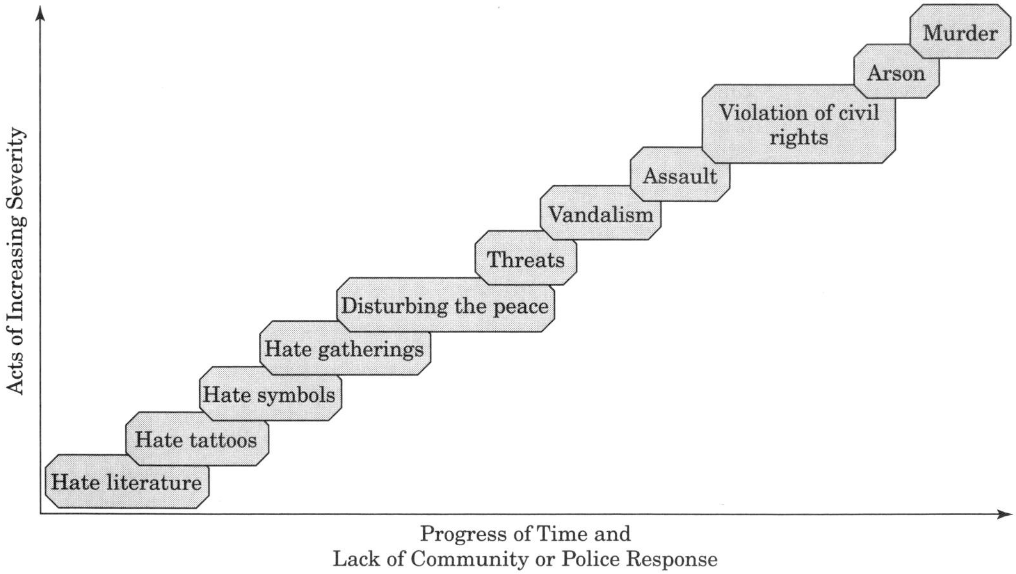

Figure 14.2 Hate-Crime Continuum (Adapted from the IACP.)

SOURCE: Kären M. Hess and Henry M. Wrobleski, *Police Operations*, 3rd ed. Belmont, CA: Wadsworth Publishing Company, 2003, p.340.

actual or perceived by the perpetrator; and any similar incidents in the same location or neighborhood that show a pattern may exist.

They should also consider whether the victim was engaged in activities promoting his or her group or community; whether the incident coincided with a holiday or date of particular significance to the victim's group; any involvement by organized hate groups or their members; and the absence of any other motive such as economic gain.

As noted by the U.S. Department of Justice's Community Relations Service, hate crimes are occurring with increasing frequency and more visibility and hostility in institutions of higher learning than in any other area ("College Campuses . . .," 2000, p.11). As Wessler and Moss (p.1) note: "When a hate crime occurs on a college campus, the ideal of a university as a place for learning and growth is ruptured." They (p.7) report: "Some of the most common problems in responding to hate crimes are that police are inadequately trained; students, staff, faculty and administrators do not report the crimes; and administrators do not adequately disseminate information to the campus community." Many colleges and universities have responded to hate crimes on campus with broad-based public condemnation of bias, prejudice and violence, including an open letter from the president or dean to the campus community and meetings open to the entire campus community. Several schools have implemented peer diversity education groups that promote understanding of diversity on campus.

The Center for the Prevention of Hate Violence at the University of Southern Maine has initiated the Campus Civility Project to address bias, prejudice and harassment. As Wessler and Moss (p.13) describe: "Administrators, faculty, staff and student leaders (such as resident advisors and captains of sports teams) participate in three-hour workshops that help them develop a fuller understanding of the harmful effects of degrading language and slurs. Most important, the workshops also provide participants with practical skills for intervening in low-key ways when students engage in conduct that demeans, degrades or frightens others."

In addition to concern about hate crimes on college campuses, law enforcement and the communities they serve may be faced with hate crimes committed not by individuals, but by groups, one of the most well-known of which is the skinheads.

Skinhead Groups

According to Schafer and Navarro (p.2): "Skinhead groups typically consist of uneducated, young, white males between the ages of 13 and 24 who have no long-term prospects for success. . . . Fortunately, most skinhead groups are not well organized and lack the leadership structure found in the majority of street gangs engaged in 'for-profit' criminal activities."

They suggest that skinheads can be divided into two groups, criminally motivated and hate motivated: "Hate-motivated skinhead groups dedicate the majority of their time to hate crimes. Incidental to hate crimes, these hard-core skinheads commit petty thefts or sell small amounts of narcotics to support daily needs, such as food, cigarettes, and alcohol and other drugs. . . . Skinheads converge, get drunk, take drugs and, at some point, spontaneously seek out hate targets to attack. They conduct little, if any, planning before committing hate crimes."

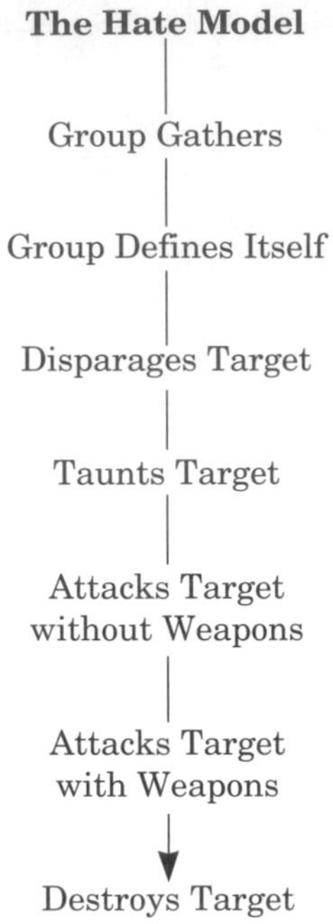

Figure 14.3 The Seven-Stage Hate Model

SOURCE: John R. Schafer and Joe Navarro. "The Seven-Stage Hate Model: The Psychopathology of Hate Groups." *FBI Law Enforcement Bulletin,* March 2003, p.1. Reprinted by permission.

Schafer and Navarro (p.3) also note: "Empirical observations show that hate groups go through seven stages in the hate process. Haters, if unimpeded, pass through these seven successive stages without skipping a stage. In the first four stages, haters vocalize their beliefs. In the last three stages, haters act on their beliefs. A transition period exists between vocalization and acting out. In this transition period, violence separates hard-core haters from rhetorical haters." The seven stages are illustrated in Figure 14.3. Whether a hate crime is perpetrated by a group or by an individual, how law enforcement and the community react to its victims is crucial.

Addressing and Preventing Hate Crimes

Law enforcement can forge partnerships with local businesses and institutions to better understand and tackle the issue of hate crimes (Paynter, p.61): "In Provincetown, Massachusetts, the police department works with area hospitals to ensure that medical professionals identify potential hate crime victims seeking treatment. In its assessment of the community, the organizations involved found that homosexual victims often were reluctant to admit they'd been victimized, even in a hospital setting. The groups coalesced around what the community was dealing with in terms of assaults and gay-bashing incidents."

The National Crime Prevention Council lists various strategies for preventing the occurrence of bias crimes in a community, such as diversity and tolerance education in schools, ongoing police–cultural organization service partnerships, rapid response to reported incidents, media campaigns about community standards for tolerance, counseling for offenders involved in hate groups and community-based dispute mediation services.

Paynter (p.61) notes that in tackling hate crimes, community policing is a vehicle to ensure victim support, community unity concerning these problems and the full prosecution of such crimes. He further asserts: "When law enforcement takes a leadership role, it plays a major part in getting citizens to stand up against hate incidents and hate crimes in their community." Creating a strong and unified voice condemning the proliferation of hate is what is needed to stamp out bias and keep it from jeopardizing public safety. One diversity trainer summarizes (Paynter, p.61): "If you're out there and you let these things happen, you might as well stop [policing]. If it escalates to the point where someone dies, people will say he did this, she did that, but WE did this because we did not say this behavior will not be tolerated."

Bouman (p.24) suggests: "[Police] can use many tactics to educate, train and empower communities to fight hate/bias crimes. Establishing and training Neighborhood Watch groups, encouraging community meetings and community problem-solving activities and supporting community efforts by involving local law enforcement agencies are just a few of the ways. . . . [They] also can train targets and victims of hate/bias crimes as responsive and preventive advocates; engage members of local community organizations to help with the response, investigation and prevention of hate/bias crimes; and help coordinate critical support services for primary and secondary victims. Vigorously responding to and investigating hate/bias crimes in the local community and using the media proactively to inform and educate the community also will generate trust for investigators within a community. On a larger scale, using national resources, programs, and models for prevention, response and healing will help revive communities."

Working with the families, friends, neighbors and communities that surround a hate/bias incident becomes as important as working with the victim. Secondary victimization induces blame, outrage or fear in a family, group of friends or community. These groups may be motivated to act in response to a hate/bias crime and retaliate in their own ways unless they are educated and provided other options for response or healing. Training victims and communities to cooperate with law enforcement and other community programs takes the control out of the hands of the perpetrator, instills confidence in the victim and community and prevents future crimes.

Other violence prevention programs are aimed at gun violence, which often manifests itself in specific types of violence that can be addressed through community policing strategies.

Gun Violence

According to the FBI's Uniform Crime Reports *Crime in the United States 2002* (www.fbi.gov/ucr/), approximately 71.1 percent of murders in the United States in 2002 involved a firearm. As President Bush acknowledged: "In America today, a teenager is more likely to die from a gunshot than from all natural causes of death combined."

Gun violence may be considered as a three-phase continuum: (1) the illegal acquisition of firearms, (2) the illegal possession and carrying of firearms and (3) the illegal, improper or careless use of firearms.

Effective gun control strategies focus on one, two or all three of these points of intervention. These strategies and programs focus on three points of intervention: (1) interrupting sources of illegal guns, (2) determining illegal possession and carrying of guns and (3) responding to illegal gun use.

Strategies to Interrupt Sources of Illegal Guns

The strategies to interrupt sources of illegal guns include law enforcement initiatives that disrupt the illegal flow of firearms by using intelligence gathered through crime gun tracing and regulatory inspections or undercover operations involving suspected illegal gun dealers. Comprehensive crime gun tracing facilitates both the reconstruction of the sales history of firearms associated with crime and the identification of patterns of illegal gun trafficking. Similarly, focusing criminal and regulatory enforcement on suspect dealers allows law enforcement to efficiently focus limited resources. Suspect dealers include those at the greatest risk of selling firearms to **straw purchasers**, that is, purchasers fronting for people linked to illegal gun trafficking.

Initiated in 1994, the Boston Gun Project includes gun trafficking interdiction as one component in their broad strategy to stop gun violence in Boston. Partners in the project include the Bureau of Alcohol, Tobacco and Firearms (ATF), the Boston Police Department (BPD), the Suffolk County District Attorney's Office and the U.S. Attorney's Office. A seasoned violent crime coordinator was assigned by ATF to pursue federal firearm arrests. Six ATF agents were also assigned to collaborate with ballistics and crime laboratories at BPD to trace recovered handguns and match them to other crimes.

Based on the ATF tracing data set, the working group established priorities for disrupting the illegal gun market. First the group prioritized investigating every trace that showed a gun with a time-to-crime of less than 30 months. Priority was also given to certain types of guns popular with youths, for example, semiautomatic handguns, those with restored obliterated serial numbers, those found in high-risk neighborhoods and those associated with gang members or territories. Priority was also given to swift federal prosecution for gun trafficking.

The project was evaluated by the Kennedy School of Government at Harvard University and found to be successful. Based on this demonstrated success, ATF launched the Youth Crime Gun Interdiction Initiative in 17 demonstration cities in 1996.

The National Crime Prevention Council suggests that regulations and ordinances on gun licensing may interrupt sources of illegal guns.

As the NCPC notes, municipal ordinances may affect the first two phases of gun violence simultaneously. However, the Centers for Disease Control (CDC) reviewed 51 studies on the effectiveness of eight major types of firearms laws on reducing the rate of violence and concluded: "[We have] found insufficient evidence to determine the effectiveness of any of the firearms laws or combinations of laws reviewed on violent outcomes. . . . This finding should not be interpreted as evidence of ineffectiveness, but rather an indicator that additional research is needed, particularly because of the huge involvement of firearms in violence in the United States" ("CDC Reports Assess Violence Prevention Strategies," 2003, p.10).

Interrupting the sale of illegal firearms also reduces the number of people possessing and carrying guns illegally.

Strategies to Deter Illegal Gun Possession and Carrying

Strategies to deter illegal gun possession and carrying include municipal gun ordinances, weapons hotlines, directed police patrols, focusing on hot spots where disproportionate amounts of crime and violence occur and focusing on individuals most likely to possess and carry firearms illegally, including gang members and probationers.

A 1992 report by the Violence Policy Center showed that the United States had more licensed gun dealerships than it had gas stations—280,000. In response the ATF implemented stiffer licensing requirements and raised the licensing fee from $30 to $200. Applicants were now to be fingerprinted and to undergo more extensive background checks aimed at weeding out unscrupulous dealers. The new requirements resulted in a 19 percent drop in the number of licensed gun dealers in three years.

This same strategy can be implemented locally if stakeholders work together to get legislation passed. For example, the East Bay Gun Violence Prevention Project was initiated by the East Bay Public Safety Corridor Partnership, a regional coordinating body formed to reduce crime and violence in response to an alarming level of gun violence among cities in the East Bay Corridor. As the OJJDP (*Promising Strategies to Reduce Gun Violence,* 1999, p.91) notes: "In 1994, faced with the presence of more than 400 gun dealers in Alameda County and 700 in Contra Costa County, the Corridor cities of Oakland, Richmond, and San Pablo began working to pass municipal ordinances to better regulate gun sales and eliminate residential gun dealers, that is, dealers who sell guns out of their homes or cars." Ordinances aimed at reducing gun violence included banning the manufacture and sale of "junk guns," requiring trigger locks at the point of sale, restricting the number of licensed gun dealers and the areas in which they can operate and placing a gross receipts tax on merchandise sold by gun dealers.

Gun interdictions may be an effective deterrent to illegal gun possessing and carrying.

A **gun interdiction** is a law enforcement–led strategy whereby local police direct intensive patrols to specific geographic areas with high rates of gun-related incidents of violence. Proactive patrols focus on traffic stops and other mechanisms to detect illegal or illegally concealed weapons and seize them. Community support for the interdiction strategy is vital because such searches and seizures can raise controversy. Community input should be sought in identifying the targeted areas to reduce the chance of charges of racial disparity should the hot spot be inhabited by members of a minority group. Gun interdictions also affect the third phase of the gun violence continuum.

Strategies to Respond to Illegal Gun Use

Strategies to respond to illegal gun use include identification, prosecution and aggressive punishment of those who commit multiple violent crimes, are armed drug traffickers or have used a firearm in a crime; intensive education; and strict monitoring of offenders.

Local gun courts that deal exclusively with gun law violations reinforce community standards against violence and ensure swift punishment of violators.

The country's first adult gun court was established in the Providence (Rhode Island) Superior Court in 1994 by a statute creating a separate gun court calendar with concurrent jurisdiction with all other superior court calendars. Within four months of its implementation, the backlog of gun-related cases was reduced by two-thirds. All cases are tried within 60 days, and most carry mandatory prison terms, including 10 years to life for a third offense. The mayor obtained support from the National Rifle Association (NRA) and from local advocates of gun control—a tricky combination.

Comprehensive Gun Violence Reduction Strategies

Comprehensive gun reduction involves partnerships through which the community, law enforcement, prosecutors, courts and social services agencies:

- Identify where gun violence occurs and who perpetrates it.
- Develop a comprehensive plan.
- Create strategies to carry out the plan.

Partners in gun violence reduction identified by the OJJDP include the U.S. attorney, chief of police, sheriff, federal law enforcement agencies (FBI, ATF, DEA), district attorney, state attorney general, mayor/city manager, probation and parole officers, juvenile corrections officials, judges, public defenders, school superintendents, social services officials, leaders in the faith community and business leaders.

The OJJDP (*Promising Strategies . . .*, p.11) suggests a somewhat more detailed outline for developing a comprehensive strategy. The steps they suggest are to (1) establish appropriate stakeholder partnerships, (2) identify and measure the problem, (3) set measurable goals and objectives, (4) identify appropriate programs and strategies, (5) implement the comprehensive plan, (6) evaluate the plan and (7) revise the plan on the basis of the evaluation. The OJJDP (p.17) identifies several characteristics of communities who have successfully implemented gun control strategies:

- The community recognizes its gun violence problems.
- Law enforcement and other key institutional administrators are enlisted as key partners.
- The collaborative has access to resources.

- The collaborative develops a comprehensive vision and plan.
- The collaborative mobilizes and sustains gun violence reduction activities.
- The collaborative develops a leadership structure.

Harris (2001, p.57) reports on five common elements found in the successful firearm crime reduction programs of the Boston Project and Project Exile in Richmond, Virginia: "(1) a coalition approach that involved all stakeholders, (2) a strategic focus on firearm-related crime, backed by an agreed-upon plan that provided mutual support for the overall goal of reducing firearm-related homicides and other violent firearm crime, (3) the vigorous enforcement and prosecution of laws related to criminal possession and use of firearms, (4) an intense publicity program designed to warn of the penalties for illegal possession or use of a firearm and (5) the support of both pro-gun and anti-gun organizations."

Other entities becoming involved in the gun violence issue are those in the medical field and health services because, as the OJJDP (*Promising Strategies . . .*, p.169) notes: "Gun violence is not only a criminal justice problem but also a public health problem." The CDC now keep statistics on gun-related injuries and deaths. The public health approach to reducing violence includes (1) emphasizing the prevention of violence, (2) making science integral to identifying effective policies and programs and (3) integrating the efforts of diverse organizations, communities and disciplines.

To be comprehensive, gun violence prevention strategies must also include educational efforts to change attitudes toward guns and violence and to promote gun safety, particularly among young people.

Reducing Access to Firearms

The Center to Prevent Handgun Violence reports more than 2.5 million children and youths currently live in homes where firearms are stored unlocked and loaded or with ammunition nearby. *Common Sense about Kids and Guns* (www.kidsandguns.org), a nonprofit group of gun owners and nonowners committed to protecting America's children from gun deaths and injuries, notes 48 percent of gun-owning households with children do not regularly make sure that guns are equipped with child safety or other trigger locks. Furthermore, although nearly 80 percent of Americans think it is important to reduce children's access to guns, approximately two-thirds of students in grades six through twelve say they have ready access to guns and could obtain a firearm within 24 hours.

Child Access Prevention (CAP) laws, or "safe storage" laws, require adults to either store loaded guns in a place reasonably inaccessible to children or to use a safety device to lock the gun if they choose to leave the weapon accessible. If a child obtains an improperly stored, loaded gun, the adult owner is criminally liable.

The primary goal of CAP laws is to prevent accidental injury by firearms. The Center to Prevent Handgun Violence states: "Research demonstrates that in the 12 states which had passed CAP laws by 1997, accidental deaths of children from firearms decreased 23% in the two years after the laws went into effect."

CAP laws also help reduce juvenile suicide by keeping guns out of the reach of children. For youths, particularly adolescents, rapid and intense fluctuations in mood are fairly common. A child going through a particularly difficult time emotionally may, with easy access to a firearm, turn a temporary situation into a permanent mistake.

Teaching Gun-Safe Behavior

When adults fail to keep firearms securely locked away or to teach others in the house, especially children, proper gun safety techniques, they place their entire family and anyone who may be in or near their house at tremendous risk. One police officer, despite educating her two young sons about gun safety and how to handle firearms, lost her older boy to an accidental shooting. He had gone next door to play with a neighbor, who had found a gun in one of the bedrooms and, while playing with it, accidentally shot his friend in the face. His mother, like many parents, had never considered asking the parents of her children's playmates if they kept guns in their house.

While the ultimate responsibility for teaching kids gun-safe behavior lies with parents, many adults themselves need coaching in this area. *Common Sense* reports 70 percent of Americans feel that more needs to be done to educate parents about how to keep their children safe from guns and on proper storage methods. Statistics indicate that the firearms used in most accidental deaths, injuries and suicides are obtained not on the street but from familiar surroundings—the homes of family or friends. According to *Common Sense,* in 72 percent of unintentional deaths and injuries, suicide and suicide attempts with a firearm of 0–19 year-olds, the firearm was stored in the residence of the victim, a relative or a friend.

Sorby and Wheeler (2002, pp.22–23) describe the Citizen Firearm Safety Program developed by the Prince William County Police Department. Each eight-hour class begins with a 90-minute lecture presented by a prosecutor who informs participants of legal ramifications of gun use and citizen liability. Additional lectures included such topics as elements of gun safety, gun safety rules, the safe use and storage of guns and special responsibilities of parents. Participants also receive numerous handouts and other visual aids and watch a live firearm demonstration. Participants rate the program highly, and it has received several awards.

Right-to-Carry Laws

Right-to-carry (RTC) concealed handgun laws are a controversial issue. One fact is clear: Such laws do increase the number of concealed weapons on the streets. The argument in favor of such laws is that it will reduce crime and simultaneously give citizens a feeling of security. Researchers Kovandzic and Marvell (2003, p.363) found "little evidence that increases in the number of citizens with concealed-handgun permits reduce or increase rates of violent crime." In commenting on this research, Donohue (2003, p.399) notes: "Kovandzic and Marvell have now put the final bullet in the body of the more guns, less crime hypothesis. . . . The addition of [their research] underscores that the weight of the evidence is now firmly behind those who have found that RTC laws do not reduce, and may even increase, the overall level of crime."

Donohue (p.403) also notes, however: "RTC laws might still prove beneficial by (1) making permit holders feel safer when out in public, (2) providing permit holders with a more effective means of self-defense and (3) reducing the costs to police departments of enforcing laws prohibiting unlicensed gun carrying."

Prevention of gun violence may greatly affect the other types of violence discussed next in this chapter: domestic violence and workplace violence.

Domestic Violence

"If ever a problem demanded a community policing approach, it is the complex and serious challenge of domestic abuse. As our sophistication about the dynamics of human behavior grows, it becomes ever clearer that family violence is a key to the expanding cycle of violence that puts all of us at risk" ("Community Policing and Domestic Violence," www.policing.com). In the words of the late Robert Trojanowicz, a community policing pioneer: "We must remember that until we are all safe, no one is truly safe."

Building trust with the victims of domestic violence is crucial. Those who have been victimized by spousal abuse, stalking, child abuse or elder abuse can sometimes be of great assistance in community efforts to prevent such victimization. This part of the chapter focuses on strategies to reduce or prevent domestic violence. In addition to collaboration among criminal justice agencies, all other stakeholders in the community need to be involved in identifying problems and working toward solutions.

Partner Abuse and Stalking

According to statistics compiled by the National Institute of Justice, one of four women in the United States says she has been a victim of domestic violence or stalking by a husband, partner or date at some point in her life ("Did You Know That . . .?" 2000, p.16). These figures are probably extremely conservative because domestic violence is often not reported to the police. According to Felson et al. (2002, p.617): "Victims of domestic violence are less likely than victims of other types of violence to call the police because of their privacy concerns, their fear of reprisal and their desire to protect offenders." Also of importance is a Department of Justice report on the National Violence against Women Survey that found 36 percent of domestic violence victims were men (Baker and Piland-Baker, 2000, p.129).

Important Research Finding

Research conducted by Moffitt et al. (2000) found that partner abuse and general crime shared the common characteristic of a trait called negative emotionality. "**Negative emotionality** is a generalized propensity for experiencing aversive affective states, including anger, anxiety, suspiciousness, and irritability. People with chronically high levels of negative emotionality are emotionally brittle; they live in a world darkened by a rapid, excessive response to minor stressors, a sense that others are malicious, and a propensity to react to even slight provocation with rage"

(Moffitt et al., p.222). Negative emotionality is a shared risk factor for both partner abuse and crime. The researchers found a significant difference between those who abuse their partners and those who commit violent crimes—a difference in constraint. Constraint is equated with self-control. According to the researchers it is about heeding societal prohibitions against expressing impulses.

Partner abuse differs from violent crime in that partner abuse is not related to constraint trait as criminal behavior is.

"In other words, the same individual who attacks someone impulsively in a bar, at a sports event, or during a robbery may use violence strategically to control his or her partner in the privacy of home" (p.223). The fact that partner violence is "strategic, painful, and willful" (p.224) has important implications for individuals working on strategies to prevent domestic violence.

Legislation to Prevent Stalking and Domestic Violence

Although several laws have been passed to prevent stalking and domestic violence, one law, the Violence against Women Act (VAWA), merits emphasis because it makes this serious problem a systemwide institutional priority. In October 2000 Congress voted to reauthorize VAWA, restoring authorization for VAWA programs for five years, with more than $3 billion in funding ("Congress Votes . . .," 2000, p.1).

Problem Solving and Domestic Violence: A Case Study

This case study is adapted from Brookoff et al. (1999, pp.113–150). In 1995 the Tennessee legislature enacted a new domestic violence law encouraging arrests and mandating the filing of reports and development of domestic violence databases. A group of Memphis police officers and doctors met to discuss their mutual frustrations about their lack of progress with victims and perpetrators of domestic assault: "Repeat 911 calls were mounting, emergency room visits for battering were skyrocketing and the batterers kept on battering" (p.113).

In response to the new law, the police asked medical personnel to accompany them on domestic violence calls to see whether a "caregiver approach," using a nonthreatening, private and caring manner, could help identify ways to improve victims' treatment and identify prevention opportunities. After patrol officers had responded and stabilized the scene, a survey team entered the home and interviewed the officers about the circumstances of the call and their decision whether to arrest. If the incident fit the legal criteria for domestic violence, victims, assailants and adult family members in the house when the police arrived were also asked to participate in the survey. In addition, medical personnel were able to help assess batterers and their victims. One predisposing factor to domestic assault the Memphis police and health care workers identified was intoxication with alcohol or drugs.

In nearly every case, the survey team delineated risk factors for future assault that could be reduced by treatment. They also identified young children apparently traumatized by witnessing the assault and in need of help (p.133). In addition they discovered several social and psychological barriers stand between domestic violence participants and the help they need.

Some victims cited economic dependence. Others had an exaggerated dependence on their batterers. Some reported their assailants had forced them into criminal activity or drug abuse as a leverage should they try to find a job or leave the relationship. The most common barrier found by the team was an assailant's drug abuse. Two-thirds had used cocaine and alcohol the day of the assault—a mixture likely to incite violent behavior. As part of their problem-solving efforts, the team collected specimens for toxicological testing from domestic assailants. Efforts were made to help them get treatment.

As is often the case when problem solving is used to address a community problem, tracking calls revealed that police had been called to the home on a previous domestic violence call in 85 percent of the cases. In 50 percent of domestic homicide cases, police had responded more than five times to domestic violence calls at the home in the previous two years. And, as is frequently the case in problem solving, additional problems are brought to light. In the case of the Memphis collaboration, officers and health care providers alike came to realize the devastating effect domestic abuse had on children who witnessed it. Such children far outnumber the direct victims of domestic assault. And if these children witness repeated episodes of family violence, they may come to believe it is normal and acceptable.

The team videotaped some of the cases, and a team doctor wrote an article based on one case called, "The Faces of the Children." In it he wrote (Brookoff et al., p.141):

> I remember one case where we were leaving a home and found a three-year-old boy who had just seen his mother badly beaten. The boy was sitting in the corner and holding the family's kitten by the throat and punching it.
>
> One of the police officers called out to the mother, "Your boy is about to kill your cat."
>
> "Oh don't worry about that," she called back. "He always does things like that when he sees the way his daddy beats me."

Animal abuse has a direct link to domestic violence.

Turner (2000, p.28) reports on a New Jersey study that found in 88 percent of families where there had been physical abuse of children there were also records of animal abuse. The research showed that two-thirds of the abusers harming animals were fathers, while the remaining third were the children themselves. She notes: "The FBI has used the correlation between childhood animal abuse and adult violence for years to profile serial killers." According to the Humane Society of the United States, "Animal cruelty is one link in the chain of family violence" (Turner, p.18).

Ponder and Lockwood (2000, p.36) suggest: "Law enforcement officials considering a program on the connection between animal abuse and family violence should start by contacting their counterparts in social service and animal protection agencies and joining their local anti-violence coalitions. These contacts can be used to develop cross-training, cross-reporting and multidisciplinary response teams."

Corporate Partnership to Combat Domestic Violence

Most executives and managers in the corporate sector have given little or no thought to the impact of partner abuse on the health and safety of their employees. Potential barriers to understanding and helping employees who are victims of partner abuse include lack of awareness, denial, embarrassment, privacy and confidentiality concerns, victim blaming, expectations of self-identification by abused women, fear of advocating for change and concern that outreach to abused women may alienate male employees, damage the company image or be too expensive.

A survey of employee assistance professionals (EAPs) found that a large majority of EAP providers had been faced with cases of partner abuse, including restraining order violations and stalking in the workplace. General policies on workplace violence exist, but few specifically address domestic violence. Among larger corporations, EAP staff use a range of practices to assist employees affected by abuse, including use of leaves of absence, medical leaves and short-term disability. The affect of domestic violence on the workplace is discussed shortly.

The Lakewood (Colorado) Police Department and Motorola joined forces to apply sophisticated law enforcement and business principles to develop new strategies for managing domestic violence cases. The partnership uses **process mapping**, a program Motorola developed as part of its quality management process. An alternative to traditional top-down methods of internal analysis, process mapping takes a horizontal view of a system and involves personnel at all levels. It uses a series of flowcharts or maps to visually depict how information, materials and activities flow in an organization and how work is handed off from one unit or department to another. It also identifies how processes work currently and what changes should be made to attain a more ideal process flow.

The process mapping program not only identifies areas for improvement but also facilitates communication between the city, police department and community. Lakewood Mayor Steve Burkholder said of the partnership: "At a time when the concept of community policing has the attention and financial support of both the public and private sectors, the partnership demonstrates what can be accomplished in the spirit of collaboration. Together, Motorola and the Lakewood Police Department are having a dramatic impact on our understanding and approach to the crime of domestic violence" (Partington, 2000, p.173).

The department has also developed a domestic violence registry, which provides responding officers with a profile of the address on a laptop including whether weapons have been involved in prior incidents and whether backup would be advisable (Youngs, 2000, p.3).

A Domestic Violence Reduction Unit

In 1992 the Portland Police Bureau identified a need to provide additional services to families. In keeping with the community policing philosophy, the agency turned to the community to help define the new programs. They consulted over 100 community leaders and groups. To design the administrative framework for their Domestic Violence Reduction Unit (DVRU), the bureau looked for models other agencies had designed. It also held discussions with the district attorney and judges as well as leaders in the battered women's movement. It was agreed that officers would not only vigorously enforce the laws but that they would also become advocates for victims. It was also agreed that they would need increased cooperation between the police and other public safety agencies to enhance reporting and enforcement.

The unit's activities are not confined to working with individual cases. It is also a source of training for other officers and for community education outside the Portland Police Bureau. In addition, the officers have provided training to over 20 other police agencies in the country. According to Butzer et al. ("The Role of Police . . .," p.9):

> The Domestic Violence Reduction Unit in the Portland Police Bureau demonstrates how acting on the values of community policing can result in the integration of fresh perspectives and new approaches into police work. Perhaps more importantly, it illustrates how implementing community policing strategies can result in a closer alignment between the police agency and the community. The community policing perspective required a conscious effort to consult with different groups within the community, and to incorporate those groups into the process of creating the DVRU, its priorities and strategies. In a democratic society such consultation with the community helps tie the police agency into the society, and helps the agency to adapt to societal changes. Community policing can make a difference, but it takes more than rhetoric: it takes real action as illustrated by the creation and implementation of the Domestic Violence Reduction Unit.

When forming partnerships to prevent domestic violence, the issue of cultural diversity between male-dominated police organizations and female-dominated grassroots advocate groups must be addressed.

S*T*O*P Violence against Women

The Department of Justice's S*T*O*P Violence against Women grant program provides money directly to states and Native American tribes as a step in helping to restructure the criminal justice system's response to crimes of violence against women. The acronym stands for *services, training, officers* and *prosecution,* the vital components in a comprehensive program for victims of domestic violence and its perpetrators. This program requires collaboration between victim advocates, prosecutors and police. Funding can provide improvements such as:

- Crisis centers and battered women's shelters serving tens of thousands of victims a year.
- Hundreds of new prosecutors for specialized domestic violence or sexual assault units.
- Hundreds of volunteer coordinators to help run domestic violence hotlines ("The Violence against Women Act . . .," p.5).

Domestic Violence Courts

Court-based domestic violence programs help victims understand court proceedings, exercise their right to prosecute their abuser and obtain referrals to services outside the court system, enhance victims' ability to make informed decisions, reducing the likelihood of additional victimization. Training for court personnel focuses on understanding victims' financial, emotional and medical needs and informing victims of their legal rights, such as obtaining a protective order or pursuing their abuser. Court programs also seek to increase cooperation among courts, police, prosecutors and community advocates for victims.

Ostrom (2003, p.105) stresses: "Success necessitates system-wide collaboration and the ongoing commitment of judges, health care professionals, the police, prosecution and citizens who witness violent acts." Researchers Gover et al. (2003, p.109) found "significantly lower rates of rearrests among defendants processed through the domestic violence court." They conclude: "The results from this study suggest that systematic localized court interventions aimed at domestic violence defendants can be effective in enhancing enforcement and improving victim safety. . . . Overall results suggest that therapeutic treatment for batterers may reduce domestic violence among convicted batterers who agree to the sentence."

Barriers to Multiagency Collaborations

Multiagency collaborations are not without their barriers. Researchers Giacomazzi and Smithey (2001, p.99) analyzed the process of a multiagency collaboration involving a large, municipal police department and other service providers working toward a solution to family violence against women. Their results suggest: "Even in an era of multiagency collaboration, one cannot presume that personnel of relatively autonomous organizations have the organizational capacity and/or the willingness among personnel to truly collaborate. Formidable barriers toward effective collaboration abound and result in a less effective process of negotiation rather than collaboration."

They (p.112) found: "Many apparent collaborative endeavors suffer from turfism: partners who consciously or unconsciously strive to remain in control, protecting their own interests." In addition (p.113): "Among human service providers and educators, there appears to be a philosophical difference regarding the solution for family violence when compared with law enforcement. Human service providers and educators exhibited a decided emphasis toward preventive activities rather than law enforcement responses." They (p.114) also state: "A variety of other barriers to the realization of the commission's goals were also reported, including perceptions of waning interest in the commission's activities, lack of organization, scheduling of meetings and unclear expectations of participants." Giacomazzi and Smithey (p.117) conclude: "The community policing context—one that encourages intraownership, democratic self-management, education and a true sense of membership—certainly appears to be a ripe environment for necessary changes to take place that would enhance collaborative efforts."

The problem of partner abuse often also involves child abuse, whether it be the trauma a child experiences witnessing such abuse or actually being physically abused as well.

Child Abuse

According to the Council against Domestic Abuse (Ziegler, 2000, p.65): "It is estimated that one-half of the men who beat their partners also abuse their children." Published studies report a 30 to 60 percent overlap between violence against children and violence against women in the same families. Although they use different

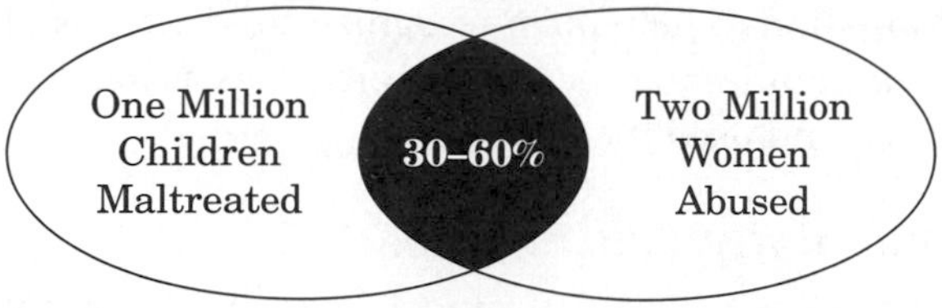

Figure 14.4 Overlap of Child Maltreatment and Domestic Violence

SOURCE: "In Harm's Way: Domestic Violence and Child Maltreatment." http://www.calib.com/nccanch/pubs/otherpubs/harmsway.htm

methods and different sample sizes and examine different populations, they consistently report a significant level of co-occurrence ("In Harm's Way . . .," p.1). Figure 14.4 illustrates this overlap.

Finkelhor and Ormrod (2001, p.1) note: "Not only are children the victims of many of the same crimes that victimize adults, they are subject to other crimes, like child abuse and neglect, that are specific to childhood. The impact of these crimes on young victims can be devastating, and the violent or sexual victimization of children can often lead to an intergenerational **cycle of violence** and abuse [emphasis added]."

Children in violent homes face three risks: (1) the risk of observing traumatic events, (2) the risk of being abused themselves and (3) the risk of being neglected.

Children Exposed to Violence

Johnson (no date) states: "[Children who witness violence] are the 'bystanders' to violence, the indirect victims, cowering, crying, wide awake even in the dead of night. Children who witness violence in their homes and neighborhoods, recent studies suggest, may not be as resilient as medical and mental health specialists once believed. It turns out that kids exposed to violence—especially the estimated 3.3 million to 10 million kids a year who've seen brutality between people they love and trust—are often as traumatized as those who are directly victimized."

Training Professionals to Recognize Child Victims

Hospital personnel, lawyers, justice system officials and psychiatrists should receive training to enable them to recognize child victims of violence and abuse, understand their special needs and act as their advocates. Law and medical schools can provide trainers. Professional associations can also cooperate in creating training programs and fostering cooperation among their members who staff key agencies.

A potential obstacle is that professionals such as lawyers and physicians may be reluctant to admit their inability to recognize and assist child victims. The American Academy of Pediatrics and the Center to Prevent Handgun Violence sponsor educational and training materials for pediatric health care professionals through the Stop Firearm Injury program. The program provides doctors and others with brochures, posters, reading lists and other information to help them recognize child victims of gun violence and refer them and their families to other service providers as needed. Thousands of physicians have received and used the materials.

The Child Development–Community Policing Model

The child development–community policing (CD-CP) model is a pilot initiative that emphasizes the importance of developing collaborative relationships between law enforcement and mental health communities to ensure that youths exposed to violence have access to a wide array of services offered in their communities.

The CD-CP model emphasizes cross-training of criminal justice and mental health professionals to develop collaborative problem-solving techniques that go beyond the reach of either "system" acting alone.

The distinction between law enforcement and child protection agencies is beginning to blur with police spending more time in noninvestigative activities and child protection workers spending more time as investigators. Their spheres of influence have come to overlap in many areas, and both have shifted emphasis from reactive to proactive responses when possible.

The CD-CP program began in New Haven, Connecticut, and has been facilitated by resources of and researchers at the Yale University Child Study Center. Specifically, the CD-CP model's training and collaboration principles include the following:

- Child development fellowships for police supervisors, which provide supervisory officers with the necessary expertise to lead a team of community-based officers in activities and services related to children and families, and create opportunities to interact with the child mental health professionals with whom they will collaborate in the future
- Police fellowships for clinicians, which provide clinicians the opportunity to observe and learn directly from law enforcement officers about the responsibilities of community-based policing, while also building collaborative relationships with law enforcement officials
- Seminars on child development, human functioning and policing strategies are offered for clinicians, community police officers and related justice practitioners that incorporate case scenarios to apply principles of child development to the daily work of policing
- Consultation services that give law enforcement the ability to make referrals and obtain immediate clinical guidance if necessary
- Program conferencing, where CD-CP police officers and clinicians meet weekly to discuss difficult and perplexing cases

Osofsky (2001, p.5) states: "Since its inception, CD-CP has intervened in the lives of more than 3,000 children and families in New Haven. In addition, CD-CP has consulted with and provided direct services to multiple school and child welfare systems in crises." Because the initiative is fairly new, it has not yet been empirically evaluated, but steps have been taken to ensure that the data collection necessary to support a rigorous evaluation of the effort is in place.

Forming a Multidisciplinary Team to Investigate Child Abuse

In the introduction of a booklet developed by the U.S. Department of Justice, the need for such a team is graphically illustrated (Ells, 1998, p.i):

> Two months before her seventh birthday in 1995, Elisa Izquierdo was killed. Over a period of months, she had been physically and emotionally abused, repeatedly violated with a toothbrush and a hairbrush, and finally beaten to death by her mother. Elisa's mother told police that before she smashed Elisa's head against a cement wall, she made Elisa eat her own feces and used her head to mop the floor. The police told reporters that there was no part of the 6-year-old's body that had not been cut or bruised. Thirty marks initially thought to be cigarette burns turned out to be the imprints of a stone in someone's ring.
>
> An investigation after her death revealed that Elisa had been the subject of at least eight reports of abuse and that several government agencies had investigated the reports. Nonetheless, Elisa Izquierdo was left with her abuser and eventual killer.
>
> Unfortunately, this failure to respond to reports of child abuse in a timely and appropriate manner has happened many times—and is continuing to happen—in probably every state in the country, and almost always for the same reason . . . there has been an appalling lack of communication and coordination among the agencies investigating reports of possible abuse.

A key to avoiding such tragedies is the formation of a multidisciplinary team (MDT) representing the government agencies and private practitioners responsible for investigating crimes against children and protecting and treating children in the community. Ells (pp.2–3) suggests that keys to forming a successful MDT are committed members who have the support of their agencies, an initial meeting during which each member's role and experience in investigating child abuse and neglect are respectfully heard, development of a mission statement and creation of a team protocol specifying the responsibilities of the members and procedures to follow.

Ells (p.3) also outlines keys to the successful operation of an MDT: confidentiality policies, conflict resolution practices to ensure core issues are aired and resolved satisfactorily and periodic self-analysis and outside evaluation as to how effectively they are performing.

Promising Service Developments for Children

Schechter and Edleson (2000) describe several "extremely promising projects" that have emerged in the past 10 years. Based on common characteristics found in these projects, the Center on Crime, Communities and Culture for the Open Society Institute makes four recommendations for communities and governmental bodies to help children experiencing domestic violence (pp.12–14):

> (1) Every community should conduct an audit of its current response systems and develop an infrastructure of protections and a range of services for children and families experiencing violence. (2) Local, state and federal legislative and administrative bodies; private organizations; and foundations should create funding

and policy mandates to support an infrastructure of community services for children exposed to family and community violence. (3) Professional organizations and training institutions should immediately establish guidelines for educational training, licensing and certification standards, continuing education and practice for those working with families exposed to violence. (4) Government agencies, private foundations, and service providers should collaborate on research efforts that enhance our understanding of children experiencing domestic violence and shed light on the impact of interventions with these families.

Workplace Violence

Crawford (2002, p.23) reports: "Workplace violence, according to one study, can cost businesses as much as $42 billion annually. The Workplace Violence Institute reports an estimated 16,400 threats are made, 723 workers are attacked, and 43,800 are harassed during an average *workday.*" Interestingly, of the occupations examined by the NCVS, police officers experienced workplace violent crime at rates higher than all other occupations (261 per 1,000 persons) (Duhart, 2001, p.1).

McDonald (2001, p.7) reports: "Homicide, workplace violence in its most extreme form, is the second leading cause of fatal occupational injury in the United States." Violence in the workplace continues to be the number one security threat for Fortune 1000 corporate security managers ("Violence in the Workplace . . .," 2001, p.42). However, Jaeger (2001, p.6) puts the problem into perspective by noting: "While it appears the frequency of workplace violence is increasing, it's still not an everyday occurrence. Statistics show you have a better chance of being struck by lightning than murdered by a co-worker."

Annually more than 2 million people become victims of violent crime at work according to the U.S. Bureau of Justice Statistics.

Podolak (2000, p.152) cautions: "Workplace violence joins phenomena such as road rage and hate crimes that are exploited to attract readers, expand political empires, or advance careers." He notes that the term *workplace violence* "is nothing more than a catch-all phrase referring to criminal misbehavior committed against people who have jobs. Those dealing with this problem should formulate a clear definition of what constitutes workplace violence."

Most study results and experts identify the driving forces behind the increase in workplace violence as being (1) an economic system that fails to support full employment (downsizing), (2) a legal system that fails to protect citizens and releases criminals from prison early due to overcrowding, (3) a cultural system that glamorizes violence in the media and (4) the universal availability of weapons.

Common motivations behind violent behavior in the workplace include robbery, loss of a job, anger from feelings of mistreatment, substance abuse and mental problems.

The typical perpetrator is a 25- to 50-year-old white male who tends to be a loner, has a history of violence and conflict with others and may exhibit signs of depression. This profile fits Michael McDermott, a shooting suspect who, in December 2000 supposedly upset by an IRS request to garnish his wages, killed seven co-workers in Wakefield, Massachusetts. McDermott is white, age 42 and had an angry outburst in the accounting department the week before over the prospect of losing some of his wages. McDermott gave up to police without a struggle.

Jaeger (p.74) notes: "Many employees who have committed fatal attacks gave clear, early warning signals that were not adequately addressed by their employers." Warning signs included unusual fascination with weapons, a display of unwarranted anger, irrational beliefs and ideas, feelings of victimization, talk of hurting self and others, substance abuse, inability to take criticism, constant complaining, attendance and productivity problems and past threats or acts of intimidation.

Workplace violence shares many characteristics with school violence. School violence is, in fact, a form of workplace violence for school staff.

Characteristics common to workplace violence and school violence include the profiles of the perpetrators, the targets, the warnings, the means and the pathways to violence.

Nicoletti et al. (1999) note: "The perpetrators are frequently described as 'loners' with poor social skills, who are often obsessed with violence and weapons. . . . The targets of choice . . . include authority figures, women who have rejected them and peers who are in conflict with them. . . . The shared motives of the killers is revenge. Perpetrators often bring an arsenal of weapons and will kill anyone who stands in their way."

Workplace Violence and Domestic Violence

Sometimes it is harassing phone calls to an employee or an angry spouse bursting into the workplace threatening violence or actually assaulting the partner. It may include homicide. According to May (2000, p.42), domestic violence may also include physical assaults that affect an individual's ability to perform job functions. He notes: "Domestic violence costs hundreds of millions of dollars in health-care costs, mostly paid by employer benefits." Corporations are increasingly raising the profile of battered women and encouraging individuals, businesses and communities to take action to prevent domestic violence.

Workplace Violence and Hospital Emergency Rooms

A strategy some communities are using to reduce the violence often experienced in hospital emergency rooms by violent patients and visitors is to train the staff in violence prevention. A survey of 103 hospitals in Los Angeles and other urban areas of California found that nearly 60 percent of hospital staff had been injured by visitors or patients. Hospital administrators might develop partnerships with physicians, nurses and staff to understand past events and devise training strategies and security policies to prevent further incidents. Administrators should also seek assistance from the police or other crime prevention and security specialists who can assess security issues. Although this strategy can be expensive, partnerships with law enforcement might reduce the training expenses.

Preventing Workplace Violence

Most security experts dealing with preventing workplace violence recommend forming a team. Braverman (1999, p.41) suggests the workplace violence team be composed of stakeholders representing a range of functions, including health and safety, legal, human resources, labor relations/employee relations, employee assistance, union and operations. Ideally the team would also include professionals from outside the workplace such as law enforcement representatives, health care professionals and the like. The team should consider not only physical measures to increase the security of employees but also developing clear, fair procedures for terminations and layoffs. Other policies aimed at preventing workplace violence might include zero tolerance for harassment, preemployment screening, substance abuse screening, no weapons on the property and the right to search personal property (Partington, p.6).

Doherty (2002, p.133) notes how community policing can help address workplace violence: "The model of community policing has served our citizens well in three out of four areas: homes, streets and schools. It may now be time to embrace our local workplaces as 'neighborhoods.' Employers should feel free to report workplace violence to local law enforcement, and businesses should be allowed to share information with police when necessary. Toward that end, police must work with security professionals to convince management to fully report workplace violence and to develop mutually agreed-on risk reduction plans. Doing so will benefit employees and enhance the company image by showing management's commitment to a safe work community."

Terrorism: An Overview

Terrorism is the deliberate creation and exploitation of fear to bring about political change. All terrorist acts involve violence or the threat of violence committed by nongovernmental groups or individuals. Terrorists seek to frighten and intimidate a wider audience, such as a rival ethnic or religious group. Terrorist groups typically have few members, limited firepower and few organizational resources. Rather they rely on dramatic, often spectacular, bloody, hit-and-run violent acts to attract attention to themselves and their cause (*Encarta Encyclopedia*).

Terrorism is by nature political because it involves acquiring and using power to force others to submit to terrorist demands. Terrorist attacks generate publicity and focus attention on the organization behind the attack, creating their power. Terrorists typically attempt to justify their violence by arguing that they have been excluded from the accepted process to bring about political or social change. They claim terrorism is their only option. Whether one agrees with this argument often depends on whether one sympathizes with the terrorists' cause or with the victims of the terrorist attack. The aphorism "One man's terrorist is another man's freedom fighter" underscores how use of the label *terrorism* can be highly subjective depending on one's sympathies. However, terrorist acts—including murder, kidnapping, bombing and arson—have long been defined in both national and international law as crimes. Even in time of war, violence deliberately directed against innocent civilians is considered a crime (*Encarta Encyclopedia*).

Terrorism has occurred throughout history for a variety of reasons: historical, cultural, political, social, psychological, economic, religious—or any combination of these. Democratic countries generally provide more fertile ground for terrorism because citizens' civil liberties are legally protected, and government control and constant surveillance of its citizens' activities is absent (*Encarta Encyclopedia*).

National governments have at times aided terrorists to further their own foreign policy goals. State-sponsored terrorism is a form of covert warfare, a means to wage war secretly through the use of terrorist surrogates (stand-ins) as hired guns. The U.S. Department of State designates countries as state sponsors of terrorism if they actively assist or aid terrorists, if they harbor past terrorists or refuse to renounce terrorism. They have designated seven countries as state sponsors of terrorism: Iran, Iraq, Syria, Libya, Cuba, North Korea and Sudan. Although the former Taliban government in Afghanistan sponsored al-Qaeda, the radical group led by Saudi exile Osama bin Laden, the United States did not recognize the Taliban as a legitimate government and thus did not list it as a state sponsor of terrorism (*Encarta Encyclopedia*).

Borum (2003, p.17) notes: "The terrorist attacks on America on September 11, 2001, shocked millions who perhaps before did not realize there were people in the world that would take such violent actions, even those resulting in their own deaths, against innocent civilians." Borum (pp.7–8) suggests that terrorists go through four observable stages to develop their ideologies. First an extremist individual or group identifies some type of undesirable economic condition (poverty, unemployment) or social condition (government-imposed restrictions on individual freedom, lack of order). Second, they view the undesirable condition as an injustice—it does not happen to everyone; therefore, it is not fair. Borum (p.8) notes: This holds true for some people in Middle Eastern countries who see the United States as a caricature of affluence and wasteful excess. For those who are deprived, this facilitates feelings of resentment and injustice.

Third, extremists seek to place the blame. Someone has to be responsible and pay, leading to the fourth step, viewing those to blame as bad or evil. Doing so helps facilitate terrorist actions in three ways according to Borum: (1) the aggression becomes justifiable, (2) the targets are dehumanized and (3) the extremists attacking the bad guys become the good guys, sometimes even martyrs. This process of ideological development is illustrated in Figure 14.5.

Definitions of Terrorism

Definitions of terrorism vary. As the Terrorism Research Center (www.terrorism.com) notes: "There is no single, universally accepted definition of terrorism. Even different agencies of the US government have different working definitions." The Terrorism Research Center also notes that most definitions have common elements.

Common elements in definitions of terrorism include (1) systematic use of physical violence—actual or threatened—(2) against noncombatants (3) but with an audience broader than the immediate victims in mind, (4) to create a general climate of fear in a target population (5) to cause political and/or social change.

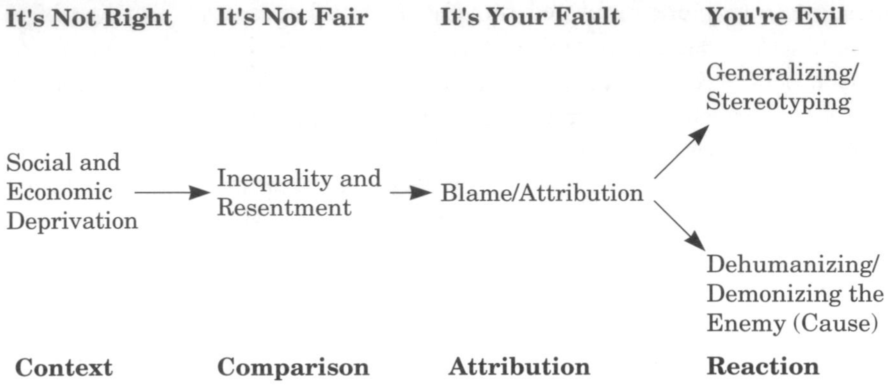

Figure 14.5 The Process of Ideological Development

SOURCE: Randy Borum. "Understanding the Terrorist Mind-Set." *FBI Law Enforcement Bulletin.* July 2003, p.9. Reprinted by permission.

The Terrorism Research Center uses the FBI's definition of terrorism: "Terrorism is the unlawful use of force or violence against persons or property to intimidate or coerce a government, the civilian population, or any segment thereof, in furtherance of political or social objectives."

The FBI classifies terrorism as international or domestic.

International Terrorism

International terrorism is foreign based or directed by countries or groups outside the United States against the United States. The 9/11 attack brought an immediate response. The 1990s saw terrorist attacks against U.S. military installations in Saudi Arabia and embassies in East Africa. According to Rogers (2000, p.84): "Osama bin Laden is on the FBI's 10 Most Wanted List in connection with the August 7, 1998 bombings of U.S. Embassies in dar Es Aalaam, Tanzania and Nairobi, Kenya. Osama bin Laden represents a new breed of terrorist capable of anything from biological warfare to spreading a computer virus." Unfortunately, he was capable of much more as Americans learned on that fateful September day. Since then the government has been extremely aware of the threat of international terrorism and has shifted its focus from a war on drugs to a war on terrorism. Literally. The Taliban was virtually obliterated in Afganistan. And the war continues. However, the number of *domestic* terrorist attacks is almost double the number of international acts of terrorism.

Domestic Terrorism

According to Scoville (2003, p.44): "You don't have to look overseas or at foreign residents to find terrorists threats to America. . . . Domestic terrorist groups may be regional, national or isolated, with numbers as large as several hundred or as few as four or five. These people are motivated, dedicated, usually heavily armed, and you [police officers] represent the government and the status quo that they abhor."

Domestic terrorists are motivated by very specific issues, such as opposition to legalized abortion or nuclear energy, or the championing of environmental concerns and animal rights. They hope to pressure both the public and its representatives in government to enact legislation directly reflecting their particular concern. Among the most active groups are the Animal Liberation Front (ALF), the Environmental Liberation Front (ELF—ecoterrorists), white supremacy groups such as the Ku Klux Klan (it is still alive and functioning), Skinhead groups and antiabortion groups. As Pitcavage (2003, p.32) stresses: "Domestic extremism is still a potent threat." Some are even so brazen as to publicize their agendas on the Internet. In addition terrorist-friendly Web sites provide extremists with a wealth of information about manufacturing low-cost, high-yield bombs.

The Police Response/Responsibility

On October 16, 2001, a little over a month after the devastating attacks on America, Glasscock, then president of the IACP, sent a letter to police departments throughout the country. In it he wrote: "The war against terrorism isn't limited to actions overseas, or even restricted to military actions. The fight against terrorism begins in our own back yards—our own communities, our own neighborhoods—and police chiefs need to prepare themselves, their officers, and their communities—the people they've sworn to protect—against terrorism."

In December, then IACP President Berger testified before the Senate Governmental Affairs Committee, noting that the 16,000 state and local law enforcement agencies in the United States—and the 700,000 officers they employ—patrol the streets of our cities and towns daily, and as a result, have an intimate knowledge of those communities they serve (Voegtlin, 2002, p.8).

The Police Executive Research Forum also issued a draft outlining local law enforcement's role in preventing and responding to terrorism (*Local Law Enforcement's Role . . .*, 2001, p.1), whose opening sentence states: "The nation is embarking upon a new and vigorous fight against terrorism, and local police agencies must be full partners in these efforts." The draft (p.3) also states:

> Federal law enforcement cannot do it alone. Local police can and will play a critical role in gathering intelligence on suspected terrorists and knowing what to do with that information. Many have critical information about individuals living in their communities.
>
> Local police agencies are uniquely qualified to assess community concerns and fears that are critical to effective intelligence gathering. This is especially true in light of the effects and progress of community policing and its emphasis on citizen engagement, partnerships, trust, information sharing and collaborative problem solving.

The keys to combating terrorism lie in information to be obtained at the local level, sharing that information and interoperability should an attack occur.

Hindsight reveals that many clues to the attack on September 11 existed, but they were fragmented, never put together, just as a jigsaw puzzle cannot be completed without all the pieces. Seemingly insignificant information may be the one missing piece to put together an impending terrorist attack. As Rehm and Rehm (2000, p.40) stress: "The local officers will be a critical element in the overall success of incident control and containment since they will have the most data on the area, offenders and early activities." The local officers, in turn, will rely on citizen information.

According to Chapman et al. (2002): "A successful response to terrorism involves an array of activities, many of which are reliant on human intelligence gathering activities and productive partnerships between local law enforcement and other agencies." They note: "In recent years technological advances have resulted in vast improvements in data gathering techniques. These technologies include in-field laptops, automated computer aided dispatch systems (CAD), enhanced records management systems (RMS), 311 systems and geographical information systems (GIS). Collectively, these tools enhance the ability to collect and warehouse large amounts of data and thereby increase the potential for identifying threats, protecting or "hardening" potential targets from criminal activity."

It is not sufficient to simply gather data. It must be shared systematically with neighboring law enforcement agencies and also different levels of law enforcement (i.e., local, state and federal) and other institutions, such as schools, hospitals, city departments and motor vehicle divisions.

Lip service is being given to information sharing at all levels. Then FBI Director Mueller (2001, p.12) stated: "I want to let you know how deeply committed the FBI is to working with you to ensure the safety and security of your communities now and in the futures." However, a General Accounting Office survey concluded that federal coordination of the numerous information sharing efforts currently underway in the nation's cities and states is lacking and the risk of missing critical information on the movement of terrorists still remains a major problem two years after terrorists attacked the World Trade Center and the Pentagon ("GAO Survey . . .," 2003, pp.12–14). This same concern was expressed by Senator Joseph Lieberman in a report by the Senate Governmental Affairs Committee (2003, p.3): "America's safety demands that state and local officials, especially law enforcement and public safety professionals, our front line defenders, are fully engaged in the war against terrorism. Yet almost two years after the September 11, 2001, terrorist attacks, Government Affairs Committee (GAC) minority staff found that these officials are being asked to fight the war against terrorism with incomplete and unreliable access to one of the most potent weapons in the homeland security arsenal: information . . . These information gaps pose a significant challenge for the federal government and leave the American people at unacceptable risk."

Prevention efforts are crucial, but preparedness is also crucial. The September 11 attack highlighted the importance of communications **interoperability**—the compatibility of communication systems such as EMS, fire and rescue, and police, and across levels of government. In addition, 311 systems can provide an avenue for citizens to contact local law enforcement, provide tips and obtain accurate information about ongoing events. Such an avenue is crucial if partnerships with the community to prevent terrorism are to be formed.

Partnerships to Prevent Terrorism

Partnerships among government agencies, including law enforcement agencies, are obviously critical and have been addressed. But broader partnerships are needed. As Delattre (2003, p.87) observes: "The question of effective partnerships has *deserved* our attention for at least half a century, and it *demands* our attention now."

The Police Executive Research Forum is fully supportive of community policing, including its emphasis on problem solving. Executive Director Wexler (2003, p.3) stresses: "To truly protect our communities from terrorism, we must enlist them as partners in our fight to prevent the next attack." Forum President Olson has stated: "From a national security standpoint, community policing could well be our number-one line of defense" (Nislow, 2001, p.1). Bucqueroux and Diamond (2002, p.1) also contend: "Community policing is our best bet against terrorism."

Giannone and Wilson (2003, p.37) describe one community policing effort in the fight against terrorism, the Community Anti-Terrorism Training Initiative or CAT Eyes program: "The CAT Eyes program was designed to help local communities combat terrorism by enhancing neighborhood security, heightening the community's powers of observation and encouraging mutual assistance and concern among neighbors. It has the following purposes:

- Watch for terrorist indicators, not peoples' race or religion.
- Teach average citizens about terrorism.
- Educate and empower citizens.
- Set up a national neighborhood block watch program.
- Educate school children."

The private sector can also be an important partner in the war against terrorism. In a summit on Homeland Security, Cilluffo, director of policy for the Office of Homeland Security stated: "The war on terrorism knows no boundaries, and the private sector is on the front lines in this war. Washington must work with private industry to build partnerships" ("Summit Focuses on Homeland Security," 2003, p.1). Local community policing efforts should also be included in such partnerships.

Beyond the Beltway: Focusing on Hometown Security (2002, p.iii) states: "For years, local police departments have used community policing techniques against crime and have engaged their communities in those efforts. Those same tactics can be transferred to the terrorist threat." This report (pp.v–vi) stresses: "An effective national domestic preparedness strategy must look beyond the Department of Homeland Security to the needs and roles of responders in our hometown." It suggests involving local mental health personnel and looking beyond the Centers for Disease Control, engaging hometown CEOs, working together as a region and educating the local media.

As partnerships are formed it is important to consider the words of Melekian (2002, p.1): "In the post September 11 world, our greatest challenge is not dealing with terrorists. Rather it is finding the balance between enhancing security and maintaining liberty." Gathering information about possible "sleeper" terrorists among us must not infringe upon individual rights to privacy or civil liberties. Nor should individuals of Middle Eastern descent by singled out for "special observation." Some communities are experiencing an increasing number of hate crimes and illegal bigotry targeting people of Middle Eastern descent and those of the Muslim faith. Community policing efforts should develop innovative approaches to community mobilization, including strategies such as community mediation to help engage the community in a positive manner and channel citizens' desire to get involved.

Bucqueroux and Diamond (p.6) note: "Few people outside the field know about the pitched battle for the heart and soul of policing that has raged over the past decade. It is said that people get the police they deserve. If we are to maintain recent reductions in violent crime and uncover the terrorists living among us, while preserving the civil rights that make our society special, we must insist on community policing now more than ever before." Addressing terrorism in this way presents a dual challenge described by Wexler (2001, p.vii): "The events of September 11, 2001, have changed the role of local police in America—perhaps forever. Local law enforcement faces the challenges of assuming more responsibility in countering terrorism threats while continuing to address crime and disorder. Success will depend on their ability to build on strong community-policing networks for information exchange and to maintain a collaborative problem-solving approach to crime amid high anxiety and crisis. Now more than ever, departments need to adhere to community problem-solving principles to decrease crime and disorder in their communities, increase their departments' efficiency, and strengthen their relationship with citizens."

The dual challenges in combating violence facing community policing are countering terrorism while continuing to address crime and disorder.

A Problem-Solving Partnership in Action

"Domestic Violence Intervention Project: Charlotte-Mecklenburg (North Carolina) Police Department." A 2002 Herman Goldstein Award Winner.

The Problem

The problem was an apparent increase in domestic assaults in the Charlotte-Mecklenburg Police Department's Baker One District.

Analysis

Analysis of domestic assault reports showed that the average victim had filed nine previous police reports, most involving the same suspect but sometimes crossing police district boundaries. Many of the prior reports were for indicator crimes—offenses such as trespassing, threatening and stalking. Within the Baker One District, most repeat call locations were domestic situations. Further analysis suggested the desirability of regarding the victim and suspect as "hot spots" instead of the traditional fixed geographic location.

Response

Baker One officers developed a tailored response plan for each repeat offense case, including zero tolerance of criminal behavior by the suspect and the use of other criminal justice and social service agencies. A Police Watch Program and a Domestic Violence Hotline voice mail system for victims were implemented. Officers developed detailed case files and created a database with victim/offender background data. The database tracks victims and offenders as moving "hot spots" from one address to another and across district boundaries.

The officers felt building on existing partnerships with other components of the criminal justice system was critical to intervene effectively in these cases. They established a stronger partnership with the district attorney's office to achieve increased evidence-based prosecution. The department's research showed many of the offenders had prior criminal records and were frequently still on probation. The Baker One officers reached out to Community Corrections, the probation and parole officers for Mecklenburg County, to garner their support and understanding of the concept and to help them focus on the behavior of domestic violence suspects who were in violation of the terms of their probation and/or parole.

A variety of stakeholders developed these intervention tactics, including domestic violence investigators and counselors, prosecutors, probation officers and practitioners in social programs that offer services to domestic violence victims and offenders. The social services agencies participating included NOVA, Victim Assistance, Legal Services of the Southern Piedmont and the Battered Women's Shelter. All agreed to work with Baker One in dealing with these complex cases. Guidelines were established to provide as uniform a response as possible to each case.

Assessment

Repeat calls for service were reduced by 98.9 percent at seven target locations. Domestic assaults decreased 7 percent in Baker One while rising 29 percent in the rest of the city. In 105 cases with indicator crimes, only three victims later reported a domestic assault. Only 14.8 percent of domestic violence victims in the project reported repeat victimization, as opposed to a benchmark figure of 35 percent. No Internal Affairs complaints were generated by officer contacts with suspects.

SUMMARY

Causes of violence may include ready availability of guns, drugs and alcohol; a desensitization to violence; disintegration of the family and community; social and economic deprivation; and increased numbers of children growing up in violent families. A problem-solving approach to preventing violence must attempt to identify the underlying causes of specific violent situations that threaten a community before solutions can be devised.

Developing effective prevention tactics will require long-term collaborations between criminal justice and juvenile justice practitioners, other social service agencies and evaluation researchers. Strategies for general violence prevention include public dialogue and community mediation, corporate support for antiviolence projects and addressing violence as a public health problem.

Hate can be classified into two categories: rational and irrational. The majority of hate crimes are motivated by racial bias, are crimes against persons and use intimidation.

Gun violence may be considered as a three-phase continuum: (1) the illegal acquisition of firearms, (2) the illegal possession and carrying of firearms and (3) the illegal, improper or careless use of firearms. The National Crime Prevention Council suggests that regulations and ordinances on gun licensing may interrupt sources of illegal guns. The NCPC suggests that gun interdictions may be an effective deterrent to illegal gun possessing and carrying. It also suggests that local gun courts that deal exclusively with gun law violations reinforce community standards against violence and ensure swift punishment of violators.

Partners in gun violence reduction identified by the OJJDP include the U.S. attorney, chief of police, sheriff, federal law enforcement agencies (FBI, ATF, DEA), district attorney, state attorney general, mayor/city manager, probation and parole officers, juvenile corrections officials, judges, public defenders, school superintendents, social services officials, leaders in the faith community and business leaders.

Domestic violence is another type of problem in most communities. It is encouraging that constraint trait is related to only a person's criminal behavior, not to abuse of a partner. Therefore, most domestic abuse is seen as acting consciously rather than impulsively, making treatment efforts more likely to be successful. Animal abuse has a direct link to domestic violence. When forming partnerships to prevent domestic violence, the issue of cultural diversity between male-dominated police organizations and female-dominated grassroots advocate groups must be addressed.

Children in violent homes face three risks: (1) the risk of observing traumatic events, (2) the risk of being abused themselves and (3) the risk of being neglected. The CD-CP model emphasizes cross-training of criminal justice and mental health professionals to develop collaborative problem-solving techniques that go beyond the reach of either "system" acting alone.

Yet another type of violence challenging communities is workplace violence. Annually more than 2 million people become victims of violent crime at work according to the U.S. Bureau of Justice Statistics. Common motivations behind violent behavior in the workplace include robbery, loss of a job, anger from feelings of mistreatment, substance abuse and mental problems. Characteristics common to workplace violence and school violence include the profiles of the perpetrators, the targets, the warnings, the means and the pathways to violence.

Common elements in definitions of terrorism include (1) systematic use of physical violence—actual or threatened—(2) against noncombatants (3) but with an audience broader than the immediate victims in mind, (4) to create a general climate of fear in a target population (5) to cause political and/or social change.

The FBI classified terrorism as international or domestic. The keys to combating terrorism lie in information to be obtained at the local level, sharing that information and interoperability should an attack occur. The dual challenges in combating violence facing community policing are countering terrorism while continuing to address crime and disorder.

Discussion Questions

1. Explain why some experts recommend a problem-solving approach to violence prevention.
2. What is the public health model of violence prevention?
3. Why do gun interdiction strategies frequently lead to charges that the police have targeted the minority community, and what can be done to allay such concerns?
4. Explain the difference researchers found between those who are violent to their partners and those who commit violent crimes against others.
5. What risks exist for children who live in homes where domestic violence occurs?
6. Corporations are suggested in this chapter as partners in violence prevention. Why would corporations have any interest in prevention or their ability to affect it?
7. Name some likely types of people who might pose a risk of violence in a workplace.
8. Discuss the aphorism "one man's terrorist is another man's freedom fighter." What kinds of examples can you think of that confirm this statement?
9. What can local law enforcement agencies do to prevent terrorism? What about communities? Will community partnerships have any effect on terrorism? How realistic do you think it is that any of these will affect terrorism?
10. Discuss any instances of hate crimes in your community. Your state. Does your state have mandatory reporting laws for hate crimes?

InfoTrac College Edition Assignments

- Use InfoTrac College Edition to help answer the Discussion Questions as appropriate.
- Research gun violence statistics in the United States, and compare what you find to that of other industrialized nations. How can the differences be explained? Be prepared to share your findings with the class.
- Research either family violence or workplace violence. Write a brief (3 or 4 page) report on the topic of your choice, and be prepared to share the key points with the class.
- Select one of the following articles to read and outline.
  - "Best Practices of a Hate/Bias Crime Investigation" by Walter Bouman
  - "The Seven-Stage Hate Model: The Psychopathology of Hate Groups" by John R. Shafer and Joe Navarro
  - "Project Exile: Combating Gun Violence in America" by Brian A. Monahan and Tod W. Burke
  - "Citizen Firearm Safety Program" by Trevin R. Sorby and J. B. Wheeler
  - "Murder at Work" by Jane McDonald
  - "Understanding the Terrorist Mind-Set" by Randy Borum

Community Project

Working in a group, design a crime/violence prevention plan for your educational institution or a place of business. Include likely partners/stakeholders, an overview of any previous crimes or violent incidents and identification of challenges and strategies to address them. Also include a critical incident response plan. Where could you find information about designing such a plan (e.g., prior crime history, maps of facility, current prevention plan, hours of operation and accessibility, the policy on employee dismissals, how student/employee complaints are handled and the like)?

References

Baker, Thomas E. and Piland-Baker, Jane. "Domestic Violence: The 'Enigma Call.'" *Law and Order,* October 2000, pp.129–138.

Beyond the Beltway: Focusing on Hometown Security. Cambridge, MA: John F. Kennedy School of Government, Harvard University, September 2002.

Borum, Randy. "Understanding the Terrorist Mind-Set." *FBI Law Enforcement Bulletin,* July 2003, pp.7–10.

Bouman, Walter. "Best Practices of a Hate/Bias Crime Investigation." *FBI Law Enforcement Bulletin,* March 2003, pp.21–25.

Braverman, Mark. "Seven Steps to Preventing Workplace Violence." *Access Control & Security Systems,* June 1999, pp.41–42, 47.

Brookoff, Daniel; Crews, Walter; Cook, Charles S.; and Thompson, Terry. "Responding to Domestic Violence: A Collaboration between the Police and the Medical Community." In *Problem-Oriented Policing,* Vol. 2, edited by

Corina Sole Brito and Tracy Allan. Washington, DC: Police Executive Research Forum, 1999, pp.113–148.

Bucqueroux, Bonnie and Diamond, Drew. "Community Policing Is Our Best Bet against Terrorism." *Subject to Debate,* January 2002, pp.1, 6.

Butzer, David; Bronfman, Lois Martin; and Stipak, Brian. "The Role of Police in Combating Domestic Violence in the United States: A Case Study of Domestic Violence Reduction Unit, Portland Police Bureau." www.ncjrs.org/policing/role161.htm

"CDC Reports Assess Violence Prevention Strategies." *NCJA Justice Bulletin,* October 2003, pp.10–11.

Center to Prevent Handgun Violence. www.handguncontrol.org

Chapman, Robert; Baker, Shelly; Bezdikian, Veh; Cammarata, Pam; Cohen, Debra; Leach, Nancy; Schapiro, Amy; Scheider, Matther; Varano, Rita; and Boba, Rachel. *Local Law Enforcement Response to Terrorism: Lessons in Prevention and Preparedness.* Washington, DC: Office of Community Oriented Policing Services, 2002.

"College Campuses Are Easy Targets for Acts of Hate." *NCJA Justice Bulletin,* June 2000, pp.11–12.

Common Sense about Kids and Guns. Washington, DC. www.kidsandguns.org

"Community Policing and Domestic Violence." www.policing.com/articl/cpanddv.html

"Congress Votes to Reauthorize Violence against Women Act." *Criminal Justice Newsletter,* October 24, 2000, pp.1–2.

Crawford, Jay. "When Employee Stress Turns Violent." *Access Control and Security Systems,* February 2002, pp.23–24.

Crime in the United States 2002. Washington, DC: Federal Bureau of Investigation, 2002. www.fbi.gov/ucr.htm

Delattre, Edwin. "Reflection on Successful Partnerships." In *Protecting Your Community from Terrorism: Strategies for Local Law Enforcement, Vol. 1: Local-Federal Partnerships,* edited by Gerald R. Murphy and Martha R. Plotkin with Edward A. Flynn, Jane Perlov, Kevin Stafford and Darrel W. Stephens. Washington, DC: Office of Community Oriented Policing Services and the Police Executive Research Forum, 2003, pp.87–92.

"Did You Know That . . .?" *Security Management,* October 2000, p.16.

Doherty, Stephen. "How Can Workplace Violence Be Deferred?" *Security Management,* April 2002, pp.132–134.

"Domestic Violence Intervention Project: Charlotte-Mecklenburg (North Carolina) Police Department." In *Excellence in Problem-Oriented Policing: The 2002 Herman Goldstein Award Winners.* Washington, DC: Police Executive Research Forum, 2002, pp.19–25.

Donohue, John J., III. "The Final Bullet in the Body of the More Guns, Less Crime Hypothesis." *Criminology and Public Policy,* July 2003, pp.397–410.

Duhart, Delis T. *Violence in the Workplace, 1993–99.* Washington, DC: Bureau of Justice Statistics Special Report, December 2001. (NCJ 190076)

Ells, Mark. *Forming a Multidisciplinary Team to Investigate Child Abuse.* Washington, DC: U.S. Department of Justice, November 1998. (NCJ-170020)

Felson, Richard B.; Messner, Steven F.; Hoskin, Anthony W.; and Deane, Glenn. "Reasons for Reporting and Not Reporting Domestic Violence to the Police." *Criminology,* August 2002, pp.617–630.

Finkelhor, David and Ormrod, Richard. *Offenders Incarcerated for Crimes against Juveniles.* Washington, DC: OJJDP Juvenile Justice Bulletin, December 2001. (NCJ 191028)

"GAO Survey Finds Terrorism Information Sharing Efforts Need Improvement." *NCJA Justice Bulletin,* September 2003, pp.12–14.

Giacomazzi, Andrew L. and Smithey, Martha. "Community Policing and Family Violence against Women: Lessons Learned from a Multiagency Collaborative." *Police Quarterly,* March 2001, pp.99–122.

Giannone, Donald and Wilson, Robert A. "The CAT Eyes Program: Enlisting Community Members in the Fight against Terrorism." *The Police Chief,* March 2003, pp.37–38.

Glasscock, Bruce D. "Letter to IACP Colleagues," October 16, 2001.

Gover, Angela R.; MacDonald, John M.; and Alpert, Geoffrey P. "Combating Domestic Violence: Findings from an Evaluation of a Local Domestic Violence Court." *Criminology and Public Policy,* November 2003, pp.109–132.

Harris, Steven R. "Model Guidelines Help Agencies Join Forces to Combat Violent Firearm Crime." *The Police Chief,* September 2001, pp.57–65.

"In Harm's Way: Domestic Violence and Child Maltreatment." www/calib.com/nccanch/pubs/otherpubs/harmsway.htm

Johnson, Caitlin. *Hidden Victims: Caring for Children Who Witness Violence.* Online: Connect for Kids, Guidance for Grownups, www.connectforkids.org.

Jaeger, Sandy. "The Age of Rage." *Security Technology & Design.* February 2001, pp.6, 74.

Kovandzic, Tomislav V. and Marvell, Thomas B. "Right-to-Carry Concealed Handguns and Violent Crime: Crime Control through Gun Decontrol?" *Criminology and Public Policy,* July 2003, pp.363–396.

Lauritsen, Janet L. and White, Norman A. "Putting Violence in Its Place: The Influence of Race, Ethnicity, Gender and Place on the Risk for Violence." *Criminology and Public Policy,* November 2001, pp.37–59.

Lieberman, Joseph I. *State and Local Officials: Still Kept in the Dark about Homeland Security.* A report by the Senate Governmental Affairs Committee Full Minority Staff, August 13, 2003.

Local Law Enforcement's Role in Preventing and Responding to Terrorism. Discussion Draft. Washington, DC: Police Executive Research Forum, October 2, 2001.

May, Johnny. "Workplace Violence: A Tragedy in the Making." *Access Control & Security Systems,* October 2000, pp.42–43.

McDonald, Jane. "Murder at Work." *Risk Management,* March 2001, p.7.

Melekian, Bernard. "Balancing Act: Security vs. Liberty." *Subject to Debate,* June 2002, pp.1, 4.

Moffitt, Terrie E.; Krueger, Robert F.; Caspi, Avshalom; and Fagan, Jeff. "Partner Abuse and General Crime: How Are They the Same? How Are They Different?" *Criminology,* 2000, pp.199–232.

Mueller, Robert S. "Responding to Terrorism." *FBI Law Enforcement Bulletin,* December 2001, pp.12–14.

Nicoletti, John; Zinna, Kelly; and Spencer-Thomas, Sally. "The Dynamics of 'Schoolplace' Violence." *The Police Chief,* October 1999, pp.74–92.

Nislow, Jennifer. "Secret Weapon against Terrorism? Chiefs Say Community Policing Is an Ace in the Hole." *Law Enforcement News,* October 15, 2001, pp.1, 10.

Osofsky, Joy D. *Addressing Youth Victimization.* Washington, DC: Coordinating Council on Juvenile Justice and Delinquency Prevention Action Plan Update, October 2001.

Ostrom, Brian J. "Domestic Violence Courts." *Criminology and Public Policy,* November 2003, pp.105–106.

Partington, George. "Partnership Combats Domestic Violence." *Law and Order,* July 2000, p.173.

Paynter, Ronnie L. "Healing the Hate." *Law Enforcement Technology,* April 2000, pp.52–61.

Pitcavage, Mark. "Domestic Extremism: Still a Potent Threat." *The Police Chief,* August 2003, pp.32–35.

Podolak, Andrew G. "Is Workplace Violence in Need of Refocusing?" *Security Management,* June 2000, pp.151–152.

Ponder, Claire and Lockwood, Randall. "Programs Educate Law Enforcement on Link between Animal Cruelty and Domestic Violence." *The Police Chief,* November 2000, pp.31–36.

Potter, Roberto Hugh and Krider, Jeanne E. "Teaching about Violence Prevention: A Bridge between Public Health and Criminal Justice Educators." *Journal of Criminal Justice Education,* Fall 2000, pp.339–351.

Promising Strategies to Reduce Gun Violence. Washington, DC: OJJDP Report, 1999.

Rehm, M. K. and Rehm, W. R. "Terrorism Preparedness Calls for Proactive Approach." *The Police Chief,* December 2000, pp.35–43.

Responding to Hate Crimes: A Police Officer's Guide to Investigation and Prevention. Arlington, VA: International Association of Chiefs of Police, 1999.

Rogers, Donna. "FBI Adds New Division to Prevent and Combat Terrorism." *Law Enforcement Technology,* May 2000, pp.84–66.

Schafer, John R. and Navarro, Joe. "The Seven-Stage Hate Model: The Psychopathology of Hate Groups." *FBI Law Enforcement Bulletin,* March 2003, pp.1–8.

Schechter, Susan and Edleson, Jeffrey L. *Domestic Violence and Children: Creating a Public Response.* Open Society Institute's Center on Crime, Communities and Culture, 2000.

Scoville, Dean. "The Enemy Within." *Police,* September 2003, pp.44–50.

Sorby, Trevin R. and Wheeler, J. B. "Citizen Firearm Safety Program." *FBI Law Enforcement Bulletin,* April 2002, pp.22–23.

"Summit Focuses on Homeland Security." *ASIS Dynamics,* January/February 2003, pp.1, 12.

Terrorism Research Center. www.terrorism.com

Turner, Nancy. "Animal Abuse and the Link to Domestic Violence." *The Police Chief,* June 2000, pp.28–30.

"The Violence against Women Act: Breaking the Cycle of Violence." www.ojp.usdoj.gov/vawol/laws/cycle.htm

"Violence in the Workplace Still Number One Security Threat for Fortune 1000 Corporate Security Managers." *Security Products,* July 2001, pp.42–43.

Voegtlin, Gene. "IACP Testifies on Local Law Enforcement Role in Homeland Defense." *The Police Chief,* February 2002, p.8.

Vogel, Brenda L. "Perceptions of Hate: The Extent to which a Motive of 'Hate' Influences Attitudes of Violent Crimes." *Journal of Crime and Justice,* 2000, pp.1–25.

"We're Not Gonna Take It." *Law Enforcement News,* September 15, 1999.

Wessler, Stephen and Moss, Margaret. *Hate Crime on Campus: The Problem and Efforts to Confront It.* Washington, DC: Bureau of Justice Assistance, October 2001. (NCJ 187249)

Wexler, Chuck. "Foreword." In *Solving Crime and Disorder Problems: Current Issues, Police Strategies and Organizational Tactics,* edited by Melissa Reuland, Corina Sole Brito and Liusa Carroll. Washington, DC: Police Executive Research Forum, 2001.

Wexler, Chuck. "Policing a Multicultural Community." *Subject to Debate,* July 2003, p.2.

Youngs, Al. "Colorado P. D. Gets Tough on Domestic Violence." *Subject to Debate,* November 2000, pp.1, 3–5.

Ziegler, Stephen J. "Battered Women: Why Do They Stay?" *Police,* October 2000, pp.64–66.

CHAPTER 15

What Research Tells Us and a Look to the Future

The best way to predict the future is to create it.

—Peter Drucker

Do You Know?

- What is at the heart of experimental design?
- What issues are raised by experiments in criminal justice?
- Whether the American Society of Criminology supports experiments in criminal justice?
- What assistance is available to departments wishing to conduct experiments?
- What percentage of distributed surveys is required to validate an evaluation?
- What features characterize the structure of successful community-oriented police departments?
- What patterns of community policing exist in the United States?
- Whether the citizen complaints generated by community policing and traditional policing differ?
- What effect community policing is having on crime statistics?
- What other types of statistics might be more helpful?
- Whether community policing helps build stronger communities?
- Whether the COPS program has been successful?
- What strategies research shows do work? Do not work? Hold promise?
- What two views of the future Bucqueroux provides?

Can You Define?

administrative density
coercive isomorphism
experimental design
horizontal differentiation
implant hypothesis
instrumental knowledge
isomorphism
mimetic isomorphism
normative isomorphism
random assignment
refraction
two-wave survey
zeitgeist

Introduction

"Over the past 10 years, community oriented policing (COP) has become the dominant theme of organizational change in law enforcement" (Zhao et al., 2003, p.387). They (p.389) suggest: "Community policing has become a dominant force behind contemporary police innovations designed to reduce crime throughout the United States." How can departments determine which of these ideas and programs are effective? Why is research important, and what pitfalls might be encountered? What has been learned that will affect community policing efforts in the future?

This chapter begins with a discussion of why research is important, what experimental research involves and some legal and ethical problems to consider. This is followed by an examination of a commonly used "research" tool, the survey. Next is a description of what limited research tells us about the structure of successful community-oriented policing departments and what patterns of community policing can be found around the country. Then the chapter discusses crime statistics and what they can and cannot tell us about the success of community policing. After that the question of whether community policing helps build stronger communities is addressed, followed by an evaluation conducted on the COPS Office. Next is a summary of what research has found to work, not to work and to hold promise. The discussion of research concludes with a look at the role of scholarly research in guiding community policing implementation and what other factors might be influential. The chapter concludes with two possible futures for law enforcement.

In many jurisdictions bike patrols are being used extensively. A bicycle unit provides high visibility, accessibility and increased mobility. It is estimated that twenty fully equipped bikes can be purchased for the price of one police car.

The Importance of Research

Oakley contends: "Choosing social policy interventions on the basis of well-designed experimental tests is a prerequisite of a democratic and equitable society" (2000, p.326). Feder et al. (2000, p.398) concur: "Experiments offer us the most clear and unmistakable evidence on the effectiveness of an intervention."

Experimental Design

At the heart of **experimental design** is the random assignment of individuals to experimental and control conditions.

Boruch et al. (2000, p. 351) define **random assignment** as "dependence on a random number table or machine-generated random number that indicates the particular treatment group to which an individual or entity will be assigned." Slavin (2003) asserts: "Random assignment to experimental and control groups is the gold standard of research." Whether a person is a member of the treatment group or the control (no treatment) group is purely a matter of chance. Boruch et al. (p.339) note that in an experiment assessing the effectiveness of arrest on domestic violence, it is possible that the majority of people assigned to the arrest group could be primarily black and the no arrest group primarily white, which is "likely to offend political as well as ethical sensibilities." To eliminate this problem, the randomization might be within blocks, that is, a pair consisting of one black and one white: "Within pairs, an individual is selected with a .5 chance to be put into the treatment group; the second becomes a member of the control group."

Although support for experiments is strong, Cordray (2000, p.401) cautions: "Randomized field experiments can provide trustworthy evidence about the effects of interventions. But investigators have limited control over important features of the field experiment (e.g., program implementation, receipt of intended and unintended services, retention of participants in the study). Unchecked, these factors can limit the technical adequacy and utility of the study."

Experiments in criminal justice are not without critics. Feder et al. (p.398) suggest: "Randomized experiments engender suspicion, making it difficult for the researcher to conduct the research." In addition, experiments in criminal justice have raised important issues.

Experiments in criminal justice raise ethical issues as well as privacy issues.

The ethical issue centers around denying those in the control group "treatment." This was tested in 1997 when the American Society of Criminology (ASC) executive board was convinced to take a stand on the desirability and ethicality of randomized experiments in evaluation research. As Short, Jr. et al. (2000, p.296) explain, the ASC received a letter from Professor Feder of Florida Atlantic University for a friend-of-the-court brief in support of her NIJ-funded evaluation of a court-mandated counseling program for domestic offenders in Broward County. Her experiment called for a randomly assigned group of men in an experimental group to be placed on one-year probation and participation in a 26-week batterer counseling program and a control group of men who received only the one-year probation. The Broward County prosecutor's office sought an injunction against Dr. Feder's experiment on legal and ethical grounds: "(a) judicial misuse of discretion (a legal issue) and (b) that it was unethical to deny treatment based on chance (random assignment)."

The ASC conducted an e-mail poll, which resulted in "virtually unanimous" support for Dr. Feder's request.

The ASC concluded: "The principle is that random assignment to treatment options is the best scientific method for determining the effectiveness of options" (Short, Jr. et al., p.296).

Support for experimental research is also attested to by the formation of the Academy of Experimental Criminology (AEC) in 2000, with Lawrence Sherman as its first president (Feder and Boruch, 2000, p.291). Feder and Boruch (p.292) state: "There is little disagreement that experiments provide a superior method for assessing the effectiveness of a given intervention. However, although the number of experiments in criminal justice has grown in recent years, experiments continue to be underutilized."

Dunford (2000, p.433) suggests: "Because of the difficulties associated with employing experimental group–control group research designs, researchers continue to conduct nonexperimental evaluations of interventions of all kinds, producing findings that are impossible to accurately interpret." He also cautions: "The results are quite likely to lead to mistaken conclusions—conclusions that may have serious consequences."

Assistance in experiments in criminal justice is available through the NIJ's Locally Initiated Research Partnerships in Policing.

In this initiative, partners share responsibility throughout the entire project, jointly selecting an area of interest to the department (locally initiated) and collaborating on the research design, implementation and interpretation of findings. Started in 1995, the NIJ partnership program currently has 41 projects. Usually the partnerships involve a local police department or other law enforcement agency and a local university. Often graduate students are used and can receive credit for research projects.

At the heart of the partnerships is the Action Research Model, illustrated in Figure 15.1. The cyclical, multistep process starts with nomination of a research topic, continues with development and implementation of the research design and ends with communicating and applying the findings.

Impediments to Experimental Design Petrosino et al. (2000) note: "Despite the millions of dollars of public funds that are invested, few outcome evaluations and experiments seem to be conducted. . . . When asked why this was the case, the research managers noted the objections of their bosses. . . . Many were listed, but three are worth paraphrasing:

1. We know our programs work; why evaluate them?
2. We know they are not harming anyone, and see number 1 above.
3. If the program helps a single child, it's worth it. Why evaluate?"

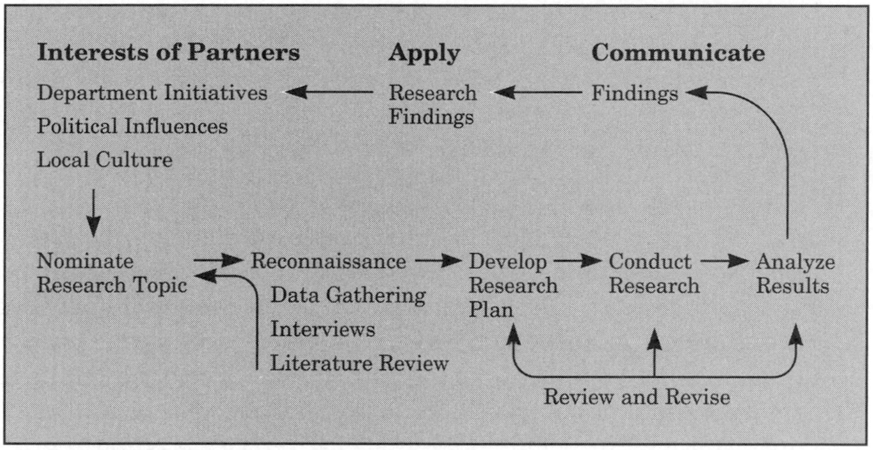

Figure 15.1 The Action Research Model

SOURCE: Tom McEwen. "NIJ's Locally Initiated Research Partnerships in Policing Factors that Add up to Success." *National Institute of Justice Journal,* Issue 238, January 1999, p.7. Reprinted by permission.

Petrosino et al. caution: "Failure to evaluate ignores a long history of admonitions about failed policies and the potential for harmful effects. Not only could ineffective programs divert money and attention from more successful interventions, they could also cause more harm than good. A program may certainly help one child but hurt two in the process. . . . One of the more egregious examples in the history of potentially harmful justice programs is Scared Straight." They (p.356) assert: "Scared Straight, at least from the data presented here, is likely a harmful program that more often than not leads to increased crime and delinquency in our communities. We conclude that rigorous evaluations are needed to identify harmful interventions."

When Experimental Designs Are Appropriate According to Weisburd (2000, p.191): "Experimental designs are not appropriate for every evaluation study in criminal justice. Nonetheless, experiments are possible in many circumstances and can provide a powerful tool for developing criminal justice policy" Weisburd cites eight principles to help researchers and practitioners assess when experimentation is most feasible:

1. There are generally fewer ethical barriers to experimentation when interventions involve the addition of resources.
2. There are generally fewer objections to experiments that test sanctions that are more lenient than existing criminal justice penalties.
3. Experiments with lower public visibility will generally be easier to implement.
4. In cases where treatment cannot be given to all eligible subjects, there is likely to be less resistance to random allocation.
5. Randomized experiments are likely to be easier to develop if the subjects of intervention represent less serious threats to community safety.
6. Experimentation will be more difficult to implement when experimenters try to limit the discretion of criminal justice agents who traditionally act with significant autonomy and authority.

7. It will be easier to develop randomized experiments in systems in which there is a high degree of hierarchical control.
8. When treatments are relatively complex, involving multiple actions on the part of criminal justice agents, experiments can become prohibitively cumbersome and expensive and accordingly less feasible to develop.

In addition to considering these principles, Thacher (2001, p.387) asserts: "Recent research about policing often aspires to emulate the model of medical research—randomized experiments designed to establish conclusively what works. This approach to scientific research produces **instrumental knowledge** about the best means to a given end, and it can contribute usefully to many important debates in policing, but by itself, it cannot speak to the full range of concerns relevant to criminal justice practice, which is characterized by a great variety and ambiguity of values. Police will benefit from instrumental knowledge [knowledge about the best means to a given end], but they will also benefit from better forms of practical reasoning." Information about what works and what does not can be obtained in other ways, including through well-designed surveys.

Surveys

One commonly used method to evaluate the effectiveness of a strategy is the survey—either in person, mailed or phoned. Sometimes a **two-wave survey** is used, the first wave consisting of a pretest before a strategy is implemented and the second wave a posttest after the strategy has been implemented for a given amount of time.

Other times surveys are used to determine what citizens feel a neighborhood's main problems are or how effective residents feel the police in their neighborhood are.

To validate an evaluation conducted by survey, 60 percent of distributed surveys must be returned.

Travis III et al. (2000) conducted research on the impact of citizen surveys by police on public attitudes. Their results indicate that such surveys may lead to lower ratings of citizen satisfaction with the police. They (p.100) suggest two possible reasons for this result. First, citizens may be generally uncomfortable in the presence of the police and be suspicious of an unsolicited police contact. Another possibility is that they may question the professionalism of the police, that is, think the police are not sure of what they are doing. It might be comparable to going to a physician and having the physician ask, "What's wrong with you and what should I do to help?"

Travis III et al. suggest that this negativism might be alleviated by phoning those to be surveyed in advance to alert them of the upcoming interview and telling them of the purpose. They (p.101) also suggest: "A wiser strategy might be to use less intrusive techniques such as mailed or telephone surveys." They conclude: "Although there is some commentary that door-to-door surveys of citizens by the police can improve police–citizen relations, it now appears that such surveys are at least equally likely to damage those relations." Departments wishing to use surveys might benefit from the Bureau of Justice Assistance's free report, "A Police Guide to Surveying Citizens." They might also want to consider the use of case studies to support how a program is working when describing it to the public or when applying for funding.

Case Studies

According to Scott et al. (2003, p.411): "Much of what we know about community policing comes from case studies of community policing in various cities. These case studies are diverse in their goals, design, length and richness of detail. Collectively, they provide much needed information about the stated purposes of community policing, in particular, places, strategic and structural components of community policing, implementation process and obstacles, and, occasionally, results. . . . Case studies frequently provide readers with a strong sense of knowing what community policing is like." They (p.410) conclude: "Case studies may represent a valuable source of data for testing the theoretical propositions related to community policing. The utility of this approach depends on the extent to which case studies assess coproduction interactions between police and residents."

Community policing is based, in part, on the coproduction of social order through the rearrangement of police-based social control and neighborhood-based social control (Kerley and Benson, 2000). Scott et al. (p.411) note: "Case studies frequently provide readers with a strong sense of knowing what community policing is like." They (p.412) also note: "Case studies have generally been used for two broad purposes. First, they are often used to explore and describe phenomena, or to provide sufficient evidence to pose concepts and possible relationships. Second, they are also used, with less frequency and effectiveness, in measuring concepts and testing relationships. Although the second use is less recommended than the first, case studies can be employed in this way, especially when the phenomena of interest are very complex, difficult to separate from context, and difficult or impossible to manipulate. . . . Community policing would appear to be one area wherein the second use of case studies may have potential and therefore, where the limits of that application should be carefully explored."

Scott et al. (p.433) contend: "Using prior case studies as a database for measuring new concepts and examining relationships among variables appears to hold some promise. . . . When reading case studies . . . one could have reasonable confidence in the following kinds of statements about police–community interaction:

- The kinds of steps taken by the police in a neighborhood to provide accessibility, improve responsiveness, and increase communication with residents (identification).
- The nature of issues or problems that residents and the police were addressing in a neighborhood and extent to which those improvement steps included problem-solving characteristics (improvements).
- The kind of steps that the police took to encourage civic engagement by residents (encouragement).
- The kinds of decisions about the neighborhood that residents contributed to and the balance of decision making by police and the residents (participation).

- The kinds of organizations that the police interacted with in the course of identification, improvement and encouragement activities and the contributions made by these other organizations (coordination)."

Scott et al. (pp.433–434) also contend that one can be fairly confident in the following statements:

- Whether or not identification efforts extended over the entire neighborhood and included most of the residents (the dispersion of identification)
- Whether or not improvement steps were concentrated (such as around business property) or widespread in a neighborhood (the dispersion of improvements)
- Whether the improvement steps were narrowly focused in crime and public safety or were more broadly gauged (the scope of improvements)
- Whether coordination occurred with a wide variety or a narrow segment of organizations important to the neighborhood (the scope of coordination)

Research Findings on Community Policing Departments

Woodyard (2003, p.39) describes how the Tampa (Florida) Police used a combination of surveys and departmental data to evaluate their community policing efforts using a "triad approach to service-oriented evaluation per squad that addressed community involvement, citizen satisfaction and TPD productivity." To assess community involvement by TPD patrol officers, each sergeant completes a detailed report for each of his squad's community/civic initiatives throughout the year. Patrol officers earn points based on predetermined criteria. To assess community satisfaction, surveys are mailed twice a year. To assess productivity, shift commanders' daily activity logs are used to compare squads, with neighborhood demographics and types of arrests in each district being considered to help "level the playing field."

Research has shed light on the structure of successful community-oriented police departments, on patterns of community policing currently found in the United States and on the difference in citizen complaints between community policing departments and traditional police departments.

The Structure of Successful Community Policing Departments

Anthony (2000) reports on research comparing the structural dimensions of community-oriented police departments to traditional departments. The research suggests that community-oriented police departments exhibit **isomorphism**, that is, they have similar structural characteristics.

> Community-oriented police departments differ in structure from traditional police departments in that their organization is less complex, their decision making less centralized and their administration less dense.

A sample of 20 community-oriented police departments was compared to a control group of 10 traditional police departments. Data obtained from the 28 surveys returned showed that community-oriented police departments had less complex organizations based on three variables: (1) commissioned specialization is lower, (2) civilian specialization is lower and (3) horizontal differentiation is lower. **Horizontal differentiation** refers to the degree to which an organization's tasks are broken into functionally distinct units. In short, community-oriented police departments have reduced the level of hierarchy.

Community-oriented police departments are also less centralized based on six variables: (1) lower vertical differentiation (decentralized decision making), (2) reduced span of control of the chief executive, (3) reduced span of control of the patrol first-line supervisors, (4) lower commissioned supervisor to patrol officer ratio, (5) participation of first-level police officers in developing the strategic plan and (6) participation of first-level police officers on committees.

The third major difference in structure is in **administrative density**, that is, the ratio of all employees to supervisory personnel. Community-oriented police departments have increased the ratio of employees to supervisors.

Community Policing Activities Engaged In

McEwen et al. (2003, p.111) report on the percent of departments engaging in community policing activities, summarized in Table 15.1. None of the departments responded that they performed all 12 activities to a great extent. Giving geographic responsibility to patrol was the only activity that a majority of departments (51 percent) reported doing to a great extent. Citizen police academies and neighborhood meetings were also engaged in to a great or moderate extent in the majority of departments.

Patterns of Community Policing in the United States

Maguire and Mastrofski (2000, p.4) explore the dimensionality of the community policing movement using four national data sets collected between 1993 and 1997. They first review the literature on this area, summarizing the key dimensions of community policing identified by various researchers. For example, Skolnick and Bayley (1988) identified four dimensions: community-based crime prevention, reorientation of patrol activities, increased police accountability and decentralization of command. Bayley (1994) identified four dimensions: consultation, adaptation, mobilization and problem solving. Bratton (1996) identified the three P's: partnership, problem solving and prevention. Rohe et al. (1996) also identified three dimensions: shared responsibility, prevention and increased officer discretion. Roth and Johnson (1997) identified four dimensions: problem solving, community partnership building, preventive interventions and organizational change. Finally, Cordner (1997) identified four dimensions: philosophical, strategic, tactical and organizational.

Common patterns found in community policing in the United States include crime prevention, problem solving, partnerships, shared responsibility and decentralization.

Maguire and Mastrofski, like Anthony, also found isomorphism occurring across the country, that is, departments tending to become similar in structure. They (pp.10–11) identify three types of isomorphism: mimetic, coercive and normative.

Table 15.1 Percent of Departments Engaging in Community Policing Activities

Activities	*Great Extent*	*Moderate Extent*	*Limited Extent*	*Not at All*
Gave geographic responsibility to patrol	51	26	16	8
Have a citizens police academy	48	10	13	29
Conduct beat/neighborhood meetings open to the public	32	35	21	12
Opened neighborhood substations	26	19	18	37
Adopted problem-solving techniques	22	33	31	14
Developed information systems to support problem-solving	17	31	37	16
Conduct citizen surveys on a regular basis	17	23	37	24
Decision-making occurs in lower ranks	16	45	36	4
Developed evaluation criteria for determining success of community policing	14	22	43	22
Decentralized detectives	10	11	18	61
Changed communications center procedures on how citizen calls are handled	9	24	36	31
Eliminated one or more ranks	5	7	13	75

SOURCE: Tom McEwen, Deborah Spencer, Russell Wolff, Julie Wartell and Barbara Webster. *Call Management and Community Policing: A Guidebook for Law Enforcement.* Washington, DC: Community Oriented Policing Services, July 10, 2003, p.111.

Mimetic isomorphism occurs when an organization copies or imitates another. **Coercive isomorphism** occurs when organizations adopt something due to pressure either from the state or other organizations, with probably the greatest source of coercive isomorphism being the U.S. Justice Department, which controls billions of dollars in funding. **Normative isomorphism** results from professionalism, with influences coming from such organizations as the Police Executive Research Forum and the IACP.

In addition to isomorphism, however, Maguire and Mastrofski (p.9) also found **refraction**, which they explain: "is the term used to describe how light rays and energy waves are deflected from their straight paths when they pass from one medium to another (such as through a prism). The variety of forms of community policing found throughout the country are the result of the United States having more autonomous police agencies than any other country in the world." They (p.11) contend: "With thousands of police executives throughout the United States making very different and often conflicting decisions, the net effect will be a refractive community policing movement."

In short, refraction results in fragmented implementation nationwide while isomorphism results in a one-size-fits-all approach to community policing. Maguire and Mastrofsi (p.15) suggest:

> The early stages of a reform movement like community policing might be characterized as refractive, with local agencies adopting its various aspects or portions as dictated by local contingencies. Later, as the movement becomes more institutionalized, the diffusion process might be characterized as isomorphic, with agencies jumping on the bandwagon based on institutional concerns for legitimacy rather than other, more technical concerns.

Citizen Complaints

Hickman et al. (2000) investigated whether community policing generates greater numbers and different types of citizen complaints than traditional policing. They followed graduates of a 1995 Philadelphia Police Academy class, the first to produce officers hired and trained under the Community Oriented Policing Services Accelerated Hiring, Education, and Deployment (COPS AHEAD) program. After three and one-half years, they obtained the official complaint records from the Philadelphia Police Department for officers in the experimental and the control group. Their results failed to support the hypothesis that community policing would result in a higher number of complaints.

Community policing and traditional policing officers generated a similar proportion of complaints, similar types of complaints and a similar number of complaints.

Their research raised an interesting question—what does the record on zero tolerance show? Commissioner William Bratton attributes the decrease in crime in New York City to the adoption of zero tolerance (for disorder and criminal activity) and the use of the COMPSTAT program. However, many scholars argue that although zero tolerance may satisfy short-term interest in law and order, this approach may return the police and the community to a relationship of conflict.

Community Policing, Evaluation and Crime Statistics

The effectiveness of community policing is often measured using crime rates for a given jurisdiction. Dropping crime rates would indicate success. As discussed earlier, many attribute our nationally decreasing crime rate to the implementation of community policing throughout the country. Others, however, suggest that is just one factor. Other factors include the robust economy, a graying population and fewer teenagers. Rogers (1998, p.43) suggests: "There is a direct correlation between the number of officers on the street and the decline in crime." The COPS office has added thousands of officers, but whether these officers are implementing community policing strategies is not as clear.

When using reduction in crime as a measure of community policing's effectiveness, the question often arises as to whether crime is simply displaced—moved to another community. In addition, if crime is, indeed, prevented, how do you measure what does not happen?

Crime statistics are seldom sufficient to understand the extent and character of a particular strategy's impact. Most research on community policing strategies shows only modest and statistically insignificant effects on crime rates, drug abuse and trafficking and fear of crime.

If departments want more effective approaches to evaluating community policing efforts, they must incorporate community-wide information in the process. It is especially important to use data collected and maintained by public and private agencies other than law enforcement agencies.

To evaluate the effectiveness of specific community policing strategies, police departments should consider data from the health care system (especially emergency rooms), schools, housing and licensing departments and community surveys.

To evaluate the effectiveness of family violence prevention programs, the number of abused women referred by medical personnel to shelters may be a more reliable indicator of program success or lack thereof than the number of domestic violence arrests. Strategies aimed at youths might use data on truancy, suspensions and expulsions as one means of measuring effectiveness.

Moore et al. (2002) address the challenge of measuring police performance. They (p.72) contend that performance should be evaluated by what citizens should value in their police department from both an individual and a group perspective. Table 15.2 presents an example of the types of values that might be measured.

They (p.132) suggest how statistical measures may be associated with identified valuable dimensions of police performance, as summarized in Table 15.3.

Table 15.2 What Citizens Should Value in Their Police Department

	Principled Values	***Instrumental Values***
Social Perspective	*Enforce the Law Faithfully and Impartially* Call offenders to account Reduce brutality and excessive use of force Allocate police resources fairly Reduce corruption Distribute burden of protection between private and public fairly	*Enhance Safety and Security* Reduce crime and victimization Reduce fear Reduce public disorder Increase efficiency and cost effectiveness Increase traffic safety Provide emergency medical/social services
Individual or Group Perspective	*Engender a Sense of Fair Treatment* Among particularly situated groups Among those obligated by police	*Provide High-Quality Customer Service* Quality of customer service: Individual evaluation Quality of customer service: Group evaluation

SOURCE: Mark Moore with David Thacher, Andrea Dodge and Tobias Moore. *Recognizing Value in Policing: The Challenge of Measuring Police Performance.* Washington, DC: Police Executive Research Forum, 2002, p.72. Reprinted by permission.

Finally, they (p.161) report on how performance measures were used in six COPS case studies and whether the importance of the measures was negotiated with authorizers (see Table 15.4).

The crime rate was one of the least important performance measures in these cities. Interestingly, Portland rated more measures as high priority than other departments and was also the only department to have negotiated performance measures prioritized with authorizers.

Several researchers have suggested that law enforcement not concentrate on crime statistics but rather focus on whether community policing efforts are able to build stronger communities—a major goal of the philosophy.

Table 15.3 Statistical Measures Associated with Valuable Dimensions of Police Performance

	Performance Dimensions	***Statistical Indicators***
	Reduce criminal victimization	Reported crime rates
		Victimization rates
	Call offenders to account	Clearance rates
		Conviction rates
	Reduce fear and enhance personal security	Reported change in levels of fear
		Reported changes in self-defense measures (levels and types)
	Guarantee safety in public spaces	Traffic fatalities, injuries and damage
		Increased utilization of parks and other public spaces
		Increased property values
	Use financial resources fairly, efficiently and effectively	Cost per citizen
		Deployment efficiency/fairness
		Scheduling efficiency
		Budget compliance
		Overtime expenditures
		Civilianization
	Use force and authority fairly, efficiently and effectively	Citizen complaints
		Settlements in liability suits
		Police shootings
	Satisfy customer demands/ achieve legitimacy with those policed	Satisfaction with police services
		Response times
		Citizen perceptions of fairness

SOURCE: Mark Moore with David Thacher, Andrea Dodge and Tobias Moore. *Recognizing Value in Policing: The Challenge of Measuring Police Performance.* Washington, DC: Police Executive Research Forum, 2002, p.132. Reprinted by permission.

Table 15.4 Use of Performance Measurement in COPS Case Studies

	Albany	*Riverside*	*Fremont*	*Knoxville*	*Lowell*	*Portland*
Overall Importance of Performance Measurement	LOW	MED-LOW	MED	MED	MED	HIGH
Negotiated with Authorizors?	NO	NO	NO	NO	NO	YES
	Crime rate				COMPSTAT	COMPSTAT -like
			Reduce emphasis on arrests	Repeat offender tracking	COMPSTAT	Recidivism in some project evaluations
	Part II crimes/ General city ordinances		Reduced emphasis on arrests		Repeated citizen surveys	Repeated citizen surveys and project evaluations
		Workload reviews/ overtime expenses		Workload reviews		Workload reviews
		Early warning system			Early Warning System/ COMPSTAT	Early warning system
		Neighborhood watch activity	Citizen surveys in some project evaluations/ neighborhood watch activity		Repeated citizen surveys	Repeated citizen surveys

SOURCE: Mark Moore with David Thacher, Andrea Dodge and Tobias Moore. *Recognizing Value in Policing: The Challenge of Measuring Police Performance.* Washington, DC: Police Executive Research Forum, 2002, p.161. Reprinted by permission.

Community Policing and Strong Communities

Kerley and Benson conducted such a study using data from a comprehensive community policing study conducted in Oakland, California, and Birmingham, Alabama, from 1987 to 1989.

> Research findings (p.46) indicate that community policing strategies do not have strong effects on community processes.

Kerley and Benson (p.64) discuss the **implant hypothesis**, which asks whether collective citizen action by a small group of neighborhood residents, for example, neighborhood-watch groups, can make a difference in the attitudes and behaviors of local residents. They suggest that the implant hypotheses might be proven true if community policing efforts meet two criteria: (1) stimulation of community processes be made the main goal and outcome measure of community policing programs and (2) police seek to more actively involve community residents in the strategies. They reason that crime rates and fear should be secondary goals and outcome measures:

> The reasoning for this is straightforward. If stimulation of community processes is the intervening variable between community policing programs and reductions in crime rates and fear, it would follow that it should be the primary goal and outcome measure of community policing programs. Unfortunately, given the current state of crime-centered politics and evaluation, this has not been the case.

Such a shift in focus might also be considered when evaluating the success of the COPS program.

Evaluation of the COPS Office

Zhao et al. (p.389) report: "Over the past 8 years, the COPS Office has awarded grants to law enforcement agencies totaling more than $7 billion, providing funding for more than 114,000 community police officers. They describe the three categories of COP grants: (1) hiring grants, (2) MORE (Making Officer Redeployment Effective) and (3) innovative grants. The MORE grants may be used by law enforcement agencies to acquire new technology and civilian personnel.

A national evaluation of the effect of COPS grants on crime from 1994 to 1999 (Zhao and Thurman, 2001, p.2) was very positive.

Preliminary findings in a national evaluation of the effect of COPS grants on crime reported that after controlling for other factors, COPS hiring initiatives have resulted in significant reductions in local crime rates in cities with populations greater than 10,000 and that the COPS innovative grant programs have had significant crime reducing effects for the entire population of COPS grantees.

It is difficult to estimate the actual additional number of officers on the street because some leave while others are added, comparable to an open house event. The number of people at the open house at any one time will be significantly fewer than the total number of people coming through. The researchers found that the COPS program "provided fuel, but not the launch pad, for the nationwide proliferation of community policing tactics between 1995 and 1998" ("Urban Institute Declares . . .," 2000, p.3).

The report notes a high participation level by high-crime jurisdictions, with 50 percent of all COPS awards going to 10 percent of police agencies with the highest number of murders in the years studied ("Urban Institute Evaluation . . .," 2000, pp.9–10).

What Works, What Doesn't and What's Promising

Sherman et al. (1998) reviewed more than 500 prevention program evaluations meeting minimum scientific standards and conclude that there is minimally adequate evidence to establish a provisional list of what works, what doesn't and what's promising as of late 1996.

What Works

Sherman (1999, p.143) summarizes the key findings on what works.

What works: increased directed patrols in street-corner hot spots of crime, proactive arrests of serious repeat offenders, proactive drunk driving arrests and arrests of employed suspects for domestic assault.

Sherman et al. list other strategies that work.

- For infants: Frequent home visits by nurses and other professionals
- For preschoolers: Classes with weekly home visits by preschool teachers
- For delinquent and at-risk preadolescents: Family therapy and parent training
- For schools:
  Organizational development for innovation
  Communication and reinforcement of clear, consistent norms
  Teaching of social competency skills
  Coaching of high-risk youths in "thinking skills"
- For older male ex-offenders: Vocational training
- For rental housing with drug dealing: Nuisance abatement action on landlords
- For high-risk repeat offenders: Monitoring by specialized police units or incarceration
- For convicted offenders: Rehabilitation programs with risk-focused treatments
- For drug-using offenders in prison: Therapeutic community treatment programs

The Urban Institute's evaluation of the COPS program also found some statistically significant effective strategies among grant awardees.

What also works: joint crime prevention projects with local businesses, citizen surveys to obtain information about residents' views on crime problems, incorporating probation officers into problem-solving policing initiatives, late-night recreation programs to give youths an alternative to gangs and criminal activities, new rules designed to increase officers' time on the beat and give them more discretion and employee evaluation measures to give credit for community policing work by officers.

What Doesn't Work

According to Sherman's summary of key findings, several strategies, some very popular, do not work.

What doesn't work: neighborhood block watch, arrests of some juveniles for minor offenses, arrests of unemployed suspects for domestic assault, drug market arrests and community policing with no clear crime-risk factor focus.

The list of what doesn't work is extensive: gun "buyback" programs, community mobilization against crime in high-crime poverty areas, police counseling visits to homes of couples days after domestic violence incidents, counseling and peer counseling of students in schools, Drug Abuse Resistance Education (DARE), drug prevention classes focused on fear and other emotional appeals (including self-esteem), summer jobs or subsidized work programs for at-risk youths, short-term nonresidential training programs for at-risk youths, diversion from court to job training as a condition of case dismissal, increased arrests or raids on drug market locations, storefront police offices, police newsletters with local crime information, correctional boot camps using traditional military basic training and "Scared Straight" programs whereby minor juvenile offenders visit adult prisons. Also found to be ineffective were shock probation, shock parole and split sentences adding jail time to probation or parole; home detention with electronic monitoring; intensive supervision on parole or probation; rehabilitation programs using vague, unstructured counseling; and residential programs for juvenile offenders using challenging experiences in rural settings.

What's Promising

Sherman's summary of what is promising includes seven strategies.

What's promising: police traffic enforcement patrols against illegally carried handguns, community policing with community participation in priority setting, community policing focused on improving police legitimacy, zero tolerance of disorder (if legitimacy issues can be addressed), problem-oriented policing generally, adding extra police to cities (regardless of assignments) and warrants for arrest of suspect except when police respond to domestic violence.

Again, Sherman et al.'s research revealed an extensive list of promising practices including proactive drunk-driving arrests with breath testing (may reduce accident deaths), community policing with meetings to set priorities (may reduce perceptions of crime), police showing greater respect to arrested offenders (may reduce repeat offending), polite field interrogations of suspicious persons (may reduce street crime) and higher number of police officers in cities (may reduce crime generally).

Also seen as promising were gang monitoring by community workers and probation and police officers, community-based mentoring by Big Brothers/Big Sisters of America (may prevent drug abuse), community-based after-school recreation programs (may reduce local juvenile crime) and battered women's shelters (may help some women reduce repeated domestic violence).

Other promising strategies were "schools within schools" that group students into smaller units (may prevent crime), training or coaching in "thinking" skills for high-risk youths (may prevent crime), building school capacity through organizational development (may prevent substance abuse), improved classroom management and instructional techniques (may reduce alcohol use), Job Corps residential training programs for at-risk youths (may reduce felonies) and prison-based vocational education programs for adult inmates (in federal prisons).

Still other promising strategies cited include moving urban public housing residents to suburban homes (may reduce risk factors for crime), enterprise zones (may reduce area unemployment, a risk factor for crime), two clerks in already-robbed convenience stores, redesigned layout of retail stores (may reduce shoplifting), improved training and management of bar and tavern staff (may reduce violence, DUI), metal detectors (may reduce skyjacking, weapon carrying in school), street closures, barricades and rerouting (may reduce violence, burglary) and "target hardening" (may reduce vandalism of parking meters and crime involving phones).

The last six promising strategies are "problem-solving" analysis unique to the crime situation at each location, proactive arrests for carrying concealed weapons (may reduce gun crime), drug courts (may reduce repeat offending), drug treatment in jails followed by urine testing in the community, intensive supervision and aftercare of juvenile offenders (both minor and serious) and fines for criminal acts.

Sherman (p.143) suggests areas in which research is lacking: "Gang prevention, for example, is a matter about which we could not find a single impact evaluation of police practices. Police curfews and truancy programs lack rigorous tests. Police recreation activities with juveniles, such as Police Athletic Leagues, also remain unevaluated."

As departments and those interested in community policing consider specific strategies, they should take heed of what Laycock (2000, p.3) stresses: "You need to know what works where and why. This question is central to the present agenda. In my view, nothing works everywhere, but something will work in every jurisdiction. That is why the where and why are important. You need to know the principles that determine what works and that will enable you to replicate successful initiatives in your own jurisdiction."

A Look toward the Future

Chief Richard Overman, Delray Beach, (Florida) Police Department presents a vision of the police department of the future: "We will be an organization that is fully trained and culturally acclimated to a partnership approach with the rest of the community to resolve problems, not only crime problems, but also problems involving social disorder and quality of life issues" (Dale, 2000, p.117). Dale reports on the results of a survey completed by police chiefs participating in a panel to discuss the most important concerns in the next decade. Six concerns were prominent:

1. Employment—Hiring and retaining professional, ethical, educated, culturally diverse personnel
2. Budget—Competitive salary, unions, grants, taxes
3. Technology—Internal/external communication, training, managing technology
4. Crime—Juvenile, elderly, white collar, computer, drugs
5. Growth—Population, diversity, geographic, build-out
6. Quality-of-life issues—Effective community policing, strategic management planning

Youngs (2003, p.97) reports on the joint effort of the Society of Police Futurists International and the FBI-sponsored Futuristics and Law Enforcement: The Millennium Conference. They identified five areas of concern that must be addressed: (1) the future of technology and its effect on law enforcement, (2) the future of leadership and management in policing agencies, (3) future crime/future law, (4) the future of policing practices and philosophies and (5) the changing face of America—demographics and policing.

Youngs (pp.98–101) suggests: "Agencies must have proactive planning programs to monitor trends, discuss and develop new strategies, and facilitate and respond to emerging trends. Law enforcement must form a variety of partnerships with both public and private entities due to lack of knowledge and resources with which to combat cyber crime and manage diversity. Non-law enforcement and administrative functions will be privatized and outsourced while traditional duties and responsibilities are handled by law enforcement. . . . Management styles will change emphasizing leadership ability and interpersonal relationship building. . . . Citizen involvement will increase and be paramount. Community policing will incorporate process mapping to a higher degree. . . . Citizens will be able to log on and track crime in their neighborhoods and vote on issues affecting them. . . . Terrorism will take many forms, such as attacks against the infrastructure through computer networks, weapons of mass destruction, genomic or genetic terrorism attacking food production and preparation, and traditional random violent attacks. . . . Citizens are likely to trade some civil liberties for protection against terrorism and cybercrime. . . . It could be that by 2050 society will have a new generation that deals with the process of change in a way that allows rapid growth without the chaos each technological development now brings."

Youngs (p.98) provides a time line prediction of trends that those responsible for planning for the future might want to consider (see Figure 15.2).

During the closing plenary session at the NCJA's National Forum 2003, panelists were asked to look to the year 2010 and communicate their visions for the future of criminal justice, including the issues that criminal justice decision makers might be facing at that time. "Overall, panelists saw improved access to technology for the public safety community, with movement away from 'cookie cutter' approaches in policing toward more intelligence-driven policing. At the same time, law enforcement will deal more with the globalization of crime, and it will be even more important then, than now, for jurisdictional boundaries to be broken and regional governance models to be developed. In 2010 criminal justice will have overcome the interoperability obstacle; improved national information sharing and data analysis; and learned to 'do more with less' through the leveraging of resources, use of technology (to solve/forecast crime and track/monitor/identify offenders), and increased private sector partnerships to help protect the public" ("National Forum's Final . . .," 2003).

Panelist Kim Allen, cabinet secretary for public protection for the Metro Louisville (Kentucky) Government, presented the truism that technology comes to law enforcement last, while those who get in first and use it for illegal purposes have incredible opportunity to operate with little risk of exposure: "Hopefully, the next seven years will provide law enforcement with the opportunity to finally catch up." Her vision of the criminal justice system in 2010 includes improved information sharing by law enforcement, "computerized justice" and increased access to real-time information. Cyberterrorism will become more attractive as security of physical targets tightens. Crime will increasingly be driven by technology and will have far-reaching consequences. The nation will experience increases in violent and

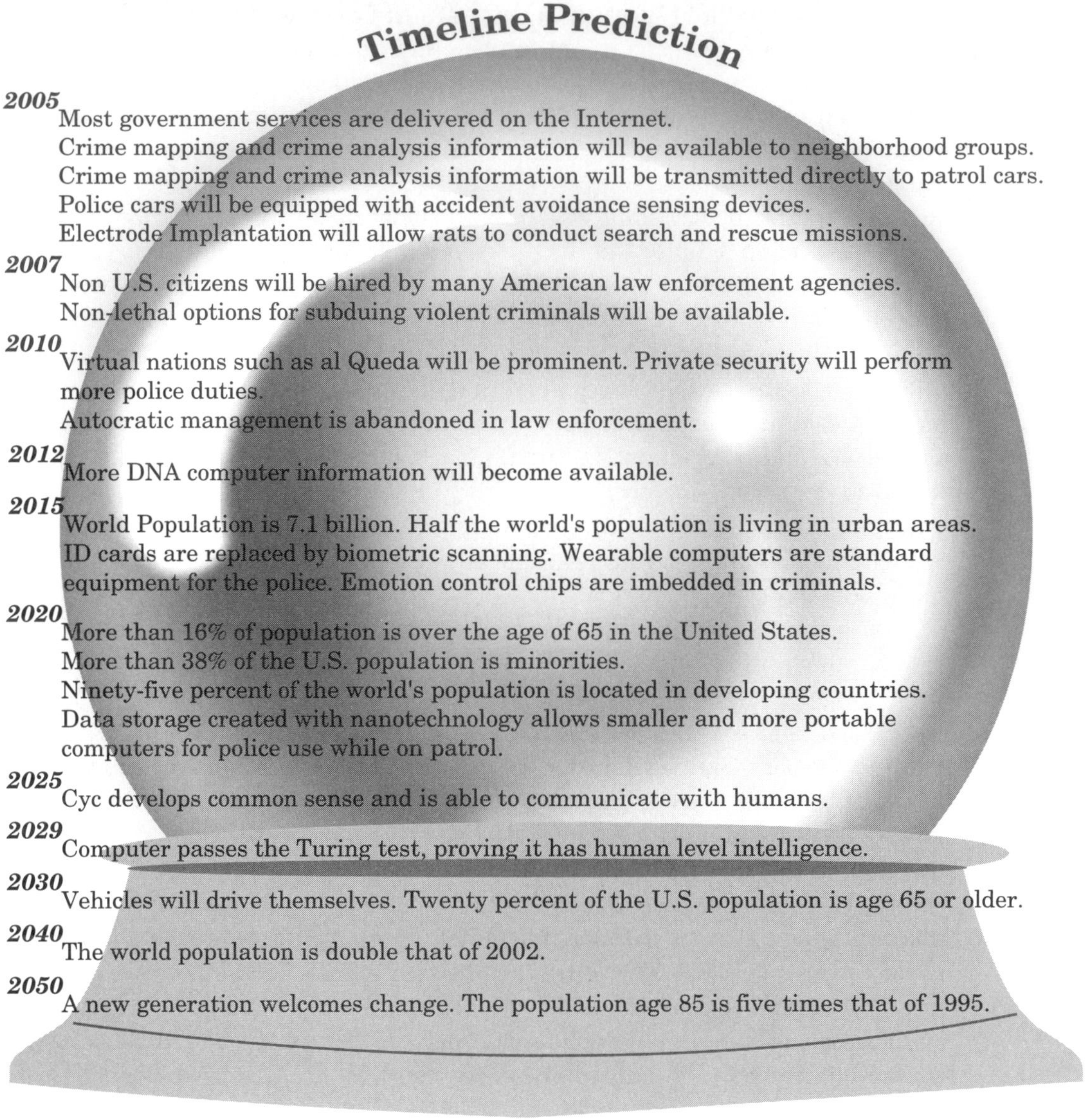

Timeline Prediction
2005
Most government services are delivered on the Internet.
Crime mapping and crime analysis information will be available to neighborhood groups.
Crime mapping and crime analysis information will be transmitted directly to patrol cars.
Police cars will be equipped with accident avoidance sensing devices.
Electrode Implantation will allow rats to conduct search and rescue missions.
2007
Non U.S. citizens will be hired by many American law enforcement agencies.
Non-lethal options for subduing violent criminals will be available.
2010
Virtual nations such as al Queda will be prominent. Private security will perform more police duties.
Autocratic management is abandoned in law enforcement.
2012
More DNA computer information will become available.
2015
World Population is 7.1 billion. Half the world's population is living in urban areas.
ID cards are replaced by biometric scanning. Wearable computers are standard equipment for the police. Emotion control chips are imbedded in criminals.
2020
More than 16% of population is over the age of 65 in the United States.
More than 38% of the U.S. population is minorities.
Ninety-five percent of the world's population is located in developing countries.
Data storage created with nanotechnology allows smaller and more portable computers for police use while on patrol.
2025
Cyc develops common sense and is able to communicate with humans.
2029
Computer passes the Turing test, proving it has human level intelligence.
2030
Vehicles will drive themselves. Twenty percent of the U.S. population is age 65 or older.
2040
The world population is double that of 2002.
2050
A new generation welcomes change. The population age 85 is five times that of 1995.

Figure 15.2 Timeline Prediction

SOURCE: Alan C. Youngs. "Law Enforcement in 2003 and Beyond." *Law and Order,* April 2003, p.98. Reprinted by permission.

property crime, fueled by the tight economy, urban poverty rates, large numbers of criminals being released from prison and a growing youth population.

Thomas O'Reily, administrator for the New Jersey Department of Law and Public Safety, opened his remarks by observing that those who do not read history are bound to repeat it; that is, if we continue to do what we always did, we will get what we always get. Among the changes he hopes will occur by 2010 are that the current structure of government no longer will be relevant, particularly at the local, county level; the quality of justice will improve, with issues of racially biased policing, adjudication and corrections addressed; policing will become increasingly intelligence driven; and there will be a greater investment in prevention.

Philip Ramer, director of intelligence for the Florida Department of Law Enforcement, expressed optimism that the public sector will catch up with the private sector technologically, with greater intelligence sharing and information analysis, and regional governance models will emerge, especially as this relates to communications interoperability.

Paul Wormeli, vice president of PEC Solutions, notes that seven years is not long enough to see any significant changes in the criminal justice system. He contends that the **zeitgeist**—the general intellectual, moral, cultural or "spirit" of the times—will not change until we are ready, but we must first have the will, opportunity and means. Wormeli outlines the three drivers: change, opportunities and challenges, and impacts on the criminal justice system as it moves toward 2010.

Drivers of change:

- The economy, which has forced reallocation of resources and caused declining revenue for public service
- The war on terrorism, which is now driving much of the workload in criminal justice and has further reduced resources
- Technology, which has helped lower costs, while providing greater capabilities for protecting public safety

Opportunities and challenges:

- Broadband access, both wireless and wired, crucial for interoperable voice and data systems
- Collaboration
- Virtual enterprise information systems
- Decision making based on information

Impacts on the criminal justice system:

- Increased efficiency, which will result in fewer redundancies and the elimination of job position
- More intelligent decision making through national information sharing and data analysis
- Improved quality of justice

Community Policing: Still a Philosophy or a Reality?

Bucqueroux (2000, pp.1, 3–4, 9) suggests that in the future, in a perfect world, community policing would be the cornerstone for a new community criminal justice system, part of the "new paradigm" of community-oriented government: "It didn't take long for average citizens to see that 'locking up the bad guys' was not always the best answer. Politicians who once ran on 'three strikes and you're out' now embrace collaborative, community-based solutions."

However, many departments have accepted the rhetoric of community policing, but not the philosophy itself. And then Ecstasy hit hard among middle-class youths and affluent, suburban parents demanded that the police do something other than locking up their children. Some chiefs even blamed community policing for being too soft on crime. The police response in affluent neighborhoods was different from what they employed in urban hot spots: sweeps, crackdowns, battering rams and overhead helicopters. The new surge of arrests led to another massive overcrowding of prisons.

Black activists, long angry that penalties for crack cocaine (for which blacks were more likely to be arrested) were much harsher than those for the powdered form of cocaine preferred by the white middle class, became even angrier as they saw the disparity in the way Ecstasy users in urban and suburban neighborhoods were treated. Rumors began to fly about an impending race war, surging through the Internet around the country. Many of the "new breed" of officers left the department as departments reverted to the military mode to be ready for any uprisings. Bucqueroux (p.4) says: "Two-track policing—different for rich and poor, urban and suburban, white and everyone else—became an increasingly stark reality."

Bucqueroux envisions two possible futures for law enforcement: one where the community policing philosophy pervades the criminal justice system or one where two-track policing exists.

She (pp.4, 9) urges: "The choice between these two futures is rapidly upon us. As new problems emerge, a series of small and large decisions will make the difference between a future where police embrace an inclusive and collaborative model or succumb to the illusory promise of solving crime and disorder problems through aggressive military-style repression." She concludes:

> The future we will inherit should not be decided by a coin flip between these two simplistic visions. Real solutions demand real changes. Those who know the checklist of changes that community policing demands must not only tell the community what it takes for meaningful reform, but they must find the courage to challenge the prevailing wisdom inside and outside the department when it is clear that the emperor is naked. The choice of whether or not community policing will be allowed to fulfill its potential will dictate the future, and the choice is ours to make.

Summary

At the heart of experimental design is the random assignment of individuals to experimental and control conditions. Experiments in criminal justice raise ethical issues as well as privacy issues. The ASC concluded: "The principle is that random assignment to treatment options is the best scientific method for determining the effectiveness of options." Assistance in experiments in criminal justice is available through the NIJ's Locally Initiated Research Partnerships in Policing. Surveys are commonly used by police departments. To validate an evaluation conducted by survey, 60 percent of distributed surveys must be returned.

Research has found that community-oriented police departments differ in structure from traditional police departments in that their organization is less complex, their decision making less centralized and their administration less dense. Common patterns found in community policing in the United States include crime prevention, problem solving, partnerships, shared responsibility and decentralization. It has also been found that community policing and traditional policing officers generated a similar proportion of complaints, similar types of complaints and a similar number of complaints.

Crime statistics are seldom sufficient to understand the extent and character of a particular strategy's impact. Most research on community policing strategies shows only modest and statistically insignificant effects on crime rates, drug abuse and trafficking and fear of crime. Research findings indicate that community policing strategies do not have strong effects on community processes.

Preliminary findings in a national evaluation of the effect of COPS grants on crime reported that after controlling for other factors, COPS hiring initiatives have resulted in significant reductions in local crime rates in cities with populations greater than 10,000 and that the COPS innovative grant programs have had significant crime reducing effects for the entire population of COPS grantees.

A study of over 500 research efforts identified what works, doesn't work and holds promise. What works: increased directed patrols in street-corner hot spots of crime, proactive arrests of serious repeat offenders, proactive drunk-driving arrests and arrests of employed suspects for domestic assault. What also works: joint crime prevention projects with local businesses, citizen surveys to obtain information about residents' views on crime problems, incorporating probation officers into problem-solving policing initiatives, late-night recreation programs to give youths an alternative to gangs and criminal activities, new rules designed to increase officers' time on the beat and give them more discretion and employee evaluation measures to give credit for community policing work by officers.

What doesn't work: neighborhood block watch, arrests of some juveniles for minor offenses, arrests of unemployed suspects for domestic assault, drug market arrests and community policing with no clear crime–risk factor focus.

What's promising: police traffic enforcement patrols against illegally carried handguns, community policing with community participation in priority setting, community policing focused on improving police legitimacy, zero tolerance of disorder (if legitimacy issues can be addressed), problem-oriented policing generally, adding extra police to cities (regardless of assignments) and warrants for arrest of suspect except when police respond to domestic violence.

Bucqueroux envisions two possible futures for law enforcement: one where the community policing philosophy pervades the criminal justice system or one where two-track policing exists.

Discussion Questions

1. What future predictions does Bucqueroux make for community policing?
2. What percentage of returned surveys is required for validation and why?
3. Researchers have identified many strategies that work to decrease crime. Name and discuss three of these strategies.
4. What is the implant hypothesis? Describe it in detail.
5. Why do crime and arrest statistics fall short of explaining the success or failure of a particular strategy? What other kinds of data should also be looked at?
6. Discuss the importance of research in criminal justice.

7. Some police agencies conduct citizen surveys to gauge public attitudes toward the police. Discuss the impact different methods of conducting surveys can have on the results.
8. How does the availability of funding affect patterns of community policing within police departments?
9. What organizational and structural differences exist between traditional police departments and those that are engaged in community policing?
10. What is a two-wave survey, and when might it be appropriate to use?

InfoTrac College Edition Assignments

- Use InfoTrac College Edition to help answer the Discussion Questions as appropriate.
- Crime researchers in Canada have formed the Network for Research on Crime and Justice, which allows researchers to network and share knowledge, avoid duplication of effort and build on existing findings. The network's Research in Brief page on the Web site includes results from the U.S. Department of Justice research on the continued decline of serious crime levels in 1999. Discuss the measures used in this research and the sources of the data. Also explain what NCVS and UCR mean.

Community Project

Design and conduct a survey (campus, neighborhood or law enforcement agency). Surveys can be conducted on a wide range of topics, including fear of crime, crime reporting, police attitudes, community attitudes and victimization surveys. Some ready-made surveys may be available from the Office of Community Oriented Policing Services and other community policing or crime prevention Web sites.

References

Anthony, Stavros S. "The Structure of Successful Community-Oriented Police Departments." *The Police Chief,* November 2000, pp.69–73.

Bayley, David H. *Police for the Future.* New York: Oxford, 1994.

Bayley, David H. *Policing in America: Assessment and Prospects. Ideas in American Policing,* Washington, DC: The Police Foundation, February 1998.

Boruch, Robert F.; Victor, Timothy; and Cecil, Joe S. "Resolving Ethical and Legal Problems in Randomized Experiments." *Crime & Delinquency,* July 2000, pp.330–353.

Bratton, W. J. "New Strategies for Combating Crime in New York." *Fordham Urban Law Journal,* Spring 1996, pp.23, 781–795.

Bucqueroux, Bonnie. "Two Views of the Future of Community Policing." *Subject to Debate,* 2000, pp.3–4, 9.

Cordner, G. W. "Community Policing: Elements and Effects." In *Critical Issues in Policing: Contemporary Readings,* 3rd ed., edited by R. G. Dunham and G. P. Alpert. Prospect Heights, IL: Waveland, 1997, pp.451–468.

Cordray, David S. "Enhancing the Scope of Experimental Inquiry in Intervention Studies." *Crime & Delinquency,* July 2000, pp.401–424.

Dale, Nancy. "Survival Strategies for the Next Decade." *Law and Order,* October 2000, pp.116–122.

Dunford, Franklyn W. "Determining Program Success: The Importance of Employing Experimental Research Designs." *Crime & Delinquency,* July 2000, pp.425–434.

Feder, Lynette and Boruch, Robert F. "The Need for Experiments in Criminal Justice Settings." *Crime & Delinquency,* July 2000, pp.291–294.

Feder, Lynette; Jolin, Annette; and Feyerherm, William. "Lessons from Two Randomized Experiments in Criminal Justice Settings." *Crime & Delinquency,* July 2000, pp.380–400.

Hickman, Matthew J.; Piquero, Alex R.; and Greene, Jack R. "Does Community Policing Generate Greater Numbers and Different Types of Citizen Complaints than Traditional Policing?" *Police Quarterly,* March 2000, pp.70–84.

Kerley, Kent R. and Benson, Michael L. "Does Community-Oriented Policing Help Build Stronger Communities?" *Police Quarterly,* March 2000, pp.46–69.

Laycock, Gloria. "Becoming More Assertive about Good Research." *Subject to Debate,* July 2000, pp.1, 3–4.

Maguire, Edward R. and Mastrofski, Stephen D. "Patterns of Community Policing in the United States." *Police Quarterly,* March 2000, pp.4–45.

McEwen, Tom; Spencer, Deborah; Wolff, Russell; Wartell, Julie; and Webster, Barbara. *Call Management and Community Policing: A Guidebook for Law Enforcement Cops.* Washington, DC: Office of Community Oriented Policing, July 10, 2003.

Moore, Mark; Thacher, David; Dodge, Andrea; and Moore, Tobias. *Recognizing Value in Policing: The Challenge of Measuring Police Performance.* Washington, DC: Police Executive Research Forum, 2002.

"National Forum's Final Plenary Session: 'Fast Forward—What Can We Expect?'" *National Criminal Justice Association Justice Bulletin,* August 2003, pp.1, 12–13.

Oakley, Ann. "A Historical Perspective on the Use of Randomized Trials in Social Science Settings." *Crime & Delinquency,* July 2000, pp.315–329.

Petrosino, Anthony; Turpin-Petrosino, Carolyn; and Finckenauer, James O. "Well-Meaning Programs Can Have Harmful Effects! Lessons from Experiments of Programs such as Scared Straight." *Crime & Delinquency,* July 2000, pp.354–379.

"A Police Guide to Surveying Citizens." Bureau of Justice Assistance. www.ncjrs.org

Rogers, Donna. "Community Policing and the Crime Rate." *Law Enforcement Technology,* October 1998, pp.42–44.

Rohe, W. M.; Adams, R. E.; Arcury, T. A.; Memory, J.; and Klopovic, J. *Community Oriented Policing: The North Carolina Experience.* Chapel Hill, NC: The Center for Urban and Regional Studies, 1996.

Roth, J. A. and Johnson, C. C. *COPS Context and Community Policing.* Presentation at the American Society of Criminology, San Diego, CA, November 1997.

Scott, Jason D.; Duffee, David E.; and Renauer, Brian C. "Measuring Police-Community Coproduction: The Utility of Community Policing Case Studies." *Police Quarterly,* December 2003, pp.410–439.

Sherman, Lawrence W. "Policing for Crime Prevention." In *Criminal Justice: Concepts and Issues: An Anthology,* 3rd ed., edited by Chris W. Eskridge. Los Angeles: Roxbury Publishing Company, 1999, pp.131–148.

Sherman, Lawrence W.; Gottfredson, Denise C.; MacKenzie, Doris L.; Eck, John; Reuter, Peter; and Bushway, Shawn D. *Preventing Crime: What Works, What Doesn't, What's Promising.* National Institute of Justice Research in Brief, July 1998.

Short, James F., Jr.; Zahn, Margaret A.; and Farrington, David P. "Experimental Research in Criminal Justice Settings: Is there a Role for Scholarly Societies?" *Crime & Delinquency,* July 2000, pp.295–298.

Skolnick J. H. and Bayley, D. H. "Theme and Variation in Community Policing." In *Crime and Justice: A Review of Research,* Vol. 10, edited by M. Tonry and N. Morris. Chicago: University of Chicago Press, 1988.

Slavin, Robert E. "A Reader's Guide to Scientifically Based Research." *Educational Leadership,* February 2003, pp.12–16.

Thacher, David. "Policing Is not a Treatment: Alternatives to the Medical Model of Police Research." *Journal of Research in Crime and Delinquency,* November 2001, pp.387–415.

Travis, Lawrence F., III; Novak, Kenneth J.; Winston, Craig N.; and Hurley, David C. "Cops at the Door: The Impact of Citizen Surveys by Police on Public Attitudes." *Police Quarterly,* March 2000, pp.85–104.

"Urban Institute Declares COPS Program a Partial Success." *Criminal Justice Newsletter,* September 15, 2000, pp.3–4.

"Urban Institute Evaluation of the COPS Office." *Subject to Debate,* September 2000, pp.9–10.

Weisburd, David. "Randomized Experiments in Criminal Justice Police: Prospects and Problems." *Crime & Delinquency,* April 2000, pp.181–193.

Woodyard, Adele. "Tampa Police Measure Community Service." *Law and Order,* April 2003, pp.38–42.

Youngs, Alan C. "Law Enforcement in 2003 and Beyond." *Law and Order,* April 2003, pp.96–101.

Zhao, Jihong "Solomon" and Thurman, Quint. *A National Evaluation of the Effect of COPS Grants on Crime from 1994 to 1999.* Washington, DC: Office of Community Oriented Policing Services, December 2001.

Zhao, Jhog "Solomon"; Scheider, Matthew C.; and Thurman, Quint. "A National Evaluation of the Effect of COPS Grants on Police Productivity (Arrests) 1996–1999. *Police Quarterly,* December 2003, pp.387–409.

Epilogue

Traditionally, the driving forces of change in police work have been legislative and judicial mandates. Though no Miranda-like decisions are coercing change today, a fundamental shift in the way officers do their jobs is taking place in departments across our country. Why is this happening? Profound changes in our world have occurred and are forcing police departments to adapt. These changes are forever shifting the way American institutions respond to the external environment. Those most profound trends are:

- Public expectations. We have more educated Americans now, than at any time in our history. As a result, they know how governmental systems work and that the "squeaky wheel gets the grease." Consequently, there is an ever-increasing demand by Americans to have a say in the way all levels of government operate.
- Worker expectations. Pyramidal-shaped organizations cannot rely on traditional order-giving tactics to enhance worker productivity and effectiveness. In public and private sectors, today's workers are demanding to have a say in the decisions that will affect them.
- Technology. Technological advances give line personnel an array of information previously unavailable to them. Consequently, they are capable of making some work decisions once restricted to supervisors and managers. Hence, technological advances have increased the importance of line workers.
- Commitment to the value of diversity. The most effective partnerships will be those that capitalize on the diversity within the community and within the police department.
- Strategic alliances/partnerships. From NAFTA to the Saturn automobile, government and private industry are increasingly reliant on developing synergies created by strategic partnerships. Likewise, the partnership component of community policing is emulating this trend that is occurring on a much broader scale.

This text has presented an enormous amount of information about community policing organized into chapters, which may tend to lose sight of the big picture. To bring closure to the topic, Commander Michael Nila, formerly with the Aurora (Illinois) Police Department, has graciously provided a commentary on two basic requirements to successfully implement community policing: making diversity an integral part of the effort and engaging the community.

DIVERSITY—AN INTEGRAL PART OF COMMUNITY POLICING

As policing in America changes from traditional to community policing, the critical challenge is to change the relationship between the police and the community. Namely, communities at risk—our poor, our youths, our elderly and our minority communities. The "us versus them" mentality that exists between the police and the community often prevents officers from willingly engaging citizens in the neighborhoods we spend the greatest amount of our time policing.

In any typical urban setting, the police very often have an adversarial relationship with citizens whose background, culture, economic condition and race are very different from their own. Too often, the police see citizens in at-risk neighborhoods as "the enemy" while the community views the police as an "invading army." Rarely, until the community policing movement took root, did the police proactively and sincerely cultivate positive relationships and truly commit to resolving problems in at-risk neighborhoods.

Progressive police agencies today recognize that embracing a community policing philosophy means making a commitment to improving police/community relationships and changing the police culture, often the greatest barrier to true police-community partnerships. The growing commitment to diversity is exemplified by the increasing number of police agencies who include "diversity" in their official organizational values such as in Aurora, Illinois:

> We value diversity, and commit to nurturing a welcoming environment of inclusion, in which we recognize the unique skills, knowledge, abilities and backgrounds of all people as our strength.

Diversity is a term often misunderstood by police officers who consider diversity initiatives intrusive, unnecessary, often accusatory and an opportunity for "finger pointing." Through aggressive diversity discussions and training, coupled with a strong diversity/ harassment policy, and most important, a commitment from top management to a "managing diversity" concept—police departments are changing the internal culture and their external relationships.

In the past, inclusion of diversity in the workforce reflected legal requirements, moral imperatives or social responsibility. As is clearly evident today, all organizations are in the throes of the explosion of a diverse workforce; and it is the police in any community who have the most contacts with a wider range of diverse people than any other profession.

Today, community policing makes managing diversity critical to success and, simply, is good management! Managing diversity is a philosophy developed by Dr. Roosevelt Thomas who established the American Institute for Managing Diversity at Moorehouse College in Atlanta, Georgia. Recognizing that the changing face of America, driven by rapidly growing minority and immigrant populations, would lead to increasingly diverse organizations, Dr. Thomas moved beyond affirmative action and quota systems. He developed a philosophy of diversity that focuses not only on understanding and respecting differences, but goes further by creating an environment where all people can contribute to their maximum potential. As described by one diversity student, "Managing diversity is about getting 100 percent out of 100 percent of our people."

All organizations must realize that diversity does not stop at ethnicity and gender. Instead, diversity must include developing understanding, acceptance and respect of all differences including lifestyle, sexual preference, geographic origin, style of dress, hobbies, habits, interests, physical differences and so on. Diversity is about developing an environment of inclusion where those who are different from the mainstream are made valuable contributors to any organization's success.

While managing diversity is critical to organizational success and maximizing productivity, the concept holds true for communities as well. Only when the police and the community both understand and respect each other can true collaboration take place. Maximizing any community's "human capital" requires everyone's involvement and commitment.

Changing the police culture, changing the police perception of the community and the community's feelings toward the police is a difficult, challenging undertaking. If the culture does not support the desired behavior change, the culture must be addressed. While difficult, this can be achieved if the commitment is made.

One success story in diversity initiatives is the Reno (Nevada) Police Department, which began community policing in 1987 under Chief Robert Bradshaw. Chief Bradshaw boldly reorganized the department under a community policing philosophy. He also recognized that community policing and cultural diversity could not be separated. With equal emphasis, Bradshaw directed massive community policing and cultural diversity training for all personnel. The result—in Reno today, police officers view diversity as a way of life that is critical to community policing, as exemplified by one Reno sergeant who stated: "The driving motivation to diversity is community policing—developing all community resources as partnerships through understanding."

While focusing on the internal culture is important to changing police officers' behaviors, so too is developing proactive initiatives that change citizens' perceptions of the police and one another. In Aurora, Illinois, community policing officers have developed a number of outreach strategies to overcome barriers with the minority community such as:

- A Spanish Citizens Police Academy that targets Hispanic community members and teaches police topics while providing information that facilitates community involvement and assimilation.
- Diversity training conducted for citizen groups that patrol and take proactive steps to address crime and disorder problems in the neighborhoods. This prevents the tendency to "pick on" the minority element in the community simply because they are the neighborhood "newcomers."
- Police-sponsored neighborhood festivals and community events that bring minority neighborhoods together with mainstream neighborhoods in celebrating the community's diversity.

Effectively managing diversity programs that work to change the culture and behaviors of all those within the organization must include the following components:

- An internal audit to assess organizational health as related to diversity issues such as employee relations, perceptions of employees to minorities, inappropriate jokes and cartoons, and so on.
- A strict harassment/diversity policy that is adhered to.
- Nonconfrontational introductory training (4–8 hours), which should be a soft sell to diversity, emphasizing the need for agency-wide commitment.
- Advanced training (ongoing training in 4-hour blocks) that addresses specific racial issues in the community, historical issues, gay/lesbian issues and sexual harassment concerns.
- Specialized needs training that focuses on the needs of specialized units such as Field Training Officers, Gang Officers, Community Policing and Recruiting. Each specialized area has a unique role to fill that heavily affects minority relations and internal cultural issues.
- Establishing an organizational commitment to diversity through developing a core set of organizational values that reflect a diversity commitment and living that commitment through every decision and action.

Organizational change begins with a vision articulated throughout the organization which, over time, begins to change an organization's very heart, soul and culture. In developing a foundation for organizational success and a vision for the future, progressive police leaders will include effective diversity programs that target internal behaviors and attitudes and external relationships with all segments of the community. The key to community policing lies in the strength of our diversity commitment and our ability to successfully engage our communities.

COMMUNITY POLICING AND COMMUNITY ENGAGEMENT

The two core components of community policing are community partnerships and problem solving. A community policing philosophy demands that the police develop partnerships with all components of our communities to facilitate community problem solving. Police officers do not generally resist problem solving—however, it is difficult to overcome the unwillingness of officers to engage the community. Community partnerships demand that the police actively engage the community if problem-solving efforts are to be effective.

To analyze why community engagement is difficult, consider barriers that may prevent police/community partnerships:

1. The police culture may promote an "us versus them" mentality, which by its very nature inhibits building trust and positive relationships with citizens.
2. The police have accepted the responsibility for crime in our communities and have become the crime experts and openly resist citizens' efforts to assist with crime issues.
3. The police rarely make any efforts to understand the very people with whom they spend the majority of their time policing. The profile of the average officer is very different than the profile of the citizens who make up the neighborhoods demanding continuous police services. The two profiles illustrate a clash of cultures, values, expectations and accepted behaviors, which results in an unwillingness and inability to partner with our citizens. It is human nature to resist the unfamiliar: the unknown makes us uncomfortable, and what makes us uncomfortable, we tend to avoid.
4. Our citizens often perceive the police negatively, and the police have an equally negative perception of the citizens whose problems we are asking them to solve through partnerships.
5. Community organization and mobilization attempts by the police often lead to frustration due to citizens' apparent unwillingness to get involved and to work with the police. Police view the reluctance to "get involved" as apathy and quickly lose interest. The common refrain becomes, "If they don't care, why should we?" Police officers must have patience and be persistent in building trust and confidence in our citizens.
6. Police often fail to realize how much the police need the community, and the community has a narrow view of the police role in their communities.
7. The reality of policing is that the police cannot resolve crime and community issues alone. The police simply do not have enough presence, resources or skills to address the challenges our communities are facing today. Partnering with the community and enhancing citizen involvement ultimately increases our numbers, resources and skills, making policing safer and easier.

We often hear police chiefs state that the police are "empowering the community," when in fact, it is the reverse. Sir Robert Peel, in his nine principles of modern policing, addresses that fact stating that the police receive their authority from the public; and he succinctly addresses the partnership issue with this principle:

> To maintain at all times a relationship with the public that gives reality to the historic tradition that the police are the public and the public are the police; the police being the only members of the public that are paid to give full-time attention to the duties that are incumbent on every citizen in the interest of the community welfare and existence.

Most of Peel's principles of modern policing actually address the importance of community support and participation if the police are to be effective. Community engagement means that the police must begin:

- Talking to, listening to and collaborating with citizens.
- Valuing sharing information with citizens.
- Valuing all people and all groups in the community.
- Replacing an "us versus them" mentality with "we."
- Replacing "we do it for" with "we do it together."
- Reorganizing policing as a service, and citizens and the community as our customers.
- Allowing the community to identify problems and solutions.
- Bringing the community into the department to help define mission, vision, values and priorities.
- Developing and working with civilian advisory councils.

When we think of community, we must think of all the community stakeholders and the many communities and neighborhoods within the larger community. Community policing has a strong neighborhood focus where beat officers work to instill a strong sense of shared community and responsibility for one another. It means providing customized policing services to all neighborhoods.

The goal is to recapture a sense of community that appears to be lost in today's communities. Neighborhoods are no longer caretakers for their fellow neighbors. In fact, we are becoming a "nation of strangers" where neighbors do not know or interact with neighbors or the community as a whole.

If we are to regain a sense of community, then we must instill a sense of community in our neighborhoods—we accomplish this by developing a sense that citizens can affect what is occurring in their lives and neighborhoods.

The community partnership process involves the police, government and the community collaborating, not when a problem arises, but as a way of conducting daily business. In community policing communities, the collaboration is continuous, ongoing and leads to constant communication and an environment of trust. The greater the extent of collaboration, the more effective partnerships will become. The goal of community policing is to enlarge the area of community collaboration. If community collaboration is to be successful, the following conditions must exist: (1) a common need, purpose and/or vision, (2) recognized leadership to guide the process, (3) a perception that personal involvement can make a difference and (4) information available about how to realistically change the existing conditions.

Citizens in community policing communities are more likely to willingly, enthusiastically support the police and engage in active partnerships activities such as:

- Participating in Neighborhood-Watch Groups.
- Participating in Business-Watch Groups.
- Attending Citizen Police Academies.
- Serving in citizen patrols coordinated by the police.
- Serving on citizen advisory councils at the neighborhood and community-wide level.
- Working with the police to identify and resolve community or neighborhood problems.
- Helping to develop policing philosophies and strategies including mission, vision, values and priorities.
- Organizing and working with teen and youth organizations.

For community policing to be successful, the police must overcome barriers to partnerships. We must work to actively engage all aspects of our communities and aggressively pursue a sense of "community" in our neighborhoods. Only by policing with the community can we effectively solve community problems.

Glossary

Number in parentheses indicates the chapter in which the term is introduced.

acculturation—A society takes in or assimilates other cultures. Also called *assimilation.* (6)

ADA—The Americans with Disabilities Act of 1990. (6)

administrative density—The ratio of all employees to supervisory personnel. (15)

Alzheimer's disease (AD)—A progressive, irreversible and incurable brain disease with no known cause and affecting four million elderly Americans; the classic symptom is memory loss. (6)

analysis (in SARA)—Examines the identified problem's causes, scope and effects; includes determining how often the problem occurs, how long it has been occurring as well as conditions that appear to create the problem. (4)

anticipatory benefit—Criminals may be deterred even before a prevention effort is implemented. (8)

assessment (in SARA)—Refers to evaluating how effective the intervention was; was the problem solved? (4)

assimilation—A society takes in or assimilates various other cultures to become a "melting pot." Also called *acculturation.* (6)

attention hyperactivity deficit disorder (AHDD)—A common disruptive behavior disorder characterized by heightened motor activity (fidgeting and squirming), short attention span, distractibility, impulsiveness and lack of self-control. (6)

bias—A prejudice that inhibits objectivity; can evolve into hate. (6)

bias crime—A criminal offense committed against a person, property or society that is motivated, in whole or in part, by an offender's bias against an individual's or group's race, religion, ethnic/national origin, gender, age, disability or sexual orientation. Also called *hate crime.* (14)

bias incident—Use of bigoted and prejudiced language; does not in itself violate hate crime laws. (14)

bifurcated society—The widening of the gap between those with wealth (the "haves") and those living in poverty (the "have nots"), with a shrinking middle class. (3)

binge drinking—Five or more drinks in a row during the previous two weeks. (11)

body language—Messages conveyed by how a person looks, moves and gestures. (6)

broken window phenomenon—Suggests that if it appears no one cares about the community, as indicated by broken windows not being repaired, then disorder and crime will thrive. (3)

bullying—Name calling, fistfights, purposeful ostracism, extortion, character assassination, repeated physical attacks and sexual harassment. Also called *peer child abuse.* (12)

call management—Calls are prioritized based on the department's judgment about the emergency nature of the call (e.g., imminent harm to a person or a crime in progress), response time, need for backup and other local factors. Also called *call reduction.* (7)

call reduction—Calls are prioritized based on the department's judgment about the emergency nature of the call (e.g., imminent harm to a person or a crime in progress), response time, need for backup and other local factors. Also called *call management.* (7)

call stacking—A process a computer-aided dispatch system performs in which nonemergency, lower priority calls are ranked and held or "stacked" so the higher priorities are continually dispatched first. (7)

change management—The development of an overall strategy to review the present state of an organization, envision the future state of the organization and devise a means of moving from one to the other. (5)

closed drug market—Dealers sell only to people they know or who are vouched for by other buyers. (11)

cocoon neighborhood watch—Focusing on only those living around at-risk places rather than an entire neighborhood. (10)

coercive isomorphism—Occurs when organizations adopt something due to pressure either from the state or other organizations. (15)

collaboration—Occurs when a number of agencies and individuals make a commitment to work together and contribute resources to obtain a common, long-term goal. (7)

communication—The transfer of information and understanding from one person to another. (6)

communication process—Involves a sender, a message, a channel, a receiver and sometimes feedback. (6)

community—The specific geographic area served by a police department or law enforcement agency and the individuals, organizations and agencies within that area. (3)

community justice—An ethic that transforms the aim of the justice system into enhancing community life or sustaining communities. (3)

community mobilization—Includes improved communication and joint policy and program development among justice, community-based and grassroots organizations. (13)

community policing—A philosophy or orientation that emphasizes working proactively with citizens to reduce fear, solve crime-related problems and prevent crime. (1)

community relations—Efforts to interact and communicate with the community—team policing, community resource officers, school liaison officers. See also *public relations.* (1)

conditional threat—The type of threat often seen in extortion cases; warns that a violent act will happen unless certain demands or terms are met. (12)

contagion—Suggests that when offenders notice one criminal opportunity they often detect similar opportunities they have previously overlooked; crime then spreads; the broken window theory is an example. (10)

conservative crime control—Comes down hard on crime; wages "war" on crime and drugs. (11)

CPTED—Crime Prevention through Environmental Design—altering the physical environment to enhance safety, reduce the incidence and fear of crime and improve the quality of life. (9)

crack children—Children who were exposed to cocaine while in the womb. (6)

creativity—A process of breaking old connections and making useful new connections. Often synonymous with innovation. (4)

crime-specific planning—Uses the principles of problem solving to focus on identified crime problems. (4)

criminal gang—A group of people following a common code of conduct, having common beliefs and identifiers, existing in a semistructured organization or hierarchy and attempting to accomplish their goals through criminal activity. (13)

crisis behavior—Results when a person has a temporary breakdown in coping skills; not the same as mental illness. (8)

critical mass—The smallest number of citizens and organizations needed to support and sustain the community policing initiative. (9)

cross-sectional analysis—A research method whereby data are analyzed by area rather than by individuals responding. (9)

cultural conflict—A theory that suggests that diverse cultures sharing the same territory will compete with and attempt to exploit one another. (6)

cultural pluralism—A theory that suggests there are many melting pots; some groups are comfortable in one pot; other groups are comfortable in another. (6)

culture—A collection of artifacts, tools, ways of living, values and language common to a group of people, all passed from one generation to the next. (6)

cycle of violence—Violent or sexual victimization of children can often lead to these victims becoming perpetrators of domestic violence as adults. (14)

DARE—Drug Abuse Resistance Education—a program aimed at elementary-age school children, seeking to teach them to "say no to drugs." (9)

decentralization—An operating principle that encourages flattening of the organization and places decision-making authority and autonomy at the level where information is plentiful, usually at the level of the patrol officer. (2, 3, 5)

deinstitutionalization—Refers to the release of thousands of mentally ill individuals into society to be cared for by family or a special network of support services. (6) Also refers to efforts to release incarcerated youths through parole and community programs. (9)

demographics—The characteristics of a human population or community. (3)

developmental assets—Forty ideals, experiences and qualities established by the Search Institute to "help young people make wise decisions, choose positive paths, and grow up competent, caring and responsible." (12)

diffusion—Occurs when criminals believe that the opportunity blocking of one type of criminal activity is also aimed at other types of criminal activity. (10)

direct threat—Identifies a specific act against a specific target and is delivered in a straightforward, clear and explicit manner. (12)

disability—A physical or mental impairment that substantially limits one or more of a person's major life functions. (6)

discretion—Freedom to make choices among possible courses of action or inaction, for example, to arrest or not arrest. (2)

discrimination—Showing a preference or prejudice in treating individuals or groups; failing to treat equals equally; a behavior based on an attitude or prejudice. (6)

displacement—The theory that successful implementation of a crime-reduction initiative does not really prevent crime; instead it just moves the crime to the next block. (4)

diversion—Turning youths away from the criminal justice system, rerouting them to another agency or program. (3) Finding alternatives to placing juvenile status offenders and delinquents in detention facilities. (9)

DOC model—Dilemmas-Options-Consequences—Challenges officers to carefully consider their decisions and the short- and long-term consequences of those decisions, with the goal of fusing problem solving and morality. (4)

drug gang—Smaller than other gangs; much more cohesive; focused on the drug business; strong, centralized leadership, with market-defined roles. (13)

EBD—Emotionally/behaviorally disturbed. (6)

effectiveness—Producing the desired result or goal; doing the right things. (4)

efficiency—Minimizing waste, expense or unnecessary effort; results in a high ratio of output to input; doing things right. (4)

8% problem—Refers to the fact that 8 percent of youthful offenders commit more than half of all repeat offenses and over half of them are under 15 years of age when they first offend. (12)

empathy—Truly understanding another person. (6)

empirical study—Research based on observation or practical experience. (9)

empowered—Granting authority and decision making to lower level officers. (2, 3, 5)

ethnocentrism—The preference for one's own way of life over all others. (6)

experimental design—Research method involving the random assignment of individuals to experimental (treatment) and control (no treatment) conditions. (15)

fetal alcohol syndrome (FAS)—The leading known cause of mental retardation in the western world; effects include impulsivity, inability to predict consequences or to use appropriate judgment in daily life, poor communication skills, high levels of activity and distractibility in small children and frustration and depression in adolescents. (6)

flat organization—Typical pyramid organization charts have the top pushed down and the sides expanded at the base. In a police department, it means fewer lieutenants and captains, fewer staff departments, fewer staff assistants, more sergeants and more patrol officers. (2, 3, 5)

formal power structure—Includes divisions of society with wealth and political influence: federal, state and local agencies and governments, commissions and regulatory agencies. (3)

frankpledge system—The Norman system requiring all freemen to swear loyalty to the king's law and to take responsibility for maintaining the local peace. (1)

gang—An organized group of people existing for some time with a special interest in using violence to achieve status. See also *street gang* and *youth gang*. (13)

gateway theory—Teaches that milder illicit drugs—such as marijuana—lead directly to experimentation with and an addiction to hard drugs such as crack cocaine and heroin. (11)

geographic profiling—A crime mapping technique that takes the locations of past crimes and, using a complex mathematical algorithm, calculates probabilities of a suspect's residence. (4)

geographical diffusion of benefit—Properties immediately adjacent to where an intervention was implemented also experience a reduction in crime. (8)

ghetto—An area of a city usually inhabited by individuals of the same race or ethnic background who live in poverty and apparent social disorganization. (3)

graffiti—Painting or writing on buildings, walls, bridges, bus stops and other available public surfaces; used by gangs to mark their turf. (13)

Guardian Angels—Private citizen patrols who seek to deter crime and to provide a positive role model for young children. (9)

gun interdiction—Local police direct intensive patrols to specific geographic areas with high rates of gun-related incidents of violence. (14)

hate crime—A criminal offense committed against a person, property or society that is motivated, in whole or in part, by an offender's bias against an individual's or group's race, religion, ethnic/national origin, gender, age, disability or sexual orientation. Also called *bias crime*. (14)

hedonistic/social gang—Only moderate drug use and offending; involved mainly in using drugs and having a good time; little involvement in crime, especially violent crime. (13)

heterogeneous—Involving things (including people) that are unlike, dissimilar, different; the opposite of homogeneous. (3)

homogeneous—Involving things (including people) that are basically similar, alike; the opposite of heterogeneous. (3)

horizontal differentiation—Refers to the degree to which an organization's tasks are broken into functionally distinct units. (15)

hot spots—Locations where most crimes occur. (4)

hue and cry—The summoning of all citizens within earshot to join in pursuing and capturing a wrongdoer. (1)

human relations—Efforts to relate to and understand other individuals or groups. (1)

hybrid gang—Characterized by mixed racial and ethnic participation within a single gang, participation in multiple gangs by a single individual, vague rules and codes of conduct for gang members, use of symbols and colors from multiple—even rival—gangs, collaboration by rival gangs in criminal activities and the merger of smaller gangs into larger ones. (13)

hyphenated American—Tendency to include ethnic background in a person's nationality—for example, Italian-American, Polish-American—illustrating America's tendency to pluralism or a multicultural approach. (6)

impact evaluation—Determines if the problem declined. (4)

implant hypothesis—Asks whether collective citizen action by a small group of neighborhood residents, for example, Neighborhood-Watch groups, can make a difference in the attitudes and behaviors of local residents. May be proven true if community policing efforts (1) make stimulation of community processes the main goal and outcome measure of community policing programs and (2) lead police to more actively involve community residents in the strategies. (15)

incident—An isolated event that requires a police response; the primary work unit in the professional model. (4)

incivilities—Occur when social control mechanisms have eroded and include unmowed lawns, piles of accumulated trash, graffiti, public drunkenness, fighting, prostitution, abandoned buildings and broken windows. (3)

indirect threat—Tends to be vague, unclear and ambiguous; the plan, the intended victim, the motivation and other aspects of the threat are masked or equivocal. (12)

informal power structure—Includes religious groups, wealthy subgroups, ethnic groups, political groups and public interest groups. (3)

infrastructure—An established network of community-based organizations and community leaders. (10)

innovation—A new way of doing something, often synonymous with creativity. (4)

instrumental gang—Main criminal activity is property crimes (most use drugs and alcohol but seldom sell drugs). (13)

instrumental knowledge—Knowledge about the best means to a given end. (15)

interoperability—The compatibility of communication systems such as EMS, fire and rescue, and police and across levels of government. (14)

isomorphism—Similar in structural characteristics. Isomorphism results in a one-size-fits-all approach to community policing, in contrast to refraction. (15)

jargon—The technical language of a profession. (6)

justice model—Views lawbreakers as responsible for their own actions; in comparison to the medical or welfare model. (3, 9)

killer phrases—Judgmental, critical statements that serve as put-downs and stifle creativity. (4)

kinesics—The study of body movement or body language. (6)

leakage—Occurs when a student intentionally or unintentionally reveals clues to feelings, thoughts, fantasies, attitudes or intentions that may signal an impending violent act. (12)

learning disability—One or more significant deficits in the essential learning processes. (6)

least-effort principle—Concept proposes that criminals tend to commit acts of crimes within a comfort zone located near but not too close to their residence. (4)

liberal crime control—Emphasizes correctional policies and broader social reforms intended to expand opportunities for those "locked out" of the American dream; wages "war" on poverty and inequality of opportunity. (11)

macrosocial—Referring to the big picture; the macrosocial environment includes the amount of social capital available as well as existing diversity, including economic diversity. (14)

magnet phenomenon—Occurs when a phone number or address is associated with a crime simply because it was a convenient number or address to use. (4)

marketing mix—All of the agency's tools that it uses to influence a market segment to accomplish its objectives. (8)

mediation—The intervention of a third party into an interpersonal dispute, where the third party helps disputants reach a resolution; often termed alternative dispute resolution (ADR). (4)

medical model—Sees those who break the law as victims of society, not responsible for their own actions; sometimes called the welfare model, in comparison to the justice model. (3)

mental illness—A severe mental disturbance that results in substantially diminished capacity to cope with the ordinary demands of life. (8)

mental locks—Ways of thinking that prevent creativity. (4)

microsocial—Referring to the smaller picture; the microsocial environment focuses on smaller units such as the family. (14)

mimetic isomorphism—Occurs when an organization copies or imitates another. (15)

misinformation synergy—Significant distortions in print and broadcast news result in a misinformed public and misguided power structure. (8)

mission statement—A written declaration of purpose. (2)

moniker—A nickname, often of a gang member. (13)

negative contacts—Unpleasant interactions between the police and the public; may or may not relate to criminal activity. (2, 7)

negative emotionality—A generalized propensity for experiencing aversive affective states, including anger, anxiety, suspiciousness and irritability; emotional brittleness causing a rapid, excessive response to minor stressors, a sense that others are malicious and a propensity to react to even slight provocation with rage; a shared risk factor for both partner abuse and crime. (14)

networking—Building and maintaining professional relationships for mutual interest. (6)

news media echo effect—The theory that the media have the power, through their coverage of isolated, high-profile cases, to influence the operations of the criminal justice system and even the disposition of individual cases. (8)

NIMBY syndrome—"Not in my backyard"; the idea that it is fine to have a half-way house—across town, not in my backyard. (3)

911 policing—Incident-driven, reactive policing. (2)

nonverbal communication—Includes everything other than the actual words spoken in a message, such as tone, pitch and pacing. (6)

normative isomorphism—Results from professionalism, with influences coming from other organizations involved in the same profession. (16)

open drug market—Dealers sell to all potential customers, eliminating only those suspected of being police or some other threat. (11)

opportunity blocking—Changes to make crime more difficult, risky, less rewarding or less excusable; one of the oldest forms of crime prevention. (10)

organizational development—Includes special police units and special youth agency crisis programs. (13)

organized/corporate gang—Heavy involvement in all kinds of crime; heavy use and sale of drugs; may resemble major corporations, with separate divisions handling sales, marketing, discipline and so on; discipline is strict, and promotion is based on merit. (13)

Pager Information Network (PIN)—A system to simultaneously notify all the media. (8)

PAL—Police athletic league—developed to provide opportunities for youths to interact with police officers in gyms or ballparks instead of in a juvenile detention hall. (8)

panel analysis—A research method where data are analyzed by individuals responding rather than by area. (9)

paradigm—A model or a way of viewing a specific aspect of life such as politics, medicine, education and the criminal justice system. (1)

paradigm shift—A new way of thinking about a specific subject. (1)

paradox—A seemingly contradictory statement that may, nonetheless, be true; for example, the less one has, the less one has to lose. (2)

participatory leadership—A management style in which each individual has a voice in decisions, but top management still has the ultimate decision-making authority. (2, 3, 5)

party gang—Commonly called "party crew"; relatively high use and sale of drugs, but only one major form of delinquency—their flexible turf is called the "party scene"; crews compete over who throws the biggest party, with alcohol, marijuana, nitrous oxide, sex and music critical party elements. (13)

patronage system—Politicians rewarded those who voted for them with jobs or special privileges; prevalent during the political era. Also called the *spoils system.* (1)

peer child abuse—Another term for *bullying*—name calling, fistfights, purposeful ostracism, extortion, character assassination, repeated physical attacks and sexual harassment. (12)

perp walks—The police practice of parading suspects before the media, often simply for the publicity provided by news media coverage. (8)

PIO triangle—Three components encompass (1) what happened, (2) what responders are doing and (3) how the public (or a portion of it) will be affected by both number 1 and number 2. (8)

place—A very small area reserved for a narrow range of functions, often controlled by a single owner and separated from the surrounding area. (10)

plea bargaining—A practice in which prosecutors charge a defendant with a less serious crime in exchange for a guilty plea, thus eliminating the time and expense of a trial. (3)

police culture—The informal values, beliefs and expectations passed on to newcomers in the department; may be at odds with the formal rules, regulations, procedures and role authority of managers. (2)

police–school liaison program—Places an officer in a school to work with school authorities, parents and students to prevent crime and antisocial behavior and to improve police–youth relationships. (9)

posttraumatic stress disorder (PTSD)—A persistent reexperiencing of a traumatic event through intrusive memories, dreams and a variety of anxiety-related symptoms. (6)

poverty syndrome—Includes inadequate housing, education, and jobs and a resentment of those who control the social system. (6)

predatory gang—Heavily involved in serious crimes (e.g., robberies and muggings) and the abuse of addictive drugs such as crack cocaine; may engage in selling drugs but not in organized fashion. (13)

prejudice—A negative judgment not based on fact; an irrational, preconceived negative opinion. An attitude that may result in discriminatory behavior. Also called *bias.* (6)

privatization—Using private security officers or agencies to provide services typically considered to be law enforcement functions. (3)

proactive—Anticipating problems and seeking solutions to those problems, as in community policing. The opposite of reactive. (1)

problem-oriented policing (POP)—A department-wide strategy aimed at solving persistent community problems by grouping incidents to identify problems and to determine possible underlying causes. (4)

problem-solving approach—Involves proactively identifying problems and making decisions about how best to deal with them. (4)

process evaluation—Determines if the response was implemented as planned. (4)

process mapping—A method of internal analysis that takes a horizontal view of a system, in contrast to the traditional vertical view; involves personnel at all levels and uses flowcharts to visually depict how information, materials and activities flow in an organization; how work is handed off from one unit or department to another; and how processes work currently and what changes should be made to attain a more ideal process flow. (14)

professional model—Emphasized crime control by preventive automobile patrol coupled with rapid response to calls. The predominant policing model used during the reform era (1970s and 1980s). (1)

progressive era—Emphasized preventive automobile patrol and rapid response to calls for service. Also called the *reform era.* (1)

protective factor—Predicts a decreased probability of later offending; often considered to exist at the opposite end of the scale from risk factors but not always necessarily so. (10)

PSAs—Public service announcements. (9)

psychopath—A category of violent individuals who tend to be socially inept loners, like the "Trench Coat Mafia" kids. In contrast to a sociopath. (12)

psychosocial—Factors that refer to individual psychological characteristics such as temperament and self-identity. (14)

public information officers (PIOs)—Officers trained in public relations and assigned to disseminate information to the media, thereby providing accurate, consistent information while controlling leaks of confidential or inaccurate information and managing controversial or negative situations to the department's benefit. (8)

public relations—Efforts to enhance the police image. (1)

pulling levers—Refers to a multiagency law enforcement team imposing all available sanctions on gang members who violate established standards for behavior. (13)

qualitative data—Examines the excellence (quality) of the response, that is, how satisfied were the officers and the citizens; most frequently determined by surveys, focus groups or tracking complaints and compliments. (4)

qualitative evaluations—Assessments that are more descriptive and less statistical; the opposite of quantitative evaluation. (12)

quantitative data—Examines the amount of change (quantity) as a result of the response; most frequently measured by pre/post data. (4)

racial profiling—A form of discrimination that singles out people of racial or ethnic groups because of a belief that these groups are more likely than others to commit certain types of crimes. Race-based enforcement is illegal. (6)

racism—A belief that a human population having a distinct genetically transmitted characteristic is inferior; also refers to discrimination or prejudice based on race. (6)

random assignment—Dependence on a random number table or machine-generated random number that indicates the particular group to which an individual or entity will be assigned. Whether a person is a member of the treatment group or the control (no treatment) group is purely by chance. (15)

rave—A dance party with fast-paced electronic music, light shows and use of a wide variety of drugs and alcohol. (11)

reactive—Responding after the fact; responding to calls for service. The opposite of proactive. (1)

recidivism—Repeat offending. (3)

reciprocity—A cooperative interchange; each party in the effort has something to offer and also something to gain from the relationship. (9)

reform era—Emphasized preventive automobile patrol and rapid response to calls for service. Also called the *progressive era*. (1)

refraction—The bending and deflection of light rays and energy waves from a straight path as they pass from one medium to another (such as through a prism). The term is used to explain the fragmented implementation of community policing in the United States due to the abundance of autonomous police agencies and the thousands of police executives throughout the country making very different and often conflicting decisions. In contrast to isomorphism. (15)

representing—A manner of dress to show allegiance or opposition to a gang; uses an imaginary line drawn vertically through the body. (13)

response (in SARA)—Acting to alleviate the problem, that is, selecting the alternative solution or solutions. (4)

restorative justice—Advocates a balanced approach to sentencing that involves offenders, victims, local communities and government to alleviate crime and violence and obtain peaceful communities. (3)

risk factor—Predicts an increased probability of later offending. In contrast to a protective factor. (10)

risk factor prevention paradigm—Seeks to identify key risk factors for offending and then implement prevention methods designed to counteract them. (10)

road humps—Short, narrow raised portions of the road that can be crossed safely only at lower speeds—more appropriate in parking lots than on roads emergency vehicles might travel. (10)

scanning (in SARA)—Refers to identifying recurring problems and prioritizing them to select one problem to address. (4)

scavenger gang—Loosely organized group described as "urban survivors"; prey on the weak in inner cities; engage in rather petty crimes but sometimes violence, often just for fun; members have no greater bond than their impulsiveness and the need to belong; have no goals and are low achievers; often illiterate, with poor school performance. (13)

school-associated violent death—A homicide, suicide, legal intervention or unintentional firearm-related death in which the fatal injury occurred on the campus of a functioning elementary or secondary school in the United States, while the victim was on the way to or from regular sessions at such a school, or while the victim was attending or traveling to or from an official school-sponsored event. (12)

selective enforcement—The use of police discretion, deciding to concentrate on specific crimes such as drug dealing and to downplay other crimes such as white-collar crime. (2)

serious delinquent gang—Heavy involvement in both serious and minor crimes, but much lower involvement in drug use and drug sales than party gangs. (13)

social capital—Refers to the strength of a community's social fabric and includes the elements of trustworthiness (citizens' trust of each other and their public institutions) and obligations (expectation that service to each other will be reciprocated). Two levels of social capital are local (found among family members and citizens and their immediate, informal groups) and public (found in networks tying individuals to broader community institutions such as schools, civic organizations, churches and various levels of government, including the police). (3)

social contract—A legal theory that suggests that for everyone to receive justice, each person must relinquish some individual freedom. (3)

social intervention—Includes crisis intervention, treatment for youths and their families, outreach and referral to social services. (13)

social opportunities—Include providing basic or remedial education, training, work incentives and jobs for gang members. (13)

sociopath—A category of violent individuals usually characterized as bullies—outgoing and manipulative, instigating fights; a type of violent leader. In contrast to a psychopath. (12)

sound bites—Good, solid information stated briefly, i.e., 7 to 12 seconds. (8)

spoils system—Politicians rewarded those who voted for them with jobs or special privileges. Prevalent during the political era. Also called the *patronage system*. (1)

stakeholders—Those people who have an interest in what happens in a particular situation. (7)

statistically significant—A predetermined level at which the results of a study would not occur by chance; most common level is .05, meaning the results would occur by chance no more than five times in one hundred. (9)

status offenses—Actions by a juvenile that would not be crimes if committed by an adult, for example, truancy or smoking cigarettes. (9)

stepping stone theory—Teaches that milder illicit drugs—such as marijuana—lead directly to experimentation with and an addiction to hard drugs such as crack cocaine and heroin. (11)

stereotyping—Assuming all people within a specific group are the same, lacking individuality. (6)

strategic planning—Long-term, large-scale, futuristic planning. (5)

straw purchasers—Weapons buyers fronting for people linked to illegal gun trafficking. (14)

street gang—A group of people whose allegiance is based on social needs and who engage in acts injurious to the public; the preferred term of most local law enforcement agencies. (13)

street justice—Occurs when police officers use their discretionary powers to simply talk to or warn youthful offenders, talk to their parents or make referrals to a social service agency; may also involve roughing up offenders. (9)

suppression—Includes tactics such as prevention, arrest, imprisonment, supervision and surveillance. (13)

sympathy—An involuntary sharing of another person's feelings of fear, grief or anger. (6)

syndrome of crime—A group of signs, causes and symptoms that occur together to foster specific crimes. (3)

synergism—Occurs when individuals channel their energies toward a common purpose and accomplish what they could not accomplish alone. (10)

systems thinking—A conceptual framework that recognizes the contribution of each component to a system (i.e., everything affects everything else); thinking in terms of the whole rather than the individual parts. (5)

target hardening—Refers to making potential objectives of criminals more difficult to obtain through the use of improved locks, alarm systems and security cameras. (10)

tattling—Something done to get someone in trouble, in contrast to telling or reporting to keep someone safe. (12)

territorial gang—Associated with a specific area or turf and, as a result, gets involved in conflicts with other gangs over respective turfs. (13)

terrorism—The unlawful use of force or violence against persons or property to intimidate or coerce a government, the civilian population or any segment thereof, in furtherance of political or social objectives (FBI). (14)

"thin blue line"—The distancing of the police from the public they serve. (1)

tipping point—That point at which an ordinary, stable phenomenon can turn into a crisis. (3)

tithing—A group of 10 families. (1)

tithing system—The Anglo-Saxon principle establishing the principle of collective responsibility for maintaining local law and order. (1)

traffic calming—Describes a wide range of road and environment design changes that either make it more difficult for a vehicle to speed or make drivers believe they should slow down for safety. (10)

transition management—Overseeing, controlling and leading the change from an organization's present state to its future state. (5)

TRIAD—A three-way partnership among the AARP, the International Association of Chiefs of Police (IACP) and the National Sheriffs' Association (NSA) to address criminal victimization of older people. (7)

turf—Territory occupied by a gang, often marked by graffiti. (13)

two-wave survey—Study method where the first wave consists of a pretest before a strategy is implemented, and the second wave consists of a posttest after the strategy has been implemented for a given amount of time. (15)

veiled threat—One that strongly implies but does not explicitly threaten violence. (12)

victim compensation programs—Programs that help crime victims cope with crime-related expenses such as medical costs, mental health counseling, lost wages and funeral or burial costs. (6)

victim/witness assistance programs—Provide services such as crisis support, peer support, referrals to counseling, advocacy within the justice system and, in some cases, emergency shelter. (6)

vision—Intelligent foresight; starts with a mental image that gradually evolves from abstract musings to a concrete series of mission statements, goals and objectives. (5)

white flight—The departure of white families from neighborhoods experiencing racial integration or from cities experiencing school desegregation. (3)

working in "silos"—Agencies with common interests work independently with no collaboration. (7)

youth gang—A subgroup of a street gang; may refer to a juvenile clique within a gang. (13)

zeitgeist—The general intellectual, moral, cultural or "spirit" of the times. (15)

zero tolerance—A policy of punishing all offenses severely, no matter how minor the offense. (12)

Author Index

Subject Index

Photo Credits

Page 4, ©David Young Wolff/PhotoEdit; **Page 27,** ©Getty Images; **Page 50,** ©Jonathon Nourok/PhotoEdit; **Page 77,** ©Brenda Ann Kenneally/CORBIS; **Page 104,** ©AP Photo/Daniel Hulshizer; **Page 136,** ©Greg Smith/CORBIS SABA; **Page 174,** ©Reuters/CORBIS; **Page 210,** ©AP Photo/Matt Houston; **Page 246,** ©Bob Daemmrich/PhotoEdit; **Page 286,** ©AP Photo/Brad C. Bower; **Page 318,** ©Michael Newman/PhotoEdit; **Page 351,** ©Will Hart/PhotoEdit; **Page 387,** ©Mark Richards/PhotoEdit; **Page 423,** ©Dennis MacDonald/PhotoEdit; **Page 464,** ©A. Ramey/PhotoEdit.